To: Bill and Darlene

With best wishes to
a great couple

John Stevens

No Ordinary University

The History
of a City
Set on a Hill

John C. Stevens

Edited by Charles H. Marler

Abilene Christian University Press
Abilene, Texas

A·C·U
PRESS

ACU Station, Box 29138
Abilene, TX 79699

Printed in the United States of America

Dust Jacket Design, Fritz Miller
Book Design and Typesetting, Mark Houston

Library of Congress Card Number 98-74874
ACU Press, Abilene, Texas
ISBN 0-89112-031-9

1,2,3,4,5

TABLE OF CONTENTS

Introduction

Don Morris, for the last chapel speech of his life, September 27, 1973, chose the subject "The How and Why of Abilene Christian College." He gave a brief history of the beginning of the school, along with its aims and purposes. Toward the end of his ten-minute address, flawlessly delivered, he used a five-word sentence that has been quoted more often than anything else ever said in chapel. "This," he said, "is no ordinary college." Coming from somebody else, the words might not have been so impressive. But everybody there knew he had given his life to build that kind of college. Three and a half months later, he collapsed on the campus, and although valiant efforts were made to revive him, he was gone.

This book is dedicated to his memory and titled *No Ordinary University: The History of a City Set on a Hill.*

Why should I be the one to undertake to write this history?

First, counting from the time I enrolled as a freshman in the fall of 1934 – and found that my first class was with Professor Don Morris in public speaking – I have been acquainted with the school for more than sixty years. After receiving the bachelor of arts degree in 1938, I was away from the campus for several years, preaching in East Texas, serving as an Army chaplain with an infantry division during World War II, and doing graduate study in the field of history. In the fall of 1948, I became a member of the history faculty and have been here ever since except for one long session and three summers of leave during doctoral studies at the University of Arkansas.

Second, I have known every president of this school, including its years as Childers Classical Institute, 1906-20, Abilene Christian College, 1920-76, and Abilene Christian University.

The founding president, A. B. Barret, 1906-8, was in retirement in Henderson, Tennessee, when I had a brief visit with him during the Freed-Hardeman College lectureship in 1941.

I do not say that I knew him well, but at least I had the opportunity of meeting him.

The third president, Robertson L. Whiteside, 1909-11, was not a close friend, but I met him, shook hands with him, read his writings, heard him speak, and saw him in action during the debates between J. Frank Norris and Foy Wallace Jr. in Fort Worth in 1934. He was Wallace's moderator. So I met and observed him, but I would not say that he would have remembered me.

With all the others, I had close contacts and genuine friendships, including H. C. Darden, the second president, who befriended me when I was a young preacher in East Texas in the late 1930s and early 1940s.

This does not say that the history of a university is wrapped up in the office of the president. The faculty may well be a more crucial factor. Without a strong faculty, whose members are dedicated to their calling and committed to the ideals and purposes of the institution, what the trustees and the president do may be only "sound and fury, signifying nothing."

And certainly, without a predominantly Christian student body through the years, the history of this institution would probably have been quite different indeed. In his "How and Why" chapel speech, Dr. Morris said, "You have to have a special kind of students to have a Christian college." I firmly believe that.

With that said, however, a president truly is in position to put his stamp on the institution of which he is chief executive, and I believe each president of Abilene Christian has left his imprint. So this history is divided into eight key presidential eras, and I think the reasons for doing that will be seen as we move along.

Abilene Christian University has had, since its beginning as Childers Classical Institute in 1906, ten presidents and one acting president: A. B. Barret, 1906-8; H. C. Darden, 1908-9; R. L. Whiteside, 1909-11; A. B. Cox, acting, 1911-12; Jesse P. Sewell, 1912-24; Batsell Baxter, 1924-32; James F. Cox, 1932-40; Don H. Morris, 1940-69; John C. Stevens, 1969-81; William J. Teague, 1981-91; and Royce Money, who began serving in 1991.

A word of explanation about the acting president seems to be in order. James F. Cox was elected to the chief executive office in the spring of 1911. But he explained in his unpublished autobiography:

In the early spring of 1911 I was offered the presidency of Abilene Christian College, then known as Childers Classical Institute. I accepted it and worked through the summer, getting ready for the opening of school in September. I had put the buildings and grounds in good order and had done some advertising. Prospects were good for a successful school year, but just two days before the fall opening I was called to the bedside of my wife at her mother's in Midway. She was dangerously ill and remained so for more than a year, so my brother, Dr. A. B. Cox, ... was left in charge of the school. ... I was not present even one day while the school was in session.

The board turned to James F. Cox again in 1932, and he served heroically as president during the difficult days of the Great Depression, 1932-40.

I am sometimes using the word "school" because, although it was first an institute, then a college, and finally, a university, it was always first and foremost a school.

JOHN C. STEVENS
June 1998

Acknowledgments

Among the sources I have used in writing this book are the following:

Abilene Reporter-News, 1907-98. The newspaper has through the years provided excellent coverage, whether it was called *Abilene Reporter, Abilene Daily Reporter, Abilene Morning News,* or *Abilene Reporter-News.* There are no file copies for the period from November 23, 1905, to April 3, 1907, because of a fire; hence, the account of the opening of the school in September 1906 has to be put together from other sources. Microfilm of later issues of the paper is in the Brown Library.

ACU Today is an attractive and factual publication and an excellent source of information about the present decade with a good deal of background information.

Adams, Walter H. *Serving Abilene and the World for 80 Years – A History of the University Church of Christ.* Abilene: University Church of Christ, 1981. The Adams history of the University Church was valuable for understanding the beginning of ACU.

Banowsky, William Slater. *The Mirror of a Movement: Churches of Christ as Seen through the Abilene Christian College Lectureship.* Dallas: Christian Publishing Co., 1965. Good insights.

Board of Trustees Minutes, Abilene Christian University, 1906-98. Basic information was drawn from these records, the originals of which are in a vault in the Administration Building.

Catalogs, Abilene Christian University, 1906-98. Catalogs of the school from 1906 to the present are in Special Collections in the Brown Library. These catalogs provide official historical information.

Childers materials. John W. Childers, of whom little has been written and without whom the dream of starting a school in Abilene in 1906 might have been abandoned, gained more publicity in New Mexico than in Texas. Colonel Childers and his wife moved there in 1907, not long after the opening of Childers Classical Institute. A 1912 publication by C. S. Peterson, Denver, Colorado, *Representative New Mexicans,* available through interlibrary loan from the University of New Mexico, provided the biographical information and the only good photograph found of Childers. An interlibrary loan also gave access to volume I of *A History of New Mexico, Its Resources and People,* published in 1970 by Pacific States Publishers of Los Angeles and containing information about Childers. A scholarly article by Thomas J. Mabry, "New Mexico's Constitution in the Making – Reminiscences of 1910," appeared in the *New Mexico Historical Review,* April 1944, with some background on Col. Childers's important work in drafting the constitution, which was essential to New Mexico's admission as a state to the United States in 1912. An article by Reuben W. Heflin, "New Mexico Constitutional Convention," appeared in *New Mexico Historical Review* in January 1946, recounting the tragedy involving a son of the colonel.

The Christian Chronicle, published in various cities after its initial operation in Abilene, has given good coverage to Abilene Christian since the newspaper's founding in 1941.

Coffman, James Barton. *Tales of Coffman.* Abilene: ACU Press, 1992. This highly readable account of a remarkable life includes highlights of the approach to James G. Hardin.

Cosby, Hugh E. *The History of Abilene.* Abilene: Cosby, 1955. The Cosby work was useful in providing background information.

Cosgrove, Owen. "The Administration of Don Heath Morris at Christian College." Doctoral dissertation, University of North Texas, 1976. Cosgrove did conscientious research. A copy of the Cosgrove dissertation is in the ACU Brown Library Special Collections.

Craig, Earl. "The Development of Abilene Christian College." Master's thesis, West Texas State Teachers College (now West Texas A&M University), 1940. A copy of this good work is in the Special Collections of ACU's Brown Library.

Duff, Katharyn. *Abilene on Catclaw Creek: A Profile of a West Texas Town.* Abilene: Reporter Publishing Company, 1969. The Duff book was useful in providing background information.

The Firm Foundation of Austin, Texas, gave good coverage to Abilene Christian through the years.

Edwards materials. Cartons of materials with exhaustive details of the William B. Edwards case are in Special Collections in the Brown Library.

Freeman, William Webb. "A History of the Campbell Movement and Its Educational Institutions." Master's thesis, Southern Methodist University, 1933. Webb, a member of the faculty of Abilene Christian, 1918-21, wrote a massive, 834-page thesis in which he gave a good deal of attention to the early history of Abilene Christian. Freeman's firsthand knowledge of the Sewell years makes his work indispensable.

Gospel Advocate of Nashville gave good coverage to Abilene Christian through the years.

Leach, Max, and Don Morris. *Like Stars Shining Brightly.* Abilene: Abilene Christian College, 1953. The Morris-Leach book is the only published history of the university and is valuable as a self-styled personal story rather than a full-scale history.

Marler, Charlie; Cheryl Bacon, and Malissa Endsley, eds. *AnswerBook,* 9th ed. Abilene: ACU Department of Journalism and Mass Communication, 1997. This reference book is alphabetically arranged and includes information about all phases of campus life.

Martin, Conny McDonald, ed. *McDonald Muster – A Family History of William Alex McDonald.* Lubbock: Scumble Publishers, 1986. Martin's history of the McDonald family contributes much to the understanding of the beginning of ACU.

Masten materials. Cartons of materials with exhaustive details of the F. O. Masten case are in Special Collections in the Brown Library.

McCann, Forrest M. *Hymns and History: An Annotated Survey of Sources.* Abilene: ACU Press, 1997.

McFerrin, J. B. *Caldwell and Company: A Southern Financial Empire.* Nashville: Vanderbilt University Press, 1969. The Caldwell Company of Nashville, which brokered the 1929 bond issue for the college, saved the day for construction on the new campus. McFerrin is excellent in describing that company's rise and fall. Another good source is the October 29, 1979, issue of *The Nashville Banner* published fifty years after Black Tuesday, which presaged the worst depression in the history of the United States and the possible foreclosure of Abilene Christian College. The *Banner* headline summarized the sad story: "Caldwell Lost It All in '29 Crash." *The Tennessean* of Sunday, May 18, 1980, also included much information on the collapse of the Caldwell companies.

The Optimist, 1912-98. The first issue of the student newspaper came out in 1912. A copy of the first issue is in the Brown Library Special Collections. Unfortunately, succeeding issues until the fall of 1919 are missing. Starting as a monthly publication in 1912, it was a weekly by 1919, and most issues since that time are intact in Special Collections, the periodicals section, and/or on microfilm. For the past two decades, the paper has been published twice weekly during long sessions. Through the years, it has been a really good student publication and is an indispensable source.

Presidential Papers, Special Collections, Brown Library. The papers of the various presidents of the university, which are in the archives, were interesting and informational, and, in fact, indispensable.

Prickly Pear, 1916-97. The university yearbook was begun in 1916, and all volumes are available in the Brown Library.

Richardson, Rupert N. *Famous Are Thy Halls.* Abilene, 1964.

Roach, Kenneth. "John Christopher Stevens: A Study of His Presidential Administration at Abilene Christian University, Abilene, Texas, 1969-1981." Doctoral dissertation, University of North Texas, 1994. Roach did conscientious research. A copy of the Roach dissertation is in the Brown Library Special Collections.

Robbins, Mae. "History and Analysis of Donations to Abilene Christian College, 1948 to 1960." Master's thesis, Abilene Christian College, 1960. The Robbins thesis is full of good information about several major gifts.

Roberts, R. L. Jr. This retired Abilene Christian librarian is a recognized authority in the history of Churches of Christ, especially in Texas.

Schwarz, Becki Bennett. *Bennett: A Texas Family.* Denver City, Texas: Lazy E Press, 1991.

Scruggs, Guy A. "The History of Abilene Christian College." Master's thesis, Hardin-Simmons University, 1944. The Scruggs thesis is valuable especially for his interviews with J. E. McKinzie and others connected with rescuing the school in the 1930s. Copies are in the Special Collections section of the Brown Library.

Sherrod, B. *Is It Worth It?* Austin: Firm Foundation, 1971. B Sherrod's firsthand account of the Edward Ranch deal and other items is invaluable.

Smith, Lawrence L., Papers. Transcriptions of taped interviews with a large number of ex-students and others, 1974-80. ACU Brown Library Special Collections. Smith began tape recording interviews with people whose memories went back many years in early 1974 and stayed with the work until the evening of his fatal heart, attack September 9, 1980, in Colorado City, Texas.

Taylor County Clerk's Office, Taylor County Courthouse. Records of real estate transactions and of matters dealing with the courts were essential to the history.

Telephone interviews, 1996-98. Scores of people who had various roles at the school were interviewed or simply asked for information about various topics

Young, Matt Norvel. *A History of Colleges Established and Controlled by Members of Churches of Christ.* Kansas City: Old Paths Book Club, 1949. For his section on Abilene Christian, Young interviewed A. B. Barret, J. P. Sewell, J. F. Cox, and others who had knowledge of the school since its beginning.

I decided early on not to use footnotes. There would have been page after page of citations from local publications and a great deal of material from my personal memory, reaching back to the fall of 1934. Rather, I have tried to include in the text itself information about my sources for the benefit of future researchers.

Many people helped in getting materials for this book. The outstanding Brown Library staff was most cooperative. A special measure of appreciation goes to Erma Jean Loveland, who has charge of Special Collections, and to her assistant, Denise Inglis. If a piece of information is in existence, these librarians can find it if anybody can. Special thanks goes to Terry Browder, J. E. Smith, Chuck Erwin, and the staff of the Taylor County Clerk in rounding up records from the Taylor County Courthouse.

Thanks to James and Frances Fulbright and Bill Hilton for reading the material, offering suggestions and corrections, and saving me from making some mistakes. And thanks to Dr. Cheryl M. Bacon for providing a fresh pair of eyes of the final proofreading work.

Thanks to Chancellor William J. Teague for especially valuable help in writing the Masten section. Thanks to Glenda Knight for expert work in preparing the manuscript for the editor and to my good wife and partner, Ruth, for reading every line and offering constructive suggestions and encouragement.

To President Royce Money for giving me the challenge to get this job done, I am especially grateful.

To the Office of Marketing and Public Relations, headed by Michelle Morris, and with such stalwarts as Malissa Endsley, Ron Hadfield, and Garner Roberts, thanks for multifaceted help, including selections of pictures – thank you, neighbors.

Finally, to Dr. Charlie Marler for serving as editor of the book. Charlie has read and reread the manuscript, has pointed out important subjects I had left out, has rearranged paragraphs and chapters where the sequence demanded it, and has corrected an occasional misstatement of fact. I say, "Thanks, Charlie, your name as editor on the cover of the book makes it stronger."

JOHN STEVENS
June 1998

CHAPTER ONE

ESTABLISHING THE SCHOOL

Part of Murphy's Law is "Before anything can be done, something else must be done first." So before we arrive in Abilene, we must start with Denton. And before we meet Allen Booker Barret, we must start with Jesse Parker Sewell.

Early in the twentieth century, leaders of Churches of Christ in Texas were busy starting Christian schools. They called the schools "colleges," but they were not really on the college level. At one time or another, small Christian colleges existed at Bonham, Gunter, Lingleville, Lockney, Sabinal, and Terrell. Earlier, Add Ran College in Thorp Spring had gone with the Disciples of Christ when a split occurred in the Campbell-Stone Movement toward the end of the nineteenth century.

In 1904, an opportunity came to start a first-class college with the potential to become a university. The place was Denton. The prime mover was Jesse Parker Sewell. He was a native Tennessean, born in Viola, Tennessee, January 21, 1876. At the age of fifteen, Jesse enrolled in Viola Normal, a teacher training school. The next year, his father moved the family to Corsicana, Texas, where he preached for the church.

Jesse stayed with an uncle in Nashville because eye specialists were working to save his vision. They were successful, and after six months, he joined his family in Texas, where he spent two years in Corsicana, working and getting experience as a preacher. When he was eighteen, he went back to Tennessee to attend the Nashville Bible School operated by David Lipscomb and James A. Harding. His attendance, with some interruptions, spanned a four-year period. The school offered no degrees; however, its students received an excellent education in Bible, literature, history, Greek, philosophy, mathematics, German,

French, Latin, and natural science – a liberal arts education. It became David Lipscomb College in 1918 and David Lipscomb University in 1988.

Sewell was a diligent student and became a lifelong learner. Along the way he accumulated a library consisting of several thousand volumes, which he ultimately donated to the Abilene Christian University library.

Three good things happened to Sewell in his four years in Nashville Bible School. First, he grew into a dynamic, power-ful, and persuasive preacher of the gospel and a great church builder. Second, he met a young woman from Bonham, Texas, by the name of Daisy McQuigg. She was a graduate of Carlton College in Bonham and was furthering her education at Nashville Bible School. Sewell graduated in the spring of 1898, and June 1, 1899, he married Miss McQuigg in Bonham. Third, he determined to do something significant in the field of Christian higher education. As Daisy McQuigg Sewell wrote later in life: "When he and I met in college, I found the ambi-tion of his heart to be to build a college of the highest rank where girls and boys, while being taught the ordinary branches of learning, would be filled with faith in Jehovah."

After marriage to Daisy, Sewell joined the McQuiggs in the grocery business, the largest retail business in Bonham. He also preached for the Church of Christ there for a time. While see-ing it grow, Sewell heard that the church in Sherman, about thirty miles away, was in trouble, in danger of losing its build-ing because of insufficient finances. He offered to make the trip to Sherman each weekend to preach on Sundays free of charge provided the church would agree to use the entire contribution to pay off the debt. The proposal was accepted. Within a year, the debt was paid, and the building was filled each Sunday.

Early in 1902, the Sewells moved to Dallas, where he began preaching for the Pearl and Bryan Church of Christ, an old congregation that had hit upon hard times. Within three years he built up the membership from sixty-five to 350. Although the Sewells rejoiced in the church growth that occurred wher-ever they worked, Daisy McQuigg Sewell declared that their vision of building a Christian college never wavered. While they were living in Dallas, the opportunity of a lifetime, they thought, presented itself. The place was Denton.

Denton would be an ideal location, about thirty miles from Fort Worth to the southwest and Dallas to the southeast. The city had a population of about five thousand; the Church of

Christ had a membership of some 300. Denton was already the home of two thriving state institutions of higher learning – North Texas Normal College, now the University of North Texas, and the College of Industrial Arts, now Texas Woman's University.

A third college, John B. Denton College, had been established by a group of Denton businessmen who were stockholders. Apparently, they soon learned that a college is generally a non-profit business, so it folded, leaving a seven-acre campus and a new brick building. The stockholders gave it free and clear to members of the Church of Christ for a Christian college.

Jesse Sewell took the initiative. As Mrs. Sewell described it, he arose from a sickbed and put together a board of trustees and a faculty. It was named Southwestern Christian College and was slated to open in October 1904. Writing in *The Firm Foundation* of August 2, 1904, Sewell declared that he had been working for six years for the establishment of such a school. This would have taken him back to his student days at Nashville Bible School when he met Daisy McQuigg and the two of them decided that their major goal in life, or, as she expressed it, "our vision, our dream, our castle in the air," was the establishment of a strong Christian college "of the highest rank."

Chairman of the board of the new Southwestern Christian College was William B. Gano of Dallas, a graduate of Harvard Law School and a member of the Pearl and Bryan Church. He was later noted as grandfather of the wealthy and eccentric industrialist and movie maker, Howard R. Hughes Jr. The law firm of Gano, Gano, and Gano was one of the most prestigious in Dallas. Sewell and Gano had worked together in framing the charter for Gunter Bible College in 1901, but apparently both knew that Gunter would not be the place for building a Christian university. Denton, they thought, was the place.

The board offered Sewell the presidency of the new college, but he rejected the offer, agreeing, however, to serve as secretary and treasurer. Daisy Sewell signed on as a teacher of art. The school opened in the fall of 1904 without a president but with the dean of the faculty, a physician, Dr. H. G. Fleming, in charge.

A major blow struck in the middle of the first year. Secretary-treasurer Sewell was diagnosed as a victim of tuberculosis and was advised by his physician to move immediately to a higher and dryer climate. Hence, he resigned and moved to San Angelo in West Texas, leaving Mrs. Sewell to complete her year as a teacher in Southwestern Christian College.

For 1905-06, the board made an agreement with A. G. Freed of Henderson, Tennessee, to lead the college as its president. He was an experienced college administrator and laid great plans for the school, but he had hardly begun his work when his health broke. Freed was seriously ill most of the year, recovered, tried it for another year, but then went back to Tennessee.

So the vision of Southwestern Christian College at Denton as the university that would be supported by members of Churches of Christ in Texas began to grow dim. The firebrand of the movement lay in San Angelo trying to overcome tuberculosis, and the college's president had returned to Tennessee because of health problems. The board was unprepared for the challenge of fund raising, maintaining facilities, faculty hiring, student recruitment, and constituency development necessary to support the operation. A later effort was made to revive the college, but this will be dealt with at the proper time.

One member of the faculty at Southwestern stood ready to pursue the dream of a Christian university elsewhere. He was a young history instructor who had signed on with President Freed in September, but after Freed's illness, he resigned in December to travel west. His name was Allen Booker Barret.

He was born near Covington, Tennessee, July 15, 1879. After graduation at age sixteen from the public schools of his home county, he enrolled as a student in West Tennessee Christian College, which in 1897 became Georgia Robertson Christian College and is today Freed-Hardeman University, in Henderson, Tennessee. After three and a half years there, he transferred to Nashville Bible School. Along the way he availed himself of a good liberal arts education but no degree. The absence of a college degree never seemed to stand in his way because he served as president of three colleges and taught Bible courses at the University of Texas, which waived the faculty degree requirement because of his broad educational background.

At age twenty-two, he married Exie Carroll. A year later, 1902, the Barrets moved to Texas, where he could do the work of an evangelist while living in Denison. He chose Denison probably because, in addition to having a strong Church of

Christ, it was a busy railroad center. From there he could catch a train to anywhere. At that time an evangelist had four transportation options for traveling: afoot, by horseback, horse-and-vehicle, or by rail. For longer than local jaunts, rail was much preferred.

While Barret lived in Denison, his friend Charles Heber Roberson paid him a visit in the summer of 1903. One day, while they were riding in a buggy, the conversation shifted to starting a Christian school. Barret suggested West Texas as a likely place for the new school. Roberson agreed. However, another opportunity arose that temporarily sidetracked the West Texas idea.

To continue their work of evangelism, the Barrets moved from Denison to Dallas and placed membership with the Pearl and Bryan church where Jesse P. Sewell was preaching. Thus Barret came into contact with the Denton opportunity. It appeared that this might be the opportunity for which he was looking. He could work with Sewell in building Southwestern Christian College.

Barret took time out from his evangelism in September 1904 to serve for a limited time as financial agent for Southwestern Christian College, which opened that month. In the fall of 1905, with the coming of A. G. Freed to the presidency of Southwestern Christian College, he had an opportunity to join the faculty at Denton as a professor of history. He eagerly accepted because he had studied under Freed at Georgia Robertson Christian College and looked forward to teaching under his leadership.

Then came Freed's disabling illness and the consequent floundering of Southwestern Christian. No doubt, the troubled situation stirred Barret to act on the discussion he and Charles Roberson had had a couple of years earlier in 1903. The sum of that conversation pointed Barret and Roberson to West Texas as an area in which a Christian college should be located.

The Charles Roberson who played a significant role in starting Abilene Christian University was born in Robersonville, North Carolina, February 28, 1879. He was thirteen when the Roberson family moved to Tennessee. At nineteen he enrolled in Georgia Robertson Christian College, where he met Allen Barret and became his lifelong friend. Although Barret left Georgia Robertson and transferred to Nashville Bible School before earning a degree, Roberson stayed at Georgia Robertson and earned both bachelor's and master's degrees. He then taught and served as principal of a Tennessee school for four years before moving to Abilene in the summer of 1906.

After Roberson's 1903 visit to Texas, some changes occurred in the life of each man. In Texas, Barret found the opportunity in the field of Christian education for which he had been looking. Hence, it appeared that he would have to look no farther west than Denton for a Christian college to work for and serve. Meanwhile, in Tennessee, Roberson married Miss Eudora McCorkle, in January 1905, so he was not necessarily interested in moving west.

Pivotal fate, however, dealt a blow to each man. In Texas, the new Christian college situation for Barret was not working out because of the serious illness of Southwestern's President Freed, and in Tennessee, Roberson's bride became ill and died in late 1905. So both men again looked westward.

Barret resigned his position with Southwestern at midyear and readied himself to look for a school location. Two friends of Barret were interested in talking with him. Price Billingsley had put together a congregation of the Church of Christ in Abilene and believed it would be a good location, and Jesse P. Sewell was ready to go all out for a Christian college in San Angelo. Barret decided to visit three West Texas towns, all served by railroads – Abilene and two towns on the Colorado River, San Angelo and Ballinger.

In Abilene, Barret met with church leaders and leading businessmen. He was well received but made no commitments pending completion of his rounds. In *Like Stars Shining Brightly*, Max Leach and Don Morris recalled Barret's vivid description of what happened in connection with San Angelo and Ballinger which left Abilene as the choice. Barret rode the train from Abilene to San Angelo. He was in a passenger car attached to the rear of a freight train. En route, he stepped out on the coupling platform at the back of the car to get a good look at the wide open spaces, and the West Texas wind blew his hat off.

Upon arriving in San Angelo, he thought that it would be improper to go bareheaded to a meeting with a group of West Texas ranchers and business leaders, but he had only enough money to buy a cap. Thinking that would be better than no headgear at all, he made the purchase. He described his appearance before the committee of businessmen and ranchers: "All the time I was talking to the committee, I had the feeling of a lack of warmth there. That is, they were definitely cool to me, and to my proposition. I think that they must have thought that a man that didn't know any better than to wear a cap wouldn't know enough to run a school."

Years later, Mrs. Sewell wrote: "The first year we were in San Angelo, Brother A. B. Barret, a college mate, moved by a desire to build a Christian college, came to see us. He and my husband presented to the Chamber of Commerce our plans. That city did not choose to take advantage of the opportunity. Mr. Sewell was sorely disappointed."

After the cool reception in San Angelo, Barret stopped in Ballinger on the way back to Abilene. He was received well, but he thought the drinking water tasted so bad that no college could prosper with such a drawback. So Abilene won his favor.

When Allen B. Barret returned to Abilene after the visits to San Angelo and Ballinger, he set to work with determination to build a Christian school. He found a congregation of the Church of Christ small in number but led by an unusually strong group of individuals who were anxious to develop a school. The church had been organized and meeting regularly for only three years. Some twenty years earlier the church had suffered division, and the people who were known as the Church of Christ, or "conservatives," or "non-progressives," simply did not function as a church for a while after the division.

A young couple, Albert F. and Cornelia McDonald, moved from East Texas to a farm in Tuscola, south of Abilene, in 1889. They were members of the Church of Christ. Soon, they and two families from Buffalo Gap began worshiping together in south Taylor County in a blacksmith shop. In 1890, McDonald bought 160 acres of land in west Abilene along Catclaw Creek and the Texas and Pacific Railroad. Soon the family moved to Abilene to live near good schools for their children. They found other members of the Church of Christ and started having church services in their home. Occasionally, a visiting minister preached for them.

In 1903, Price Billingsley came to Abilene. He was a powerful preacher, although not schooled as were Barret, Sewell, and Roberson. In fact, he wrote about himself, "Never attended school a day." He was described as a man who lifted himself by his own bootstraps. He was brilliant, eloquent, opinionated, indefatigable. Beginning January 1, 1901, at age twenty-three, he kept diaries, journals, and notes of his actions, words, and thoughts, eventually some 720 handwritten volumes by 1957.

He gave these volumes to the archives of the Brown Library at Abilene Christian University in 1958, along with his library of more than 1,000 volumes. He lived in Abilene from 1904 to 1911 and died in 1959 at age eighty-two.

Billingsley's first gospel meeting in Abilene – the one that resulted in the organization of what is now the University Church of Christ – took place in September 1903. A. F. McDonald made arrangements for a meeting house. The meeting opened Monday, September 14, and ran through September 27. Good interest was shown. The recorder for the church, Dabney Harvey, wrote that after the Billingsley meeting, on the first Sunday in October 1903, "a body of Christians agreed to keep house for the Lord." They met on that day in the county courthouse and by the next Sunday had, according to Harvey, "bought us a house" to be used as a meeting place. On the second Sunday in November, elders and deacons were chosen. The elders were J. W. Childers, H. E. Myers, and a Brother Roberts. Deacons were I. E. Mauldin and Dabney Harvey.

Harvey's statement that the church "bought a house" is somewhat mysterious. Dean Walter H. Adams, in his history of the University Church of Christ, said he found no record at the courthouse of a transfer of property to the church. It is known that the house was at South Sixth and Chestnut streets, or, as Hugh Cosby nails it down in his *History of Abilene*, 541 Chestnut.

Courthouse records show that J. W. Childers bought the property in 1904, filed his deed for record in 1906, and deeded it to his wife as her separate property in 1910. At her death in 1929, it was left to her son, W. H. Childers, and, in 1937 it was acquired by the Salvation Army. The Salvation Army added a new chapel to the property and used it for the next fifty years. It was sold to the First State Bank in 1984, and the space was cleared to make room for the bank's drive-in tellers. The sale to the bank made it possible for the Salvation Army to launch a campaign to build a larger and more up-to-date facility in another location.

Apparently, J. W. Childers, one of the elders of the new congregation, bought the property and made it available to the church pending a permanent arrangement. The interior walls of the six-room residence were removed, thus making a small auditorium available. By the time Barret came along, it was nearing capacity, which may help explain why, in his deal with

Barret, Childers was insistent on getting a permanent meeting place for the church on the campus of the college. The church was meeting in his property, which he could convert to a rental residence if he could make an arrangement for the church to meet elsewhere.

A. B. Barret, thus, was dealing with a small but growing church in Abilene. Mrs. Mary Niblack, daughter of the McDonalds, wrote that the church started with about twenty members but quickly grew to 100. Barret specifically cited such "wide-awake" men as McDonald, Col. Childers, and an up-and-coming banker by the name of W. H. "Henry" Free.

Billingsley wrote about the rapidly growing Abilene church in his diary in June 1905 and about "preaching day and night," "baptizing most every day," "doing my best preaching and work," and services that were "grander each succeeding time." July 2 he noted that the meeting had closed with "30 additions." He was paid $95. Billingsley wrote, "all things good and pleasant."

The diaries of Billingsley also tell the story of the tremendous amount of work he and other preachers were doing in the area surrounding Abilene. Although the Church of Christ in Abilene was making a new start after moribund years, nearby communities – Anson, Albany, Merkel, Trent, Sweetwater, Nugent, Clyde, and a number of others – had thriving congregations that apparently had avoided the problems that had afflicted Abilene. Their support meant much in the founding of a Christian school in Abilene. Billingsley's influence with all of these churches and his friendship with Barret undoubtedly helped open some doors. His diary entry for January 31, 1906, reads simply, "Barret is making things happen here."

However, an early threat to the unborn school was a brief but sharp disagreement between Barret and Billingsley. Something that Barret said or did caused Billingsley to accuse him of being a "digressive" – a theological liberal – which in a conservative fellowship was almost the kiss of death. But after fuller discussion, Billingsley changed his mind about the matter and came out with a public retraction and, in effect, an apology, published in Joe Warlick's *The Gospel Guide* of September 1, 1906. His diary entry for August 15, 1906, reads, "Trouble settled between Barret and myself today."

Barret did not simply shrug off the Billingsley criticisms. In a letter to *The Gospel Advocate*, January 1907, he wrote:

> By this time I am sure that the brethren have learned that the

reports that went out about the school at Abilene just before
our opening were false. It seems very strange to me that apparently good men would circulate such foolish and unfounded
things about our work here. Those things have been sifted, and
the uninformed brethren have access to the proof of the incor-
rectness of those reports. Of course they injured the work some
and prejudiced some against the school. But we opened with
good attendance, and there has hardly been a week but what we
enrolled new students ....

Barret, the twenty-seven-year-old preacher with a dream an
older man might have been too cautious to follow, was the ideal
person to approach the church and the business community in
Abilene with such a proposal. He was devoted to the cause of
Christ, completely serious in his purpose, and he had a keen
sense of humor and a booming laugh. At the opening of the
second session of the school, September 10, 1907, one of the
speakers at chapel was E. B. Bynum, prominent Abilene businessman and a leader of the Chamber of Commerce. Bynum's
comments showed the warm feelings of the business community: "Fifteen months ago I was introduced to the president of
this educational institution. I liked him ... He is a short, ducky
sort of fellow, like myself. He has not only looked good, but
made good." Max Leach interviewed Barret in 1949. He was
broken in health but could still enjoy a good chuckle. For
instance, when the conversation got around to his deceased
parents, J. H. and Bella Barret and the contributions they had
made to his character, he said, "I got too much of the human
side." When he died in 1951, his longtime friend and co-worker, Charles Roberson, wrote about him for *The Gospel Advocate,*
mentioning his enjoyment of hunting, fishing, and camping.

The rapport established with Abilene people enabled Barret
in the very beginning of his West Texas work to write a glow-
ing report to *The Firm Foundation*: "I have been here two
weeks and have succeeded splendidly."

This brings the story to Col. John W. Childers, who played
a significant role in the early days of the Abilene Church of
Christ, Abilene Christian University, and in the long-term relationship of the University Church of Christ with the campus.
Childers was a land speculator. He bought and sold property.
One needs only to consult the deed records at the Taylor
County courthouse in Abilene to see how many transactions he
was involved in through the years. Although in 1906 he had
been in Abilene only five years, he was already recognized as

one of the leading citizens of the community with the ability to move into a new situation and quickly become known and influential.

Col. Childers had an interesting background. Born in Williamstown, in Grant County, Kentucky, September 19, 1841, he came to Texas with his parents when he was fourteen, settling in McKinney, north of Dallas. When he was eighteen, he began farming for himself in Wood County, of which Quitman is the county seat. He was twenty years old when the Civil War broke out. He served in the Confederate Army – Company K, 5th Texas Cavalry, Sibley's Brigade – and became sergeant of his company. The war ended before his twenty-fourth birthday, so he hardly had time to become an actual "colonel," but he was thereafter respectfully called by that honorary title.

During the war he married Martha Gunter. The year was 1864; he was twenty-three; she was sixteen. After the war they resided in Wood County, where he farmed from 1865 to 1874, and then in Cooke County, of which Gainesville is the county seat. There he farmed and bought and sold land from 1874 to 1901. In 1898, he was elected by voters in Cooke County to represent them in the Texas legislature. He attended the regular session of the twenty-sixth Legislature from January 19 to May 27, 1899, and a called session from January 23 to February 21, 1900. After his one term in the Texas legislature, he and his wife moved to Abilene in 1901. He was sixty years of age.

The next year a tragedy occurred in the Childers family. Their marriage had been blessed by six children – three sons and three daughters. In March 1902, their youngest son, J. W. Jr., born in 1869, was involved in a shooting scrape in Silver City, New Mexico. He killed prominent attorney Thomas Heflin. The case was tried in Las Cruces, and Childers was acquitted. A juror was reported as having said after the trial: "We did not discuss the evidence. We thought he was guilty, but we were told that he was a very rich man and was going to live here, and that all the ladies in the courtroom were friends of his wife and had come to see him acquitted, and that the judge and the lawyers wanted us to acquit him."

Later, young Childers was accused of making an attempt on the life of Thomas J. Mabry, editor and publisher in Clovis, New Mexico, and was killed by the town marshal while resisting arrest. This story is probably irrelevant to the current discussion, except to point out that members of the Childers family were considered wealthy and influential.

In 1907, Col. Childers left Abilene for a few years and moved to New Mexico, where he became the first mayor of Texico. In 1910, he was a member of the convention drawing up a constitution for that soon-to-be state. In that convention he was described as "one of the irreconcilables" but at the same time as "a man of integrity." In other words, he was not always easy to deal with, but he was not ignored or overlooked. He was a large man, striking in appearance.

Reuben Heflin, a relative of the lawyer whom J. W. Childers Jr., had killed in Silver City, wrote an account of the constitutional convention. He said that Col. Childers sat immediately in front of him and was somewhat concerned to be sitting with his back toward a relative of the man his son had killed. However, Delegate Heflin, who described Childers as "an elderly man of powerful build," added that "Delegate Childers bore an excellent reputation and was considered a man of integrity."

Two or three years after helping New Mexico gain admission to the Union as a state, Col. and Mrs. Childers moved back to Abilene. When he died on July 13, 1918, the *Abilene Reporter* began its news story with these words: "Colonel J. W. Childers, for seventeen years a leading citizen of Abilene died at the family residence in Abilene Saturday afternoon, July 13, 1918, at five o'clock, after an illness of five years' duration."

Now to return to 1906 and Barret. Col. Childers owned a property on North First Street, bounded on the west by Graham Street, on the north by North Second, and on the east by Victoria Street, some five acres of land, "more or less." In the middle of the block was the Childers home, a large, comfortable, story-and-a-half house. The value of the property was set at $9,000. Barret asked him if he would consider reducing the price and selling it to the school.

The Colonel agreed to sell it to "trustees of the Church of Christ" for $6,000 to be paid to him and $750 to be paid to the church. In effect, Col. Childers was donating $3,000 – $2,250 to the school and $750 to the church by way of Barret. Because there was no federal income tax in 1906, the question of how much could be claimed as a charitable donation was not a factor. The fact is that the colonel simply reduced the price of his property by $3,000. Barret counted the sum of $2,250 as a donation. He was required to pay $750 to the church. No further mention is made of this $750. Possibly, the $750 enabled the church to restore the property at 541 Chestnut to residential status so that the Childers family could keep it as investment property.

Hugh Cosby's 1955 *History of Abilene* was well researched on most points. He had access to the memory of Henry Free, who was treasurer of the church in 1906, and to Don Morris, who was careful with the facts of history. But when Cosby wrote this paragraph he had bad information: "After Childers Classical Institute was founded, the original church house was sold for $1,000. This money was given to the school with the provision that the school chapel would be used for the congregation's place of worship."

This could not have been the case because the church had never owned the property, and in fact it was not sold. It remained in the Childers family for three more decades. It is altogether possible that the church made a contribution to the school to help pay for utilities and maintenance, inasmuch as the church was receiving free use of the auditorium and classrooms, but the donation was not a requirement. As will be seen, the original deed to the property stipulated the right of the church to meet on the campus, and the church did so, on the old campus and then on the new campus, for nearly a half-century before opening its own house of worship in 1952.

Back to the school: for the nearly five acres of land and his spacious home, Col. Childers required no down payment. True, the deed mentioned "three thousand dollars cash paid receipt of which is hereby acknowledged," but that was the amount Childers was "donating" in reducing the price. For the balance of $6,000 he agreed to accept six $1,000 notes with one note to be paid each January 1 for six years, beginning the first day of January 1908. Hence, Barret would have nearly two years to raise the $1,000 for his first payment, a generous deal for the soon-to-be school. Interest would be at the rate of eight percent per year on the unpaid balance, and interest due would be paid annually. The deed makes no mention of the $750 Barret was to pay to the church, probably because that was a side agreement. It was a good deal for Barret. It was also a good deal for the church, which was outgrowing its small church house on Chestnut, and could, as soon as an auditorium was built, start meeting on the campus.

In a *Firm Foundation* article, February 27, 1906, Barret mentioned some of the conditions accompanying the transaction: first, a high-grade literary college would be established in which the Bible would always be taught; second, the Church of Christ worshiping in Abilene would be privileged to hold its meetings in the college auditorium, as long as it should choose to do so; third, the name of the school would be "Childers Classical Institute"; fourth, trustees would be members of the Church of Christ "in good standing, who worship as the Bible directs"; and fifth, a "sufficient" building would be constructed for school purposes, and when completed it would be turned over to A. B. Barret and his brother, W. S. Barret. They would operate the school, keep up the property, pay all expenses, and share in whatever money might remain.

The deed was executed February 12, 1906. It contained the stipulations Barret had mentioned plus some strengthening; for example, where Barret's article said the name would be "Childers Classical Institute," the deed stipulated that it would always wear that name and in the event it should be determined advisable to incorporate under the laws of the State of Texas, the name of the corporation would be "Childers Classical Institute."

Another requirement of the deed was that the property with its improvements "shall be kept insured for the benefit of said J. W. Childers in an amount which shall at all times equal the amount of unpaid purchase money due said J. W. Childers." This would later be seen as a significant requirement. The building would be built of brick or stone and would be ready by September 15, 1906. The deed made clear that the ownership of the property would be contingent upon observing the conditions listed.

So Professor Barret had himself a campus. It was actually just a good-sized city block, less than a grandiose arrangement, but people were proud of it.

Nothing was said, at least in print, about the principal shortcoming of the location: it was across the street from the main line of the Texas and Pacific Railroad. Long freight trains hauling merchandise between the Atlantic and Pacific coasts rumbled through at intervals throughout the day and night. Passenger trains ran frequently, too. In the early twentieth century, there were few automobiles and no truck lines. Roads were mostly unimproved and narrow. The railroad was supreme. Classes at Childers Classical Institute frequently had to stop while a train passed. Nevertheless, great teachers and outstanding students were drawn to the tiny campus from 1906 to 1929, and the results were very good indeed.

Professor Barret also had himself a board of trustees. Before the execution of the deed, he had secured the agreement of five respected church leaders to serve as trustees of "the Church of Christ." They were to receive and hold the property and to see to it that the terms of the transaction were faithfully kept. Two of the trustees were from the Abilene Church of Christ: A. F. McDonald and W. H. Free. The other three were J. P. Sharp of Merkel, J. H. Deaver of Buffalo Gap, and J. S. Manly of Peters Chapel in Nugent. They constituted the entity to which J. W. and Martha Childers could deed their property.

The trustee group was obviously a temporary entity. Inasmuch as Churches of Christ are strictly congregational in nature, with no organization beyond or above the local congregation, no group of five men from four different congregations could actually be "Trustees of the Church of Christ." So they functioned as an ad hoc group which would hold the property until an adequate brick building could be erected to serve as an administration and classroom facility, with an auditorium large enough to accommodate daily chapel for students and faculty and regular assemblies of the Abilene Church of Christ. Once these goals were accomplished, McDonald, Free, Sharp, Deaver, and Manly would turn over the property to the Barret brothers, and they would run the school. The trustees of "the Church of Christ," having turned the school over, were to disband, to be succeeded by a Board of Trustees for the school. Barrett implied this arrangement in his *Firm Foundation* article.

The seven months between Monday, February 12, and Monday, September 10, 1906, when Childers Classical Institute opened, was a period of an amazing amount of activity. Money had to be raised among members of the Abilene Church of Christ, Abilene business people, church members of outlying towns, and the brotherhood at large. In addition to the required brick building, employment of a faculty was a priority. Students had to be recruited. A catalog was needed. A charter would be necessary. A corporation must be established. A Board of Trustees for the school would have to be available when the time came to receive the campus from the trustees of the Church of Christ.

The first person recruited for the faculty was Barret's dependable friend Charles Roberson. As soon as Roberson could close his school year in Tennessee and move to Abilene, he came. His bride of less than a year had died just a few months before. He was ready to move. He would be in Texas three years before he would marry Miss Katherine Moyers of Ferris, Texas. Roberson arrived in Abilene in time to make some trips with Barret, soliciting funds and students. Owning bachelor's and master's degrees and a record as a teacher and a principal of a school in Tennessee for the past four years, he contributed significantly to the preparatory phase.

Traveling by train and horse-and-buggy, Barret, sometimes Mrs. Barret, Roberson, and perhaps W. S. Barret, although no further mention of him occurs after the *Firm Foundation* article, secured gifts from 195 individuals in Nugent, Thorp Spring, Merkel, Colorado City, Snyder, Hamlin, Rule, Trent, Sweetwater, Loraine, Roscoe, Dunn, Westbrook, Sagerton, Rochester, Haskell, Stamford, Avoca, Anson, Clyde, Baird, Putnam, Moran, Cottonwood, Rising Star, Granbury, Weatherford, and Fort Worth. Given the modes of transport available, obviously, they took on a difficult task to cover that much ground and see that many people in such a short time with so many other things to be attended to. Also, for every donor, they must have encountered a number of non-donors and "maybe later" responses.

The largest single cash gift from outside of Abilene was $250. One gift was valued at $500. It consisted of two lots in Merkel. There is no record of how much money the lots actually brought when they were sold. Total cash gifts from outside of Abilene amounted to $3,500. In addition, members of the Abilene church subscribed $5,000, including the $2,250 property gift by Col. Childers. The Abilene business community came in with sufficient pledges and gifts to complete the fundraising needed for the brick building required by terms of the Childers deed.

"On a cold, damp day in March 1906, the basement for the administration building . . . was dug." Thus began a story in *The Optimist* some twenty-three years after the fact. The author of the story was Paul Southern, editor of the paper. He had the opportunity of interviewing several people who were present when the digging took place. T. G. Moore of Abilene was contractor for the building, which cost approximately $8,000, but that did not include finishing the basement. Six months after construction was begun, the building was far enough along that school opened September 10. Three classrooms out of the ten were ready by opening day. The auditorium was usable, equipped with 150 opera chairs, which left space for fifty or so folding chairs so that 200 people could be seated "in a tight squeeze." The other classrooms were opened one by one; the basement was left unfinished until 1911.

Dimensions of this first administration building were forty-eight by forty-eight feet. This would amount to 2,304 square feet of floor space on each of two floors, or a total of 4,608 square feet, a small building for its many functions. Henry Eli Speck arrived on the campus in 1912 to begin his work as a faculty member and dean of the college. He later reported that his first involuntary exclamation was "Do you call this a college?" By that time the school was known as Abilene Christian College, but Dean Speck said he could understand why the students referred to it as "the Abilene Chicken Coop."

Of course, there was no such thing as air conditioning. On hot days, with all windows open, a long freight train cruising through town about 300 feet away could pretty well shut down classes. A writer in *The Optimist* gave a vivid description:

> To the Texas and Pacific railroad goes the honor of disturbing more classes than any other contraption in west Abilene. Hundreds of students have been saved the embarrassment of saying, "I don't know," by the drawn-out whistle of a mile-long freight train. For many years, counting the cars in a freight train served as the chief entertainment for bored psychology students. Many a night's sleep has been punctuated by the sharp blasts of a fleeting passenger train.

Surely, the little "chicken coop" administration building was modest, but to A. B. Barret it was grand. It was incorporated into a much larger administration building erected in 1919, but the entire structure was burned to the ground in 1929. Thousands of bricks from the burned structure were moved to the new campus in 1929 and stored in an out-of-the-way room in Bennett Gymnasium. When the magnificent Biblical Studies Building was erected in 1989, President William J. Teague came up with a plan of allowing friends of the university to donate to the cause by designating memorial bricks in honor of people they wished to recognize. Two pillars of these bricks with names attached can be seen today in the Hall of Servants of the Biblical Studies Building.

A day before registration at the new college, Charlie McLaughlin, from Dickens County, Texas, arrived with his father in a buggy and was told by Charles Roberson, registrar and secretary-treasurer, that because he was on hand he might as well go ahead and register, which he did. Thus he was the first student to enroll in the new institution. He attended two years before transferring to the University of Texas. McLaughlin was disappointed when his CCI credits were not accepted for transfer to the University of Texas because the young school was not accredited and not actually a college, but he was a lifelong supporter of Abilene Christian. Two daughters – Estelle, who married Robert Johnston, and Charlotte who married Harry Whitlow – graduated from the college. His oldest daughter – Wanda, who married Russell Seacat – attended Texas Tech, but taught for a while in Abilene Christian High School. The youngest – Wynetta, who married J. Q. Carter, attended ACU for three semesters and finished her degree at Texas Tech.

Monday, September 10, 1906, the prodigious labors of A. B. Barret and associates had brought about a school. Just seven months had elapsed since J. W. and Martha Childers had signed a deed conveying their home and a city block of property encompassing it to "trustees of the Church of Christ" for the purpose of establishing a school. In compliance with conditions outlined in the deed instrument, a brick building had been constructed for multi-purpose usage – administrative offices, classrooms, and auditorium. It was unfinished, but it could be used. Some twenty-five students registered Monday.

Opening chapel was conducted Tuesday morning, September 11, at ten o'clock. An overflow crowd of more than 200 was on hand. W. H. Free led the opening hymn, "All Hail the Power of Jesus' Name." This hymn has been used at every opening since that time. Free himself led the song every year until 1948 except one when it was necessary for him to be away from the city. President Barret spoke, stating his firm conviction that "What man has done, man can do." Charles Roberson spoke on the need to stress fundamentals in educating the whole person. Representatives from the city of Abilene welcomed the school to the community.

An unusually well-qualified faculty was on hand. President Barret taught Bible. Charles Roberson was secretary-treasurer and taught classes in English, mathematics, and spelling. A University of Texas graduate, James Franklin Cox taught mathematics and science. He was a few months older than Barret and Roberson. He had two years' experience as president of Lingleville Christian College, as well as teaching experience in Texas public schools. Edwin F. Hoover, with a bachelor's degree from Trinity College, Durham, North Carolina, now Duke University, offered languages: Greek, Latin, French, and Spanish. Evelyn Carroll, a sister of Mrs. Barret, taught primary and elementary grades. Mamie Rattan was a teacher of history, English, and Latin. She resigned at midyear because of low enrollment. Lucretia Creath, a business school graduate, taught the intermediate students and commercial subjects.

Looking back on that first year, James F. Cox, while president of Abilene Christian College thirty-three years later, described the first faculty as "an unusually strong one for the times .... Few institutions of higher learning ever had better faculties for taking care of their first prospective student bodies."

Barret and Roberson and the splendid faculty must have been quite disappointed by the first-day registration of only twenty-five. However, before the year was too far gone, other students arrived, pushing the total first-year figure to eighty-five. Even that was not high enough to permit things to go as planned. Cox said, "... it became necessary for the president, who was financing the school, to pay the faculty and other running expenses largely out of his own pocket." Furthermore, the president found it expedient to quit teaching classes so that he could devote his full time to raising money to keep the school solvent. That was not an unusual step for a college president to take.

The first student body, although small in number, came from families who were destined to be represented in the school from that time to the present. Although Childers Classical Institute was an academy, not a college, it was no ordinary school. For example, Otis Marion Reynolds arrived on campus November 1, 1906, and enrolled in the first class. He was twenty-two years old. O. M. had not had much opportunity to go to school. He said that when he enrolled in Childers Classical Institute he did not know "a verb from an adverb, an adjective from a hole in the ground." He studied at Childers for three years, during which time he said that he served as "official janitor" and "official song leader." Later on, he was a student for another year. Although he did not intend to become a preacher when he first enrolled, he developed into a very successful one; hence, he referred to himself as the first student of Abilene Christian to become a full-time preacher. His children, grandchildren, and great grandchildren have attended the university through the years.

Roy Estes enrolled in 1906. In all probability, at least one member of the Estes family has studied at the university every year since 1906. Four members of the Cranfill family were in the student body, and the Cranfill name has been well represented at Abilene Christian through the years. The McDonald family was represented by Kirby, Mary, and Eula. In succeeding years other members of the family of A. F. McDonald matriculated in the school, and during all of the years since, if the names were collected of the McDonalds, Niblacks, Pruitts, and Martins, among others, there would be a large aggregation. Leslie Hays began a dynasty. So did Lon Harvey. Viola, Wilner, and Earl Zellner represented a strong Christian heritage. Ada Sikes began a tradition among Sikes family members.

Albert Moore, son of board chairman T. G. Moore, was a 1906 student. Twenty-one years later, a niece of Albert, Ann Arnold, enroledl and two years later married Arthur M. "Tonto" Coleman, a 1928 graduate. Tonto Coleman became one of America's best-known and respected figures in the field of university athletics. He was in great demand as a speaker nationwide. He concluded his active career with service as commissioner of the Southeastern Conference. Children and grandchildren of Ann and Tonto Coleman have continued in the Abilene Christian tradition.

An outstanding member of the class of 1906-7 was Beulah Cain. She was born in 1880; hence, she was twenty-six when she enrolled in Childers. She attended only one semester before dropping out of school because she had a boyfriend back home in Cottonwood, Texas. They had been courting since she was nineteen. When she was forty-four, they married. He was Major Andrew Arvin. In 1980, on her 100th birthday, she was a special guest at chapel in Moody Coliseum on the campus of Abilene Christian University. She explained to members of the student body that she and Major Arvin took so long to marry because they both worked and did not have time for it. She was in high spirits and excellent health. Her trademark was waving a white lace handkerchief. She was a crowd pleaser, and the students loved her. In subsequent years, when Mrs. Arvin paid her annual visit to chapel, the coliseum was a scene of students waving white handkerchiefs with her. The students drove her around and into Moody Coliseum in a golf cart, called a "Beulah Buggy." She died at the age of one hundred eight in 1988. Her husband preceded her in death at age ninety-six in 1977.

The students in 1906 and later became a major factor in the survival of the school with Spartan facilities. Students enjoyed the school. At least, the great majority did. Some did not. In his catalog issued at the beginning of the second year, President Barret wrote,

> The past year was our first, but we consider it well spent. We enrolled quite an excellent body of students who did much good work. Of course we lost some pupils during the year. Two were expelled, some quit because they were not willing to conform to the regulations of the Institute, others were compelled to return home.

But for the most part great camaraderie developed. For example, when the administration building was not ready to be connected to city water, members of the student body formed a bucket brigade each morning to relay buckets of water from a well on the Ed S. Hughes property about two blocks from the campus. Guy Scruggs, in his 1944 thesis, "The History of Abilene Christian College," characterized this as "rollicking fun." With or without luxuries, students enjoyed the campus, and parents were glad to send their children to the academy. The capable teachers were better trained than the average public school faculty of the time. Daily chapel brought students and faculty together. Musical programs, athletic contests, dramatics, and visiting lecturers prevented boredom.

Young women were required to wear uniforms. "The Institute has adopted a beautiful gray uniform for the girls," according to the catalog. "The boys will likely select theirs this fall. The girls' uniform, complete, will not cost over $15.00." Parents, if not the students, appreciated the economy, but no record is found that the boys ever got around to selecting their uniforms.

With the many blessings, along came problems. The money shortage never disappeared, but money was not the only problem. In fact, in its first year of operations, problems plagued the little school. Price Billingsley's criticism of Barret had worked out amicably, although scars remained. Billingsley was present for the opening of school and was pleased. Later, he served on the faculty.

Then a problem arose that caused J. S. Manly, a key member of the trustees, to refuse to continue serving. Manly had made the largest cash donation to Barret's initial fund drive among congregations outside of Abilene. He was a respected elder of the church at Nugent, which was the leading congregation in the drive to support the building of a Christian school in Abilene. Borden Manly Jr., a grandson of J. S. Manly, says members of the family do not know what the problem was, and neither Barret nor Manly left a written record explaining the situation that developed.

However, based on interviews with Barret thirty-seven years later, Norvel Young understood that the problem arose over an issue that very well could have been avoided. Young, after writing that "a difference arose between the president and one of the original trustees," explained in a footnote to his *History of Christian Colleges*: "At the first formal meeting of the board, Barret had all the former actions of the board rescinded. Then a motion was made to accept the charter with the five trustees listed. The objecting trustee was omitted from this new list and thus was excluded from the board."

Seemingly, from this clear language, although other problems may have existed between Manly and Barret, the deciding factor was the business of rescinding all former actions of the board. What would this do to the solemn commitments the board had made to Col. and Mrs. Childers? What effect would it have on the hundreds of people who had made donations to the trustees for a specific purpose? It does seem that the wording was unfortunate.

Granted, the "trustees of the Church of Christ" had to be nothing more than a temporary group – an ad hoc situation. Here were five men, members of four different congregations, calling themselves "trustees of the Church of Christ." Who gave them the right to be "trustees of the Church of Christ"? With the congregational form of church government in which no hierarchy above the local congregation is recognized, the only Church of Christ of which anybody can be a trustee is the congregation to which he belongs.

No doubt, Barret understood this. He implied it in his letter to *The Firm Foundation*, February 27, 1906, when he said that when a suitable building was erected and the school was ready to start, the trustees would turn the property over to him and his brother to operate. Then, as the case turned out, he would need a Board of Trustees for the school, and that would be the continuing, self-perpetuating body. All he needed temporarily was an entity to which Col. Childers could deed his property for school purposes.

Maybe Manly understood that, and maybe he did not. But one can see that as a responsible businessman and church leader, he might have thought that rescinding all actions of the ad hoc board would repudiate the arrangement with Col. Childers regarding the kind of a school required, the qualifications of board members, and other parts of the agreement on the basis of which the property had been deeded to the trustees.

Nearly a century later, it seems that a better choice of words would have been to "ratify and affirm" all actions of the previous board. That board had done nothing that needed repudiation or rescission. Clearly, the principals needed to draw a line of demarcation between the temporary board and the permanent board, but repudiation, in retrospect, appears unnecessary.

Barret had apparently from the beginning expected the five-man group to reconstitute themselves as the continuing board of Childers Classical Institute. Hence, the same men would govern the school. Four of them agreed to continue, and they did continue. But Manly was not one of the group. Maybe he did not choose to serve, or maybe, because of the controversy, he was not invited. At any rate, he was not on the new board. Some historical writings about Abilene Christian University mention the "original trustees," leaving off J. S. Manly, but the fact is he was a member of the actual original board. That board played such an important role in the founding of the university that he should not be forgotten. Regardless of the cause of Manly's discontinuance, members of his family have served as faithful patrons of the school through the years.

Manly was replaced by T. G. Moore, who was elected first chairman of the new board and served faithfully for five years. J. P. Sharp was chairman pro tem of the first meeting. When the newly designated board had its first meeting November 3, 1906, the agenda called for these items of business: Rescinding all former actions of the board "so far as trustees, etc. and begin anew so far as proceedings of business," adoption of a charter, naming officers of the board, deeding the property to the corporation as soon as the charter could be filed with the Secretary of State, insuring the property, and other business.

When the trustee problem had been dealt with, a considerably more ominous one arose. School had been underway only nine weeks when a disturbing letter was sent to each of the five "trustees of the Church of Christ." The letter was from the prestigious Abilene law firm of Leggett and Kirby. The November 19, 1906, letter was not addressed to the trustees of

Childers Classical Institute but to the original "trustees of the Church of Christ":

> Col. J. W. Childers has retained us to institute suit for the purpose of canceling the deed made by him and his wife ... because of the breach of some of the conditions named in said deed. We have stated to Col. Childers that we very much dislike to bring a suit which will involve this matter in litigation, and he has finally consented that we may take the matter up with the trustees named in said deed to ascertain if the matter can be adjusted .... We are also requested to say to you that if you join in any conveyance of this land to any person or corporation, that we are instructed to hold you personally liable for any damages which may accrue thereby.

What had gone wrong? For a young school to cross wires with a significant donor was undesirable. The school had just lost from its trusteeship its largest cash donor from outside of Abilene. Now the man who had made the campus possible on favorable terms was threatening a lawsuit. Meanwhile, a college building had been constructed, a faculty employed, and students recruited. The campus was bustling with activity. The credibility of the new school and, to a certain extent, of the Churches of Christ over a wide area of West Texas was at stake.

When Max Leach interviewed A. B. Barret in 1950, Barret told Leach that one of the notes was past due, hence the lawsuit came about. Certainly if anybody should have known what the trouble was, Barret should have known. But at the time of the Leach interview, Barret was aged, in very poor health, and had served as president of three other colleges after leaving Abilene. Factually, his answer did not fit the circumstances; Childers did not hold a past due note against the trustees or the college.

When Norvel Young interviewed Barret in 1943, he was told that Barret and Childers had had a disagreement in the local church, with the result that "Childers lost influence in the local church and afterward sued the institute to regain his property." Barret's recollection for Young, most likely, accurately described the situation.

Whatever was the cause, the facts seem indisputable. When the property was deeded to the trustees, Col. Childers took six notes for $1,000 each as his compensation. The transaction occurred February 12, 1906. The first note was due and payable January 1, 1908. The letter from the attorneys, dated November 19, 1906, was written thirteen and a half months before the first note was due. So the debt could not have been the problem.

Minutes of the Board of Trustees meeting of February 11, 1907, include this language: "... the matter of the suit then pending, Col. Childers vs. Trustees, was discussed and agreed to employ J. M. Wagstaff to represent us in court." The firm of Leggett and Kirby had been unable to work out a settlement satisfactory to Col. Childers. The Board of Trustees was girding for battle at the courthouse with an elder of the church, or at least one who had been an elder of the church.

The minutes of the trial in the District Court make clear what the court's judgment was:

> *J. W. Childers vs. A. F. McDonald, et al.* On this the 12th day of March, 1907, ... the evidence having been introduced by both parties, and the court having considered the evidence and being of the opinion that there was no issue of fact to be determined by the jury and that all facts necessary for the determination of the case were undisputed and that the judgment should be for the defendants, the court instructed the jury to bring in a verdict for the defendants, which the jury did, in accordance with the instruction of the court.

Also, by the time the trial took place, the first year's interest on the notes was due. It had not been paid. The court noted that fact, but commented that interest due on the notes had been offered to Col. Childers, but he had refused to accept it. If he had accepted the interest payment he would have been validating the school's good faith in keeping the terms of the deed. The court added that the school had been ready at all times to pay the interest when it was due. So at the time, neither the principal nor the interest on the notes was due.

The school was victorious over the Colonel. The court instructed the defendants to recover from the plaintiff all costs they had expended in connection with the trial, so the Colonel had to pay for the school's lawyer. The judge further commented on two points as a matter of record: first, the Colonel ostensibly filed the suit because the trustees had not kept the property insured as specified in the deed, but, second, the real design was to declare all six notes due and payable immediately or recover the property.

To all appearances, the property was insured against fire well before the trial took place. Minutes of the first board meeting, November 3, 1906, include this paragraph: "The board agreed that the property or the buildings be insured against fire and that A. F. McDonald was appointed to have said buildings insured." Although no later notation showed that McDonald actually secured the insurance, the character and integrity of the man leads to the assumption that he did. At least the judge was satisfied. It would appear, however, that during a period of the construction the building perhaps was uninsured. Because no loss had been sustained and because the building was insured well before the trial began, that question became immaterial. A man who was a friend of Christian education, and who had done much for the church and the school, had filed a suit over a problem that no longer existed.

The defendants whom Col. Childers was suing were A. F. McDonald, J. H. Deaver, T. G. Moore, J. P. Sharp, J. S. Manly, W. H. Free, W. H. Childers, A. B. Barret, and Childers Classical Institute. W. H. Childers was the Colonel's son. How did it happen that he was against his father and on the side of the school? Unless the court made an egregious error, the document reveals a division in the Childers family ranks. It will be seen shortly that W. H. Childers was the man who quickly ironed out one last problem between the Childers family and Childers Classical Institute a dozen years after his father's death. Apparently, he remained on good terms with his father in spite of being a defendant in the suit.

Indeed, things were not always serene between the original benefactor and the institute that bore his name. In fact, when the district judge rendered his verdict, attorneys for the Colonel gave notice of appeal to the Second Supreme Judicial District at Fort Worth. However, a review of cases considered by that court does not reveal that the appeal was ever perfected.

The 1907 lawsuit was not the last controversy between Col. Childers and the Board of Trustees. When the first $1,000 note became due and payable in January 1908, it was not paid. Childers immediately declared all six notes due and payable. In its meeting of January 28, 1908, the board met the issue head on. A resolution was passed unanimously, agreeing and admitting that the Colonel's claim was correct: the six notes plus interest were due and payable, and the board assumed full responsibility.

The problem was that certain Abilene individuals had bought the notes from Childers. The offer the board now made to these individuals was to increase the interest rate on the notes from eight percent to ten percent "from this date to the holders thereof if demanded." Apparently this resolution and the willingness to pay ten percent interest "on demand" satisfied the holders of the notes, and the board did not have to come up with the cash immediately. In defense of Col. Childers's action at this time, he was acting not only in his own interest but also on behalf of the note holders. Possibly, he had endorsed the notes in selling them to fellow Abilenians, so he was looking after his own business, too.

The name Childers Classical Institute was never used very much. For the opening of the second session in 1907, the institute ran an advertisement in the local newspaper with President Barret's picture and a photograph of the campus and the heading in bold letters, CHRISTIAN COLLEGE. In small print underneath were the words Childers Classical Institute. During the third year of its history, President H. C. Darden, who succeeded Barret, had a handout printed with this headline, "The Abilene Christian College Needs ...," and proceeded to list the needs without any mention at all of the name Childers. And at the opening of the fourth session, in 1909, the *Abilene Daily Reporter*, in its first-page story, said, "The Childers Classical Institute, better known as Christian College, entered on the fourth year of its life today."

When James F. Cox became president in 1911, he recommended, and the board concurred, that the school be called The Abilene Christian Training School. The charter name was still Childers Classical Institute. When Jesse P. Sewell became president in 1912, he announced that work was beginning immediately to make the school a junior college, and his first catalog was headed "Abilene Christian College – Charter name: Childers Classical Institute." That was the only way from that time on that the name Childers would be used at all. In 1920, the charter was amended to make the name officially Abilene Christian College. In 1976, a charter amendment changed the name to Abilene Christian University.

Official openings of the school were covered each year by the *Abilene Daily Reporter*, but unfortunately no copies of the September 1906 newspapers exist for a record of the first official opening. Apparently, a fire destroyed file copies of the newspaper between November 23, 1905, and April 3, 1907. Possibly Col. and Mrs. Childers were honored at the first chapel. During the years after 1906, the *Abilene Daily Reporter* front-page coverage of the official openings never mentioned the Childers' presence. This may have been because, as already mentioned, they moved to New Mexico soon after selling their home to the school. The 1907 Abilene city directory does not include J. W. and Martha Childers although it does list their son, William H., who was a cattleman. By 1914 the city directory shows J. W. Childers back in his Abilene home on North Fifth Street, where he was listed each succeeding year until his death in 1918, "after," as the story in the *Abilene Reporter* said, "an illness of five years duration." It is possible that during those years he was not able to attend campus functions.

When he died, the funeral service was conducted in his home with the Masonic Lodge in charge. News coverage mentioned no one from the college or the Church of Christ as having a part in the service. Not a word was said in the newspaper story about the role he had played in the beginning of Abilene Christian College. People who remember Jesse P. Sewell, who was president of the college in 1918, and Henry E. Speck, who was dean, would know that if there had been any way of establishing warm and cordial relationships with the original benefactors, these men would have done it. Unfortunately, an estrangement seemed to have existed.

Martha Childers died October 10, 1929. She had signed her will just two weeks earlier. It was filed in the office of the Taylor County clerk. Paragraph five reads: "I have a controversy with Abilene Christian College with reference to the title to the original property conveyed by my husband to Childers Classical Institute. ... I here appoint my son, W. H. Childers, ... To settle this controversy, and whatever settlement he makes shall be binding upon my heirs and devises ...."

Seemingly, Mrs. Childers nourished no particular animosity because she called for all of her heirs to accept the settlement that her son would work out. W. H. Childers evidently had no problem because January 31, 1930, he reached this settlement with the trustees of Abilene Christian College, which was filed February 2 for record: "Whereas, on the 12th day of February, 1906, J. W. Childers and wife, Martha Childers ... conveyed to ... [the trustees] certain lands ... and whereas certain restrictions were made in said original deed, ... that the college or school shall always be known as Childers Classical Institute ... Now therefore in consideration of the premises and of the payment of $4,000 to Rose Childers, independent executrix ..., we, W. H. Childers and Rose Childers ... do here now release the lands described from any and all restrictions of every kind that were retained in the deed ...."

Actually, the trustees repaid the Childers estate the original price reduction of $3,000, which the Colonel had made in selling his home place to the trustees, plus $1,000. The estate was repaid the $2,250 donation to the school and the $750 donation to the church. The deal was good for all concerned. Col. Childers had done a great service in providing a foothold for what has become Abilene Christian University. The foothold was the needed start. If he had not made it possible for A. B. Barret to start a school on a shoestring, Barret might have failed in his attempt to start a school in Abilene. And the colonel did a favor for the Church of Christ in providing a place for the church to use for its assemblies and classes through the years on the college campus. That also proved to be a blessing to the school for nearly a half-century.

The trustees undoubtedly broke a covenant with Childers when they changed the name to Abilene Christian. However, the trustees made amends and restitution to all concerned in 1930. Members of the Childers family accepted the arrangement. A great-niece of Col. and Mrs. Childers fills an important staff position on the campus in the late 1990s; she is Mary Womack, academic adviser in the Department of Education. Another great-niece of the colonel is Jan McCoy, a 1960 graduate. She and her husband, Burl, and their two sons and daughter, constitute a noted singing group and a loyal ACU family. Burl was a member of the university coaching staff for years. A third great niece, Joy Crouch, has recently moved to Abilene after years of mission work in Austria and Bosnia. The Childers family and Childers Classical Institute always will have an important place in the genesis and history of Abilene Christian University.

As President A. B. Barret was getting ready for the second year of Childers Classical Institute, also known as Christian College, he had a positive outlook. In the catalog prepared for the 1907-8 session, he commended the excellent students of the first year. He admitted that the year had not been successful for all students. He wanted to get the message out that "[w]e have no room for idlers. This is no place for those who have nothing to do but to spend money and have a good time." Most of the students, however, thought it was a great place.

To Barret's first-year faculty, he added the Klingman brothers: George, who was to be dean of Bible and professor of sacred literature, sacred history, philosophy, and German; and

William, to teach sight singing and serve as librarian. George Klingman was an especially gifted preacher, teacher, and writer. He and his wife loved students and enjoyed entertaining them in their home. With bachelor's and master's degrees from Transylvania University and with his knowledge of Hebrew, Greek, and church history, he was a powerful influence on his students. One chink in his armor was his doctor of philosophy degree from something called Carnegie University of Dover, Delaware. When the late Lawrence Smith checked into the credentials of Carnegie, he found that it was a mail order, or correspondence, school, short-lived, and soon closed for failure to pay taxes. That, however, was a minor problem and had nothing to do with his great influence. Almost three decades would pass before a member of the faculty would hold a recognized Ph.D. degree; he was Walter H. Adams, who received the degree from Columbia University in 1932.

The 1907-8 catalog extolled the attractiveness of the campus, the strength of the faculty, and the high quality of life in Abilene, which Barret and other city leaders called the "Athens of the West," and "a quiet, clean, moral little city of about ten thousand inhabitants." Where a shortcoming existed, President Barret put the best face possible on it. For example, students had no dormitories to live in. To be sure, the Childers home, which came to be known as the White Cottage and was the president's residence, could also accommodate about a dozen young women. Mrs. Barret prepared their meals. Male students and most of the females had to find lodging with families in the neighborhood. But instead of lamenting and apologizing for the lack of dormitories, the catalog stated, "We have no dormitories and we desire none. We have 'homes' under the management of Christian families. Thus we offer our pupils the influences of well-ordered homes ... far better than crowding too many into one building. The morals are superior and the students enjoy better health, for the food is more carefully prepared." Another paragraph stated, "Young ladies can find homes nearby where they can make their board, etc., by assisting with the housework. Young men can find many ways to make expenses."

The *Daily Reporter* devoted six of the eight columns on page one of its edition of September 10, 1907, to the official opening of the second year. The story noted that "while the chapel was filled, all in the audience found comfortable seats and the exercises were most enjoyable." After the devotional, President

Barret gave a short address, in which he said: "Somewhere in Texas there will be located the strongest of the colleges of the Non-Progressive Christians, and believing that a school is what the teachers make it, we expect to have that college located at Abilene. I love Abilene and it is my earnest desire to see that class of college at Abilene." Then he mentioned a fact of life: "The board realizes that Abilene has not done what she should have done and I know she has not done what she is going to do."

After the president's speech, Mr. Marion Zellner made comments. Barret introduced him as "a wealthy citizen attracted to Abilene by the advantages of this college"; four Zellner students were enrolled in the school. Then musical numbers were performed by teachers of the Western School of Music, with which the college was affiliated because it had not yet added art and music to its own offerings. Finally, on an optimistic note, the second year was declared officially in session.

Prospects were good for a great second year. The news that seventy students enrolled on the first day of registration was reported by the Abilene newspaper, which said registration was expected to reach more than 100 on the second day of registration. Front page *Abilene Daily Reporter* coverage on Wednesday, September 11, 1907, included this appraisal: "The college president and trustees are all men who believe in doing much and saying little and have surprised Abilene citizens by their accomplishments." Actually, during that second year, enrollment reached one hundred thirty. Things seemed to be going well.

But a t midyear, President Barret shocked the school community with the announcement that he was resigning as president at the end of the year and moving to Denton. He would become president of Southwestern Christian College, which would be renamed. Although he had said at the beginning of the year that he expected Abilene to become "the strongest of the colleges" sponsored by members of the Church of Christ, he had returned to his original conviction that Denton would be the place. Losing Barret was not the only bad news. The trustees learned that he was taking key members of the faculty with him. Charles Roberson, George Klingman, and Edwin Hoover were going to Denton. James F. Cox had left after the first year.

Even though Barret had said, "We shall continue our work, overcome all difficulties, and know not the word 'fail' until our efforts are crowned with success," he was giving up on Abilene as the principal university among Texas Churches of Christ. Abilene would play a smaller role, he explained in a *Firm Foundation* article, March 10, 1908: "Some one will ask, what about Abilene? Of course, we who have been here shall go to Denton, but it is purely for a greater work than we can hope to do here.... In fact, we intend that this shall be a correlated school with the one in Denton. The school will sustain a preparatory course that will place its graduates into the Denton university, or any other of equal rank."

What had brought about this change in Barret's thinking in so short a period? First, as Norvel Young pointed out in his *History of Christian Colleges*, "Barret was primarily a promoter and found it difficult to endure the tedious task of coordinating the efforts of both board and faculty."

Second, some serious problems had arisen during the year and a half Barret had been in Abilene. The difficulty with Col. Childers resulted in the lawsuit seeking to reclaim the property, a court victory for the school which nevertheless left some scars.

Third, another problem cost the fledgling school the support of board member J. S. Manly. Another board change came about when M. L. Hays of Clyde replaced J. H. Deaver, who resigned in July 1907. In 1908, J. P. Sharp resigned and was replaced by M. Zellner, who had moved from Loraine to Abilene. The original board had consisted of two trustees from Abilene – McDonald and Free – and three from outside Abilene – Manly from Nugent, Deaver from Buffalo Gap, and Sharp from Merkel. All three of the non-Abilene board members were now off the board. Probably the difficulty of travel to meetings was part of their problem – perhaps the total problem.

Fourth, Zellner added somewhat to Barret's problems. He was a man of considerable wealth and was respected as an independent thinker. He was inclined to be critical of Barret's administration. Barret brought this out in his 1943 interview with Norvel Young. A major issue was money; the school was strapped for cash. Barret's deal with the board was that he would take in all of the money that came from tuition, fees, and donations, and pay out all of the money that had to be paid out – teachers' salaries, building upkeep, utilities, or whatever. It was a bad business deal.

He went into the real estate business to try to make money to help keep the school going. For example, the *Abilene Weekly*

Reporter of April 5, 1907, listed the following transactions: "A. B. Barret to J. F. Clark, lots 1 & 2 in Block E, city of Abilene, $2,000; A. B. Barret to Mrs. Fannie Harvey, lots 14 & 15, block 23, city of Abilene, $500; A. B. Barret and wife to Abraham Bergman, part of lot 1, block 24 Harris addition to the city of Abilene, $6,500." Records at the county courthouse reveal quite a number of such transactions.

Barret was a promoter and a salesman. Because he drew no salary or expense money as president, he was not necessarily lining his own pockets; he was paying the bills for the school, that is, most of the bills. At the second meeting of the Board of Trustees, February 11, 1907, the five members agreed to sign a note to the Citizens National Bank for a loan to cover some operating expenses of the school. Barret agreed to raise the money, and the board agreed that he should receive a commission of ten percent on all funds raised. Times were hard, and money was difficult to raise. Barrett undoubtedly was embarrassed by the January 1908 overdue notes controversy with Col. Childers.

Into this situation came the people of Denton. Southwestern Christian College was in its fourth year of operation. The trustees reported that they were ready to make it into a university. They offered Barret the presidency. They would use existing facilities during the first year but would proceed to buy additional land near the campus, designate twenty-five acres for campus, plat the balance, sell city lots, and use the proceeds to erect buildings for the university. The city of Denton had agreed to give dollar for dollar up to $30,000, which was a considerable amount of money for the time. "Southland University," the school's new name, would have a College of Arts and Sciences, a College of Sacred Literature, a School of Expression and Oratory, and, later, other colleges and schools. "I am sure we need just such work as is proposed," Barret wrote in *The Firm Foundation* article, "and that we now have the best opportunity for it that we have ever had."

The situation looked bright for Denton but dismal for Abilene. The doomsayers, however, had to reckon with two factors.

First, students and their parents liked the little school and the spirit of excitement on the campus. The two literary and debating societies and athletic events had raised much of this excitement. The catalog stated, "It is not our purpose that our students shall run wild over athletics as some do, but we want them to have enough training to make them strong and to keep them well." The place was always buzzing with activities. Musical programs were enjoyed by the students. Drama had a small stage in the auditorium and made the most of it. Parents and students were pleased with the good teachers. People were moving to Abilene to put their sons and daughters in the school.

Second, the Board of Trustees comprised strong men who were not about to let the school shut down. Just as the board took charge of the notes due to Col. Childers, so the board assumed its rightful responsibilities in keeping the school going – a significant development. Up to this point the board had been a rubber stamp for Barret's proposals. After all, the school was his idea. He had engineered the deal that gained a campus. He had persuaded the initial group to serve as trustees. Now he was moving on. And the board moved in. In its meeting of February 29, 1908, the board graciously accepted Barret's resignation and passed a resolution of appreciation "for the great interest he has taken in building up the work at this place and the success he has made."

So at the end of the school year, Allen B. and Exie Barret moved away. The *Daily Reporter* of May 12, 1908, carried a page one story: "The college has had a successful year and the session ends with everything in good condition. President Barret has accepted the presidency of Southland University in Denton and will move there June 1. ... George A. Klingman will preach the closing sermon for the school in the chapel hall next Sunday night. His subject will be 'She Hath Done What She Could.'" Maybe this was the logical valedictory to Barret's first speech two years earlier, "What Man Has Done, Man Can Do."

The Denton university did not work out. In 1909, Barret and Roberson moved to Cleburne and organized Clebarro College; "Clebarro" was a name derived from a combination of the names "Cleburne-Barret-Roberson." The pair operated Clebarro jointly for four years, after which Barret left it to Roberson and moved to Austin to promote the Bible Chair for the Church of Christ at the University of Texas. After working at that task, he returned to Tennessee to do evangelistic work for the rest of his active life. In 1943, he tried to resurrect Burritt College at Spencer, Tennessee, which he described as "the oldest college conducted by members of the churches of

Christ in the world." He would call it the Burritt-Barret Bible School. Registration was set for September 8, 1943, but students did not come. Abilene remained the enduring legacy of Barret's life.

Seemingly, after the announcement of Barret's departure, a contact about the presidency at Abilene was made with James F. Cox, who had been a member of the first faculty in 1906. He was now serving as president of Lingleville Christian College. Cox wrote to J. S. Manly to report on how the Manly son, Borden, and daughter, Ruth, were doing in school at Lingleville, and closed his letter by asking, "How are things shaping up at Abilene? What do you think of my leaving here and taking that school?" Unknown to Cox, the board had the day before made its decision in another direction, voting to employ H. C. Darden, superintendent of schools at Clyde, as president of Childers Classical Institute. The board offered him the same deal Barret had had: "The contract with Prof. Darden being that we lease him the school building and dormitory free of rent, that the school be run according to provisions of charter, that he is to select teachers, pay teachers, advertise the school, and pay for advertising, pay for fuel used by the school, keep the place in repair, etc. and as compensation for this he is to receive what the school brings in or pays."

Henry Calhoun Darden was an excellent school man, both as a teacher and an administrator, and he was persuaded to accept the presidency of the school. He enjoyed thereafter telling that he was one college president who had never attended a day of college.

Born in Alabama in 1868, he was eighteen months old when his mother died. His father, who had served as a surgeon in the Confederate Army, moved to Texas with his eight children. The doctor had been a slaveowner in the old South and was seeking a new life in Texas. When Henry, known by the nickname "Hal," was only seven years of age, his father died, leaving a hundred books in his library. Young Hal went to live with an uncle. He attended school for three months, learned to read and write, and went through the second reader. At another time when he spent time with a sister, he attended school for two weeks. These two short periods were his only schooling until he was eighteen years of age because he lived where schools were not operated. But he developed a love of reading between the ages of seven and thirteen as he read through his father's library, which consisted mostly of classics, poetry and prose.

When he was eighteen, Darden got a job paying $20 per month. He saved his money, soon enrolled in Rockdale High School in Texas, and completed high school in two years, graduating in 1889 at age twenty-one. Then he moved west to work on a ranch, but soon he came down with a fever and while convalescing heard that a teacher was needed at a school in Jones County, just north of Abilene. He applied for the job even though he did not have the qualifications the school trustees advertised. But he was a strapping six-footer, and the trustees had had trouble at the school and wanted somebody who could control the students. The trustees hired him, and he spent the rest of his life in the school business. In later years, his scholarly and professorial demeanor led to his always being called "Fessor." But he never went to college.

Darden brought in Robertson L. Whiteside as his co-worker at the new school in Abilene in 1908, which proved to be a wise decision. Whiteside was a well-known preacher, teacher, and writer. The Darden year as president of Childers Classical Institute was a good if not spectacular one. Enrollment was up. His years in public schools had given him insights into how to interact with a community, which enhanced the school's cordial relationships with Abilene. Although Darden was unaccustomed to the rigors of having to raise money, with Whiteside's help, he tried and realized some success.

A story in the *Reporter* of January 25, 1909, explained the situation: "For some time the Christian College of this place has been in need of $8,000 to pay off the balance due on the building and property of the school. The trustees, after carefully considering the matter, decided that they could raise half of the amount needed and asked that Abilene raise half. A committee is at work on the matter today…. This school is worth much to Abilene and we cannot afford to lose it. A number of our very best families are here because of this school."

Then a statement crept into the story showing the naiveté of the men in charge: "The school will be put on a basis where it can never be run in debt again." The pledge reached a little too far; college presidents discover that carrying out a promise a school will never run a deficit is nigh unto impossible. For one thing, a faculty has to be hired ahead of time for students who may not enroll in the numbers anticipated. Still, every effort to run a school on a balanced budget must be exerted, and over a period of years the budget must be balanced.

The Abilene committee went to work, and one month later, the *Daily Reporter* announced victory in its February 25, 1909, edition. All but $260 of the $8,000 goal had been raised, which was expected within a few weeks. The newspaper further described the relationship of the school and the community: "As an evidence that church lines ... cut no figure with Abilene citizens when the general interest of the town is at stake, the committee who raised the money was composed of members of Methodist, Baptist, Presbyterian, Christian, and other denominations of the town." This "general interest of the town" rule has characterized the relationship of Abilene with the school through the years.

The cooperation of the business community with the Board of Trustees made it possible to retire the original Childers notes and to take care of some other obligations. The importance of that fund-raising effort at that particular time in the history of the small school could hardly be overstated. Patrons of the school demonstrated strong loyalty everywhere. For example, when Nora Powers Hendrix observed her 100th birthday in February 1992, the *Abilene Reporter-News* ran a front page feature story about her life. She told of how her widowed mother, Ida Bell Foster Powers, ▄▄ ran a boarding house for male students in order to send her children to the school. The catalog for 1908 included Stephen, James, Nora, Zene, and Georgia Powers as students.

In February 1909, the board reviewed Darden's work and unanimously approved offering him the position for another year on the same terms under which he was currently serving. He accepted. However, between February and May, as he explained it later to a newspaper reporter, drouth and depression threatened enrollment, and illness had struck his family. Hence, he decided he had best return to the public schools. So, at the end of one year as president of Childers, he left, with the goodwill of all concerned. He spent the rest of his career, until retirement in 1940 at age seventy-two, in the public schools of Texas. For the last twenty-four years he was principal of the school at Call, a small lumbermill town in East Texas, where he was described as "one of its oldest and best loved citizens." His granddaughter, Mrs. Valrie Darden Bullington, is an alumnus and lives near the campus today with her husband, Wally, who was head football coach at the university and athletic director 1969-88.

With Darden's resignation, the Board of Trustees turned to R. L. Whiteside, who had been brought in as Darden's co-worker. Whiteside accepted on the same terms that Barret and Darden had already found infeasible. He stayed with the job two years, beginning with the fall semester of 1909 through the spring of 1911. He was also minister of the College Church of Christ, for which service he was paid $12.50 per week. The third president of Childers Classical Institute was a scholarly man. Born in Middle Tennessee in 1869, had a limited early education, but at the age of twenty-one he studied a year in West Tennessee Christian College and then enrolled as a member of the first class in the Nashville Bible School. He was a successful preacher and a prolific writer for church publications. In later years, his books had wide circulation.

During the Whiteside presidency, enrollment grew modestly, and with the help of his small preaching income and the fact that his wife kept boarders, he was able to pay his teachers and keep the school going. That the trustees left it up to him to run the school is attested by the fact that the board did not meet between May 21, 1909, and February 13, 1911. At least, no minutes of a meeting have survived.

The fact that the board probably failed to meet did not stop the board members from actively supporting the school. For example, A. F. McDonald sold most of his land along Catclaw Creek and the Texas and Pacific Railroad and gave the money to the school. The amount was $12,000, the largest gift received by the institution during the first half-dozen years of its existence.

Unfortunately, because of the peculiar type of contract the Board of Trustees had with the early presidents, record keeping was not of the quality to recognize sacrificial and generous gifts such as McDonald's. Gifts to help them run the school went to the presidents, who were above enriching themselves (it is known that each of those early chief executives had to give up the job when he ran out of money). Also, donors had no need to substantiate a gift because the era preceded the income tax, charitable giving credit, and the necessity for an annual audit.

McDonald Muster, the family history edited by Conny McDonald Martin and published in 1989, described the A. F. McDonald commitment, and Don Morris referred to it in 1973, saying it "saved the college." Albert Fitzgerald McDonald undoubtedly served the key role in organizing the Abilene Church of Christ; yet when the first group of elders and deacons was selected, he was not one of them. Maybe he was not asked to serve; maybe he declined to serve. He was listed by Barret as one of the three up-and-coming men of the Abilene church and was one of the five trustees in getting the college started. Yet he never served as chairman of the board. When Colonel Childers filed his suit against the board, the suit was styled *J. W. Childers v. A. F. McDonald, et al.*, another probable indicator of his leadership position among the trustees.

Another member of the McDonald family made a distinct contribution to the lore of student life during the Whiteside administration. Alex McDonald was a son of A. F. and Cornelia McDonald. On the day he was scheduled to graduate from intermediate school, he was walking with a group of boys past the administration building while a group of first graders were scuffling. The president, at his desk, called to him through a window, "Alex, see if you can stop those first graders from fighting." Alex yelled back to the president, "Stop 'em yourself, Rabbit Legs."

When he saw President Whiteside get out of his chair and move toward the door, Alex and the boys with him started running. He never came back to get his graduation certificate. Years later, when he was a leading businessman of Lubbock and for twenty years an elder of the Broadway Church of Christ in Lubbock, he was occasionally reminded by children and grandchildren of his gaffe in President Whiteside's presence.

During the Whiteside administration, the school sponsored a Special Bible Study Week during the first week of January 1910. President Whiteside invited Price Billingsley and C. R. Nichol to present lessons. Before this date similar weeks had focused mainly on the students' needs, but Whiteside invited preachers from far and near to come to the 1910 meetings. Approximately fifty preachers attended and participated in discussions. The Bible study was conducted again in January of 1911, and G. H. P. Showalter, editor and publisher of *The Firm Foundation*, took careful notes during the 1911 session and published them. These sessions were forerunners of the influential Abilene Christian Lectureships, which were officially launched in 1918.

In February 1911, the Board of Trustees met after a twenty-one-month hiatus. All members were present: T. G. Moore, chairman; A. F. McDonald; M. Zellner; M. L. Hays; and W. H.

Free, secretary. First item on the agenda was "the matter of a president for the school." Whiteside was elected to serve for a third year. He was called before the board and notified. He accepted, but three months later, he resigned. The board accepted his resignation even though a petition signed by "some patrons and pupils" asked him to reconsider.

In a letter to Don Morris in 1949, Whiteside explained why he could not reconsider:

> Those were hard years in West Texas. I remember ... we had another drouth in 1908, and you know the effects of a drouth hold on for a long time after the drouth is broken.... Of course I was faced with the same battles that my predecessors had. The only income for teachers' salaries and for our own living was out of tuition. If there weren't enough students, or if they couldn't pay, it was the teachers and the administration who were hurt .... It was common for me to work from 6 a.m. to 10 p.m. those first months .... My wife kept boarders and this paid the food bill. I also preached for the college congregation and the small salary they paid me was a great help. But times got worse, rather than better, and the church could no longer pay me a regular salary, but gave me what was left when the incidentals had been paid. Mrs. Whiteside and I had three children in school then, and we were both then, and are now, firm believers in a Christian education being the only kind of an education.

He stayed on at the school as a teacher, and, without the burdens of the presidency, he was able to do more preaching, for which there was some financial support.

At the board meeting, May 16, 1911, the trustees amended the charter, increasing membership from five to nineteen, with seven instead of a majority required for a quorum. This extended the geographic reach of the board somewhat although no member lived more than two counties away from Abilene. Among the men added after this action were J. S. Arledge of Maryneal and Jesse P. Sewell of San Angelo, two trustees destined to fill unique roles in the future of the institution. During the board's May meeting, T. G. Moore's resignation from the board was accepted, with J. B. Cranfill replacing him as a member and M. Zellner replacing him as chairman.

The May 16 meeting also resulted in the appointment of James F. Cox as president of the school. The board departed from the pattern used for the first three presidents by contracting to pay Cox a $1,500 per year salary, and, in return, "Jas. F.

Cox is to give his entire time, discharging the various duties as president of the school."

President-elect Cox announced that the school would be known as Abilene Christian Training School because the name would be more in line with what it actually was. It was not a college – at least, not yet. He did not recommend a change in the charter name; hence, it was technically "Abilene Christian Training School – Charter Name: Childers Classical Institute."

Under Cox's leadership, during the summer of 1911, the basement of the administration building, which had been left unfinished in 1906, was readied for use, which meant a fifty percent increase in space available for educational purposes. Even with this much-needed addition, the total square footage of the administration-classroom-auditorium building was about two-thirds the size of the Zona Luce Building on the present campus.

The Abilene newspaper was optimistic for the future of the school. August 13, 1911, it reported: "Dr. Cox comes to Abilene fully qualified to head such a promising and enterprising educational institution as the Christian Training School." The paper also reported that two graduates of the State University, A. B. Cox, the president's brother, and Prof. Carl A. Gardner would join the faculty, and Miss Mary McDonald would lead the primary department. The newspaper added the encouraging news that every dollar of indebtedness against the campus had been paid and that the school was on "a broader and firmer basis," undoubtedly made possible by the McDonald gift, along with others.

At this point, a real blow hit the school; the newly-elected president explained: "... Prospects were good for a successful school year, but just two days before the fall opening I was called to the bedside of my wife at her mother's in Midway. She was dangerously ill and remained so for more than a year, so my brother, Dr. A. B. Cox ... was left in charge of the school and he and the other teachers ran it. I was not present even one day while the school was in session."

Because Mrs. Cox was still very ill at the beginning of 1912, Cox resigned as president of Childers Classical Institute to accept the post of superintendent of the Midway School. So the Abilene Christian Training School in 1911-12 operated without the president who had done so much hard work in preparation for it.

A. B. Cox, who was acting president during the year, later earned his doctorate at the University of Wisconsin and was for years director of marketing at the University of Texas. At Abilene Christian he was obviously in a temporary position and launched no vigorous moves. Enrollment was low. When the board met in the fall of 1911, the report showed sixty-five pupils enrolled. It would have been understandable if the board had voted to shut the school down.

In its meeting of January 18, 1912, however, the board voted to elect Jesse P. Sewell president for the ensuing year. The offer was a salary of $125 per month, but Sewell came to the next meeting April 22, 1912, with a proposal that the board turn the school over to him and Carl Gardner on essentially the same terms as Barret, Darden, and Whiteside, except that he wanted it for five years.

The board accepted the proposal and in fact reinforced it with some words of their own, according to Sewell's report,

> Now, Brother Sewell, we've been losing money every year on the school. As trustees, we've been having to put up money to pay the teachers and to close out the debts at the end of the year and we've lost all the money on the school that we are going to lose .... Our proposition is, we'll turn the property over to you and we'll back you morally and every way we can, but you finance it .... We're telling you in advance, we're not going to make up any losses.

The board talked straight, but J. P. Sewell could handle straight talk. He could give it out and also take it. He agreed to take the job for five years, with Carl Gardner as the dean.

Sewell started to work in the summer of 1912. In 1917, when his five-year term was up, he was elected to another five-year term on the same basis. In 1922, the president and the board agreed to another five-year term. But before that term was over, he found it necessary for health and other considerations to retire. His was a brilliant college presidency. He never drew a salary during his twelve-year term. As he said to Joseph Jones, "I financed Abilene Christian College without having any assistance from any others. I've owed these banks here as much as $15,000 at one time, with nobody else on the note except me. But from the very beginning this school began to grow."

He admitted, however, that the Board of Trustees helped him more than his words had indicated. When he announced plans, soon after taking office, to build a dormitory for the women, which would be the first building program since the original administration building in 1906, he solicited and received grants from the business community of Abilene. "Most of the trustees put in a thousand dollars apiece on this new building," Sewell said, "and, when we built it, enthusiastically supported it." A donation of $1,000 was a generous gift at the time, which illustrated the trustees' willingness to help, but they were not yet ready to assume the main burden. In time, that would change.

CHAPTER TWO

SAVING THE SCHOOL

If ever the man and the moment met in the history of Abilene Christian University, the phenomenon occurred when Jesse Parker Sewell moved in as president in the summer of 1912.

After midyear of 1904-5, when the onset of life-threatening tuberculosis forced Sewell to give up his work as treasurer of Southwestern Christian College at Denton, he had lived in San Angelo, ninety miles southwest of Abilene. He operated an insurance agency, in which he did very well financially, and preached on Sundays with his usual success. In 1906, he tried to help Barret establish his school in San Angelo, but the business community failed to promise the kind of support either Barret or Sewell thought was necessary. In June 1911, during the James F. Cox presidency, Sewell was elected to the Board of Trustees of Childers Classical Institute, or, as it was called that year, Abilene Christian Training School. The next year, at age thirty-six, he was elected its president. He purchased a two-story house near the North First Street campus and moved to Abilene.

Daisy McQuigg Sewell came as his full partner. The offer from the Board of Trustees fulfilled the dream the couple had shared since their days as students at Nashville Bible School. Daisy Sewell was listed in the catalog of 1912-13 as a teacher of art and Bible. The WACU Museum has several of her paintings, and one of her paintings is on the north wall of the President's Dining Room in the McGlothlin Campus Center. She was also dean of women. She was no ordinary dean, however – Daisy Sewell was extraordinary. She was in effect executive assistant to the president.

"Those were the days when your case could be appealed from the president of the college to a higher court – that of Dean of Women," wrote Jean Martin, later to be Mrs. R. L. Sanders, in a 1943 *Optimist* biographical sketch about the unique dean. The story was based largely on stories told to her by her parents, Edwin and Jewel McDonald Martin. Jewel was the daughter of A. F. McDonald, one of the founding trustees.

To complete the office of the chief executive, Inez Norton was hired. During the summer of 1912, newly selected President Sewell preached at Floydada, on the high plains of West Texas, where he baptized Miss Norton, a recent high school graduate. He persuaded her to enroll in Abilene Christian College, and Mrs. Sewell employed Inez as her secretary. Years later Inez Norton commented about Daisy Sewell's generosity: "Sister Sewell had inherited, from her mother's estate, a small fortune. I was in her office when she wrote the check which closed out that account. She broke down and cried ... [and] she said to me, 'Inez, that is the last of the money left to me by my mother. I have given it all to Abilene Christian College. I am glad I had it to give. I believe it will do good after I am gone ... but what will I do for money now?'"

Jesse P. Sewell needed a strong wife. He was physically frail. As a child he had "sieges of fever and pneumonia." At age fifteen he attended Viola Normal in Tennessee. He weighed only eighty-seven pounds. After Viola he attended Nashville Bible School but left during his senior year because of ill health. As an adult he fought off tuberculosis. He was never blessed with good health. About five feet seven inches tall, he never weighed more than 125 pounds. But he had the heart and the courage of a born leader. He had a strong voice and could speak so as to be heard by a large audience without the aid of a public address system. He had what Renaissance people called "terribilita" – the ability to inspire awe. He was also much longer-lived than anybody would have predicted. He died July 4, 1969, at age ninety-three, with body worn out, but mind still sharp. During his long lifetime, he was blessed with two good wives. Daisy McQuigg Sewell died in 1944. He married Maxie McDuffie Runnels of San Antonio in 1948, and they were blessed with twenty-one years together.

Someone said that when Dr. Samuel Johnson completed his monumental *Dictionary of the English Language*, he commented, "I knew very well what I was going to do; I knew very well how to do it; and I have done it very well." That could be said of Jesse P. Sewell in connection with his aims for Abilene Christian College. In fact, late in life he said, with a grin, "I was conceited enough to think maybe I could do it just a little better than anybody else." In 1962, at age eighty-six, he spoke to an overflow crowd at the opening convocation for the fall semester of the college. This excerpt shows that he knew what he was going to do:

> Fifty years ago, at 8:30 a.m., 1912, I presided at my first opening exercise as president of the institution. During the twelve years that followed, I supervised the activities of our young college. I was working under a definite and controlling purpose. And that purpose was to have part in the development of a college in Texas with very exact and precise characteristics. In my mind and on my heart was a college with a philosophy and practices definitely different from the philosophy and practices of the average college. It must be a standard, fully accredited college of liberal arts. It must maintain a Department of Bible and Religion right along with all of its other departments. The Department of Bible and Religion must be strong, vital, scholarly, and deeply spiritual. Attractive enough that it would, in the very nature of what it was to be, become the foundation on which all other things in the college rested and about which all of the activities of the institution circulated. The philosophy under the control of which we were working, I repeat, called for a Christian college of Liberal Arts.

First, in 1912, he announced that it was to be a college. His good friend and predecessor James F. Cox had changed the name of the institution from Abilene Christian College to Abilene Christian Training School because that was what it was. Sewell was not criticizing Cox, but he changed the name back to College because that was what it was going to become – a full-fledged, accredited junior college. To be sure, the charter name was still Childers Classical Institute, but that would be changed officially in 1920.

Second, Sewell put together a strong faculty. Carl A. Gardner, a graduate of the University of Texas, was named dean of the college and professor of English, history, and economics. He was the first dean of the college. George Klingman had been dean of Bible but not of the entire faculty. Gardner later liked to recall that he washed windows ("The school could not afford a janitor," he said) and coached debate, baseball, and basketball in addition to being the dean – all for $85 per month. R. L. Whiteside, former president, was persuaded to stay on as vice president and professor of Bible, Greek, and philosophy. D. A. Faubus became head of the commercial department. Forty years later, his son, Dr. Overton Faubus, became a member of the Business Administration faculty and served for thirty-three years, chairing the department, 1963-80, gaining it widespread recognition, and laying the foundation for its current status as a college. His son-in-law, Dr. Jack Griggs, is the dean of the College of Business Administration today. Arthur Curry taught mathematics and science and was also in charge of athletics. Jessye Pauline Stevens was instructor in Latin, German, and expression. Lillie Carns Kelton taught piano, and Mary McDonald, daughter of A. F. McDonald, was principal of the primary department. (During the Christmas season of that year, Miss McDonald was married to Thomas Augustus "Gus" Niblack of Lubbock.) President Sewell installed his father and mother, Mr. and Mrs. W. A. Sewell, in the White Cottage, the original Childers home, with Mrs. Sewell as matron for the girls who stayed there. The students called them Father and Mother Sewell.

Third, in addition to recruiting a strong faculty, President Sewell had worked diligently at recruiting students. The catalog for 1913-14 reported that from first to last, 207 students were enrolled during 1912-13 – the first Sewell year. That was three times the enrollment of 1911-12. Great morale was exhibited by the students, faculty, trustees, and parents. *The Daily Reporter* was enthusiastic:

> Never before in the history of the school has there been such an interest shown on the part of the trustees, out of town friends, and citizens of Abilene. A large number of families have moved to Abilene for the benefit of the school, and the enrollment will be the largest in the school's history.

Fourth, Sewell and Gardner went to work to establish accreditation as a junior college with the University of Texas, which was the highest accreditation a Texas school could achieve at the time. An agreement was made that if the school could meet the standards by June 1913, the work of the year 1912-13 would be accredited retroactively. A vigorous campaign for funds enabled the school to meet the goal, and an "A" rating was achieved, which meant that the university would accept credits transferred in from Abilene. In 1914, full junior college standing was achieved.

Fifth, while busily engaged in developing an accredited college, Sewell left no doubt as to the Christian commitment of the institution. In the first catalog, he said, "No student can graduate from Abilene Christian College without a thorough course in the Bible." Every student studied Bible. Every student attended daily chapel exercises, where students and faculty participated in singing, prayer, Bible reading, and devotional messages. Campus life was permeated with spiritual influences.

Sixth, while all of this was going on, Sewell marshaled an all-out effort to expand the physical facilities of the campus. As in 1906, the campus comprised the small administration building, containing classrooms, auditorium, and offices, and the Childers house – the White Cottage. This did not mean that preceding presidents had disregarded the need for expansion. Darden had spearheaded a drive to raise money to pay the school out of debt, including the original notes to Childers. Whiteside had started bringing to the campus outstanding preachers as a beginning of what would become the Lectureships, which acquainted the brotherhood with the school. Cox had secured funds to complete the basement of the Administration Building, which meant fifty percent more floor space for that facility. More – much more – was needed.

The first project was a new dormitory for women. The result was Daisy Hall, named for Mrs. Sewell, who devoted the last of her inheritance to help build it. The White Cottage was moved to a new location on campus so that Daisy Hall could be built on that prominent spot. It provided an attractive, modern home for fifty or so young women. Quarters were included for President and Mrs. Sewell, who sold their house to help pay for the dormitory. A library room was situated adjacent to the president's suite, where his 600-volume library could be available for use by the students. On the ground floor was built a cafeteria, which served the residents of Daisy Hall and other students, including the men. The ground floor also had space for the Department of Domestic Science.

An all-out drive for funds enabled the completion of this first addition to the original campus during the 1914-15 session. Inez Norton, later Mrs. D. B. Rambo, described an unusual contribution by the students to the success of the campaign for funds: "During the summer of 1914 ... students of Abilene Christian College chopped cotton, cooked for threshers, worked on threshing crews, picked cotton in the late summer and early fall, and did any work that they could find to do to earn five, ten, twenty-five dollars. This money was not to pay tuition next fall, but to donate... toward the building of the new dormitory...."

When the women occupied Daisy Hall, a dozen or so men were given the privilege of living in the White Cottage with Father and Mother Sewell.

Athletics presented some problems for the new president. In August 1912, the first issue appeared of *The Optimist*, the student newspaper, with Arthur Slater of Clyde as editor and publisher. Featured in the first issue was an article by faculty member Arthur Curry in which he expressed great hope for athletics: "We hope to have good football, basketball, and baseball in their respective seasons. Track and tennis teams may work throughout the year.... I delight in this work, because I can see its practical and far-reaching results. I hope the students will enter into it enthusiastically and help me to accomplish the things I have mentioned above."

Coach Curry was doomed to disappointment. Although athletics, especially baseball, had played a big role on campus since the first year of the school, it had not yet come up against a president like Jesse P. Sewell. Maryanne Baxter, who married Johnny Wallace and died in 1995 at age 101, told the story of Sewell versus athletics in a January 21, 1977, letter to Lawrence L. Smith. Maryanne came from Clyde, enrolled in 1911, continued in school until 1914, and with Corrie Acuff was chosen by President Sewell to select the school colors, purple for royalty and white for purity. Maryanne wrote:

> The boys wanted to play football and they played a few games, without the aid of pads or uniforms, with the Abilene High School. This was brought to a sudden halt when "Prexy" overheard one of the boys, "Little Punk" Burns, yell, "kill 'em!' and 'give 'em hell!" The game was immediately called off and Prexy said that we didn't need to play games that encouraged us to talk like that and caused us to want to hurt someone!

Consequently, intercollegiate or interschool athletics was out, a great disappointment to the students and to the general public. *The Daily Reporter* got into the act with a story mildly lamenting the fact that Christian College was not "playing the game this year." Although this was the situation, President Sewell prepared his catalog for the upcoming school year, 1913-14, and under the heading "Athletics," he wrote that "clean, honest athletics will be encouraged to a moderate degree." But he was referring to contests among clubs on campus. In the next paragraph, headed "Match Games," he spelled out his policy: "Last year we consented, against our judgment, to allow our boys to play match games of ball with different teams in Abilene. We gave it a THOROUGH, FAIR TRIAL, and our opinion is stronger than before that match games, with outside teams, are an injury in several ways, and of absolutely no benefit from any viewpoint. We will not allow them in the future."

Were athletic contests with other schools dead? Not exactly. *The Daily Reporter* came out with a surprising story in its edition of February 3, 1913:

> There was joy in the Christian College camp – baseball camp at any rate – when it was announced that the ban on match games with other schools in athletic contests had been removed. The authorities of the school (for good reasons) so far in the athletic life of the college this year have not allowed contests of any kind to be played with outside schools, and now that this has been removed the students are taking all the keener interest in athletics. The action of the authorities was announced Friday.

This change in policy posed a bit of a problem. The catalog for the coming school year, 1913-14, was already in print with the announcement that prohibited "match" play with other schools. The policy was changed before it officially became effective if a policy is merely an opinion until it gets printed in the official catalog of the institution.

The athletic incident showed one great characteristic of President Sewell: even though he could be stern and apparently inflexible, he could change directions when he saw he had been in the wrong. Perhaps Daisy Sewell had a private conversation with him.

The student body went all out in support of the new policy. *The Daily Reporter's* story about the first baseball game confirmed student interest: "Before a large crowd of enthusiastic spectators, Draughon's Practical Business College defeated Christian College on the latter's grounds Thursday afternoon by a score of 4 to 3. At all points the game was tight and there was scarcely any loose playing, although this was Christian's first match game of the season." This game was played February 27, 1913. It takes a spirit of optimism to schedule a baseball game in Abilene in February. A baseball game with Simmons College in April brought this comment in the *Reporter*: "The Christian students turned out almost en masse, and with the addition of the Simmons students, things were made lively throughout." Although baseball and basketball were back on the campus, football did not make it back until-several years had elapsed, and track and field had not yet been introduced.

In the spring of 1916 a new publication, the college annual, appropriately named the *Prickly Pear*, appeared on campus. Bellah Philpott, later a member of the English faculty, was editor, and Hollis Manly, later a long-time trustee, was athletics editor. He was the same Hollis Manly who, along with his brother, "Babe," or Cline Manly, was described by Dean Carl Gardner as "pretty rowdy" – so rowdy in fact that the dean would not let them room together or even stay at the same house. Hollis stayed with Mrs. Dabney Harvey, and "Babe" lived with the Gardners. One day, "Babe" came by the dean's office and reported, or confessed, that he had chloroformed Hollis. However, Hollis woke up sniffling, and went on with no apparent ill effects. That first *Prickly Pear* included a picture of the track squad and baseball and basketball teams – but no football team.

In 1920, the *Prickly Pear*, with Inez Norton as editor and Sewell Jones as athletics editor, carried a photograph of a sixteen-man football squad with an attention-getting narrative:

> For the first time in her history, A.C.C. permitted the boys to participate in intercollegiate football. A few of our best friends feel that she has made a great mistake. The President of the institution himself was once of this opinion, but when he saw that we could shod our feet with leather cleats without removing the 'gospel of peace,' when he saw that our loins were 'girded with truth' in spite of the fact that they were padded with khaki and cotton, when he saw the 'breastplate of righteousness' shining underneath the shoulder pads, when the 'helmet of salvation' held its own, when he saw that a man could, by the clean and friendly spirit with which he handled the football, make use of 'the sword of the spirit,' he willingly offered his support.

In calling the 1919 season the first year for intercollegiate football, athletics editor Jones was technically correct. The 1912 game that was unceremoniously canceled was with Abilene High School and therefore not an intercollegiate contest. Furthermore, it must be remembered that in the first Sewell semester, ACC was still almost altogether an academy even though called a college.

The first football season was an abbreviated one – four games. ACC won two and lost two. As soon as the season was over, the student body, with the president's blessing and cooperation, started a campaign for funds with which to purchase land that could be used as a playing field. In fact, the students, in chapel and on the campus and with letters back home, came up with $6,300, with which they purchased the land and built Wildcat Park across the railroad west of the campus.

Neighboring Simmons College had abandoned football two years before Sewell came to Abilene Christian. In 1910, the Simmons quarterback and captain, after discarding his helmet during a game, was tackled hard and thrown to the ground on his head. The resulting concussion led to a coma and his death. President J. D. Sandefer, who ruled Simmons very much as J. P. Sewell was to rule Abilene Christian, announced the discontinuance of the sport, and it was out for several years. The difference between Sandefer's ruling and Sewell's was that ACC banned match play in all sports, but at Simmons only football was outlawed. Also, Sandefer restored football before Sewell did.

Administrative changes came faster than football to the Sewell campus. At the end of the second year of his administration – the eighth year of the institution – some changes took place. For example, Dean Gardner resigned. He continued as a friend of the college and was close to President Sewell. His salary was $85 per month, but, as he said in an article written many years later, "Sewell's was less." Gardner had done a great job for the college, especially in his contacts with the University of Texas, of which he was a graduate. He went on to earn his master's degree at Texas, doctoral studies at Columbia and New York University, and to have a distinguished career in education.

When Gardner left, a young man whom he had been instrumental in bringing to the campus stepped into the dean's position. He was Henry Eli Speck, twenty-nine years old, newly married to Willie E. Wallace, daughter of Foy E. Wallace Sr. Speck came to the faculty in 1913 after receiving his bachelor's degree from the University of Texas. During his first year he was head of the Commercial Department. Thereafter, he was listed as professor of mathematics, or mathematics and science. He served with distinction as dean from 1914 to 1924.

Speck had a unique educational background, which may have helped him relate so well to the student body. Born in 1885 in Llano County, he never studied in a school with more than one teacher until he was eighteen. When he was nineteen, he began teaching at Pack Saddle Mountain School. From there he interspersed teaching with attending college for the next nine years, graduating from the University of Texas just in time to sign on with Childers Classical Institute. When he resigned in 1924 to move to Southwest Texas State Teachers College in San Marcos, the student newspaper, *The Optimist*, paid him this tribute: "Throughout the years that he has been at Abilene Christian College it can be safely said that he has not made an enemy in the student body. Even those students who have felt the discipline which was necessarily part of his work have left his office feeling that they got a square deal. As an ardent supporter of athletics as well as other branches of student activities he has almost become the idol of the boys of the institution."

Dean Speck was a vital part of the Sewell administration. The trio of J. P. Sewell, Daisy Sewell, and Henry Speck guided the college to senior college status and to recognition as a leading institution of higher education in Texas. He contributed much to the human qualities of the campus. The students admired and respected President Sewell. They admired, respected, and loved Dean Speck. He served not only as dean but as ombudsman. He could appreciate student viewpoints while maintaining and enforcing basic commitments of the institution. The dean took a leave of absence in February 1920 for the balance of the school year and through the summer months to complete work on a graduate degree at the University of Denver. Two hundred students showed up at the railroad station to see him off. According to *The Daily Reporter*, "They sang their songs and gave the dean a few college yells as expressions of their esteem and best wishes," surely to a sense of interest among his fellow passengers on the Texas and Pacific.

The Speck family has continued to be represented on the faculty through the years. Dr. Henry E. Speck Jr. served as a Bible professor, 1959-1988, and is an elder of the University Church of Christ. Mrs. H. E. Speck Jr. – Dr. Beatrice "Bea" Speck – taught in the Department of History during the same years and chaired the department in 1980-84. She is in demand as a speaker and is active in church, university, and community. Their son, Henry E. Speck III, with an Oxford doctorate, is director of the university's World Class program.

The Sewell years had much to do with founding the spirit of activism on the Abilene Christian campus, in contrast with the isolationism – insofar as political and governmental affairs are concerned – to be found on some campuses related to Churches of Christ at that time. Although he grew up under the instruction of spiritual giants such as David Lipscomb and James A. Harding at the Nashville Bible School, he did not share their beliefs in voting, running for office, and serving in the military. In his book *Civil Government*, Lipscomb wrote of the tragedy of the American Civil War: "... the years of sectional strife, war, bloodshed, destruction, and desolation swept over our land, and the spectacle was presented, of disciples of the Prince of Peace, with murderous weapons seeking the lives of their fellowmen.... It took but little thought to see that Christians cannot fight, cannot slay one another or their fellow men...."

From that base, Lipscomb went further. He reasoned that if the Christian could not himself fight, he could not vote to make another person fight. Hence, the Christian does not vote at all because he cannot know in advance whether the person he is voting for will use his position to bring about war or support war. The Christian's duty is to pay his taxes, obey the laws, and pray for the government to protect the rights of its citizens to live "quiet and peaceable lives in all godliness and honesty." Lipscomb was so highly respected and revered that not many members of the Church of Christ disagreed with his position.

However, when the United States declared war against the Imperial German government in 1917, Sewell made arrangements to establish a Student Army Training Corps on the campus of Abilene Christian College. Forty-three young men enlisted. They were paid thirty dollars per month, were issued government equipment, and were under military discipline all the time. Besides the courses required in English, French, German, mathematics, history, and government, the students were allowed to take Bible courses if they so desired. Under this program, the enrollment in the fall of 1918 was fifty percent larger than in the previous year.

Norvel Young states, "In appreciation for the school's patriotic cooperation the city of Abilene gave the college a gift of five thousand dollars." At the same time, some 200 miles north of Abilene, the leadership of Cordell, Oklahoma, forced the board and administration of Cordell Christian College to close their doors and leave town because they had so steadfastly refused to be involved in combat during the war. A later effort to revive Cordell Christian College was short lived.

Webb Freeman, a faculty member at Abilene Christian during those years, wrote: "The most unusual thing in the whole college, considering it is a Christian school, is the appearance of the S.A.T.C. unit in full uniform. The military leader is Lieutenant Hankey. Those numbered are in all exclusive of the lieutenant, forty-three. There are fourteen other names added, referring to men participating but not represented in the pictures given. Paul Witt was sergeant.... President Sewell was one of the most loyal citizens to be found anywhere."

D. L. Petty, second editor of *The Optimist* in 1912-13, was the first former student to die in the military service of his country. He died in action in Germany in World War I.

After the war, as before and during the war, Sewell continued his pattern of active participation in governmental and political affairs. He was not a leader in partisan politics, but he did speak out on questions having to do with the public interest. For instance, he went all out for the adoption of the Eighteenth Amendment – the Prohibition Amendment to the Constitution. In January 1919, he attended a meeting in Dallas of the Anti-Saloon League and was appointed to a committee of five "to organize the forces of Texas and to put the Prohibition Amendment over in good style." He was elected to the Board of Directors of the Anti-Saloon League of America and met with the group in Washington, D. C.

Now and then, President Sewell's activism in political affairs, such as the effort to legislate prohibition and the sponsorship of a military unit on campus during the World War gained for him some notoriety. For example, on Sunday evening, November 5, 1922, ten knights of the Ku Klux Klan in full regalia marched into the auditorium and down the aisle to where President Sewell stood before the congregation. The leader of the group made a short speech, telling how much the Ku Klux appreciated Sewell and the school and asked him to accept a check for $25 for the school and a similar check for himself. In the early 1920s the Klan was revived in Texas, and Abilene was no exception. The Klan's appearance at the college was typical; *The Daily Reporter* is full of reports that the Klan appeared unannounced in all different types of churches of Abilene to make small gifts. The tactic tended to compromise the churches and their ministers and apparently was designed to gain community approval of the Klan. Some oral versions of the incident at Abilene Christian, concocted later, would have it that the fearless president expressed in no uncertain terms his disapproval of the Klan and told them to get out. But Wendell Bedichek, who wrote the story for *The Optimist* did not mention any such response, and Ernest Walls, who was present and who today in his nineties remembers the incident clearly, says that the president merely said, "Thank you," and set the checks aside to be used in a better cause. The Klan members took their departure.

The Sewell years brought about a good deal of building and land acquisition for campus expansion. From the very beginning of his tenure, the president was making plans for a larger administration building. Enrollment had outpaced existing space, and various temporary arrangements were made. Classes could be conducted in various situations, but an immediate priority was housing for men. In June 1917, a contract was let for a new dormitory for men "of brick, concrete, and hollow tiling," with two stories and twenty-six rooms. It was named Zellner Hall, in honor of the family that had done so much for the school. By 1919, it was necessary to convert Zellner to women's housing, and a one-story frame building called the Emergency Hall was thrown together for the men. Also, the White Cottage was once more available for the men. In 1920, a third story was added to Zellner.

In 1918, President Sewell and the board were able, after several years of hard work, to contract for the construction of a new administration building. The 1906 building was incorporated as the east wing of the new facility. The new auditorium, with a main floor and a balcony, could seat approximately 1,000, whereas seating capacity in the old building had been about 200. *The Optimist*, in January 1919, published a picture of the new building with this commentary: "Contains a large auditorium, library and study hall, two offices, and twenty rooms." The official dedication was January 12, 1919.

Two major building projects remained to be accomplished on the five acres "more or less" of the old campus. First was the men's dormitory that had been promised for some years. It was named McDonald Hall in honor of founding trustee and generous donor A. F. McDonald, who died in August 1924. It was ready, with its fifty rooms, for the beginning of the fall semester in 1924. With the opening of McDonald Dormitory, the White Cottage – the Childers homeplace – that had served valiantly as a rooming place for men and women alternately, was razed. The 1925 *Prickly Pear* commented: "The tearing down of the White Cottage marked the passing away of the oldest landmark on the college campus. This old domicile of various people once stood where Daisy Hall now is, and was a prominent building when A.C.C. first opened." One *Optimist* poet expressed himself with regard to the White Cottage:

"The wind whistles under it,
"The paint's wearing off of it,
"The boys are getting tired of it,
"What will you do about it?"

Emergency Hall – better known as the Mule Barn – was converted from a dormitory for men to a dining hall. One more permanent building needed to be constructed on the crowded acres, and quite a story is connected to the solution.

Abilene Christian students had no place to play basketball except outside, and the students decided to do something about it. The A Club was founded by Professor G. C. Morlan during the 1916-17 school year. Its motto was "We live to serve." Men were chosen for membership based on character, leadership, and service. This group led the student movement to build a real gymnasium. The project was conceived in 1922. For basketball, after 1920, the team played on an outdoor wooden floor with a screen wire cage around it. It was called the "Wildcat Cage," with no cover, just a floor, no chairs, no benches. Spectators stood outside the cage.

The Optimist of October 18, 1923, published this story:

> The A Club timed the opening of the campaign ... for the morning after the Wildcats had won a football game. The team played Wayland College in Plainview on Friday. It was a cold day, with a Texas Panhandle wet norther blowing. The team returned to Abilene at 9 a.m. Saturday on the Sunshine Special. The student body – all 250 or 300 members – was gathered for chapel. ...

> Coach Victor Payne walked into the auditorium at the head of his players and seated himself down front. Of course, the victorious squad was given a very enthusiastic welcoming ovation. The stage was set.

> In about one hour that small student body had pledged $3,030 to the gymnasium fund.

A later *Optimist* article, May 12, 1927, gave credit to Dean Henry Speck, A Club president Don Morris, and student body president Wendell Bedichek for spearheading the drive. Three thousand dollars was a magnificent response but not enough to do the job. The next year's student body, led by Walter Adams, Harold Anderson, and Leslie Blakney, came up with an additional $2,000, and, as will be shown in the next chapter, the Board of Trustees made arrangements for the remaining funds needed. A number of young men in the student body got their physical education credit digging excavations for the foundation, helping pour concrete, and contributing to labor in various ways until the building was ready. No wonder the students were proud of the gymnasium. It was their building in a special way.

Incidentally, that student-built gymnasium is still in daily use in 1998 by the Coca-Cola Company. McDonald still stands. So does the Mule Barn. The other main campus buildings – the Administration complex, Daisy Hall, and Zellner Hall – have long been gone. Daisy was converted to a tourist court, or motel, for a while. It was called Grande Lodge. It did not succeed as a motel and was finally torn down. The big fire destroyed the Ad Building. Zellner Hall was razed, a story that will be told later.

The year 1919 was pivotal for the Jesse P. Sewell administration. That was the year Abilene Christian became a senior college and an all-out campaign was made to develop a greatly expanded campus beside the railroad tracks. In May 1919, the new catalog announced "the opening of Abilene Christian College in September 1919, as a standard four-year college" and included an explanation of how it came about. President Sewell explained:

> It was not our purpose to build a four-year college at Abilene. We were satisfied to give the service of a really first-class junior college. But we were determined to build into this junior college the very best Christian service .... We continued to add equipment and to build into our organization men and women as we found them in harmony with our ideals of Christian service....

Finally, two barriers stood in the way of offering the four-year program leading to the bachelor's degree: one additional faculty member and about $12,500 for new equipment. Batsell Baxter was the new faculty member, and the city of Abilene agreed to put up the $12,500. Students and faculty overwhelmingly supported the move to senior college status. The first degrees were awarded in the spring of 1920. Members of that first class to receive bachelor's degrees were Winnie Coons, Truman Harrison Etheridge, Gertie Horn, Silas Howell, Inez

Norton, William C. Smith, Carlos D. Speck, Irene Terry, and Hazel Watkins.

Clearly, by 1920, Abilene Christian had grown to its capacity on the small North First Street campus. A strong effort was made to obtain additional acreage nearby. Minutes of Board of Trustees meeting of May 14, 1920, contain this entry: "On motion the purchase of 30 acres of land … at $200 per acre was approved and the president of the board was authorized to execute four notes of $1,000 each in payment of same in addition to $2,000 cash consideration." President Sewell described the situation in an article published by *The Gospel Advocate* a couple of months later: "Our pressing, immediate need is the room to take proper care of the school we have now. We have recently bought thirty-five acres of ground. This ground has on it one large, handsome brick home and two modern bungalows. This gives us room to grow."

The deed records at the Taylor County Courthouse reveal that the purchased land was situated on the south side of the railroad, beginning one block west of the existing campus. The northern boundary was South First Street; the eastern boundary was Highland Street; and the initial purchase ran down to South Third Street. The western boundary was Catclaw Creek. This land would certainly have provided an adequate campus for years to come. By adding thirty acres south of the railroad tracks to the original campus of about five acres north of the tracks, plus some five acres of Wildcat Park, the college had room for solid growth.

In the catalog for 1920-21, an architect's sketch of "The Future Home of Abilene Christian College," was captioned: "This picture presents to you A.C.C. as we expect to build it on our new campus." It was a quadrangle design, with eleven large and attractive brick buildings surrounding a mall. It was, however, a bad deal. It was too close to the noise of the railroad, which would have split the campus. Its western border was Catclaw Creek, notorious for occasional flooding. The area was already developed, so there would not have been land for sale to home builders to help finance the building of the campus and to develop an ACC community. It would not have been a distinctly identifiable part of Abilene as a home for the significant educational institution that was developing.

Although minutes of board meetings do not include discussions that must have taken place, the recorded actions of the board indicate that the Board of Trustees decided within two or three years after purchasing the land for campus expansion that money to pay off debts and to help in building the new dormitory for men – McDonald Hall – was more important than campus expansion at that time. At a board meeting February 22 and 23, 1923, Otto Foster of Cleburne introduced a resolution to sell all or part of the land owned by the college south of the Texas and Pacific, and the resolution passed unanimously.

Subsequent to that action, the property was platted as "Christian College Subdivision," and the plat was filed for record with the county clerk June 5, 1923. Out of this subdivision, one block was reserved for the college, the block with the "large, handsome brick" home President Sewell mentioned in his *Gospel Advocate* article. It was built by H. O. Wooten, a pioneer Abilene buinessman, and had been the Wooten home for years. It became the beloved Shady Dell, home of the college president. Also, the college retained Wildcat Park.

After years of living in Daisy Hall, President and Mrs. Sewell had a beautiful house with spacious grounds. They could entertain the entire faculty and large groups of students. For instance, *The Optimist* carried this story in May 1924: "Three hundred people gathered on the lawn of Shady Dell ... on Wednesday evening at 8:00 to give Brother and Sister George A. Klingman and family a farewell greeting." After the Sewells, the Batsell Baxters made Shady Dell their home until the college moved to the new campus in 1929. The new home for the president could not begin to equal the beauty, spaciousness, and warmth of Shady Dell. In 1930, after the college had sold the land on which Shady Dell stood and moved out to its new location northeast of town, fire of undetermined origin broke out in the unoccupied house and practically destroyed it. *The Optimist* paid eloquent tribute:

> For many years Shady Dell was a favorite resort for students who assembled on the lawn for various functions. Numerous picnics, banquets, parties, and musicales have been celebrated in the old building and on the beautiful lawn in front. The annual banquet of the Sub T-16 used to be given there with Mrs. Batsell Baxter as hostess.
>
> News of the destruction will cause ex-students in many parts of the nation to review joyous scenes of yesteryear which were enacted on the property.

In addition to campus expansion, a tremendous accomplishment of Sewell was the recruiting of faculty members.

A fortunate selection was Miss Alma Adams, who came from Thorp Spring Christian College in the fall of 1915. She taught home economics and expression. The next year, Grover Cleveland Morlan joined the faculty, mainly because of Miss Adams. He taught Bible and history and coached athletics. He was a native of Iowa, but after joining the faculty of Abilene Christian he made his career in Abilene, Texas, until his retirement. A quiet, soft-spoken man, he was amazingly energetic and innovative. He began teaching education when that course was added to the curriculum in 1918. Four years later he organized a psychology department and became head of the combined Division of Education and Psychology. In that same year he took charge of extension work. In 1934, he became director of the summer school. He organized the A Club – the men's honor organization – and was its sponsor for many years. Along the way he earned the doctor of philosophy degree from the University of Iowa.

Within a short time after the arrival of G. C. Morlan on campus, Alma Adams became Mrs. Morlan. A few years later she was responsible for bringing her brothers, Walter and Leland "Chili" Adams to Abilene Christian College as students from Chickasha, Oklahoma. Walter Adams stayed on after graduation to fill an unparalleled role in the history of the institution – but that story will come later.

In 1917, Howard L. Schug joined the faculty and taught German, Spanish, and Latin. He was a scholarly man, vitally interested in mission work, famed for his absent-mindedness. Along the way, he earned the Ph.D. degree from George Peabody College for Teachers. One of the many stories told on Dr. Schug concerned the time he, at least allegedly, drove his car to a meeting in Wichita Falls. He returned to Abilene by bus. Remembering then that he had left his car in Wichita Falls, he went to the bus station and bought a round-trip ticket to go get it. Another was that he was walking across campus reading a book and eating an ice cream cone. Bumping into a post or a tree, he bowed and said, "Excuse me!" When the students began doing faculty takeoffs in chapel each year around April 1, Dr. Schug was a natural. The student who portrayed him had to be long of bone, thin, and large-nosed. It was helpful if the student happened to have one eye that seemed to look in another direction from the way the dominant eye was looking. A beret and wire-rimmed glasses finished the caricature.

Other significant teachers who joined the faculty during the Sewell years, most of whom stayed until retirement, were R. C. Bell, a spiritual giant who was never known to begin a Bible class without a word of prayer; Jewell Watson, who gave generations of students a love of great literature; W. Earl Brown, who made history come alive for students who were willing to read and study and talked over the heads of those who were not; Paul C. Witt, who developed the sciences so that Abilene Christian gained national respect for its high standards; Elizabeth Nelson, instructor of mathematics, later beloved dean of women, and still later, librarian; Lylian Arledge, who with Mrs. Morlan constituted the Department of Home Economics; Batsell Baxter, whose joining the faculty in 1919 as professor of natural sciences, made possible, insofar as adequate faculty was concerned, the achievement of senior college status; and James F. Cox, who returned as professor of education in 1920.

The recitation of these names is not meant to ignore the talented men and women who taught here for a while and then moved on. George Klingman, Walter W. Freeman, Charles R. Brewer, Lorrin G. Kennamer, and others made great contributions to hundreds of students through the years. For example, Professor Morgan Higdon Carter came from Tennessee to start a sociology program in the fall of 1923. The 1924 *Prickly Pear* paid him a compliment at the end of his first year of teaching: "Mr. Carter has succeeded in building up a very interesting department and his courses have proved to be very popular, in a measure, with the student who is looking for a course that will require full time and overtime. There is no loafing in the sociology department now." That was a clear message for students who preferred to loaf to stay away from sociology. On the other hand, students who took sociology expecting an easy subject, without a doubt found it can be fun to study.

Students who came during the Sewell years made significant accomplishments during their careers. No wonder. President Sewell made it clear that he would not put up with anything less than serious students. Consider these paragraphs from the catalog for 1918-19:

ARE YOU WANTED?

It would be ideal if a school could be found in which there were no sports, dudes, idlers, shallow-brains, busybodies in everything except that for which they were sent to school. We are anxious to help, but if you are "going off to school" to see how much of "the old man's money" you can spend; or if you think you must slip out at night and see how many fool things you can learn; or if you think a little learning a dangerous thing, and are going to fight against getting any at all, or if your shoes are too highly polished to put under a study table, your hair too well combed to run your fingers through, your trousers too well pressed to sit any place except in the parlor; or if you have too many suits to stay in your room, please allow us to save you money, time, and embarrassment. A.C.C. has no place for you, and will not suffer the student body to associate with you. Experience has taught us that we can do such students no good. We are not opposed to students looking neat, clean, and tidy. Taste and common sense are encouraged in dress.

Of course, that paragraph was not likely read by prospective students. It was "Prexy" talking to West Texas parents who were looking for a place to send their sons and daughters where there would be some controls. It must have worked at the time because each year the enrollment was higher than before.

Sewell's successes also included the Abilene Christian Lectureship, which had its official beginning in 1918. As Bill Banowsky pointed out in his book on the Lectureship, presidents of Abilene Christian from the beginning made a practice of inviting outstanding preachers to speak on the campus. But until 1918, such occasions had been mainly for the students. Beginning with the period January 7-11, 1918, the Lectureship was an all-out undertaking to bring people from all over the brotherhood to Abilene for an intensive week of preaching, Bible teaching, singing, and fellowship. To be sure, it was also an excellent way to get families better acquainted with the college. The Abilene Christian Lectureship would be for years the largest gathering of members of Churches of Christ in the world. It was not designed as a meeting of delegates or anything of that nature. The college had complete respect for the congregational system of church government; hence, no resolutions were passed, and no effort was made by the college to control the churches. The Lectureship was a service to churches and families.

A situation arose during that very first Lectureship that was scheduled to become a tradition. A headline in the local paper on the last day of the week's program told the story: "BLIZZARD DOES HEAVY DAMAGE ONE DEGREE ABOVE ZERO." However, a blizzard did not interfere too much with the scheduled events, except that the last evening's service was canceled because of the inability of the speaker to reach Abilene.

The twelve years of the Sewell presidency were also years of change in student life. What had begun in 1906 as an academy called Childers Classical Institute had become, first, an accredited junior college in 1914 and, then, an accredited senior college in 1919. For several years, academy and training school students outnumbered the college students. The academy was a strong four-year high school, with a principal and a good corps of teachers. The training school, which during some years was called "the practice school," consisted of the first seven grades. After 1919, a student could start with the first grade and go through to the bachelor's degree on the campus of Abilene Christian College.

An essential factor in keeping the institution alive and growing through the years was an active campus life. The principal student activity from the beginning, whether as players or spectators, was athletics. Baseball was the first sport, and, until the 1920s, the main sport. Basketball came next, although there was no gymnasium until 1925. For years, basketball was played first on a dirt court and beginning in 1921 on a wooden deck with net wire around it to keep errant passes from bouncing too far afield. A lot of basketball was played on this court. Match games with other schools, even in January and February, were played in "the cage," as the open-air court was called, although arrangements were made when extreme weather occurred for games to be played in Simmons College's Marston Gymnasium. When games were played at Simmons, large numbers of ACC students traveled by city trolley to root for the team.

For years, football was played primarily on an intramural basis and in a limited way. In 1907, with a thirteen-man squad, some match games were played, mostly at the high school level, but with two games involving Simmons College's second team. Homer Scarborough played fullback and coached the team. He reported that team members furnished their own uniforms and chipped in to buy a football. In 1912, an effort was made to play football games with other schools, but then came President Sewell's ban. Football came back to stay in the fall of 1919. Guy Scruggs relates the experience a group of eager supporters of football had when they tried to go big time:

> In 1920, Abilene Christian College, like many other colleges before that season and since, was the victim of a few enthusiastic friends who thought that the way to attain renown in ath-

letics was to hire a team. "Arrangements" were made with about a score of young men, most of whom had played on outstanding college and high school teams.... Not a game was lost.

When the subsidized football team went to Brownwood to play Howard Payne College, the president went with the players. According to *The Optimist,* he "endeared himself to every man on the team." At halftime, he informed the team that they were all to be his guests for dinner. When J. P. Sewell took a position, there was no going half way. He who had once condemned intercollegiate football had become its most prominent booster.

"After the football season, however," Scruggs reported, "most of the members of the football team withdrew from school. The practice of subsidizing athletes had been both a success and a failure." Scruggs went on to describe what happened next: "In 1921, the team was not subsidized and the results were disastrous." However, when Vic Payne came aboard as coach, the Wildcats resumed their winning ways. Thereafter, for more than two decades, help given to athletes carried with it some job responsibilities. Football and basketball players and track men worked on the grounds, cleaned buildings, washed dishes in the cafeteria, or did other bona fide work in exchange for room and board and/or tuition. During the 1920s and 1930s, costs were so low that students could literally "work their way through." After World War II, as enrollments burgeoned and costs escalated, athletic scholarships were granted in keeping with regulations of the Texas Conference, of which Abilene Christian was a member. Alignment with athletic conferences was begun during the Batsell Baxter years. The Wildcats were members of the Texas Intercollegiate Athletic Association, 1924-33; the Texas Conference, 1933-54; the Gulf Coast Conference, 1955-57; independent, 1957-63; the Southland Conference, 1964-73; and the Lone Star Conference, since 1973.

Tennis was played early by interested individuals, both men and women. Intercollegiate track for men had its beginning in 1922 and rapidly became a headline maker for the college. Track did not fully come into its own, though, until after the Sewell years, which is not to say that President Sewell was opposed to track. It simply was not on the high priority list.

Women took an active role in athletics during the Sewell years. The 1922 *Prickly Pear* showed the nine members of the women's basketball team with their coach, Mr. Lanier, and this paragraph: "These girls are real basketball players, capable of giving any girls' team in the state a hard fight." The 1920 annual carried a picture of the women's basketball teams of the Hardings and the Zellners and a shot of the college's women's volleyball team. The 1921 annual published a picture of the interclass basketball champions for both men and women. As a concluding bit of testimony that athletics and physical exercise at Abilene Christian consisted of activities for women as well as men, the 1920 annual featured Miss Elizabeth Nelson's Hikers, all women, getting what was probably the best exercise of all – a vigorous hike.

Sports were vital to campus morale. The non-participating students, at least, had sports and student athletes for whom to cheer. When the Wildcat Sports Hall of Fame was established at ACU in 1986, the first group of athletes honored included Esker "Eck" Curtis, the most outstanding of the Sewell era athletes. He played quarterback and ran track. After graduation in 1925, he had a distinguished coaching career at the University of Texas-Austin and is honored in the Texas Sports Hall of Fame.

The adoption of a mascot for the college occurred in 1919, when intercollegiate football, baseball and intramural sports came to need a playing field. The student body of about 185 college students became excited about the possibility of raising money to buy land for an athletic field, property that lay along South First Street and on either side of Catclaw Creek, two or three blocks west of the campus. The A Club challenged the other clubs on the campus to join in a contest to see who could raise the most money for the project. The winner would get to name the park. It was a spirited contest, especially between the top two contenders, the A Club and the West Texas Club. The West Texas Club came out on top by a narrow margin. The West Texans called for nominations from the student body for the name of the park. The top two suggestions were "Antelopes" and "Wildcats," and "Wildcats" won. After fourteen years without a mascot, ACC teams became known by the name "Wildcats," and their home park was named "Wildcat Park."

The money raised by the students was sufficient to buy the five acres of land, fence it, and erect a small covered pavilion for spectators. After the excitement of having Wildcat Park for football and baseball games, in 1923 Sam Cox of Ozona, Texas, donated to the student body a live, young wildcat, which had been captured on his ranch. An *Optimist* story expressed appreciation:

> Much interest has been shown by the students recently in the wildcat which occupies a cage on the campus near the college tailor shop. The animal is the official mascot of the Abilene Christian College teams and was presented to Coach Victor Payne by Mr. Sam Cox of Ozona, who captured the animal near his home. The specimen is a good one and serves the local teams as an ideal mascot, being entirely peaceable until molested and then giving vent to unrestricted wrath in a noisy manner…. As yet, the mascot has not been named.

Later the wildcat was named "Bob Thomas." Unfortunately, captivity was not a good thing for young Bob. Within a year he was dead. He was buried "with pomp and ceremony" on the campus. Dean Speck and several students made talks.

The school colors selection history is less clear than the adoption of the Wildcat as mascot, and a group of Sewell era alumni have competed with earlier alumni for the honor. O. M. Reynolds wrote that during 1908-9, while H. C. Darden was president, a group of students met as a committee for the purpose of making the colors selection. Committee members were Reynolds, Bertha Glass, Lizzy Parmelly, Arthur Slater, Beal Lanier, and Claude Sikes. They met in the southeast upper room of the Administration Building and came up with the recommendation that the official colors should be purple and white. On the other hand, Maryanne Baxter, later Mrs. Reba "Johnny" Wallace, declared that during the 1912-13 session, she and Corrie Acuff, later Mrs. Lawrence Brasher, were walking across the campus one day when President Sewell saw them and asked them to take on an important task for the school. He wanted them to come up with a recommendation for school colors. They selected purple and white. In an interview with Lawrence Smith, Mrs. Brasher gave substantially the same account that Mrs. Wallace gave, adding that they looked through the Bible in selecting white for purity and purple because that was the color of the robe placed on Jesus at his crucifixion.

Because O. M. Reynolds, Maryanne Baxter Wallace, and Corrie Acuff Brasher were all so precise and definite in their descriptions of what had happened – they named names and

gave the place of meeting in each case – it seems fair to conclude that each was in the right about the matter. During the
years, 1909 to 1911, the situation on the campus was not con-
ducive to remembering just what decisions had been made.
When Maryanne Baxter came in 1911, apparently nothing
showed that school colors had already been chosen. Probably,
the Reynolds committee's recommendation had simply been
lost in the shuffle. From 1908 to 1912, five individuals had
moved into the president's office, including Sewell, who did
not know colors had been chosen. It is interesting, however,
that both groups came up with purple and white, which have
served athletics and academic regalia purposes very well
through the years.

The roots of "O Dear Christian College," the alma mater,
likewise go back to the Sewell era. Maryanne Baxter Wallace;
Ruby Christian, later Mrs. Lloyd Wilson; and Inys Whiteside,
daughter of the third president of ACC, wrote the first school
song, titled "Dear Old Abilene." The first stanza, as quoted in
the 1920 *Prickly Pear*, was:

> Dear old Abilene
> Where we are often seen
> Beneath the skies of blue.
> Dear college – here's to you.
> We'll give our college yell
> And all our praises tell,
> With many a heart sincere,
> Our college dear.

This song failed to take hold. When Grover Cleveland
Morlan arrived as a new faculty member in September 1916, he
soon introduced an adaptation of a college song used at
Highland Park College in Iowa. He had matriculated there as
an undergraduate. Morlan's adaptation, named "O Dear
Christian College," was rearranged by Leonard Burford of the
Music Department in 1934 and has served as the alma mater
through the years:

> O dear Christian College, we love you,
> Our dear Alma Mater today;
> Like the stars shining brightly above you,
> Your fame shall shine brightly for aye.
> To you we'll prove faithful and loyal

While ever upholding the right,
And gladly we'll give forth the royal
Three cheers for the purple and white.
CHORUS
Then we'll pledge our love to Christian,
To her is honor due.
While we gaily sing let praises ring
For our alma mater true.

The second and third stanzas are not often used:

We gathered while safe in your keeping
Bright jewels of wisdom and truth,
Preparing life's field for the reaping,
Improving the days of our youth.
Whenever the call comes for service,
We'll answer with hearts true and right,
In home, shop, field, pulpit, or office,
We'll honor the purple and white.

Still upward and onward we're pressing
To win the great battle of life,
True courage and brave hearts possessing,
We'll never grow faint in the strife.
And when our life's journey is ended
And sunset is shrouded by night,
In the warm afterglow we'll see blended
The beauteous purple and white.

Another tradition of the Sewell era was the literary societies, now long dead. They complemented athletics as focuses of student life in the early years of the college. During the second year, 1907-8, two literary societies were organized. Otis M. Reynolds, a student during the first year and for several years thereafter, and a loyal alumnus for the rest of his life, described the beginning of these societies. He said that Professor Charles Roberson gave them their names, the "Argos" and the "Argens." Every student in school understood that he or she would be an Argo or an Argen. The societies competed in athletics, oratory, debate, quartet singing, and the sponsorship of lyceum numbers. Students were not assigned to a society; they were recruited, within the limitation that each club was expected to have approximately half of the student body, and every student was required to belong to one society or the other. Hence, the beginning of heavy competition was no doubt in the recruiting of new members.

In 1913, the literary societies voted to change their names. One group chose to be the "Harding Literary Society," honoring James A. Harding, co-founder of the Nashville Bible School, which was President Sewell's alma mater. The other group chose the name "Zellner," honoring ACC board member and benefactor M. Zellner. The Hardings and the Zellners played a vital role in making campus life interesting to the students. Competition for members was keen.

In the fall of 1921, the Hardings came out swinging. This message appeared in *The Optimist*:

> The Hardings are the smaller of the two societies in the number of members. Our members are from the plain every day student body and are sociable, industrious, and loyal. If you are looking for an aristocratic society you will not stay with us, but if you are looking for a bunch who will love one another and love the school, a bunch who will be kind and altruistic toward their sister society members, you will find just that type of folks among the Hardings.

The Zellners' message on the same page was, sure enough, more aristocratic and low-key: "We cherish the highest ideals of society work. We want to make the society spirit one of sportsmanship. Friendly animosity is desirable as long as it remains on the proper plane."

As the college continued to grow in enrollment, however, and as smaller social clubs and other types of student organizations began to come along, interest in the two campuswide organizations waned, and by 1925 the students simply failed to organize themselves into the two groups. Other types of clubs filled the void. They were smaller and more specialized. Perhaps closer friendships resulted. But there was never again the same breadth of interest as characterized the Hardings and Zellners – the Argos and the Argens. Never again would the intensity of competition in intellectual and cultural matters or in intramural sports rival the intensity of the literary societies, 1907-25.

With the continued growth of the student body in the Sewell era, pressure increased for more student input into campus life. The first breakthrough came with the organization of a Student Council by the young women of Daisy Hall. The *Prickly Pear* for 1921 printed the pictures of twelve Student Council members with this explanation: "The Daisy Hall Self

Government was organized last fall when it was learned that Brother and Sister Sewell approved of young people learning to govern and control themselves. We are glad that we were the first to follow their suggestion, and have tried to show the faculty that Student Self-Government is a success, and would be good for the entire school. We have made a few mistakes, but have profited by them and have grown stronger. We feel that this experience has accomplished much good and that we are better fitted for homemakers, since having studied the problems of self-government."

The next year, the women of Zellner Hall joined the movement, and a Student Council represented both dormitories.

Toward the end of that year, the student body as a whole voted to establish a representative group called "United Student Activities." It emphasized that the group had "no powers concerning the government of students," but it could "elect and control" the managers of different student activities.

During the 1922-23 session, Wendell Bedichek of Abilene was athletic manager, which meant that he had a major responsibility for scheduling contests in football, basketball, and baseball. Edwin Martin of Lubbock was forensic manager, with responsibility for lining up debates, oratorical contests, and other events involving speaking activities. Bedichek was also editor of *The Optimist*, which meant that he was a very busy man. In a summer of 1922 issue of the paper, he detailed some of his woes: "Athletic manager Wendell Bedichek has been at work since the close of school in an effort to get the schedule for next fall's football season into a definite form. He has been in communication with several colleges and universities of the state but has not as yet made final arrangements for any games save the one with Canyon Normal which is to be played on Wildcat Field on October 21st. Most of his efforts have been diverted toward obtaining a team to play the Wildcats at the West Texas Fair on September 30...."

Athletic manager Bedichek, however, had an exciting schedule arranged by the time the students arrived in September. Admittedly, the game with the Stamford American Legion was not exactly intercollegiate competition, but the fact that the Stamford group was composed of ex-college players, including some all-stars, challenged the Wildcats before they came out with a 7-0 victory. Also, the game with the Segal All-Stars of Breckenridge represented desperation scheduling, but the Wildcats felt good about a 16-0 victory. The October 14 game with Cisco Junior College resulted in a romp for the Wildcats, 70-0. But the student body, a large number of whom went to Cisco by train for the game, enjoyed it immensely.

No doubt, forensic manager Edwin Martin was busy, too, but he was not having to deal with so many people nor with such intense emotions as Wendell Bedichek. Incidentally, these first two student managers, elected by the students, went on to unusually distinguished professional careers. Bedichek was managing editor of the *Abilene Reporter-News*, filled other important roles with the Harte-Hanks news organization, and was associated with the Texas Research League in Austin. Martin – Dr. Martin – was featured in a *Houston Chronicle* story in 1955 under the headline "Neighbor of Note: He Has Helped Teach Millions." The *Chronicle* story mentioned Martin's high office in the United States Armed Forces Institute during World War II, helping millions of men and women in the service continue their education. He was stationed at the Pentagon. The event that triggered the *Chronicle* story was his appointment in 1955 as assistant superintendent in charge of Houston high schools, a position he held for years as superintendents came and went.

By 1923, the college was ready for a full-fledged Students' Association. Wendell Bedichek, who was vice president of the senior class, was the first president of the Students' Association. He was also the head yell leader. Don Morris, who was president of the senior class, was the vice president of the Students' Association and was assistant yell leader. The newly created association was said to have functioned efficiently during the year, providing a vehicle through which "the students have expressed themselves frankly, in resolutions, with regard to things pertaining to the welfare of the college and student body."

Walter Adams was forensic manager of that first Students' Association. He would be its president the next year. Seven years after Adams was president of the Students' Association, he would be dean of the college and would serve in that capacity until 1969 – thirty-seven years. Eight years after Morris was vice president of the Students' Association, he would become vice president of the college, and eight years after that he would become president of the college, to serve in that capacity for twenty-nine years – until 1969. Those two men were earmarked beginning in their student days for the top leadership roles in the institution. Joined by Lawrence L. Smith, who was business manager, then called "bursar," from 1928 to 1969 – forty-one years – they became a most effective and respected administrative team.

Joining the Students' Association to fill the void left by the death of the Hardings and the Zellners, clubs of various kinds sprang up. Geographic clubs, representing various states, counties, and regions helped combat homesickness, no doubt. Special interest groups, such as the Press Club and the Dramatics Club, flourished. And then were born the social clubs, the pride of many and at the same time the bane of not a few through the years. Three social clubs that were organized during the Sewell years are still functioning. The first two clubs in that category were GATA and Ko Jo Kai. During the three decades from 1920 to 1950, the GATAs customarily included with their group photograph in *The Prickly Pear* the words, "oldest social club on the campus, organized January 16, 1920," or similar language. The Kojies generally were content to have the wording, "one of the oldest social clubs on the campus."

In the 1952 volume of the annual, however, the Kojies began to challenge the GATA claim to seniority. On the GATA page was the traditional language, "organized January 16, 1920," and "oldest social club." But the Kojie page, facing the GATAs, contained a bit of a challenge to the seniority claim of the GATAs:

> Ko Jo Kai... was organized in the year 1920, and was known as the High A Club, because it was composed of a group of girls with high ideals. Due to the similarity in name to the honor club, the A Club, the girls were asked to change the name of the club the following year. The girls considered many names before deciding on the name Ko-Jo-Kai, which in Japanese means "a little group of women."

By the time the 1956 annual came off the press, the Kojies had delved further into their history and were ready with their official claim to seniority: "Back in 1919 there was a club on the old campus called the Hi-A Club. The next year the girls in the club changed its name to Ko-Jo-Kai, a Japanese name that means 'a little club of women.'" So it can be seen that the Kojies have a rationale for claiming to be the oldest club if it is conceded that a group can change the name and still be the same organization. The institution that has been Childers Classical Institute, 1906-1920; Abilene Christian College,

1920-1976; and Abilene Christian University since 1976 could hardly disagree with the proposition that a name change does not change the basic institution. Also in the 1956 yearbook, the GATAs still proclaimed themselves the oldest social club on the campus. In recent annuals, both clubs – and other clubs – have given more emphasis to their constructive service projects through the year.

GATA (Girls Aid to Athletics) had as its original purpose "to aid and entertain home and visiting athletes." An example of how club members functioned is found in connection with a basketball game between the Wildcats and Howard Payne College in the winter of 1922. *The Optimist* reported it:

> The members of the Howard Payne basketball team were very favorably impressed by A.C.C. ... While here the boys from Brownwood were entertained by the girls from Girls' Aid To Athletics. This organization of girls has done much to engender a friendly spirit in the athletes of different colleges toward A.C.C.

The entertainment consisted of taking the young men to a musical performance on campus by Thurlow Lieurance and Company, specializing in Indian music. Before long, however, the club adopted and espoused broader interests. A later annual explained that the initials came to stand for "Girls Aiming Toward Achievement." The GATA fountain is one of their achievements on campus.

Ko Jo Kai was organized with the announced purpose of enjoying life, later amended to include "exchanging gossip, discussing styles, the college administration, prospective exams, and new plots for further entertainment." Still later Kojies espoused "the purpose of creating closer bonds of friendship and loyalty to the school, stimulating social activities, and bringing its members to a greater appreciation of the real values of life."

For the men during the Sewell years, Sub T-16 brought social clubs to the campus. The prime movers in founding this club were John Paul Gibson, later a successful pediatrician in Abilene and a longtime trustee of the university, and Walter Adams, later the peerless dean of the university. Dean Adams has given a firsthand account of how it came about in 1923:

> I do recall that it was during this year that the first men's social club was organized, the Tuscarora, later Sub T-16. John Paul Gibson ... was really responsible for its being organized. John Paul came by my room in the yellow cottage one Saturday

afternoon and suggested we get several of our friends and go to Elm Creek west of Abilene and have bacon and scrambled eggs that evening. He asked me to contact certain boys and he would get in touch with others. As I recall, about ten or twelve boys showed up, including one, George Klingman, Jr., who had been in the navy. He entertained us by telling some tall tales about the navy and particularly about the good ship Tuscarora with its thirteen decks and straw bottom. During the course of the evening someone suggested we organize a club and we proceeded to do so. It was natural that we should name the club "The Good Ship Tuscarora." Since all ships have skippers, first and second mates, quartermasters, captains of the head, etc., we proceeded to select such from our number, and thus was born the first men's social club in the history of the college.

The Good Ship Tuscarora ran aground during its first year and was kicked out of port. With certain improvements, commitments, and promises, it was allowed to recharter as a submarine – Sub T-16. Through the years the men of Sub T have been frequent visitors to the dean's office, but as of this writing, the crew seems to have the situation in good shape.

Through the years other social clubs have come on line, and some have gone, but these three – GATA, Ko Jo Kai and Sub T-16 – were started during the Sewell years and are still on campus.

Students with great senses of humor always make campuses interesting places for their administrators, faculty, and classmates; such was true of the students of the Sewell-Speck era. For instance, there was J. C. "Jakey" Brown. In honor of his graduation in the spring of 1924, he sent invitations to all of his relatives and friends. At last, with two invitations left over, he determined not to waste one, so he sent one to movie star Mary Pickford in Hollywood and addressed the other one to "The Honorable Cal Coolidge, The White House, Washington, D. C." Neither responded. In later years, Jake Brown had a successful career as a rancher in northwestern New Mexico and southwestern Colorado. He was a church leader and a benefactor of Abilene Christian University and died at age ninety-two in 1995.

Another personality of the period was D. B. "Happy" Rambo. He enjoyed telling of the time that Dean Speck started a campaign on campus to call students by their given names instead of nicknames, and especially if they were on the daily chapel programs. He thought more formality would lend dignity to the occasion. Once, when "Happy" was slated to lead the chapel singing, Dean Speck could not think of "Happy's" name. Rambo stared innocently ahead. Finally, in exasperation, the dean said, "Aw, 'Happy,' get up here and start the song."

And Don Morris told the story of the frizzed hair of Gustus A. Dunn Jr. The rumor was out that his fellow residents of the Mule Barn, led by football star Alfred "Fats" Collins, were planning to shave Dunn's head. President Sewell called the hulking plot leader into his office and appointed him to be Dunn's bodyguard for the next few days. When he asked Collins if he would accept the assignment, "Fats," who needed all the points he could accumulate with the president, replied, "Yes sir, Brother Sewell, I sure will." He later declared it to have been the most burdensome assignment he had ever been given – but Gus kept his hair.

Embedded in the history of students at Abilene Christian University, is the story of the Southwestern Company of Nashville, Tennessee. This company, which is still strong – and larger than ever – dates back to the immediate post-Civil War period. It had no connection with Abilene Christian College until early 1922, when sophomore John Paul Gibson encountered the company. Gibson, of Washington, D.C., enrolled as a freshman in the fall of 1921. He had planned to attend college in Nashville, but he changed his mind after hearing Jesse P. Sewell speak in Washington. President Sewell happened to have a copy of the *Prickly Pear* with him, so he let young Gibson look through it. John Paul did not take long to make his decision. He said, "President Sewell offered me a job. I had been working for a railroad and therefore had free transportation. Then, when I saw pictures of all those good-looking girls in the annual, my mind was made up, and so I came."

President Sewell followed through, as he always did, with the job. John Paul found himself washing dishes in the college cafeteria at twenty-five cents per hour – not bad for a college freshman at the time. He was grateful for the job and worked at it throughout the year. During the year, however, he saw that he would not be able to meet all expenses with what he was making. He knew that his parents were not in position to help him. He needed a better-paying job, or at least an additional source of income.

A lawyer and his wife whom he had known in Washington moved to Abilene, so he paid them a visit. In the course of conversation, he told them his problem. His friend said to him, "Why don't you sell Bibles for the Southwestern Company of Nashville? I did, and paid my way through law school." The school year was nearly over by that time, but his friend wrote to the Southwestern Company about him, and he received through the mail a sample case and some literature from the company. During the summer of 1922, he tried selling Bibles in his family's neighborhood in Washington, D.C. He did this without attending one of Southwestern's sales schools. He simply studied the literature and became familiar with the samples in the case. He devised his own system of selling, which was simply to walk up to the front door, knock, and politely undertake to show the samples of his Bibles.

Gibson was surprised and delighted with his success. The company's established plan, spelled out in the literature, was for the salesman to take orders, attempt to get as much down payment as he could arrange, and deliver the books later in the summer, at which time he would collect the balance due, or else not leave the book. It should be understood that in those days, the Bible salesman did not have a car, so he could not have an inventory of books with him. Toward the end of the summer, the established procedure was to buy, borrow, or hire an old vehicle of some kind and take his deliveries to the customers. He would notify the customers ahead of time – via postal card – of the projected date and time of his arrival with their books.

Gibson did so well – on paper – with his neighborhood sales that he wrote the college that he would not need his dishwashing job for the next year. Some other needy student could have that job. Unfortunately, at delivery time he was surprised at how many of his customers did not have the money to take their order. Thus he did not have enough money to pay all of his college expenses, and he had already forfeited his campus job. He came up with an alternate plan. He took his trusty sample case and sold Bibles in Abilene after classes and on Saturdays, and he began taking a friend with him to sell. That friend was Walter Adams. Adams was so impressed with Gibson's smooth approach that he tried it himself and found he could sell Bibles. Gibson got a sample case for him. Adams became a member of Gibson's "team," which meant that John Paul got a small commission on everything Walter sold. Don Morris joined up, as did Burton Coffman, Wendell Bedichek, Ernest Walls, Lawrence Smith, and many, many others.

Teams of salespersons began selling in the summers in Texas, Tennessee, Virginia, West Virginia, Ohio, and elsewhere. The practice was for a person to sell during one summer and, then, for the next summer get himself a team. Professors at Abilene Christian began to notice how many of their students were making more money by working in the summer than the teachers made teaching in the college nine months of the year. Bible selling helped many a young man – and some young women – pay their way through college and get some marvelous experience along the way.

As for the student who got the whole business started – John Paul Gibson – he worked his way through medical school with his Southwestern sample case. After graduation from medical school, he was doing an internship in a hospital at fifty dollars per month, so, to support his family, he kept his sample case in the car with his medical kit. At a tribute dinner for Dr. Gibson in 1974, Dean Adams spoke of those days and stated that since 1923 some 2,000 Abilene Christian students had sold Bibles for Southwestern. Dr. Gibson, during fifty years of medical practice in Abilene, including ten years as the college physician and professor of health education, led many people to Christ by personal visits. His conviction was "Anybody who can sell Bibles can do personal work."

In the 1930s Otis Gatewood took the lead in selling Bibles and recruiting people to sell. One of his recruits was Fred Landers, who made a career with Southwestern, and in whose honor people of the company established an endowed scholarship at Abilene Christian University. Jim Samuel came as a shy young man from California and became sales manager for the company. Abilene Christian University students still go on the Southwestern summer safaris, although not in the numbers that once characterized the business. With so many hundreds, and in fact thousands, involved through the years, it would not be practical to start naming them. Undoubtedly, their children and grandchildren have heard, or will hear, their stories of the experience.*

By 1923-24, the Sewell era had run its course. In the days of the Roman Republic, when dark days and difficult times beset the republic, officials of the city-state would appoint a dic-

---

*I am grateful to R. D. Tyler of the class of 1937 for information on the Southwestern Bible Company. Tyler sold Bibles for several years. I sold in the summer of 1936, with some success.

tator to come in and take total charge and straighten things out. He would be given a specified time frame to get the job done, and then he was to go back to whatever he had been doing when he was called to the dictatorship. The famed example was Cincinnatus. He was plowing in his field when messengers came calling him to take charge. All ordinary laws were suspended for the duration of the dictatorship. The dictator had the power of life or death over people. He made government more efficient, collected the taxes, paid the bills, and at the end of six months went back to his plowing.

The comparison does not say that J. P. Sewell had all the characteristics of a dictator. He respected the faculty and the students. He and Dean Speck were partners in the administration. He and Daisy McQuigg Sewell were partners in everything. He was a humble servant of Jesus Christ. At the same time, however, he was a man of strong convictions. For twelve years he presided over Abilene Christian College with a firm hand. That was the understanding he had with the Board of Trustees when he took the job. The trustees were weary of having to look for a new president every year or two. They were tired of the constant struggle for bare survival. They wanted somebody who could take charge and let the board set policies with assurance that there would be an executive who could run the school as it was supposed to go. He saved the school – not only saved it, but made it an institution of quality. When he took the reins in 1912, it was Abilene Christian Training School – not a college at all. Some sixty-nine students, none of them college students, were enrolled. The last year he was president 525 students, about 300 of them college students, were enrolled.

The time had come, however, for the Board of Trustees to have a more significant role in running the institution. During the years since 1912, the board had matured. In 1912, the board was in a position of weakness, pleading for a strong leader to take the school and do something with it. Board members were worn out from confrontation with financial crises. By 1924, however, the board members were wanting more input into how things went with the school.

Obviously, some disagreements developed between the president and the board. President Sewell had desired to move the campus to a thirty-five-acre tract south of the railroad tracks. The board vetoed the plan and voted to sell the land. During that same meeting, the board commended O. E.

Phillips, who had been employed as fiscal agent, "for his work in getting financial affairs out of the chaotic condition in which he had found them when he took charge as Fiscal Agent." This would seem to have been a rather significant criticism of the presidential office.

The time came for Jesse P. Sewell to go. He submitted his resignation December 27, 1923, but the board did not accept it. He asked for a special meeting of the local board December 31 and insisted that his resignation be accepted. Again the board demurred. But the next day, January 1, 1924, at a called meeting the board passed this resolution:

> whereas J. P. Sewell has offered his resignation as president of Abilene Christian College and has contended that it is best for the school and him, giving as his reasons the condition of his health and the excessive heavy burden of the office;
>
> We, the members of the board present, after much deliberation and prayer, do this day accept Brother Sewell's resignation at his request, to take effect at the close of summer school, 1924.
>
> We feel that we owe to Brother and Sister Sewell a debt of gratitude that cannot be paid in money for the untiring service and sacrifice they have made to build this institution. We know that hundreds of boys and girls from many lands owe to them much for their knowledge of the Lord and their fitness for life.
>
> Brother and Sister Sewell have done for Abilene Christian College that which no one else could do or did do; to give them up is painful and a loss that seems irreparable, but upon the urgency of the request we feel compelled to act now, both in justice to Brother Sewell and the school.

The news impacted the students and faculty like a bombshell. *The Optimist* carried a plaintive but loyal editorial:

> The idea of a man other than Jesse P. Sewell presiding over the administration of the college affairs seems strange to the students. It has been so long since another man has been in the place that not more than half a dozen who are connected with the school locally were here at that time. He has been the builder of the college. He has guided the ship through the storms and now he feels that his work is finished. The builder is now handing up the duties and burdens to another.

The editor went on to say, "Students must stand behind the Board. The Board must stand behind the faculty. The faculty must give its best at all times."

The fallout from the Sewell resignation included the departure of Dean Henry Eli Speck. He had been a key factor in maintaining a great spirit among all students on the campus as the dean of the college. He supervised a smoothly run program of campus life while heading up the academic program. President Sewell, because of uncertain health, was absent from the campus scene much of the time. His frequent illnesses did not keep him from promoting the school, but he was a somewhat distant figure insofar as the students were concerned. Consequently, Dean Speck bore the responsibility for the day-to-day operation of the campus. He did it with skill and grace.

One lengthy illness of the president occurred while the dean was taking a semester's leave of absence for further graduate study. On the first page of the *Daily Reporter*, on January 12, 1920, there was this revealing but somewhat mystifying story:

> From his sickbed at Abilene Christian College, President Jesse P. Sewell stated Monday that he would be one of two hundred Abilene citizens to give ten dollars each toward raising the $2,000 still due the college on Abilene's promise of financial aid.
>
> The money is badly needed just now to care for additional expenses incurred in connection with purchasing new equipment. Two thousand dollars is the sum needed to round out Abilene's contribution.
>
> Mr. Sewell has been ill since Christmas, confined to his bed most of the time with something resembling a nervous breakdown. His condition Monday morning was unimproved.

The president, apparently, had been indisposed for almost three weeks with an undiagnosed illness. *The Optimist* followed up with an article three and a half weeks after that, with this sentence: "Brother Sewell came to chapel Friday [January 30] for the first time since his illness."

The editor of the *Prickly Pear* ran this melancholy comment that year: "Feb. 3. I just don't see how I'm going to stand it. Our Dean has gone. Of course we all love Bro. Baxter, but we want Bro. Speck to be here too." Baxter, who was in his first year on the faculty, had been named acting dean during Speck's leave of absence."

When President Sewell resigned, he recommended Dean Speck to replace him. The Board of Trustees did not choose to follow his recommendation but chose Batsell Baxter to be the next president. Sewell made no attempt to conceal the fact that his recommendation had not been followed. In a chapel speech after the vote of the board, he told students and faculty, "In the beginning I made a recommendation. This recommendation has not been met with...." Then he graciously continued: "I am glad that a man in whom I have absolute confidence has been selected for this responsible position." Thus although he had recommended Speck, he gave a ringing endorsement of Baxter.

Dean Speck undoubtedly was disappointed. He would have been a great choice. But Batsell Baxter was also an excellent choice. A statement made by Sewell in that chapel speech probably explained the situation. He said, "From the time that I came to the definite conclusion that the time had arrived for a reorganization of Abilene Christian College on another basis, that my resignation was necessary, I have been interested not for myself but for the welfare of the college.... As we look forward to a new administration for the college, and know that the college must be reorganized entirely, it is a serious matter." The key words of the speech were, "the college must be reorganized entirely." Up to that time the president had borne the entire burden of running the school. He had raised the money, collected tuition, room, board, and fees, paid the faculty, kept up the property, and added buildings. The board had helped, but the board ordinarily met once a year and ratified the actions of the president. That had to change. The president had worn himself out and was not constitutionally equipped to know how to turn loose of the way he had been running the school, day and night, year-round, for twelve years. On the other hand, the board comprised a group of men who were vigorous, successful in their own businesses, and ready to take the reins. The time had come for the trustees to take over the role that trustees should fill in an educational institution and to let the president be the chief executive in carrying out his responsibilities under the oversight of the board.

Dean Speck had been Sewell's partner in running the school for a decade. Conceivably, trustees thought he would contiue Sewell's methods as president. Perhaps Baxter would be more adaptable to the changes they wanted to make and for which the time had come. After considering the situation, Speck also decided that the time had come for him to move along. Two months after Sewell's resignation, Speck announced that he, too, would leave the school, saying he believed he could be of more service to humanity elsewhere. Some years later, he wrote about the college, "She has never taken a forward step nor risen to greater influence but that my heart has beaten faster and my joy has been greater." Shortly after his resignation, he announced that he had accepted a position as dean of men at San Marcos Normal College, now Southwest Texas State University, where he dealt, on a friendly basis, with such students as Lyndon Baines Johnson, who was working his way through college and whose job-seeking was aided by the dean of men. Dean Speck often returned to the campus as a speaker and as an honoree.

He was always a friend of the college.

Speck was gone, as was the man who represents the quintessential meeting of the man and the moment in the history of the university – Jesse P. Sewell.

CHAPTER THREE

Moving the School

The Sewells were out. The trustees were in. The change was revolutionary. Since 1906, the trustees had been primarily a group of advisers to the presidents. Additionally, when a president found it necessary to leave the work, it fell the trustees' lot to locate a successor. They had done a good job of that. Three presidents and one president-elect who did not get to serve had come and gone. The fourth president, Sewell, was in the process of leaving.

The situation that confronted the board in 1924 was different from previous changes of the presidency. This time, the board would set a salary for the president and take responsibility for the development and ongoing of the school.

This is not to say that the trustees had not helped finance the college through the years. In his 1961 interview with Joseph Jones, President Emeritus Sewell said that he had financed Abilene Christian College for twelve years without "any assistance from any other source."

In the same interview, however, he said that when he started to build a dormitory for the young women, the first building project since the little "chicken coop" Administration Building in 1906, the trustees gave generously to the cause and "enthusiastically supported it." So it is not fair to the memory of the great and good men who served on the board from the beginning of the school to say that they had not paid dearly for the privilege of serving. They gave, but they had never officially assumed responsibility for building and perpetuating the school.

Now – in 1924 – they were doing just that.

President-elect Batsell Baxter explained the situation in a Lectureship speech a month after he had been selected to take over the post the next August:

> Today the institution is on the most stable basis it has ever been. The trustees have taken over the debt against the school. They have assumed responsibility for the running expenses of the school. They have promised that the program for growth and development shall go steadily forward.

President Baxter reaffirmed this position a month later in an article in *The Optimist* for the benefit of students and faculty:

> The Board of Trustees, for the first time in the history of the school, has assumed the financial obligations for the maintenance of the school. Heretofore, this has rested solely on Brother Sewell. It means a great deal to have thirty-five of the best business men of the church behind the institution. The board is to be commended for putting the school work on this business basis. This has put renewed confidence into every branch of the work.

Five years later, in remarks at the official opening of the gleaming new campus northeast of town, President Baxter reaffirmed the commitment of the trustees, as quoted by W. W. Freeman:

> A number of the men who are on the Board of Trustees have broken their backs financially for Abilene Christian College. Now perhaps you wonder what contributions I have made to the financial development of the school. The biggest thing I have been able to do with this Board of Trustees is to let them alone and let them do it. They have managed the building program; I have managed the school.

Even though Batsell Baxter usually refrained from overstating or understating a case, he did in fact fail to give himself the credit he deserved in working with the trustees. A reading of the minutes of the Board of Trustees will show that from year to year the president was involved in fund raising in cooperation with the board. He did not spend all of his time on the campus. He helped raise money, and he managed very carefully all that came under his care. When the college was primarily a presidency, the trustees helped the president. Likewise, when the time came that it was primarily a trusteeship, the president worked hand in glove with the trustees. Fund raising was never a monopoly operation.

Baxter was a native Texan, born in Tom Bean, November 17, 1886. He grew up in the neighboring city of Sherman, to which his parents moved when he was a year old. After graduating from Sherman High School, he lived and worked for two years on a farm, where he acquired the ability to use tools and do hard physical labor. The next two years he worked as a reporter for the *Sherman Daily Democrat*, experience that gave him a facility for writing concise columns. He wrote regularly, throughout life, especially for *The Gospel Advocate*. As president of the college, he wrote materials promoting the school and used them as advertising. This helped build enrollment to new records.

In 1908, he went to Tennessee to enroll in Nashville Bible School, the school that Barret, Whiteside, and Sewell had attended. By the time he enrolled, it had begun awarding bachelor's degrees, which it had not done while the aforementioned three ACC presidents attended the school. In 1911, Baxter accomplished two goals: he received the bachelor of literature degree from Nashville Bible School, and he married his sweetheart from Sherman High School, Frances Faye Scott. The newlyweds moved to Corsicana, where he preached for the Church of Christ for a year, and then to Thorp Spring, where he served as professor of English in Thorp Spring Christian College. Halfway through the year the dean of the college resigned, and, though he was the youngest member of the faculty, Baxter was named dean.

After four years at Thorp Spring, the Baxters moved to Cordell, Oklahoma, where he served for two years as dean of Cordell Christian College during the World War. With the closing of the college at Cordell, he was out of a job, so he moved his family back to Texas. He had completed a bachelor of arts degree at Texas Christian University in 1917, and in 1919 he received a master of arts degree from Baylor University. In that same year, he was the additional faculty member who was needed to qualify Abilene Christian to move up to senior college status, so to Abilene the Baxters came. He had been in Abilene for five years – as a professor of history and of biology and, for a short time, as acting dean while Dean Speck was on leave of absence for graduate study – when the board elected him as president.

The Baxter presidency was an era of good feeling. The board and the president worked together harmoniously. The only disagreement on record involved efforts of the trustees to raise the president's compensation. Minutes of the meeting of February 24 and 25, 1926, show an interesting situation: "Moved, seconded, and unanimously voted to give Mrs. Baxter two lots in the college addition – to her estate only as her separate property, separate and apart from that of her husband. This is to show an appreciation of the board to Brother Baxter for the work he did at the beginning of his administration without pay and for the traveling expenses that he paid out of his own salary. Brother Baxter refused to accept this is [sic] the reason for this action." So although Batsell Baxter could be stubborn, the board came up with a way to bypass his reluctance to accept increased compensation. Mrs. Baxter was a practical person. She accepted the property. A year later, the board again voted to raise the presidential salary, and Baxter refused to accept it. This time he prevailed. Perhaps he exhorted the board not to try any more end runs.

Baxter was an unusual president in more ways than one. He liked to do maintenance work. He was a mechanic at heart. Jerome Reese, son of board vice president J. C. Reese, and later a successful orthodontist, told Lawrence Smith of his work as a campus maintenance man while a student: "I was a repairman, and Brother Baxter told me anytime I got into trouble to come in by the back door of his office and peek in and let him see me. Then when he got through he would come in and talk to me. If I had any problem he would help me out. I never did run into a problem that he couldn't help solve."

Reese told of the time a water cooler failed in the Administration Building. President Baxter always kept some tools in his desk drawer, so he went with Reese to repair the water cooler. They took it apart, put it back together, and it worked. Reese also told of the time he and other student workers were laying sidewalks on the campus in the summer. They had worked since seven o'clock in the morning, and it was approaching six in the afternoon. They had poured the last batch of concrete into the forms and were getting ready to trowel it to a smooth finish when the president came along. "If you fellows are tired and want to go in, I'll finish the walk for you," he said. They accepted his offer with alacrity. He took a trowel and finished the walk in a professional way.

Not only was he good with the tools of the carpenter, the plumber, the bricklayer, and the cement finisher, he was also a good cook. His son, the late Batsell Barrett Baxter, who became one of the all-time great preachers among Churches of Christ, wrote, concerning his father in the kitchen, "He assisted mother in the kitchen, in the preparation of meals. His special forte was the cooking of meat." However, to keep his father from looking too good, Batsell Barrett added in "I Remember My Dad" in a 1979 *Gospel Advocate*, "After the meal, he was through, however, for I never remember seeing him with a single dish."

Faye Baxter too had a great deal to do with the good feeling and the popularity of her husband with the students. She was an accomplished artist, and her paintings became cherished gifts. In the 1927 and 1928 issues of the *Prickly Pear*, her picture was included in the faculty section, and she was given the title of "Preceptress of A.C.C." Just what the job description for that title might have been was not made clear. She did carry on her work with all parts of the college community with dignity and grace.

The congenial and practical working relationship between the Board of Trustees and the president was complemented by a similar board-faculty feeling. During the meeting that resulted in the employment of Baxter as president, the board received seven recommendations from the faculty. Before 1924, some history of faculty-to-board communication dated back to 1911 when faculty members presented a petition asking help in persuading President Whiteside to withdraw his resignation. But the record shows no faculty initiative quite so bold as the seven recommendations presented before the Baxter hiring. Maybe that was because the faculty realized the board had hitherto been fairly unconcerned about the operation of the institution.

At any rate, the faculty presented seven recommendations.

Numbers one through five and number seven were unanimously adopted. Number six did not rate a mention in the minutes. Number one was perhaps the result of knowledge that the board was taking control as never before and the faculty felt constrained to advocate restraint: "We feel that the President should be the head of the school. In order to do this, he should be able to name his own dean, registrar, and bursar. Both these and all other members of the organization should be under the control of the president. ... The president should, with the approval of the board, select the members of his organization." Article two was a bold one: "There should be no decrease in the faculty salary budget. In case the income of the school is not sufficient to make needed repairs, pay the faculty, and replace necessary equipment, then the trustees should make up the deficiency at the end of each quarter. The yearly budget should be agreed upon by the board and president at each annual meeting of the board." No doubt, some of the trustees swallowed hard at this recommendation, but unanimously approved it. When the Great Depression struck, a few years later, the board could not completely live up to this stipulation; in fact, faculty salaries were reduced in mid-year. But when that time came, all parties understood.

Articles 3, 4, and 5 were bland recommendations advocating businesslike procedures in operating the school. Article 6 was not even described in the minutes, but article 7 showed that the faculty, the administration, and the board members were all on the same page insofar as the basic purpose of the school was concerned: "The ideals for which Abilene Christian College now is pledged should be maintained, namely, Bible study and spiritual development should be supreme. Standard educational work should be done. In all of our work, we should strive to place the emphasis on the fact that it is ABILENE CHRISTIAN COLLEGE."

The era of good feeling and high campus morale was reflected in student enrollments. During his third year as president, Baxter wrote in his report to the board, "We are handicapped greatly for lack of room. The new building which is being planned will relieve this situation for classrooms, but not for dormitories, in which we are badly crowded." This fact was the predominant problem confronting the board and the president during the latter half of the decade of the 1920s.

The trustees had taken charge of the situation, no doubt about it. They usually met twice a year for a few hours, but now they took on new life with the realization that they controlled the destiny of the college. An *Optimist* story reported that the meeting when Baxter was elected president went on all afternoon, Wednesday, January 23, 1924, and into the evening, after a break for dinner, until one o'clock in the morning. Reconvening at nine o'clock that morning and continuing until noon, "the entire membership," the story read, showed "a greatly increased interest in the affairs of the college."

Furthermore, although the board had already announced that there would be no meeting in February, even though that was when the annual meeting was ordinarily held, it was agreed that the board would meet in February for possibly three or four days. The trustees had never been involved in so much activity.

The results were progressive and even radical.

For one thing, the board decided to go ahead with construction of a dormitory for men. Zellner Hall, built in 1917 as a dormitory for men, had been turned over to the women in the fall of 1919, and the men had been moved to a wooden building called Emergency Hall, but soon nicknamed the Mule Barn. A promise had been made to the men then that a new dormitory would be built for them. Five years later, after an ongoing effort to raise the money to build a men's dormitory had been talked about, written about, and no doubt prayed about, the men still lived in the Mule Barn.

During the February meeting of 1924, the board instructed the local board to put together a combination of donations and loans and build the dormitory and have it ready for occupancy by the fall. Furthermore, as part of the contract, Emergency Hall was to be remodeled, enlarged, and converted to a modern, well-lighted, well-equipped kitchen and dining hall. That was all the authorization the local board needed. Plans were finalized, money was arranged, a frame residence occupying the planned location of the new building was moved, a contract was let, and construction got under way on a three-story brick dormitory with rooms for a hundred men, plus an apartment for the dormitory supervisor. The building was ready when school started in September. Only the third floor had new furniture; floors one and two had furniture moved out of Emergency Hall. No complaints about this detail were registered. And the student body had a dining hall to replace the basement of Daisy Hall, long outgrown.

At first, *The Optimist* referred to the new dormitory as Sewell Hall, apparently the name the board planned to give it. However, just a month before the new dormitory was scheduled to open, the man died who, more than any other person, had been responsible for establishing, or reviving, the Church of Christ in Abilene, and who had led the way in receiving A. B. Barret and encouraging him to start a school. He was Albert Fitzgerald McDonald. His death on August 16, 1924, caused the trustees to rethink the situation. At the annual meeting during the next February, J. C. Reese moved and W. H. Free seconded, and the board voted unanimously to name the new dormitory McDonald Hall. No more appropriate name could have been memorialized. The completion of McDonald Hall was hailed by *The Optimist* as "the greatest change that has been made on the campus since the erection of the new administration building."

Another decisive action taken by the board was praised by the student body. The gymnasium, which had been started by the students, financed to a great extent by student contributions – and what they could wangle from parents, grandparents, and friends back home – and constructed with the help of student volunteers, fell somewhat short of being usable. The board immediately made arrangements for needed funds and gave instructions to do the job. After playing basketball since 1906 on a dirt court and a plank floor laid on the ground, but still al fresco, the students at last competed in a real gymnasium, with brick walls, a good roof, a solid concrete subfloor, a smooth wooden floor over that, and seats for spectators.

The first game played in the new Wildcat Gym was against the Buffaloes from West Texas State Teachers College in Canyon, now West Texas A&M University. The date was March 2, 1925, a Monday evening. The 1925 *Prickly Pear* reported that the building was packed before the first whistle blew. The Wildcats lost to the Buffaloes, but "A.C.C. fans will never forget the fight that was put up."

In spite of the great change the new men's dormitory made on the campus, it did not solve the space shortage. A couple of years after the opening of the new dormitory, gymnasium, and dining hall, the campus newspaper was lamenting the crisis:

> At present dormitories are overflowed. The administration building, which was enlarged in 1921 by adding a small wing to the original college building, is worse crowded than the student boarding halls. At some periods of the day two or three classes must be held simultaneously in the auditorium. Others are held in dormitory parlors and in almost every possible space.

The trustees had already recognized this, but a period of time was required to think in big terms. The first idea was to build a large new administration building. At the annual meeting in February 1926, a motion was presented and passed unanimously that a joint meeting be sought with elders of the College Church of Christ. The purpose of the meeting would be to determine whether the college and the church could pool resources to build an auditorium with a seating capacity of not less than 2,000 and preferably 2,500, with classrooms adequate for the church, which could be used by the college during the week. There was no notation as to just where on the crowded campus such a building would be located. No record exists that such a meeting was conducted, but presumably the joint trustees-elders meeting occurred with the two groups in agreement because within three weeks a building committee was appointed.

Before long, a deal was made with the Abilene Chamber of Commerce that promised success for the campaign. The chamber people promised to canvass the Abilene business community and raise $75,000 if members of the Church of Christ and the college community would match it. By November, a board meeting elicited the information that members of the church had already come up with pledges totaling $52,000, with seventy-five prospects still to be interviewed. On the spot, the trustees voted to underwrite the remaining $23,000, and so notified the chamber leadership. The chamber people, soliciting the business community, were not as far along with the campaign as the church members were, but all seemed confident of reaching the goal. An architectural firm had already come up with a sketch of the proposed new building, and the picture was run in *The Optimist* of October 7, 1926.

Everything seemed to be moving along on schedule. January 13, 1927, *The Optimist* came out with a page one story: "... Ground is to be broken by the first of February or soon thereafter, and the trustees think the building will be ready for use by next September."

Then came the annual meeting of the general Board of Trustees, February 24, 1927. The meeting began in a routine manner. Twenty-two of the thirty-five members were present. After the reading of the minutes of the previous annual meeting, it was unanimously voted to extend President Baxter's contract for another three-year term, with a 16.6 percent salary increase. A parenthetical insertion in the minutes explained, "This increase was afterwards refused by Brother Baxter." An *Optimist* headline told the reaction of the students in chapel to Baxter's reelection: "CHOICE OF BAXTER FOR PREXY GETS DEAFENING OVATION." A resolution was passed unanimously, ratifying and affirming all actions of the president of the board, J. S. Arledge, and/or the vice president of the board, J. C. Reese, in signing "deeds, conveyances, and other instruments for and in behalf of Abilene Christian College."

At this point, the board minutes reveal that a motion was on the floor to amend the charter regarding membership on the board. Article VI, which specified that the board would consist of "thirty-five members" would be amended to read "thirty-five male members." The minutes do not show that any females were candidates for membership on the board. Insofar as the record shows, the board did not debate the motion. The minutes say, "Carried unanimously." But nothing happened. Before an amendment to the charter could become official, it would have to be filed with the Texas Secretary of State in Austin and become a matter of public record. Several meetings of the Executive Committee of the board occurred during the twelve months after the annual meeting of February 27, 1927, but the amendment was not mentioned. When the annual meeting of February 1928 took place, the minutes were read, and it is presumed that the action of the year before was mentioned, but the action was not affirmed, reported, or overturned.

The probability is that if and when Chairman Arledge and Secretary Free went to see Judge J. M. Wagstaff about preparing and filing the amendment with the Secretary of State, Wagstaff, who had been the school's attorney since the Childers suit of 1906, would have reminded them that Article VI of the charter stipulated just two qualifications for trustees: membership in the Church of Christ and residence in the state of Texas. Then Wagstaff would no doubt have mentioned the language of Article XII: "This charter shall never be changed as to qualifications of Board of Directors defined in Article VI of this charter but in other respects said charter may be amended as occasion may require and all donations to this corporation and institution of learning shall be given, and shall be considered in law to have been given on this condition." In other words, the number of trustees could be changed but not the qualifications. With these two qualifications in mind, the board was expected to use good judgment in selecting the best people possible to join them as trustees. Seventy years later a change was made in the Texas residency requirement, but this required a lengthy judicial process and will be discussed in chapter eight.

As it turned out in 1984, Mary Frazier Clark was the first woman added to the board. The charter did not need to be amended because it had since the beginning made board membership available without restriction as to gender. Mrs. Clark and the women who later have joined her on the board – Mary Prudie Brown, Dr. Janice M. Massey, Jane Varner Beard, Virginia Palmer Chambers, Jennifer Haltom Doan, Barbara Bates "Barbie" Johnston, and Melinda Ann Worley have all represented new strength for the board. So the "males only" motion was only a 1927 diversion.

Also, at the 1927 meeting, all of a sudden, with no fanfare or buildup, a surprise was introduced. The minutes read: "Moved by Otto Foster, seconded by T. A. Russell, that it is the sense of this Board of Trustees that the local board offer the property upon which the present buildings are erected for sale during a term of thirty days, the price to be $250,000. Carried unanimously." Talk about a sudden change of direction! From discussing and planning a new administration building, the board had voted to sell the entire campus! Some discussion may have occurred before or after the motion was presented, but there is no positive indication of it. It may be inferred from by the words of the motion: "It is the sense of this board." It is understood that a good secretary, which Henry Free certainly was, includes only actions and not side discussions, facial expressions, or any other extraneous matter in the minutes. That could be said of Free and of F. B. Shepherd, secretary pro tem for that particular meeting. Apparently Shepherd took the notes of the meeting, but the minutes seem to have been written and were signed by Free.

President Baxter apparently was taken by surprise, for in his report to the board during the same meeting, he wrote, "We are handicapped greatly for lack of room. The new building which is being planned will relieve this situation for class rooms but not for dormitories, in which we are greatly crowded." So the president was confidently expecting the new administration building to get under way, and now the board had passed a resolution, without a dissenting vote, to sell the campus.

Otto Foster, who entered the motion, was a successful pharmacist from Cleburne. Over the years he owned or shared ownership in a progression of pharmacies. The late Don Morris described him as one "who gave much money over the years; he gave to every need." In the 1960s his six-figure gift made possible the expansion of the present science building. The trustees voted to name the facility "The Otto and Mattie Foster Science Building."

But Otto Foster was more than a man with money. He had a vision of what Abilene Christian College ought to be and become. He was the man who had entered a motion four years earlier, in 1923, to sell all the land – some thirty-five acres or so – that the college had acquired south of the railroad tracks. That was the land President Sewell had thought would be an acceptable site for campus expansion, but Foster had larger aspirations for the college. So that particular tract was registered with the city as "Christian College Subdivision of Part of Blocks 16 and 17 of the Harris Addition to the City of Abilene" and sold to ready buyers, with lots, streets, alleys, and utilities all laid out. Profits made from this action helped put the college in position to do some larger things.

Foster did not have in mind a particular site for the new campus. He left the initiative for that up to people who knew Abilene better than he did. But he knew that a facility that would include an auditorium seating from 2,000 to 2,500 people, plus classrooms adequate for church and college, should not be built at the existing location, and he knew that the college did not yet own a suitable location. So in the absence of a good plan, he moved the abandonment of a bad plan, which meant that the board would have to start out from ground zero to locate, acquire, and build a campus. How long that would take was anybody's guess.

T. A. Russell, who seconded Foster's motion, was an Abilenian. He was in the homebuilding, ranching, and real estate businesses. When he died in 1969, the local newspaper reminded its readers that in one year – 1919 – he had built 100 homes. He built many more after that. Mr. and Mrs. Russell had reared three children of their own, plus four adopted children of relatives who had died. They made it possible for all seven children to attend Abilene Christian College. Tom Russell was accustomed to thinking in large terms and launching big projects.

The action of the board in voting unanimously for the Foster-Russell motion was somewhat surprising. Just two years earlier they had made possible the completion of a gymnasium that the students worked so hard to get. They had seen, just two and a half years earlier, the completion of a men's dormitory that had taken five years to accomplish. The existing administration building was only eight years old. It does seem that some board member would have arisen to say, "Hold on a minute. Before we give all of this up that we have come by with such a sacrifice, let's look around us for expansion room."

Actually, the motion simply called for a thirty-day period during which the local board would offer the campus for sale for $250,000. A literal interpretation would be that if no sale was made during that time, the deal was off. In fact, Foster followed with another motion, to the effect that "the building committee advertise for bids on the new building within the next thirty days, the authority to be given said committee to reject any or all bids." This motion too was approved unanimously. Regardless of conditions attached, the board had made up its mind to abandon the campus and seek a new location. There would be no turning back.

As soon as word got around that the college was looking, a site became available. Roy T. Denman owned a tract of land in west Abilene – west of Cobb Park and Catclaw Creek – which he proposed to develop as residential property. He offered to give ten acres to Abilene Christian College plus $25,000 cash from the sale of lots. The board expressed some interest, but all of the disadvantages inherent in the property south of the railroad tracks would have gone along with the Denman property except that the noise from the railroad would not have been so pronounced. And even though Denman would have been willing to offer a larger piece of land than ten acres for a campus, it would have been too small. Even so, the board voted to place $1,000 in escrow as forfeit money to hold the offer open for at least three months.

Meanwhile, efforts to sell the campus resulted in no sale. A meeting was arranged with a committee representing the city and the public schools. Abilene was looking for a location for a new junior high school. Abilene trustees of the college were anxious to explore the possibility that the city might buy the campus for that purpose. They offered the campus to the city for $160,000, with the provision that the college would raze the dormitories and use the bricks and such other materials as might be usable to rebuild at the new location. After all, a junior high school would not need dormitories. The administration building and the new gymnasium would go to the school district.

Discussions revealed no interest on the part of the public school officials in the proposal, so it was dead, which was a stroke of providence for what was to become Abilene Christian University. If the public schools had snapped up the offer, the trustees would have felt strong pressure to accept the Roy

Denman offer, which would have been a bad choice for the long-term growth of the university.

Mother Nature also entered into the decision not to proceed further with the Denman offer. The heavens opened, and a big rain fell on the Catclaw Creek watershed. That famed waterway, which is normally dry, or nearly so, became a torrent and flooded most of the area the trustees were thinking about. That clinched the decision, according to Katharyn Duff in *Abilene on the Catclaw*. As it was, Mr. Denman had $1,000 that he would not otherwise have had. And he still had his property intact.

Now began a significant effort on the part of another city or two or three to attract the college. San Angelo, Wichita Falls, and Dallas were all mentioned. San Angelo made the one really concrete offer. Burton Coffman's *Optimist* got hold of a story and ran it, no doubt with the approval of President Baxter and the board chairman: "It became known publicly yesterday that a delegation of businessmen and city officials from San Angelo had conferred Saturday evening [April 30, 1927] with city school trustees [local board]. The visiting delegation declared that if A.C.C. is to be moved from Abilene, San Angelo wants it. An informal offer of $250,000 and a 100-acre campus is understood to have been made."

That was one version of the offer. On the other hand, Guy Scruggs had the opportunity of talking to the principals involved in the negotiations. Arledge, Reese, McKinzie, Free, Russell, and others were available for interviews. His version was that the San Angeloans spoke in terms of 1,280 acres on the outskirts of the city, plus $50,000 cash. One explanation for the difference in the two accounts might be that Scruggs was talking to men fifteen years later. It was an attractive offer. Fact is, though, nobody wanted to move.

Although selling the old campus was no longer a decisive factor, it was a job that still needed to be done. A reading of the minutes traces the course of attempts to sell the campus. The February 24, 1927, Foster motion would allow thirty days for somebody or some entity to snap up the whole campus, with all of its improvements, for $250,000. A meeting three weeks later, after the public schools had shown lack of interest, set the maximum price at $250,000 and the minimum at $200,000. Three years later the minutes read: "Motion by J. C. Reese, seconded by E. L. Crawford, that the Chair appoint a committee to sell the old campus for a price of $50,000 or more. Motion carried." It should be pointed out, however, in connection with the latter entry from the minutes that in the meantime the Administration Building had been destroyed by fire. And the Great Depression had struck.

For a number of months after the college moved, the Highland Church of Christ continued to meet in the gymnasium. For the first winter after the college moved to its new location, the basketball team had its regular workouts in the old gymnasium because Bennett Gymnasium was not completed until the spring of 1930.

Ten days after the latest board vote on the old campus, the property finally sold to W. F. Sims, a Hillsboro friend of board member J. E. McKinzie, who announced that the sale was for "more than $50,000." Minutes of the Board of Trustees do not give any more detail than that. An unspecified down payment was made, and notes totalling $31,000 and backed by a lien on the property were accepted. The college sold the notes to J. M. Radford, an Abilene businessman who had befriended the college.

Sims converted Daisy Hall into a tourist court, called Grande Lodge. It was operated for a number of years, was allowed to run down, reverted to the Radford estate, and was sold finally to the Texas Coca-Cola Bottling Company. The company tore it down and replaced it with storage warehouses. April 23, 1934, the board voted to sell or demolish the gymnasium and Zellner Hall. The gymnasium was marketable and was ultimately acquired by the Texas Coca-Cola Company, but there was no market for a brick veneer dormitory that had sat vacant for five years, so it was demolished. On the old campus today, three facilities still stand. McDonald Hall is now an apartment project, privately owned. The gymnasium is in excellent condition, being used by the Coca-Cola Company primarily to store cans for recycling. Emergency Hall, the Mule Barn was used for years by T. S. Lankford Garment Company, with dozens of workers operating machines. It was later a classroom facility of the Texas State Technical Institute, now Texas State Technical College, but is currently vacant.

Charles W. Bacon was president of the Abilene Chamber of Commerce. He was vitally interested in the growth of Abilene Christian College. He labored diligently to get the support of the entire business community for the development program. To him it was a matter of dollars and cents, in addition to the contributions the college could make to the religious, cultural, and educational climate of the city and environs.

One day he was talking with J. C. Reese, vice chairman of the ACC board. They were in Bacon's office, on the top floor of the Alexander Building, at North First and Pine Streets. Bacon arose from his chair and said to Reese, "Come over here to the window." He pointed to a wide strip of rolling land northeast of the city and said,"That is a wonderful place for Abilene Christian College." He was pointing to a section of land 2.3 miles from the downtown post office. It was beyond the eastern city limits, which in general coincided with the Abilene and Northern railroad track running north and south just west of Cedar Creek. Cedar Creek was similar to Catclaw in that at times it would flood and cover dozens of acres with unwelcome water. But although the land Bacon was talking about started at the east bank of Cedar Creek, it rose significantly in elevation east of the creek, which would prevent flood waters from covering the site that Bacon was suggesting. In fact, what Bacon was talking about could and would be called "The Hill."

Reese immediately went out to see the property; he walked around and saw all kinds of possibilities. He went back and said to his colleagues of the local board, "This is the place." One by one and in groups the other board members went to see the property. When Dee Rambo was visiting from Huntsville, Reese took him out to see the place. Other out-of-town trustees were given the tour.

A special meeting of the general board was called for August 1, 1927. Twenty-one members were present. First, they discussed plans in considerable detail. Then the entire board made an inspection trip of the proposed location. At six o'clock, board members were guests of the Abilene Chamber of Commerce at a banquet. The hosts admitted they were still some $4,000 short of their goal but assured the board members they would reach it.

A formal vote to buy the property was not under consideration. Instead, the local board received authorization to go ahead with the best deal that could be made for the new campus. Friday, August 19, members of the local board – J. S. Arledge, W. H. Free, Dabney Harvey, Harvey Hays, G. C. Helvey, C. T. Hutcheson, J. E. McKinzie, J. C. Reese, and T. A. Russell – voted to buy 680 acres.

Of this land, 200 acres belonged to Mr. and Mrs. Edward Adams, 160 acres were owned by Mr. and Mrs. W. E. Hughes and Mrs. M. M. Mayfield and family, and 320 acres were the property of Mrs. Xenia Adams Miller. The boundaries of the 680 acres were Cedar Creek on the west, Ambler Avenue – although it was not yet so known – on the north, Griffith Road on the east, and East North Tenth Street on the south. The land was essentially a square. Actually, it was a section plus an additional forty acres on the northwest. The forty-acre portion was involved because the channel of Cedar Creek did not run exactly north and south. It was a magnificent piece of property for a college campus with room for a whole new subdivision of the city.

Total cost of the land was $119,600. The board proudly announced that the entire deal had been consummated without the payment of a commission. After all, trustees Tom Russell and Henry Free were realtors. They could handle real estate transactions. People living in the vicinity were good neighbors. They showed their appreciation for the college by donating parcels of land adjoining the purchased acreage. For example, Mr. and Mrs. J. R. Griffith donated fourteen acres across from the northeast corner. Other donors of land included Oscar Harris and wife, the W. E. Floyds, R. R. Calfees, T. C. Campbells, J. A. Kings, C. D. Brummitts, Ola B. and E. M. Hunter, and a number of others. Donations ranged from one acre up to fourteen. They added up to 121 acres, giving the Board of Trustees 801 acres with which to work.

Announcement of the deal was made in time to make page one headlines in the local papers Sunday, August 21, 1927. The

Reporter-News called it "the most important step ever planned by Texas educational leaders in the Church of Christ." The news story pointed out that as soon as the deal was made, $81,500 worth of lots was sold. "Only 60 acres of lots will have to be sold," the story declared, "to pay for the land. This will leave 620 acres of land in the purchased part and all of the donated land – all clear of debt." Monday's paper continued the story by describing the automobiles lining the road to Hamby. When some in the crowd showed confusion as to which land had been purchased, one of the trustees mounted the running board of his car and made a speech explaining it. That, no doubt, was J. C. Reese.

Tuesday's *Reporter-News* editorialized: "Our friends the trustees of Abilene Christian College have gone quietly about the business of putting over one of the most important and far-reaching movements in the history of education in West Texas." The *Abilene Times*, another city newspaper of that time, said in its page-one story: "Through the work done by President Baxter and his co-workers, the institution will be able to reserve a campus of a hundred acres, sell off lots sufficient to pay for the buildings needed, and still have hundreds of valuable acres left for future needs, endowment, or whatever course may be decided on." Although the *Times* missed the true situation in crediting the president and his co-workers with the splendid accomplishment, it correctly analyzed the long-range program and plan. This master stroke was not a presidential accomplishment. Appraising, negotiating, and consummating a project of this nature required people who were accustomed to operating in the business world. This is what a good board of trustees can do, and this pivotal decision and purchase was made by trustees.

Thirty-five men served as trustees then. Eleven lived in Abilene and constituted the local board. The other twenty-four came from twenty-one cities, towns, and small villages, with only two localities having more than one member each, Dallas, three and Sweetwater, two. All trustees were required by charter to be residents of Texas and members of the Church of Christ in good standing with a local congregation.

Most of the talking in board meetings was done by the Abilenians – most, but not all. It has already been seen that two of the farthest reaching motions in the history of the institution were initiated by Otto Foster of Cleburne: first, the 1923 motion to sell the thirty-five acres that had been accumulated south of the railroad tracks for future campus expansion and, second, the 1927 motion to sell the campus.

Other outspoken trustees from outside of Abilene included Judge Allen D. Dabney of Eastland, a noted attorney. He was not known to repress an opinion or a judgment. Judge W. O. Kenley of Wichita Falls spoke out less frequently than did Judge Dabney. George W. Birchfield of Fort Worth was a wealthy man. He gave generously and could lend the school $100,000 even when he was not in position to give the whole amount. R. H. McKay of Ferris was a noted banker, valued for his insight into sound financing. J. B. McGinty of Terrell had the ability to contribute to meetings of the group. In fact, all of the board members contributed to the strength of the board and consequently were able to back up their commitments to building up Abilene Christian College.

The general board leaned on the eleven-member local board to do a great deal of the work. Three of them were the movers and shakers of the local board: Arledge, Reese, and McKinzie.

J. S., or James Shaffer, Arledge was a rancher. His ranch was at Maryneal, Nolan County, south of Sweetwater. He was elected to the board in 1911 and served as chairman or president of the board, 1916-1933. He moved to Abilene in 1913 so that his children could attend Abilene Christian College. When the opportunity came for Abilene Christian to make the big move, he sold his ranch and worked full time for the college. He took charge of the sale of lots and, in fact, became fiscal agent for the college. His ready smile, diplomacy, and courtesy in dealing with people made him a good chairman.

J. C., or James Cannon, Reese was an independent oil operator. He was a wiry man who stood not more than five feet seven inches tall and weighed no more than 130 pounds. He possessed seemingly boundless energy and knew how to put together business deals. He had moved his family from Mineral

Wells to Abilene in 1923. He had served on the board since 1918, and at the time of the big move he was vice chairman of the board. Because of being self-employed in business, he was able to devote a great deal of time to work for the college – and he did just that.

The third member of the trio was J. E., or John Edward, McKinzie. He came to Abilene from Hillsboro, where he had grown up. In Hillsboro he had been in cattle raising, real estate, and insurance and had served two terms as tax assessor-collector of Hill County. He had been a member of the board since 1919. When Batsell Baxter was elected president in 1924, he persuaded McKinzie to move to Abilene and operate the food service for the college. This did not preclude his continuing to be a member of the board because he was not an employee of the college. He had a contract to provide food service for students at prices stated in the college catalog. The contract provided that he was to be paid eighty percent of what the college collected for board. For this he was to furnish the food and pay all labor costs.

The college was fortunate to have McKinzie on the campus full time. Don Morris wrote concerning him, "He could be at home and converse intelligently and profitably with almost anyone under any circumstances. McKinzie was at ease with anybody – a bank president, business leaders in Abilene or nationally known business leaders. Such people soon saw that he was a keen thinker and natural leader."

Over the years some criticism of the arrangement occurred because it appeared to some people that McKinzie was profiting from his position as a trustee. Similar criticism was leveled at Arledge and Reese because, at one time or another, each was on a modest salary from the college while devoting full time to the college. In the case of all three men, it was probably providential that they were available, as will be discussed later.

W. H., or William Henry, Free was an invaluable member of the board. He was in a category by himself. Having been a trustee since 1906, he was frequently called on if a question concerning the earlier actions of the board or questions of interpretation of the original charter came up. He was the authority on finances. He had been secretary-treasurer of the board since the beginning of the school; he was treasurer of the College Church of Christ for thirty-five years and was in banking for a quarter of a century. He wrote about himself: "My only hobby is trying to serve my community, having served every civic organization in the city, from public school board on down or up as the case might be, and on the side collecting old coins and golfing."

Other members of the local board – E. L. Crawford, Harvey Hays, Dabney Harvey, G. C. Helvey, C. T. Hutcheson, T. A. Russell, and C. A. Wade – were all dependable men and faithful trustees, but they had to devote time to their personal businesses and could not spend as much time working directly for the college as Arledge, Reese, and McKinzie were in position to do. As events developed, it was necessary for the local board members to do most of the work. During the months of construction, President Baxter said that the local board met "sometimes once a week, often every night, especially during the press of the work." The president knew because he usually met with them. Seven members constituted a quorum. Sometimes they had to go home because they could not bring together a quorum.

It was natural, therefore, that the local board assumed a great deal of responsibility and authority. The thirty-five-member full board did not actually vote on some very important matters but delegated them to the local board. For example, in the purchase of land for the new campus – a truly major decision – the unanimous board vote was "that the local board be empowered with full authority to make the best arrangements possible for a new campus in Abilene." That was undoubtedly the only way great things could have been accomplished. Down the road, however, there was bound to be a backlash against the power of the local board.

Taking control of the school in January 1924, these trustees moved it from a cramped little campus to the wide-open spaces northeast of town with an acreage of one hundred sixty times larger. They decided to call the new subdivision Abilene Heights and successfully petitioned Abilene to take Abilene Heights into the city limits.

The trustees had hit upon the best plan they could have come up with for building a campus and providing an endowment within a relatively short timeframe. Such a project required a large scale to be successful. With 801 acres of land to work with, they hired an engineer to come up with a plat showing land to be set aside for campus, an area for commercial development, hundreds of lots for residential purposes, plus streets, avenues, boulevards, alleys, parks, and whatever other categories of land use were necessary for the building of a successful subdivision. H. J. Bradshaw was employed as engineer of the project. It did not take long for him to devise a plan that the trustees and the city approved.

A major question facing the leaders was "Will the lots sell?" Indicators that made the planners optimistic that the lots would sell were the continuing expansion of Abilene, the growth of Abilene Christian College, and the increase in members of Churches of Christ in the city. The college and related churches had grown strong enough that an auditorium seating between 2,000 and 2,500 was needed, and with both the Chamber of Commerce and the local newspaper commenting about the many people who were moving to Abilene because of the college, the market for the new subdivision seemed, no doubt, secure.

The weeks after August 19, 1927, the date the trustees decided to buy the land, were filled with activity. Decisions were made promptly and followed up. Minutes of meetings convey something of the excitement and the sense of accomplishment of the men who were devoting so much time to the project.

Negotiations were undertaken with the city for two major streets to be built out to the subdivision, including bridging Cedar Creek. It was raw ranch land, with tall grass, weeds, and lots of rocks. An existing road ran along the north boundary of the land – Hamby Road, which is now Ambler Avenue. An eastward extension of North Tenth Street from the two city cemeteries, running along the south boundary of the property, was needed. Conversations with the city led to widening of the street between the Cedar Hill cemeteries to make possible East North Tenth Street.

The college also needed a major street running from the downtown to the campus. The first idea was that North Sixteenth Street might be extended eastward to the new location, but some obstacles canceled that idea. The final decision was to connect with North Thirteenth Street at its beginning point two blocks west of Cedar Creek and let it move in a northeasterly direction across the creek and up the hill. The new street was named "College Drive." After crossing the creek it would blend into East North Sixteenth and would also swing around to merge with what would have been East North Seventeenth, except that the name College Drive was given to the main approach to the campus.

The numbered streets in Abilene Heights from Tenth through Twenty-third were called "East North" because their counterparts within existing city limits started numbering at the east city limit and moved westward. The Abilene Heights streets running east and west corresponded in name and numbering with existing city streets, hence, the somewhat unusual designation of East North as a prefix to the numbered streets. The street running into the addition from north and west was called Lincoln Drive. The proposed new boulevard south from the campus to East North Tenth and north from the campus to Hamby Road was named Washington Boulevard. The northerly extension was ultimately incorporated into the campus. Streets running north and south in Abilene Heights were named alphabetically: Avenues A through F. Avenues A and B were never developed, and Avenue C was swallowed up when Cedar Crest Drive was developed and extended southward from East North Sixteenth to East North Tenth.

The naming of the Abilene Heights thoroughfares was not very imaginative but exhibited the true, pragmatic American character. The trustees, who were terribly busy businessmen, should probably have referred the naming of streets to the English faculty. One can imagine Shakespeare Boulevard, John Milton Drive, and Chaucer Avenue, instead of D, E, and F.

The campus itself would lie between East North Sixteenth Street on the south and East North Eighteenth on the north – two blocks – and between Campus Court on the west and Avenue F on the east. It was a small campus – slightly more than twenty acres. After all, the trustees had been thinking in big terms when they bought the land, but they were not used to a large campus. A comparison of the twenty acres or so of that campus plan with the more than 300 acres in the new campus illustrates the reality that these decisions left ample room for expansion when the time came.

Great optimism blossomed, but the board realized that lots do not sell themselves. So the board members asked the chairman, J. S. Arledge, to become fiscal agent and take charge of selling the lots. They voted to pay him a modest salary and furnish a car and expenses for his work. This arrangement was later criticized by some because the charter forbade payment for serving on the board, except for expenses of travel to and from board meetings. The records fail to reveal that any board member ever was paid for such expense. Arledge was not being offered a salary as a board member; the offer would make it possible for him to devote his full time, working day and night, to sell those lots. Legal counsel to the board, J. M. Wagstaff, gave his opinion that the arrangement was within the terms of the charter.

The urgency to sell lots rested on the cold, hard facts: 680 acres of land had cost the college a total of $119,600, and it was now necessary to construct a number of new buildings all at once. Because of the distance involved between the old and new campuses and lack of transportation, the trustees found it infeasible to erect one building at a time on the new campus and have some classes on the new campus while keeping some on the old campus. The move from the old campus to the new location would have to happen all at once. So over a short period of time, plans were developed, bids were sought, and contracts were awarded for eight new buildings: an administration-classroom complex, auditorium, men's dormitory, women's dormitory, educational building for the training school and academy, a combination dining hall and light housekeeping unit, a gymnasium, and a president's home. An entirely new campus had been contracted for on the plain east of downtown.

Total cost of all of these buildings plus equipment and furnishings was approximately $600,000. In the 1990s, with multi-million dollar building projects, this seems to be a modest sum of money, but one must remember the decades of inflation since those days. The task was breathtaking for such a small and financially limited group of people.

The moment was a uniquely exciting time in the history of the college. Paul Southern, experienced editor of *The Optimist,* wrote this appraisal of the Abilene Heights development: "In addition to the school buildings proper under construction, innumerable homes are going up, constituting probably the greatest single project Abilene has ever known. ... This mammoth building project is of inestimable benefit to Abilene. It has given employment to workers in all building trades lines, who in turn have spent their money with Abilene businessmen. To J. C. Reese goes the honor of being the first to build in the new ACC addition. ... It is estimated that approximately 250 men are at work on and around ACC campus at the present time." In an earlier issue of the paper, Southern wrote that it was the dream of the trustees "that some day Abilene Christian College would grow to be a university."

The trustees received some significant help from generous individuals during those years. In 1928, Mr. and Mrs. J. N. Luce of Spur, Texas, offered to the college 640 acres of land valued at $40 per acre or a total of $25,600, in return for a six percent annuity for as long as either of them should live. The board accepted the offer with gratitude and named the educational building on which construction was ready to get underway for Mrs. Luce – the Zona Luce building. Mrs. Luce lived until 1970. The college faithfully paid that annuity for forty-two years. At about the same time, Mr. and Mrs. E. D. Chambers of Afton, Texas, gave $10,000 in vendor's lien notes in return for a five percent annuity. The newly planned light housekeeping unit and dining hall was named Chambers Hall in their honor.

Annuities have done much for Abilene Christian University through the years. In the earlier days, the board used the money for the purpose at hand, but in later years, actuarial tables have been followed, and on each annuity a substantial reserve has been set up to ensure the timely payment of all interest due. Annuities are good for both donor and recipient.

The recipient has a percentage of the gift that can be used for the need at hand, and in the long run the remainder of the principal will be available. The donor of the annuity receives a donation credit according to actuarial tables, plus an assured and regular source of income on a lifelong basis, or for a specified length of time if the donor prefers. The donor also receives the satisfaction that comes from helping worthy causes. Abilene Christian has never defaulted on an annuity obligation.

In 1929 also came a gift that would ultimately be worth millions to the school, but at the time it was assigned a value of approximately $15,000. Mr. and Mrs. L. P. Bennett of Denver City, Yoakum County, Texas, gave two sections of land, 1,280 acres, to the college in exchange for tuition for their children. A brief effort was made to sell the land because the money was sorely needed. Fortunately, the land did not sell. In 1931, the Bennetts deeded an additional half-section, making a total of 1,600 acres for the college. Through the years, they gave additional mineral interests. Its later consequences would be significant. Although the Bennett land was not immediately worth very much insofar as cash flow was concerned, it did provide the college additional collateral for necessary borrowing.

With these and other gifts in hand, however, the trustees still expected that the big revenue producer for the college was the sale of lots in Abilene Heights. The first public sale of lots was conducted Thursday, December 8, 1927. Five hundred lots were offered for sale out of 160 acres of the 801-acre tract. All of the sixteen commercial locations were sold at auction in forty minutes time. These lots went at an average of $987 each. More than one-fourth of the residential lots were sold at prices ranging from $400 to $1,000, depending on size and location. Most purchases were financed over a period of time.

With the vigorous leadership by J. S. Arledge, lot sales continued briskly. He prepared a message to church members everywhere summing up the sales effort: "This is the prettiest addition in Abilene. [It] is located on a high hill overlooking the town and surrounding country; the water runs in every direction off the campus, where there are now being built seven new, modern, fireproof school buildings, all of the same architectural design and color. ... Now this is nice and wonderful to enjoy. But what I started out to tell you is ... that when it is finished we are going to owe about $200,000. The only way we have of paying for this is to sell the balance of these lots. Now we are not asking you for a donation. We are only asking you to make an investment in these lots, in the best close-in addition, in the best town in West Texas. ... Now is an opportunity, as one good brother stated it, 'to help Christian education without it costing you anything.'" Then Arledge outlined the terms: ten percent down and ten percent every six months with eight percent interest on the unpaid balance.

A few weeks after the sale of lots in Abilene Heights began, a late night event of Sunday, January 27, and the early morning of January 28, 1929, resulted in a sudden, unexpected, and unwanted infusion of cash into the building program. Paul Southern and Homer Hailey, student preachers and seniors in the college, were returning to Abilene after midnight from preaching appointments. They were traveling in Hailey's automobile. As they crossed the tracks from South First to the campus, they saw flames shooting from the Administration Building. They went to Daisy Hall and aroused Elizabeth Nelson, dean of women. She called the fire department, and the department responded quickly. The fire was too far ahead of them. The building was a total loss. Cause of the fire was never determined.

The Optimist of that week described the disaster:

> Within a few minutes after the announcement of the fire, hundreds of students and residents living near the college arrived to watch the firemen and to render aid. College boys assisted the firemen in dragging the hose, and in wetting surrounding buildings to prevent spreading of the fire.

> All permanent records of the students were saved, President Baxter stated following the conflagration. About one-half of the books in the library were saved by the students. All of the biological equipment was totally destroyed. Three pianos and one saxophone were destroyed.

Emotions swept over the students and faculty.
The Optimist continued:

> Sadness pervaded the campus Monday as students and faculty members gazed upon the lonely brick walls and upon the mass

of charred ruins within them. Many students met on the lawn and reviewed conversations and scenes which took place in the old Ad building during former years.

Monday the eyes of every student and patron of the school turned toward the new buildings under construction on the college's new campus northeast of the city. These buildings, however, will not be completed until sometime in the summer, hence cannot be used for this crisis.

From San Antonio came a poignant message from Mrs. Jesse P. Sewell. After reviewing the dream that she and Mr. Sewell had shared as a young couple to "build in Texas a Christian college, where God's word would be taught to every student every day," she wrote:

> The building that was burned was the home of that dream. Every brick was dear to our hearts. ... I remember the long, long drought. The earth was parched and bare; the sky had been like brass for months. We needed room more than I can tell you, but the people wouldn't give money to buy it. The clouds began to gather and for months we hoped and prayed for rain, and it came. I remember when we were standing by a window in Daisy Hall watching it pour from the sky, and giving our Heavenly Father thanks for the great blessing. I turned from the window and sat down at a table, saying, "Now, Jesse, you can get the money for the new building."
>
> I am so glad the new building is going up. It will far surpass the old in size, beauty, and convenience, but it cannot be loved like the old which was built by small gifts given at great sacrifice.

An unknown student correspondent wrote this appraisal of the fire:

> It was the largest fire that Abilene has ever known, and we hope it is the largest fire that she will ever know. ... I was impressed by the part that the students took in assisting to combat the raging fire, to save records, books, and furniture. Some stood on the roofs of surrounding buildings, ready to fight any blaze that might start there, while others donned heavy slickers to help the firemen handle the heavy water hose. The students did not wait for anyone to take the lead or to suggest anything, but they broke through the library windows to save as much of the library as they could, and to save the trophies, which were kept in a case in the reading room. They kept cool heads; not all of them tried to get into the library, but just a few. The others formed a double line leading from the windows of the library to a place of safety from the fire. Books were speedily passed down this line, and more were saved in this manner than would have been saved by any other method. Back to the front of the

building: the flame had reached the office, and it looked as if the records and the files of the office of the dean, president, and registrar would be completely destroyed. Our president led the way and the students followed to save the valuable records and files.

One positive aspect of the fire was that insurance from the burned building was more than enough to pay for the new Sewell Auditorium going up on the new campus, and some humor helped occasionally. Edward Washington "E. W." McMillan was preacher for the College Church of Christ. He was also head of the Bible Department. At the Sunday evening service before the fire, he preached an unusually fiery sermon. He claimed he was working diligently to keep his audience awake. The next day he was out looking over the charred ruins, thinking of where he had stood just a few hours before and preached the gospel. A ranchman who had moved to Abilene so his children could attend the college put an arm around his shoulder and said, "Brother McMillan, that was a good sermon last night. I knew when you finished if that sermon did not set something on fire I would be unable to see why."

And before long, President Baxter was roasted at a civic club luncheon. Everything was set up as if it were a live radio broadcast. An individual came to the microphone, introduced himself as President Baxter, and announced that he would speak on "Why I Burned the Ad Building." It took the president a few moments to appreciate the humor.

The trustees, however, had to confront the serious, immediate problem of where to have classes. Simmons University, McMurry College, Draughon's Business College, and the Chamber of Commerce offered the use of classrooms. So did downtown churches, including Baptist, Methodist, and Presbyterian congregations. The trustees expressed appreciation to all but thought it would be impractical to ask students to walk the distances from the campus that would be necessary if any of these facilities were used. Public transportation was not practical, and few students had automobiles.

So the board decided to build a temporary wooden building to take care of the situation. As planned, the long, narrow building would have six classrooms and offices for president, dean, bursar, and registrar. It was anticipated that the $2,000 building could be thrown up in a matter of days. Three hundred arm chairs and an equal number of folding chairs were secured to meet the emergency. While the temporary administration building was under construction, the gymnasium was being utilized overtime. Several classes, chapel and church services were conducted in it. The basement of Daisy Hall plus the parlors of all three dormitories were reserved for classes.

The trustees promised quick results in providing a temporary building. Sure enough, within ten days, classes were meeting in the new building. Workmen endured sleet and snow to get the job done. The board also promised that the new lumber being used for this building would be used on the new campus.

All sources of liquidity combined, including donations, insurance money and down payments on lot sales, however, would not meet cash flow requirements of construction on the new campus. Fairly early in the process the board came up with an educated estimate that between $160,000 and $200,000 long-term financing would be required. The money was needed quickly. Construction workers, contractors, and suppliers could not afford delays in payment. An extensive search of long-term borrowing possibilities began. In May 1929, trustee George Birchfield of Fort Worth offered to lend the college $100,000 for five months to meet pressing bills. The offer was accepted with gratitude.

In August 1929, an agreement for long-term financing was made with the Caldwell Company of Nashville, Tennessee. The loan was for $200,000, with a discount of $12,000, meaning that the college would receive $188,000 to retire the Birchfield loan at its maturity and to meet construction payments. The Caldwell deal called for the college to come out with a ten-year bond issue for $200,000. The bonds would bear six percent interest from September 1, 1929; two years would elapse before the first payment would be due. That would be September 1, 1931. Each September 1 thereafter through 1941, payments would be due on this schedule:

1930 – Interest only due ($12,000); total: $12,000

1931 – $7,000 plus interest ($12,000); total: $19,000
1932 – $8,000 plus interest ($11,580); total: $19,580
1933 – $9,000 plus interest ($11,100); total: $20,100
1934 – $10,000 plus interest ($10,500); total: $20,500
1935 – $11,000 plus interest ($ 9,960); total: $20,960
1936 – $11,000 plus interest ($ 9,300); total: $20,300
1937 – $12,000 plus interest ($ 8,640); total: $20,640
1938 – $13,000 plus interest ($ 7,920); total: $20,920
1939 – $14,000 plus interest ($ 7,740); total: $21,740
1940 – $15,000 plus interest ($ 6,300); total: $21,300
1941 – $90,000 plus interest ($ 5,400); total: $95,400

Total principal payments were $200,000; interest was $112,520; the total obligation created was $312,520 over a twelve-year period in return for immediate cash amounting to $188,000, not an undue burden. A report to the board at its annual meeting on February 23, 1929, showed that sales of lots up to that date amounted to $197,545. Most lot purchasers had bought on the time-payment plan, meaning ten percent down and, the trustees hoped, ten percent every six months, plus eight percent interest on the unpaid balance.

In addition to revenue from lot sales already made, unsold lots in the subdivided portion of Abilene Heights had a book value of $161,515. Admittedly, lot sales had slowed considerably since the white-hot beginning of the campaign, but there was still a market. In addition, 490 acres more could be subdivided. Surely the trustees controlled enough resources to pay all remaining obligations incurred in moving the campus, including the land purchased, the eight buildings erected, and all other expenses, and have enough left over to begin a permanent endowment fund.

By some sort of miracle the new campus was ready for use in September of 1929 – not as early in September as had been the hope, but still in September, which was the promise. Five of the buildings were ready: Administration, Zona Luce, Zellner Dormitory for women, McDonald Dormitory for men, and Chambers Hall, which had the dining hall on the main floor and light housekeeping rooms for women on the top floor. There was a basement that would not be finished for several years to come. Sewell Auditorium was not completed, but it was usable. Bennett Gymnasium was just getting underway and would not be completed until toward the end of the school year.

One other facility was not complete, the main artery from downtown – College Drive. It was far enough along, however, that the city could open it temporarily, especially for the activities of the next five days. Afterward, College Drive was shut down pending completion, which was not long off.

Freshmen began enrolling Friday, September 20. The first service of the College Church was on Sunday morning, with E. W. McMillan preaching to an overflow crowd estimated at 1,800. Not all of the permanent seating had been installed, but folding chairs accommodated the crowd. "All Hail the Power of Jesus' Name" was the opening song, led by Henry Free. President Emeritus Jesse P. Sewell led the prayer. Then, as the news account goes, McMillan spoke briefly. Alumni who remember "Prexy" Sewell's propensity for leading long prayers (up to twenty-seven minutes by Paul Southern's watch) probably will smile when reading that the preacher chose to make his sermon brief. McMillan's sermon dealt with obstacles that had been overcome by Nehemiah in rebuilding the walls of Jerusalem and restoring Jewish worship. He made an appropriate comparison to difficulties that had been successfully dealt with in the big move.

After the service, all students and visitors were invited to be guests of the college for lunch in the new dining hall. J. E. McKinzie, board member and operator of the dining hall, was accustomed to thinking in large terms, so one can be assured that he and his staff were ready for the crowd. Special guests for the weekend were some 300 alumni. Walter Adams, faculty member and president of the Alumni Association, had declared it Homecoming Weekend. He presided at the luncheon, and he and faculty member Don Morris and newspaperman Wendell Bedichek all spoke – briefly, enthusiastically, and to the point.

Then board vice chairman J. C. Reese was introduced. He explained the new drive to establish the 10,000 Club. The goal of the club was to enlist 1,000 ex-students and friends of the college to seek ten individuals each who would pledge ten dollars each, payable over a three-month period. The money raised would go toward paying for the new buildings and expenses incidental to moving the campus. It was to be a love offering for their Alma Mater. If successful it would quickly add $100,000 to the college coffers. More than 100 exes signed up on the spot. Because of the Great Depression that set in just a month later, the 10,000 Club did not reach the goal, but thousands of dollars were contributed to create a good start in educating alumni to support their school.

The 10,000 Club introduced the greater Abilene Christian constituency to a young man who obviously had a great future with the college: Don Heath Morris. He was twenty-seven years old, a 1924 graduate of the college. He had taught history and speech at Abilene High School from 1924 to 1928 and had then joined the faculty of Abilene Christian College. He taught courses in public speaking and education and was coach of debate, which had always been a significant activity, but which under his sponsorship was destined to more significance than ever. He was named general campaign manager and was busy lining up his organization and increasing the membership of the 10,000 Club.

Thirty-six years later, Batsell Baxter, then teaching Bible at David Lipscomb College in the twilight of his career, spoke to a group in Bennett Gymnasium during the February lectureship. He expressed admiration for the progress the college had made and was making and said that from the days of his presidency the trustees had marked Don Morris as a future president and Walter Adams as a future dean of the college.

On Monday, September 23, the alumni meeting continued, with speeches by President Emeritus Sewell and long-time Dean H. E. Speck, among others. Both men expressed strong support for the college and congratulated the board, administration, faculty, students, alumni, and total constituency on the progress that was so evident.

The next morning, Tuesday, September 24, at ten o'clock, official opening exercises were conducted. With more than 1,000 students and patrons present for the exercises in Sewell Auditorium, J. E. McKinzie presided. Henry Free led "All Hail the Power of Jesus' Name," and President Baxter gave the invocation. After the devotional, the mayor of Abilene, Thomas Hayden, welcomed the students and, while he was speaking, announced that he was becoming a member of the 10,000 Club. The mayor received wild applause.

The next speaker was Charles Bacon, the Chamber of Commerce president who had played such a key role in site selection for the new campus. Greetings were heard from Dr. Oscar Henry Cooper, president of Simmons University, and Dr. J. W. Hunt, president of McMurry College. Board chairman J. S. Arledge read a brief history of the school. President Baxter concluded the program by declaring the twenty-fourth session officially open.

The glorious five-day campus inauguration gave way to student registration Tuesday afternoon and Wednesday morning. Classes began meeting Wednesday afternoon. Enrollment was down somewhat from the previous year. The problem was not with the college but with the academy and the training school, both of which suffered enrollment drops; in fact, they were about half the size of the previous year. The problem was that many parents who had been sending their children to the school when it was in their neighborhood were not in position to transport them to and from the new location. Nobody was discouraged or surprised by that.

Surprise, shock, and discouragement began to displace the euphoria on the new campus. *The New York Times* of Wednesday, October 30, 1929, carried a banner headline on page one: "STOCKS COLLAPSE ... BUT RALLY AT CLOSE CHEERS BROKERS." The story called the day before, Tuesday, October 29, "the most disastrous day in the stock market's history" and added, "Billions of dollars in open market values were wiped out as prices crumbled." Later in the story a one-sentence summary explained the problem: "Hysteria swept the country and stocks went overboard for just what they would bring at forced sale."

This was the Great Crash. Trouble had besieged Wall Street for the past eight days. Monday, October 21, panic selling of stocks set in so fast that the ticker tape could not keep up; by Thursday, October 24, reports said that eleven well-known speculators had committed suicide. The stock market crash did not necessarily cause the Great Depression, but it was a forceful signal that all was not well with the economy. However, even with the stock market situation, concern was low-key in Abilene, Texas. The *Abilene Daily Reporter* did not carry a front-page headline about it. In fact, there was a small story on page three with the heading "OPTIMISM HOLDS SWAY IN NEW YORK STOCK MARKET." The next day a story on page nine was headlined "ROCKEFELLERS BUYING STOCKS AND PRICES START UPWARD."

Immediately after the stock market crash of October 29, 1929, and the deepening depression that followed, Abilene Christian College people tried to go on with business as usual. High on the agenda was an open house. The original plan called for open house to be staged in conjunction with the official opening of school September 24, 1929. However, because some of the new buildings were not quite finished, notably Sewell Auditorium, open house had to be postponed. The buildings were usable, at least by sections, for classes, administrative offices, and chapel, but they were not yet ready for showing.

Finally, however, the great day was set for Sunday afternoon, January 19, 1930. Everything was ready except Bennett Gymnasium, on which construction was just getting underway. All of Abilene, and in fact all of West Texas, was invited to visit and tour the campus between two o'clock and six o'clock in the afternoon. More than 2,000 people came, a steady stream of people during the four hours set for the occasion. An *Optimist* writer did the counting and reported that at one time 190 automobiles were parked in front of the campus.

The tour started at the Administration Building. President and Mrs. Baxter and board member E. L. Crawford and wife stood at the main entrance and welcomed all visitors. Student guides were on hand. Visitors were taken to the administrative offices, where they found Dean Cox, registrar Clara Bishop, and bursar Lawrence L. Smith at their welcoming stations. Visitors were shown the classrooms with their new furniture on the main floor and the third floor. The third floor also was the home of the college library, much of which had been rescued from the burning Administration Building on the old campus. Then they toured the ground floor to see where the well-equipped biology, chemistry, physics, and foods laboratories were located, as well as the extension department.

From the Administration Building the touring group moved across to the Zona Luce Education Building, home of the training school, which was the elementary school, and academy, which was the high school. W. H. "Henry" Free, only charter member of the board still serving as a board member, was receiving guests there, along with W. C. Sikes, academy principal, and Essie Rambo, training school principal. Instructors were also on hand to greet visitors.

Next, the visitors were escorted to Zellner Hall, the dormitory for women. Board chairman J. S. Arledge was on duty there, along with board member T. A. Russell and Elizabeth Nelson, dean of women and instructor of mathematics. All seventy-five rooms were open, and the girls were there to greet the people. At Chambers Hall, there were two receptions. One was on the main floor, which was set aside for the college dining hall and kitchen. Mr. and Mrs. J. E. McKinzie were doing the honors. The refreshments there were a welcome part of the tour. The top floor was set aside for light housekeeping for women. Elishia Deane Walker, biology instructor and hostess, showed visitors the twenty rooms of that facility. McDonald Dormitory for men featured two trustees, Dabney Harvey and G. C. Helvey, in addition to the supervisor and the residents, with their rooms all presentable.

The last stop of the tour was Sewell Auditorium, with seating for 1,280. The dream of a 2,000- or 2,500-seat auditorium had been modified, but it was still a great facility. Its excellent acoustics for chapel singing, arrived at accidentally, for no acoustical engineer was involved in the planning, will be remembered as long as people are alive who attended chapel exercises in Sewell during the years from 1929 to 1968. Moody Coliseum was completed in 1968 and could accommodate the entire student body and faculty for daily chapel. As of this writing, Sewell is serving nobly as the home of the Theatre Department. Because the stage is so much larger than in the original auditorium, and because seating has been reconfigured for dinner theatre, seating capacity is now about one-fifth of what it was as an auditorium. The university will continue to utilize Sewell after the grand new $10 million fine arts center, in the planning stages in 1998, is completed.

An *Optimist* article pointed out two unique features of this college auditorium. It contained a baptistry and a nursery because it also was used for meetings of the College Church of Christ until 1952, when the church moved into its own facility across the street from Sewell. Hosts and hostesses welcoming the tour at Sewell included trustee Harvey Hays, faculty member Don Morris, speech arts instructor Mary Hale, and the director of fine arts, Miss Pat Malone. The basement of the auditorium, under the stage, had fine arts studios and practice rooms.

The afternoon had been triumphant, but the toughest days in the history of the college lay ahead.

Whatever were the factors that brought on the Depression, the results were soon seen. In 1930, 1,300 banks over the nation closed their doors. During the next two years, 3,700 more closed. The Federal Deposit Insurance program did not exist in those days. Depositors lost their money or had it tied up while the banks were scrambling to salvage losses and reopen. Unemployment increased from 1,000,000 during the boom years to 13,000,000 very quickly. Personal incomes in the United States fell almost by half; hysteria gripped the nation.

The Great Depression struck Abilene Christian College full force. Property sales fell to near zero. Many persons who had bought lots and had made a ten percent down payment could not keep up the payments and had to return the lots. The trustees were land rich and cash poor. President Baxter made reference to the problem in his report to the board in February 1931:

> I realize that the board is heavily burdened in trying to pay for the land and buildings. You have had some disappointments in receipts that would have disheartened a less courageous body of men. The financial condition of the country, with the stagnation of lot sales, the depletion of donations, and failure in pledge payments have made a situation which, if we did not

know its merits, would look like bad management on the part of the local board.

But Baxter was constrained to point out some problems the president's office also faced: he had heretofore managed to keep a balanced budget in operating the college with tuition monies, fees, and the small margin from room and board. But that precarious balance had changed. He was behind some $20,000. Eight thousand of this was owed to J. E. McKinzie and the dining hall. The college also owed Central State Bank $10,000.

Baxter had on hand some $30,000 in assets on paper. Students had signed notes to the college for their bills for tuition, fees, room, and board. These notes were for a total of $30,000, "three-fourths of which," he declared, "are good." Some of the notes were backed up by school warrants, which teachers in some public schools were being paid in lieu of cash. Teachers could use these warrants at some grocery stores and other places of business that could afford to hold the warrants until the school district could redeem them with cash, but Abilene Christian College was not quite in that shape.

A year later, February 1932, Baxter made his last annual report to the board. Deep discouragement was evident:

> During the past two years ... the administration for the first time since I became president eight years ago, has been unable to pay the running expenses from the receipts from board, room, tuition, and fees. I had an agreement with the Board at the time I became president, that all salaries would be made up by the Board. It seems that to spend money for this purpose is a violation of the strict construction of the charter. Also, the Board is unable to do this for financial reasons.

The charter provision to which he was referring is Article IX, which reads:

> All donations and paid subscriptions to this corporation shall constitute a permanent fund, and no part of it shall ever be used, save and except for three purposes, to wit: First, to procure a suitable site for the college; second, the construction, furnishing, and equipment of suitable college buildings; third, an endowment or investment fund – i.e., a fund to be invested by the Board of Directors in bonds, mortgages, real estate, or otherwise, so as to produce an income; and all of the expense of this corporation and institution of learning shall be paid out of the income of the college.

Apparently somebody on the board had just lately discovered article nine and had told the president that the board could not help him with expenses of the school because donations could be used only to buy land for campus, erect buildings, or put aside in endowment. From the beginning of the corporation, however, the very men who adopted the charter did not so understand it. In fact, contracts with Presidents Barret, Darden, Whiteside, and Sewell had always been that the president received all the money that came in – from donations or otherwise – and paid out all that had to be paid out, and the president did not have to worry about whether the money came from tuition or donations.

Furthermore, there is such a thing as "living endowment." The desires of the donor have to be considered – or an institution may run out of donors. Living endowment is donating the equivalency of the income that could be earned from endowment instead of donating the principal.

The charter argument was not a very sound one. The one, however, that was backed up with all kinds of data was the second reason Baxter mentioned to explain why the board could not help with his problem: "Also, the board is unable to do this for financial reasons."

At any rate, President Baxter was discouraged; maybe fatigued would be a better word. He added this note:

> Last year faculty salaries were cut ten percent, the president's salary fifteen percent, after the first month. This year the president and faculty are voluntarily turning back half of our salaries to the wiping out of our deficit. One cannot run on this way for any great length of time. In addition to this, faculty members are nearly all paying on pledges or lots to help the school.

Two good witnesses as to the hardships faculty members endured during the early days of the depression are Walter Adams and E. W. McMillan.

Adams, with his wife and young daughter, Dewby, moved to New York City to begin work on his doctorate at Columbia University in the fall of 1930. The Board of Trustees had adopted a policy of paying half salary to teachers working on doctor's degrees. The problem was that there was not a member of the faculty who had the doctorate; hence, accreditation was out of the question. Adams was promised $100 per month during his stay in the big city. It is amazing what $100 would buy at the time. He received the check the first three or four months, but "as a Christmas present" he received a letter from President Baxter in December saying that the college could not send any more money. Walter Adams was not the sort who could be dissuaded by bad news. He got a job working two nights per week at the 23rd Street YMCA in New York City, continued preaching on Sunday for the small congregation meeting in the Pythian Temple, borrowed some money from a cousin, W. C. Stripling of Fort Worth, borrowed money on his life insurance, and stuck it out.

By September 1931, he had completed residence requirements at Columbia and was back in Abilene to teach. Shortly, President Baxter called the faculty together and announced that all would have to get by with half salary. This meant $100 per month for the Adamses, and the house they were renting cost them $30 per month. "But," as he says, "with my preaching occasionally, refereeing football, and Louise teaching voice and directing the choruses, we made it fine."

E. W. McMillan was another one who would not be whipped down by tough times. He recalled,

> The school appointed me as chairman of the Bible Department. Everybody felt good. New campus, buildings, new equipment, new everything. We were on our way. Many of us bought or built new homes. But we had barely started in the fall of 1929 when that historic depression hit – and the bottom fell out of just about everything. I was teaching full time and preaching for the College Church on a full-time basis. ... The school and church gave me just about ten percent above what they would have paid if I had been just at one job. Now when that depression hit, the college announced that they would have to cut salaries fifty percent; and the church announced they had to cut salaries forty percent. I didn't quarrel with it.... All of us were trying to find somebody who would give a little money to the college .... I would go to a church I knew ... make a speech, see some individuals, and beg and look sad. I didn't have to put it on – I did feel sad; that's the way all of us working survived.

November 28, 1931, Batsell Baxter submitted his resignation as president of Abilene Christian College. He requested that it be effective as of June 1, 1932. At that time he would become president of David Lipscomb College, Nashville,

Tennessee. He certainly did not have to leave. The board supported him. Faculty members trusted him. Not many college presidents could go before a faculty and announce a plan for fifty percent downsizing of salaries and then be able to say to the Board of Trustees that the faculty had voluntarily taken a cut.

Baxter resigned perhaps because of fatigue. Maybe he was looking for a college that had not risked everything on building a whole new campus in the wide open spaces. Maybe he was looking for a college whose charter did not seem to say that a board could buy land for a campus, build buildings, and set up long-term endowments, but could not help educate its students, sustain its faculty, or come to the aid of its president. On the other hand, Batsell Barrett Baxter, who adored and admired his father, said that one criticism of him was that all through life "he moved too much." He did not ever stay at one place very long. The fact is that after two years as president of Lipscomb, the Baxters were back in Abilene, where he was head of the Bible Department. Batsell Barrett also said about his father: "One of his finest qualities, an ability somewhat rare, was his ability to 'come down the ladder of success gracefully.' It is comparatively easy to go up the ladder of success with good grace, but to step aside gracefully and let others take one's place, to step into the shadows with good spirit, is relatively rare."

After three years in the Bible Department at Abilene Christian, he went to California for two years as the first president of George Pepperdine College, now Pepperdine University; then taught in the Bible Department of Harding College, now Harding University; served a second term as president of Lipscomb in 1943-46; and the last ten years of his life was chairman of the Bible Department at Lipscomb.

Regardless, he was another right person at the right time for what Abilene Christian needed, and academic and campus life during the Baxter years was a rich tapestry.

The sciences were at the threshold of significant growth when the new campus was built. The plan for the new three-story Administration Building was clear. The top floor was reserved for general classrooms. The main, or second floor, was set aside for administrative offices and classrooms. The ground floor was occupied by the Science Department. The Science Department consisted of biology, chemistry, and physics, with mathematics thrown in. Physics was a new offering in 1929 because of considerable demand, especially from pre-medical students. Paul Chandler Witt was head of the Science Department. He taught chemistry and the new physics offerings, and, if necessary, biology. Elishia Deane Walker taught biology, and President Baxter was available for advanced courses. Elizabeth Nelson taught mathematics.

No matter what the plan was for the use of the new Administration Building, an adjustment was soon needed. The ground floor could not accommodate all three of the sciences plus mathematics. So it was decided that chemistry would have to go. Besides space considerations, chemistry was too odoriferous an operation to be housed in the Administration Building. A solution was available. The trustees had vowed when they threw up the temporary building on the old campus after the fire that the new lumber, hardware, doors, windows, and roofing would be used on the new campus. The temporary frame building was moved to the new campus, located south of Chambers Hall and east of McDonald Dormitory, and became the home of the chemistry program for the next seventeen years. It was too large a structure to be moved intact, so it was sawed into three sections, loaded onto flatbed trucks, transported to the new location, and reassembled with some modifications. It was officially named the Chemistry Building, but soon became known as the Chem Shack.

Department head Paul Witt bought lots directly across East North Sixteenth Street from the Chemistry Shack and built his home because of the location and his understanding that when the time came for a new facility for science, it would be at the same spot. As things turned out, when the new building was erected, in 1945-46, it was located farther west than he had anticipated, but that was a minor disappointment for him, for the following reason: With the Chem Shack, whenever freezing weather occurred, which was not too often, but often enough, Dr. Witt took personal responsibility for moving to his house across the street all of the chemicals that might be ruined by freezing. There they would remain for the night and then be transported back to the shack when the stoves were lit by day. Talk about dedication! When the new science building was built in 1947 with central heat, he no longer had to transport chemicals, so being near was not as essential as it was during the years of the Shack.

In spite of its plethora of shortcomings, the Shack served valiantly through the years and was the subject of considerable merriment, and some snobbery, in the student press. The *Prickly Pear* never published a photograph of it in the campus buildings section from year to year. Occasionally, in snapshot sections, it appeared in the background or from the air, but it was never identified. Apparently, editors of that publication or, more likely, faculty sponsors were embarrassed by the Chem Shack, the poor relative of the new campus. And yet some of the most distinguished research on the campus was done there.

R. D. Tyler, a 1937 graduate of the college, served as a chemistry instructor under Dr. Witt. He wrote a good description of the shack from which so many distinguished chemistry majors graduated:

> The exterior consisted of one inch by twelve inch boards running horizontally around the building; the interior was lined with one by twelves nailed on horizontally. There were no screens on the doors or windows. The roof was covered with black tar paper with a coat of tar to keep it from blowing off. Through all the years it was used it never had a paint job. It was hot in the summer, cold in the winter; no air conditioning and only open flame gas heaters. The wind seemed to blow all the time; air circulated under the floor and through the knotholes and cracks in the floor. Space was rearranged so that there were two large classrooms, two offices, two store rooms, and one balance room.

Tyler added, "Although we had other classes in the new brick buildings, we were never envious of the other classrooms, and we were proud of our own Chem Shack. Dr. Witt kept us all busy and we were one big happy group; we had picnics, and Mrs. Witt had us over to their home."

So many success stories could be related in connection with the Chem Shack era, but one story will suffice. Malcolm E. "Mac" Pruitt came out of the small town of Hamilton, Texas, in the fall of 1937 and enrolled in the small, 650-student, unaccredited Abilene Christian College. He graduated in 1941 with a bachelor of science degree and a chemistry major. He went to work for Dow Chemical Company, headquartered in Midland, Michigan. He rose through the ranks to become director of research for Corporate Dow, with some two thousand persons, including approximately fifty Ph.D.s in chemistry, working under his direction – and his bachelor's degree in chemistry from Abilene Christian was the only earned degree he ever had.

When the hallowed, maligned, appreciated but ridiculed Shack was razed in 1947, with the completion of the new brick, concrete, and steel science building, an *Optimist* obituary concluded with these sentiments: "After many years of service and with its very foundations being shaken many times with the vibrations of many explosive experiments, and once with a fire, its walls and desks covered with the carvings of bygone generations, it is gone. And all that we can say in farewell is, 'Goodbye, little chem shack, goodbye.'"

Paul Witt and W. Earl Brown, two faculty members during Baxter's administration, bring to mind the deal President Sewell worked out with them concerning their futures. "Prexy" Sewell was always thinking of the future of Abilene Christian College. This does not mean that he had a monopoly on thoughts about the future. All presidents of Abilene Christian have thought of the future, but President Sewell specialized in it. In the graduating class of 1922 were two young men of whom he made a special request. They were Witt and Brown, both English majors.

Witt came to Abilene in 1916 as an eighteen-year-old high school student to enroll in the ACC Academy. After graduation from the academy, he enrolled in 1918 in the college. He was interested in science but found no science major available. So he majored in English and minored in chemistry, with most of his chemistry being taken at Simmons College. During his college years, he was an all-around student. Distinguished in his academic work, he was also president of the A Club and a member of the men's glee club and of the college quartet. He played violin in the orchestra and was a member of the yell team. He lettered in baseball, participated in debate, and was sergeant of the Student Army Training Corps during World War I. He was preparing to go overseas when the war ended. In 1920, as a junior in college, he became bursar of the college and continued in that capacity until graduation and through his first two years of teaching.

He received the bachelor of arts degree in 1922. Along the way, President Sewell had a heart-to-heart talk with him and convinced him that his place in the Kingdom of God was to prepare himself to teach science at Abilene Christian College. Witt was interested in mission work, but Sewell pointed out the variety of students he would be able to influence in preparing scientists with a Christian faith for the world. He considered that mission work. Witt bought it.

Paul Witt's teaching was a lifelong ministry. Hundreds of students were built up in the Christian faith while pursuing studies in science. He completed the bachelor's degree work in chemistry at Simmons in 1925, the master's degree at the University of Texas in 1927, and the doctor's degree at the University of Colorado in 1938. His doctoral dissertation was a study of the sulfa drug, which, when first introduced, caused numerous deaths. His study showed what caused the drug to be poisonous and led to its development as a so-called miracle drug that was safe to take. His work became nationally known, and he received many honors. Witt was a full-time faculty member for forty-five years and part time for four more.

William Earl Brown was another young man for whom President Sewell had other ideas. He majored in English with plans to go to the Lubbock area and teach in the public schools. But "Prexy" prevailed upon him to plan for doctoral studies in history and to head up that department. So Brown completed his master's degree in history at the University of Colorado in 1926, returned to his teaching at Abilene, took the year of 1927-28 for residence work at Johns Hopkins University, returned to Abilene for a period of years while continuing his research, then took another year in Baltimore. He completed all of his work, including his dissertation, and turned it in to await word from his major professor – his faculty adviser. It developed that his major professor was retiring, leaving him in the hands of a new adviser. A new committee was appointed. The decision of these professors was that he would have to start over with another subject. Tired, broke, dejected, he returned to Abilene and never was awarded the doctorate for which he had labored so diligently. No matter, he was a great teacher throughout his forty-four-year tenure and a true Christian.

A number of other strong faculty members came to the college during the Baxter years.

Jewell Watson was head of the English department, 1929-59. Dr. James Culp, who succeeded her as department head in 1959, credits her with giving her students an unusually strong foundation in the Anglo-Saxon language and in the historical surroundings of great literary works. She was a strong classroom teacher and influential in campus life. She lived for eighteen years on the third floor of Zellner Dormitory for women and served as assistant to the dean of women.

Edward Washington McMillan was persuaded to move to Abilene in 1928. He had a double assignment: preacher for the College Church and head of the Bible Department at Abilene Christian College. He was involved in a very successful ministry at Cleburne when the invitation came for him to move to Abilene. Cleburne wanted him to stay; Abilene wanted him to move. The way he settled that problem was typical of the faith he transmitted to his students. He simply asked the elders at Cleburne and the elders in Abilene to get together and decide where he should serve. He promised he would be happy with their decision. The two groups amicably agreed he should move to Abilene, where he could teach hundreds of students in the college and preach for the College Church of Christ. He did some of the greatest work of his life during the next several years.

Burnya Mae Moore was one of the most energetic and versatile faculty members to come aboard during the Baxter years. With a degree in vocational home economics from Texas Woman's University in Denton, she joined the faculty of Abilene Christian in the fall of 1928, teaching textiles and clothing. She taught for the next forty-seven years, retiring in 1975. Along the way, she acquired a master's degree from

TWU and did summer work at Columbia University in 1936 and the University of Chicago in 1945. In addition to classes in textiles and clothing, she taught design arts, foods and meal planning, first aid, home nursing, time and money management, and child care. After World War II, she conducted seminars for returning veterans and wives dealing with furnishing and decorating campus housing.

She was chairman of a project to publish the *Women of ACU's Cookbook*, an outstanding success. Money from cookbook sales went to scholarships. Activities in the community included the Business and Professional Women's organization, the American Red Cross, and the American Association of University Women, of which she was treasurer for many years. She served annually as a judge of projects at the West Texas State Fair and was active in other community affairs. She left her home to the university to be sold and the proceeds used to improve the museum in Jennings House, a project of the Women for ACU. Her former home presently houses the Abilene Higher Education Authority, which makes possible attendance of hundreds of students yearly. The university provided funds to improve the museum.

Elishia Deane Walker arrived on campus in 1926 to teach biology. After the move to the new campus in 1929, it was noticeable that the stray cat population of The Hill was depleted annually during certain laboratory assignment periods in her anatomy classes. Occasionally, an overzealous, or under-conscientious, student would snatch a feline that was not actually a stray. This caused commotion and was ultimately abandoned. Nowadays, animals for laboratory purposes are ordered from approved sources and arrive on campus in a preserving solution. Miss Walker was a diligent teacher who expected her students to be diligent. Woe betide the student who tried to get by with an exhibit of East Texas grasshoppers, which had been collected by somebody else, in a West Texas biology class.

Jasper Willie Treat graduated from the college in 1928 with a degree in Spanish. During his senior year he was president of the Students' Association. Through the 1928-29 school year, he taught in the high school at Colorado City. In the fall of 1929, he began teaching in the Foreign Language Department of ACC, and for the next forty-seven years he taught Spanish, French, and, when there was sufficient demand, Italian. He spoke all three languages fluently. His doctorate was from the University of Texas. In 1976, he and his wife, Mildred Sellers Treat, were honored by the Abilene Exchange Club with its Golden Deeds Award "for nearly a half-century of working with the poor and underprivileged here and in Mexico." He devoted his life to working with Spanish language churches and died February 17, 1998, at age 90.

W. M. Yowell was quiet, unassuming, and gentle in manner. He came to the faculty in 1927 with a background of teaching in Christian colleges: Harper in Kansas, Thorp Spring, Harding, and David Lipscomb. He had taught one summer at Southwest Texas State Teachers College and had been a school superintendent. In Abilene, he taught courses in sociology and psychology. After eighteen years on the faculty, he suffered a heart attack and died at age sixty-four.

Irma Kennamer Christian grew up in Woodville, Alabama, which was not large enough to have a high school. When time came for Irma and her brother, Clyde, to go to high school, they were sent to Nashville, where an older brother, Lorrin G. Kennamer, was teaching in David Lipscomb College. In Lipscomb High School, she became a pen pal of a girl in England. This developed into a lifelong friendship, which led to many trips to England and the rest of Europe. It also whetted her appetite for the study of geography, which happened to be her older brother's preferred subject.

In 1923, L. G. Kennamer signed on to teach geography at Abilene Christian. Besides his wife and two children, he brought along his two younger siblings as college students. Going to school winter and summer and working to pay her way, Irma graduated in 1928. The same year, she began a thirty-five-year career of teaching the fourth grade at Abilene Christian Training School. Her favorite subjects were Bible and geography. In 1930, she married C. A. Christian. He earned a living for his family, so that his wife could use her teacher's salary to travel and see for herself the great historic places so she could describe them vividly to her students. Before long, she began teaching geography to teacher education majors enrolled in the college. The result was a large number of young teachers who were enthusiastic about geography and history during a time when these two important subjects were being neglected in many schools. Her brother, L. G., taught at ACC for five years; she stayed a lifetime. As this is being written, she is ninety, going strong, and attending chapel daily.

Mary Coffee Locke came in 1928. She taught art for a decade: ceramics, oils, pastels, woodcarving, china, and charcoal. She moved to Abilene to send her son and two daughters to college, took in boarders, and taught art, for which she had a special talent. She had been trained in art but did not have a college degree. So, while teaching, she finished her bachelor's degree and took postgraduate study in California.

During the first two years of the Baxter administration three men, teacher-coaches, arrived at ACC. They were destined to have an influence for good larger than life, on campus and beyond. They were coaches Asbury Bratten Morris, Guy Scruggs, and J. Eddie Weems.

Morris came in the fall of 1924 as head coach of football, basketball, and baseball, and athletic director. He also was head of the Physical Education Department and taught a full load of classes in that department. Morris was a graduate of Texas A&M with a major in agriculture, a field in which he planned to make his career. He was a natural-born athlete. Out of high school, he was recruited for Texas A&M by football coach D. X. Bible. Standing five feet seven inches tall and weighing 150 pounds, his lifelong weight, he became the star quarterback for the Aggies. He led his team to a victory over Centre College in the first of what was to become the annual Cotton Bowl games, January 2, 1922. In addition to his quarterbacking, he was the place kicker, hailed by the A&M annual as "the boy with the million-dollar toe." He was also shortstop on the Aggie baseball team, captain of the team for one year, and for two years led the Southwest Conference in hitting and runs scored.

After graduation from college in the spring of 1923, he played professional baseball in the Western Association in Ardmore, Oklahoma, in the summer and taught and coached at Greenville High School for one year before being recruited by

President Baxter as a faculty member of Abilene Christian College. In 1924, ACC had just been admitted as a member of the Texas Intercollegiate Athletic Association, so it could be expected that the competition would be tough. Morris's teams were always competitive even when they did not win championships, which they did win often enough. But the greatness of "Coach," as he was known through the years, was measured by far more than his coaching ability. What he accomplished in the lives of so many hundreds of students who played for him, and those who simply knew him on campus, was beautifully summed up in a note sent to him on the occasion of his retirement in 1982 by John Wooden, longtime head coach of basketball at the University of California at Los Angeles:

No written word, no oral plea
Can teach our youth what they should be;
Nor all the books on all the shelves.
It's what the teachers are themselves.

After eighteen years, Morris turned head coaching responsibilities in football over to his ex-student A. M. "Tonto" Coleman. In 1955, he relinquished all coaching duties and concentrated on his job as athletic director. In 1969, he became athletic director emeritus and began using his vast and favorable acquaintanceship with Abilene Christian alumni to promote the A. B. Morris Athletic Fund. Hundreds of ex-students echoed the sentiment of one alumnus who said, "Coach Morris is one fund raiser whose annual phone call I look forward to receiving." In recognition of his unusual life, he was elected to four sports halls of fame: ACU, Texas A&M, the National Intercollegiate Athletic Association, and the Intercollegiate Directors of Athletics.

Coach had not been on campus long before he met Rebecca McKay. They were married in 1925. Their son, Charles, who died in December 1997, was a noted athlete who played under his father, with no special favors extended, and had a distinguished career in athletics, including many years as an executive of the National Association of Intercollegiate Athletics. Rebecca Morris was a faculty member in the Speech

Department for many years and is today as avid a supporter of ACU athletics and of the fine arts as she was during her husband's lifetime.

Guy Andy Scruggs also came in 1924 as an assistant coach. He taught in the academy, and, because he was only a junior college graduate, he took college courses that would lead to a bachelor of arts degree in 1927. Later, he earned a master's degree in 1944 from Hardin-Simmons University, climaxed by a commendable thesis titled "The History of Abilene Christian College." Scruggs was born in Mississippi but was brought to Texas as a two-year-old by his parents. He grew up near Don Morris of DeSoto and A. B. Morris of Wheatland; in fact, he went to high school at DeSoto. After graduation, he attended Thorp Spring Christian College, completed his two years at Thorp in 1919-21, passed his state examination for a permanent teacher's certificate, and went to Munday, Texas, to play semi-pro baseball. While there, he was hired to teach in the Munday schools. With a teaching job, he gained the approval of Sam Allen to marry the Allens' daughter, Bess, whom he had courted at Thorp Spring. Previously, Allen, a genuine old-time West Texas rancher, had taken a dim view of his daughter's association with a baseball player. In fact, he described Guy as the only man he had ever known who "got paid to play."

Bess, having graduated from Thorp Spring and having passed her state examination for a permanent teacher's certificate, joined her husband in teaching. During his third and her second year at Munday, two opportunities arose. First, a Saint Louis Cardinal scout asked him if he would be interested in a major league baseball contract. Scruggs was of course intrigued. He was quite a pitcher. But a second offer intervened. Scruggs was instrumental in getting President Baxter as graduation speaker for Munday High School. While there, Baxter offered him a job teaching in the academy and helping with coaching duties for the college. The Scruggses moved to Abilene in the fall of 1924.

The Morris-Scruggs combination was a success from the beginning. Both men were Christian gentlemen around the clock. They respected the athletes, and the athletes respected them. In later years, an amazing percentage of athletes became successful in their careers, leaders in the church, and loyal alumni, many of them trustees of Abilene Christian University.

Through the years, Scruggs had various duties, including the head coaching job for baseball, tennis, and badminton. He served as principal of Abilene Christian High School. He was a member of the physical education faculty of the college. He did his work well. During a four-year period, 1928-32, he was away from the college, working on the family ranch near Christoval. The story behind that was that his father-in-law had a goal of providing a good ranch for each of his children – three sons and two daughters. He helped his oldest son homestead a ranch near the Mexican border. He owned land near Lamesa and more in Terrell County, plus the home place and a ranch which he bought adjoining it – enough for all the Allen offspring. He planned to give the home place to Bess and Guy Scruggs. So Guy thought it wise to learn ranch management from a man who knew the business, an outstanding opportunity.

All seemed to be going well until a speaker from Abilene Christian College came to talk on the subject of "Christian Education" for the church the family attended. During the course of the sermon, Allen looked at his son-in-law and saw tears running down his cheeks. The next day, while they were out on the range, he said, "Guy, I do not understand why a man would rather work at a college than run a ranch, but I believe that is what you want to do, and I will certainly understand." So ended the Scruggs' interlude of ranching. Allen was a longtime trustee of Abilene Christian College. Among his gifts to the college was the valuable Allen Farm, which is now part of the campus. Guy Scruggs spent his life being a genuine friend to students; he was happier with students than with cattle.

The third great coach who came during the early years of the Baxter administration was J. Eddie Weems. He was employed in 1925 as head of the English Department and track coach. He was outstanding as an English teacher and did miraculous things as a coach. Born April 13, 1896 (he liked to emphasize that it was Friday the thirteenth), at Temple, he was somewhat delayed in his educational attainments. He was twenty-two when he graduated from Temple High School. His schooling had included one year in the academy of Thorp Spring Christian College, 1915-16, while Batsell Baxter was dean of the college. From Temple High School he enrolled in Texas Christian University where he lettered in track four years and majored in history. After receiving his bachelor's degree in 1922, he stayed a year longer and earned a master's in Bible. With such a background he spent forty years as an English teacher of great repute. During all of those years he was proud of the fact that he never missed a class because of illness.

Weems found the track program practically non-existent at ACC, but he developed it to the point that he became known as the father of track and field at ACC. Between 1925 and 1937, his track teams won thirteen TIAA titles and shared another. Among the young men he coached to stardom were Elmer Gray, James "Sonny" Cowan, Hulan Armstrong, Chester Keagy, Howard Green, James Vickery, Dyle Vaughn, Clarence Nelson, Ross Dawkins, and Elmer and Delmer Brown. Weems was noted for his chapel speeches with their precise diction and no wasted words. He loved to preach, "without pay, and rarely for more than expenses," as one admirer wrote. "He seemed to prefer smaller churches unable to afford or to attract a full-time minister."

In 1937, Weems resigned and went to California to join the faculty of newly established George Pepperdine College, where he taught English and continued to turn out great track teams. With the onset of World War II, he left California and returned to his Texas ranch, a 280-acre enterprise between Waco and Temple. Back in his home state, he was a tutor in English at the University of Texas for a while and then taught and coached track at Austin High School for a year. With the end of the war, he returned to Pepperdine for five more years and then came back to Texas. He taught and coached track at TCU from 1955 to 1962 and put in the closing years of his teaching career at Abilene Christian. When he retired at age sixty-nine, he was honored and presented this certificate, which was signed by B Sherrod, chairman of the board; Don H. Morris, president; and Walter H. Adams, dean:

TO J. EDDIE WEEMS

Coach and Teacher of English.
For your exemplary Christian character;
For your quiet and modest sincerity;
For your faith in the Bible as a practical guide for living,
And for your love and respect for the English language
This Scroll is presented.
As the Father of track at Abilene Christian College,
As a coach concerned more with how the game was played
than with the final victory, you will be long remembered.

Sunday morning, July 11, 1976, seventy-nine-year-old J. Eddie Weems and his wife, Anna, left their home in Temple to drive to the small town of Upton, where he preached twice a month. There was a collision, and J. Eddie and Anna Weems were killed instantly. The Weems record will be remembered as long as there is an Abilene Christian University.

To emphasize the difference between athletics of the Baxter and early Morris era and in the 1990s, a story in *The Optimist*, January 8, 1931, brings up an interesting fact about basketball: "The Cats promise to have one of the best teams this year that has ever worn the Purple and White. Full equipment was issued to the following men last week: Pippen, Powell, Reese, Lawrence, Allen, White, Day, Reynolds, Hill, Wortham, Alexander, Carter, and Cooper. The Wildcats have one other thing this year that is the answer to every coach's prayer, and that is plenty of height on the floor. If Coach Morris starts the same lineup against the Indians that he did in the scrimmage with the Cowboys, the team will average six foot with the exception of one man, and if he puts Wortham on the floor in the place of Reese, the club will reach the half-dozen mark all the way around." Those six-footers gave a good account of themselves that season, excluding four losses to Texas Tech and TCU. Today, a six-footer is considered short.

Selecting students to mention in this history is difficult because so many outstanding men and women persevered during the Great Depression. One of the strong contributing factors to the survival of Abilene Christian College during the dark era was the continued vigorous enrollment. In the September 1929 registration – the last enrollment before Black Tuesday – 517 resident students registered, and 293 students were taking courses by correspondence, which G. C. Morlan had made into a large program. A year later, with the depression in full swing, the number of resident students dropped by sixty, but the number taking courses by correspondence increased by 185. The low point of enrollment was the fall of 1932, with 405 resident students and 485 studying by correspondence. Thereafter, resident students kept growing in number, reaching and maintaining the mid-600s during the 1930s. Many of the students of the 1920s and 1930s completely worked their way through ACC. Their parents did not have the money to send them.

For instance, Leslie George Huff enrolled in September 1926. He had worked on the farm and saved his money, so he was able to write a check for his tuition, room, and board for the fall semester, but that left him with only four dollars, not enough to buy books. In those days the college did not have classes on Mondays, in deference to preachers from both student body and faculty who went out to preach on weekends and sometimes needed a day to return to the campus. Classes met Tuesday through Saturday morning. Huff got a job with the J. C. Penney store for Mondays and Saturday afternoons. Then he landed an evening shift, which sometimes went all night, at a milk processing plant and so was able to pay his way through college and maintain a respectable bank account. He also graduated with his class on schedule in 1930, cum laude, with a mathematics major and had time to meet Eunice Swope from Killeen. They were married in August after his graduation. It is no wonder that he had a successful career as a teacher in the public schools of Texas and in the insurance business, culminated by his founding of American Founders Life Insurance Company in 1954. He was honored as the Alumnus of the Year in 1962.

This era also marked the beginning of medical school admissions for Abilene Christian graduates. Before 1925, most male graduates went into preaching, teaching, business, or ranching. The female graduates went mostly into teaching.

In the graduating class of 1921, one student had made up his mind to go to medical school. He was James Delma Mabry. During his student days, he was known as Delma, but afterward, in his medical practice, he went by his initials, Dr. J. D. Five Mabry children came from Penelope, Texas, to enroll in the college. The first two – a daughter, Tolula, and her brother, Delma – enrolled in the fall of 1917. The youngest of the Mabrys, Artemis, enrolled in the fall of 1935. In 1918, an epidemic of influenza claimed many victims, including Tolula Mabry, who was in her second year of what was then a junior college. The 1919 *Prickly Pear* included a picture of her, with these words underneath: "The richest toll of the Spanish Influenza. Died December 9, 1918." Her mother was also a victim of the epidemic. They died within two days of each other. Delma Mabry said that the deaths of his mother and his sister helped him to decide to study medicine.

When he graduated in 1921, he went to Wyoming and taught school for a year. Then he was admitted to the University of Texas Medical School in Galveston. Apparently, he had to do some extra work because of Abilene Christian's lack of a pre-medical program at the time. He graduated in 1928, did his internship at Hermann Hospital in Houston, and remained on the staff there. When he died at age fifty-one, a Houston newspaper article described him as "one of the top surgeons on that hospital staff."

The graduating class of 1925 produced the first three candidates for medical school who went on to complete their degrees and launch their careers as physicians. The three future physicians were John Paul Gibson, Chester Callan, and Sam Ogle Jones. Gibson was the student who compiled an outstanding record as a Southwestern Bible salesman as already discussed.

Chester Callan came as a freshman from Rotan in the fall of 1921, graduated with a natural science major, and entered the University of Texas Medical School at Galveston. After graduation from medical school in 1929, he interned at Scott and White Hospital in Temple and then opened his office in his home town of Rotan, population of about 2,000. He was active in the practice of medicine there for the next fifty-three years.

In October 1948, Dr. Callan was the subject of a feature article in *The Saturday Evening Post* under the heading "We Need More Country Doctors." He was named the Country Doctor of the Year. He was a busy doctor, mayor of the town for a term, and was a twenty-six-year member of the Lions Club. A priority was his service as an elder of the Church of Christ, and he was a member of the Board of Trustees of ACC from 1938 to 1976.

Sam Ogle Jones, a brother of Mrs. J. C. Reese, also was a member of the class of 1925. He was called "Cowboy" in college. He graduated from Vanderbilt University's School of Medicine and spent his career in Centerville, Tennessee.

The first woman pre-medical graduate of Abilene Christian College to complete her medical degree and devote her life to the practice of medicine was Mildred Cariker. She came as a freshman from Nacogdoches in 1928 and graduated in 1932. She studied at the University of Texas Medical Branch in Galveston. She served as a pathologist with the Mayo Clinic in Rochester, Minnesota, for eighteen years. After that, she was in Dallas for a period and then completed her career as the only pathologist in the East Texas city of Marshall.

According to the records of the Biology Department, the first Abilene Christian College student to complete dental school was Jerome Reese. He was a 1931 graduate who attended Baylor Dental School in Dallas. Graduating in 1934, he established an office in Abilene and served for several years as the college dentist. Reese went into military service in the dental corps in 1941 and served five years. After World War II, he specialized in orthodontistry and moved to San Angelo. He was a lifelong supporter of his alma mater and served for a quarter-century as an elder in the Colorado and Jackson Streets Church of Christ.

Another career area in which Abilene Christian alumni began to excel was government service. From the freshman class enrolling in the fall of 1924, two students were destined to play important roles in the highest levels of the United States government.

Rita Foster was from Cleburne, daughter of longtime board member Otto Foster. An English major, she graduated in 1927.

She taught for two years in Clarendon Junior College and married Frank Stocking. In 1934, they moved to Washington, where he went to work for the United States government. He died in 1940. She decided to stay in Washington with her young son, Soxy. Mrs. Stocking began working in key government positions. Among her assignments were four years in the White House during President Harry Truman's administration, where she was secretary to John Steelman, assistant to the president. After her White House years, she was administrative assistant to Oveta Culp Hobby, secretary of Health, Education and Welfare under President Eisenhower. She completed her government career with HEW and was named Abilene Christian's Alumnus of the Year in 1972.

Omar Burleson came from Anson and enrolled as a freshman in the fall of 1924. He spent only one year as a student in Abilene Christian, but he later served as a trustee for forty years and was Alumnus of the Year in 1970. After graduation from the School of Law at Cumberland University in Tenn-essee, he had various jobs, including service as county attorney and then county judge of Jones County, an eighteen-month stint as an agent of the Federal Bureau of Investigation under J. Edgar Hoover, and an assignment with the United States Navy during World War II in the Pacific. In 1946, he was elected to the United States Congress. The people of the Seventeenth Congressional District continued to elect him, so that he served thirty-two years in the House of Representatives. At retirement, he was seventh ranking member of the House

In addition to teaching, medicine, and government, alumni from the Depression era were succeeding in widely varied fields.

Dean Walling came from Amarillo in 1926 and graduated in 1930. During his senior year he was hitchhiking – the travel method of choice in those days for college men – to Oklahoma. A kind gentleman stopped and offered him a ride. The man was Henry Salvatori, who was with Geophysical Services, a Dallas company. The upshot of that chance hitchhiking encounter was that Walling went to work for Salvatori's company. When Salvatori left the Dallas company in 1933 to found Western Geophysical in California, Dean went with him, became a vice president in 1938, executive vice president and manager of operations in 1948, and president of the company in 1959. Dean and Thelma Bernard Walling made the initial gift of $200,000 in the mid-1960s toward a coliseum. That gift triggered the Design for Development, which brought in $10.8 million that made possible the erection of Moody Coliseum, Gibson Health and Physical Education Center, the McGlothlin Campus Center, the Foster Science Building expansion, Walling Lecture Hall, and the Herman and Margaret Brown Library, and launched the college into a whole new era of growth. He was Alumnus of the Year in 1959.

James Burton Coffman burst onto the scene as a freshman from Potosi, Texas, in the fall of 1923. As a student he participated in virtually every activity on campus, except athletics. He was editor of *The Optimist* for two and a half years. He was president of his sophomore class. As a senior he was president of the Students' Association, the Press Club, and the Glee Club; a member of the college quartet, the A Club, Sub T-16, and the ACC band. He was on the debate team for four years. He had a distinguished career as a preacher of the gospel, climaxed by his work with the Manhattan Church of Christ in New York City 1954-71. Before his retirement in 1971, he wrote commentaries on Matthew and Hebrews; after retirement he wrote on all the remaining books of the Bible – thirty-seven sizable volumes in all. The Coffman commentaries were at first published by the Firm Foundation Publishing House, but rights were acquired by the ACU Press in 1983. Sales of Coffman commentaries are being extended to areas outside the United States. He was Alumnus of the Year in 1971.

Alfred Eugene "Poly" Wells, Outstanding Alumnus of 1973, came to the campus in 1927. He was a graduate of Polytechnic High School in Fort Worth. In high school he had been a four-sport letterman in football, basketball, baseball, and track. In each sport, each year, he was awarded a bright orange sweater with a big black letter "P" on it. Having a rather limited wardrobe on the ACC campus, he wore these sweaters when weather required. It did not take the students long to call him "Poly." Graduating in 1931, he began a career as a teacher and administrator in Texas public schools that extended over the next forty-three years. During the last twenty-three years, he was superintendent of the Abilene Independent School District – the longest tenure any superintendent of the Abilene school system has ever had. In 1932 he married his ACC fiancee – Zieta Guest.

Elden Busby, Leslie Huff, Paul Southern, and Roy Stone were all 1930 graduates. Busby was editor of the *Prickly Pear*, with Huff as his business manager. Southern was editor of *The Optimist*, with Stone as his business manager. Even though it was the year the Great Depression struck, both publications sold so much advertising that the editors and business managers, who were allowed by the college to split the unlikely profits, did very well financially. In fact, the word went out that they made more money than some faculty members. For the next year, the college changed the policy in favor of fixed stipends.

Predictably, all four went on to successful careers, Huff as the founder of American Founders Insurance and Busby and Stone as distinguished educators in Fort Worth schools. Busby was superintendent of schools for a time, and Stone was assistant superintendent in charge of high schools after serving as principal of two schools. Southern became a distinguished professor of Bible and Greek and 1951-70 head of the Bible Department at Abilene Christian College.

D. Lloyd Nelson and Hugh M. Tiner were outstanding men of the class of 1929. Nelson was editor of *The Optimist* during the 1927-28 school year; Tiner was business manager of the *Prickly Pear* for 1928-29. Both had an opportunity to enroll in the graduate school of Stanford University at the end of the fall term in 1928 and took it. Tiner made a deal with Leslie Huff to finish the year in his job and have the job for himself the next year. Both Tiner and Nelson completed doctor's degrees at Stanford. Tiner was the second president of Pepperdine University, and Nelson was for many years a Pepperdine trustee while serving as a professor of educational administration at the University of Southern California. He was for some years chairman of the board at Pepperdine.

Ernest Walls was a member of the class of 1926. He went through the ninth grade in a rural two-teacher school and finished his high school work in the Abilene Christian Academy.

He then continued through college. During his freshman year, 1922-23, while serving as class president, he paid his way by milking cows. In the summer of 1923, however, he sold Bibles for the Southwestern Company. He was so successful that he sold each summer through 1926 and did not have to work at anything but school work during the long sessions. The *Prickly Pear* of 1926 paid him a rare compliment:

> President of the Senior Class, the Students' Association, and the A Club, Walls has been the unquestioned leader among the students of '26. Not of the garrulous type, he talks only when necessary, but when he speaks one may be certain that something worthwhile has been said. A character of sterling quality, coupled with an attractive personality, has brought him the trust and friendship of faculty and students alike.

Besides putting in his time in the military during World War II, he worked his way up in the Houston school system. During his last seventeen years, he was personnel director for all of the elementary schools, "responsible for hiring all teachers at the elementary level," quite an assignment in Houston.

Lee Duckworth married Eula Pratt of Eliasville, Texas. To them were born five daughters. Duckworth was a teacher in small one- and two-teacher schools. Early on, he made two decisions: first, that he would never undertake to teach his own children in the school room and, second, that he wanted his children to attend Abilene Christian College. So when the first daughter, LaVerne, was ready for school, he left teaching and went into the grocery business. His first store was in Newcastle, north of Breckenridge, Texas. Then he opened a store in Breckenridge. The first daughter entered Abilene Christian in the fall of 1926, and the others came in their turn: Leola, Irene, Estelle, and Jo Bill. In fact, from the fall semester of 1926 through the spring of 1939, there was always a Duckworth daughter in the student body, and sometimes two. In 1928, the Duckworths decided to move to Abilene, so they opened a store at North Eighth and Hickory Streets. Later, they had stores also at 373 Walnut and 1282 South Second. All five of the daughters graduated from the college, and all but one married ACC schoolmates. LaVerne's husband was not an alumnus of the college. He was, however, a strong Christian and a church leader. Their grandson, Bob West, is now a member of the Board of Trustees.

Sam Davis Tatum came from Tennessee. He came to Abilene after graduating from David Lipscomb College, which was then a junior college. He earned the bachelor of arts degree from Abilene Christian in 1927 as an English major. In ACC he was a debater, a winner in oratory, and a member of the Glee Club. After Abilene, he enrolled in the University of Tennessee Law School. With law degree in hand, he passed the bar examination and set up shop in Nashville. He must have been a natural-born judge because almost from the beginning of his law practice he served as special judge in Criminal Court and special chancellor in the Chancery Court in Domestic Relations. On June 1, 1939, he became judge of the Juvenile Court of Davidson County, metropolitan Nashville, and filled that post for almost twenty-eight years – in fact, for the rest of his life. He suffered a heart attack and died in February 1967 while still in office.

Judge Tatum spoke on the 1956 Lectureship of Abilene Christian College. His topic was "In the Nurture and Admonition of the Lord." In his lecture, he stated: "Since I became Judge of the juvenile Court of Davidson County, I have tried approximately 14,500 youngsters under the age of seventeen for violating the law in that jurisdiction. Of that great host, in only two instances did fathers and mothers go to Sunday School and church regularly with their children." With Judge Tatum, the courtroom was a place dedicated to rescuing young lives. He devoted his life to what he considered a cause.

Baxter era athletes and coaches are well represented in the ACU Sports Hall of Fame, which was inaugurated in 1986. Coaches A. B. Morris, Guy Scruggs, and J. Eddie Weems joined these athletes in the hall:

Theo Powell, '28, is described in his citation as "one of the greatest – if not the greatest – of all-around athletes in ACU history." He earned some fourteen varsity letters in four sports – football, basketball, baseball, and track.

A. M. "Tonto" Coleman, '28, competed for the Wildcats in football, basketball, and baseball. After several years of coaching at the high school level, he moved into the college ranks, coaching at ACU, the University of Florida, and Georgia Tech. He concluded his career as commissioner of the Southeastern Conference. He was named ACU's Outstanding Alumnus of 1966. He is a member of the Texas Sports Hall of Fame.

Dalton Hill, '28, was a four-year letterman in football, and also competed in basketball, baseball, and tennis. He was all-conference center in football in the Texas Intercollegiate Athletic Association in 1926. He was later known as one of the outstanding tennis coaches in Texas.

Garland "Goober" Keyes, '32, was a star quarterback and a top pole vaulter. The citation mentions the first football game ever between Abilene Christian and McMurry. Keyes scored on punt returns of fifty and thirty-four yards and a run from scrimmage of seven yards. The score was 24-0.

L. A. "Tiny" Adams, '32, starred in football and track and field. He was an all-TIAA tackle, set TIAA records with the shot put, and led the Wildcats in discus and javelin.

Elmer Gray, '32, "was the first student-athlete from Abilene Christian to compete in the Olympic trials in track and field." He was the first ACU athlete to run under fifty seconds in the quarter mile. He ran on winning relays at the Texas, Kansas, and Drake Relays. The ACU track stadium is named for him.

Lee Powell, '33, was a four-year letterman in both football and basketball. After graduation from college, he coached for a time in Kentucky and in 1936 took over operation of Old Hickory Clay Company of Paducah, Kentucky. He was named the ACU Alumnus of the year in 1963, and in 1984 he received an honorary doctor of laws degree from his alma mater. Dr. Greg Powell, grandson of Lee and Dorris Powell, is the distinguished chairman of the Chemistry Department at ACU.

Charles A. "Lefty" Reynolds, '33, entered college at sixteen, played freshman basketball and tennis, and then earned three letters each in basketball and tennis. By the time he was nineteen he had used up his eligibility. He was all-conference as a senior. As a junior, he was the conference scoring leader. He went on to a career of school administration. He was superintendent at El Dorado, Texas, for nine years and at Brady for twenty-three years. He served for years as an elder of the Brady

Church of Christ. His father was Otis M. Reynolds, a member of the first class of Childers Classical Institute in 1906.

Admittedly, profiling a handful of teachers and a small list of outstanding students overlooks hundreds of students and a number of teachers who went about their business and lived lives of important service in the vineyard of the Lord. The ones headlined in this section were simply representative of the great body of teachers and students who helped build Abilene Christian.

Always in the background during the Baxter years and the Depression were two other much less well-known builders – business corporations that played a definitive role in building and saving Abilene Christian College: the Missouri State Life Insurance Company of Saint Louis and the Caldwell Company of Nashville.

The first was the Missouri State Life Insurance Company. When the Abilene Christian trustees took over from President Sewell in 1924, they decreed that the dormitory for men that had been talked about for several years but not built would be built and ready for occupancy within seven months. The general board authorized, and, in fact, instructed the local board to raise all the money they could and borrow the balance. So application for a sizable loan was made to the Missouri State Life Insurance Company.

The company had Abilene representatives – the W. J. Behrens Agency. Behrens family members were strong supporters of Simmons College, but they were also good friends to Abilene Christian. Moreover, Hollis L. Manly, a graduate of Abilene Christian and destined to be an effective trustee for many years, was a special representative for the life insurance company. The loan was negotiated for $22,500, payable over a five-year period. This would complete the financing of the new dormitory for men and make it possible to remodel Emergency Hall, the Mule Barn, into a modern kitchen-dining room facility for all the students.

Payments on the loan were made as scheduled. By February 1928, the principal of the note was down to $16,500. Everything looked promising for the note to be fully paid on time by February 1931. Four years after the loan from Missouri State was negotiated, the Caldwell Company of Tennessee came into the picture.

In the spring and summer of 1929, the Abilene Christian College trustees were desperately looking for a long-term loan of $200,000 to meet fast-mounting obligations on the new campus that was under construction, and they turned to the Caldwell Company. The company began as a Nashville investment banking firm, but it developed over time into a conglomerate, headed by Rogers Caldwell. The company controlled more than fifty banks from the Gulf of Mexico to the Ohio River. It had branch offices in twenty cities, including New York and Chicago. It also owned newspaper interests, coal mines, oil companies, trust companies, dairies, laundries, grocery stores, and dress shops. J. B. McFerrin wrote a book, *Caldwell and Company: A Southern Financial Empire*, in 1969. He wrote that Caldwell bought insurance companies "like new suits." Among the insurance companies was Missouri State, acquired in 1926.

No doubt, it was the good record Abilene Christian had with Missouri State that brought the Caldwell Company and the college together. At any rate, the company agreed to originate and underwrite a $200,000 Abilene Christian College bond issue, which would provide immediate cash for the college. The Board of Trustees resolution authorizing the execution of "any and all instruments which may be necessary to the final completion of the issue of Two Hundred Thousand Dollars in bonds of Abilene Christian College" was approved by the board October 18, 1929. Abilene Christian received $188,000, and Caldwell got $12,000 for its fee. Caldwell then sold the bonds at par to various companies and some individuals. The major purchaser of the bonds was Missouri State Life, the Caldwell subsidiary and a satisfied creditor of the college. To back up the bond issue, the college gave a deed of trust to its entire campus, "together with all buildings and all additions and betterments which may, from time to time, be placed thereon; and all fixtures, furnishings, furniture and equipment, which may be placed in the building, or buildings, situated thereon, whether such buildings now exist or are hereafter erected." Also included in the mortgaged property was a thirty-five-acre tract tentatively set aside as a park, now the location of Sherrod Apartments.

Eleven days later came Black Tuesday, October 29, 1929, which heralded the beginning of the Great Depression. Fifty years after Black Tuesday, a writer for *The Nashville Banner* – a man who knew Rogers Caldwell well – summed up what happened in one sentence: "When the stock market crashed, Caldwell's empire came down like a house of cards."

It is idle to speculate what would have happened if the trustees had experienced a month's delay in making the deal with Caldwell. The trustees received their money and went on with construction. All was well in Abilene – for the moment. But not in Nashville, not even for the moment, says the *Banner* article: "The collapse of Caldwell & Co. triggered the financial ruin of hundreds of companies in the South and threw the Tennessee state government into panic. 'We thought at first we could maneuver our way out,' Caldwell said. 'In late 1929 we still had cash. But outside events were felt here. Businesses I was counting on went down. There was no stemming the tide.'" When the Depression came, Caldwell became one of the most controversial personalities in the state. When teachers were not paid because state funds had vanished in Caldwell's banks – when mills and stores were shut down and children went hungry – Tennesseans blamed Rogers Caldwell. He was later indicted – but subsequently exonerated – on three counts of fraud and misappropriation of funds.

The collapse of Caldwell meant also the ruin of Missouri State Life Insurance Company – but not immediately. The superintendent of insurance for the state of Missouri did not declare the company in receivership until 1933. But the company was doomed. For a while, people in Abilene, Texas, did not seem to realize what bad news Black Tuesday really was. Before long, however, it became obvious that Abilene Christian College was in trouble. Sales of lots virtually stopped. People who had bought lots, paying a down payment and financing the balance, began turning the lots back. Not only was the college not going to be able to make its payments on the $200,000 bond issue, but it still owed $14,000 to Missouri State Life on its 1925 loan. If readers of *No Ordinary University* consider that amount a paltry sum, they can take calculators in hand and figure, say, a ten percent, yea, even five percent inflation factor per year from 1931 to the present and arrive at an idea of the size of the problem. The trustees requested an extension of the Missouri State loan, and the company granted it. The college was given five additional years, down to January 1, 1936, to pay the remaining balance, with an interest rate of seven percent.

Another major purchaser of Abilene Christian College bonds was Life and Casualty Insurance Company of Nashville. Principal owner of this company was A. M. Burton, a good friend of Abilene Christian College and a major donor to David Lipscomb College. Life and Casualty was not a Caldwell property. It stayed strong despite the depression. The Fourth and First National Bank of Nashville – a Caldwell bank – also bought Abilene Christian College bonds, as did other companies and a number of individuals. When Missouri State Life folded in 1933, its policyholders were reinsured by General American Life Insurance Company of Saint Louis. General American took over the company's assets and obligations. As McFerrin says, it took care of policyholders, but stockholders lost their investment.

The year 1933 also appeared for a while to be the year of doom for Abilene Christian College. However, trustees of the college, working skillfully with officials of outgoing Missouri State and incoming General American, and with other bondholders, and with the support of hundreds of friends of the college, came up with a solution that was satisfactory to all concerned, which was a matter for leaders of the James F. Cox years.

When the Great Depression struck, what had once appeared to be so brilliant now appeared to have been not very prudent, and the fallout brought on by critics of the board set up events that brought about significant turnover in board membership during the next era. Judge Allen D. Dabney, of Eastland, a board member since 1917, summed up the situation in 1932:

> Had times remained normal, there would have been a thousand homes built on this hill. $390,000 of notes would have been paid, or practically retired, but since adverse circumstances have

come our way, we are now meeting circumstances where we must fight together and work together .... The county is broke; the state is broke; the nation is broke; the world is broke. We could not help it.

From Austin came a letter signed by five leading men of the Church of Christ, including G. H. P. Showalter, editor and publisher of *The Firm Foundation*. It was mailed to all members of the Board of Trustees, plus about a dozen other people, not named. It concerned rumors that were making the rounds of the brotherhood to the effect that the trustees were not running Abilene Christian College according to the terms of the charter, nor were they running it prudently. According to the letter, two highly influential members of the board – George Birchfield of Fort Worth and Judge R. O. Kenley of Wichita Falls – had quit the board because of the way things were going. And a man who was still very much on the board, Otto Foster, said to his fellow board members, "This thing has grown and grown, and it is in every town outside of Abilene." A not-too-subtle threat was embedded in the letter:

> The affairs of Abilene Christian College, a chartered institution in the state of Texas, are subject to investigation by the Attorney General's department in Austin should the possible need for such investigation be placed before the Attorney General. Certainly we have no present idea of making complaint, but it is not at all improbable from the information which we have at hand, that in an extremity due to failure of the Board of Directors to take seriously some matters herein contained, such procedure may, perforce, be resorted to.

The chairman of the board took the matter so seriously that he scheduled a meeting involving the signers of the letter and the full board. The date set was February 24, 1932. A stenographic reporter was employed to get a verbatim record of everything said during the meeting. Only one of the five signers appeared for the meeting. He was Dr. Albert Deveney, an elder in the church, a respected physician, and a friend and patron of the school, but who was very much concerned and wanted to know the truth about the matters contained in the letter. It was reported that editor Showalter was en route, but the decision was made to proceed with the meeting, with Dr. Deveney as the spokesman for the letter writers.

The first rumor was

> That certain members of the board are receiving compensation for services rendered the school in flagrant violation of Article VII of charter, which reads, "No member of the Board of Directors shall ever receive any reward whatever for his services except that all expenses actually incurred by members of the Board in attending to its meetings may be paid by order of the Board of Directors."

That rumor had some basis. The part about compensation was true. Both chairman Arledge and vice chairman Reese had been compensated for certain services. Arledge had been put on the payroll as far back as August 1, 1927, in order that he might work full time plus overtime in developing the new Abilene Heights and in advertising and selling lots. He sold his ranch and devoted himself wholeheartedly to the project. And nobody could have done it as well as he did. He had checked with the attorney who had represented the school since its beginning – J. M. Wagstaff – and had been told that he could be paid for certain professional services and still be a board member. It was not a violation of the charter. He was not being paid for his service as a board member. After all, he had been a member of the board since 1911, and chairman since 1916, and had never been paid, even expenses, and had not desired or expected such.

Vice chairman Reese had been put on the payroll by vote of the board in September 1929, when the bond issue was being arranged with the Caldwell Company. It was obvious that a continuous program of soliciting donations would be necessary in order to meet the requirements of the bond issue, and no better person could have been found for that job than the peppery little vice chairman who never met a stranger.

Henry Free spoke to the issue. He had been a board member since the beginning of the college in 1906, and as secretary of the board through the years, and as a banker, he had a clear remembrance of fiscal matters especially. He had driven to Merkel to see former board member J. P. Sharp, the only other living trustee of the original five. The two of them had signed an affidavit to the effect that when the charter was adopted in 1906, the question arose of whether a trustee could be compensated by the school for professional services rendered separate and apart from being a trustee. They affirmed that all members of the board, in consultation with their attorney, held the view that such was within the terms of the charter.

So that question was left about where it was. If there had been a violation of the charter, it was most assuredly not a flagrant or intentional violation. Dr. Deveney said he would return to his fellow signers and give a favorable report. He still thought it would be best for a trustee to resign before going on the payroll for any purpose, but he was convinced that all concerned had been honest in the matter. Since that time, however, board members have not been on the payroll while continuing as members. Those who have been added – as administration, faculty, or staff – have resigned as trustees in accepting such an assignment.

The second rumor was

> That at the time you were putting board members on the payroll you were dismissing from the faculty men who had been with the institution for years and against whose scholarship or character no breath of suspicion had been, or could be, raised, because of a lack of funds.... At the same time, you paid ... $7,200 in the maintenance of athletics....

On this issue President Baxter was the spokesperson. The following exchange between Judge Dabney, who could not help acting like the attorney that he was, and President Baxter, whose responses were terse, no-nonsense, and to the point, is of interest. Dabney asked the questions; Baxter gave the answers:

Dabney: "Why was it necessary to let out some of the faculty?"

Baxter: "Because we had not the money to pay."

Dabney: "Why did you let out any teachers at all?"

Baxter: "Because of the depression."

Dabney: "If it had not been for that, you would have kept them on?"

Baxter: "Part of them I would."

Dabney: "Did you let out teachers ... in order to pay athletes?"

Baxter: "I do not pay athletes."

Dabney: "Is it not a fact that this year ... other schools let out quite a number of their faculty?"

Baxter: "Yes."

Dabney: "Why did you let out certain faculty members?"

Baxter: "I let out those whom we could do without the easiest."

Dabney: "Did you let your personal feelings enter into it?"

Baxter: "No, not at all. It was only a matter of efficiency."

Dabney: "Did you let out anybody because of dislike?"

Baxter: "I had one man on the faculty several years ago that I let out because of his unfortunate tactics."

Dabney: "Your whole procedure down to the present time was for the ultimate good of the school, was it ... ?"

Baxter: "Yes, so far as I understood it."

Baxter explained further the deal with athletes. Certain athletes were assigned jobs on the campus, along with other students. The president himself assigned the jobs and held the assignees responsible for doing the job. Such things as work in the kitchen or on the campus had to be done by somebody, and if athletes needed the work, could do it, and did do it, they were used. They were not paid in cash but were given credit on their school expenses. Baxter named names of athletes he had dismissed from their jobs because of nonperformance, just as was true with other students.

Dr. Deveney had no further problem with that issue. The third rumor was "That an enormous debt of several hundred thousand dollars has been placed against the property ... disregarding the provision of Article XI of the charter, which reads: 'that this corporation shall never contract any debt which shall exceed twenty-five percent of the value of the college property ....'"

Vice Chairman Reese took this one on. He explained that, with the cash and pledges that were on hand when the new campus was planned, with the value of the land and the new campus buildings, with notes amounting to approximately $100,000 signed by people who had bought lots on the time payment plan, plus gifts that had come in, including Luce, Chambers, and Bennett donations, the debt was not at all unreasonable when contracted. Judge Dabney came out with his homily on the Depression and suggested to Dr. Deveney and his friends: "We are all building for the generations to come, and this plant is but a monument of faith in the living savior and for the purpose of molding character [and] great men in the Kingdom of Christ. Oh, gentlemen, do not knock us but get behind and push." J. B. McGinty declared that it was imperative that Abilene Christian College succeed, "not because it is Abilene Christian College or because it is located at Abilene, but for Christian education, the greatest thing, aside from the church, that we can engage in."

The next charge was that no adequate audit had ever been made. Chairman Arledge mentioned two audits, which seemed to satisfy that situation. Dr. Deveney said, "That sounds like a real audit."

Finally, the matter of the number of trustees required to be present in order to have a quorum was discussed. The criticism was as follows:

> The school as originally organized had under its charter a board of five members, a majority of whom constituted a quorum. Later, the board by amendment was increased to nineteen and seven constituted a quorum. Then later the board was increased to thirty-five members and still seven constitutes a quorum. To our minds this is a most dangerous provision. The effect has been to give the members of the board in the vicinity of Abilene the full powers of the board.

Board members who spoke to this point expressed willingness to have a larger number for a quorum but pointed out that during the tense times of construction, it would have been almost impossible to transact business if a larger number had been required.

At the conclusion of the long meeting, Dr. Deveney expressed support for the college. He still had reservations about paying trustees for any service to the school, and he advised them to re-examine the charter to determine whether they were in violation. But they already had the word of the two surviving trustees who adopted the charter in the beginning, plus the opinion of competent legal counsel, and there was hardly a reason for them to change their opinions.

However, a 1997 revision of the charter and bylaws makes it possible for a trustee to serve in other capacities, for which there is compensation, without resigning the trusteeship. It is no longer a subject dealt with in the charter but is in the bylaws, as follows: "Trustees as such shall not receive any salaries for their services as Trustees ... but nothing herein contained shall preclude any trustee from serving the corporation in any other capacity and receiving compensation therefor."

The trustees had carried the day. Two weeks after the board meeting, editor Showalter carried a ringing endorsement of the work of the college in his "Editorial Observations: The board of regents of Abilene Christian College has been criticized. Many complaints have been made, and rumors of mis-management, incompetency, and even of dishonesty have been circulated. Recently a document was placed in the hands of the board reciting these facts and detailing some of the criticisms and complaints and calling for such action on the part of the board that would clear the school, restore confidence among its supporters, and intensify the zeal and interest on the part of those who are friends of this great institution of learning. ... I am happy to announce in these columns, that upon the invitation of the board of regents I sat in their meetings, listened to their deliberations and made diligent inquiry regarding each and every one of the charges ... and am happy to report that all of these matters are without support so far as facts are concerned. To say that these brethren have not made mistakes would be to assume that they are not human, but I am fully assured and convinced that their conduct has been honest and their efforts sincere and unselfish.... May this great work and every other kindred endeavor be crowned with the success that the Lord's work merits...."

So, what started as a potential crisis was turned into commendation. The local board had carried the day. Without such driven individuals, the school would have stayed over by the railroad tracks. The local board had wrought miracles. But they had incurred some opposition along the way, and it would not quite go away. Five years to the day after the intense meeting concerning the rumors, Arledge, Reese, McKinzie, Crawford, Hays, and Russell of the local board all resigned from the board. Otto Foster of Cleburne would join them. A new generation of board members would take over. At least Henry Free would still be there to fill in the gaps in their history lessons. But that would not happen until February 24, 1937. In 1932, they still had two big tasks to perform: they had a new administrative team to inaugurate, and they could not afford to leave office until they had found a solution to the indebtedness into which they had plunged the institution by their boldness – even their audacity, so to speak.

Chapter Four

Rescuing the School

When, in the fall of 1931, Batsell Baxter announced his resignation as president, effective June 1, 1932, the Board of Trustees had only one nominee to replace him: James Franklin Cox, who had served as dean of the college for the entire time of the Baxter presidency. He was the logical choice. Cox had been elected president once before, in 1911, but had been unable to serve. However, as a faculty member since 1920 and dean since 1924, he had shown the same dedication and ability as when he had been a member of the first faculty in 1906.

As the decision worked out, it was not exactly a vote of confidence– through no fault of Cox's. The board elected Cox to fill the remaining year of Baxter's term, and a motion was made before the board to appoint a search committee to look for a president. It seemed to President-elect Cox that he might simply fill the post until a president could be appointed. The motion included a provision that a majority of members of the search committee be from outside of Abilene, indicative of some friction between the Abilene and out-of-Abilene members. No doubt it was because the Abilene members had been meeting so regularly and trying so desperately to come up with ways and means of rescuing the school that they were not keeping the other board members informed. After discussion, the motion was withdrawn, but it was still in the minutes.

Cox assumed responsibility for finances of the college May 1, 1932, and moved into the president's office June 1. He was the first president of the college to be more than forty years of age at the beginning of his term of office. A. B. Barret, founding president, was only twenty-seven – half of Cox's age – when he started the school. Darden and Whiteside were both forty when they took on the presidential responsibility. Sewell was thirty-six; Baxter thirty-seven. Cox was fifty-four.

One of the first steps the new president took was to appoint three young and vigorous men as his top administrative associates. Don Morris, at age twenty-nine, became vice president. He would be in charge of public relations, public information, recruiting of students, and fund raising. He would also continue to teach and to coach debate.

Walter Adams was named dean of students. He was twenty-eight. In naming him dean of students instead of dean of the college, President Cox explained to him that his own appointment might be temporary; hence, he was holding the job of dean of the college for himself if that should prove to be the case. In that event, Adams would still be dean of students and would not be demoted. As it turned out, Cox was elected unanimously to a full three-year term the next year. Apparently, however, he forgot to change Adams' title until five years later, which was no problem for Walter Adams, who went merrily along as dean of the whole bailiwick – and education teacher.

Lawrence Smith was twenty-eight. He was named bursar. He had done that job under President Baxter. He was responsible for receiving and disbursing all of the money that came from student tuition, fees, room, board, and such auxiliary enterprises as the college might have. He did not handle or supervise debt service for the three tracts of land that had been bought or the bond issue obligation. Trustees had their own office for that. The bursar was responsible for the payroll and all campus-related expenses. The job required tact, good humor, patience, and forthrightness. For example, if the college could not meet its payroll on time, teachers and staff who did not have funds to tide them over could see the bursar for advances against the salary that was due. If fifteen or twenty dollars could furnish necessities until payroll money was available, Lawrence Smith was the man to see. One-on-one negotiating made severely limited funding stretch as far as possible while not letting people go hungry or lose their homes. A budget was nonexistent. It was the art of the possible.

These three administrators whom President Cox appointed to work with him would stay together for the next thirty-seven years, providing a quality and stability of leadership almost, if not altogether, unheard of in college and university circles.

The administration was a tremendous plus factor. In fact, the time had come for another shift in the operation of the school. From the beginning and through the Sewell administration, responsibility for operations, planning, and development had belonged to the president. With the end of the Sewell administration, the total burden of responsibility for planning, expanding, and developing the institution had been taken over by the board while the president was left free to superintend on-campus operations as the general rule.

Such an arrangement made the Great Move possible; it would probably not have taken place without such a plan. The arrangement also incurred the Great Debt. Every brick, stick of furniture, laboratory utensil, dining hall and kitchen setup, and library book was mortgaged. The trustees, and especially the local board, were nearing exhaustion – financially as well as physically. The time had come for a strong administrative team to take initiatives in planning and development as well as operations, and, in concert with and under policies approved by the board, to move the entire program forward as a unit.

The Cox administration established a great working relationship with the board. The same was true with regard to the faculty and the student body. The dignified president could count on winning incoming freshmen over when he recited "When Rubenstein Played the Piano," the story of Jud Browning, who went from the country to visit New York City. Jud found himself attending a piano concert by the famed pianist. Halfway through the program, Jud was so carried away that he jumped up and shouted, "Go to it, Rube!" He was immediately flanked by two policemen. They let him stay with promises of no more outbursts, but Jud later said, "It would have taken more than two policemen to drag me away." As an encore, Cox would recite "A Letter from Sam." He would occasionally remind the entire student body in chapel to "hoe your row to the end." Most of the students in the 1930s understood that old cotton patch admonition. They knew they had a friend in the presidential office. Toward the end of his tenure, an appreciation dinner honored President Cox; the favors were miniature hoes.

The early 1930s were not all doom and gloom; some really bright spots shined through. One was student enrollment. Regardless of hard times, students kept coming. For the first year of the Cox administration, enrollment of resident college students was twenty percent above the previous year – from 405 to 485. The next year enrollment increased twenty-six percent to 614. Throughout the decade, the figure was well up into the 600s, with the exception of 1938-39, when the total number of students fell to 557. The next year the number was back to 626. And most were "hoeing their rows to the end." Beginning in 1936-37, when the large freshman classes had worked their way up, more than 100 students graduated each year – until World War II.

Nearly all of these students needed financial help. Many of them – maybe most of them – wound up owing the college substantial sums. Bursar Smith had each student sign a note with some sort of payment plan. He never charged a note off as a bad debt. Most paid. If a student had a touch of larceny in his heart and thought he could ignore a note he had signed, he might be brought up short some years later, when applying for a loan to buy a house, to find a question mark about his credit. An ex-student called the bursar one day, complaining about his debt and his credit rating. He said, "Why, that's such a piddling amount – if I weren't over here on the other side of town I could write you a check for that right now." Smith's reply was. "Where are you? I'll come and get it." He was not above going himself.

Another note of optimism was the faculty. During the 1930s some strong teachers were added to the force.

Charles Roberson came back. He had been with Cox on the first faculty in 1906. For Cox's first year as president, Roberson was back to stay. Two years later, Batsell Baxter returned. He had resigned as president in 1932, but in 1934 he was back to teach Bible – which was his first love.

W. R. Smith resigned from the Board of Trustees to accept appointment to the faculty. With his background as a public school superintendent and a junior college president, he was a strong addition to the education department, teaching school administration and classes in history. When the practical field of Christian education was added to the traditional department of Bible, W. R. Smith was the logical person to name as its head.

Gilmer Belcher came to teach education, mathematics, and history, with his Ph.D. from George Peabody College for Teachers. September 16, 1998, marks his 100th birthday, and he still has a memory that would do credit to most people a half-century younger.

Marcus Mullings was a strong addition in mathematics, with a Ph.D. from the University of Cincinnati.

Paul Southern was a powerful addition to the Bible faculty. At this writing, he is ninety-seven and has not lost his gift of oratory or his enjoyment of a bit of humor.

Leonard Burford was added to teach voice in the music department. During the summer before he started his teaching, President Cox saw him and said, "Leonard, we need an a cappella chorus. You start one." By the time school began, he had twenty-six voices lined up. The chorus became a famed feature of Abilene Christian.

Arthur M. "Tonto" Coleman came as a coach. He also taught courses in history, government, and physical education. In addition to being one of the all-time great coaches, he was an excellent teacher.

D. W. Crain was added as band director and a teacher of music. With practically no budget, he built a first-rate organization and paved the way for later directors to develop the Big Purple. Some years ago he and one of his students who later became a noted director of the Big Purple – Douglas Fry – were voted into the Texas Bandmasters Hall of Fame.

Norene Watson, who became Mrs. Dewey Davis, came to teach piano and the theory of music and began a forty-year career with Abilene Christian.

W. M. Dowell played a valuable role in developing the Department of Physical Education. His wife, Vera, served for a time as college nurse and taught classes in physical education.

Margaret Ehresmann was an articulate and lively addition to the speech faculty.

James E. Freeman was a powerful addition to the department of business administration. Lawrence Smith was the lone teacher of business from 1929 to 1936 and needed help. Freeman also played a vital role in acquiring Camp Barkley facilities to accommodate the great surge of students after World War II.

Retta Scott Garrett taught a generation of students to love and to feel the emotional impact of great literature and was the faculty adviser of the *Prickly Pear*.

Homer Hailey was one of the most popular Bible teachers and a powerful preacher.

Hosea Lewis joined the faculty to teach classes in mathematics and physics. He knew how to challenge students of a non-scientific bent.

There was much room for optimism and hope for the future: a spacious new campus, a strong Board of Trustees, a vigorous administration, an excellent faculty, and an outstanding enrollment picture. Abilene Christian College was truly a viable institution.

One problem that would not disappear was the Great Debt. The college owed for nearly everything, including the original 680 acres of land on the Hill. That should not have been the case, but it was. The Great Depression played havoc with the Abilene Heights plan.

A heartbreaking decision was made that the college had bought too much land and needed to get out from under some of it. In May 1932, the local board passed a resolution appointing J. S. Arledge, J. E. McKinzie, and T. A. Russell as a committee "to negotiate with Edward Adams, Mrs. Xenia Miller, and others who have past due notes, and make such settlements as they deem best for the best interest of the school." Of the landholders referred to, the best chance was to persuade Mrs. Miller to take her land back, which was the half-section, or 320 acres bounded on the west by Avenue F, on the north by the Albany highway, on the east by Griffith Road, and on the south by East North Tenth Street. It was a splendid property, but if the college could not pay for it, something had to be done – and quickly.

Three months later, the committee reported success in dealing with Mrs. Miller. The original purchase price for her land had been $44,000, including a debt of $3,200 that she owed on the land. The college had made a down payment of $5,000, signed vendor's lien notes for $35,800, bearing eight percent interest, and assumed the note she owed to Realty Trust Company of Dallas. The college was not in arrears on payments because payments were not scheduled to start until January 1933. There was some past due interest. The college offered to pay her $1,000 cash to take back her land, minus 12.21 acres that had been sold for $2,100 to West Texas Utilities Company for an easement for power lines. She would reassume the Realty Trust Company obligation of $3,200 plus past due interest. In return, she would hand over to the college seven vendor's lien notes in the aggregate amount of $35,800 and forgive past due interest thereon, and the deal would be closed. She agreed to go along with the deal. But, although Mrs. Miller had a right to repossess her land in toto, she voluntarily decided to give the college credit for what had been paid. She deeded back to the college some 12.9 acres on the east side of Avenue F – free and clear. In the deed she stated two conditions: first, if the college should go into bankruptcy within three years, the land would revert to her, and, second, it could not be sold with the proceeds to be used on existing indebtedness. The college did not go bankrupt within three years, or ever.

There was a sequel though. Not too many years passed before trustees and administrators regretted having had to give up the land. Repeated efforts were made, especially after World War II, to buy back the land, but Mrs. Miller was not interested. In the early 1950s, the board of the Abilene Independent School District and Superintendent A. E. "Poly" Wells purchased land from her for a campus for Taylor Elementary School. But Abilene Christian was not able to negotiate a land purchase.

In 1951, the Texas Highway Department bought twelve acres from Mrs. Miller as a right-of-way for a new road to run between Ambler Avenue and East South Eleventh Street, which was named Stadium Way. It was renamed Judge Ely Boulevard on December 17, 1974. The routing of that thoroughfare left

Mrs. Miller with thirteen acres west of the new road and adjoin-ing the 12.9 acres she had deeded to Abilene Christian in 1932. On February 20, 1952, she sold it to the college for $1,000 per acre. The new thirteen-acre acquisition, combined with the 1932 gift of land made a nice strip of approximately twenty-six acres, strategically located. This is the strip of land on which today stand Gardner and Sikes Dorm-itories, the Mabee Business Administration Building, the Central Plant, the Biblical Studies Building, a large parking lot, eight tennis courts, plus the three indoor, air-conditioned courts in the Teague Center which is not on the Miller land, and A. B. Morris Hall.

The Miller solution was minor compared to the $200,000 bond issue. Two payments of principal and interest had been missed. The bond indenture included this paragraph:

> One of the conditions of said deed of trust and of this bond is that if default shall be made in the payment of any of said inter-est coupons, or in the payment of principal hereof, or in the payment of any of the bonds, principal or interest …. then the principal of this and all the other bonds secured by such deed of trust shall become forthwith due and collectible.

Although the board was supposed to have twelve years from September 1, 1929, to retire the series, the entire amount of principal and interest was now due.

In his first report to an annual meeting of the board February 23, 1933, President Cox declared that the only rec-ommendation he would make to the board for the remainder of the year was to go all out to take care of the bonded indebt-edness. He acknowledged that the college owed the Edward Adams family and the Hughes and Mayfield families for the 200 acres and the 160 acres that had been bought from them. But he suggested that the bonded indebtedness be taken care of first. Until this was cleared up and the campus freed of the lien, he saw no hope of accreditation or needed construction, such as a suitable building for chemistry.

As for the board, it faced a makeover itself. J. S. Arledge, who had presided for sixteen years with skill and tact, announced his retirement – not from the board but from the chairmanship. He said, "I am resigning in favor of a younger

man, and I want to nominate J. E. McKinzie in my stead."
McKinzie was elected unanimously, and three vice chairmen
with him: J. C. Reese and E. L. Crawford, both Abilenians, and
J. B. McGinty of Terrell. Seven new trustees, who would have
much to do with the future growth of the school, were elected:
B Sherrod of Lubbock, D. B. Rambo of Huntsville, J. B.
Collins of Big Spring, and four Abilenians, Clyde Echols, H. C.
Harvey, G. L. Jennings, and J. E. Manly. Hollis L. Manly was
named secretary, replacing W. H. Free, who had been doing the
minutes for twenty-seven years. New chairman McKinzie was
ready to spend practically full time on the major problem. He
had people who could run the kitchen and dining hall in his
absence, and he was ready to serve. Some complaints about
having the food service of the college in the hands of the chairman of the board were registered, but in this case, it would
seem providential.

Several new roads of help seemed to be leading toward
Burkburnett, Texas, a few miles north of Wichita Falls, the last
stop of any consequence before the Red River and Oklahoma,
and the scene of a sizable oil strike in 1919. A Burkburnett citizen by the name of John G. Hardin had been wealthy before
oil, with several thousands of acres of good wheat land, but his
wealth was multiplied when oil was found under his land.
Hardin had a cousin who was closely connected with Abilene
Christian College; in fact, she lived across the street from the
campus. She was Mrs. Mary Jane Rambo. Her daughter, Essie
Rambo, a graduate of the college, was principal of Abilene
Christian Training School. Mrs. Rambo's son, D. B., also an
alumnus and board member, was a J. C. Penney store manager
in Huntsville and husband of the former Inez Norton, who
worked for years as assistant to Jesse P. Sewell during his presidency.

Mrs. Rambo was not necessarily close to her cousin, but she
circulated the word about him. He had been a Baptist. His first
wife, who had died young, was a member of the Church of
Christ. He was married to a second wife, who was a generous
person. They had no living children. Mr. Hardin had had two
children by his first wife and one by his second wife, but none

survived. It was a remote chance, but in 1929, trustees McKinzie and Hollis Manly went to Burkburnett and had a brief visit with Mr. and Mrs. Hardin. Guy Scruggs, who got his information in a 1944 interview from McKinzie, described the meeting: "McKinzie said that both Mr. and Mrs. Hardin were very hospitable and gave them a hearty welcome and told them that it was their plan to give all their earthly possessions to some cause, and not leave it for lawyers and courts to settle. They told McKinzie and Manly, however, that they were not yet ready to start giving away their estate."

Later, McKinzie and Reese went to Burkburnett to see Ross Reagan, city manager and a member of the Church of Christ. Reagan told them that Hardin was in the process of making a sizable gift to the city of Burkburnett and that therefore it would probably not be a good time for solicitation. He also said that Hardin had decided to make no gifts without a recommendation from his nephew and banker I. E. "Ike" Harwell and Jack Chatham, a Burkburnett lawyer. That arrangement had been made after a gift to Buckner Orphan Home. After all the publicity from that gift, he had been besieged by requests. To gain some privacy and peace of mind, he had stipulated that all requests for help would have to go through Harwell and Chatham, and he would not talk to people before they had been cleared by these two men. Reagan also broke the news to the Abilenians that in order to reward the two men for the time they would have to spend dealing with applicants, Hardin would authorize them to charge a brokerage fee for each grant made. In other words, if Abilene Christian should be cleared to receive a grant of $200,000, the college would have to be prepared to pay perhaps $20,000 to Harwell and Chatham. McKinzie and Reese saw no problem with that.

From that point, the situation seemed stalled for a year or two. In 1931, a miraculous opportunity to see Mr. Hardin himself developed. It started in the fall of 1930. Thelma "Sissy" Bradford was teacher and head of the home economics program at Burkburnett High School. Burton Coffman was the new associate minister of the Tenth and Austin Streets Church of Christ in Wichita Falls. Coffman had met Sissy Bradford six years earlier when, as a college student, he was selling Bibles in

Oklahoma. He went to the Bradford home on a farm near Chickasha and met Thelma and her sister, Lolabel. Both young women had completed the sophomore year at Oklahoma College for Women. Both were going away to college in the fall: Lolabel to Abilene Christian College, where her aunt, Alma Adams Morlan, was the wife of the head of the Education Department, and Thelma to North Texas State Teachers, where an aunt was the wife of the dean of the college. Besides having an aunt to live with in Denton, Thelma needed to go to North Texas to get her vocational home economics degree.

After the visit to the Bradford home in 1925, Burton saw Sissy once when he was on a debating trip as a college senior to North Texas State. Sissy happened to be a spectator at one of his debates. No doubt, she was rooting for North Texas. In the fall of 1930, Burton learned that evangelist Horace Busby, who had for years been a favorite preacher on the campus of Abilene Christian, was preaching in a meeting at Burkburnett, so he drove there to hear him. Much to his surprise he saw Thelma Bradford there. He rushed up to her and boomed, "Where have you been all my life?" That started a courtship that resulted in their wedding the next May. The new Mrs. Coffman resigned her job at Burkburnett, and the Coffmans set up housekeeping in Wichita Falls.

Some time later, J. C. Reese was in Wichita Falls and dropped by to see the Coffmans. He mentioned the trustees' contacts with Mr. Hardin and that they could not get an appointment with Mr. Hardin and were not making progress with his front men. It turned out that Mr. Hardin was a member of the Burkburnett school board and that customarily the home economics students and their teacher prepared and served meals to the trustees at their meetings, or, at least, some of their meetings. Mr. Hardin had been especially complimentary of Miss Bradford, now Mrs. Coffman, and her students for the way they handled those occasions. Thelma "Sissy" Coffman telephoned her former superintendent and asked him if he would call Mr. Hardin and ask him if Miss Bradford's new husband might come by with Mr. Reese from Abilene and visit with him for a few minutes. The appointment was arranged, and Burton writes, in his autobiography, *Tales of Coffman*,

"Within twenty minutes we had his pledge to save Abilene Christian College." The rescue, however, was not quite that easy. More than two years of careful negotiations followed before the deed was done, but the meeting was a significant step along the way.

An Abilene businessman who had been a true friend of the college through the years provided the suggestion that, building on what had already been done, made the deal possible. The man was J. M. Radford. He pointed out that holders of the Abilene Christian bonds would probably be happy to settle for considerably less than the face value of the bonds. After all, since 1929, when the two hundred $1,000 bonds had been issued, sharp deflation had changed the economy. Prices had fallen. People were glad to get fifty or sixty cents on the dollar. Sometimes, they would take a third.

Next, he suggested that good municipal and utility bonds were selling for as low as eighteen cents on the dollar. It might be possible to trade such securities for the college bonds at an even exchange. In other words, the college might buy a $1,000 municipal bond, for, say, $250. That $1,000 bond would be exchangeable for an Abilene Christian $1,000 bond. If held to maturity, it would be redeemed for the full face value by the issuing agency. The individual who had put up the money for the college to buy the municipal bonds would get for his money the Abilene Christian bonds. He would hold those until the college could get in a position to pay off those bonds – probably not at full face value but at a high enough rate to repay the friend who had made it possible. The municipal bond could be held to maturity and would then be paid off by the issuing agency for full face value – $1,000. If the individual needed his or her money in a hurry, the bond would have to be sold at the market discount. Radford was thinking of putting up the money himself if he had assurance that the Abilene Christian investors were willing to make the exchange, but his death was the end of that possibility.

However, he had planted the thought in the minds of McKinzie and company. Somebody else had planted a thought in the mind of the chairman of the board. October 1, 1933, a letter from the General American Insurance Company of St.

Louis came to chairman of the board McKinzie. It stated that there would be a meeting of the holders of Abilene Christian College bonds in the offices of the company October 17. Representatives of the college were invited, indeed, expected, to attend. The letter stated that bondholders were discussing asking the courts to appoint a receiver who would operate the college in the interest of the bondholders. That would not, of course, have been a wise agenda. On more sober reflection the bondholders would probably have rejected that procedure. Nobody could operate more efficiently than the existing administration of the college. Besides, if the college were taken away from members of the Church of Christ, who would have comprised its constituency? Could they have given it to the State of Texas? Was there any other kind of business that could use a college campus? It would have been unwise, however, for the trustees to ignore the possibility of a receivership. Besides, this might be the spark needed to motivate action.

After conferring with the local board at a called meeting, McKinzie and Hollis Manly went to Burkburnett. They were fortunate in getting an opportunity for a lengthy discussion with banker Harwell and later with attorney Chatham. Both men were impressed with the Radford suggestion, but they said that Hardin would not put out any cash to buy municipal bonds. And the chance for a cash gift to the college was nil. Finally, McKinzie asked if Hardin might already have some bonds in his portfolio that would not sell at face value. Harwell checked and came back with a list of Joint Stock Land Bank Bonds. These were bonds that had the backing, though some-what indirect in nature, of the federal government. They were sometimes called "quasi-government bonds." They were good bonds and were selling at about half price. The Abilenians said the college would pay a six percent annuity on the face value of the bonds if Hardin liked the idea. Harwell and Chatham said they would discuss the matter with Hardin and report. McKinzie and Manly returned to Abilene.

The next day about noon, Harwell called to say Hardin was interested. Harwell suggested that McKinzie ask the St. Louis people to postpone the meeting for two weeks to give time for working out the proposal. That was done. More meetings and discussions took place between Abilene and Burkburnett. It was finally agreed, first, if the St. Louis people were willing to go with the plan, and, second, if the Abilene Christian people could meet Hardin's conditions, he would consider furnishing land bank bonds with a face value of $160,000, with the proviso that $20,000 of the Land Bank bonds would go for brokerage to Harwell and Chatham.

The plan to be presented to St. Louis was that land bank bonds with a face value of $140,000 would be exchanged for Abilene Christian College bonds with a face value of $200,000, with all past due interest on the Abilene bonds forgiven by the bondholders. Counting the approximately $33,000 in interest and past due interest that would be forgiven, the bondholders would be getting approximately sixty percent of their money back. And that was not a bad deal in terms of 1934 dollars as compared with pre-depression 1929 dollars. That was entirely acceptable to the St. Louis group. Then came the difficult part: negotiating an agreement acceptable to the Hardin people. A letter from Harwell, dated December 30, 1933, specified the requirements:

1. The bonds must be used to clear all lien indebtedness against the college campus and buildings.

2. An annuity agreement was to be signed whereby the college would pay $9,600 per year to Mr. and/or Mrs. J. G. Hardin as long as either lived, with $4,800 for the first six months to be paid in advance, and thereafter $800 per month.

3. The annuity was to be backed up by "a first and only lien" on the campus grounds and all buildings of the institution, together with a chattel mortgage lien upon all fixtures on campus grounds and in buildings.

4. One-half of the gross revenues of the dormitories must be "impounded and held until there is a surplus of $2,400 over any amount that may be due under said annuity agreement."

5. The college must "secure pledges, agreements, and legal obligations" of twice the yearly requirement of the annuity payments, and such pledges, legal obligations, and agreements must be kept current throughout the life of the annuity. In other words, the college must have good pledges of $1,600 per month to make certain that the $800 obligation to the Hardins

could be kept current. That meant that if a person who had made a pledge had to drop out, there must be a replacement. Securing pledges was not just a one-time process.

6. The Administration Building was to be named in memory of Mrs. Cordelia Hardin, first wife of J. G. Hardin, and Mrs. M.A.T. Adams, her mother, "who were members of the Church of Christ."

7. It all had to be done before February 15, 1934 – just six weeks from the date the letter was written.

Abilene Christian's trustees agreed with the terms and set to work. The immediate challenge was to secure the pledges. Vice President Don Morris was put in charge of this detail. He organized a pledge-raising campaign that utilized trustees, preachers, preacher students, and friends of the college throughout Texas and in neighboring states. Pledges ranging from a high of $100 per month to "less than a dollar a month" were secured, and the deadline was met. Acknowledging that "innumerable others" helped in the drive, Morris' office listed these workers who were "outstanding in the recent six-weeks' work": J. D. Harvey, Colorado City; Robert C. Jones, Amarillo; Fred C. Ross, Ballinger; Roy Lanier, Waxahachie; Perry Wilmeth, Cleburne; S. N. Allen, Christoval; Leslie Huff, Belton; R. T. Martin and B Sherrod, Lubbock; Lee McCaleb, Anson; Ellis McGaughey, Elk City, Oklahoma; D. B. Rambo, Huntsville; I. G. Etheridge, Dallas; and W. R. Smith, Baytown.

The campaign was the most thorough job of canvassing the brotherhood of Churches of Christ that the college had ever done. Pledges of more than $19,000 per year were obtained. Benefits of having carried on such a grass roots effort so successfully went considerably beyond obtaining the Hardin gift.

While the campaign was going on, J. E. McKinzie and his son, John, traveled highways and byways of Kentucky, Tennessee, and Mississippi, locating owners of the $20,000 of Abilene Christian College bonds who were unable to attend the St. Louis meetings and arranged to trade bonds with them.

The victory announcement was made during Lectureship to a packed house in Sewell Auditorium on Thursday evening, February 22, 1934. Enthusiasm was so great that a group of young men began clanging the bell that had been used to call students to meals through the years – and cracked it. That made it somewhat reminiscent of the Liberty Bell in Philadelphia. It did represent freedom for the college. The bell is now on display in front of the Women for ACU Museum.

President Cox allowed himself to get so carried away that on the spot he announced a holiday for the next day – but Lectureship went on as scheduled through Friday evening. He also declared that the gift had saved the school, and nobody disagreed. Word got out – and in fact, the front page story in *The Reporter* so stated – that the gift had cleared the school of all indebtedness. That, however, was not the case. Sizable debts remained, but the debts that were collateralized by a lien on the campus, buildings, furnishings, and fixtures, were all paid. The campus was still mortgaged. One lien had replaced the other. But the Hardin lien had a termination date down the line.

Mrs. John G. Hardin – Mary Catherine Hardin – died on September 5, 1935. She was a fine person. It was her insistence that the Administration Building be memorialized to Cordelia Adams Hardin and to Cordelia's mother that clinched that part of the deal. Hardin's death came December 16, 1937. He lacked one day of having lived forty-six months after the annuity became effective. The college had paid the annuity ahead of schedule – as always – up until January 17, 1938. The Hardin Estate trustees refunded the January payment of $800. Because his death occurred one day before the annuity date, the trustees refunded the December payment also. That meant a net of forty-five months of annuity payments at $800 per month – $36,000 – paid by the college to settle the original $200,000 bond issue, plus some $33,000 interest. Furthermore, inasmuch as Harwell and Chatham had accepted $20,000 of the land bank bonds as their brokerage fee, the annuity payments also had taken care of that.

Finally, because Don Morris' team had rounded up gifts ranging from $100 per month down to less than a dollar, totaling more than $70,000, the college actually came out more than $30,000 ahead. None of the donors asked for a refund of donations. As soon as the annuity payments were terminated, Morris' office mailed back to all donors their signed pledges and thanked them for having helped so magnificently. During the forty-six months, approximately 10,000 receipts had been mailed. Naturally, some of the trustees thought that the drive had been so successful that it might as well continue in building up some endowment. But it was thought best to sign off on that project and let new planning begin for an endowment campaign. The college could bask in the good will that had been created. Many other campaigns would mark the future – some for a great deal more money – but none would be more successful.

Now, surely enough, the campus was freed from mortgage.

> At the annual meeting of the board in February 1936, President Cox came up with a revolutionary development. His cover letter explained it: For the first time in the history of Abilene Christian College the President is submitting to the Board a budget. You will note that this budget is balanced, and that there is a gross surplus of several thousand dollars. For four years, I have fixed salaries, cut expense here and there, have paid every dollar I promised, and have always closed the year with a surplus. I have paid the faculty just as much as I could, but they have always been underpaid.

> This year I am proposing a definite salary increase and a definite stipulated amount for each of the items in the list of expenditures for 1936-37, but I am making provision for additional income by increasing certain fees and adding other fees as are needed as the "traffic will bear."

The old days of regular negotiating with the bursar on even such items as blackboard erasers were ending. Finances would be on a much more predictable basis. However, a fallback paragraph signaled to teachers that they should not yet go out and buy new automobiles: "Every effort will be made to pay every item in full, but in case it can't be done, the teachers will be asked to take a discount."

Board chairman McKinzie had established such good rapport with J. G. Hardin that he came up with the idea of negotiating a loan for $40,000 from the Hardin estate for retiring some old pre-1929 debts. These were debts that the college should not have had to pay, and yet they were honest obligations. For example, when the old campus was sold to W. F. Sims, he made a down payment and signed notes for the balance. The college sold the notes to J. M. Radford, but, in order to make the sale for cash, followed the customary practice of endorsing the notes. Sims went broke. Radford died. His estate demanded payment, and the college owed the money. But the Radford estate was willing to settle for considerably less than the face value of the notes. The loan was arranged. The Bennett ranch and 232 lots in Abilene Heights were put up as collateral. Hence, for $40,000 cash, McKinzie was able to make satisfactory settlement of $78,122 of old indebtedness. He hoped to get the $40,000 loan added to the annuity obligation, but that could never be done. The college took care of the loan in a propitious manner.

While all of the heavy sessions of the Board of Trustees were going on dealing with the very existence of the institution, another type of problem came up for board notice. Minutes of the local board meeting on May 17, 1934, contain this notation:

"A motion made by T. A. Russell, seconded by Harvey Hays, that the Board of Trustees recommend to President Cox that every boy connected with the tying of cows in the Administration and Auditorium buildings be suspended from school, and that in order to reenter school, each boy be required to make acknowledgments in chapel." Some subjects are best left with no further discussion. This momentous problem was not solved until a year later, when the board outlawed "staking [in the official minutes the word is spelled 'steaking'] cows and other stock in the college campus." Even the president's cow could no longer feast on the green grass of the campus. Lawn mowers would have to do all of the work.

The board had performed heroic deeds, but not without a price. Tension was in the air when the full board met. John McKinzie was such a dominant personality that he was wearing out his welcome as board chairman. He could think on his feet. For example, in the Hardin negotiations, when it became clear that Hardin was not going to spend any money buying low-priced bonds of any kind, it was McKinzie who wondered if the Hardin portfolio might already contain such bonds. It was McKinzie who volunteered that the college would be glad to pay a lifetime annuity to the Hardins and a brokerage fee to Harwell and Chatham. He did not have time to confer with the general board on details worked out in closed-door negotiations. His fellow board members understood this, no doubt, but they nonetheless would have preferred a more easygoing leadership, even though such might have been ineffectual.

In the annual meeting in February 1936, President Cox took the unusual step of lecturing the board members on their behavior. He made a plea to every board member to "forget personalities and unite in one great effort to make a finer and better Abilene Christian College." Vice President Don Morris read McKinzie's report to the board, showing that during the three years of the McKinzie chairmanship the indebtedness of the college had been reduced by more than $275,000, and that the total debts still owed amounted to $90,000. The report suggested that during the next year the board should undertake a number of projects calculated to wipe the slate clean of all indebtedness of any kind, except, of course, the Hardin annuity, which was still in process of being paid monthly, but which was backed up by good pledges.

When the time came for election of officers of the board, Chairman McKinzie stated that he realized mistakes had been made along the way, and he asked to be excused from the meeting while the voting was taking place. Vice Chairman Reese took over. The minutes report, "After many incomplete motions it was moved by T. A. Russell, seconded by R. Martin, that W. H. Free be elected president of the board for one year. Motion carried unanimously." McKinzie, like J. P. Sewell twelve years earlier, had saved the school – with help, of course – but he was somewhat domineering along the way. After three years as chairman, he was out, and the calm, steady, tactful thirty-one-year member, Henry Free, was the new chairman. Free was an excellent choice.

One year later, February 1937, members of the board were shocked when McKinzie, Reese, Arledge, Russell, and Crawford resigned from the board. All were Abilenians. One trustee from outside of Abilene joined them in resigning. He was Otto Foster, from Cleburne, a frequent critic of board actions, but always a staunch supporter of the college. The resignations were not on the agenda. The secretary failed to record the matter in the minutes. No action was taken. Six weeks later, however, a meeting was called of the general board, which was unusual for that time of year. After several items of routine business were taken up, a motion was read "[t]hat the seven resignations submitted orally by members of the board in the February meeting be accepted. Motion carried."

Along with acceptance of the resignations, a sincere resolution of appreciation for the work they had done and a request were adopted: "We who remain on the board want each of you who resigned to know that your services and sacrifices for A.C.C. shall not have been in vain.... Furthermore, we beg of you to cooperate with us now in our efforts to carry on and to build a greater Abilene Christian College." They did cooperate. There was no soreheadedness. In the annual meeting of the next year, the group unanimously approved a resolution of appreciation for J. C. Reese "and all other former board members for their willingness to cooperate with the board."

Seven Abilenians still held membership on the board after the Big Five departed. The remaining Abilene trustees were solid and dependable, but quieter. Henry Free was chairman. Hollis Manly was secretary. Others were Sam Bacon, Clyde, H. C. Harvey, G. C. Helvey, C. T. Hutcheson, G. L. Jennings, and J. E. Manly. These men gave Abilene good representation.

One other action by the board took place in the summer. The contract with McKinzie to operate the dining hall was canceled after thirteen years. The food service was taken over by the college, and a manager was employed with a straight salary.

In reading the minutes of board meetings after the resignations, a change of emphasis can be detected. The administration moved into more prominent participation. For example, from the summer meeting in 1937:

> President Cox made his semiannual report to the Board, a copy of which is filed with the minutes. J. E. Freeman, Fiscal Agent, made a report as to what progress is being made concerning the book setup as to all properties owned by the college. Mr. Freeman stated the assets and liabilities of all properties would be completed within a short time. Vice Pres. Don H. Morris made a report concerning the Hardin Annuity account.

The administration was coming into full partnership with the board – keeping the records, organizing the forces, initiating recommendations. In fact, more and more, fund raising came to be focused on the office of the president of the college.

President Cox's report included a recommendation concerning how the board would operate. Instead of having a local board and a general board, he recommended a board committee system:

1. An Executive Committee of five, made up of the president of the board and two members of the board appointed by him, and the president and vice president of the college;

2. A Finance Committee consisting of the president of the board, two members of the board appointed by him, the vice president of the college, and the fiscal agent;

3. A Budget Committee, consisting of the president of the board, two members of the board appointed by him, the bursar, and the president of the college;

4. A Building and Grounds Committee, consisting of the president of the board and two members of the board appointed by him, the chairman of the faculty committee on buildings and grounds, and the bursar;

5. An Education or Teachers Committee, consisting of the president of the board and two members of the board appointed by him, the president of the college, the dean, and the director of the summer school.

The recommendation was accepted with an amendment that appointments of board members to the various committees be approved by the full board. This arrangement seemed to work very well, but with the onset of World War II and gasoline rationing, gradually the local board became the executive committee.

The 1930s were great years to attend Abilene Christian College. Toward the end of his presidency, James F. Cox listed notable facts about the college:

"1. It is the largest college in the world owned and controlled by members of the Church of Christ.

"2. It requires more credit in the Bible text for the bachelor's degree than any other college in the world known to us.

"3. It is the only standard, class A, senior college in the state that is maintained without any endowment.

"4. It is the only senior college in Texas and one of the very few in the world that built an entirely new plant all at one time and moved into it.

"5. It is one of the very few colleges in the country that paid all of its bonded indebtedness during the depression.

"6. No other senior college in Texas showed such a rapid growth in its student body from 1931-32 to 1934-35 – almost 56%. During the same period, the salary payroll more than doubled – another remarkable achievement."

Admittedly, it took a genuine optimist to list item number three as any sort of a plus factor. However, if a college does not have something that is very much needed, it must be acceptable to brag about how the college manages to survive without it.

Three major disappointments for President Cox were failure to gain membership in the Southern Association of Colleges and Schools, to build a new library building, and to replace the Chem Shack with a science building. He worked diligently, especially on the drive for the library, but in the summer of 1936, a board resolution decreed, "In view of the present drought and because the campaign to raise funds for a new library building has failed to pay expenses," the effort was discontinued.

Regrettably, a new library was then unattainable. However, a major improvement in the library was made during the summer of 1936. Since the 1929 move, the library had occupied space on the east side of the third floor of the Administration Building. The library had outgrown that space, and, as President Cox pointed out to the Board of Turstees, the top floor of the Administration Building was not designed for the heavy load that books represented. When the decision was made in the summer of 1936 to cancel the drive for a new library building that would hold 100,000 volumes and space for 300 library patrons at one time, an alternative plan was imperative. Chambers Hall was chosen as the new home of the library, where it would reside until 1969.

First, the basement, or first floor, of Chambers was finished so that the food service operation could be housed there. Up to then, food service had occupied the main floor, and light housekeeping units had been maintained on the third floor. Then the main floor was made ready so that the library could be moved from the Administration Building. Light housekeeping continued on the third floor until 1949, when the library took that over.

At the annual meeting of the Board of Trustees on February 22, 1939, President Cox made this announcement: "With an initial gift of $2,500 on February 1, 1939, Sister E. F. Woodward, of Houston, Texas, has established the Harley Woodward Foundation for Christian Evangelism in memory of her son, Harley Woodward, who was killed in an airplane wreck about three years ago." The Woodward fund has been used through the years for loans to students who needed short-term help in order to complete their education for Christian service. The loan fund has a unique record in that no loan made from it has ever gone unpaid. The modest interest charged for loans has augmented the fund considerably through the years. The 1997 audit showed the assets of the fund at $55,225. The usefulness of the fund and the way it has been administered through the years was a factor in a gift announced in 1998, the largest gift in the history of the university, a story that is told in chapter eight.

During the summer of 1939, President Cox decided he had hoed his row just about to the end. He composed an eloquent letter to the board dated August 24, 1939, and timed to coincide with the semiannual meeting of the board:

> Dear Brethren: Almost eight years ago, when Brother Baxter resigned, you offered me the presidency of Abilene Christian College. I accepted this great honor and this great privilege for service in good faith, realizing, in a measure, at least, its heavy duties and responsibilities, with its consequent disappointments and worries. The burdens, the problems, and the responsibilities have indeed been great. I have done the best I could, and now I believe it is best for me and for the college to turn the office back to you and ask you to permit me to be just a teacher again in A.C.C. without any administrative duties.

He stated that it was his desire to complete his term by June 1, 1940, but expressed the hope that the board would elect his successor in time for the two of them to work together on plans and budget for 1940-41. He would not, of course, presume to suggest to the board whom they should select to succeed him, but he did give a broad hint: "It is my judgment that you should elect a strong, vigorous man in his prime, a Christian of course, and an educator, a good mixer, a tireless worker, one who knows and loves the ideals of Abilene Christian College. We have such in our faculty, and so it is my hope that you do not go outside the faculty to find your next president."

The Board of Trustees was in session. The letter was read. The resignation was accepted with expressions of appreciation and gratitude for the work that had been done. The formal resolution of appreciation for President Cox was prepared later. The trustees felt no need for a presidential search committee. Only one person was nominated, and he was elected to be the seventh president by acclamation. Don Heath Morris was the first alumnus to serve as president. He would take office two and a half months before his thirty-eighth birthday.

The transition from Cox to Morris was smooth, as all presidential transitions have been at Abilene Christian. The Morrises had been renting Cox's home while the Coxes lived in the president's home on the campus. When Morris took over as president, he and his family moved into the president's home, and the Coxes returned to their home. Cox happily taught courses in Bible and Christian education for the next eleven years, retiring in 1951, at the age of seventy-three. When he was presented to students and faculty in chapel Saturday morning, April 21, 1951, the audience was not aware that he was giving his farewell address. But as he spoke on the topic "What Abilene Christian College Means to Me," it became apparent that it was his farewell. The Reporter-News gave page one coverage. The story included this paragraph: "As the tall, white-haired Bible professor uttered his closing remarks, tears were flowing from the eyes of students and faculty and they rose to give him an unusual ovation." He died September 30, 1968, at the age of ninety.

Other memorable people in the Cox presidential era indelibly etched university history with traditional tales, such as the stories of the Bennett family, J. E. McKinzie, Sheriff Burgess, the Burford family, and Clara Bishop.

Becki Bennett Schwarz wrote a few years ago an excellent volume titled *Bennett: A Texas Family*. Her grandparents, L. P. and Ruth Bennett, owned several thousand acres of ranch land in Yoakum County, which is as far west as one can go on the South Plains of Texas and remain in Texas. The western boundary of Yoakum County is the New Mexico line. The Bennetts were blessed with a large family – four sons and four daughters. It was a country of vast distances and thin population. Because they insisted on education for their children, traveling to and from school was a problem.

They tried different arrangements. They hired a tutor to live on the ranch and run a school in a small line-rider camp house. Later, they helped establish a school at a place called "Sligo," which helped. When the two older children were ready for high school, the Bennetts made arrangements for them to room and board with some people in Brownfield. Then they bought a place in Lubbock so the family could be together during the school year. In 1927, they moved to Abilene so their school age children could attend Abilene Christian Training School, the academy, or the college – whichever was needed.

The latter 1920s were not too kind to people in the cattle business – even before the Great Depression struck – so, in 1929, the Bennetts made a trade with Abilene Christian College. They gave two sections of land – 1,280 acres in exchange for tuition. Six of the eight Bennett offspring attended ACC. At the time, the gift was assigned a book value of $15,000, and the trustees showed their appreciation by naming the new gymnasium, which at the time was described as "the finest in West Texas," for them. Little did the auditors dream of the millions of dollars the land would ultimately be worth to the college's endowment. Another half-section was given in 1931, making the total ACC Yoakum County holdings 1,600 acres.

The Great Depression nearly caused the Bennetts to lose their ranch and all that was on it. Heavy losses in cattle forced

Bennett to borrow a good deal of money from the Agricultural Livestock Finance Corporation of Fort Worth. He had to put the ranch up as collateral. Finally, he had to sign a deed of trust conveying the ranch to the Finance Corporation. The corporation joined the First National Bank of Lubbock in advertising it for sale at auction. The sale of all 8,320 acres of it was scheduled for October 1, 1935.

One hope remained: oil. A company from Fort Worth had a drilling lease on the ranch, but oil was selling at such a low price that incentive to drill was low. In the fall of 1935, however, drilling got under way. Joe Childers, an Abilene attorney who represented Bennett, persuaded the bankers to postpone the sale thirty days. The day before the drillers were scheduled to reach the depth that would show whether there was oil or not, Abilene Christian's board chairman, J. E. McKinzie, joined Bennett, and the two of them sat up all night talking and praying. Of course, the acreage that had been given to the college would not have been involved in the sale because when it was donated, it was free and clear. But McKinzie was sincerely interested in his friends, and, besides, he knew that if oil was found on the Bennett acres, the ACC acres would not be far behind.

The drilling produced a gusher. The ranch was saved. ACC would soon realize oil profits from its Bennett land.

L. P. Bennett was a member of the Abilene Christian Board of Trustees from 1941 until his death in 1956. His son, Gene, father of Becki Schwarz, served from 1952 until 1977. He was a lifelong supporter of the university. He died June 25, 1998. His wife, Vera, and their two sons and two daughters, are all loyal alumni. If trading tuition for Bennett ranch land was not the best trade Abilene Christian ever made, it certainly ranks very close to whatever was.

Another storied character who entered the ACC scene in the 1930s was J. S. Burgess. In 1934, Lawrence Smith and James F. Cox persuaded Burgess to go to work for the college as caretaker of the new campus. He was certainly a colorful personality. He was fifty years of age when he began work on the campus. He retired thirty-four years later. Burgess was born in

Kansas on February 10, 1876. As he explained, he went to school only through the fifth reader, so it was certain that he would go to work for a college. When he was twenty-one, he went into "Indian Territory," as he called Oklahoma – and as it was – and married "the prettiest girl in the Territory." In 1904, they came to the Abilene area and a few years later moved into the city. For years, he worked as a policeman, fire fighter, parks worker, street worker, and even a stint as health inspector.

Then came the invitation to work on the new campus, which was unattractive and treeless with the exception of mesquites. Burgess went to work planting trees. Pecan trees were his specialty. He was assigned some student workers, and he saw to it that they earned their money. Douglas Fry was one of the number. He and Lawrence Smith together described the Burgess method of planting. First, he would have his student worker, or workers, dig a hole about four feet square. It was hard work. The ground was hard and rocky. When the hole was as deep as the students – using shovels, crowbars, and other weapons – could be reasonably expected to dig, Burgess would take over. He would place a half-stick of dynamite, with a long fuse attached to it, in the hole. He would place an old blanket over the hole, to catch and partially hold the rocks that would be blown out.

Then he and any others who were around would retire to a safe distance – as far as his fuse would permit. If the planting happened to be taking place close to the street, he would have somebody stopping traffic. Then there would be a terrific explosion, with rocks, dirt, mud, and the blanket flying into the air. Then the pecan tree would be placed into the hole, and the place would be filled with dirt, rocks, tin cans, and other materials. He did not want all dirt because it would pack into a solid substance and prevent enough water from reaching the roots. The system worked. Those large pecan trees are still a blessing to the campus, more than a half-century later.

Some time before he retired, he was asked how many trees he had planted. He did not know, but he said he had recently counted and there were about 130 pecan trees and forty sycamores. He said, however, that he had planted more than that number, but the college through the years had to dig some of them up to make room for buildings. He always regretted seeing one of his trees dug up. He did not count mesquite trees.

Burgess also sowed grass, planted and cared for flowers, raised the flag of the United States every morning, and lowered it in the evening. After some years, when he became too old to do all of the things he had been doing, he took on the assignment of night watchman. That is when the students nicknamed him "Sheriff." Occasionally, he had his shotgun and fired it into the air if he suspected a prowler might be hiding somewhere. Once, he approached the dean of men with one shoe in hand. He said, "Last night, I found a fellow hiding in the bushes outside the girls' dormitory. I knew I couldn't catch him, so I fired my shotgun into the air. He ran so fast he ran out of this shoe. I thought maybe he would come by looking for it." The dean replied, "Sheriff, I can assure you nobody will come by asking about a shoe. But we can keep it on display for a while as a memento."

On one occasion when Sheriff was too ill to take care of his morning duties of unlocking the doors and lighting the fires in the offices and classrooms, someone had to go to his house to get the key for the building. The president of the college could be absent for a week at a time, and few people would know the difference. But the absence of Sheriff for one morning stopped the operation of the school. Then it followed, wags said, that Sheriff was more important than the president. On the occasion of his retirement, the *Reporter-News* story about him called him "philosopher, lover of nature, fountain of wisdom, and confidant of thousands of students through the years."

Sheriff and the food service were constants in the lives of students, and probably they could not have had a better food service during the 1920s and 1930s than the family-style meals served by J. E. McKinzie.

He was an unusual person. Born in Tennessee in 1882, he was brought to Texas as a small child. His family settled in Hill County. As a young man, he worked in a butcher shop and became skilled in the trade. Later, he went into insurance and real estate and served two terms as assessor-collector of taxes for

Hill County. On the side, he always ran some cattle.

When the McKinzie family moved to Abilene, he brought eight Holstein cows with him. He leased a box car, put cows in one end and furniture in the other, and shipped them by rail. He leased 160 acres in the vicinity of today's Dyess Air Force Base. Meeting the train in Abilene, he and his sons herded the cows down the road to the pasture. That was the nucleus of his dairy operation. He also raised hogs and furnished milk, butter, bacon, ham, and sausage for his campus enterprise. When the move to the new campus came in 1929, he leased from the college the 320-acre Miller land. After the land was deeded back to Mrs. Miller, he leased from her. He had another half section between East North Tenth Street and the railroad, which is now the Radford Hills area, and 250 acres near Elmdale. He built up quite a herd – about 100 head of milk cows – and some beef cattle.

After working with McKinzie for seven years, President Baxter paid him this tribute: "As manager of the dining hall, he has given me sympathetic and wholehearted cooperation. The financial hardships have not diminished the amount of food on the tables. He has not allowed his financial worries to hinder the very enviable record of having run a college dining hall for seven years with almost universal satisfaction to the student body.... I have never worked with a better yokefellow. His free-hearted and accommodating spirit has endeared him to both faculty and students." Lawrence Smith, in a 1980 interview with McKinzie's son, Fred, added his tribute: "He was very patient and never complained to us. Once in a while, he would come to me and say, 'Lawrence, I need a thousand dollars.' I would visit with him a while and get him to settle for $500."

Students talked about being fed a lot of beans and mashed potatoes. Maybe that helped explain their good health. Some students had never before enjoyed cornmeal mush for breakfast, but they had that privilege under McKinzie. A bowl of hot cornmeal mush, with a bit of butter, a spoonful of sugar, and some milk could convince even the most skeptical. Meals were served family style at tables for four and tables for six. Seating was assigned, with an effort made to achieve a gender balance at each table. If more food was needed, someone at the table would hold an empty bowl up, and a student worker would retrieve it and bring it back full. A full syrup pitcher was always at each table for each meal. At mealtime, students lined up outside the hall until the bell was rung and the doors opened. They quickly went to their assigned places and stood until a bell sounded to quiet everyone. The student who had been selected to offer thanks for the meal did so, and the "chowing down" began.

The food service generally provided employment for twenty or twenty-five students, and thus helped many a student work his or her way through college. When the Board of Trustees decided, in 1937, to take over the food service and hire a manager, a careful check of the books revealed that over the past thirteen years, the college owed McKinzie $32,670.

The trustees voted unanimously to make a fair settlement of the account, and a satisfactory deal was worked out. He received from the college:

1. Ten "Better Than Gold" certificates, worth $600 each. These were certificates that he could present to children or grandchildren (or whomever he chose) when they were ready for college. A gift of $600 would pretty well take care of a semester's expenses, considering how low the cost was for tuition, room, and board at the time.

2. Four tracts of land, valued at $2,425.

3. Cash for $2,075.

4. A promissory note of the college, for $15,000, providing for regular monthly payments and five percent interest on the unpaid balance. Payment on this note was completed by 1941.

5. Cancellation of obligations he had to the college for lots in Abilene Heights, for a value of $1,657.

Finally, he expressed his own desire to cancel or forgive the last $5,513 of the college's debt to him.

McKinzie was out – out of the chairmanship, off the board, and out of the dining hall. He had, however, left his mark.

After a couple of years looking after his cattle, he was appointed district supervisor of the oil and gas division of the Texas Railroad Commission, with headquarters in Abilene. When World War II came to an end in 1945, the college was ready to begin its first new permanent structure since the 1929 move. It was to be a dormitory for women. When Don Morris told McKinzie that the trustees wanted to name the building for him, he requested that it be named in honor of his wife, who had meant so much, in her quiet way, to the building of Abilene Christian. So the new dormitory was named Bess McKinzie Hall. He did not live to see the new building completed. A heart attack took him on May 26, 1946. Don Morris described him as "another example of the right man coming into leadership at the right time."

Another family whose victory over adversity inspired thousands of students through excellence of life and the musical arts was the Burfords. An admirer wrote: "The J. L. Burford children – Leonard, Jack, and Mable – were cheerful, confident, purposeful, musical, blind, and a blessing to the community of which they were a part." Mable explained how this came about: "Our parents instilled in us that we had to do something for ourselves." Born with a condition known as retinitis pigmentosa, they were destined for blindness. They refused to give in to it. Leonard's pronouncement was "Blindness is, at the worst, a nuisance." They were musicians, teachers, builders, organizers, and managers. They had a constructive philosophy and an optimistic outlook. They always seemed excited about some project they had underway.

Leonard was the oldest, born September 6, 1906 – the week before Childers Classical Institute officially opened. His mother started teaching him to play a reed organ early in life. By the time he was eleven, he could play more than 300 hymns and sing all of the parts to each one. His musical education was greatly advanced when Pat Malone joined the Abilene Christian faculty in 1919 as instructor in piano. His studies in piano with Miss Malone and in voice with Myrtle Dunn helped prepare him for his thirty years on the music faculty, including twenty-four years as department head. Completing his bachelor's degree at ACC in 1925, he later earned master's and doctor's degrees at Columbia University. His contributions to music at Abilene Christian College were great indeed. Singlehandedly, he upgraded singing among Churches of Christ.

Although Jack and Mable were not members of the faculty, their contributions to the college through the years, and their success as teachers of piano and violin students ranked alongside standards achieved by their older brother. This section, however, deals with the extracurricular activities of the Burfords, and particularly of Leonard.

He had a complete, power-equipped shop in his home. He worked with table saws, belt sanders, and drill presses. He could rip boards to the desired dimensions. He could drive nails without smashing a finger. It bothered his neighbors to hear him sawing and hammering in utter darkness. He and Jack had to remember to turn a light on in their workshop at night – not for their benefit, but for the concerned neighborhood. When he needed a new fence for his back yard, he built it. Because this work was usually at night, he tried to remember to turn on the floodlight. He liked to go bowling. He enjoyed bicycling. He acquired a bicycle built for two. He would do the pedaling. All he needed was someone to control the handlebars. He looked forward to going to the gymnasium to shoot the basketball from the free-throw line.

When he decided that the community should be able to enjoy opera, he suggested to Rex Kyker of the Speech Department that they do one. Kyker's response was, "All right, Leonard, you select the opera, and we'll do it." Burford chose "Aida." One skeptic commented, "How can these two men direct us in an opera when Burford can't see and Kyker can't sing?" "Aida" was so successful that the pair produced seven more operas.

When Burford was headed for New York City for graduate school, he decided to get a guide dog. Ronald was a magnificent animal. He helped Burford in New York, but when they returned to Abilene, Burford was seen leading the dog around the campus. He made such a pet of Ronald that he ruined him as a guide dog.

He was an enthusiastic member of the Lions Club and was the regular pianist for their weekly meetings. He and Jack and Dr. Clinton Adams formed a trio called "Three Blind Mice." Leonard played the piano, Jack the violin, and Adams utilized a harmonica and an electronic instrument called a "claviolene."

They performed for civic clubs and wherever people wanted unusual entertainers. Their repertoire ranged from the classics to "My Darling Nellie Gray."

When Burford was fifty-one, he married Mary Titsworth, hostess of Nelson Dormitory. They were a happy couple. He died in 1961, at age fifty-five. He had done a lot of living during his years.

When Clara Bishop confronted the strong, self-confident men of the 1930s Board of Trustees, they found they were dealing with a tough-minded little woman and had more than they could handle gracefully. Bishop was a forty-three-year-old widow with three daughters when she came to Abilene Christian College to work as President Sewell's secretary in 1921. In 1902, she had married William James Bishop, and the two of them had set out for Japan to do mission work. They spent a number of years in Japan and loved the work and the people. Their three daughters were born there. In 1913, Bishop became a victim of tuberculosis and had to come home. Clara and the girls stayed in Japan to look after the work there. In time, an urgent message reached her, asking her to come home. Her husband was in critical condition. She closed down their operation as fast as she could, and she and the daughters boarded a ship for America. Her husband died before she arrived.

She had to go to work to support the family. She knew the Sewells. By going to work for President Sewell, she could earn a modest living and arrange for her daughters' educations. In 1924, she became secretary to President Baxter. Two years later, she was named registrar of the college. She also had oversight of the business office. When Lawrence Smith signed on as bursar of the college, he was at first under the direction of Mrs. Bishop.

Her crisp, businesslike manner of dealing with people rubbed some people the wrong way. Although the trustees ordinarily did not concern themselves with personnel matters, they decided to get involved. They decided that Mrs. Bishop should go. In a meeting April 4, 1935, by a vote of eight to four, the Board of Trustees decided not to renew her contract for the next year. President Cox was to notify her. He chose to do it by writing a letter rather than by personal confrontation.

She wrote an eloquent letter to the board, and President Cox read it to the members. It was written with restraint. She said she was not bitter, but shocked. Nobody had ever told her anything was wrong. Nobody had suggested to her that she needed to do things differently. Nobody had even yet told her what was wrong or needed improvement. She admitted that she did not coddle students, for, as she said, "This school is a character-building institution." She realized that some faculty members had probably criticized her, but she reminded board members that a job like hers would naturally bring on some criticism. She told the board, "Not one of you would cast off even a dumb animal that had worn itself out in your service, to live or die, survive or perish." The board voted unanimously to keep Mrs. Bishop. She retired sixteen years later, at age seventy-three.

Two significant off-campus events of the Cox era have left colorful stories, the role of an *Optimist* business manager in the renaming of Simmons University and the marching of the Wildcat Band in the inaugural parade of Governor W. Lee "Pappy" O'Daniel in Austin.

The late Dr. Rupert Norval Richardson was a nationally noted Texas historian. He was an alumnus, a long-time faculty member, and, for ten years, president of Hardin-Simmons University in Abilene. Some years ago, he wrote a history of Hardin-Simmons titled *Famous Are Thy Halls*. He told the story of how John G. Hardin's good deed for Abilene Christian College helped Hardin-Simmons, a Baptist university: "It was in 1934, that word came to Simmons University that Burkburnett farmer-oilman John G. Hardin was planning to leave his fortune to philanthropy, and that he favored Baptist causes. Solon Featherston of Wichita Falls, always loyal and alert in the interest of the university, acquainted Dr. J. D. Sandefer, president of Simmons University, with the situation and secured for him an interview with Mr. Hardin."

Richardson tells of Dr. Sandefer's visit with Hardin, and of how encouraging Hardin was, but he made no commitment, similar to the ACC experience with the farmer-oilman. Friends who knew Hardin best told Dr. Sandefer that he could not be hurried. So back to Abilene Sandefer came, with assurance from people who were close to the Hardins that they would let him know when the time was ripe for him to return to Burkburnett for a visit.

The HSU historian continued: "While we were thus marking time, a bit of news that reached us quite casually one day chilled us like the first whiff of a January norther. The bearer of the news, strangely, was no other than the business manager of the Abilene Christian College student newspaper, who breezed into our office one afternoon to sell Hardin-Simmons University an advertisement. And why should Hardin-Simmons be advertising in the Abilene Christian College *Optimist*? Oh, this was a special issue; the Burkburnett-Wichita Falls capitalist, John G. Hardin, was making a generous gift to Abilene Christian College, supplying some $200,000 to purchase the bonds outstanding against the college, thus securing for it a new lease on life. Surely, Simmons University would want to congratulate Abilene Christian College on this good fortune."

The outcome of the *Optimist* business manager's call was that after the good people of Simmons recovered from shock, they did take a large advertisement, as did McMurry College, the Methodist institution across town. The special edition of the *Optimist* came out on Thursday, February 22, 1934, to coincide with the big announcement.

Richardson wrote: "Now we had nothing but the kindliest feelings toward Abilene Christian College. The two institutions had never been regarded even as rivals, and there had certainly never been any jealousy or rancor between the two."

What Simmons people could not understand was why a prominent Baptist layman would ignore the needs of a university supported by his own church in favor of one related to Churches of Christ. However, they later learned that he had given in memory of his first wife, who had been a member of the Church of Christ. Then the Baptists of Texas quit waiting for a call from Burkburnett. They got busy, rallied their troops, and went to Burkburnett. Two months after the Abilene Christian announcement, they had their own announcement: $200,000 on an annuity basis, with a ten percent brokerage fee for Harwell and Chatham.

The story went further, however. Just as, for Abilene Christian, the suggestion of taking some half-priced bonds from the Hardin portfolio and counting them at face value opened the door, so the Simmons people came up with the idea of adding the name "Hardin" to the name of the university. They did it before any additional Hardin commitment beyond the initial $200,000, but in the long run, it paid off. Hardin-Simmons received a much larger gift, described at the time Dr. Richardson wrote his 1964 book as "the greatest benefaction from any one source" in the history of the university.

Thus, the business manager of Abilene Christian's student newspaper, the *Optimist*, turned out to be a good neighbor. Reuel Lemmons, later a long-time trustee and editor of the *Firm Foundation*, was that business manager.

The Wildcat Band story was told by Leon Henthorn, of the class of 1940. The band, now known as the Big Purple, was invited to march in the inauguration parade of W. Lee O'Daniel as governor of Texas in January 1939. O'Daniel, who was president of a flour-milling company before getting into politics, was infamous for using the song "Please Pass the Biscuits, Pappy" as his theme song. Two buses transported the group to Austin. Late in the evening, they headed back to Abilene, with the girls in bus number one and the boys following in bus number two, which was driven by band director D. W. Crain. Suddenly, about midnight, all of the occupants of bus number two were jarred awake and found that the bus was on its side, skidding down the highway. The driver had dozed off and had jerked awake to find he was headed for a culvert. He over corrected, and the bus flipped over on its side, with the consequent skidding.

When all hands had scrambled out of the wreckage, it turned out that only one person was injured. James Malcolm Smith had an artery cut in his forearm. They were not far from Brownwood, so he hitched a ride into the city, got the arm patched up, and was able to rejoin the group when the relief bus came through. The wrecked bus was straddling the highway, so band members built a bonfire to keep warm and to flag down any approaching traffic. Nevertheless, a farm pickup ran past the warning and plowed into the wrecked bus. The driver of the pickup had dozed off. Luckily, neither he nor his wife was injured. After a time, a wrecker arrived and shoved the bus in two pieces – chassis and seats and the roof – off to the side of the road and into a borrow ditch, thus opening the road to traffic. Henthorn had lost his glasses, but when the wreckage was cleared from the highway, somebody looking at the debris shouted, "Here's someone's glasses." They were Henthorn's – unbroken.

Later, some students went back to Brownwood and to the scene on the highway. They managed to pile the roof onto the chassis, and Charles "Skeeter" Dick drove the wreck to Abilene. The picture of the wreck, which was printed toward the back of the 1939 *Prickly Pear*, raised the question, "How could anybody drive a heap like that?" In Henthorn's annual, a note signed by Louie Welch, who was a member of the group and later five-term mayor of Houston, read, "We have lived together, and if Something Bigger Than Man hadn't helped, we'd have died together. Your roommate, Louie."

In every decade, some students become alumni newsmakers while most of the people are going about their lives quietly, serving God and mankind. Leading newsmakers during the Cox administration were Jack Pope, Hettie Lee Ewing, Louie Welch, Marguerite Anderson, LeMoine Gaunce Lewis, Jack Pearl Lewis, Olan L. Hicks, Reuel Lemmons, Norvel Young, Batsell Barrett Baxter, Carl Spain, W. B. West Jr., A. Clifford Thornton, John W. Holton, and Robert Wilson Holton.

Jack Pope, '34, earned a law degree from the University of Texas in 1937 and then practiced law and put in some time in the United States Navy during World War II before beginning, in 1946, a thirty-eight-year career as a judge in Texas courts. This included four years as a district judge, fifteen years as a Court of Civil Appeals justice, and nineteen years as a justice of the Supreme Court of Texas. During his last two years on the

Supreme Court, he was chief justice. He was a member of the Abilene Christian Board of Trustees, 1954-83, and has been a Senior Board member since 1983. The Alumni Board named him Alumnus of the Year for 1964. ACU awarded him an honorary doctorate in 1981. An endowment, the Jack Pope Fellows Program, offers scholarships to students preparing for public service. He is respected as a legal scholar and as a person of integrity. He has often said, "Nobody is worthy of being a judge in Texas courts who is not willing to be defeated in the next election."

When he was on the bench, the judge generally had a stern visage. He had, however, another side, as Leon Henthorn related: "During the time Jack Pope was a Justice on the Supreme Court, he assisted in little dramas in Bible School at the University Avenue Church of Christ. One of the most vivid memories of my daughter, Barbie, is of the Judge as the bleating 'lost sheep,' on all fours, going down the basement hallway in the church building." Judge Pope and his wife, Allene, stay busy in retirement with church work, speaking, writing, and arranging and cataloguing his papers.

Hettie Lee Ewing graduated with the class of 1937. By the time she enrolled in the college in 1934, she had already done several years of mission work in Japan. She devoted fifty-five years of her life to that work. During World War II, she came home to the United States, served as a translator for the United States government in various places, and helped relocate Japanese families coming to this country. As soon as the war was over, she returned to work with the people whom she desired to serve. Frank and Della Pack visited her in Japan, and Dr. Pack wrote an article in the *20th Century Christian*, explaining why she was so effective: "She determined to live as they lived, to follow their customs insofar as they did not conflict with God's will, and to maintain a lifestyle in keeping with the ordinary Japanese people among whom she lived and worked."

Louie Welch, '40, was elected to five consecutive terms as mayor of Houston, fourth largest city in the United States. After ten years as mayor, he retired undefeated and was named mayor emeritus for life. His path to political popularity was somewhat unusual. Mac Bedichek described it in the spring 1966 issue of *Horizons:* "In the arena where public interest is too often sacrificed to expediency, Welch believes in the integrity of the public man – he should do what he believes to be right, regardless of the political cost.... When confronted with a knotty problem, the mayor invariably asks, 'What would be the right thing to do?'" He was a member of the Board of Trustees, 1953-85, and has been on Senior Board since 1985. He was chosen as Alumnus of the Year 1965 and was awarded an honorary doctorate in 1981. In 1983, friends endowed the Louie Welch Chair for Business Administration.

Marguerite Anderson, '37, made significant contributions in building the Abilene Christian library – its holdings, staff, and service. Anderson came as a freshman in 1933 and was assigned to work as a student assistant in the library. She was on the job when the library was moved from the third floor of the Administration Building to the main floor of Chambers Hall in the summer of 1936. When she graduated in 1937, she was invited to remain as assistant librarian to Elizabeth Nelson. When Nelson retired because of ill health in 1942, Anderson became head librarian and served with distinction for the next eleven years. The war years were not the most favorable period for library expansion, but the collection grew steadily. With the doubling and trebling of enrollment after the war, more space was a desperate need. In fact, it was a prerequisite to accreditation, which had long been a goal. In 1949, she supervised library expansion to include the top floor of Chambers, almost doubling the space. When she resigned to enter private business in Abilene in 1953, her friend Callie Faye Milliken was chosen to succeed her. Milliken's story comes later.

LeMoine Gaunce Lewis, '36, became in 1941 the first ACU graduate admitted to the Harvard University Divinity School. He received the S.T.B. degree in 1944 and the Ph.D. in 1956. He became a legendary professor of Bible and church history at Abilene Christian, teaching from 1949 until retirement in 1986. From 1959 through 1966, he was director of the Bible Teachers Workshop, which was begun by G. C. Morlan in the summer of 1956 and has served the church most usefully since that time. Lewis was a true scholar and always in demand as a preacher. After retirement from the classroom, as he was preparing for wider service to the brotherhood, he was struck down by cancer and died in 1987.

Jack Pearl Lewis, '41, followed his brother, LeMoine, in enrolling at Harvard. He received the Ph.D. in 1952. Thus, he became the first Abilene Christian graduate to receive the doctorate from Harvard because his brother, LeMoine, took out a few years for teaching large classes and grading papers at Abilene Christian. Jack went straight through to the doctoral degree. He also earned a doctorate from Hebrew Union College. His career has been spent as a distinguished professor at the Harding University Graduate School of Religion in Memphis, Tennessee.

All five of the children of LeMoine and Jack Lewis have Ph.D. degrees. Once, during a family reunion in Abilene, a reporter from the local newspaper got word of it and called to speak to "Dr. Lewis." Six of them were in one room, so the reporter was asked to be specific. They were truly a scholarly family.

Olan L. Hicks, '32, and Reuel G. Lemmons, '35, earned distinction in the field of Christian journalism. Hicks founded the *Christian Chronicle* in Abilene during World War II. It was a unique and exciting paper because its primary purpose was to report what was actually happening among Churches of Christ and to give some attention to religious news in general. Mission work was emphasized. It continues as one of the most influential publications among Churches of Christ and in 1998 is published by Oklahoma Christian University.

Lemmons became editor of the venerable *Firm Foundation* at the beginning of 1955. Through his clear, powerful writing and his preaching and lecturing, he became one of the most influential voices among Churches of Christ. In his last *Firm Foundation* editorial, August 23, 1983, he wrote: "For twenty-eight years and eight months we have pled for unity, and not division." He was a trustee of ACU from 1953 to 1984 and was a Senior Board member from 1984 until his death in 1989. He was Alumnus of the Year for 1969.

Norvel Young, '36, Batsell Barrett Baxter, '37, and Carl Spain, '38, transferred from David Lipscomb College to

Abilene. All three were highly successful as preachers and educators.

Young, after a long ministry with Broadway Church of Christ in Lubbock, became president of George Pepperdine College in Los Angeles in 1957, when that institution was going through some difficult times. For four decades, as president, chancellor, and chancellor emeritus until his death in 1998, he filled a vital role in the spectacular growth of Pepperdine University. He was also board chairman of *20th Century Christian*. When the Abilene Christian Alumnus of the Year award was begun in 1958, he was the first recipient. He was an ACC trustee before beginning his work on the West Coast.

Baxter, son of the fifth president of Abilene Christian, became head of the Speech Department at David Lipscomb College in 1945. He held that position for eleven years, during which time he served a term as president of the Southern Speech Association and of the Tennessee Speech Association. When his father, who had been head of the Lipscomb Bible Department for ten years, died, in 1956, he was invited to fill that post. He resigned as head of the Department of Speech to become head of the Bible Department. He filled that position with distinction until his death in 1982. For twenty-five years, he also preached for the Hillsboro Church of Christ in Nashville and was the speaker for the *Herald of Truth* television and radio series. He was known throughout the nation and beyond. He was Alumnus of the Year for 1961.

Spain came from a ministry with the Central Church of Christ in Houston to join the Bible faculty at ACU in 1954. He taught in the Bible Department for thirty years, retiring in 1984. A great favorite with students, he rendered an especially significant service to the college and to the Church of Christ brotherhood in his speech on the 1960 Bible Lectureship, which is discussed in chapter five.

W. B. West Jr., a member of the class of 1934, was a true scholar. After years of teaching and graduate study, he became chairman of the Bible Department at Harding College in 1951. When the Harding Graduate School of Religion was established in Memphis in 1958, he became dean of the school. With his leadership, the Graduate School attracted a strong faculty and developed an outstanding program.

A. Clifford Thornton, '34, was Alumnus of the Year for 1977. He was a trustee for years and is in 1998 on the Senior Board. He was in the upper echelon of several major corporations, the last being the Eaton Corporation of Cleveland, Ohio. In addition to his success in the business world, he is another example of a successful person who remembered his roots. Wherever he and his family lived, they were strong members of the church and servants in their communities.

John W. Holton, '39, was Alumnus of the Year for 1978. In addition to his bachelor of arts degree from Abilene Christian, he earned his law degree from National University in Washington, D. C. In 1942-43, he was legislative assistant to Congressman Sam Rayburn of Texas. After three years of service in the United States Navy, he returned to work as legislative assistant to the congressman. In 1952 he became administrative assistant to Speaker Sam Rayburn and continued in that capacity until Rayburn's death in 1961. He was then appointed as an assistant to the new speaker, Congressman John McCormack of Massachusetts, until the end of that Congress in 1962. After that, he became senior government relations counselor for the American Bankers Association and continued in that work until retirement. For thirty-five years he served as an elder of the Sixteenth and Decatur Church of Christ in Washington, during which time he took responsibility for endorsing ministers from Churches of Christ as candidates for the military chaplaincy. His widow is the former Katherine Roberson, daughter of the Charles Roberson who worked so closely with A. B. Barret in founding Childers Classical Institute. He died in December 1997.

Robert Wilson Holton, '41, younger brother of John Holton, created quite a stir on the campus in the fall of his freshman year. The *Reporter-News* of November 6, 1937, announced that he was one of four persons chosen from 6,573 tested in the Southwest in the Metro-Goldwyn-Mayer search for talent to go to Culver City, California, for additional movie tests and prospects for options. It was quite an honor. People on the campus were thrilled, but there were forebodings.

Prayers were offered for this eighteen-year-old Daniel in the den of lions. Holton went to California, wrote about all the great movie stars whom he met, and enjoyed considerable success in pictures and especially in television. He was announcer for the long-running *Loretta Young Show*. He stayed true to his Christian convictions. To illustrate how highly his faith was respected, he was selected for the leading role in a full-length film on the life of Jesus, "Day of Triumph." His Hollywood name was Robert Wilson. Perhaps he would have been a bigger name if he had been willing to go along with some of the movies that were made. Through the years, he served two congregations – one in California and one in Texas – as an elder. When the *Herald of Truth* television series was launched, he was announcer. As a member of Prestoncrest Church in Dallas, he often read a selection from the Bible at the Sunday morning service. In the 1970s he recorded the entire *New Testament – New International Version* – on tape. He died December 9, 1996, leaving his wife of fifty-seven years, the former Mary Louise Ladd; a son, Ladd, of Fort Worth; and a daughter, Mary Lee, whose husband, Dr. Charles Mattis, is a professor of biology at Abilene Christian University and has a practice of dentistry in Abilene.

Wildcat Sports Hall of Fame honorees from the Cox era left their marks on the fields and arenas of play.

Howard Green, class of '35, was one of the first group of nominees when the Hall of Fame was begun. He was chosen in 1934 to tour the Orient as a member of the United States track team. The group left San Francisco August 12, aboard a Japanese steamer. During the next four months and twelve days the team participated in meets in various cities in Japan, Manchuria, Korea, the Philippines, and Shanghai. By the time the Shanghai meet occurred, Howard complained mildly because the team had been separated to appear in more places. He wrote, "Due to the dividing of our team, there were only four of us left to compete. I ran, and won both the 100- and 200-meter races. Our relay team was really a joke, being composed of a shot putter, a miler, and a 5,000-meter runner besides myself, but we won it, even with this unique combination." The 1935 *Prickly Pear*, which ran Howard's report, summarized the situation in these words: "Perhaps the glory of Christian has been carried farther and sent to loftier heights and greater fame by Howard Green, than by any other one individual student."

Robert L. "Squib" Carruthers, '37, was an all-conference center in football. He was the university's nominee for the *Sports Illustrated* silver anniversary all-America team in 1961. After graduation with a degree in education and history, he coached and taught in high schools for some years and then had a successful business career. Over the years, he served as an elder for Churches of Christ in Houston, San Angelo, and Austin.

W. E. "Mose" McCook, '38, was a tri-captain and four-year letterman in football and a two-year track and field letterman in the sprints, relays, and long jump. After graduation, he coached at Brownfield, Ozona, and McCamey and then entered the sporting goods business. His citation reads, "He never had a losing season as a high school football coach, and he coached Ozona and McCamey to their first district and bi-district championships." His son, Charles, came along as a Wildcat quarterback in the 1960s.

Kendall "Ace" Jones, '39, was cited as "one of the most versatile athletes in ACU sports history." He was a three-year letterman in both basketball and tennis and won the Texas state badminton championship in 1939. He was twice named an all-conference guard in basketball. During his three years, the Wildcat records were 9-3, 16-2, and 12-5. After graduation, he served in the U.S. Navy, winning the all-Navy singles tennis championship one year and the doubles championships three years.

Thurman L. "Tugboat" Jones, '40, was "one of the top fullbacks" in Abilene Christian history. After his college days, he played professional football for two years with the old Brooklyn Dodgers before entering the ranks of high school coaches. His Highland Park team beat Abilene High School for the state championship. He later was athletic director at Midland before retiring. His twin sister, Judy, is the wife of Garvin Beauchamp, who was head football coach and dean of students.

Garvin V. Beauchamp, '41, was an all-conference lineman. After service in the United States Navy during World War II, he came back to his alma mater as assistant football coach and became head coach in 1950. In that year, ably assisted by coaches Oliver Jackson and Bill McClure, he led the Wildcats to the only undefeated, untied record in the history of the university. The team went on to victory over Gustavus Adolphus College in the Refrigerator Bowl in Evansville, Indiana, 13-7. The Wildcats won in spite of the fact that when quarterback Ted Sitton faked a handoff to Alton Green and slipped it instead to Bailey Woods, the referee, thinking Green had the football, blew the whistle when Green went down, while Woods went lugging the ball across the Gustavus Adolphus goal line. Although the call was flagrantly incorrect, the officials disallowed the touchdown. They did, however, give Alton Green credit for a five-yard gain – and Green had not touched the football. A few plays later, Sitton tipped the referee off, saying, "We're calling that play again." The referee said, "Don't get smart with me, or you'll be sitting on the bench." Sitton simply said, "Well, we're calling it again." He did, and the play worked for another touchdown, and this time the referee allowed it. Later, the referee admitted to sportswriters that he had never seen a more deceptive quarterback. Beauchamp was head coach through the 1956 season and became dean of students. In 1969, he became vice president for campus life and filled that job admirably until retirement in 1988. The amphitheater by the Biblical Studies Building is named for Garvin and Judy Beauchamp. He was for years an elder of the University Church.

Helmuth E. Stromquist, '41, lettered four years in football. He was twice named all-conference end, was awarded honorable mention all-America in 1938, and was third team all-America in 1939. He was a career Air Force man, retiring with the rank of colonel.

Leon Reese, '41, was an all-Texas Conference basketball player in 1940-41, and, as his citation reads, "a pioneer of the one-handed jump shot in collegiate basketball in the Southwestern United States." He was also a three-year letterman in tennis. An Abilene sportswriter wrote of him, "There isn't much an opponent can do in the way of defense when Reese is hot with his jumping push shot." During his senior year in Abilene Christian, he was president of the A Club, the Alpha Chi Scholarship Society, and the Business Administration Club, in addition to being vice president of the Students' Association. He is the son of long-time Board of Trustees vice chairman J. C. Reese and the father of Dr. Jack Reese, who was named dean of the College of Biblical Studies in 1997. Leon Reese was an Abilene businessman through the years and is a long-time elder of the University Church.

From the early days of Childers Classical Institute and Abilene Christian College, debate was a significant activity on the campus. Debates between the Hardings and the Zellners drew large crowds. In the 1920s, with the attainment of senior college status, intercollegiate debating assumed a position of considerable importance. When Don Morris and Walter Adams teamed up in the early twenties, nobody could beat them. Other prominent debaters were Roy Cogdill, Waldo Proffitt, Aubra Banowsky, John Paul Gibson, Burton Coffman, John F. Wolfe, Abner Morris, Henry Hogg, Ernest Walls, Everett O'Dowd, Comer Clay, Foy Moody, Evelyn Arceneaux, and LaVerne Dennis.

When Walter Adams was appointed to the faculty after his 1925 graduation, he became debate coach until Don Morris took over with the fall semester of 1930. Morris continued as debate coach throughout the decade of the '30s. During the first year under Morris, Comer Clay and C. W. Cecil were first team. Clay was later a long-time member of the faculty at Texas Christian University, and Cecil went on to become a major general in the United States Air Force. Other capable debaters were Elton Abernathy and Garnett Wilks. Wilks went into banking, and Abernathy became a faculty member of Southwest Texas State University. The *Prickly Pear* for 1931 gave notice of a rising young speaker: "Jack Pope did excellent work in both debating and oratory, won a majority of his debates, and represented A.C.C. in oratory. Although Jack is just a freshman, he certainly does put up good arguments." Representing the women that year were Willa B. Sloan and Margaret Wolf, both of whom received praise from the staff of the *Prickly Pear* for their work.

By the next year, Pope and Cecil had established themselves as the number one team. Abernathy and Jack Bates were strong. And a newcomer to the campus was Trine Starnes, who teamed up with Fred Crabtree. Starnes was destined to become one of the all-time campus greats in debate, oratory, and extempore speaking. He was also a capable editor of the *Optimist* in 1934-35 and president of the Students' Association. He dedicated his life to preaching the gospel. He was so effective in his chosen work that he and his wife, Malissa, are memorialized in the Trine and Malissa Starnes Center for Preaching and Evangelism in the south wing of the Biblical Studies Building. This helps emphasize that a continuing primary purpose of the College of Biblical Studies is to prepare gospel preachers for their work.

Other students who achieved notable successes in debate during the 1930s were Reuel Lemmons, Norvel Young, Batsell Barrett Batsell, Hope Reed, May Ree Harrison, Wanda Mayfield, LeMoine Lewis, Raymond Kelcy, Mardell Lynch, John Stevens, Gaston Cogdell, Nick Craig, Eugene Debs Smith, Elizabeth Nelson, Martha Copeland, Olive Jane Wilson, Burnya Mae McHam, and Dudley Faver, who went on to become a major general in the United States Air Force. The 1937 *Prickly Pear* reported, "John Stevens and Mardell Lynch started the season off by winning the Baylor University tournament, the largest debate tournament in the Southwest. This was something no other A.C.C. team had ever done." By the time 1939 rolled around, Don Morris, with increasing responsibilities, was ready to turn the sponsorship and coaching of debate teams over to an energetic and hard-working young faculty member, Fred Barton.

On the eve of the 1940s, the college community had said goodbye to significant leaders and some wrenching times. It now found itself with a flavored by a group of new members who would live up to the heritage left by strong, visionary trustees; a young, seasoned administration of Morris, Adams, and Smith; a pioneering, well-prepared faculty; an enrollment stabilized at about 650 dynamic, eager students; a new but unique, small campus; a sound financial statement; and a growing group of successful alumni and friends. The college was ready for the Morris years and the test of World War II and the post-war boom years.

CHAPTER FIVE

ADVANCING THE CHANGELESS

Don Morris began his work as president of Abilene Christian College on June 1, 1940. His inauguration was scheduled for the fall, but his work began in June. In government, officials must be sworn in – inaugurated – before they are empowered to act. In academe, however, a newly elected president normally assumes responsibilities of office several weeks or months before the big inaugural day. The custom has a practical side to it. The officeholder has an opportunity to test the water – and be tested – before going to the expense of an inauguration. But, when Don Morris took over and was inaugurated at Abilene Christian College, his tenure lasted for twenty-nine years.

Scant notice was given to the June 1 presidential transition in the local press, which was almost totally occupied with war news from Europe. By the time of the Morris move into the presidential office, Adolph Hitler, with his Nazi blitzkrieg, was on the way to liquidating France and completing the conquest of continental Europe. He had already annexed Austria and Czechoslovakia. He had defeated Poland, Norway, Denmark, Belgium, Luxembourg, and the Netherlands. He had a ten-year non-aggression pact with the Soviet Union. Italy was his ally. Spain and Portugal had fascist governments and were sympathetic toward the Nazis. Mussolini of Italy was planning to take over southeastern Europe, including Yugoslavia and Greece. Switzerland and Sweden were officially neutral. The United States was held back by its twin policies of isolationism and neutrality. Hitler was making plans for an all-out invasion of

Britain, the last nation on earth with the potential to resist him at that time. With the United States at war's door, the editors at the *Reporter-News* made a reasonable choice in giving little attention to the June 1 administrative change at Abilene Christian College.

However, when the time arrived for the official opening of the fall semester, September 11, 1940, ACC was page-one news again in the local press. Abilene mayor Will Hair greeted the record number of students, saying, "Whether you think so or not, the fact that this is a Christian institution, where the Bible is taught along with the arts and sciences, is a great asset to you. Ours is the only pure democracy left in the world, and its continuance depends upon the degree to which the people follow the Christian religion." Today, many would say that the mayor was politically incorrect in his statement, but he called it as he saw it in those days. Although he was not a member of the Church of Christ, he was a true friend of the college. He predicted that the new ACC president would be "one of the greatest the college has ever had" and added, "He has a big job this year in following James F. Cox, whom I consider one of the best men I have ever known."

Garvin Beauchamp was president of the student body for that year. He had been elected with a landslide vote of ninety percent of the students. His campaign platform was plain and simple: "I am 100 percent for Abilene Christian College and everything for which it stands." He followed the mayor at the podium and exhorted the incoming students to make the most of their opportunities. Robert C. Jones, a Wichita Falls minister and an alumnus, spoke to the new students on behalf of the Ex-Students Association. He said that he had preached in twelve states and had never visited a community where he did not find friends of ACC. Harvey Scott, minister of the College Church of Christ, urged the students to find a church home in Abilene. Board chairman Henry Free led the crowd in singing the traditional hymn, "All Hail the Power of Jesus' Name." Immediate past-president Cox read Paul's sermon on Mars Hill, and, after the prayer, the new president, Don Heath Morris, declared the thirty-fifth year of Abilene Christian College in session.

The next page-one story for the new administration was the official inauguration of the seventh president of the college. The occasion was Homecoming chapel, Saturday, November 9, 1940. An estimated throng of 2,000 crowded into Sewell Auditorium for the ceremony. The *Abilene Reporter-News* described the grand occasion:

> The trustees, members of the faculty, members of the graduating class of 1924, of which Morris was president, and those of 1923 and 1925 – his own college mates – and the members of the present student council followed the presidential party in a processional from Hardin Memorial Building into Sewell Auditorium to open the program.

Vice President W. R. Smith presided. Trine Starnes, class of 1935, led the prayer. Chester Kenley, class of 1924, read from the Bible. Henry Free led singing. Fred Barton, president of the Ex-Students' Association, spoke about the appropriateness of having the inaugural at the Homecoming chapel: "Since the beginning of this school more than thirty-four years ago, 9,000 men and women have moved through its halls as students, and seven men have served it as president. But not until now has a president been selected from among the ranks of its ex-students. It is therefore especially fitting that at this annual Homecoming of ex-students, the chapel program should be designed to do honor to that one of our number who has recently been so honored...." After Barton's address and singing by the A Cappella Chorus, directed by Leonard Burford, board chairman Free gave the charge to the new president, concluding with the admonition "to remember, strive for, and lead the faculty and students in the accomplishment of the great ideals for which Abilene Christian College has stood throughout the history of its existence."

Concluding the program was the speech by the new president. He spoke of the separate but interrelated roles of students, faculty, trustees, and patrons of the school, concluding with this admonition, which was from his heart:

> Here shall we have an institution where our sons and daughters may receive training in the arts and sciences and in those branches necessary for successful business and professional life, and at the same time have that which is transcendently more important, the stabilizing, inspiring, saving influences of

Christian teaching and associations. To this end let us today dedicate all that there is or shall be about our institution.

Morris was a natural for the presidency. Born on a farm near DeSoto, Texas, August 13, 1902, he came from pioneer Dallas County families on both paternal and maternal sides. Dallas County was organized in 1846. The Morris family arrived in 1849, and the Nance family in 1852. Grandfather David Nance's memoirs of the Civil War have been preserved for posterity in history professor Benny Gallaway's excellent book *The Ragged Rebel*. Nance was a strong believer in education. He did not have much opportunity to go to school while growing up, but after the war, he sat in on classes at Add-Ran College. He was not trying to earn a diploma; he simply wanted to learn. Later, his daughter, Annie Laurie, and her husband-to-be, Byrom Palmer Morris, attended Add-Ran. They became the parents of Don Morris.

So Don Heath Morris came from a significant background of belief in education, and not just education, but education with a Christian foundation. After graduating from DeSoto High School in 1918, he attended Thorp Spring Christian College from 1918 to 1920, graduating with junior college credentials and a teacher's certificate. After two years of teaching Latin and mathematics in Red Oak High School, near DeSoto, he came to Abilene Christian College in the fall of 1922 to complete his bachelor's degree. After his 1924 graduation, he signed on to teach history and speech and to coach debate at Abilene High School. He was a respected and popular teacher. During his four years at Abilene High, he had the privilege of teaching and coaching sons and daughters of leading Abilene citizens, who would themselves in time become community leaders. Such contacts helped solidify the good standing of Abilene Christian in the community.

During his first year at Abilene High, November 1, 1924, he married his college fiancee, Alberta Allen of Waxahachie. He early gave her the descriptive and loving nickname of "Team." He never did accept credit for accomplishments by himself. Leaving Abilene High School in 1928, he joined the faculty of Abilene Christian College to teach English and public speaking. When James F. Cox became president in 1932, he nominated

Morris as his vice president. From that time on, there was little doubt, if any, as to who would be the next president.

In addition to his formal college training, he had gained fund-raising experience, which is indispensable to a college president. In late 1929 and in 1930, he was coordinator of J. C. Reese's Ten Thousand Club, which was dedicated to locating 10,000 people who would pledge ten dollars each, payable over a three-month period, in support of the college. Modest though the goal was by today's standards, the task force fell short of 10,000 because of the Great Depression, but several hundred signed up regardless of the perilous times. Then, in 1934, when the Hardin annuity came through and it was essential to get a large number of pledges to assure the monthly payments to the Hardins, Morris was named to chair the drive, which was an overwhelming success.

Morris had the character, intelligence, speaking ability, personality, and energy to get things done. He had another characteristic in a super abundant measure. He was totally dedicated to Abilene Christian College. He did not neglect his family or the church; he simply neglected to take up hobbies. When an *Optimist* writer interviewed him during his first year as president, her concluding question concerned his hobbies. He thought a minute, smiled, and said, "Abilene Christian College is my hobby." That was the unvarnished truth.

He had a "Team" at home, and he put together a strong administrative team on the campus, individuals who believed in teamwork. W. R., for William Roy, Smith, a 1921 graduate of the college, became vice president. As a college student, Smith had studied for a year and a summer at the University of Texas and two years at North Texas State Normal College before transferring to Abilene Christian for his senior year. His master's degree was from the University of Texas. He went into school administration, as did many of the graduates of Abilene Christian in its early degree-granting days. His experience included serving as a public school superintendent and president of a public junior college. As vice president, he was in charge of campus property, publicity, and student workers, which was a real challenge. Without a superintendent of buildings and grounds, student labor was the resource used to maintain the campus. During the early war years, downtown businesses also had a great demand for student workers, which Smith coordinated. His experience in management and his great patience kept the college-business community relationship, which depended upon the punctuality and reliability of student workers, under control.

Walter H. Adams was an experienced dean with graduate degrees from two great universities, Stanford and Columbia. He was charged with overseeing the entire educational program. His expertise in dealing with faculty, students, accrediting agency representatives, people involved in teacher certification, and the many other intricacies of the educational program became legendary. He was called a "Dean's Dean."

Lawrence L. Smith had been running the bursar's office since his student days. He was responsible for the annual budgeted operational income and expenses, student accounts, and the negotiation of notes with students who were graduating but would have to have some time after graduation – maybe years – to pay their past-due bills. He was also responsible for the collection of notes.

James E. Freeman, the only non-ACC graduate in the administration, was in charge of the trustees' office, with the title of fiscal agent. He had oversight of college off-campus property, such as the Bennett ranch and the Luce and Chambers properties. He was also administratively responsible for sales, trades, and repossessions of lots in Abilene Heights and was custodian of funds in the trustees' office.

The Morris administration began with an all-time record enrollment. In the fall of 1940, 652 college students arrived on campus. That academic year was an outstanding one in spite of considerable anxiety about the war in Europe. In September, the Congress adopted the first peacetime military draft in the nation's history. The law called for the registration of all men between the ages of twenty-one and thirty-five for a year of military service within the United States. Numbers of students enlisted before being drafted, thus choosing their branch of service. The navy was the choice for many. The air force was not yet a separate branch of the military, but Naval Aviation and the Army Air Corps were options. And then Lubbock offered a special attraction.

Col. T. L. Gilbert was commanding officer of Lubbock Army Airfield. His daughter, Jacquelin, was a graduate of the college – class of 1939. Because the colonel was developing his command in order to turn out a large number of instrument-rated multi-engine pilots, he came to the campus to persuade a considerable number of young men to enlist before being drafted. He wanted them in his command because he believed Christians made good soldiers. Dozens of students enlisted. Some spent all of the war years in Lubbock, turning out pilots. Others, after a time, were given overseas assignments. Because a number of the recruits took brides, the Broadway Church of Christ in Lubbock, and no doubt other congregations, had a sudden augmentation of young couples. One faculty member – speech instructor Fred Barton – had already been drafted and was in the process of being assigned. Col. Gilbert made arrangements for him to transfer to Lubbock. So far as is known, the colonel was never disappointed in any of his Abilene recruits.

With war clouds building, enrollment for the fall of 1941 dropped seven percent from the previous year, which was not bad, considering the draft and the fact that many young men were volunteering. Then came the decisive blow. December 7, 1941, Pearl Harbor brought the United States officially into all-out war with as nearly unanimous nationwide support as had ever occurred. The *Optimist* reported student response:

> When the first news bulletin was flashed, Sunday, Boys' dorm was electrified. From the western, third-floor hall boys marched raggedly but spiritedly downstairs to the tune of, "You're in the Army Now." Scantily-clad figures dashed up and down the corridors, yelling, "Meet you in Tokyo."

> Reaction to hostilities in Girls' dorm was almost the reverse of that in Boys'. Every radio clicked on with the first report and remained on as coeds listened in stunned silence until late at night. Several girls with sweethearts or brothers in or near the fighting broke down.

After the declaration of war, the draft was expanded. The student newspaper tried to see a humorous side of the subject.

In the issue of February 13, 1942, a front-page, boxed article was titled "Draft Party Monday," which said:

Feel that draft?

All men who reached their twentieth birthday before December 31, 1941, and any who will not have attained their 45th by February 16, 1942, are respectfully invited by the United States Government to attend a function in their honor to be held in the auditorium from 7 a.m. to 9 p.m. Monday.

Presiding at the guest book will be J. E. Freeman, school fiscal agent, who will supervise and assist each 'guest' in the registration of such information as name, age, address, etc.

A birth certificate is not wanted.

This "party" is not just for students. Every man on the hill who meets the age requirements – including professors – is urged to attend ....

By the way, penalty for dodging the registration includes a penitentiary sentence."

Five hundred seventy-two students enrolled in ACU for the fall of 1942, and one year after that the number fell to 451. The war years were difficult years, but several steps were taken to deal with the enrollment decline.

First, in recognition of the fact that the smaller student body was mainly the result of the shortage of men, the men's dormitory, McDonald, was converted to a dormitory for women, and the men were assigned to the top floor of Chambers Hall. Since 1929, this floor had been reserved for some twenty young women each year who desired to do light housekeeping. That meant room on campus for twenty men instead of 150, and for 300 women instead of 150. The additional dormitory facilities for women helped keep enrollment at a reasonable figure.

Second, because income from student tuition and fees was off by about a third, it was necessary to step up fund-raising efforts. An all-out drive was made to pay off the entire indebtedness of the college. Although enrollment was lower, money out among the constituents during the war years was more plentiful than it had been for years. Never since its establishment in 1906 had the college been completely out of debt. So the administration and the board decided that if they were unable to recruit more students, they would at least recruit more money and pay off all indebtedness. Then, with the end of the war the college would be in condition to get students again. The result of that decision was that with all the disturbing news about wartime conditions, President Morris was able to report great news to the board in February 1943: "Let's have the good news first. We are out of debt. There is not an acre of ground or piece of equipment which the college owns which is not altogether free today of any obligation. The last note was paid last Wednesday. All of the bills of the college are paid up to date.... A conservative estimate would be that approximately 9,200 individuals have made contributions to Abilene Christian College within the past seventeen months." Never in the history of the college had so many people been involved in its support.

Third, a necessary step during the lean war years was a downsizing of faculty and staff, accomplished with as little hurt to employees of the institution as could have been experienced. Of the thirty-eight faculty members, several were granted leaves of absence for military service. Fred Barton became a lieutenant in the Army Air Corps, stationed in Lubbock. Coach A. B. Morris, head of the Physical Education Department, joined the navy as an instructor in physical education with the rank of lieutenant. A. M. "Tonto" Coleman, coach and instructor in the Department of Social Sciences, became a lieutenant in the Army Air Corps, teaching aircraft identification. Hosea Lewis, of the Physics Department, was named a regional supervisor with the Civil Aeronautics Administration. R. T. Clark, Biology Department, was commissioned an ensign in the navy. Dr. John Paul Gibson, who had served as college physician and professor of health education since 1933, resigned in 1943 to devote full time to his medical practice in Abilene. J. W. Treat, Department of Foreign Languages, went on half-salary while on leave completing his doctoral studies at the University of Texas. Maynet Thomas Baley, English, was granted leave of absence for health reasons. Mona Sieh resigned as a music instructor to accept an offer in public school music. Elizabeth Baxter, director of the

Extension Department, was given leave during 1942-43 and then resigned to take a government job. Her work was taken over by Dr. G. L. Belcher. In fact, most of the positions of men and women who were granted leave or resigned were assumed by remaining faculty members, who, with smaller classes, were willing to take on extra jobs.

Fourth, intercollegiate athletics was a casualty of the war. The last football game played during the fall of 1942 was the Homecoming game with Austin College. It was played Saturday, November 21. The Wildcats won, 53-0. Because of transportation problems and the draft, the Texas Conference schedule of intercollegiate athletics was canceled until further notice. The next football game was played at Homecoming, October 20, 1945. World War II was officially over. The game was with Tarleton, and the Wildcats "won a moral and statistical victory," but lost the game, 19-0, according to the *Optimist*. The last intercollegiate basketball game of the 1943 season was on Friday night, February 26, 1943. The Cats lost to Howard Payne, 42-40. The next intercollegiate basketball game was January 7, 1946, with Hardin College of Wichita Falls, and the Cats lost, 45-40.

Fifth, the 1945 Lectureship was canceled at the request of the Office of Defense Transportation. The request was "that all group meetings requiring travel for more than fifty persons and scheduled to occur after February 1, 1945, be canceled. It was bigger and better than ever the next year.

Sixth, during the war years special courses of study were added to serve the needs of the times. For example, Dean Adams reported several such courses as being offered in the spring of 1942: army paper work and shorthand, a speedup course in business administration; weaving and handwork in home economics; medical corps first aid and nursing methods in physical education; radio engineering and trigonometry in mathematics; and civil pilot training for ten students each semester.

Professor Hosea Lewis was the ground instructor for the pilot training. He was assisted by R. D. Tyler, who had already received a rating to teach ground school, but who took the course in order to get flight training. C. J. Collier coordinated flight instruction for ACC students. Ground school included eighty-five hours of instruction, and flight training involved forty hours of flying lessons. With President Franklin D. Roosevelt's request for American industry to turn out 50,000 airplanes per year, a great demand for pilots was foreseen, and the colleges and universities of America were expected to help provide them.

In the fall of 1940, the first group of ten students for the program was selected, nine men and one young woman, Annette Price, who later married Charles Mosman. Price passed and received her pilot's license. She spent the next eighteen months getting her degree while working in the bursar's office and as part-time secretary at the Abilene airport, building flying time, and, after graduation, getting married. At that time, the Army Air Corps was not yet ready for women pilots, but with her husband inducted into the corps and assigned to the Naval Air Station at Hensley Field in Dallas, she secured a secretarial job there. When her commanding officer learned of her pilot's credentials, he asked whether she might be interested in giving instrument training for pilots, using the new link trainer. Her response was, "Lead me to it." For several years she was busy helping turn out hundreds of instrument-rated pilots for intercontinental and transoceanic flights. Dudley Faver was another member of that first class. He went on to a career in the Air Force and retired as a major general. R. D. Tyler became a flight training supervisor in Oklahoma.

The military was claiming a large number of the men of the student body. In his semiannual report to the board in August 1943, President Morris stated that about eighty-five young men had withdrawn from school during the previous twelve months to enter military service. In spite of that, the twenty spaces in Chambers Hall were filled, ten men were assigned to the Bradshaw Apartments, which the college had rented, and others were being placed in private homes. The regular dormitory for women, Zellner, was totally occupied, and McDonald dormitory, which had been built for men but had recently been remodeled and turned over to the women, was comfortably filled.

In July 1944, President Morris wrote a statement for a brotherhood publication explaining the college's contribution to the war effort:

> Bonds and stamps have been on sale on the campus since the beginning of the war. A salary deduction plan for the purchase of bonds by ACC faculty members has been in operation since that plan was inaugurated by the government. This past year ACC faculty members invested between eleven and twelve percent of their total salaries in war bonds. This is all very little. What amounts to much is that approximately eight hundred ACC boys, four of them faculty members on leave, are in the Service. Twelve of them have given their lives in service to the nation; others are missing. The college is proud of these eight hundred boys. I have indicated such, many times, in chapel, in speeches in various parts of the state, and on at least one state wide radio hookup. Our nation is engaged in a gigantic effort to subdue lawless men and nations on the earth. All should cooperate wholeheartedly and fully in this great task.

The position taken by the college and its president during World War II was in line with that adopted by President Sewell and the college during World War I.

The girls of Cadettes, a social club, with their sponsor, Mrs. G. C. Morlan, adopted as a project the preparation of a service flag, six feet wide and eight and a half feet long. On a background of white, bordered by red, a blue star was mounted for every student and ex-student who was involved in the military service during World War II. Mrs. Morlan prepared the flag. The Cadettes affixed the stars. Each name was given a number, and with that number, the star for that individual could be located on the flag. When word of the death of a person in service came to the registrar's office, that information was passed on to the Cadettes, and a gold star replaced that particular blue star.

By the time the war was over and the latest information was assembled, 1,088 stars were mounted. Forty of them were gold. These numbers do not necessarily represent all students and ex-students who were involved in the war. It is understandable that the registrar's office possibly did not receive word of all alumni in military service. According to the records of the Jennings Museum, the gold star list on the service flag included these men: Elbert Alvis, Joe W. Boyd, J. W. Burns, Raymond Burroughs, Ray DeBusk, Dan Finch, Lloyd Freeman, Ted Hale, Edwin Hampton, Harold Haun, Freeman Holly, Robert Hornbaker, Al Hunter, C. W. Johnson, R. B. Kendrick, Robert King, James Emmett Lee, Dudley Lemmon, C. D. "Sticks" Lovelace, John Middleton, Glen "Cy" Moore, John D. Moore, Bruce Munday, Wyatt Oliver, Homer Osborne, Austin Parrish, Earl Proctor, David Pursch, Reginald Reynolds, Henry Roberson, David Rose, Charlie Scarborough, Gene Allen Scruggs, Paul Sherrod, William Smith, Hulen Stromquist, Oliver Wyatt, Charles Yates, Gene Young, and Nick Young.

The flag hung in Sewell Auditorium so that every day students, faculty, and guests attending daily chapel, and every Sunday, the hundreds of people assembling for services of the College Church, were reminded of classmates and alumni who had served. When Moody Coliseum was opened in February 1968 and became the location for daily chapel, Sewell was scheduled for remodeling. The service flag was removed and stored in the president's office. When the Women for ACU opened the Jennings House Museum across the street from the campus in 1966, the flag was placed on a wall of the museum, where it has been a major attraction. In 1998, the flag was taken down for some needed repairs because it was showing the ravages of a half-century of exposure. Plans are to encase it in plexiglass or some other protective covering and mount it in a permanent location.

Each of the forty gold stars could be the subject of an essay, but these biographical sketches about two men represent the group in this book.

Paul Sherrod Jr., of Lubbock, was killed in Leyte in December 1944. He had been a student from 1939 to 1942. On his body was found a clipping from an *ACC Bulletin* printed in 1943 and reprinted in the *Optimist* of November 26, 1943. The article was a message the college hoped students would learn. The fact that Paul carried the clipping with him into battle shows how deeply students can be influenced by their years on the campus. Author of the article was Max Leach, and it was titled "The Promise of Abilene Christian College to

Its Students of the Past, of the Present, and of the Future." It read:

> Since the past is gone, and the future is yet to be, this promise is to you, student of the present.
>
> Believing first that the Christian life is the only life to be lived, I will do all that is in my power to help you to live as a Christian.
>
> Believing that the greatest characters that have ever lived are the humble, the serving, the unselfish, I will do my best to inspire you and to educate or mold your life around these qualities.
>
> Believing that you are average, rather than a genius or a moron, I will devote most of my attention to you, and will plan my work for you and will exist for you.
>
> Believing that not riches, nor power, nor worldly glory, nor fame, nor pride of life constitute success or contribute to the happy life, I will not try to make of you a stuffy intellectual or a learned snob, but will give you an education that is useful in the living of a life among men, and towards spending eternity on the banks of the River of Life.
>
> Believing that you are an individual, having your own hopes and fears, abilities and limitations, talents and defects, I will treat you as such – loving you, cherishing you. You will not be just a number or a name in my roll book.
>
> Believing that your soul is precious in the sight of God, I will aid your development as a Christian and cause you to be well-pleasing to him.

Gene Allen Scruggs, another casualty of the war, was the son of Coach and Mrs. Guy Scruggs. He grew up on the campus. When he began the first grade, he was in the Abilene Christian Training School, and he never went to school anywhere except on the Abilene Christian campus. He was a junior in the college when he was drafted. He had been in the Army seven and a half months when he was killed in action April 1, 1945, just inside Germany near the Remagen bridge. He was nineteen. In Dr. Paul Witt's remarks at a memorial service for Gene Allen in Sewell Auditorium, Witt read from a small Bible that Scruggs had with him when he was killed. In it was an outline of a talk he had made to a church near Fort Leonard

Wood, Missouri, where he was stationed before being sent overseas during the waning days of the war in Europe.

The war would not last always. While it was going on, the Morris administration worked diligently to prepare for the future. In an early report to the board, the president estimated that he had been absent from the campus from one-third to one-half of the time. Since gasoline rationing limited travel by automobile, he utilized travel by railroad, bus, and an arrangement called the "travel bureau," which requires some explaining. Every day, the local newspaper, and no doubt newspapers everywhere, carried in the classified section notices under the heading "Travel Oppor." Notices would read, for example:

"AAA Travel Bureau: Share expenses plan. Late model cars to all points daily. Ph. 2-9123."

"Going to Houston. Want two passengers. Call 9349."

"WANTED: ride to San Antonio, Corpus. Saturday night or early Sunday. Call Mrs. Crider, 6226."

"Three passengers wanted to Williamsburg, VA. Ph. 6727."

"WANTED: Three passengers to Sioux City, Iowa. Leaving Monday p.m. 418 Jeannette."

No doubt about it, the travel bureau plan was an economical way to travel. The passengers were diverse sorts of people. A not infrequent problem was with some who wanted to drink while they rode. Morris told about riding in the back seat with two men who apparently were friends. One was drinking rather heavily and fell asleep. His billfold fell out of his back pocket, and his buddy helped himself to a five-dollar bill. By the time they arrived at their destination, the inebriate was awake. Before getting out of the car, Morris, with his big voice, spoke authoritatively to the thief: "Give this fellow his money." The thief, who pretended to be such a good friend to the drinking man, protested that he did not have the man's money, but Morris said, "I saw you take it and I'm saying, 'Give it back.'" The miscreant sheepishly handed over the five.

Another such incident is related by Morris' daughter Jackie Warmsley:

> Again, three men were packed into the back seat with Morris in the middle. One of the men kept taking a bottle out of his

pocket for a nip. Morris was watching him but not saying any-thing. Finally, the man asked him, "Are you a preacher?" The answer was "No." Shortly, the man, aware of the Morris expression of disapproval, asked, "What do you think I ought to do with this whiskey?" The answer was, "If I were you, I'd throw it out the window." The man chuckled and said, "I'm not that drunk."

These stories demonstrate that a college president had to be thoroughly dedicated to his work to put up with such means of getting around to see friends of the school and enlist their support. The work paid off. Hundreds of new friends were gained and old ones strengthened.

One of the early steps Morris and Jimmy Freeman took was to make a deal with the Farmers and Merchants National Bank, now the First National Bank, for a line of credit so that, barring extreme emergencies, it would not again be necessary to miss or delay a payroll. After all, faculty and staff members of the institution were working for modest compensation to begin with; they should not have to do without. With the number of friends increasing, and with finances in better shape, it was no longer such a risky proposition to make short-term loans at the bank.

Plans were made for the new science building. In 1929, the commitment had been firm that the chemistry shack would be temporary, but a decade and a half later it was still in use. During the war, building was impossible because materials were unavailable. But preparations were underway for construction of two projects just as soon as possible. A science building and a dormitory were truly needed. The dormitory could be for either women or men. If for women, the men would get McDonald back. If for men, the women would keep McDonald. As things turned out, with the end of the war, enrollment zoomed up so rapidly that the women kept Zellner and McDonald and got the new dormitory and still were short. The men were housed for a number of years in wooden army barracks and in apartments and in spare rooms on the Hill. But they were housed, and the institution grew.

Don Morris saw it coming. His report to the Board of Trustees in February 1945 was made while the war in Europe still raged and while plans were being made for a massive invasion of Japan. He reported that college enrollment for the 1944 fall semester had been 485. For the spring semester which was currently under way, enrollment was 443. In September when the board met for its semiannual session, the war was over. Registration for the fall semester of 1945 showed a total of 614 college students, with late registrants still arriving. His analysis of the registration revealed an interesting situation. Of the 614 students already registered, 329 were freshmen. During the peace years, 1929-40, the average freshman class constituted forty-two percent of the total student body. If the size of the freshman class in coming years should remain that large, an enrollment of approximately 800 could be expected. Housing would become a problem because the college had only 320 dormitory spaces on campus, and housing in Abilene Heights was strictly limited. The Great Depression had struck just as the subdivision was being marketed, and during wartime construction had been virtually impossible.

Another problem was identified. Of the 329 freshmen, there were 214 women and 115 men. Historically, the apportionment had been about half and half. The young men were still in the process of being released from the service. Morris presented the board with a carefully reasoned scenario, reminiscent of the old debate coach helping his charges develop their cases: "This means that if conditions change so that the boys can enter school, as they undoubtedly will, and if other conditions remain as they are, and if future freshman classes are only the size of this fall's freshman class with the boys added, and if the proportion of freshmen and upperclassmen should remain constant, we should have a thousand college students within the next two or three years." Lest somebody should point out that Morris undershot the mark – enrollment within three years was closer to 2,000 than 1,000 – let it be said that the old debate coach always advocated taking the conservative side in making forecasts and estimates, or, in fact, in running the college.

The trustees could have decided to set a ceiling of, say, 650 students, which was the highest prewar number, and insist on being an exclusive private institution. Some schools did that.

But that was simply not the thinking of the Morris administration or the Board of Trustees. Having laid the groundwork, Morris now presented the challenge: "Large additions in facilities must be provided before the fall term of 1946 or it will be impossible to accommodate the students for that semester! In order for additional dormitory space to be had by the fall semester of 1946 construction should begin within the next few weeks."

With the wholehearted cooperation of all elements of the college community – board, administration, faculty, alumni, and students – activity and accomplishments during the next twelve months were almost unbelievable.

The science building was the first permanent structure to be built since the campus was opened in 1929. The official ground breaking ceremony for it took place June 12, 1945. Dr. Paul Witt turned the first spadeful of earth. It was not finished by the time school opened in September 1946, but, as the *Optimist* pointed out, classes were able to move into nine "not entirely completed" classrooms to "the tune of hammers." Before long, the scientists had their dream building, which has been added to and improved over the years.

Construction of the new dormitory for women was begun January 4, 1946. It was not ready for occupancy when the students arrived in the fall of 1946, but it was ready the next fall. With an all-time record enrollment in 1946, the girls doubled up. In McDonald and Zellner, with approximately seventy-five rooms each, designed for two to the room and preferably one, with two small closets to the room, four girls were assigned to each room, with four bunk beds in place. *The Optimist* ran a picture of one of the rooms, with this descriptive sentence: "The four sardines squeezed from left to right are: Vell Dagnell, LaJuana Payne, Mary Margaret Crowder, and Nell Borch." Hence, the 220 or so girls who would have been assigned rooms in the new dormitory, had it been ready, were simply doublebunked. They put up with such arrangements because they were young, excited about having friends, and hoping for better things ahead. Also Abilene girls were not allowed to live in the dormitories that year. Even though they had looked forward to being away from home and "on their own" in the dormitory, they would have to wait another year. But they spent a good deal of time visiting in the dormitories, which made the four-person rooms sometimes even more crowded. Study, obviously had a better chance in the library.

All the male students who showed up in 1946 were accommodated, as Leach described in *Like Stars Shining Brightly:*

> Frantically, the college sought for rooms and more rooms to keep this vast overflow of students. People who had never before been landlords rented out a room and sometimes two rooms. Faculty members with space in their houses or garage apartments could make almost as much out of rentals as they made out of teaching. The whole hill became a beehive of rooming houses....

Another phenomenon which would provide housing for men and many other so called "temporary solutions" for the college began in 1945 and continued into 1946, making the campus look somewhat like a military post. With the closing of Camp Barkeley, twenty miles southwest of Abilene, a large number of buildings became available. Because of the indefatigable work of Don Morris and some trustees, ACC became the recipient of apartments for 170 couples, rooms for 400 single men, and cottages for thirteen teachers and their families. In addition, sizable buildings were obtained for classrooms, teachers' offices, a maintenance facility, and a miscellany of other purposes. The college would finance the moving but would be reimbursed by the Federal Public Housing Administration.

Then came the job of physically moving the buildings from Camp Barkeley to the ACC campus. Leach gave details of the process: "The wheel horse on this job was vice president W. R. Smith. He had to do as much finagling on his end of the deal as president Morris did on his. There were highway right-of-ways to be secured for moving of the monstrous buildings; telephone, telegraph, and electric wires to be raised and lowered; an army of carpenters to be secured – all kinds of problems, piling helter-skelter on each other. J. E. Freeman, fiscal agent of the college, handled the business end of the projects."

Milton Fletcher tells about the night watchmen for the project. When he was a student, W. R. Smith hired him, Chris Clark, Chet Bogle, Dan Cabe, and A. C. Greene as night watchmen for the Barkeley materials in early 1946. After discharge from the military, they were set to resume studies that fall. Smith hired them to do duty from dusk to dawn seven days a week to guard the mass of materials hauled in from Camp Barkeley. There was not any place to store the materials except on the campus grounds. Some buildings were whole and others had been cut into two or more parts and were waiting to be set on foundations and reassembled. There were doors and windows, lavatories, commodes, urinals, sinks, pipes for plumbing, electrical wiring, light fixtures, and stacks of lumber. These materials were strewn about the campus as if a tornado had hit. A great pent-up demand on the part of the public for building supplies made all of the materials piled onto the campus a temptation to nighttime marauders. The five veterans were assigned the job of keeping them away. Each man was armed with a billy stick, a flashlight, and mosquito repellent.

McKinzie dormitory was under construction, and the basic framework was in place. One of the five men, taking turns, was always on watch from the top of the unfinished dorm. Intruders could take only one street from town out to the Hill, East North Thirteenth, which at the railroad track became College Drive. The watchman on the wall could easily see over Sheriff Burgess' young pecan trees the headlights of traffic heading toward campus. He would alert his colleagues on the ground, and they positioned themselves to meet the midnight or early morning visitor. The watchmen had no firearms, but the visitor did not know that. A flashlight shining in one's face and an authoritative veteran's voice inviting the visitor to vacate the premises was invariably effective. The midnight visitors traffic was light but heavy enough to keep the watchmen on their toes and to convince the college administration that they were needed. By the fall of 1946, the Army buildings were mostly ready.

Three decades slipped by before the last of the barracks was removed. They served a noble purpose. In no way could the school have accommodated the thousands of students who came in the postwar period without them. Life in the men's barracks, the married couples' barracks, and the hutments is good today for stories told to children and grandchildren. Charles G. Anderson of the class of 1955 gives a good description of life in the plywood hutments, which were located where the McGlothlin Campus Center now sits. He and Margie Newhouse were married between semesters in February of his senior year. As Charles says, they did not have the money or time to go away for their honeymoon, so they were married in the chapel of the College Church and drove around the campus to their hutment. He described their new home: " ... A hut was divided into two rooms with plyboard. The bed filled up one whole room with a small bathroom adjoining it. We could sit at our dining table and reach the refrigerator, stove, and just about any place in the room. We had a small couch on one side. We covered our hut with morning glory vines in the summer of '55. Other students liked to slip up to the side of a hut and slap on it really loud to awake anyone sleeping. This was done especially when they knew honeymooners had moved in. When the West Texas wind blew, the huts would shake, and we feared they would blow away. In the spring, when the thunderstorms and tornados came, we usually abandoned the huts and went to the dormitory or Administration Building until the storm passed over." The Andersons were going to college on the G. I. Bill. When their first son was on the way, they moved into an apartment. That son, Dr. Charles G. "Chuck" Anderson Jr. is now a distinguished Abilene physician. No wonder he is a success; he got his start in an ACC hutment.

Dean Adams accomplished the greatest work of his academic administration in his recruitment of faculty during the enrollment explosion of the post-World War II years. From an official enrollment of 481 in 1944, the student body surged to 673 in 1945, a forty percent increase, and to 1,453 in the fall of 1946. This was an increase of one hundred fifteen percent over the previous year and three times the enrollment of just two years earlier. The dean was making telephone calls, writing letters, and sending telegrams to people far and near, looking for prospective teachers. He had help from the president, the vice president, and department heads, but his was the primary responsibility for securing faculty. He called upon preachers and elders of churches and alumni and friends to help in the search for teachers. He studied transcripts, read reference letters, and personally interviewed nearly all of the teachers who were interested in considering a faculty position at ACC.

In addition to seeking men and women with the proper academic credentials, he was looking for faithful Christians. As a professor whose classes had always attracted students, he was looking for teachers who could communicate, who could have a positive and helping attitude toward students, and who could wholeheartedly support the mission and purpose of Abilene Christian College. His success in building a strong faculty helped guarantee the continued growth of the student body through the years. By the time of his retirement from the dean's office in 1969, some 3,026 students were enrolled for the last full year of his administrative service.

A survey of teachers who came and stayed at least ten years and who were recruited from 1945 through the year 1968-69, will remind alumni of some of the greatest teachers in their academic careers. They are listed here year by year:

1945 – Orval Filbeck, education, and Bill W. Davis, music.

1946 – Garvin Beauchamp, physical education; Dewey Davis, agriculture; Floyd Dunn, chemistry; Oliver Jackson, physical education; Catherine Kenley, education; Chris Kyker, dramatic arts; Rex Kyker, speech; Haven Miller, foreign language; Ruth Rambo, business; JW Roberts, Bible; Mima Ann Williams, English; Marie Wilmeth, home economics; and Woodrow Wilson, Bible.

1947 – John Anderson, music; James Burrow, history; T. W. Colby, agriculture; Clara Mae Ellis, English; and E. D. Shelton, English.

1948 – F. M. Churchill, agriculture; Orbie Grimsley Gilbreth, education; Mary Hale Harlow, library; Donice Hawes, home economics; A. Z. Hays, education; Lena Hays, math; John P. Lewis, Bible; Lowell Perry, speech; Bellah Philpott, English; John Stevens, history; Norman Whitefield, art; and Roy Willingham, biology.

1949 – Lewis Fulks, speech; LeMoine G. Lewis, Bible; Bill McClure, physical education; Frank Pack, Bible; Kenneth Rasco, English; and J. D. Thomas, Bible.

1950 – Gaylan Collier, speech and dramatic arts; J. R. Endsley, biology; Gay Golden, library; L. D. "Bill" Hilton, business; Keith Justice, agriculture; Frank Rhodes, history; Ralph Smith, history; and Heber Taylor, journalism.

1951 – Holbert Rideout, Bible.

1952 – James Culp, English; Overton Faubus, business; and J. C. McCurdy, business.

1953 – Douglas Fry, band and music; Robert Johnson, Bible; and Paul Rotenberry, Bible.

1954 – Weldon Barnett, education and psychology; Edward Kirk, education; Callie Faye Milliken, library; Zelma Odle, English; Carl Spain, Bible; and M. D. Williamson, industrial education.

1955 – John Bradford, chemistry; Eugene Clevenger, Bible; Bill Decker, Bible; George Ewing, English; Dwain Hart, physical education; Charles Marler, journalism and mass communication; Luther Marsh, psychology; Joe Marshall, English and golf; Bert Mosier, industrial education; Martha Mosier, business administration; Jerry Mullins, health, physical education, and recreation; Dee Nutt, health, physical education, and recreation; Thomas Shaver, history; and Jayne Whitaker, English and speech.

1956 – Clyde Austin, psychology; Weldon Bennett, Bible; Edward Brown, speech; Norris Campbell, psychology; Sally Cauthen, chemistry; Ima Clevenger, speech; Earl Clevenger, business administration; William Fryer, psychology; Clinton Hurley, English; R. L. Johnston Jr., Bible; Russell Lewis, education; Lila Nutt, health, physical education, and recreation; Chapin Ross, speech; Everett Taylor, library; Les Wheeler, health, physical education, and recreation; and William Wright, business administration.

1957 – James Bradford, math; Paul Faulkner, Bible; Vernon Moody, music; Kathryn Taylor, library; Martha Tipton, music; Bob Whitaker, English, psychology, and social work; and Ray Whiteside, education and psychology.

1958 – Brent Green, art; Charles Coleman, speech; Mina Coleman, music; Benny Gallaway, history; Neil Lightfoot, Bible; Tommy McCord, chemistry; Roy Shake, biology; and Gerald Wilson, biology.

1959 – Troy Caraway, art; Joyce Curtis, physical education; M. L. Daniels, music and assistant band director; Alvie Davis, chemistry; Beatrice Speck, history; and Henry E. Speck Jr., religious education.

1960 – Rollie Blondeau, music; Don Drennan, assistant business manager and business administration; S. E. McReynolds, math; and Woodard Robbins, math.

1961 – Carl Brecheen, Bible; Gene Evans, math; John Little, biology; Mae Robbins, business administration; Harold Wilkinson, education; and Willie Wilkinson, history.

1962 – Tony Ash, Bible; Everett Ferguson, Bible; Don Lewis, chemistry; Earle McMillan, Bible; Eva Thompson, home economics; and David Williams, English.

1963 – Jerry Drennan, industrial education; Martha Gaines, health and physical education; Tim Mason, agriculture; Ron Rathbun, music; and Ben Zickefoose, health and physical education.

1964 – B. J. Humble, Bible; Burl McCoy, health and physical education; Talmage Minter, art; Clark Potts, journalism; Joe Spaulding, history; Bonnie Walker, library; and George Walton, English.

1965 – Dwight Caughfield, math; Edwin DuBose, agriculture; Edwin Enzor, Jr., speech; Preston Harper, English; Bennett Hutchinson, chemistry; Troy Mark Jones, foreign language; Gary McCaleb, business administration; John Robinson, history; and Ludene Slatton, English.

1966 – Juanita Avinger, education; William H. Avinger, education; Ina Green, psychology; Harold Lipford, education; David Merrell, English; Marianna Rasco, home economics; R. L. Roberts, Jr., library; and William Clark Stevens, biology.

1967 – Curt Dickson, physical education; Emma Sue Findley, English; Chantrey Fritts, education; George Gurganus, Bible and missions; David Hughes, math; Beth McLeskey, physical education; Wilma Marshall, English; Thomas Olbricht, Bible; Margie Pistole, business administration; Waunette Shaver, education; Ted Sitton, physical education; Gary Thompson, government; Douglas Warner, business administration; and Kenneth Williams, biology.

1968 – Leroy Baker, business administration; Jack Boyd, music; George Carter, English; Pauline Dunn, music; Marian Hurley, English; Jeannette Lipford, music; Forrest McCann,

English; Don Smith, physical education; and Charles Trayler, music.

1969 – Donald Altman, business administration; B. E. Davis, mass communication; Addie Felts, physical education; E. Milton Findley, education; Ed George, music; Charles Ivey, physics; Loreta Kelley, home economics; Jimmy Rix, business administration; and Cleddy Varner, physical education.

The Texas Conference was officially reorganized at a meeting in Dallas on Saturday, December 8, 1945. Lt. Cdr. A. B. Morris was out of the Navy and back on campus, prepared to resume duties as athletic director, head coach of basketball, and head of the Physical Education Department. Capt. Tonto Coleman was released from the air force and was ready to resume coaching track and football and teaching classes in history and government. While the subject of coaches is under consideration, it should be said that Capt. Fred Barton had completed his air force assignment and was prepared to teach his classes in the Speech Department and coach debate.

Through the years, the college was fortunate in having strong men as chairmen of the Board of Trustees. When the board was constituted in 1906, J. P. Sharp was president pro tem long enough to see T. G. Moore added to the board and elected president, as the office of chairman was called at the time, except in the minutes. Moore served until May 1911. At that time M. Zellner took the gavel and was chairman until his death in 1916. Then came J. S. Arledge, who held the post for sixteen and a half years. He steered the board through the years of the move to the new campus and the launching of Abilene Heights as a subdivision and then through the first three and two-thirds years of the Great Depression.

J. E. McKinzie was next, from February 1933 until February 1936. Those were trying years, with the school threatened with foreclosure. It was saved from that possibility by the Hardin gift.

After the turbulence of the McKinzie era, which was not the fault of any one person or any group of persons, W. H. Free held the reins for six years. He was a calm and steady leader. He could look back over those years with pardonable pride when he wrote his final report to the board:

> It has been my privilege to serve as a member of the Board of Trustees ... since the beginning. Of the original five charter members, I am the only one left. For many years I served as your secretary. Then in 1936 you elected me as your president. At that time the future of the college was very uncertain. There was not only a lack of harmony in the board but bitter internal strife. This, together with the external forces working against the school, plus a large indebtedness ... made for a dark picture indeed ....
>
> Today, gentlemen, that picture is different. Today the board of trustees ... are unified in their efforts to see that the school shall continue to serve our boys and girls. There is the utmost harmony and friendship between the members. And apparently all the external forces which would do harm to the good name of the school have been silenced and the people, especially members of the church, are coming to realize more and more the need for Christian education. Today, the campus, with all of the buildings and equipment, all of the lots and acreage which the college owns near the campus, are free of debt – a condition which has not existed since its beginning.

The last sentence of W. H. Free's final report to the trustees was, "So let us all work together in peace, harmony and Christian love."

Free was succeeded by E. D. Chambers, who with his personable but strong-willed wife, Julia, was one of the most generous and stalwart supporters of the college. Chambers chaired the board just one year, from February 1942 to February 1943. In January 1945, Mr. and Mrs. Chambers added to their generous record of giving to the college by donating from their savings out of a lifetime of farming and ranching $140,000. Of that amount, $65,000 was to go toward costs of the new dormitory for women – provided the college raised from other sources $60,000, which was done – and the balance was to be kept as endowment for the Bible Department and missions. Mr. and Mrs. Chambers, who had no children, died within a week of each other in July 1945.

J. B. Collins, Big Spring businessman and an ex-student of the college from the Sewell days, was the next chairman, 1943-47. A gift of land he and his wife made to the college was a crucial factor in the accreditation endeavor.

After Collins, B Sherrod of Lubbock, a trustee for thirteen years, was elected chairman and held the post for twenty years, 1947-67. B Sherrod was a large and impressive man, six feet three inches tall, healthy, and possessed of boundless energy. He was successful in business, an elder of the Broadway Church of Christ, and he fitted naturally and comfortably into leadership roles. As a youth he had attended Gunter Bible College for a time and was sold on the idea of Christian education. After one year as chairman, he told his fellow trustees that either they would have to elect a new chairman or he would have to sell his business interests and devote full time to the work of building the college and the church in Lubbock. The board reelected him chairman, and he went about the work of disposing of his businesses.

So began the Sherrod-Morris partnership, a time of incredible growth and solid undergirding of the institution. A principal contribution of Sherrod to the program was his insistence that while the college would never look down on modest donations, a great deal of time would have to be devoted to soliciting large gifts – big money. This kind of work took time and patience. To be sure, there had been some large gifts – the Bennett ranch and the Hardin and Chambers gifts, for example – but such were needed in much greater numbers. And that was the area in which he wished to work, along with the president.

In this new initiative, Charles Damron, city manager of Childress, Texas, was employed to be director of development. There had been fund raisers earlier in the history of the school, but the plan now was to establish a development office and go about cultivating prospects in a systematic, well-organized way. Damron came on board in January 1948. Joyce Whitefield was appointed director of alumni files and development records. She began developing information about great numbers of people and their areas of interest.

Sherrod, Morris, and Damron began a campaign of traveling across Texas, visiting alumni and church and business leaders. They came to the conclusion that the college needed the services of a firm that specialized in the business of helping charitable institutions organize development programs. They came up with the name of the John Price Jones Company of New York, which had been in the business longer than any other company in the nation and had a reputation as tops in the field. A visit to New York by the three resulted in contracting with the Jones company to work with Abilene.

The Abilenians were quite surprised when the man sent to West Texas by the Jones company was an Englishman by the name of James Powell-Tuck. There was some doubt as to how this would work out, but not for long. "P-T," as he soon came to be called, began intensive interviewing of board members, administrators, faculty, and a selection of students to get the feel of the place. As a member of the Church of England, he was not accustomed to the informality of chapel, but he liked it. He was a stern taskmaster. As Damron said in a Lawrence Smith interview, "He had to have a good secretary. He had spitfire speech and speed, and he wanted everything done correctly and when he asked for it, not five minutes later." So Damron employed a young Englishwoman by the name of Betty Tomkins, later Mrs. Ray Whiteside, as the secretary. Betty Whiteside could keep up with anybody. She later served as secretary to Dean Adams and as administrative assistant to Presidents Stevens, Teague, and Money, and in 1998 is still on the job.

While Powell-Tuck, Damron, and Whitefield were building staff and files and soliciting trustees, administrators, faculty, and, yes, students, on the assumption that outsiders cannot be successfully approached until the insiders show their faith in the cause, Sherrod and Morris were approaching major prospects. One of the first was a big-time West Texas rancher.

On a Sunday in June 1947, President Morris and Chairman Sherrod scheduled a meeting in San Angelo of friends from southwest Texas. Twenty or so men responded. After church services, they went to the Cactus Hotel for lunch with alumnus host Chester Kenley of San Angelo. After lunch, Sherrod and Morris outlined needs of the college and spoke of the development program that was in the planning stage. The guests were asked for the names of prospects whom the chairman of the board and the president might visit. In the discussion, one name came up that was to lead to one of the largest gifts in the history of the school. Toward the close of the meeting, Houston Burcham, a businessman from Fort Stockton, spoke of a man he had known about ten years who had large land holdings about fifty miles southeast of Fort Stockton. He was an elderly bachelor, a virtual recluse, but he might become interested in ACC. His name was William M. "Bill" Edwards.

A quarter of a century later, at a luncheon at which Houston Burcham was recognized, along with some others who helped bring representatives of the college and Mr. Edwards together, Don Morris reminisced:

> I remember very well that morning, just as the church service started, I noticed Houston Burcham, patron of the college and businessman from Fort Stockton, walk in. He had driven 163 miles to come to the meeting, and that impressed me. There was a lot riding on that drive by Houston Burcham that day.

The next month after the San Angelo meeting, Sherrod and Morris drove to Fort Stockton to see Burcham. They found him at his feed and seed store and invited him to go to see Mr. Edwards with them. He told them more about Edwards, but said he thought it would do no good for him to go with them. He said that he really was thinking that Edwards was not a prospect, and he did not want to be responsible for wasting their time and money in seeing him. They assured him that they were prepared to take their chances, and so he wished them well. They found Edwards at his ranch house, sitting under a chinaberry tree. Morris said, concerning that tree: "I have read of the Charter Oak in Connecticut, a shrine of liberty, but for Abilene Christian College, I'll take that chinaberry tree in Pecos County, where we first shook hands with William M. Edwards on that sunny afternoon."

Edwards was sitting out of the hot July sun on a small wooden bench he had made. Sherrod and Morris stood and talked with him for about fifteen minutes. Sherrod led the way by telling him that they had not come to ask him for a donation but wanted to give him some information about the college and its students. The visit was brief. Edwards gave no indication of any interest, but he invited the two gentlemen to come to see him at any time. It was difficult for Don Morris to conclude the visit and leave without any kind of solicitation, but he did. Of course, when he returned to Abilene he wrote Edwards, thanking him for his courtesies and expressing the hope to visit again. And he put him on the list to receive literature.

They went back to visit him in October, finding him too busy to see them this time. He apologized and invited them to come again. So within two months, they tried it again. Thereafter, during the next seven years they called on him ten or twelve times. They learned of his work habits. He would arise at four in the morning and work until about two in the afternoon. Then he would sit in the shade and rest and read for the balance of the day. He had a good library. Morris wrote concerning his books: "The walls of his room were lined to the ceiling with them." That room is worth describing. The ranch house was occupied by a couple who had helped him on the ranch for years, Mr. and Mrs. Nieves Subia, a Mexican couple. Edwards lived in one room. It was octagonal in shape and had walls of concrete. In addition to his books lining the walls floor-to-ceiling, he subscribed to a number of magazines, including the *Saturday Evening Post* and *National Geographic*. He kept his files of the old *Literary Digest*. He kept up pretty well with world affairs. He enjoyed reading Zane Grey's western novels and had a set of *Encyclopedia Britannica*, which he consulted regularly.

Over the years, the three men became good friends and discussed a number of topics, but there was not much talking about his estate. In his autobiography, *Is It Worth It?*, Sherrod tells about the first glimmer of light after seven years of visits:

> On the next trip we made to see him, he did tell us that he had no heirs that he wanted to leave his holdings to, as they lived differently from the way he lived, and in some prior years there had been some hard feelings on [the part of] some of the members of some of his family. Therefore, he did not feel obligated to leave them anything. That was the very first encouragement we had from him, as we felt he would leave it to someone and it may as well be to the college.

One event that changed the picture somewhat was Edwards' January 2, 1953, purchase of an additional ranch, 13,118.7 acres of land, to add to his existing holdings of

28,721 acres, making his ranch properties total 41,839.7 acres. Morris always chuckled when he told of the time he asked, "Would you mind telling us how much land you own, Mr. Edwards?" Slowly the answer came, "Well, it's about 41,839.7 acres." He had always paid cash for land, but this time he incurred an indebtedness of $295,750, which was a sizable debt for a seventy-six-year-old man to incur. However, he had an abundance of collateral for the debt. He had for many years said that his goal was to own 100 sections of land free of debt. This new purchase made his holdings nearly sixty-six sections – two-thirds of his goal. He needed to pay the indebtedness with no delay. Payments were to be $22,500 per year, plus interest.

This new land, known as the Mitchell ranch, included a palatial rock house which J. C. Mitchell had built. It had 5,900 square feet of floor space, twelve rooms, walls fifteen inches thick, and a tile roof. In 1968, when Sherrod wrote his book, he estimated that replacement cost would be $225,000. He was probably conservative in his estimate. It had a rock fence around it, built of the same type of stones that were in the house. Edwards moved from his octagonal room to the new ranch headquarters, but he used only two rooms, leaving the rest of the house for his ranch foreman and wife. Furthermore, he kept a tarpaulin on his bed in the new house. It had been his cover for so long, why change? It was two years after he moved into the big new house before he had electricity from the Rural Electrification Administration brought in. His explanation to Sherrod and Morris was, "It wasn't economical, and lanterns had done the job well for me in the past." He had a telephone installed, but never answered it. In two years he used it only twice. Both times, he was calling for a truck to come and get the wool that was ready. He was truly a pioneer.

The new purchase provided an opening for negotiations. Sherrod told the story:

> In 1954, after we had visited Mr. Edwards some seven years, off and on, and not pushing him, but letting him make up his own mind what he wanted to do, we asked if he would be interested in deeding the ranch to us, and his retaining a full life estate, if we would pay him $25,000 per year to help get the ranch paid out while he lived.

240 – Advancing the Changeless

The laconic reply was that he would think about it.

A few days later, the two men were back at the ranch and asked him if he had thought about the proposition. Without hesitation he replied that he had thought about it a lot. He said that if they could make the offer $50,000 per year, he was ready to trade. Sherrod replied that they would have to get approval of the Board of Trustees, but they would not let much time pass before getting him an answer. With unanimous approval of the board, the deal was made. On December 15, 1954, Edwards deeded to the college his entire land holdings, including all of the minerals to which he had title, while reserving a life estate for himself. In return, the college agreed to pay $50,000 each year, beginning December 15, 1955, on the principal of the indebtedness, and would continue to pay that amount annually until all indebtedness was eliminated. For his part, Edwards would pay the interest and continue to enjoy all income and pay all expenses in connection with the operation of the ranch.

The deed was recorded in both Pecos and Terrell counties. The original was placed in the college's vault, where it is today. The college made payments on schedule – $50,000 on December 15 of 1955, 1956, 1957, and 1958. As far as anyone connected with the college knew, everyone was satisfied with the deal that had been made, including the Edwards nephews and nieces. Indebtedness on the land was rapidly reduced. Edwards was able to continue living just as he had lived before the deal was made. Then, in October 1958, he suffered a stroke and was never able to speak again. The County Court in Fort Stockton recognized a nephew as guardian, and the couple moved into the ranch house. The first indication that all was not well came when the guardian leased the entire ranch for an unreasonably low price, with an option for a long-term renewal at the expiration. The county judge recognized the lease as valid. College officials realized that if such a lease were allowed to stand, they had wasted $200,000 on the deal. At any rate, it was decided that until the matter of ownership of the land was cleared up, the college would make no more payments on the indebtedness.

Edwards died June 9, 1959. Family members who had moved in on the ranch refused to vacate the premises; hence, the college had to sue for possession and to revoke the "sweet-heart lease" that had been executed. The case was in the courts for several years. Family members, who had not said anything against the deal during the almost four years that had elapsed between his deeding the ranch and his stroke now claimed that their uncle was of unsound mind and that he had been unduly pressured by the representatives of Abilene Christian College. Sherrod described the courtroom scene:

> Statements were made before the jury that President Morris and I were two of the biggest liars, crooks, wrongdoers, taking advantage of an old man, and robbing the heirs of their just dues, and many a statement that was hard to take without doing anything about it.
>
> On one occasion when it had been extremely bad, after the judge had called for a 15-minute rest, I walked to his desk and asked him, in a rather loud voice, what the fine would be just to batter in the faces of the lawyers. He said not to do anything in his court but wait for them outside. I never did do anything, but my Irish blood sure did boil when they got so rough on us.

The college lost the case at the district court level. Jurors ruled that Edwards was of sound mind but had been subjected to undue pressure. Sherrod said that in talking with some of the jurors later, he was told that they just did not want to see the property go to the college. The case was appealed to a higher court. Some friends of the school thought the college should compromise and settle the case out of court, but members of the Board of Trustees were convinced that Edwards had known what he was doing and had done what he wanted to do. Because he was dead, the college had a moral obligation to defend his right to do what he had wanted to do with his property. This was a lesson that was not lost for others who had in mind willing or deeding estates to ACC. It helped them know that, after they were gone, the college would be faithful in trying to see to it that their decisions would be respected.

The Court of Civil Appeals for the Eighth Supreme Judicial District of Texas rendered its decision on September 23, 1961. The entire estate went to the college. The family member who had been recognized as administrator of the estate was ordered to pay all court costs, and the administrator was ordered to pay the college rent for the time that had elapsed since the death of Edwards.

The estate was placed in the permanent endowment fund of the college. From oil and gas leases and cash bonuses for those leases, payments for seismographing damages, grass and hunting leases, and, in recent years from natural gas production, the estate has produced some $8 million as endowment income. In addition, more than $3 million has been added to the endowment fund from sale of land. The university still owns 10,040 acres of the original estate. The Edwards estate has helped make it possible for Abilene Christian University to grow and serve students from around the world.

While the Edwards story was ongoing, other significant gifts came in response to Sherrod-Morris contacts. For example, there was the Mabee Foundation of Tulsa, Oklahoma, and Midland, Texas. During the 1930s, Sherrod had traded a business he owned in Big Spring for a nine-section ranch in Reagan and Upton counties and soon acquired five more sections, making his landholdings about 9,000 acres. In the early 1950s, Sunray Oil Company of Tulsa took an oil lease on the ranch. One day, while Sherrod was in Tulsa, trying to learn when the company was planning to drill, he visited with Paul Taliaferro, general counsel and executive vice president of the company. In the course of their conversation, he mentioned the work he was doing with Abilene Christian College. Sherrod told of Taliaferro's response:

> He asked why we did not go and see the Mabee Foundation and Mr. Frank Stickle. He told me they had a lot of money to give away and that the Mabees' foundation was one of the richest in the state of Oklahoma…. Dr. Morris and I made a trip to Tulsa in a few days and had a luncheon date with Mr. Stickle, who was chairman of the Mabee Foundation. We told him of our desires and needs – a boys' dormitory. He said, "Why not a girls' dormitory?" We told him we had to take the boys' dormitory away from the boys and give it to the girls, and now the boys had nothing but the old Army barracks and we needed it for a boys' home. He said without too much more talk, "I see no reason why we can't do that for you; we have made most of what we have in West Texas."

In short order, a formal application was made, and the Mabees agreed to send their contractor, Al Ward, to Abilene to superintend construction. The foundation paid all costs except the architect's fee, landscaping, and furniture. The result was Mabee Dormitory, built to house some 312 residents, which was ready by the fall of 1953. In October of that year, for the formal dedication of the dormitory, Mr. and Mrs. Mabee, along with the foundation trustees and Paul Taliaferro, flew in from Tulsa. Mabee spoke in chapel and, with his sense of humor and words of wisdom, made a hit with the students. The Mabee Dormitory gift was the first of a series. John Mabee died in 1961, but his nephew, Guy Mabee, Guy's son, Joe, and other directors of the foundation have continued as generous benefactors in connection with virtually every building project on the campus.

A short time after the first Mabee gift, a dormitory just like Mabee Dorm was built and named "Edwards" after the great West Texas rancher who had given so much to the college he never even visited.

Farms and ranches were the main sources of development of Abilene Christian College during the twenty years of B Sherrod's board chairmanship. He spoke the language of farmers and ranchers. He never tried high-pressure tactics. He never begged. He did not speak from a standpoint of desperation. He simply told the story of Abilene Christian College, what was happening, and what was needed. People he visited trusted him. He and Don Morris were an incomparable team. Sherrod at six feet three and Morris at five feet eight, stocky of frame and with a deep and pleasing voice, got the attention of the high and mighty and of people of low estate. The results spoke for themselves.

Some humorous stories came out of their thousands of miles of travel together. For instance, once they spent the night in Fort Stockton, which had only one available motel room. They always arranged for a single room for each, but on this occasion, they had to sleep in the same room. About midnight, Sherrod called the office and asked the desk clerk about any possibility of another room. The clerk asked abruptly, "Are you fellows having trouble?" Sherrod explained that his colleague was snoring so loudly he could not go to sleep. The clerk expressed regrets but assured him that all the spaces on the premises were occupied, whereupon, Sherrod dressed, left the room quietly, and got in his car to try for a nap. Sometime later, Morris awoke, saw that he was the only occupant, went outside and found Sherrod trying to sleep in the car. After considerable discussion, Morris persuaded Sherrod to go into the room and take his turn in the bed, and Morris spent the rest of the night in the car. They vowed never to repeat that night. They traveled in the same car but could not sleep in the same room. Sherrod usually drove the car; anybody who ever rode with Morris understood.

Once in Washington, D. C., they walked past the Blair House. President and Mrs. Truman and guests were staying there while the White House across the street was being refurbished. Secret Service guards stood on duty, with their dark suits, white shirts, and frozen features. Sherrod, in his friendly West Texas fashion, gave a wave of his hand and said, "Howdy, fellas." They were visibly taken aback, but after a moment's hesitation, returned his greeting with slight smiles. Another time, when they were in New York City, they went to a symphony concert. Sherrod was weary and could not, he thought, keep from squirming. Suddenly, a New Yorker sitting behind him, commanded in a loud voice, "Sit still!" Sherrod, who was seldom intimidated, vowed that he froze in place throughout the rest of the program.

Sherrod's habit of forthrightness occasionally brought him trouble, such as the time Don and Alberta Morris spent the night with B and Ezzie Sherrod in their spacious home at Lake Buchanan – the home in which every room had a large window looking out onto the beautiful lake that came up to the backyard. During breakfast the next morning, Sherrod made the comment, "I declare, Mother, I believe you didn't have your usual good luck with the biscuits this morning." Mrs. Morris had to admit she had made the biscuits. The Morrises and the Sherrods were such good friends that they all enjoyed a good laugh – except the embarrassed B.

Gifts, primarily of land, continued to come. For instance, Sam Hardwick of Lubbock left the college in his will a section of good wheat land southwest of the city. Mr. and Mrs. John W. Catchings of New Mexico gave a ranch in return for a five percent annuity. The ranch was valued at $120,000 and sold for $135,000. Mr. and Mrs. Walter Williams lived near Lubbock. Sherrod told about meeting them:

> One time I stopped by their place and was invited into their home. I had not been there very long until I mentioned the college to them and about what and how we might be able to work out a deal with them. He replied that they had been talking only the night before about what they were going to do with what they had, as they wanted it to go to some worthy cause.

The upshot of that visit was a 200-acre farm that sold for $500 per acre cash.

Among other ranches donated to the college were the Shelby Green property in New Mexico, the Joe Bozeman lands in Reeves and Lamb counties, and the F. E. and Martelia Gardner properties that have produced millions for the endowment of the school. Other members of the Board of Trustees also worked in behalf of the college. J. H. Richards of Fort Worth was the key man in introducing Mr. and Mrs. W. O. Carter of Fort Worth and Godley to the college. For many years, the Carters operated in downtown Fort Worth a cafeteria, which specialized in delicious home cooking. They bought land with their earnings, and their gifts to Abilene Christian were generous indeed.

By the 1950s, the time had ripened for the college to seek membership in the Southern Association of Colleges and Schools. This accreditation had been on the agenda throughout the Baxter and Cox years and the first decade of the Morris years, but was not a challenge during most of the Sewell years because no regional accreditation agency was in operation. During Sewell's early years, a Texas college with credits acceptable to the University of Texas, or, toward the end of the period, to the Association of Texas Colleges and Universities, was considered accredited.

By the 1920s the regional accreditation movement replaced state accreditation. Colleges and universities of a region set up an association, standards, and an accrediting procedure handled by the educational establishment itself rather than leaving it up to the government. Hence, the nation was divided into regions, with each region to accept the list of accredited institutions of the others. The Southern Association of Colleges and Schools covered Alabama, Florida, Georgia, Kentucky, Louisiana, Mississippi, North and South Carolina, Tennessee, Texas, and Virginia. Standards were high. Dean Cox and later Dean Adams made a point of attending annual meetings of the association. They took part in workshops and business meetings and, over the years, developed a good working relationship with educators and administrators from all eleven states of the group.

For years, Abilene Christian was on the approved non-member list of the Southern Association. So far, so good, but that was not enough. Graduates of the college applying for admission to graduate school at Harvard, Stanford, Columbia, Vanderbilt, or other universities often found they were admitted only on probation. If a student could do the academic work, probation was not particularly bad, but it did not help one's self-image or respect for the educational institution from which he or she had graduated.

Principal barriers to accreditation were lack of endowment, an insufficient number of faculty members with doctoral degrees, and inadequate faculty compensation. Until 1946, a problem area was the pitiful facility for chemistry. In spite of the fact that Paul Witt and associates were turning out an amazing group of outstanding scientists, the old Chem Shack with its cracks in the floor, fire hazards, and too many other inadequacies to mention, had been a major concern. But the new science building had remedied that deficiency. Furthermore, the faculty was being strengthened, and compensation was better. The main problem was lack of endowment.

A great asset came along after the end of the war. James Bryan "J. B." Collins of Big Spring had served on the Board of Trustees since 1933 and was board chairman 1943-47. In the early days of World War II, he acquired thirteen acres of vacant land adjoining an airfield under construction on the west side of Big Spring. In haste for housing for its new base, the military built 162 apartments on the Collins land and then notified him that condemnation proceedings would get under way so that the government could buy the land from him. Collins wrote the federal judge in whose court the process would take place that he did not desire to sell the land but would grant permission for the government to use it as long as necessary. Consequently, plans for condemning the property were abandoned, and a lease for one dollar per year was arranged.

With the end of the war the military turned the property over to the Federal Public Housing Authority. The FPHA was making arrangements to destroy the housing and return the land to the owner. In his Lawrence Smith interview in 1976, Collins said that he learned the government was making such housing in some places available to educational institutions. He asked President Morris whether the college might be interested in the facility as rental property and received the expected enthusiastic affirmative answer.

Morris and Sherrod went to Washington to check into possibilities. At the FPHA, they were told that in building such facilities, and thereby competing with private enterprise, the government promised communities that it would raze the buildings when the emergency ended. However, the ACC men were told that if they could get support from citizens of Big Spring for preserving the property, the government could go along. It was suggested that they should obtain letters from the Big Spring Chamber of Commerce and civic clubs. Because the city was experiencing a housing shortage, securing the letters was easy. Armed with the letters, Morris and Sherrod went back to Washington, and with the invaluable aid of Speaker Sam Rayburn, West Texas Congressmen Omar Burleson, George Mahon, and O. C. Fisher, and the new but influential Texas Senator Lyndon B. Johnson, legislation was passed by both houses of Congress and signed by President Harry Truman authorizing the transfer. The very day the college received title, the Korean conflict broke out, and all subsequent transfers were frozen. Sherrod and Morris were just in time.

The government let the housing stay rather than tear it down, and J. B. Collins gave the land, valued at $1,000 per acre, to the college. The project was called "Ellis Homes," was appraised at $603,524, and was promptly assigned by the board to the endowment. In the president's report to the board September 25, 1950, he announced that the new addition made the total endowment principal more than $873,000. He added: "It is believed that the net income from Ellis Homes will amount to approximately $27,000 each year. This will make our endowment income from invested endowment approximately $49,000 per year and will leave $35,000 in living endowment necessary to meet the Southern Association endowment requirements.

He added that the Alumni Association had asked for the privilege of raising the $35,000 per year and that the Abilene Christian College Foundation would guarantee the funds. He admitted, however, that the foundation's guarantee might not be acceptable to the Southern Association. As the situation developed, he was correct in that assessment. The foundation did not have the assets to guarantee the living endowment income.

B Sherrod and J. C. Rigney, another Lubbock trustee, stepped in. After the college was voted in as a member of the Southern Association, December 6, 1951, the board voted this resolution of appreciation during its meeting of February 18, 1952:

> resolved: That the Board of Trustees of Abilene Christian College go on permanent record as being deeply appreciative of the generous act of brethren B Sherrod and J. C. Rigney and their wives in pledging one-half million dollars worth of real estate to guarantee the endowment of the college for three years. We recognize this liberal act as the decisive factor in our being elected to membership in the Southern Association of Colleges and Secondary Schools.

According to the records, their guarantee did not cost the two men the properties that had been set aside. Alumni and friends of the school came through. But their guarantee represented total trustee commitment. Morris spoke of the instrument by which the guarantee was made and the reply of the chairman of the Southern Association visiting committee, "I see nothing wrong with this, and it looks to me like you're in good shape."

When Sherrod retired as chairman of the board, February 20, 1967, he and his wife were honored by the entire ACC family. the *Optimist* ran a two-page spread with text and pictures. One photograph was of the Sherrods and the Morrises. Another showed Morris and Sherrod in academic regalia with the Sherrod's daughter, Wildring B – Mrs. Bryan Edwards – between them. Another showed Sherrod and F. O. Masten of Sudan, whose story will unfold later. Don Morris was quoted: "Sherrod has given more time to ACC and other institutions like it than any other man I know. As chairman of the board he has given more time, and at his own expense – he's never been paid a dollar for anything he has done for the college. At the time of the Edwards trial in Fort Stockton, he spent seven weeks of his time there."

February 21 was declared Sherrod Day on the campus, with a grand luncheon and praises and expressions of appreciation. Members of his family were present: his wife, Ezzie; his daughters, Wildring B and La Wanda – Mrs. Louis Murfee – and some grandchildren. The *Prickly Pear* for that year was dedicated to him. A full-page photograph was opposite a page of large print, written by one of the student editors.

> In dedication to B Sherrod: Abilene Christian College is what it is today because of your personal dedication to the cause for which it stands. In 20 years as chairman of the Board of Trustees, you have seen and helped the College grow as never before. This spring the number of graduates alone will approximately equal the College's total enrollment when you became a board member in 1933. This year's graduates will receive their degrees virtually in the shadow of buildings under construction – mute testimony to your effective working for the physical growth of the College. Here, on the eve of a new era, you have chosen to retire as Chairman of the Board. Dedication like yours will be an example to us, our children, and our children's children.

In 1973, when apartments designed to accommodate 224 students were built in what had once been known as A Club Park, the entire area was designated Sherrod Residential Park. These apartments have been occupied at capacity since their opening. When the Don H. Morris Center was built a few years later, the major southeast wing was set aside as the Sherrod Hall for Family and Consumer Sciences.

Sherrod was succeeded in 1967 as board chairman by Willard Paine, class of 1948, the first alumnus of the college to serve in that capacity. Paine was president of the First State Bank of Monahans. He fitted comfortably into the leadership position to which he was elected by his fellow trustees. He was in office for the transition of the college presidency from Don Morris to John Stevens in 1969.

The student enrollment expanded dramatically in the immediate postwar years, 1945-48. In the fall of 1946, head count of enrollees jumped to 1,453, more than double the previous year's number and three times what it had been just a year before that. The president and dean searched diligently for qualified faculty. The vice president and fiscal agent feverishly worked to provide housing, classrooms, and faculty offices. The bursar staffed the business office to serve the lines of students paying bills or trying to make financial arrangements.

In the fall of 1947, 1,649 students enrolled, and the next year 1,689. Of that number, 554 were veterans attending on the G.I. Bill. A widely held assumption was that enrollment gradually would drift back to, say, 1,000, but still ahead of peak prewar years. In a report to the board in February 1949, Dean Adams presented a paper quoting national studies of probable future college enrollments. He cited indicators that enrollment would likely level off as the veterans finished their work but that by 1960 increases would occur again. He concluded with the opinion of many people that whether the enrollment would increase was a moot issue, but that the important question was "How many students do we want?" He continued,

> There is a wide difference of opinion on this point. There are those who believe that we should admit all who want to enroll and strive to provide the necessary facilities for them. On the other hand, there are those who believe that we should decide on the number of students we can best serve and limit our enrollment to that number. Each plan has its advantages and disadvantages.

The question was laid before the board. Because the charter required all board members to be members of the Church of

Christ and residents of Texas, a vote for enrollment limits stood little chance. Church members and Texans were expansionists to the core. Board members were willing to set academic and other requirements that might preclude the admission of some students, but they were not disposed to set an arbitrary limit. Probably most trustees agreed the situation would take care of itself with the decline of the number of veterans to be served. This position seemed validated when only 1,547 students signed on in the fall of 1949, a decline of 142 from the previous year. During the next two years, the slide continued partly because of the Korean conflict. Thereafter, the upward trend set in again, and the Board of Trustees came to know that expansion of permanent facilities and endowment on a hitherto undreamed of scale would have to take place if the demand was to be met.

Dean Adams, other academic leaders, and the trustees soon responded to the post-World War II enrollment expansion and new and varied needs of a larger student body with the addition of four departments and a school – agriculture, industrial arts, psychology, journalism, plus the graduate school by 1955.

In 1944, the Department of Agriculture was established. This step was taken in response to a growing demand, which received enthusiastic support from the Board of Trustees, many of whom came out of the world of farming and ranching. H. W. Gist was employed to head the new department. With bachelor's and master's degrees from Texas A&M, he had been a vocational agriculture teacher for nine years and had then moved to Kingsville as professor of agriculture at the Texas College of Arts and Industries. He was chairman of a State Committee for Postwar Planning for establishing young men in farming. He also chaired the State Lone Star Committee for Farming. He had impeccable credentials. The board even authorized the fiscal agent to buy materials and build a residence for the chairman of the Agriculture Department. It was indeed a spacious house.

To show unusual support for Gist and the agricultural operation, Mr. and Mrs. S. N. Allen gave the college a farm located diagonally across the highway from the existing 100-acre farm situated north of Zellner Dormitory and representing the undeveloped portion of Abilene Heights. The Allen farm comprised 114 acres. The board voted to approach Mrs. Xenia Miller concerning buying back from her the entire tract that had been turned back to her in 1932. This did not succeed. The L. P. Bennetts made a cash donation of $5,000 toward operational expenses of the farm. Numerous donations of property and livestock, as well as cash, were made to the program. The Agriculture Department was indeed launched with genuine enthusiasm.

But something went wrong. Nine months after Gist began his work with ACC, this notation was entered into the minutes of the Board of Trustees: "The resignation of H. W. Gist, head of the agriculture department, was announced and received with regret." After further discussion, this resolution was adopted unanimously: "That brother Gist be given an opportunity to withdraw his resignation provided he will agree to work harmoniously with the personnel of the college and under the direction of the Agriculture Committee. If he does not wish to withdraw his resignation, it will be accepted as of July 1, 1945." Gist apparently made amends. He continued his job through the 1945-46 academic year. Leroy Fry was employed as farm manager, and enrollment in the new department was good.

When the summer of 1946 arrived, the administration and the board had had enough. Although Gist offered to stay, provided he could have a contract for five years, he was notified he would not be retained. Dewey Davis, superintendent of schools and teacher of agriculture at Seminole, Texas, accepted the post as head of the department. T. W. Colby joined the faculty in 1947. F. M. Churchill came in 1948. J. Keith Justice was added in the 1950s. Since 1946, when it was provided offices in one of the Camp Barkeley buildings called the "Ag Annex," the department has functioned effectively and now is housed in the refurbished Zona Luce Building as the Department of Agriculture and Environment. The department operates some 900 acres of land as laboratory. It is staffed by a strong faculty with doctoral degrees in various fields of agriculture and the environment. Dr. Glenn Davis is chairman.

In 1953, the Department of Industrial Arts came along. Owen T. "Skipper" Shipp was the first chairman, and, for the first year, the only teacher in the department. A war surplus building from Camp Barkeley was moved from the site on which the new dormitory for men was to be built and remodeled into a home for the new department. The catalog statement introducing the department read, "The department is well-equipped with new machinery, new hand tools, and every effort is made to keep up with the changing materials and methods." In 1954, Delwin Williamson joined the faculty, and the next year, when Shipp moved over to the Development Office, Bert Mosier and Gerald Jackson were hired. Courses offered included woodworking with hand tools and machines, mechanical drawing, engineering drawing, and crafts, and the department graduated students ready to teach industrial arts in public schools.

One of the most enthusiastic students in this popular department was Mrs. Don Morris. She had natural talent for woodworking, and with the courses she took, she became adept at turning out beautiful pieces of furniture and other items. In 1959, her oldest grandson, Jimmy Lawson, had knee surgery and had to use crutches for a while. He was twelve. The Morrises had eight younger grandchildren, who were so interested in using Jimmy's crutches that they became quite a nuisance to him. For Christmas that year, their grandmother made eight pairs of crutches, a pair to fit each child. The Morris clan had a unique Christmas season with nine grandchildren crutching around the house and neighborhood. The younger ones would not go anywhere without them.

The department is now known as Industrial Technology, which offers computer-aided drafting, flight training leading to the private pilot's certificate, manufacturing technology, electronics, engineering drawing, and an array of sophisticated and highly developed subjects. Dr. Jerry D. Drennan succeeded Williamson as chairman, and present chairman is Dr. James Clinton Cooke.

Psychology was another program that grew its way into being a full-fledged department in the postwar years. Psychology had been a part of the Education Department for years, but in the 1953 catalog, its separate status was recognized, with a suggested curriculum for psychology majors and with Dr. Max Leach as the first chairman. Today, with eleven faculty members, all with the Ph.D. degree, it is one of the departments most in demand with some 200 majors. Chairmen since Leach have been Norris Campbell, 1966-70; Ray Whiteside, 1970-77; Ed Headrick, 1977-95; and Robert McKelvain, since 1995.

Journalism became a new department of the college in the mid-1950s. From 1923 through the spring of 1951, two courses in journalism had been taught regularly in the English Department. Beginning with the fall of 1951, several new courses were added. Heber Taylor was hired as instructor, and it became a division of the English Department. By the fall of 1955, it had grown to the extent that it became a separate department, with Taylor as the first chairman. Reginald Westmoreland from the *Dallas Times Herald* was added as an instructor. The catalog said of the new department, "The field of journalism probably exerts more influence on the American people than any other, save possibly education and religion." Hence, the decision to offer a major in the field.

By the early 1960s, the teachers and the administration did not agree about the amount of support the department needed, and Taylor and Westmoreland left for other universities. Journalism was once more, for a time, a division of the English Department, and broadcasting was a division of the Speech Department under Dr. Lowell Perry. In 1967, Charles Marler, Dr. Chapin Ross, and Clark Potts proposed a new mass communication program combining journalism and broadcasting within the Speech Department. Dr. Rex Kyker, head of the latter department was interested in the national trend to change "speech" to "communication." So, in 1968, the department, which had been Public Speaking when Don Morris taught, became the Communication Department. In 1969 Dr. Burl Edward Davis became director of the mass communication division in the department.

By 1988, because of the rapid growth of the entire field of communication and the size and complexity of the Communication Department's programs, the mass communication division became the Department of Journalism and Mass Communication, with Dr. Charles Marler as chairman. Today, this department offers six programs for undergraduate students – advertising and public relations, broadcast journalism, electronic media, journalism, photojournalism, and religious journalism – and a master of science program in digital media. The department publishes the semiweekly campus newspaper, the *Optimist*, which has won the All-American rating of the Associated College Press every year since 1975. The university's annual, the *Prickly Pear*, is a publication of the department. During the last dozen years, it has earned the All-American award from the Associated Collegiate Press five times. The department also operates radio station KACU-FM, the local public radio outlet with a signal that reaches listeners within seventy miles or so. Finally, the department manages, in conjunction with the Abilene Independent School District, a television station, KUF-TV7, which can be received on campus or by off-campus people who are on the Abilene television cable system or on the Heartland satellite TV system. Opportunities for hands-on experience abound for students in the Department of Journalism and Mass Communication.

During the meeting of the Board of Trustees in February 1952 – the meeting at which official notice of accreditation was given – the board authorized the appointment of a committee to study pros and cons of beginning a graduate school. One year later, the committee made its report and recommendation. The report pointed out that many graduates, especially in the fields of preaching and teaching, had for years expressed a desire to continue with graduate studies after completing bachelor's degrees at Abilene Christian. Also, numerous graduates of state universities had expressed a desire to do graduate work at a Christian college. Hence, the committee recommended that, beginning with the summer session of 1953, courses leading to master's degrees in two areas be offered. Those fields would be Bible and education. The Graduate School would have a modest beginning, but could grow to meet future needs. Minors would be available in business administration, English, mathematics, modern languages, music, natural science, social science, and speech.

The recommendation of the committee received unanimous approval of the board. At a signal from President Morris, staff members began passing out copies of the Graduate School catalog, which had already been printed in anticipation of a favorable vote. It would have been interesting to see the disposal procedure for several hundred newly printed catalogs if the board had happened to turn down the committee recommendation, or if some cautious member had recommended a year's delay in implementing the matter, and if such a recommendation had been approved by the majority. The president may have been accused of "jumping the gun," but he knew that if the program was scheduled to begin with the summer of 1953, and approval was not gained until February 1953, he needed graduate catalogs ready for distribution immediately.

The decision to establish the Graduate School proved to be a success. For the first three and a half years, it was administered by Dr. Walter H. Adams, dean of the college, assisted by Rex Kyker, who, as director of the Summer School, became also director of graduate studies. The Graduate School grew steadily so that it was soon apparent that a full-time dean was needed. Dr. Fred J. Barton was named to that position in February 1957. Dr. Kyker replaced him as head of the Speech Department.

Concurrent with Barton's appointment came the announcement that the graduate program would be expanded to include the fields of biology, chemistry, mathematics, and physics. Throughout Barton's tenure as dean, 1957-72, followed by Floyd Dunn, 1972-84; Bruce Evans, 1984-88; Dwain Hart, 1988-89; Clint Hurley, 1989-91; Carley Dodd, 1991-98; and, beginning in 1998, Dr. Angela Brenton, graduate programs have continued to grow until at present some 700 students are enrolled in the Graduate School. Master's degrees are offered in thirty-four fields. The largest number of graduate students is found in biblical studies and missions. Other majors, in the order of popular demand, are education, psychology, organizational and human resource development, marriage and family therapy, business administration, and communication.

The only doctoral program offered to this point is the doctor of ministry degree.

The fiftieth year of Abilene Christian College was celebrated throughout the academic year beginning in September 1955. Theme for the year was "First Things First for Fifty Years." It was printed on the cover of the college catalog. It was echoed on the cover of the *Prickly Pear*. It was the subject of *Optimist* articles and editorials. Chapel speakers referred to it. In one of his most memorable chapel speeches, Rex Kyker concluded with the exhortation that the theme should not stop with fifty years, but should be extended to "First Things First Forever." The fiftieth year began with a record enrollment. For the first time the number of students surpassed 2,000, reaching a total of 2,213.

Four major construction projects were being completed as students arrived. First was the north wing of the Administration Building, known as the Bible Building. The Bible Building was paid for by the time it was finished. Total cost of the building, including furniture and campaign costs, was about $370,000. Of this amount, five gifts ranging from $15,000 up to $125,000 accounted for eighty percent of the total. Three of these were gifts of real estate which were sold and the proceeds used for the building. These three gifts were all in exchange for annuities, which meant that the college had a continuing obligation for a limited period of time. But the people at ACC had learned how to handle annuities since the days of the Hardin gift in 1934. One donation was a gift of securities, and one gift was a cash bequest. These five larger gifts had been made primarily because of contacts by Morris and Sherrod.

The drive for remaining funds needed was led by a committee consisting of John Banister, minister of the Skillman Avenue Church in Dallas; Reuel Lemmons, editor of *The Firm Foundation* in Austin; and Norvel Young, minister of the Broadway Church in Lubbock and later president and chancellor emeritus of Pepperdine University. Staff person for the campaign was a young man who was getting his start in fund raising. His name was Bill Teague. Preachers all over the Southwest helped contact people about the need. They and 7,200 donors put it over the top. President Morris was particularly pleased with these donations. He told the board, "The results of the campaign go far beyond the amount of money subscribed. I believe that it has made hundreds of new friends for the college, who will mean much to the school for many, many years."

The other three buildings – a dormitory for 312 men, a dormitory for 210 women, and a cafeteria – introduced a new dimension into the procurement of facilities to serve the ever-growing enrollments at Abilene Christian College. They were financed in another way. The federal government was making long-term, low-interest loans to colleges and universities for housing and cafeterias. This grew out of the national commitment to provide education for veterans of World War II. It was also intended by the mid-1950s to help veterans of the Korean conflict. But before veterans could be admitted to colleges and universities, those institutions had to have room to take care of them. Therefore, the Congress appropriated funds to be used by the Federal Housing and Home Finance Agency in making forty-year loans bearing interest at the rate of three percent to institutions that submitted proper applications. Buildings financed in this way could be used for all college students, not just veterans. But the need to serve veterans helped start the program.

The Board of Trustees, in a called meeting June 22, 1954, voted to apply for financing for the two dormitories and a cafeteria. Applications were prepared and filed, and the total package was approved. A bond issue was required because the law stipulated that the bonds were to be offered for sale to private investors first. If any private investor could beat the government's rate of three percent for forty years, the best bid would get the bonds. Only after the private enterprise system had had its chance would the government step into the situation and offer to buy the bonds. The government got the bond issue.

Shades of 1929! Abilene Christian College was going into another bond issue after what had happened during the years 1929-34. Two main differences, however, guided the trustees. First, the entire campus did not have to be mortgaged. A first mortgage was placed on the project itself and the site thereof. Then a first lien was placed on the gross revenues of the dormitories and the net income of the cafeteria, but as long as payments on the bond issue remained current, problems would be avoided. Second, the college had a great many more friends – including people of wealth – than was the case in 1929-34. However, the overriding reason for going into another bond issue was the determination to avoid turning down any young man or woman who met scholastic and character requirements for admission. The government loan was the quickest way to achieve what needed to be done. The loan covered all construction costs, architect's fees, landscaping costs, and interest during construction.

A great deal of construction during the winter of 1954 and the spring and summer of 1955 made for happy disruption of campus routines. Three contractors were at work. B. F. Horn Construction Company of Abilene was low bidder on the men's dormitory. Rambo Construction Company of Fort Worth won the contract for the women's dormitory. Work on each of the dormitories was underway by November 1, 1954. Rose Construction Company of Abilene was awarded the Bible Building contract on January 25, 1955, and started work immediately. Rose also got the cafeteria project and began work in March. The fervent hope was that all four buildings would be ready by the time the golden anniversary year of the college would begin in September. None of the four was finished by September although all four were nearly ready.

The status of the Bible Building meant that classes scheduled to meet in it would have to be shifted to the College Church building and Sewell Auditorium for a while. The situation of the women's dormitory meant, as an *Optimist* story reported, that some 170 young women who had reservations for the new dormitory were temporarily assigned to private homes, where they paid five dollars per week for their rooms. Some of these homes were seven or eight blocks from the campus, which meant a nice morning hike for non-auto-owners. But Mrs. W. C. Sikes, dean of women, assured the girls that their rooms would be ready "within three to five weeks." The new dormitory for men was partially ready for occupancy, but there was a short delay before full occupancy. The first meals in the new cafeteria were served on the first of November.

The four new buildings were dedicated and named at Homecoming on Saturday, November 5. The Bible Building was not named for anybody. With more than 7,200 people donating to its construction, the thought was that "The Bible" would be the most appropriate name. The dormitory for women honored the memory of Elizabeth Nelson. That for men was named for William M. Edwards. The cafeteria honored Mr. and Mrs. John W. Catchings, who in 1955 deeded their 3,040-acre ranch near Lovington, New Mexico, to the college in exchange for an annuity. It was sold four months later for $135,000. Estimated value at time of the gift was $125,000. And while they were at it, the trustees named the science building, which had been opened in 1946 but had never been named, in honor of Mr. and Mrs. Otto Foster of Cleburne. The *Optimist* noted the day before dedication, "The buildings are already in use; workmen are still applying the finishing touches."

One unique feature of the four new buildings was that they were the first buildings in the history of the college with central air conditioning. How people survived, especially during summer sessions, illustrates that people do not so much miss something they never had. Moving the cafeteria out of Chambers made it possible to turn all of Chambers Hall over to the library. A three-story library was a first for ACC, but a good deal of work had to be done before Chambers was fully converted to library use.

Five symposia that brought outstanding scholars from various parts of the nation to the campus were a distinctive feature of the fiftieth year. The first of these dealt with the subject "Progress and Perspective in Science." Dr. William Shive, head of the Chemistry Department at the University of Texas, was the visiting scholar and main speaker. The other symposia were "Experiencing the Arts," "Contemporary Religious Thought," "American Freedoms and Responsibilities at Mid-Century," and "Social Science in the Modern World," for which noted historian Boyd Shafer, editor of the *American Historical Review*, of Washington, D. C., was the visiting scholar and main speaker. All of the symposia were enthusiastically sponsored by the various departments and attracted a good deal of attention locally and in the academic world.

Unfortunately, with more than 6,000 exes and friends on campus for Homecoming, the football game was with the Mississippi Southern Southerners, who beat the Wildcats, 40-0. Coach Garvin Beauchamp offered the explanation that the Southerners had "the best line any college team of mine has ever faced" and explained that the Wildcats would have done better but for the absence because of injuries of three of his top players, Leondous Fry, Paul Goad, and Allen Merritt.

As part of the extravaganza of the golden anniversary Homecoming, Galaxy, a men's social club which was in its first year of existence, arranged to transport Big Tex from the Texas State Fairgrounds in Dallas to Abilene and the ACC campus for the week. He was sixty feet tall, wore a seventy-five-gallon hat and size seventy cowboy boots, and was made of steel, chicken wire, and papier-mâché. Gene Coleman, a freshman from Dallas, who later rose to be director of marketing at the Federal Reserve Bank of Dallas, had the brainstorm. Nearly everyone, including members of the ACC administration who approved the project, thought it was an impossible dream. Consequently, no one thought of looking into how the project would be financed.

Coleman took off a week from classes to work on the project. He secured a permit from the mayor and city council of Dallas to move Big Tex. He persuaded the Texas and Pacific Railroad Company to declare the metal in Big Tex's frame to be junk in order that the railroad could quote a reduced rate for haulage. Consequently, the frame arrived in Abilene on three railroad flat cars. A trucking company brought hat, head, hands, and boots to the campus. The man who put him together in Dallas came to Abilene for that purpose. An oil field worker with a crane was enlisted to help. Big Tex was in place from Thursday through Sunday of Homecoming weekend. He was located on the campus in front of the Administration building, facing toward downtown Abilene, from all parts of which he could be seen. He was taller than the Ad Building. As Coleman told Malissa Endsley, director of media relations at ACU, for her story in the *Reporter-News* in October 1995, "Big Tex caused quite a bit of attention. Roads leading up to the campus were just solid with cars, and hundreds of people were lined up to see him. CBS radio was there and some early TV stations and newspapers."

One small detail had been overlooked. Coleman and his principal co-promoter of the deal, Glenn Wiggins, had panhandled enough money to bring Big Tex of the Texas State Fair to Abilene, but they did not have enough money to send him back to Dallas. R. G. Meggs, a trustee from Dallas, made a plea in a board meeting for the members to donate to a "back to Dallas" fund. Ross Walker of Tyler supported the request by saying, "Let's help old brother Meggs out on this." Thereafter, trustee Meggs was referred to as "old brother Meggs," but Walker's support helped generate the cash needed to return Big Tex to Dallas.

It was truly a grand Homecoming, but for many people the highlight of the year was the seven performances of the golden anniversary pageant, *A City Set on a Hill.*

June Bearden of Lubbock, a graduate of the class of 1942, wrote the script, which accentuated highlights of the history of the college from its beginnings. Robert Page of the class of 1948 wrote original music. Lewis Fulks, class of 1948, was director and designer. "A City Set on a Hill" had seventy speaking parts. A 100-voice chorus, a thirty-piece orchestra, and a fifteen-member band furnished music for the show. Counting all actors and musicians, plus the stage crew and ticket and ushering people, some 300 students were involved in the production. Twenty-eight major scene changes were required; a trained stage crew did them efficiently.

"A City Set on a Hill" was nothing short of magnificent. The *Reporter-News* gave it a front-page, center-column review the morning after the opening performance. An editorial in the same issue paid tribute to the entire Lectureship occasion:

> The Fiftieth Anniversary Bible Lectureship will bring to "The Hill" some of the best known Church of Christ speakers and preachers in the country, and what may well be the largest number of visitors to a similar occasion in the history of West Texas – an expected 10,000.... It is no small feat to care for a crowd of that size over a period of several days, and the ACC people are due a great deal of credit for undertaking the chore.

But nothing daunts them, and nothing ever has. That is why we have seen a tiny school that began on North First Street fifty years ago grow into the dynamic educational institution 'on the hill' it is today.

The Golden Anniversary Year, 1955-56, marked the sixteenth year of the Morris presidency. At the beginning of his presidency, the seven major structures built in 1929-30 still constituted the totality of campus facilities. No new construction had been started during the 1930s, for which survival was the main challenge. For the size of the student body, only two new buildings were actually needed during that period, a science building to replace the Chem Shack and a library to replace the use of the terribly inadequate southeast portion of the top floor of the Administration Building. But new construction had to wait for better times.

During Morris' first five years – the years of World War II – new construction was impossible and, actually, unneeded because of reduced enrollments. The time to build began with the end of World War II. During the next ten years, seven major buildings were launched, amounting to more than two and a half times the total floor space of the 1929 construction, which had been considered as "one of the greatest building programs ever undertaken by any school in the South." And that was just the beginning. Within the next five years, the Citizenship Center and Gardner Dormitory were completed. The Citizenship Center was the south wing of the Hardin Administration Building – the counterpart of the Bible building on the north side. The two wings together had three times as much floor space as the original central building. Gardner Dormitory for women was the largest dormitory project yet undertaken, with room for 352 residents. It was another facility financed by bonds sold to the Federal Housing and Home Finance Agency.

At the beginning of the fall semester of 1959, the twentieth year of Don Morris' presidency, the *Optimist* paid him a rare and deserved tribute:

A young Abilene Christian College speech teacher in June 1940, was handed the reins of the college as its seventh president.

Some may have wondered whether the decision was the best one. After all, running a college was a hard and exacting job, and the speech teacher was only 37 years old, one of the youngest college presidents in the land.

Today, as he begins his 20th year of active and vital service to Christian education, President Don H. Morris has proved his salt. He passed his fifty-seventh birthday August 13th, and his hair is turning a dignified white. He has become a symbol to thousands of men and women around the globe of what can really be done with a Christian institution of higher learning.

When he took over as president in 1940, ACC had 661 students in the fall. In the fall of 1959 Abilene Christian College is enrolling nearly 2,500 students, almost four times as many.

He has been influential in helping the college grow to be the largest of 19 senior and junior colleges in the U. S., Canada, and Japan operated by members of the churches of Christ.

Since 1940 he has seen:

An increase in major permanent buildings from seven to 16, and another one planned this fall.

An increase in annual operating budget from $172,500 to $2,800,000.

An increase of the value of the physical plant from $588,300 to $5,700,000.

An increase in total assets from $873,600 to $5,700,000.

Academically, the college achieved the highest accreditation possible when it was elected to membership in the Southern Association of Colleges and Secondary Schools in 1951.

The graduate school, which now offers masters degrees in nine areas, was established in 1953.

During Morris' tenure, ACC has added departments of agriculture, psychology, industrial arts, and journalism.

All the pressures of the life of a college president haven't made him a nervous wreck. His door is still open to the bewildered freshman students who might drop in to ask a question.

His dealings with persons during his frequent necessary trips have not made him enemies. He is known and loved by ex-students and friends across the land and in many other lands.

As 1960 dawned, everything about Abilene Christian College was positive, with one glaring exception. No African-American students were enrolled in the student body. Through the years, vigorous discussion had taken place on the subject in the *Optimist*. For example, in November 1945, a column signed with the initials "D. M.," apparently written by *Optimist* staff member Delbert Matthews, carried the title "Colored Should Have Rights, But...." The writer declared, "I am not opposed to Negroes coming to ACC if ACC is equipped to care for them. I am opposed to them coming here and rooming and eating with whites. This would do more harm in the white students lost than good in the Negroes gained. A large percent of students, I fear, would be turned away to other schools." Then he came up with an ingenuous bit of reasoning: "Someone says that is racial prejudice. Whether it is or isn't, the students are gone, and we can't teach them against prejudice if we don't get them here to start with."

A strong dissent came in from ex-student J. W. Goss, and the paper ran it with the same emphasis given the original column except for the disclaimer, "The following is merely the expression of the opinion of an ex-student of ACC and does not necessarily reflect the opinion of *The Optimist* staff." The disclaimer was not attached to the column signed by "D. M." Goss wrote,

> The editorial advanced one of the most socially damaging doctrines ever advanced by Christian theology; i. e., spiritual equality does not result in social equality .... We have said in effect: "You have a soul loved by God as much as mine. Christ shed his blood for you. Heaven is interested in your obedience. You stand equal with me. But, you can't worship with me, you can't eat with me, you can't ride beside me. In a word, you can't associate with me, or enjoy the same measure of human progress."

And so the discussion went, off and on, for the next fifteen years. Some members of the board spoke out on the subject, as did some of the faculty. But most were willing to go on with business as usual. As William S. Banowsky wrote in his book *The Mirror of a Movement*,

> Of the colleges established prior to World War II by members of church of Christ, only Los Angeles' Pepperdine College was

situated outside the deep South or Southwest. As might be expected, Pepperdine was the only one of the schools to be fully integrated. Administrators at the other institutions had no cause to ponder seriously such a move.

The status quo reigned. Then, in January 1960, Floyd Rose, a young black student who desired to prepare himself for preaching the Gospel, applied for admission to ACC and was rejected. He went across town to McMurry College, a Methodist institution, and was accepted. This created a great deal of discussion, on campus and off. Here was a young man desiring to preach for Churches of Christ who could not be educated at a college operated by members of the Church of Christ. Rose could get a Methodist education, but he was not planning to be a Methodist preacher. Some of the best-known, most-noted preachers among Churches of Christ were black men such as Marshall Keeble of Nashville and R. N. Hogan of Los Angeles. They could speak on the lectureships and speak to classes, but they could not enroll as students.

President Morris and board chairman Sherrod decided to appoint a committee to study the subject and report to the board. Garvin Beauchamp, dean of students, was appointed chairman. Board members J. B. Collins and Hollis Manly and faculty members Frank Pack and Overton Faubus were named members of the committee. Beauchamp's first report to the board was given at its meeting on Saturday, February 20, 1960. He said the committee was launching a program of interviews with representatives of the board, administration, faculty, student body, and alumni. Furthermore, they planned to meet with the president of Southwestern Christian College of Terrell, Texas. That junior college had been established primarily by some members of the ACC board in order that young African Americans would have a college to attend. Southwestern seemed to be serving a good purpose, and the committee wished to explore what effect, if any, a change of policy by Abilene Christian would have on that school. Finally, the committee would secure information from other colleges in the area that had made studies of the matter. After its studies, Beauchamp would report with recommendations to the board.

The committee's work was speeded up and simplified by Carl Spain's speech on the Lectureship that began the Sunday after the Saturday board meeting. Spain was scheduled to give his lecture twice, as all speakers had to do then because crowds were so large that two auditoriums were used. So Spain spoke Wednesday morning, February 24, in Sewell Auditorium, and gave the same lecture the next day in the Hillcrest Church auditorium. His assigned subject was "Modern Challenges to Christian Morals." Spain's lecture was not exactly a surprise. The book containing all of the lectures had been on sale all week in the Lecturship tent, and no doubt the word was out that the speech was coming. Furthermore, a copy of the book had been sent to the Dallas bureau of the Associated Press a week ahead of time. This led AP to carry a daily story about the Lectureship for the first time in history. Undoubtedly, all of this helped assure standing room only for both occasions. It was a powerful sermon.

Carl Spain was born in Chattanooga, Tennessee, and reared in Alabama and Georgia. He attended David Lipscomb College while it was a junior college. After graduation, he came to ACC in 1936 and graduated in 1938. Afterward, he took a master of arts degree and a bachelor of divinity from Southern Methodist University, and the doctor of theology degree from Southwestern Baptist Theological Seminary. After several years of full-time preaching, he joined the Bible faculty in Abilene. He was a popular teacher and an outstanding preacher.

He began his lecture in a rather quiet and scholarly manner. He defined "moral," then discussed briefly "Christian Faith and Morals," and "The True Basis of Morality." This led into comments about "The Challenge of Modern Naturalism," which brought him to what was obviously very much on his heart:

> Whether we are willing to admit it or not, there are some dark chapters in the history of America … as vile as have ever been perpetrated on the face of the earth. Marching under the standard of the god of mammon and bluffing his way with ballots and bullets, the white man put his big white foot on the Negro's neck, quoted the pledge of allegiance to the flag, and piously recited platitudes about all men being born free and equal.

Spain recited an instance in which a church in his home community and for which he did some preaching refused admission of black people as guests at their services. He cited another time when some members of the church granted permission for blacks to use the baptistry and by so doing created a near-riot:

> Before the baptismal service was over, police came to put a stop to it.... The local paper took up the fight in good old 'Democratic' style. Police patrolled the area around the church building. The Lord's church was branded as a communist front organization where whites and Negroes socialized as brothers. The community systematically boycotted the business establishments of some of the Christians for months, nearly causing them to go bankrupt."

> Then he brought the lesson home to the campus: "God forbid that churches of Christ, and schools operated by Christians, shall be the last stronghold of refuge for socially sick people who have Nazi illusions about the Master Race.... A Methodist college will admit our own Negro preacher brethren and give them credit for their work. Baptist colleges in Texas will do as much. Our state universities will admit them. There is no law of our state or nation that will censor us. The Bible does not rule against it. Why are we afraid?

The reporter who covered the lecture for the *Abilene Reporter-News* wrote, "A murmur ran through the crowd as Spain made the statement. He received several 'Amens' when he added, 'If the shoe pinches, there is nothing I can do about it.'"

The *Optimist* came out with strong editorial support ten days later: "When a person takes a public stand as did Carl Spain on the question of campus integration, it is expected that he would meet much controversy. According to the scores of persons who have personally let Spain know their feelings and the 25 letters he had received by Tuesday, the stand for integration is one which should have been taken long ago." After several paragraphs, the editorial ended with a jab at the executive officers of the institution: "The administration, it appears, has been told, 'Act well your part; there all the money lies.' Hundreds of students think this absurd, and it is hoped that those responsible for it will consider student opinions."

The integration decision, however, was not for the administration to make; the issue was for the Board of Trustees to
address. Most people were unaware that a committee chaired
by Dean Beauchamp was already working on the problem when
Spain gave his lecture. One contribution of Spain's lecture to
the committee's work was to expedite the process. For example, over the next several months, the committee received 116
expressions in writing from the 135 members of the faculty, and
thirty-six letters from the forty-five board members. When any
question receives a response in writing from eighty-six percent
of the faculty and eighty percent of the board members, the safe
assumption is that something unusual stirred people to action.

Perhaps the most important contribution of the Spain lecture to the integration process was to prepare leaders of
Churches of Christ from all over the nation for Abilene
Christian's acceptance of the inevitable. People who heard him
returned to their homes and discussed his lecture.

At the Board of Trustees meeting of May 29, 1961,
Beauchamp's committee recommended as a first step that
"beginning with the fall semester of 1961, any applicant who
meets the admission requirements to graduate school be admitted." The recommendation of the committee was approved by
the board. The *Optimist* of February 9, 1962, reported:

> After more than half a century of segregation, the first Negro
> student is enrolled at Abilene Christian. Washington D. Harris,
> principal of Wallace Elementary School of Colorado City,
> enrolled Tuesday in the Graduate School for a once-a-week
> graduate education course. Harris holds both the bachelor's
> and master's degrees.

The next step came when the Beauchamp committee recommended in the spring of 1962 that "any applicant who
meets the admission requirements and who has junior standing
or above be admitted to Abilene Christian College." Concern
was expressed about coordination with the work of
Southwestern Christian College at Terrell. The committee was
mindful of the request made by the president of Southwestern,
"Let me have these young people for the first two years, and I
will get them ready for transfer to Abilene at the upperclassman
level." The board approved this second committee recommen-

dation. The report concluded with these words, "After this assignment is completed, the Committee feels it will have completed its study." The committee did a good job. Carl Spain did a good job. And the trustees responded favorably – not unanimously but by a large margin.

In the fall of 1962, Billy Curl and Larry Bonner, graduates of Southwestern Christian, enrolled as juniors in ACC.

Curl was first to register. He was a speech therapy major and a Bible minor. He began preaching each Sunday for a congregation in Colorado City, some seventy-five miles from Abilene. He says today that he was "just a kid from East Texas who was interested in getting an education and being a missionary to Africa." He had no idea of the dynamics surrounding his registration as the first full-time African-American student. President Isbell of Southwestern Christian had suggested to him that he should go to Abilene, and so he came. After graduation from ACC, he worked in Africa for ten years. When he returned to this country, he began work with the Crenshaw Church of Christ in Los Angeles and has had a successful ministry with that church for more than a quarter of a century. He is a member of the Board of Trustees of Southwestern Christian College.

Bonner was a psychology major. He carried a full load while working as a waiter at the Windsor Hotel. He graduated with the class of 1964 and has had a successful career in business. He now lives in Maryland.

Allen White, who had a bachelor's degree from Tennessee State University in Nashville, enrolled as a graduate student in music education at the time Curl and Bonner enrolled as juniors. White's wife, Shirley, registered as a junior.

In the spring of 1963, Jesse Johnson and his wife, Pat, registered as music education majors. They were graduates of Michigan Christian College, a junior college, where they had been popular student leaders. They became members of the Choralaires and then of the A Cappella Chorus and were popular on campus.

In the issue of May 10, 1963, the *Optimist* ran a full-page feature on these six students, complete with photographs and text. The headline was quite appropriate: "INTEGRATION COMES

TO ACC – QUIETLY." In other words, what some people thought would be cataclysmic turned out to be the education of six more members of the student body. They were forerunners of many hundreds to come in the years ahead.

Another participant in the integration of the college was J. C. Redd, a leading Mississippi businessman who was a member of the national board. This board consisted of individuals from states other than Texas who would make good trustees. Because the original charter required trustees to be residents of Texas, these national board members attended meetings of the board, participated in discussions, served on committees, and did everything regular board members did except vote. Redd took it upon himself to recruit and give financial assistance to outstanding African-American students from his state to attend Abilene Christian. He helped them go to college and kept in touch with them. Whenever he came to a meeting of the board or other campus occasions, he enjoyed getting together with those young people. He considered helping them one of the best opportunities of his life.

Redd found a willing co-worker in Dr. Clyde Austin, who was director of admissions and placement for the college. Austin began such vigorous efforts to recruit, educate, and then place minority students that the Office of Economic Opportunity in Washington recognized his efforts. In 1968, OEO convened a national conference on higher education for minority groups. The meeting was conducted on the campus of Pennsylvania State University. Austin was selected as one of two educators from Texas to attend the conference and share ideas.

By the fall of 1962, qualified students who were classified as juniors, seniors, and graduate students were eligible for admission regardless of race and were being recruited. However, the process would be incomplete until the third step was accomplished, the enrollment of freshmen and sophomores. This came about quietly through the avenue of science.

The Foster Science Building was erected in 1945-46 It was the first permanent structure since the move to the new campus in 1929. When the ground breaking ceremony for it took place June 12, 1945, the college had fewer than 500 students. Nobody, not even an optimist such as Don Morris, was likely to predict the enrollment of six times as many students by the 1960s. But they came. In fact, more than 3,000 of them arrived in the fall of 1965. The Foster Science facility was far from being large enough to serve growing departments of biology, chemistry, physics, and mathematics. Foster contained only 28,644 square feet of floor space; studies showed that an additional 50,000 square feet of space were needed.

The Congress of the United States had passed and the President had signed the Higher Education Facilities Act of 1963, with provision for grants of twenty-five to thirty-three and one-third percent of the cost of new facilities for science and mathematics, plus long-term low-interest loans for most of the balance. In early January 1965, President Morris presented the opportunity to fund new wings on the Foster Science Building to a meeting of the executive committee of the board and found all present in favor of applying for the grant. Inasmuch as the executive committee meeting was January 7 and the deadline for applications for that fiscal year was January 15, the application was prepared and turned in immediately. Six weeks later at a meeting of the full board, the action of the executive committee was confirmed.

Part of the application for the Foster Science Building expansion project was a statement of compliance with Title VI of the act. This statement was to be signed by officials of the institution and was to accompany the application. Title VI read as follows: "No person in the United States shall, on the ground of race, color, or national origin, be excluded from participation in, be denied the benefits of, or be subjected to discrimination under any program or activity receiving Federal financial assistance."

Integration at all levels came about at ACC, then, through the need to borrow federal monies for the Foster Science Building. African-American freshmen and sophomores began to enroll in the fall of 1963. The president of Southwestern Christian College understood and continued to recommend to his graduates that they should further their educational careers at Abilene Christian College. Actually, the Abilene move did not hurt enrollment at Southwestern Christian. The federal funds came through for the Foster Science Building project.

Integration also changed the face of athletics. Charlie Marler, then director of sports information, remembers meeting Burl McCoy, assistant track coach, outside the athletic offices the day McCoy learned of the freshman-sophomore decision. McCoy was ecstatic about how that change would broaden the horizon for recruitment of high school African-American athletes. Marler went to President Morris' office concerned about news media treatment as this development became public. Morris said the Board of Trustees wanted no publicity. Marler made the argument about shaping the story in a positive manner. Ironically, it was more of a story because of its athletic recruiting implications than earlier integration developments. Marler drafted a story for the president. He liked it and called the Executive Board to get clearance to let the story go. The *Abilene Reporter-News* ran the news release verbatim, and little or no reactions occurred.

In February 1998, Floyd Rose, the young man who had been denied admission to ACC in 1960, but who was later admitted to McMurry College and attended there in the spring of 1961, was a major speaker on the ACU Bible Lectureship. He thrilled the audience with his powerful sermon on the subject "True Unity Is Grace Unity." He spoke of the hatred that had been in his heart because of his rejection four decades earlier, but he declared he had been delivered from it and foresaw a glorious future when the word "brotherhood" will not be "merely a word at the end of a sentence," but will become the "first order of business" on every agenda.

The second African-American faculty member was John Whitley in Bible beginning in 1971. Although he enjoyed teaching, he preferred to preach full time and left in 1976. Dr. Billy Van Jones received the bachelor's degree at ACU in 1970, the master's degree at the University of Houston in 1972, and the Ph. D. at Houston in 1974. Then he signed on to teach in the Psychology Department at ACU and has completed twenty-four years on the faculty. He is a full professor. Since he completed his doctorate in record time, he has many years of effective service in the future. Other outstanding African-American teachers in the late 1990s are Brenda Van Dunk and Major

Boglin, both of whom came in 1990. Van Dunk is a member of the sociology and social work faculty. She holds the bachelor's degree from Montclair State University in New Jersey and the master of social work degree from Syracuse University. Boglin teaches in the marriage and family therapy program and has the bachelor's degree from Texas Christian University, the master of religious education degree from ACU, and the master of marriage and family therapy degree from ACU. On the coaching staff, Andrew Prince and David Merrill have been assistant basketball coaches as was Gerald Todd in football. In the late 1990s Victor Randolph and Rickie Harrison are assistant coaches of football, and Sylvia Dyer is assistant track coach and compliance officer.

In the late 1950s and early 1960s, President Morris had brought the college to a time to stop thinking of one building and one campaign at a time. The college had grown to such an extent that a planned program of development was essential. The wooden barracks that were still in use needed to go. The time for temporaries had expired.

A comprehensive plan for a ten-year program of unparalleled development grew out of these activities:

First, the Master Planning Council was established by the board in February 1958, with twenty-four members representing the various constituencies of the college. Seven of the most active members of the Board of Trustees were appointed to the council: B Sherrod as chairman; W. B. Cayce, Fort Worth; J. B. Collins, Abilene; Chester Kenley, San Angelo; Hollis Manly, Abilene; E. V. Mitchell, Midland; and Crutcher Scott, Abilene. Representing the advisory board were Leon Reese, Abilene, and Morgan Munday, Fort Worth. Jack Currey, Abilene, president of the Alumni Association, was a member. W. Earl Brown, History Department head, represented the faculty. Don Drennan, president of the Students' Association, provided able representation for the students. President Morris and Dean Adams were ex-officio members. Others from the administration and staff were Fred Barton, dean of the Graduate School; Garvin Beauchamp, dean of students; James E. Freeman, fiscal agent; Robert D. Hunter, director of alumni relations; Rex

Kyker, director of summer school; Ken Rasco, registrar; Lawrence Smith, bursar; W. R. Smith, vice president; and John Stevens, assistant president, who was co-chairman. Walter E. Burch was named director of development. His experience as a planner and writer made him a valuable resource person for the council.

Second, a massive self-study of the institution occurred over a twenty-month period from 1959 to 1961, a requirement of the Southern Association after ten years of the college's membership in that accrediting group. The study was coordinated by Dean Adams and involved the entire faculty and administration.

Third, the Southern Association site committee visitation in March 1961 and subsequent approval of ACC's self-study reconfirmed the regional accreditation.

Fourth, the university employed the John Price Jones Company once more as advisers in planning and articulating needs and goals. The Jones company also served as consultants in the fund-raising procedures that followed the planning.

Fifth, a campus planning firm – Jessen, Jessen, Millhouse, and Greeven of Austin – was contracted to plan the layout of campus and buildings. Herbert C. Crume was the company architect and planner who headed the ACC project.

Sixth, the National Development Council was created. Initial membership consisted of thirty-seven business and professional men from various parts of the nation. They were named to the council because of leadership in their business or profession, dedication to Christian education, the respect they enjoyed in their communities, and their eagerness to develop a greater Abilene Christian College. Dean Walling was named chairman.

First meeting of the National Development Council was October 24, 1963. The members discussed the Design for Development which had grown out of the five groups who had worked on its different aspects and announced that their purpose was to provide leadership in accomplishing it. At their first meeting, they were reminded of the statement attributed to Daniel Burnham, noted Chicago architect and builder of cities: "Make no little plans; they have no magic to stir men's blood and probably themselves will not be realized. Make big plans; aim high in hope and work, remembering that a noble, logical diagram once recorded will never die, but long after we are gone will be a living thing, asserting itself with ever-growing insistency."

Taking into account academic planning as achieved through the self-study, physical plant planning by the Campus Planning Study, and financial planning as developed through ten-year budget projections, the council arrived at a ten-year goal of $25,682,500. The campaign for funds would be divided into two phases. The first phase – the first three years – called for securing $10,383,000, with these new buildings to be begun: a coliseum-auditorium-physical education center; science halls; library; campus center; and a central plant and maintenance facility. In addition, money would be available for streets, paved parking, landscaping, and tennis courts. These physical plant projects would utilize approximately half of the $10,363,000 goal. The other half would be used for endowed scholarships, faculty research and equipment, faculty salaries, library books, and operational supplementation.

Dean and Thelma Walling made an initial gift to the program of $200,000 to be applied to the coliseum campaign. It was the largest single gift up to that time ever made by an ex-student of the college. It was a pacesetter, and the Wallings continued to give. This inspired others to contribute toward the goal. Within a few months, membership of the NDC grew to include 121 men and women across the nation. They began by making their own gifts; then they asked others to participate. NDC members gave $3,608,090 toward the phase one goal of $10.4 million.

The first of the phase one facilities erected was the coliseum-auditorium and physical education building. Rose and Sons, Inc., of Abilene won the contract and September 12, 1966, started the building, the most massive project in the history of the college, involving 123,000 square feet – approximately three acres – of floor space. It was completed just in time for the Lectureship – the fiftieth one – opening Sunday, February 18, 1968. The construction contract called for expenditure of $2,195,000. About half of that amount was for the coliseum and half for the physical education wing. It was necessary to keep accounts separate for the two because the physical education portion was eligible for a federal HEFA grant and loan. The coliseum was ineligible for this money because daily chapel exercises, including prayer, scripture readings, and devotional talks, in addition to annual Lectureships and other such meetings would be conducted there. By the time seating for the coliseum, classroom and office furniture for the physical education wing, architect's fees, sound system, pro rata share of the cost of building the central plant, and several other items were included, total project cost was $2,649,000.

The Wallings' $200,000 gift started the funding of the coliseum-auditorium. There were donations of $100,000 from Lee and Dorris Powell of Paducah, Kentucky; the Blakley-Braniff Foundation of Dallas; Henry Salvatori of Los Angeles, a longtime colleague of Dean Walling; and Mr. and Mrs. Doyle Thomas of Abilene. Mr. and Mrs. C. O. Wheeler, of Robstown, Texas, gave $40,000. Then a gift of $500,000 came from the Moody Foundation of Galveston. The liaison for this contact was Jack Goodman, an alumnus and businessman of Lubbock. Because of the strategic timing of this gift and with appreciation for the generosity of a foundation that had no previous relationship with the college, the trustees voted to name the facility the Moody Coliseum-Auditorium. The balance of the money needed for the coliseum portion came from gifts made by members of the NDC and others to the overall Design for Development Phase I goal. Also, some funds were available from oil leases from the Edwards and Gardner ranches.

For the physical education wing, funding came from a Higher Education Facilities grant of $444,980, plus a long-term, low-interest loan for $578,000. However, a firm pledge that would assure the payment of the bonds was needed before the college could afford to accept a loan that large. At that point, an interesting offer was made. Franchisees, associates, and suppliers of Gibson Discount Centers, which had headquarters in Dallas and stores in a number of states, donated $365,000 in cash, which, when invested, would take care of most of the payments on that bond issue. Additional gifts from Mr. and Mrs. Gibson took care of the balance. In appreciation, the board voted to name the wing the Gibson Health and Physical Education Center. A bronze plaque was installed in the south corridor, with a picture of Herb and Belva Gibson and the names of about 500 donors to the fund.

Official opening ceremonies for Moody Coliseum and Gibson Health and Physical Education Center occurred Sunday afternoon, February 18, 1968. Despite weather delays, including, as the *Optimist* reported, twenty rainy days in January and still more rain in February, the contractor readied the building just in time. Mary Moody Northen, daughter of the founder of American National Life Insurance Company and the Moody Foundation, and William L. Moody IV, grandson of the founder, were present. Mr. and Mrs. Gibson and their family members were present. Most of the other major donors were on hand. In honor of the new dome on campus, some students prepared signs reading "Astrochurch."

Seven thousand people came for the day. With chairs on the coliseum floor, approximately 5,000 crammed into the main arena. Closed circuit television had been set up in the double gymnasium, now Scruggs Gymnasium, and the single gym so that an additional thousand or so people could see and hear. Hallways were jampacked. The parking lots were unpaved, and heavy rains meant muddy parking lots. Reports said a number of church buses filled with young people for the Youth Forum that was to follow the opening ceremony simply turned back.

The program for the official opening was impressive. The ACC Concert Band, with Douglas Fry directing, opened with several numbers, followed by the Grand Chorus of the A Cappella, Choralaires, and Choral Union featuring a composition M. L. Daniels had written for the occasion. Coach A. B. Morris gave the invocation. President Don Morris paid tribute to donors who had made the building possible, introducing the major donors, and calling on Moody for his response.

After Moody's remarks and "The Hallelujah Chorus," performed by the Grand Chorus, Willard Paine, chairman of the board, thanked the Gibson donors and presented Mr. Gibson for a response. Then the chorus sang "The Lord Bless You and Keep You," and Coach Guy Scruggs led the benediction. But the benediction was not a signal for the crowd to go home.

Upcoming was the Youth Forum, the principal program for the afternoon. The man who had drawn so many people to the occasion was on hand to lead the singing. He was Pat Boone, then at his peak as a movie and television star and noted for clean living and faithfulness as a member, song leader, and Bible class teacher at the Burbank Church of Christ in California. Boone and his wife, Shirley, daughter of country and western star, Red Foley, helped make the occasion unforgettable. They had been met at the airport in rainy weather the afternoon before by 200 eager, autograph-seeking fans.

Robert D. "Bob" Hunter, assistant to the president, chaired the forum. Boone led singing. Burton Coffman, minister of the Manhattan Church of Christ in New York City, led the prayer. Ira North, minister of the largest congregation of the Church of Christ in the nation, at Madison, Tennessee, was principal speaker. A more dynamic platform party could not have been found. The Youth Forum was a resounding success.

After the forum, open house held forth until 6:30 that Sunday evening, and then the Bible Lectureship got under way at 7:30 with Texas Supreme Court Justice Jack Pope speaking on the Lectureship theme "Crowning Fifty Years," in recognition of the fiftieth year of the Lectureship at Abilene Christian College. After the evening lecture, there was a reception for the Alumnus of the Year, Orbin V. "Mel" Melton, of Burbank, California, president of WED Enterprises, a subsidiary of the Walt Disney Corporation.

Just as the Design for Development was creating concrete results from the planning and hard work that had gone into it, signs surfaced that the long and great period of leadership of B Sherrod and Don Morris was coming to an end.

During the annual meeting of the board in February 1966, Sherrod was in the hospital. For the first time since he had been elected chairman by his fellow trustees, he was not presiding. Willard Paine, vice chairman, presided. When the time came for the annual election of officers of the board, Sherrod was reelected, but this time Paine was named first vice chairman, with the understanding that he would succeed to the top post in February 1967. When the executive committee of the board met in April, it was reported that Mrs. Sherrod had called to say her husband's condition was improving. When the full board met five weeks later, the report was that he was still improving. At a board meeting on August 10, he was back and presiding. At the annual meeting in February 1967, Sherrod was in his familiar slot and fully in charge. At the place on the agenda for election of board officers, he was ready for Paine to be elected as had been arranged the year before. Paine did the gracious thing in asking Sherrod to continue presiding over the meeting in progress.

November 17, 1966, President Morris suffered a stroke which resulted in a rather extensive stay in the hospital and a period of rehabilitation. The executive committee of the board appointed an administrative committee to be in charge of operations in his absence. John Stevens, assistant president, was named chairman of the committee. Other members were Walter H. Adams, dean; Lawrence L. Smith, bursar; and Garvin Beauchamp, dean of students. Sherrod, who knew what it was to be ill and temporarily unable to function, was quoted in an *Optimist* story as saying, "During President Morris' illness, which we believe to be temporary, we feel the friends of the college would want to know that we have made plans to continue the progress of the college as usual."

The president was away from the office for almost three months. He was back on the job, however, in time for the 1967 Lectureship, which began Sunday, February 19. Meanwhile, an ominous note was sounded. Lawrence Smith, who for almost four decades had kept the school off the rocks financially, was hospitalized for an indefinite time, and the board appointed Bill Hilton, assistant bursar, to fill the post, prepare necessary reports, and keep things running on schedule in the business office – which Hilton could do. Happily, however, Smith was soon back on the job.

Lectureship in 1967 was memorable. Don Morris was back. B Sherrod retired from chairmanship of the board but not from the board. Willard Paine, the first alumnus to become board chairman, took over. An *Optimist* reporter asked the president if the change of chairmanship meant any change in board policy. Morris' answer was, "None whatever." This was true. Paine believed in the same vigorous but sound expansion of the school Sherrod had always advocated.

The new chairman, like his predecessor, was a big man. The first graduate of the college with a major in agriculture, Paine graduated in 1948. He would have gotten out earlier but for three years of military service in Europe during World War II, during which he was awarded the Purple Heart. Back in college after the war, he lettered three years in football and gained academic as well as athletic honors. At the conclusion of his eligibility, he signed a contract to play football with the Pittsburgh Steelers. However, while waiting for the time to report to training camp, he received a call from President Morris with news that Marvin Carlile, of Tulia, Texas, one of the most respected bankers in the Panhandle region of Texas, wanted to talk to him about a banking career. Carlile wanted a graduate in agriculture who could deal with farmers and ranchers. Paine liked Carlile's offer, canceled plans to play professional football, married his college sweetheart, Billie Jo West of Galveston, learned banking under a good teacher, and moved up to the presidency of the First State Bank of Monahans and then to the Citizens National Bank and Bank of the West in Lubbock. He was a natural to succeed B Sherrod as chairman of the board.

Two days after the official opening of Moody Coliseum and the Gibson Health and Physical Education Center, ground breaking, or "ground clearing," as President Morris called it, took place for the McGlothlin Campus Center. One Army hutment, which had been used for married student housing, was lifted off its foundation by a crane as the ceremonial "ground clearing." Removal of the hutments triggered nostalgia among former occupants as buyers purchased the huts for seventy-five dollars each and moved them away.

The McGlothlin Campus Center architectural planning called for 88,225 square feet of floor space, making it the second largest building on the campus, second only to the coliseum-physical education complex. The Campus Center provided space for the cafeteria, the college bookstore, the post office, meeting rooms, Students' Association offices, *Optimist* and

Prickly Pear offices, and a good meeting place "under the clock" in the mall area.

The $1.875 million project was made possible by the sons of Ray and Evelyn McGlothlin – Hal, Jack, and Ray Jr. – and Joe Corbin. A student center was high on the priority list of campus needs. The old army surplus Students Exchange could not very well handle the crush of students coming for their mail after chapel or lining up to buy textbooks at the beginning of a semester or to sell them them back at the end of the semester, or buying a snack and cold drink in mid-afternoon. Surely, something had to be done.

May 18, 1965, Fiscal Agent James E. Freeman and Assistant President John Stevens visited the office of the Federal Housing and Home Finance Agency in Fort Worth to inquire into the possibility of government financing for a student center. They were told that there was no particular problem foreseeable in connection with securing the loan. They were given materials to be completed for the preliminary application for a student center.

When this news circulated, three young and successful Abilene businessmen began to develop ideas. They were Jack and Hal McGlothlin and Joe Corbin. Hal McGlothlin was the principal spokesman. He told college officials why he was so interested in a student center. He wanted a place where students could meet and mingle, have recreational opportunities such as bowling alleys and pool tables, and relax. Also, of course, he realized the need for a larger cafeteria, a bookstore, post office, and grill. So he and his colleagues came up with a proposal for the college to consider. Their proposal called for the college to take three steps:

First, apply for and get a thirty-year, three percent Federal Housing and Home Finance loan for $1,500,000 to cover construction costs of the building;

Second, furnish from other sources the estimated $150,000 that would not be covered by the government loan, such as interim financing; and

Third, raise funds from other sources to buy furniture and equipment for the building.

The three businessmen would then put sufficient assets into a foundation to make the annual payments of approximately $76,000 for the thirty years of the life of the loan.

The trustees liked it. They knew the credibility of the men and the great need of the moment. Furthermore, the bookstore and cafeteria were both revenue-producing enterprises. The trustees could have justified borrowing money and paying it back out of annual revenues, but that would have deprived the annual budget. The McGlothlin deal was a win-win proposition. All the donors asked in return was that the center bear the name of the McGlothlins' parents and that their company, Locus, Inc., have the construction contract. The trustees had no difficulty with that. They always required competitive bids, except when one person or entity was paying the entire cost of a building. In that case, as was done with the Mabees in the men's dormitory construction, the donor could name his contractor. The architect would be hired by the college and would be responsible for drawing plans and specifications and on-site supervision of the job. Everything seemed favorable. A preliminary application for a loan was submitted. A letter arrived from HHFA acknowledging receipt of the application and with a number assigned to the project. The college was advised that further action would be unnecessary until information of the fund reservation was received by the college president.

Three months later, Stevens went by the office in Fort Worth to visit with Emma Brown, who was in charge of the office, about why no word had come. He was advised that the college should proceed with its final application. In February 1966, word came that no more loans were being made. Increased enrollments and the attractive low interest rate had created a demand far in excess of funds available. A call to Fort Worth confirmed that the announcement applied to the ACC application. Two days later, President Morris and Stevens went to see Brown, seeking clarification. They learned that the government agency had $760 million in approved applications and no money and that, even though HHFA was expecting an appropriation for the next fiscal year of $300 million, there would still be a shortage of $460 million, even if no new applications were given final approval. The Abilene Christian application was not that far along. Not even influential congressmen, including ACC board member Omar Burleson, could change that. A choice between rejecting the McGlothin offer or seeking private financing had to be made. The decision was for private financing. The best offer was by Southwestern Life Insurance Company of Dallas. When Southwestern expressed interest in making the loan, the decision was made to ask for $1,650,000 instead of the $1,500,000 that the government loan would have been. The deal involved the larger figure for twenty years at six percent, whereas the government loan would have been for $1,500,000 for thirty years at three percent. The government loan would have required payment of $76,500 per year for thirty years. Southwestern's loan – ten percent larger – would require monthly payments – $12,546 per month for twenty years. Annualized, that would almost double the payback on the government loan, but it was for more money and would pay out ten years sooner.

The whole deal was acceptable to the McGlothlin group. Their pledge was to meet payments of $76,500 per year. With assets for that purpose in a foundation, they turned the foundation over to the college. If the college decided to assume an additional obligation, they had no objection.

One of the requirements by Southwestern for making the loan was that a fee of $10 per student – a student center fee – be assessed each semester, and that fee would be used to help make payments. Ten dollars per semester was not an excessive amount, and the students had a fine campus center.

The McGlothlin group – Hal and Jack McGlothlin, with a supplement by older brother, Ray Jr., and Joe Corbin – did exactly what they promised to do, and, because some of the assets they turned over to the college continued to result in income even after the twenty-year loan was paid, in the long run the difference between the Southwestern loan and the original government offer was largely erased.

The center, named for Ray Sr. and Evelyn Trimble McGlothlin, opened on July 1, 1968. The recreational part bears the Corbin name. If the day comes that an additional level is needed, the foundation and columns are sized to accommodate the upper story.

The library rose to a place of distinction during the Morris administration. From 1906 to 1919, it was in a rather insignificant location in the Administration Building. In fact, for the first dozen years of the school, it was practically nonexistent. The little square building, forty-eight feet by forty-eight feet, with two stories, had a closet-sized space for a library. This was the Administration Building that, according to Dean Speck, caused the students to refer to the school as "Abilene Chicken Coop" instead of Abilene Christian College.

In 1917, after the school was an accredited junior college, President Sewell asked Professor Howard L. Schug to "do something" with the library. Dr. Schug later related that the president took him to a small room and showed him eight piles of books. It is difficult to imagine a scholarly professor having to be taken by the president to the school library. Probably, Dr. Schug had a so much better library in his own home that he had never bothered. At any rate, he borrowed from the librarian of Simmons College a book explaining the Dewey system of book cataloging and got busy. The first set of books acquisitioned, June 1917, was *Masterpieces of Eloquence*, donated by Sewell.

In the Administration Building enlargement of 1919, the library was given a more respectable allotment of space, although still about the size of a small classroom. In the disastrous fire of 1929, approximately half of the books were saved by efforts of faculty and students. When the move to the new campus took place during the summer, the library was assigned the space of "at least three classrooms," according to board chairman McKinzie in a report to the board in 1935, in the southeast portion of the top floor of the new Administration Building. There it remained until 1936, when it was moved to the main floor of Chambers Hall. That floor had been vacated by the cafeteria, which moved to the newly finished basement. In 1949, the top floor of Chambers was converted from housing to needed library space. Finally, in 1955, with the move of the cafeteria to the new Catchings building, next door to Chambers, the basement portion of Chambers was remodeled, and for the first time in its history, the ACC library had an entire building of its own, with 18,500 square feet of floor space.

The last major building undertaken during the Morris presidency was the Margaret and Herman Brown Library. Ground breaking for this facility took place during Lectureship in 1969, and the building was open and ready to serve the students when they arrived in the fall of 1970. The new library was four times the size of Chambers Hall.

At this point the spotlight falls on Callie Faye Milliken, a 1938 graduate of the college who became head librarian, succeeding Marguerite Anderson in 1953. Milliken was the first Abilene Christian librarian to achieve the doctor's degree in library science. She planned the Brown Library, the first building in ACU's history to be designed as a library. Two wings have been added since 1970: the John C. and Ruth Stevens Wing in 1984 and the C. L. Kay Wing opened in 1996. Dr. Milliken initiated the Friends of the Library program. The organization now numbers some 400 members, who make donations and use their influence and contacts to get others to give time, books, and money to the library.

Dr. Milliken pioneered the collections of microforms and audiovisuals. She led the ACU library into membership in AMIGOS, the regional system of the Ohio College Library Consortium. The OCLC Online Union Catalog is a merged electronic catalog of libraries around the world. It is the largest, most comprehensive, and one of the most-used databases of bibliographic information in the world. Scholars and researchers can choose from more than 30,000,000 records and half a billion location listings for materials they need. Dr. Milliken retired as director of the Library in 1977 but remained as associate director until 1986.

A stroke of fortune came to Abilene Christian College in 1957 in acquiring the copyright and publishing rights to *Great Songs of the Church, Number Two*. In his scholarly and eminently readable work, *Hymns & History*, published by the ACU Press in 1997, Dr. Forrest McCann, longtime professor of English at Abilene Christian University, includes the story of *Great Songs*. The original edition came from the presses in 1921. Compiler, editor, and publisher was E. L. Jorgenson of Louisville, Kentucky. It was the first hymnal in history with selections arranged in alphabetical order. McCann calls it "the greatest influence on the hymnody of the Churches of Christ in the twentieth century." The first printing sold out in a little more than a year. A second printing appeared the next year with a fifty-song supplement. Thereafter, new printings were required regularly. In 1937, Jorgenson came out with *Great Songs of the Church, Number Two,* containing six hundred numbers divided into "gospel songs" and "hymns." The book was printed in round-note and shaped-note editions. In 1954, Jorgenson sold printing rights to the round-note version to the Standard Publishing Company of Cincinnati and the plates for the shaped note version to the *Christian Chronicle* of Abilene.

In 1956, the *Christian Chronicle* went bankrupt. The Bankruptcy Court of the United States for the Northern District of Texas, Abilene Division, sold those rights to the hymnal that had been owned by the *Chronicle* to Frank Riggs of Odessa, Texas. Riggs was a friend and patron of Abilene Christian College; hence he offered the deal to the college, which could market the book through its bookstore, managed by James Fulbright. The contract called for the bookstore to pay to Mr. and Mrs. Jorgenson, for as long as either lived, five cents per copy on all sales. Another five cents was paid to Hope Publishing Company, and a smaller royalty was paid to Rodeheaver-Hall-Mack Company, both of which owned copyrights on a number of songs and hymns in the book.

Through the years, the bookstore sold more than a million copies. *Great Songs, Number Two* was the leading hymnal among Churches of Christ and was popular with various denominations. In 1986, *Great Songs of the Church, Revised* came from ACU Press. Some 82,750 copies have been sold. Although it is no longer the hymnal most in demand among Churches of Christ, it is still a standard of excellence in its field.

Twenty-five Morris era athletes compiled distinguished intercollegiate, Olympic, and professional records that have caused them to be selected and honored in the ACU Sports Hall of Fame. They are profiled here:

Chip Bennett, class of '70, was named Player of the Year for college division football for the 1969 season. He was a 6-3,

230-pound linebacker named to the Kodak All-America team by the American Football Coaches Association and to the Associated Press All-America team. That was pretty good for a young man who had reported as a non-scholarship football player. After completing his college eligibility, he was drafted by the Cincinnati Bengals and played in the National Football League in 1970 and 1971 before knee injuries ended his career. During his senior year in Abilene Christian, he made a perfect 4.0 record. He graduated with a bachelor's degree in business. His father and mother had graduated from ACC in the early 1940s. His father also had been an outstanding football and basketball player. His brother and two sisters are alumni of the college.

Bill Blakeley, class of '56, was outstanding in basketball. After graduation, he was head coach of basketball at the University of North Texas, Christian College of the Southwest, and the Dallas Chapparals, now the San Antonio Spurs. He is now a representative of professional athletes.

Wally Bullington, class of '53, played center on that famous undefeated, untied 1950 football team. He earned first team all-America honors, and, after graduating, entered the coaching ranks. He compiled a 40-19-1 record in six seasons as head football coach at Abilene High School. Then, in nine seasons at Abilene Christian, he had four teams that were nationally ranked and coached six first-team all-America players, including all-pro running back Wilbert Montgomery. He is now retired after a number of years with the *Herald of Truth* radio and television program.

Larry Cox was in ACC from 1962 to 1966 and was on the Associated Press All-America team after his senior year of eligibility. A 6-3, 254-pound defensive tackle, he was drafted by the Denver Broncos in 1966. He played four seasons for Denver, and then for two years he was with the Chicago Bears, the Green Bay Packers, and the San Diego Chargers before retiring from the National Football League in 1971. After that, he completed his degree requirements and went on to the master's degree from another university. He is having a successful career as a school administrator.

Paul Faulkner, class of '52, was national champion in the pole vault for the National Association of Intercollegiate Athletics during his senior year. He was captain of Abilene Christian's first track and field national championship team in 1952. He won the pole vault in 1951 and the javelin in 1951 and 1952 at the Texas Relays in Memorial Stadium at the University of Texas. He won the javelin in 1951 and the pole vault in 1952 at the Kansas Relays at the University of Kansas. During his college years he began preaching. Then he preached in Kansas and North Carolina for a few years and in 1957 returned to the campus as a dormitory director. He persuaded the dean to let him teach one freshman Bible class while taking graduate work leading to the master's degree. He was soon one of the most popular Bible teachers. After graduate work and completion of the doctor's degree at Southwestern Baptist Theological Seminary, he and Dr. Carl Brecheen teamed up in the field of marriage and family relationships and became internationally known for their Marriage Enrichment Seminar.

John Ray Godfrey, class of '68, was named to the first-team All-America in basketball for his senior year by three different groups: the Associated Press, the United States Basketball Coaches Association, and United Press International. He holds the all-time scoring record for a single game in Moody Coliseum with forty-one points, accomplished in the inaugural game in Moody, and that was before the three-point shot came along. He is now superintendent of schools in Hawley, Texas.

Alton Green was co-captain of the famous 1950 football team. A line-smashing fullback, he led Abilene Christian to Texas Conference championships in 1948 and 1950. During his playing days, ACC teams defeated such formidable opponents as Arizona State University, Southwest Texas State, the University of Tampa, and the University of Tennessee at Chattanooga. He became a successful high school coach before beginning a business career.

Pat Holder was a record-setting wide receiver on Abilene Christian's nationally ranked football teams from 1967 through 1970. He set an Abilene Christian career record by catching 155 passes during his three varsity seasons. Jim Lindsey was the quarterback who threw those passes. Today, Holder is president of one of the largest property management companies in the nation.

Paul "Ginger" Johnson was a member of Abilene Christian's NAIA national championship track teams in 1954 and 1955 and of its Gulf Coast Conference championship team in 1956. He also ran on Wildcat relay teams that claimed major titles at the Texas, Kansas, and Drake Relays. He ran the fastest mile in Texas in 1955. He is a dentist in Lubbock. Because of his emphasis on implant dentistry, he is in demand as a speaker and consultant. He is a member of the Board of Trustees of the university.

John Lawler came from Australia in 1959 and graduated in 1963. During his track career, he set the United States freshman record for the steeplechase and the Texas collegiate record for the mile. He won the Penn Relays steeplechase in 1961 and again in 1962. He was on the dean's honor roll consistently. He is chief executive officer of a group of mining companies in Australia.

Leon Lepard graduated in 1955. He was a member of the record-setting relay teams that won titles at the Texas, Kansas, and Drake Relays for coach Oliver Jackson. He lettered four years. He is now in farming, ranching, and real estate in Brownfield, Texas.

Jim Lindsey was a record-setting quarterback during the 1968, 1969, and 1970 football seasons. He earned five NCAA career records and threw for 8,521 yards, more than any quarterback in the history of collegiate football. He was selected to play in the North-South All-Star Game during his senior year. After his college career, he played in the Canadian Football League with the Calgary Stampede. During his first year he helped his team win the CFL championship and the Gray Cup. His last year in Canada was 1974, when he played for Toronto. He is president of Jim Lindsey and Associates of Fort Worth.

Robert McLeod was a winner in both football and basketball. He was an outstanding pass receiver in football. After his college career, he helped the Houston Oilers win the American Football League championship in 1961. He was also outstanding in basketball. The Hall of Fame citation says: "In basketball, McLeod rewrote the ACU record book. His records included most points (43) and most rebounds (23) in one game, best season rebound average (13.6), most rebounds in a season (368), and most points (1,607) and rebounds (1,237) in a career."

Von Morgan was first team all-America in football in both 1953 and 1954. As an end, he led the nation in 1953 in catching ten touchdown passes. He was drafted by the Philadelphia Eagles in the National Football League draft but declined in favor of attending dental school. In track, he was Texas Conference champion in the long jump. In freshman basketball, he led the team with 300 points in nineteen games in 1951-52. He was in the practice of dentistry in McCloud, California, when he met an untimely death in an automobile accident, November 13, 1984. He was inducted posthumously into the Sports Hall of Fame.

Bobby Morrow won three gold medals at the 1956 Olympic Games in Melbourne, Australia, one of which he has given to ACU. It is kept securely in a vault except for special occasions. By the time he had finished his collegiate career, he had won fourteen national sprint championships. The Hall of Fame citation gives this information about his spectacular career:

> He set or tied five world records, and he was the first man since the legendary Jesse Owens to win three Olympic Gold Medals. His many awards and honors include Athlete of the Year 1956 by *Sports Illustrated* magazine, outstanding amateur athlete James E. Sullivan Memorial Trophy in the United States in 1957, and Sportsman of the Year for 1957 by *Sport* magazine.

Morrow is a member of the Texas Sports Hall of Fame and National Track and Field Hall of Fame. His gold medals are on display at the Smithsonian Institute in Washington, D. C., and he is featured in the International Olympics Museum in Lausanne, Switzerland.

Jerry Mullins was a running back on the 1950 undefeated and untied football team. He was captain of the team the next year as a junior. As a senior in 1952, he was all-conference and won honorable mention all-America. After graduation in 1953, he coached in high school for three years and then came back to join the Wildcat coaching staff. He served on the university staff for thirty-five years before retiring.

Dee Nutt was named all-America, first team, in basketball in 1949-50. He made all-conference three times. After a brilliant playing career he was a successful coach. He was head coach at Abilene Christian from 1955 until he resigned in 1969 to coach the national team of Mexico for the 1970 Pan American Games and the 1972 Olympics. He later served as superintendent and coach at Abilene Christian High School, Westbury Christian School in Houston, and again at ACU.

Willard Paine was captain of the 1950s undefeated football team and twice won all-conference honors. He is profiled earlier in this chapter, primarily in connection with his work as a trustee.

Pete Ragus was a co-captain of the undefeated 1950 football squad. He led the team in catching Ted Sitton's passes that year. He lettered three years, was all-conference in 1949 and 1950, and honorable mention all-America. Lettering also for three years in track and field, he was a member of the undefeated mile relay team in 1951 and was captain of the team. After his 1951 graduation, he had a distinguished career in Texas high school coaching, topped by twenty-four years of service as athletic director of Lubbock public schools. He is a member of the Texas High School Coaches Association Hall of Honor.

Jim Reynolds "rewrote the record book during his three-year varsity career in basketball." He was named to all-America teams by *Sport* magazine and the Associated Press and, after his college career, was drafted by Cincinnati of the National Basketball Association, but chose instead to go in another direction. He received a bachelor of arts degree in Bible from Abilene Christian, in 1964; the S.T.B. degree in 1967; a doctor of theology from the Graduate Theological Union in Berkeley, California, in 1974; and a law degree from Southern Methodist University in 1981. He is now an attorney in Fort Worth and has been preaching for the Lake Highlands Church of Christ in Dallas since 1984.

James Segrest graduated in 1959. The ACU Sports Hall of Fame citation tells his story succinctly:

> James Segrest was a member of ACU's 440- and 880-yard relay teams which set five world records in 1956, 1957, and 1958.

He was a member of the NAIA national championship team in 1955.... Segrest was a member of the U. S. national team which competed against the Soviet Union in Lenin Stadium in Moscow in 1958. During his four years the Wildcats had a record of 52-9 in the 440 and 880 relays, and Segrest ran in all sixty-one races. Segrest went on to a rewarding career in coaching. His Monahans team won the Texas state high school championship in 1966. After becoming coach at Odessa College, his teams won eleven national junior college championships in indoor and outdoor track. In 1979 he was head coach for the United States team in the World University Games at Mexico City. He is now retired from the athletic directorship of Odessa College.

Ted Sitton was the quarterback whose passes were precise and whose handoffs were so quickly and craftily done that, in the Refrigerator Bowl in 1950, an official blew the whistle when an Abilene Christian running back was tackled, only to discover that another man had the ball and was scampering across the goal line. However, the official refused to allow the touchdown and declared the ball down where it had never been. Fortunately, the Wildcats went on to victory. He became one of the great coaches at his alma mater.

V. T. Smith Jr. was "one of the most talented running backs in the history of college and professional football," says the Hall of Fame citation. He was all-America for the Wildcats and went on to play five years for the Los Angeles Rams in the National Football League. He led the NFL in punt returns in 1949 and in kickoff returns in 1950. In track, he was a champion sprinter and javelin thrower. His son, V. T. Smith III, also played football and is having an outstanding career in high school coaching.

Wayne Walton was a 6-5, 275-pound offensive tackle who helped keep the opposition from tackling Jim Lindsey before he could unleash a pass. He also opened gaps in the opposition line when Trent Lancaster and others were running with the football. The citation, written by Garner Roberts, gives the sequel: "Wayne Walton was the highest professional draft choice in the history of ACU Wildcat football. He was selected in the second round by New York in 1971 after Giants' scouts rated him the top collegiate offensive lineman in the nation." He played for the Giants in 1971-72 and Kansas City Chiefs in

1973-74. Walton was also a champion in throwing the discus. He received the bachelor of science in business in 1971. He is now a businessman in Fort Worth.

Les Wheeler was an outstanding tackle on the undefeated 1950 football team. He was a two-time all-Texas Conference selection, and in 1951 he was all-Texas College and first-team all-America. He earned both bachelor's and master's degrees from Abilene Christian. He had a tryout with the Philadelphia Eagles. Garvin Beauchamp reported that Weeb Eubank, coach of the Eagles, said that Wheeler had great possibilities. Eubank tried to get Wheeler to stay with professional football, but, as Beauchamp said, "He had his heart set on getting married and coaching." After several years of high school coaching, he became an Abilene Christian coach and taught history classes. He was head football coach for six seasons. In 1963, he was named Coach of the Year for the Southwest region by the American Football Coaches Association. He lost a two-year battle with cancer, dying August 12, 1989, at age 58.

Bill Woodhouse earned a degree in accounting in 1960. During his four years at Abilene Christian, he twice tied the world record in the 100-yard dash. He ran on Wildcat relay teams that set world records under coach Oliver Jackson. He was an alternate member of the 1960 United States Olympic team and ran on the gold medal winning 400-meter relay team for the United States at the 1959 Pan American Games. He toured Europe with the United States national team in 1959, winning all thirteen of his sprint races. He came to Abilene from Mason City, Iowa, and has developed his career in the insurance business in Corpus Christi, Texas.

The most spectacular band concert in the history of Abilene Christian University took place on Friday evening, May 21, 1954. The place was Sewell Auditorium. The band was the Wildcat Band – not yet known as "The Big Purple." The director was Douglas "Fessor" Fry. It was the end of Fry's first year as band director.

He had been hired away from the Brady, Texas, high school, where he had won all sorts of honors for his high school band. Fry was a 1940 graduate of the college. During his college years he had worked for Sheriff Burgess in planting pecan trees on the campus. Fry reported that when Sheriff saw him back on the campus, he asked, "What are you doing around here, Fry?" When Fry answered that he had been employed as band director and music teacher, Burgess responded, "Don Morris must have a short memory."

Fry knew how to run a band. He had organizational skills and discipline. He knew how to develop a good marching band for halftime at football games. He also had an outstanding concert band, and this was his first spring concert at ACC. If some people had been making the decisions, it would have been his last spring concert. On the day of the program, the *Optimist* carried a short notice: "The ACC Wildcat Band will present its spring concert, Friday, May 21. Both heavy and lighter types of music will be played." Little did the campus newspaper know how "heavy" it would be. One of the numbers was Tchaikovsky's "1812 Overture." The reporter did not know that the grand climax, with sounds of cannon fire in Moscow, would not be the usual roll of drums but the real thing.

Fry had made a deal with a local unit of the National Guard – the 131st Field Artillery of the 36th Division – to set up a 105-millimeter howitzer at the rear of Sewell Auditorium. He had two cousins – Neil and David Fry – who were members of the unit and who had special responsibilities. David, with a walkie-talkie, was stationed off-stage with the conductor in view. Neil, with a walkie-talkie, was outside with the gun crew. As the concert band reached the exact point for the thunderous response, the conductor gave the signal to his off-stage man, who relayed it to the gun crew outside. The result was described in the next issue of the *Optimist*:

> *NOVEL BAND CONCERT CREATES DISTURBANCE.* To some it was the end of the world; to some it was a Russian attack; to some it was an explosion in the Science Building; and to some it was the dormitory going up in flames.
>
> And yet to many others it was the climax of a marvelous band concert in Sewell Auditorium. Thanks to the nine booming sounds from the National Guard cannon, last Friday's program was considered extremely effective.
>
> Indeed it was! Whole dormitories shook. Windows fell out.

Babies were awakened. Parents ran out in the street. Cars stopped. Neighborhood people called city police sixteen times and the *Reporter-News* about ten times. As far as attracting attention, the concert was a howling success. We only hope most of the reaction was favorable.

Not all of the reaction was favorable. For example, Rex Kyker, of the Speech Department, who lived a half-block south of the big noise, had just succeeded in getting his children to sleep, only to have them jarred awake by the noise. He proposed organizing a march on the president's home with a petition to fire Doug Fry immediately. However, he soon got over it and was a strong supporter of Fry and his band.

Some window panes in McDonald Dormitory, Julia Hall, and the semicircular formation over the door in the east end of the auditorium had to be replaced. Bursar Lawrence Smith had them installed and charged the band's budget. The howitzer was firing blanks instead of projectiles, but inevitably, remnants of the bags that held the powder came out and started some grass fires where the shreds fell. They were quickly extinguished by guardsmen. So ended Bonaparte's takeover of Moscow, and so began his retreat. Neither Fry nor any of his successors has tried a repeat of that notable performance.

Lawrence Leon Campbell Smith, the bursar, was a champion at economizing. He would save a dollar wherever he could. He had an opportunity once to buy, for fifty dollars, a big, black, shiny Buick that he thought would make a fine car for the president of the college to drive in seeing prospective supporters of the college. Those were the days when Buick was building cars with either three or four vents on each side of the front hood. They were simply called "four-holers" or "three-holers." The four-holer was a really big car with a big engine that purred along and got probably nine miles to the gallon of gasoline. That is what this car was.

The state had confiscated it from a drug runner in the vicinity of the Mexican border and was desirous of selling it to some good person or cause so that it would be turned from disreputable uses by unsavory characters to worthwhile purposes. One distinguishing characteristic of this car was that it had genuine leopard skin seat covers. One could imagine the risk of life and limb that had gone into acquiring the fine, large animal whose hide had gone into this work of art.

When Don Morris saw the car, he made an on-the-spot decision. Not only would he not be driving it, he would not even ride in it. When asked if he had an objection to keeping it on campus for others to drive, he somewhat reluctantly said that he would have no objection. He did suggest a couple of blankets be thrown over the seat covers. It is known, however, that some delegations who checked it out for school trips stashed the blankets in the trunk. So far as is known, it did not become a brotherhood scandal.

The Homecoming bonfire was a tradition dating back to the fall of 1927. The *Optimist* of October 13 of that year published this front page story: "ACC has never had a real Homecoming in the history of the school. Each year two reunions are held, but they have been in towns some distance from Abilene. The dreams of many a loyal student will come true November the eleventh, when a big Homecoming, fostered by the 'C' Association, will be staged in Abilene." The "C" Association comprised individuals who had earned letters in Wildcat athletics.

The feature attraction for that first official Homecoming was the football game with Texas Tech. The Wildcats won that one, 6-3. The *Optimist* of the week after the big event had this story about the first Homecoming bonfire:

> Preparatory to the Tech game, the largest bonfire ever seen in West Texas was staged on the Wildcat practice field last Thursday night.
>
> The stack of wood, paper, and boxes was carefully constructed and not just thrown together. One hundred cross ties furnished the lower ten or fifteen feet of the miniature house. Then for twenty feet above this, boxes filled with paper were added until the stack reached a height of thirty feet.
>
> Crude oil was poured on the house Thursday afternoon. Members of the football squad lit it, and in a few moments flames were leaping high into the air.
>
> Speeches were made by Coach Morris, members of the faculty,

and ex-students.

People in towns twenty miles from Abilene reported that they saw the fire. At Merkel some thought that all of Abilene was on fire.

The *Prickly Pear* for that year referred to that first Homecoming as "a gala day in the annals of history for ACC." The "huge bonfire" was "a signal for the glorious victory that was to be won the next day."

The tradition thus begun continued after the move to the new campus. Freshmen would organize and fan out across the countryside to round up old lumber, logs, and relics of various kinds and then they would build quite a pile of flammable materials within an enclosure of four poles and a network of wire to hold the materials in place.

It was strictly against the rules for anybody on those scavenging expeditions to take anything without permission. Almost invariably, however, somebody would deposit some contraband on the heap – fence posts or some material that had been placed in an alley, not for the taking, but for future use – and apologies and now and then reimbursement would be necessary.

One year, a picture of the bonfire came out in the *Reporter-News*, and the burning pile highlighted an outhouse on top. It turned out that the structure belonged to a small rural church. During the week after Homecoming, a committee representing the church came to call upon President Morris. They had him dead to rights because they had seen the photo. It obviously was an old structure, but when the president inquired as to its condition, he was assured that it served its purpose. He did the right thing. He sent a carpenter who built a brand new outhouse that was strictly state of the art for the small congregation. Members of the class of '62 owned up to the skullduggery. No wonder that class is now the leader in the Alumni Fund Campaign.

Homecoming bonfires came to an end after the 1968 celebration. The Texas Legislature passed a law during the summer of 1969 forbidding the building of an open fire. The city fire marshal announced that prosecution would follow any violation of the law. The administration of Abilene Christian did not choose to seek any kind of exemption. Pregame pep rallies on Friday night were celebrated without bonfires, and the Homecoming musical and Freshman Follies took up the slack.

In 1956, Bill Teague, executive assistant to President Morris, recommended to the president the employment of Robert D. "Bob" Hunter as director of special events. The outcome was that Hunter was added to the staff in September 1956, and immediately began coming up with fresh ideas that have meant much to students, faculty, alumni, and the general constituency of this university. When Malissa Endsley came out with a feature article about Bob Hunter in *ACU Today* in the fall of 1993, she titled it "The Mind That Roared." She quoted Chancellor Emeritus John Stevens as having said that Hunter has about a dozen new ideas a day: "About three of them will be outstanding, one will be indispensable, and the rest you could probably throw out the window." The subhead of her article read, "Bouncin' Bob Hunter is retiring after 37 years of smiling, shaking hands, making friends, and inventing some of our most cherished traditions."

Robert D. Hunter was born in Dodge City, Kansas, but grew up mainly in California. He enrolled in Abilene Christian in the fall of 1948 and graduated in 1952 with a bachelor of science degree in business administration. He entered law school at the University of Texas in the fall of that year, but with the Korean conflict still not settled and more trouble developing in Southeast Asia, he joined the navy after one semester of law school. Upon receiving his commission as an officer, he was sent to the Far East, where he served in Japan and on the *USS Midway* and the *USS Oriskany*. In 1954, he married Shirley Long, whom he had met in Austin and who happened to be with her parents in Thailand, where her father was on assignment with the State Department.

After his overseas duty, Hunter was assigned to the National Security Agency in Washington, D. C., and was completing his tour of duty there when the opportunity came to work with his alma mater. He hit the Hill with feet spinning and, after one year, was named director of alumni relations – the first full-time executive the alumni body had ever had. He was given a broad mandate:

1. To coordinate all programs of the executive committee of the alumni association with on-campus people and programs;

2. To direct the annual Homecoming program;

3. To help organize alumni clubs throughout the United States;

4. To be responsible for conducting the annual alumni fund;

5. To serve on the student life committee and help develop closer relationships among alumni and students.

In connection with the fifth of the responsibilities, he came up with an idea that changed February forever and has been copied by other institutions. The first Sing Song took place in February 1957. Clubs and all four classes were invited to form choruses and perform just before Lectureship. Twenty-three campus clubs entered, including Aggies and Sample Case Sitters, who were the Southwestern Bible salesmen. Men of the faculty got into the act. They formed a Faculty Men's Glee Club and enlisted such stellar performers as Marcus Mullings, George Ewing, Tommy Shaver, JW Roberts, Overton Faubus, W. C. Sikes, and E. W. McMillan, who was a bona fide good bass. Hunter was director. Bill Teague was master of ceremonies to entertain the crowd while the curtain was down in between the groups' numbers. Lewis Fulks was technical director. Norris Ragle had the sound system. The crowd filled Sewell Auditorium. Five judges were on hand. First place went to Galaxy men's social club. Second place went to the junior class. The show that began with one performance in Sewell Auditorium on Thursday evening before the beginning of Lectureship on Sunday is now presented in Moody Coliseum on Friday evening, Saturday afternoon, and Saturday evening for approximately 7,500 people.

A major benefit of the Sing Song Hunter created is that it involves many students. More than 1,000 take part each year. It has been good for student life, alumni relationships, and student recruiting. Students enroll each fall who have attended Sing Song since their elementary school years.

When Hunter tackled his number two responsibility, Homecoming, he approached theatre director Lewis Fulks with the idea of presenting full-scale Broadway musicals as an integral part of Homecoming. Fulks liked the idea; thus was born a series of stage productions that have dazzled and charmed Homecoming visitors and thousands of others for four decades.

The Wizard of Oz was the first of the Homecoming Musicals in the fall of 1958. Fulks built the sets during the summer but had to leave in September for an assignment at Pepperdine College in Los Angeles and to work on the doctorate at the University of Southern California. Dr. Gaylon Collier, associate professor of speech, became director of the show. A student assistant, Frank Morris, was in charge of the sets. John D. Anderson conducted the orchestra. *Wizard* played to full houses in Sewell Auditorium on Saturday evening of Homecoming and Monday and Tuesday evenings of the next week. Wilkes Berry wrote, in an *Optimist* review, "The 1958 production of *The Wizard of Oz* will be remembered and loved for years to come."

The 1959 production was *Student Prince* directed by Dr. Collier. In 1960, *Brigadoon* was staged with Dr. Rex Kyker directing. Fulks was back for the 1961 *The King and I*. He continued to produce the musicals in Sewell Auditorium until 1970, when the Abilene Civic Center was opened. The musical that year was *The Sound of Music*. The Civic Center, with twice the seating capacity of Sewell, was sold out four weeks ahead of time. More than 7,700 people attended the 1970 performances. Hunter had shaped Homecoming.

Hunter introduced the President's Circle idea during the first year of the Stevens presidency, 1969-70, including a dinner each year on the Saturday evening before the beginning of Lectureship, to bring together individuals and couples who during the previous year had donated at least $1,000 to the college, in any category or combination of categories. The members receive a specially bound book or similar memento. Donors of as much as $50,000 at one time or during consecutive years over a ten-year period are Life Members. Attendance is by invitation only. A donor's wish to remain anonymous is respected, except that donors obviously see one another at the dinner. The first President's Circle dinner was Saturday evening, February 21, 1970. It began as a rather small affair but grew steadily. The idea of the President's Circle dinner was simply to thank people for their support. It has never been a time for solicitation. The honorees have already given generously and will continue to support the university as long as it is true to its mission and purpose. The dinners had to be moved years ago to the Civic Center. The goal each year is to have an attractive setting, good meal, great program, and to adjourn in time for Saturday night's Sing Song performance.

One of Bob Hunter's most significant accomplishments was something he did not think of. He carried out an idea that others had; they just needed him to get the job done. Presidents Abner McCall of Baylor University, Norman Hackerman of Rice University, John D. Moseley of Austin College, and Chancellor James M. Moudy of Texas Christian University were among leaders of independent colleges and universities who thought some consideration should be given students attending such institutions. In their view, because Texas taxpayers pay huge sums to support state colleges and universities and to subsidize tuition for students attending them, every student who chooses to attend an independent college or university represents a considerable saving to taxpayers. The thought was that if the state could provide at least minimal help to independent college students, all Texas taxpayers would be better served.

While continuing as vice president of Abilene Christian, Hunter took on the job of executive vice president of the Independent Colleges and Universities of Texas. In that capacity he coordinated lobbying for passage of the Tuition Equalization Grant Program by the Texas Legislature in 1971. On the basis of need, approximately 1,000 Abilene Christian students per year receive grants ranging from $500 up to $2,500 annually to help pay their tuition at ACU. A similar situation exists in other universities who are members of ICUT.

Harking back to the days of his lobbying the TEG through the legislature, Hunter heeded the call of Abilene citizens in the

1980s to represent them in the Texas Legislature. He won the election in 1986, and has been reelected every other year since. He runs as a Republican, but in Taylor County, nearly everybody, regardless of party, supports him.

Another substantial Bob Hunter idea was his proposal to invite the entire alumni body to nominate individuals from among their number who represent in an outstanding way what Abilene Christian stands for and ask the executive committee of the association to select from the nominees one to be honored each year. There was debate. One viewpoint was that to select one person each year would be to overlook many alumni who were equally worthy of recognition. It was decided that to fail to honor anybody because it was not possible to honor everybody was shortsighted. It has turned out to be a great success. Alumni are delighted to have the opportunity to suggest good people who are examples of the stated mission of the University: "to educate its students for Christian service and leadership throughout the world." The first person honored as Alumnus of the Year was selected for the year 1958. He was Norvel Young, a member of the class of 1936, educator, preacher, teacher, scholar, author, and college administrator at Pepperdine University. Every year since, an outstanding man or woman has been selected and featured at a luncheon in connection with the Bible Lectureship.

Nominations come in each year. Once an individual has been nominated, he or she remains on the active list to be considered from that date forward. Information about a nominee can be supplemented at any time. The directors of the association meet each year and spend a good deal of time considering the nominations on hand. Their job is to choose one for the calendar year just completed.

From 1968-1998, thirty-nine individuals have been honored. Of that number, eighteen came out of the Baxter and Cox years. The remaining twenty-one have the signature of Don H. Morris and Walter H. Adams on their diplomas. Students whose diplomas were signed by John Stevens, Bill Teague, and Royce Money have not been out of college long enough for the Alumnus of the Year honor, but they will be coming along. The twenty-one who graduated during the Morris years are the following:

Mary Prudie Story Brown, class of 1943, the honoree for 1989, was a member of the ACU Board of Trustees from 1986 to 1994, at which time she joined the Senior Board. Her bachelor's degree was in speech and drama. She earned the master's degree from the University of Colorado and did further graduate work at the University of Minnesota. She and her husband, Glenn Brown, a pharmacist, have been active in their hometown of Stanton. She took the lead in building a museum and library there. She served as president of the National Federation of Music Clubs, which, with 500,000 members, is described as "the world's largest music-promotion organization."

Dr. Winnie Jo Sosebee Crump graduated magna cum laude from ACU in 1950. She attended Southwestern Medical School of the University of Texas and became an anesthesiologist. She was selected for the Outstanding Alumnus Award in 1982. She became a victim of cancer and died in 1995.

Robert J. Hall, class of 1951, was named for 1993. He was for many years president of the Visador Company in Jasper, Texas. He is now owner of Magnolia Investments. He has been a member of the Board of Trustees of ACU since 1972. He and his wife, Mary Ann, a 1953 graduate, have two sons and two daughters. All are ACU graduates.

Ray Hansen, class of 1953, was honored in 1992. After graduation from ACU, where he was a star football player (Oliver Jackson called him "the best downfield blocker we've ever had…. He was all elbows, knees, and feet"), he went to work for Exxon, and spent thirty-nine years with that company. When he retired, he was manager of marketing operations, dealing with 650 distributors and 8,000 retail stores. He has been on the ACU board since 1976.

Parker Henderson, class of 1950, has devoted his life to mission work. In 1958, he went to Thailand, where no Churches of Christ existed, and devoted twenty-three years to work there. In 1969, he established a School of Preaching at Bangkok. His son, Larry, now directs the school. The Churches of Christ in Thailand are growing. Henderson and his wife, Donna, left Thailand after their years of successful work and moved to

Trinidad, where he established a school of preaching. They normally spend one year out of every five in this country. While in the United States, he teaches in the Sunset School of Preaching at Lubbock. He was the Outstanding Alumnus of the Year 1980.

Ira Hill, class of 1956, is chairman and chief executive officer of White Hill Oral Technologies. For years, he managed corporate research for such companies as Tenneco Chemicals, Monsanto Industrial Chemicals, and International Flavors and Fragrances. In 1984, he decided to return to his creative role of inventor of new products. His company has since that time acquired fifteen patents. He is a member of the Board of Trustees. He and his wife, June, make their home in Locust, New Jersey. He was the Alumnus of the Year 1996.

Don C. Jackson, class of 1943, was chosen for the year 1985. At the time of his selection, he was deputy director for programs and resources of the National Security Agency. After graduation from ACU, he was in the navy for four years. He then went on to earn both the master's degree in management and the doctor's degree in economics from George Washington University. His service with the National Security Agency included an assignment as senior U. S. liaison officer at the U. S. Embassy in London and a good deal of time in the Far East. In fact, he established a congregation of the Church of Christ in Taipei, Republic of China. He and his wife, LaVerne, now live in Abilene, where he teaches in the College of Business Administration.

Oliver Jackson, class of 1942, was the honoree in 1960. Famed for his accomplishments as head track coach at ACU, 1948-63, and also for his solid work as line coach of football under coaches Tonto Coleman and Garvin Beauchamp, 1946-55, he later had a successful career in the business world. Jackson was president of the National Track Coaches Association, 1961-62. He coached Bobby Morrow, who won three gold medals in the 1956 Olympics in Melbourne, and Earl Young, who won a gold medal at Rome in 1960. He was with Billy Pemelton when he won fifth place in pole vaulting at Tokyo in 1964. Jackson had left coaching for the business world in 1963, but he still supported his athletes and Abilene

Christian University. In fact, he served on the Board of Trustees from 1974 until 1991, at which time he went on the Senior Board, where he still serves. He and his wife, Biddie, live in retirement in Abilene.

George W. "Bill" Knight, who was honored in 1979, graduated magna cum laude with a bachelor of science degree in chemistry in 1955. He earned a master of science degree at Florida State University in 1957. He returned to Abilene to teach chemistry at his alma mater before joining Dow Chemical Company at Lake Jackson, Texas, in 1961. He was a senior research scientist for Dow at the time of his retirement in January 1997. He was a co-recipient of an IR-100 Award, an industry-wide recognition of the top 100 research projects in the nation. The award was for the development of a new family of polyethylene resins. In 1991, the Dow Company presented him one of only three Herbert H. Dow Medals for his scientific contributions. He served as an elder in the Lake Jackson Church of Christ. In retirement, he and his wife, Anna, are living in Edmond, Oklahoma. Their two daughters and a son are all graduates of ACU. He is a member of the Board of Trustees.

Ray McGlothlin Jr. Alumnus of the Year for 1976, graduated with a bachelor's degree in Greek in 1949. He earned a master's degree in Greek from the University of Texas in 1951. He served as director of the Church of Christ Bible Chair in Austin until he became vice president and later president of the McWood Corporation in Abilene. McWood was "a crude oil gathering and marketing, refining and processing and oil and natural gas producing company." With his brothers, Jack and Hal, he made possible financing for construction of the campus center, which was named in honor of their parents. He was a member of the Board of Trustees of ACU from 1964 until 1995, when he became a member of the Senior Board. He was chairman of the board 1974-84. He and his wife, Kay, have lived in Abilene since 1954. Their four daughters are graduates of ACU.

Orbin V. "Mel" Melton, class of 1941, was chosen for the year 1967. After his graduation from ACU, he spent two years as a teaching assistant at the University of California at Los Angeles. From there he went to work with the Walt Disney companies, and, with the exception of two years out for military service, he was associated with Disney for the balance of his career. At the time of his selection by the alumni board, he was president of WED, a wholly owned subsidiary of Walt Disney Productions. He was heavily involved in the development of Walt Disney World in Orlando, Florida, serving as vice president for finance of that enterprise. He served as a deacon and then for many years as an elder of the Burbank Church of Christ. A victim of cancer, he died in 1982. His wife, Mary Frances, died in Los Angeles in 1998.

Nancy R. Miller, class of 1960, was chosen as Alumnus of the Year 1997. Miller has given twenty-six years of outstanding leadership as president of Christian Homes of Abilene. Her commitment to national and international adoptions has united infants with loving families. Her ministry to children, mothers, and families and her active involvement in church and community activities made her a logical choice for the honor.

Randy Nicholson, class of 1959, was honored in 1991. At the time of his selection, he was president and CEO of AutoFuel Company, a retail gasoline business with outlets in Texas, Arizona, and Hawaii. He was also chairman and CEO of AutoGas Systems, Inc. He founded E-Z Serve, Inc., a self-service auto fuel distribution business in 1971 and sold it in 1986. He grew up in Boles Home, Quinlan, Texas. By the time he arrived in Abilene to attend college, he was already assured of a job with Safeway. When he enrolled in school, a financial aid official informed him that since he had grown up in Boles Home, he was eligible for free tuition. He turned it down. He reasoned that up to that point in life, he had been given things, and now that he had a job it was time for him to start paying. So he worked forty-eight hours per week at Safeway and graduated in four years with a degree in accounting. By 1962, he had earned his Certified Public Accountant designation. At the dinner planned by the Alumni Association in his honor, he said that he credits God, his wife, Barbara, and ACU for his accomplishments. The Nicholsons were major donors to the Biblical Studies Building. He is a member of the Board of Trustees and co-chairman of the "To Lead and To Serve" campaign.

Ira North came from Tennessee to Abilene Christian in 1941, having graduated from David Lipscomb, then a junior college. He graduated in 1943 and was honored as Alumnus of the Year in 1974. In addition to his bachelor's degree from Abilene Christian, he earned the master's degree from the University of Illinois and the Ph.D. from Louisiana State University. At the time of his selection, he was pulpit minister at Madison, Tennessee, the largest congregation of the Churches of Christ in the world. He spoke to more than 5,000 people each Sunday morning. In addition to his pulpit work, he was speaker for a weekly live telecast of *The Amazing Grace Bible Class*, seen and heard on 130 radio and television stations throughout the world, including the Armed Forces Network. The Madison church was chosen Church of the Year in America by *Guideposts* magazine in 1968. Dr. North lost a battle with cancer in January 1984.

Wilson C. "Dub" Orr, the 1995 Alumnus of the Year, graduated in 1950. At the dinner at which he was presented as the choice of the alumni board, President Royce Money referred to him as "the Red Adair of the Church of Christ." This comparison of Dub Orr with the famed Houston fire fighter in the oil patch was apt because he has helped many churches solve inner conflicts. Beginning in 1934 and extending through 1952, four Orr brothers from Vernon attended Abilene Christian. All were excellent students and outstanding football players. Each in turn played center and linebacker. After graduating from ACC, Orr took a master's degree in business at the University of Texas and then became secretary-treasurer of the McWood Corporation in 1955. He was with McWood and then E-Z Serve until he retired from business in 1987 to devote himself to church work. He goes wherever invited, does not go if not invited, accepts no pay but expenses only, and has helped churches as far away as Sydney, Australia. He served twenty-six years as an elder of the Eleventh and Willis Church in Abilene. He served on the board from 1970 to 1998, when he was added to the Senior Board. He and his wife, Polly, have three sons and a daughter, all ACU alumni.

H. Lynn Packer, class of 1950, was Outstanding Alumnus for 1984. At the time of his selection, he was chairman of the board and chief executive officer of Wyatt's Cafeterias of Dallas. He took graduate work at Southern Methodist University and also at Cornell University. He joined Wyatt's in 1954. He was elected to the Board of Trustees in 1972 and succeeded Ray McGlothlin Jr. as chairman in 1984. He served effectively as chairman until 1991 and was succeeded by Don Crisp of Dallas. He remained on the board until 1998, when he moved to the Senior Board.

Willard Paine, class of 1948, was Alumnus of the year 1968. A sketch of him appears elsewhere in this history.

Joe Ritchie, class of 1959, Alumnus of the Year for 1994, is a professor and holds the Homer Nowlin Chair in the College of Agriculture at Michigan State University. After receiving his bachelor's degree from ACU, he earned his master's at Texas Tech University in soil fertility and physical chemistry. From there he went to Iowa State University and earned the doctorate in soil physics. He has become world famous as a soils scientist. In fact, one of the speakers at the tribute luncheon sponsored by the Alumni Association was Dr. Francesco Basso, dean of the College of Agriculture at Potenza, Italy. Ritchie has been a member of the National Board of ACU since 1989 and, with the recent charter amendment, is being added to the board. He is an elder of the Church of Christ in Okemos, Michigan. He and his wife, Ann, who is also an ACU graduate, have a son and daughter, both ACU graduates.

Robert Jerry Strader Sr. class of 1952, chosen in 1990, is a retired brigadier general in the United States Army Reserve. He attained that rank in 1988, the highest rank possible for a reservist in the Army dental corps. Dr. Strader is a partner in Abilene Oral and Maxillofacial Surgery Associates. At the present time he is serving as senior vice president for medical affairs at Hendrick Health Services. He is an elder of the Highland Church of Christ in Abilene and has served on the Board of Trustees since 1983. He and his wife, Patsy, have a son and three daughters, all of whom are alumni of ACU.

R. Gerald Turner, Alumnus of the Year for 1988, was a 1968 graduate in psychology from ACU. He earned master's and doctor's degrees at the University of Texas at Austin. At the time the alumni board chose him, he was chancellor of the

University of Mississippi. He was named to that post at the age of thirty-eight. He was there for eleven years, during which time, as an Associated Press story put it when he was leaving for his new assignment as president of Southern Methodist University in Dallas, "dramatic changes" were made. For one thing, he raised a great deal of money – some $110 million. The library was doubled in size, seven new academic programs were added, and other improvements were made. His work in race relations was applauded by some and criticized by others. By the time of his departure, the Confederate flag was gone, minority enrollment had doubled, overall enrollment increased, and Ole Miss had the first black vice chancellor in its history. In January 1995, he announced that he had accepted the presidency of SMU. It seemed strange that a practicing member of the Church of Christ would be chosen as the president of a Methodist university. Turner's response to that was the same that he gave at the University of Mississippi: "I will respect your freedom to worship, or not worship, if you will respect mine." His wife, Gail, is also an ACU graduate.

Dr. B. David Vanderpool, class of 1952, went from the Abilene campus to Southwestern Medical School in Dallas. He completed his doctor of medicine degree in 1956. There followed a year's internship in Shreveport, Louisiana, a four-year surgical residency at Parkland Memorial Hospital in Dallas, and two years of military service. He then set up practice in Dallas. At the time of his selection as Alumnus of the year for 1987, he was president of the Texas Medical Association. Dr. Vanderpool was a pioneer in dissolving gallstones with shock waves instead of surgery. On the day after the luncheon on campus in his honor, he was a guest of ABC's "Good Morning America," discussing the new procedure. He has served for years as an elder in the Skillman Avenue Church of Christ in Dallas. He and his wife, Margie, have a son who is an ACU graduate and a surgeon. Dr. David Martin Vanderpool gave the tribute to his father at the Alumni Association luncheon on campus in February 1987.

J. McDonald "Don" Williams, graduated cum laude from ACU in 1963. He received his law degree with honors from George Washington University in 1966. After several years in the practice of law, he joined the Trammel Crow Company in Dallas, in 1973, as a partner in overseas projects. Four years later, he became president, chief executive officer, and managing partner of the company. In 1994, he became chairman of the company. During his tenure, the Crow company became the largest real estate company in the world. Williams is involved in numerous Dallas business enterprises and is active in community affairs. He has been a member of the ACU Board of Trustees since 1981. He was a major donor and chairman of the successful national campaign for $10 million for the construction of the Mabee Business Administration Building in the mid-1980s. He is an elder of the Skillman Avenue Church of Christ. He and his wife, Judy, are parents of five children.

From 1906 until 1934 the school operated on the quarter system. For example, the calendar for 1933-34 showed the formal opening of the fall term to be on September 12. Final examinations for that term were November 29 through December 2. Registration and the winter term classes resumed January 2, and final exams were given March 3 through 7. Spring term classes began on March 10, with finals May 28-31. The summer quarter was divided into two terms. Beginning with the fall of 1934, the college went on the semester plan. The fall semester started later in September and continued until interrupted by Christmas holidays. Classes resumed after Christmas and ran for three weeks before finals. The spring semester began the latter part of January and lasted until the end of May.

During the last year of the Don Morris presidency, the calendar was changed. The fall semester began earlier, and exams were finished before students went home for Christmas. The change was popular with everybody – well, nearly everybody. There might have been a standpatter or two. Interestingly enough, the change from the term or quarter system to semesters became effective with the enrollment of John Stevens as a freshman student in the fall of 1934, and the change of the calendar to get classes completed and exams out of the way before Christmas became effective at the beginning of Stevens' freshman year as president. He deserves no credit for either one, but was glad both took place and that he was an eyewitness to history.

The annual Bible Lectureship series had its beginning in January 1918. In his book *The Mirror of a Movement*, William S. Banowsky quotes Jesse P. Sewell as saying, "The establishment of the Lectureship may prove to be the most significant accomplishment of my lifetime." He added that with the help of his wife and Dean Henry Speck, he planned the program, invited the speakers, and handled the publicity. He personally directed Lectureship during the balance of his tenure as president.

Batsell Baxter, who succeeded Sewell as president in 1924, was director of the Lectureship throughout his eight years in office. James F. Cox continued the practice of personal direction by the president. When Don Morris took office, he began by following the pattern that had been set. He had a tough time running Lectureship during the war years, with the small crowds because of gasoline rationing, tire shortages, and no automobiles being manufactured. In fact, the 1945 series was cancelled. Nonetheless, Lecture Week continued to be a major event on campus.

In 1953, as Banowsky points out, "J. D. Thomas became the first man to serve as director of the Lectureship who was not at the same time president of the college." Under his direction, attendance zoomed upward, and Lecture Week became a really big-time event. Thomas divided the various responsibilities into several areas and appointed a supervisor over each area. One area was publicity and program. Another had to do with reservations and housing for the thousands of visitors. A third area dealt with physical arrangements, dealing with such items as having a public address system if one was needed, chalkboards, podium, and whatever was necessary to help make a successful event. Someone was in charge of the major collection taken on Monday or Tuesday evening of the week. Thomas was an organizer. His expertise was perhaps a result of his experience in city management before he went off to the University of Chicago to secure his Ph.D. degree and return to teach Bible.

Under Thomas' direction, the huge Lectureship tent began to be erected each year so that booksellers and people dealing in nearly everything connected with church work could reserve space for their exhibits. The Lectureship tent became a sensation. It was said that some people who came to Lectureship never attended the lectures. They spent their time in the tent, where, in a day's time, one could see nearly everybody who was in attendance from around the world. Thomas managed the Lectureship until 1970. Carl Brecheen succeeded him and ran the annual program with outstanding success for the next twenty-four years. Bill Young was co-director with Brecheen in 1993, and Young has been director since 1994. The tent has been abandoned in favor of exhibits in Bennett Gymnasium and the Hall of Servants in the Biblical Studies Building. People from around the world continue to write "Abilene, Texas," on their calendars to reserve Sunday through Wednesday of the last full week of February each year to attend Lectureship.

A summer workshop for Bible class teachers was begun in July 1955 as the brainchild of Grover Cleveland Morlan. Dr. Morlan was a thinker, a planner, an innovator. He came up with a number of ideas that have helped make Abilene Christian University the distinctive institution that it is. The Bible Teachers Workshop was one of his best ideas. At first it was called Instructional Materials Workshop for Bible Teachers and Others Interested in Improving Instruction in the Church. It was sponsored by the Education Department and the Bible Department. The workshop began July 28, 1955, with speeches, discussion groups, and evaluation of filmstrips and other materials for teachers. It was a success. Whereas Lectureship was an event primarily for preachers, this was an event for the hard-working Bible class teachers of the churches; they were simply looking for help in doing their work.

Dr. Morlan was chairman of the panel that planned the program. He did not make an appearance on the program until the last hour, when he presided at the evaluation of the session. Other members of the planning group were Alan Bryan, LeMoine G. Lewis, B. F. Holland, and Paul Southern. For the first three years, Dr. Morlan directed the workshop, assisted by

Rex Kyker, director of summer sessions. Beginning in 1959, LeMoine Lewis was director. By that time, the meetings were beginning on Monday evenings and running through Thursday evenings. Lewis was in charge of the program through 1966. Since 1967, Carl Brecheen has been director. Bible Teachers Workshop continues to be of service to hard-working, dedicated church members.

A significant step was taken in January 1968 with the addition of George P. Gurganus to the faculty as professor of Bible and missions. Although such individuals as Howard L. Schug and J. W. Treat had for many years stressed mission work and had done a great deal of it themselves, there had not been a solid academic program designed to prepare people for what they would meet on the mission field. Gurganus had excellent academic preparation for his work. His bachelor's degree from Harding College was in the field of business administration. His master's degree from Syracuse University was in speech, and his doctor's degree from Pennsylvania State University was in cross-cultural communication and cultural anthropology. In addition, he and his wife and two daughters had lived for years in Japan, preaching the Gospel and establishing a self-supporting Church of Christ in Tokyo.

Gurganus soon recruited Wendell Broom as a fellow teacher of missions. Broom had years of experience in mission work, primarily in Africa. He added much to the program. Soon, Edward Matthews joined the group, coming from a background of work in Guatemala. Today, missions is a department in the College of Biblical Studies. There are three full-time professors in the department – Philip Slate, chairman; Edward F. Matthews; and Gailyn VanRheenen – all of whom hold doctoral degrees in missiology and have had broad experience in working for the Lord in foreign fields.

The practice of former years of sending eager missionaries into distant fields without proper preparation was similar to sending soldiers into combat without training. Like such soldiers, the missionaries did not stand much of a chance for success. Most of them would be back home before too long. Those days are gone. People doing work in difficult fields can get excellent training that will stand them in good stead in their chosen fields of work.

Garvin Vastine Beauchamp was a model of integrity, at least outwardly. He was dean of students, a member of the Abilene City Council, an elder in the College Church of Christ, and famed as a football coach of the Singing Christians before becoming dean of students. He has, however, a felony in his past, even though it was never filed for record. He stole a car belonging to Bible professor Carl Spain and was caught red-handed. The dean had a business meeting in downtown Abilene. His automobile was temporarily out of service. The college had a 1956 Ford parked in the Administration Building parking lot for use when needed for local purposes. Beauchamp was in a hurry. He went by the president's office to get the key from presidential secretary Delno, Mrs. JW Roberts. He noticed that the key did not turn too easily in the ignition, but it worked. After completing his business downtown, he was returning to the campus, thinking peaceful thoughts.

Meanwhile, Professor Spain finished teaching his class and was ready to go home, but his car was missing. It was a 1956 Ford – same make, model, and color as the one that belonged to the college. Naturally, he called the police. When Beauchamp reached the intersection of East North 16th Street and Campus Court, alongside the College Church of Christ, a police car with flashing light and siren stopped him. As the uniformed officer approached him, Beauchamp said, "What's going on?" The officer said, authoritatively, "You stay right where you are until another officer gets here." About that time the colleague arrived, and Spain was with him. Spain said to the mystified culprit, "Beauchamp, you have my car!" All was soon smoothed over. Realizing that each had a set of keys that would fit both cars made the business of driving on the campus an adventure.

One can imagine that among the considerable audience of students attracted by the excitement, there must have been several who called home that evening and started with the statement, "You can't believe who was arrested here today."

During the 1947-48 school year, a group of musicians got together and formed the Nauseating Nine. They were talented musicians who staged some outrageous but hilarious performances. Whenever they presented a concert in Sewell Auditorium, the place was packed. Glenn Wallace, preacher for the College Church of Christ, fired both barrels at them one Sunday night after shows on Friday night and Saturday night to overflow crowds in Sewell Auditorium. He said it was disgraceful to think that a group like that, with saxophone wailing, trumpet squealing, bass rumbling, and singers screeching, could draw a crowd so large that people were practically breaking down doors to get in, and paying thirty-five cents a head to get in. Here it was Sunday night, and for the church service Sewell auditorium was only about half full. (Glenn must have been present for the performance because he knew what instruments were featured and described them so well.)

Personnel of the Nine were Freddy Waddell, trumpet and baritone; Robert H. "Tex" Williams, bass fiddle; Harry Tansill, trombone; William N. "Bill" Scott, saxophone; Philip Boone, trumpet; Don McCord, clarinet; James Dean, trombone; Glynn Castleberry, who later was Mrs. Robert Page, Jean Caskey, who later was Mrs. Claude Tabor, and Kelly Martin, vocalists. Paul Moffitt was master of ceremonies. To be sure, when they did a choral number, the entire gang joined in on the vocals.

One of their most famous compositions, "Across the Street to Ivo's," celebrated Ivo Woosley's ACC Drug and Supply, across the street from the Administration Building. The proprietor was a great friend of the students, an avid booster of athletics, and tail twister at the Lions Club. The Woosleys and their daughter and son-in-law, Louise and Bob James, ran the store. It was noted for good hamburgers and other nutritious items, as well as being a place for good fellowship.

With considerable difficulty, permission has been obtained to reprint the song:

ACROSS THE STREET TO IVO'S
(Tune: "Across the Sea to Ireland")
Have you ever been across the street to Ivo's,

Well maybe just at chapel time each day.
As you listen to the clinking of the pinballs,
And greet the chapel cutters on the way. (All the Way!)*

O the breezes blowing o'er the street from Ivo's
Are scented with cigar smoke ten days old. (Ten Days Old)*
And in booths behind the loud and glaring jukebox,
The gay young hearts in laughter waste their gold. (Fool's Gold)**

Now the Dean goes there and tries to teach them his way,
And sometimes it is futile so he thinks.
But if they don't change their ways before tomorrow,
The Dean is gonna raise an awful stink. (P.U.)

Now if there is going to be some grades hereafter,
And somehow I am sure there's going to be.
Just remember when you go across to Ivo's
Your grades will be much lower than a D. (A dirty D!)**
*Add with strong feelings and emotions.
**Bass voices with descending notes.
(All rights are reserved by the Nauseating Nine. Permission to
reproduce requires signatures of all members.)

By May 31, 1968, President Morris was able to report the successful conclusion of phase I of the Design for Development. Whereas, the goal had been $10,383,000, gifts and pledges had reached the grand total of $10,858,246.88. More than 8,800 donors had participated.

The twelve-month period beginning with the fall of 1968 and running through the summer of 1969 was a fitting year for Don Morris to conclude his twenty-nine-year presidency. The Design for Development had been a complete success. A committee appointed to plan phase II of the DOD reported to the Board of Trustees:

> No college among those supported by members of the churches of Christ has received such massive widespread support in so short a period as the Phase I campaign of the Abilene Christian College Design for Development.

More than 8,800 alumni, parents, Board and Advisory Board members, and friends of the college are depended upon for research, planning, cultivation, and contact for gifts to provide the magnificent total in excess of $10.8 million committed in Phase I (1963-68).

Moody Coliseum and the Gibson Health and Physical Education Center were fully operational. McGlothlin Campus Center opened in July 1968. The two new wings of Foster Science Building, plus the Dean and Thelma Walling Lecture Hall attached to the science building, were completed by the end of the year. The Central Plant was cooling and heating all of these facilities and could be expanded as future buildings came on line.

Band director Douglas "Fessor" Fry came up with an idea that was immediately accepted: to remodel Catchings Cafeteria so that it could be used by the Music Department. Music desperately needed a building. It was divided between two barracks, one for the band and the other for the balance of the department.

Plans were drawn, and the project went out for bids. Locus Construction Company, having finished the Campus Center, got the contract. Not only was Locus low bidder, at $105,312, but the company made a voluntary refund of $20,000 on the Campus Center project. Miss Roxie Neal, of San Antonio, donated $65,000 to the music building campaign. Others came in, and funds were soon subscribed to cover the construction contract, architect's fees, furniture, and pro rata cost of being hooked up to the central air conditioning plant, all of which made the total cost of the project $140,831.

Catchings Cafeteria was now an integral part of McGlothlin Campus Center, so what had been Catchings Cafeteria was now to be the Leonard Burford Music Building. The east end was converted and has served as the home of the Big Purple band since 1969. The west end of the Catchings building was converted into the Roxie Neal Recital Hall, an excellent facility with seating for 150. What had been once the serving area became practice rooms for students. Along north and south walls were spacious studios for teachers. The refrigerated storage area became studios. The grocery storage room became an instrument storage location. The garbage room became "The Fessor's Rec Room." Band students took turns with steel brushes and steel wool, soap and water, scrubbing away remnants of what the room had once been. The Burford Music Building has long since been outgrown. Plans are being developed in 1998 for something larger and finer for the Music Department, within a center for the performing arts. Until the new facilities become reality, however, the building that was once a cafeteria has served well.

The naming of the band hall in the process of converting Catchings Cafeteria into the Burford Music Center was one of the most touchingly appropriate decisions in the history of Abilene Christian University.

William Robert Reese, who was known as "Bill," "Big Bill," and "Pete" while he was a student in Abilene Christian, 1963-67, was drum major for the Big Purple for all four years of his career here. He had been drum major for Abilene High School for three years before that and had filled the same role for Jefferson Junior High in Abilene during the three years before that. He was a natural-born leader.

He was outstanding in leading the Big Purple through half-time activities at football games in Shotwell Stadium. Packed houses in Sewell Auditorium for the Homecoming production of *The Music Man* in the fall of 1963 were ecstatic when, as the grand finale and climax of notable performances, Reese came leading the Big Purple down the aisles playing "Seventy-Six Trombones." The trombones and the rest of the band were somewhat challenged to be heard over the wild applause of the audience, but they succeeded.

In 1962, Reese joined the marines as a private and served six months of active duty before entering college at midterm in 1963. He then served in the marine reserves and eventually applied for the platoon leadership class. He spent three summers in training to qualify for his marine second lieutenant's commission, which was awarded after his graduation from college at midterm in 1967. He left Abilene on September 29, 1967, and was quickly moved into duty in the front lines in

Vietnam. He became executive officer of K Company, 3rd Battalion, 9th Marines, in January 1968.

While he was a student he married Cathy Campbell, a fellow student. They were expecting a child the latter part of March or early April. Although Bill was keeping close connections with his young family, he was not forgetting his alma mater. Right after January 1, 1968, he sent his entire paycheck of $300 to band director Douglas "Fessor" Fry, with a letter stating, "I've enclosed a little something for the Big Purple. I'm sorry it's a bit late for Christmas. Just remember that ol' Pete still remembers all the Big Purple did for him and appreciates more than dirty old money could ever tell."

When word came that Lt. Reese had been killed in action February 14, 1968, the band had played the day before for 6,000 people at the official opening of Moody Coliseum and was preparing for a regular rehearsal on Monday morning, February 19. The word had already been whispered around when director Fry walked in to begin the rehearsal. A story in the *Optimist* described the occasion:

> The room was dead still when Fessor Fry began speaking in a low and choked voice. He told us he had been that morning to see Bill's family – his parents and his wife. They had just heard of his death yesterday, though he had been dead about five days. There was little that "Fessor" or anyone could say. He asked us to rise from our seats for a minute of silence. We rose and paid that brief tribute to our lost friend, then we went out.

Not only was Bill Reese a patriot and a man of character, but he had a philosophy of life that he described in a paper written for Dr. Ray Whiteside while he was enrolled in Whiteside's human development class. It has been reproduced and quoted many times and deserves to be in this book:

> I feel that my philosophy of life is quite simple and certainly very American. I have lived a free man in a free country for almost 23 years now. I have had virtually everything I could need or want. I attend a Christian college, I have Christian parents, I have a Christian wife, and on the story goes. To my mind this leaves me with some tremendous debts to repay.
>
> The largest debt is to my God. He has given all of this to me. He has given me a strong mind and body, and a voice to sing and speak His Word. I have taken a very active part in Bible teaching, singing, and preaching, over the past years, and I shall

continue to do so. This is a very pleasant debt to repay, although I'll never make it.

The next debt is to my parents and my wife. My folks raised me in a Christian home. They taught me right from wrong. Now, as I finish college, I must excel in my chosen profession. Not only must I do well professionally, I must be a good father. My wife deserves my best along with my parents. I must strive to be the finest husband and father ever. Anything less than the best will not repay the debt.

The last debt is to the United States of America. I do not speak of politics or politicians here. My forefathers bled and died so that I could live a free man for 23 years. I believe in America. I want my sons to have the same opportunities that I have had. I want to teach others, eventually, and give them what I can for what it's worth. If I can be of some help to someone in this way, then my debt to America will be partially repaid. As for the other portion, I will be commissioned a second lieutenant in the United States Marine Corps in January. Sure, I'll probably fight. I don't want to, but my father didn't want to either.

These are my main goals in life.

No wonder the band hall is named for Bill Reese. His medals, honors, and memorabilia are in the archives of Abilene Christian's Brown Library. May his name and life and philosophy be remembered through the years to come.

The Board of Trustees in executive session November 8, 1968, received two crucial reports. The first was that Dr. Walter H. Adams, who was in his thirty-seventh year as dean of the college, had announced his intention to relinquish duties of the dean's office at the end of that academic year. An ad hoc board committee and President Morris recommended that Dr. B. J. Humble of the Bible Department be named to succeed him, effective September 1, 1969. Meanwhile, Dean Adams was to be named vice president for academic affairs for one year, at the end of which time he would become dean emeritus. The next report was that Lawrence L. Smith, who had served as bursar for forty-one years, was retiring from that office and would be succeeded by his longtime assistant, L. D. "Bill" Hilton, who would take the title of business manager. This change also would be effective September 1, 1969. Smith would become vice president for financial affairs and would work on special assignments.

At the annual board meeting in February 1969, President Morris expressed his desire to retire from the presidency, and chairman Willard Paine appointed a committee of trustees to begin a search for his successor. Chairman of the committee was Dr. J. P. Gibson. Members were Hulen L. Jackson, Gilbert T. McLeskey, B Sherrod, and John A. Wright. Paine asked the committee to come in with at least a preliminary report by the time of the May meeting of the board.

At the May 3, 1969, meeting, the board in executive session received the report of the committee. Recommendations were as follows:

1. That Brother Don Morris be elevated to the office of Chancellor of the College on September 1, 1969.

2. That, as Chancellor, he be relieved of burdens of the administration so that he may devote his great talents to representing the college at various group meetings (ex-students, preachers meetings, lectureships, etc.) and in cultivating the many friends of the College....

3. That John Stevens be appointed President of the College, to take office September 1, 1969.

At the same meeting, upon recommendation by Morris and Stevens, Garvin Beauchamp was named vice president for student personnel services, and Robert D. Hunter was named vice president for public relations and development.

It was quite a change of administration. The three men who had worked as a team for so long were moving out, and a new team was moving in.

Abilene Christian had never had a chancellor. It seemed to be a good arrangement, and so it worked out to be. There had not been a vice president of the college since W. R. Smith's retirement in 1962, and now four vice presidents would head up the four sectors of administration: academic affairs, student life, finances, and public relations. Each vice president would be responsible for an area of administration, subject to coordination with the president. In academic affairs, Dean Adams would be vice president for a year, and then Bill Humble would become vice president. In finance, Lawrence Smith would be vice president for a year and would become treasurer, and Bill Hilton would be vice president. Beauchamp and Hunter would be the other two vice presidents.

So ended the Morris administration, the longest in the history of the university and one unlikely to be equalled during the twenty-first century.

CHAPTER SIX

REAFFIRMING OUR PURPOSE

Shortly before September 1, 1969, President Don Morris, Dean Walter Adams, and Bursar Lawrence Smith moved out of their respective offices, and John Stevens, Bill Humble, and Leo Dale "Bill" Hilton moved in. The change of administrations was harmonious and smooth, which is not to say that succeeding a trio of men who had been leading the college for longer than many people could remember was easy.

People had a difficult time realizing that Morris was no longer president and chief executive, Adams was not the dean, and Smith was not the bursar. Of the 170 members of the 1969 faculty, only five – Fred Barton, Burnya Mae Moore, Marcus Mullings, Paul Southern, and J. W. Treat – had taught at the college under any president other than Morris. Only two – Treat and Moore – had reported to any dean other than Adams. No member of the 1969 faculty had ever received an Abilene Christian College paycheck from any bursar or business manager other than Smith. Several factors helped the transition and minimized the natural forebodings.

First, the three departing executives were big men. They endorsed and supported their successors. They were available for counsel – upon request – but they did not volunteer it. Happily, the new people were altogether in favor of keeping the college Christian.

Second, each of the longtime leaders had new specific and important assignments. Chancellor Morris was in position to leave his office and make contacts with friends and prospective supporters of the institution without having to hurry back for a meeting or a crisis on the campus. He accomplished some great things for the college during the remaining four and a half years of his life. Adams, with the title for one year of vice president for academic affairs, did not have to deal with the day-to-day operation of the dean's office. He agreed to oversee the self-study for the forthcoming Southern Association visit, which was a full-time job. And Smith, with the one-year title of vice president for finance, was asked to look after off-campus properties belonging to the college, including the Edwards ranch, the Gardner ranch, and numerous other properties that had been given to the college and needed the Lawrence Smith brand of oversight. Later, Smith undertook, at Stevens' suggestion, the task of interviewing ex-students and others who were acquainted with various phases of the history of the school. He did not live to write it himself, but the material he compiled has been most helpful in the preparation of this history and is available for future researchers.

Third, the new administrators had in effect been understudies for their new jobs for years. Stevens had been assistant president, working with President Morris on a day-to-day basis, for thirteen and a half years. Hilton had been assistant bursar since 1952. Humble had not been in administration but was scholarly and efficient and had the confidence of the faculty. Two other vice presidents were simply continuing their jobs. Garvin Beauchamp had completed thirteen and a half years as dean of students before he became vice president for campus life. Bob Hunter had been on Don Morris' team since 1956, and his position was now titled vice president for public relations and development.

John Christopher Stevens came from a long line of Texans through both father and mother. He was born July 15, 1918, in the small town of Richland, Navarro County, Texas. He was the son of Dr. John Christopher and Ella Hardin Stevens. His father was a physician – a country doctor. He died in 1930 when John was twelve. In 1934 Stevens enrolled in Abilene Christian College and graduated in 1938 with a major in Bible and a minor in Greek. After preaching for four years in Jasper, Texas, and one year for the Central Church of Christ in

Beaumont, he volunteered for service as a chaplain in the U. S. Army during World War II. He served with an infantry regiment in all of the ground campaigns of Western Europe, from Normandy until the end of the war.

During his time in Europe, he became more interested than ever in the study of history; hence, on returning to the states, he enrolled in graduate study at the University of Arkansas, to which state his mother had moved during the war years. After completing the master's degree in 1948, he joined the faculty of Abilene Christian College in the fall of 1948, and, while teaching and taking a fifteen-month leave of absence, completed work for the Ph.D. degree at Arkansas in 1954.

In December 1948, Stevens married Ruth Rambo, a teacher in the Department of Business Administration. Her parents were D. B. and Inez Norton Rambo, both of whom had long and prominent connections with Abilene Christian College, dating back to the Sewell years. The Stevenses have a son, Clark, a daughter, Joyce, and five grandchildren.

Vice President Hunter was asked to chair the committee for planning and carrying out the Stevens inaugural ceremonies. The committee did its work well. Results were outstanding. The date selected was Saturday, February 21, 1970, the day before the beginning of the annual Bible Lectureship, which assured a good crowd. Approximately 3,500 people were on hand. Some 208 colleges and universities and forty-nine learned societies, educational associations, and organizations were represented by the delegates. Others sent citations or plaques.

With Dr. Walter Adams presiding, the program got under-way at 10:30 in the morning in the new Moody Coliseum. First came the processional, with music composed by M. L. Daniels of the music faculty and played by the Concert Band, directed by Charles Trayler. When the presidential party entered, the audience stood and remained standing for the Ceremony of Allegiance, which featured the Concert Band, the Grand Chorus, and the Pledge of Allegiance. Dr. Batsell Barrett Baxter gave the invocation. He was chairman of the Bible Department at David Lipscomb College, son of the fifth president of

Abilene Christian, and friend of Stevens since both were students in the 1930s. Texas Supreme Court Justice Jack Pope read from the Bible. He chose a selection from I Kings ch. 3, in which Solomon asked for wisdom. Solomon's request pleased the Lord, who admonished Solomon to "walk in my ways and obey my statutes and commands as David your father did."

Six individuals then brought brief greetings. Walt Cabe represented the student body. Dr. B. J. Humble spoke for the faculty. Distinguished alumnus Louie Welch, mayor of Houston, brought greetings from the alumni. Congressman Omar Burleson and United States Senators John Tower and Ralph Yarborough brought greetings from the nation's capital. A choral tribute, "God Give Us Men," a poem by Josiah Gilbert Holland with musical arrangement by Jack Boyd, was presented by the Grand Chorus, directed by Boyd. Dr. Bevington Reed, Texas commissioner of higher education, gave the inaugural address, expressing strong support for Abilene Christian College and similar institutions.

Chancellor Morris presented the new president to Board Chairman Paine, who inducted him. The inaugural speech was thought by a few people to be somewhat radical because of this paragraph:

> ... I hope that in being a Christian college we will always be a bulwark in support of Biblical teaching and Christian living in this world. I hope also that we can always be a liberal arts institution in the finest traditions of higher education. We shall expect to continue to explore, as fully as our talents, time, and resources will permit, issues facing modern man. There are no subjects on this earth, or in outer space, or in the metaphysical realm, which we cannot study on the campus of a Christian institution of higher learning. Everybody can know our basic commitment, but I hope that people will also realize that there are no closed minds and no off-limits subjects on this campus so long as in our teaching and practice we operate within the framework of our historic commitment. We can study – and I hope with a fair and reasonable approach – even those viewpoints which might not be in agreement with our basic presuppositions. In this way we can see to it that students and faculty are aware of the currents and crosscurrents of our age and that the education to be pursued at a Christian college is highly relevant.

In retrospect, the statement seems not radical at all.

After the singing of the Alma Mater, the benediction was led by the commissioner of the Southeastern Conference, famed Abilene Christian alumnus A. M. "Tonto" Coleman. The recessional, an original composition by band director Charles Trayler titled "Onward Excellence" concluded the proceedings.

Some 1,500 people had tickets for the luncheon in the Gibson Health and Physical Education Center. The program included a delightful musical presentation by the Hilltop Singers, with Ed George directing, and greetings from a number of other dignitaries led by the presidents of Hardin-Simmons University and McMurry College. The speaker was another Stevens friend since 1934, Dr. Norvel Young, Pepperdine University president.

The greatest day in the life of a college president, some wits say, is inauguration day; thereafter, the only way to go is downhill.

However, the Stevens administration was unanimous in deciding to go all out to increase the number of students who would attend Abilene Christian College. The students were available, but they would not automatically choose to go to ACC. Several decisions were made in attempting to recruit new students.

First, going slow became the strategy for increasing charges. The word was out especially among Churches of Christ, the source of most Abilene Christian students, that Abilene was considerably more expensive to attend than other Christian colleges. However, principal competition came from the strong state colleges and universities of Texas, with their exceedingly low tuition charges. Therefore, basic student charges – tuition, room, and board – were not increased for 1970-71. For the next year, tuition was increased three dollars per semester credit hour; the general fee was increased five dollars per semester credit; but a number of nuisance fees were eliminated, such as laboratory fees. In 1972-73, the tuition increase was two dollars per semester hour, but in 1974-75 and 1975-76 tuition remained at the 1972-73 level. All of these efforts to hold the

line on costs were taking place during a time of rampant inflation. The Consumer Price Index showed an eleven percent
increase in 1974, nine percent in 1975, and continuing high
figures until 1980, when inflation reached thirteen and one-half
percent for the year. Later studies indicated that keeping tuition
and fee increases down did not necessarily affect enrollment
appreciably. At any rate, it was tried for a number of years.

Second, upgrading of campus housing was adopted as an
essential strategy to increase enrollment. The first step was
to air condition all of the older dormitories. The Mabee
Foundation made a grant of $530,700 in 1976 to make possi-
ble the renovation of Mabee Dormitory, which had been built
just before air conditioning was recognized as essential in West
Texas. The renovation involved expansion of the Central Air
Conditioning Plant, and that expense was part of the reason the
Mabee renovation cost more than the original building.
McDonald, Zellner, and McKinzie dormitories also were air
conditioned. Zellner was tied into the loop to the Central
Plant; McDonald and McKinzie were equipped with individual
window units. The president's report to the board in February
1980 contained this quotation from Garvin Beauchamp's housing secretary: "It is so pleasant to not receive all the medical
excuses requesting air-conditioned rooms." Bill Hilton's report
added that by the fall of 1979 every classroom, office, and dormitory was air-conditioned. The campus was becoming more
livable in hot weather.

Also, four new, major housing projects were undertaken.
Sherrod Residential Park, a thirty-five-acre tract, was opened in
1974 with apartment units for 224 residents. The apartments
were in two clusters – one for men and one for women. They
occupied the land originally set aside as A Club Park when the
college moved to the Hill. These apartments have always been
popular. A second new project was A. B. Morris Dormitory, a
facility for 160 men, opened in 1975 as an athletic dormitory.
Cash and pledges of $360,000 had been raised to match other
available funds. Friends and alumni thought athletes should
have a home of their own, with a member of the coaching staff
in residence. Coach Don Smith and wife, Barbara, assumed
management responsibilities. When the Smiths decided to

move into a home of their own, Coach Jerry Wilson and wife, Diane, moved in. After the Wilsons, Coach Wes Kittley and wife, Linda, served as supervisors. After a time, thinking changed, and it was decided that athletes should not be housed apart from the regular student body. Athletes joined other students, and Morris became a regular dormitory for men.

Morris Dormitory was not too much in demand for a time; in fact, for some years it was vacant. Major Boglin and Cynthia Cooke were deans of students in the office of Charles Trevathan, vice president for student services from 1991 to 1997. As dean, Boglin dealt with problems of non-traditional students living in regular dormitories. "Non-traditional" refers to older students or students with a handicap, such as blindness, who need a place other than a regular dormitory to live. And he found that more students in that category were coming to college. The thought of converting Morris Dormitory to apartments for non-traditional students occurred to him. He broached the subject; members of the administration and the board bought it; and it was done. A. B. Morris Hall became one of the most popular residence halls on the campus, with a waiting list.

In the fall of 1977, the W. C. and Vera Sikes Dormitory for 202 women was opened, the first dormitory with a private bath in every room. Sikes was built in San Antonio in independent modules of concrete and steel, weighing approximately 40,000 pounds each. After assembly by the H. B. Zachry Company in San Antonio, the modules, complete with plumbing fixtures, were trucked to Abilene and set in place on the prepared foundation. Stevens remarked to H. B. "Pat" Zachry, "That building should last until eternity." The reply was, "At least that long." The next year, a dormitory similar to Sikes was built for 252 men on the northern edge of Sherrod Residential Park. One wing was named for Lawrence L. Smith and the other for Walter H. Adams, and the complex was known as Smith-Adams. In 1997, the two-unit complex, which is separated by a living room, was redesignated as "Smith Dormitory" for men and "Adams Dormitory" for women.

Over a four-year period beginning in 1973-74, housing was provided for 838 additional students. Three of the four projects

332 - Reaffirming Our Purpose

– Sherrod, Sikes, and Smith-Adams – were financed at the three percent interest rate offered by the College and University Housing division of the Department of Housing and Urban Development. They were all revenue-producers and have paid off the loans ahead of schedule.

Third, an effective financial aid strategy was developed to increase enrollment through improving grants, loans, and work opportunities. Coach Jerry Mullins was appointed director of student financial aid June 1, 1971, and he ran that office throughout the remaining decade of the Stevens administration. Mullins was efficient, well-organized, and unfailingly courteous and helpful to students and parents. Many a student who could not otherwise have financed a college education could do so with a well-planned package of grants, loans, and part-time work.

One significant step forward was the Tuition Equalization Grant program, enacted by the Texas Legislature and signed into law by the governor on June 9, 1971. This program came into being largely through the lobbying efforts of Vice President Hunter, who also was executive director of the Independent Colleges and Universities of Texas. Thousands of students have been able to attend Abilene Christian with the aid of TEG grants since 1971.

As the years have passed, the portfolio of endowed scholarship funds has grown. Endowed scholarships as of May 31, 1997, amounted to $25,260,000. Interest earned by these endowed funds is available for merit and academic scholarships plus need-based awards. In 1970 endowed scholarships totalled only $830,000. Tuition has been increased through the years but not nearly as much as scholarship funds, which have made it possible for many students to pay the tuition.

The Federally Insured Student Loan Program was part of the Higher Education Act of 1965 and was signed into law by President Lyndon B. Johnson on the campus of Southwest Texas State University at San Marcos in 1965. FISL was not a direct government loan program. Banks were to make the loans. The student could borrow money for college purposes. The government would pay interest on behalf of the borrower while he or she was in school, so banks were assured of getting their interest payments. Nine months after graduation or "quituation," the borrower was to begin payments of principal and interest and would have up to ten years to repay the loan. Extensions were granted if, for example, military service intervened, or if a decision was made to go to graduate or professional school. In case of death, the loan was canceled. The FISL program would pay the bank note. In case of default, the government paid the bank and then began a process of collecting from the defaulter. In the eyes of outsiders, banks could not lose. But banks for the most part were usually uninterested in making the loans. Amounts were too low, payback too long, and government requirements for "due diligence" in collections before government insurance was effective were too time-consuming. Hence, the program designed to help students pay their way through college came to a virtual standstill.

Abilene Christian applied and won approval as a lender under the Guaranteed Loan Program, as FISL came to be called. The board voted to set aside considerable sums from endowment for loans, a good investment, with principal and interest guaranteed. But soon demand became so great the initial sum set aside for FISL was insufficient. Board members were reluctant to go overboard in investing the endowment in such a manner. Then, the college discovered banks would be willing and able to make the loans to students and service them during their college years if they could sell the paper before payback began and before the college graduates scattered all over the world while owing money to local banks. In consultation with a Dallas law firm and a Dallas investment firm, Abilene Christian took a leading role in getting legislation through the United States Congress, the Texas Legislature, the Taylor County Commissioners Court, and the Abilene City Council, making possible the establishment of the Abilene Higher Education Authority. AHEA had the power to issue tax-exempt bonds to secure capital to be used in buying student loan notes from banks when banks were ready to turn them over. Money became available to students and parents who needed it.

Enrollment boomed. Fall registration figures were as follows:

1969 – 3,110
1970 – 3,217
1971 – 3,311
1972 – 3,346
1973 – 3,365
1974 – 3,647
1975 – 3,830
1976 – 3,979
1977 – 4,220
1978 – 4,231
1979 – 4,372
1980 – 4,560

Then, Christian Education Sundays came into the picture. Dr. Walter Adams came by the president's office one day to offer his services in a unique undertaking. He said that if the college would secure speaking appointments for him on Sunday evenings, he would travel at no charge other than perhaps reimbursement for gasoline to various places and talk on the subject of Christian education. He was not thinking about a commercial for ACC; rather he would discuss biblical teachings from Old and New Testaments concerning parents and children. Naturally, he would mention the role that Christian institutions of higher education could play in the lives of students, but he would talk about all Christian colleges. The idea seemed sound. Various churches were contacted and were enthusiastic. The upshot was that soon Dean Adams and other members of the administration and faculty were on the road or in the air on Sundays. "Christian Education Sundays," they were called. If a congregation did not want a speaker to displace the pulpit preacher, a meeting with the high school class was arranged. Through the years, beginning with early church-related colleges in America, concerns were raised because so many colleges that started as institutions for Christian higher education gradually drifted away from their first loyalties. People at

Abilene Christian were and are determined that such shall not happen here. Christian Education Sundays were an excellent way to keep in touch with church members over the nation.

At the end of Stevens' second year in office in May 1971 meeting of the Board of Trustees, Chairman Willard Paine announced that, in keeping with a Southern Association recommendation, he was assigning board members to working committees. There would be five committees, with nine members on each committee. Jack Pope was chairman of the committee on academic affairs with Dr. Bill Humble, vice president for academic affairs, as the staff resource person. The committee on student personnel services was headed by R. V. Hardegree with Vice President Garvin Beauchamp as staff resource. Finance was chaired by Jasper Howard, and Vice President Bill Hilton served that group. The committee on public relations and development was presided over by Gilbert T. McLeskey, with Milton Fletcher, vice president for development and public relations, as resource. Finally, the committee on purpose was led by Dr. J. P. Gibson with President Stevens as resource. The staff resource person for each of these committees was responsible for providing reports to the group, taking minutes, and providing whatever assistance he could in helping the committee function.

The roles of the first four committees were self-explanatory. The committee on purpose needed some defining, and Paine charged the group:

> The function of this committee will be to review constantly any and all offices of the college operation to determine whether the underlying purpose of the institution is being fulfilled. It will be the prerogative of this committee to delve into any matter pertaining to the functioning of the institution, including the academic, student personnel services, finance, and public relations divisions, to determine how well the college is fulfilling its commitment.

At the beginning of Stevens' third year in office in August 1971, Board of Trustees Chairman Paine gave further emphasis to the importance of the working committees, as described in the minutes: "Chairman Willard Paine reviewed the activities of the five special board committees, stating that the committees were designed to carry the major work load of the board. He feels that attendance at the committee meetings is even more important than attendance at board meetings." Willard Paine made numerous contributions to the ongoing of Abilene Christian, but the leadership he provided in setting up working committees as the backbone of the board structure was one of his most valuable contributions. Since then, board members in their committees have been receiving information they have needed in order to make informed decisions, and they have had ample input into the operation and general direction of the institution.

On one other subject, Paine trod where others hesitated insofar as board membership was concerned. B Sherrod had proposed the idea of an age of retirement for board members just as for faculty, but the suggestion lay dormant. In one of Paine's first meetings, June 1, 1967, he acknowledged that the officers of the board had been instructed to come up with a recommendation. At the November meeting that year, the board voted that a member whose regular term expires after he has reached his seventieth birthday "might be elected to Senior Board Member status, with the privilege of attending meetings and entering into all discussion but with no voting privileges."

At a meeting of the board in September 1973, Paine announced the appointment of a committee to nominate a new chairman. He asked the members to be prepared to report the next February. When the time came, the committee nominated Ray McGlothlin Jr. to be the tenth chairman of the Board of Trustees, the first Abilenian to serve as chairman since 1947.

Faculty members added during the Bill J. Humble years as chief academic officer, 1969-76, and who stayed at least ten years are Jon Ashby, communication disorders; Bryan E. Brokaw, agriculture; Wendell Broom, Bible; Edward E. Coates, education; Jane Coates, education; Dan Coker, Bible and missions; Richard A. Cox, English; Addie Felts, physical education; Bo Green, mathematics; Kelly Hamby; Marsha Harper, library; Edwin B. Headrick, psychology; Billy Van Jones, psychology; F. Furman Kearley, Bible; Jean Crawford Marsh, education; Gary McCaleb, management; Paul Edwin Morris physics; Brad

Reid, management; Sarah Johnston Reid, music; Delno Roberts, library; Charles Rudolph, testing and career counseling; Paul D. Schulze, physics; Willard Tate, physical education and communication; Rollo B. Tinkler, sociology and social work; Jeff Warr, journalism and mass communication; Christian William Willerton, English; Art Williams, art; and John T. Willis, Bible and ministry.

Ed Brown replaced Humble as chief academic officer in 1976, and he served in that position until 1982. Faculty members added during the Brown years who stayed at least ten years are Cheryl M. Bacon, journalism and mass communication; Jozell Brister, management; Robert E. Brown, foreign languages; James Clinton Cooke, industrial technology; Carley H. Dodd, communication; Ian A. Fair, Bible and ministry; Charles Felix, geology; Barbara Gray, academic advancement; C. G. Gray, education; Mel Hailey, political science; Adam Hester, theatre; Wanda Montgomery Higgins, home economics and family studies; Vera Justice, accounting; Dickie Leroy Hill, exercise science and health; Dutch Hoggatt, journalism and mass communication; Arlie Hoover, history; D'Lyla Kirby, communication disorders; William Lynn Luttrell, exercise science and health; Merlin Mann, journalism and mass communication; Rusty McLen, marriage and family therapy; Archie Manis, biology; Edward F. Mathews, missions; Tom Milholland, Biblical and family studies; Royce L. Money, Bible and ministry and university president; James Ross Nichols, biology; Perry Reeves, chemistry; Ken Roach, library; Ervin Michael Sadler, physics; Virginia Sadler, art; Michael Scarbrough, music; Charles Small, management sciences; John Smallwood, computer science; Henry Speck III, history; and R. Dale Tacker, education.

The Paine-led trustees and the Stevens-led administration in the fall of 1970 were approached by the trustees of Christian College of the Southwest in Dallas and the trustees of Fort Worth Christian College, asking the Abilene leaders to assume operations on both Metroplex campuses. The request posed a difficult challenge to the Abilene Christian trustees and administration. On the one hand, the two campuses had good buildings and locations, and Abilene might introduce some innovative programs that would be impractical on the Abilene campus. On the other hand, the junior colleges were quitting because of lack of money, and even the experienced, successful Abilene team would be challenged to succeed in Abilene and Dallas-Fort Worth. Abilene Christian trustees, nevertheless, voted approval provided the Metroplex campuses paid their way without draining any money out of the Abilene budget. The operation began without any commitment as to how long it would last.

Dr. Henry E. Speck Jr. was on leave of absence from Abilene while his wife, Bea, was completing her doctorate in history at Texas Christian University. He was asked to take over as dean of the Dallas campus. Dr. Thomas A. Shaver of the Bible Department was on leave because his wife, Waunette, was working on a doctorate at North Texas State University in education. He was asked to take over as dean of the Fort Worth campus. Douglas Warner, who had been serving efficiently in Abilene as director of student financial aid and had demonstrated ability to handle financial affairs, was sent as administrative director of both campuses. His job was to see that no money was lost.

Speck and Shaver both did good jobs with limited resources. After a year, both returned to their teaching positions in Abilene, leaving Warner in charge in Dallas and Fort Worth. At the same time, Don Drennan was appointed assistant to the president in Abilene, with one of his numerous assignments being to coordinate affairs on the Abilene campus with Metroplex operations.

A similar agreement was sought with the Fort Worth police department, but to no avail. The Fort Worth campus was turned over to Fort Worth Christian Schools, and the entire Abilene Christian program in the Metroplex was now in Dallas and was called Metrocenter. After 1976 it was known as ACU/Dallas. In 1982, the decision was made for the Dallas operation to become independent of Abilene, with its own Board of Trustees, and the name was changed to Amber University. Dr. Douglas Warner is the only president the remarkably successful Amber has had, and its enrollment is limited to 1,500 students.

Dr. Warner told how the Dallas program succeeded in a 1996 report to his board:

> In all likelihood, the educational venture in Dallas would have ended in failure had it not been for a chance meeting with the head of the Dallas police department, Chief Frank Dyson, in June of 1971. The chief reported that he was very interested in upgrading the quality of the Dallas officer by sending him or her to college. However, because of the rotation schedule ... officers could not go to college in a traditional setting. Shifts rotated from day to night every 60 days.... [A] schedule was devised that would accommodate the officers' rotating schedule. The class concept became known as the 'flip-flop' schedule where the same instructor taught the same material twice – once at night and once in the day. The student could attend either section and get the knowledge needed .... The plan ... represented a new educational focus. The Dallas campus had found the working adult, and to nearly everyone's surprise the Dallas campus operated in the black financially its first year.

Shortly before noon Wednesday, January 9, 1974, Chancellor Don Morris collapsed and fell on the campus, just east of the library. He was walking from Moody Coliseum, where he had attended a meeting of preachers, to his office in the Mabee Auditorium wing of the Brown Library. Bible professor Woodrow Wilson was with him. Another member of the Bible faculty, R. L. Johnston Jr. was walking nearby and saw what had happened. Leaving Wilson and others who were coming along to look after the fallen leader, Johnston rushed to the Morris office nearby and asked Delno Roberts, who had been Morris' secretary for seventeen years and was the widow of Bible professor J W Roberts, to call an ambulance and Mrs. Morris, which Mrs. Roberts did. Johnston then ran across the campus to the chancellor's residence on Campus Court to drive Mrs. Morris to the scene. It was a very cold morning, but bystanders had shed their overcoats and covered the stricken chancellor. The ambulance arrived without delay, and attendants began applying first aid, which continued all the way to the West Texas Medical Center. Johnston drove Mrs. Morris to the hospital and stayed with her until their son, Tommy, and other family members were on hand. Don H. Morris was pronounced dead at 1:30 in the afternoon. Because registration for the spring semester was not scheduled until Friday, January 18, most students and faculty got word of the death via radio and newspapers. In his national radio broadcast Thursday morning, January 19, Paul Harvey reported, "Obituaries include Dr. Don Heath Morris, Mister Abilene Christian College. Heart attack on his beloved campus at 71."

At the next meeting of the Board of Trustees, a committee was appointed to decide on a proper memorial for Morris. The decision was unanimous for a Don H. Morris Center for the communication arts. This seemed most appropriate because Don Morris was a communicator of the highest order and the first chairman of the Public Speaking Department when it was separated from English in 1934. What started as the Public Speaking Department became "Speech" and then "Communication," but, by whatever name, it began with Don Morris. The building would come to house the departments of Communication, Journalism and Mass Communication, Art, and Family and Consumer Sciences. Also planned was a free-standing but adjacent 800-seat multi-purpose auditorium, designed especially for fine arts concerts, guest lecturers, and a large variety of special events.

Architects Tittle and Luther developed a complex that contained, including the auditorium, 116,700 square feet of floor space, second only to the coliseum-physical education complex in size. In addition to serving as the home of four academic departments, it is headquarters for the *Optimist*, the *Prickly Pear*, public radio station KACU-FM, and television studios; the division of communication disorders, chaired by Dr. Jon K. Ashby; for a time, the offices of Vice President Hunter; and the offices of Dr. Colleen Durrington, dean of the College of Arts and Sciences.

Trustees and members of the National Development Council, Advisory Board, and administration worked to recruit funds for the center. Any facility commemorating the life of Don Morris was destined to attract widespread support. Foundations responded generously. The Brown Foundation of Houston, having become acquainted with the college in giving $500,000 for the Margaret and Herman Brown Library, duplicated that gift in support of the Morris Center. The Mabee Foundation gave $250,000. The Kresge Foundation of Michigan came through with $100,000. They were friends of Milton Fletcher. The Glenmede Trust, a Pew family foundation, of Philadelphia gave $25,000. This group had become acquainted with Morris in connection with Freedoms Foundation of Valley Forge, which had honored him and the college for support of the free enterprise system. The Fondren Foundation of Houston and the Amon Carter Foundation of Fort Worth were donors. Acquaintance with the Carters later resulted in support of the School of Nursing.

A great gift came from the Cullen Foundation of Houston. Members of the Cullen family and other directors knew little about Abilene Christian College. Furthermore, most of their gifts went to good causes in the Houston area, such as the world-renowned medical center. One advantage Abilene Christian had was that the Cullens were great supporters of Houston Mayor Louie Welch, and they knew "because he told them, as he told anybody and everybody who would listen" that he was a graduate of Abilene Christian and a trustee. The mayor and Stevens made some visits and applied for a grant of $500,000. One day a call came from Roy Cullen, vice president and secretary-treasurer of the foundation, saying that the directors were willing to give $1 million if the college would agree to use half of it for the Morris Center and set up the other $500,000 in endowment to support faculty research projects. Response was, of course, affirmative. The Cullen Endowment for Faculty Enrichment has assisted many faculty members in undertaking projects resulting in intellectual enrichment and enhanced classroom teaching. This gift was the only example on record of a foundation's decision to give ACC twice as much as it had requested.

The foundation gifts were appreciated. However, a large part of the funding came from individuals and couples. Mr. and Mrs. Roy Coffee of Dallas, Mr. and Mrs. Dean Walling of Los Angeles, Mr. and Mrs. Ray McGlothlin Jr. of Abilene, Mr. and Mrs. Harrold Owen of Fort Worth, and Mr. and Mrs. Robert S. Bell of Dallas were major donors. Hundreds of gifts brought the total to approximately $5.5 million, enough money for the building contract, furniture, and equipment. Rose and Sons of Abilene were low bidders at $3,619,500. The contract was signed November 29, 1976.

The board decided to name the auditorium the Roy and Lillie Cullen Auditorium. The communication portion of the sprawling complex was named the Roy and Winnie Coffee Communication Hall. The Art Department section was named the Alice Pratt Brown Art Hall. The art gallery was named the Clover Virginia Shore Art Gallery. A column was erected outside of the main entrance designating it as the Don H. Morris Center, and a bust of Morris, sculpted by Arthur Williams, is in the foyer. Official opening of the Don H. Morris Center was September 5, 1978, four years and eight months after the revered president died on his beloved campus.

Naming the wing housing home economics, now the Department of Family and Consumer Sciences, Sherrod Hall was especially appropriate. Dr. Marie Wilmeth, the first woman faculty member at ACU to earn the doctor's degree, was chairman of the department for twenty-seven years. B Sherrod had, on more than one occasion, promised Dr. Wilmeth a good building. This was the fulfillment of his dream as well as hers.

Talk of changing from "College" to "University" dated back to the move to the new campus in 1929. However, with the crash and the Great Depression and the desperate battle for survival of the early 1930s, the idea was muted, and in fact died out. In the early 1970s, with enrollment moving steadily toward the 4,000 mark, with the growth of the Graduate School and the library, and with the growing prestige of the sciences and other academic fields, talk of a name change became prevalent once more.

Dean Emeritus Walter Adams was requested by the president to chair a special committee to study the subject and come up with a recommendation. Assistant to the President Don Drennan was named as administration resource person for the committee. Members were Dr. J. P. Gibson and Wilson C. "Dub" Orr for the Board of Trustees, Ernest Walls and Jimmy Jividen for the alumni, Dr. Mike Kemp and Dr. Bea Speck for the faculty, and Kelly Utsinger and Jeff Hicks for the student body.

Some reasons for the change were considered:

1. Many two-year institutions were dropping the "junior college" designation and were becoming simply "colleges." Abilene Christian was not a junior college.

2. Abilene Christian College was the only institution in Texas offering work above the master's degree, "the 90-semester-hour degree in Bible," known as a college.

3. "University" might make the institution more attractive to students transferring from other institutions at the junior, senior, or graduate levels.

4. Prestige of a degree from a "university" might enhance job opportunities for Abilene Christian graduates.

5. Some individuals and/or organizations would perhaps be more likely to contribute to a university than to a college.

6. Materials published by the Chamber of Commerce and other media referred to Abilene as a "city with one university and two colleges," which could be interpreted as one "big" school and two "little"schools. ACC was larger than either of the other two.

Some reasons against the change were considered:

1. Abilene Christian College, ACC, had a proud history and was well established academically and in such activities as athletics, music, and debate. Many believed that a change of name would lose much of the identification gained over the years.

2. A change of name might be construed by some as a change in the basic purposes of the institution.

3. The institution might become known as a "weak" university rather than as a "strong" college.

4. Administrative costs might increase.

5. Some people believed that institutions that do not offer doctoral degree programs should not be known as universities.

Dean Adams went about the task of chairing the committee in his customarily thoroughgoing way; it was a working committee. During the fall of 1974, the committee turned in its recommendation that the name should be changed if agreement could be reached on structure of the university. This report was submitted to the committee on purpose of the

Board of Trustees. Chairman of the committee was Texas Supreme Court Justice Jack Pope. Minutes of the meeting of the board for February 24, 1975, contain this paragraph: "Judge Pope reported on the study that had been made regarding a name change for the college. A motion was made by Judge Pope and seconded by Willard Paine that the study be continued with emphasis regarding the administrative changes that would be necessary, and that a report be made at the next board meeting." One year later, Judge Pope moved and Willard Paine seconded that the name of the institution be changed to Abilene Christian University. The vote was unanimous. The proper amendment to the charter was filed with the Texas Secretary of State, making the change official.

A message from the president of the university to prospective students and others on the mailing list read:

> IT IS NOW ABILENE CHRISTIAN UNIVERSITY! At 3:01 p.m., February 22, 1976, the name of Abilene Christian College was changed to Abilene Christian University.... We are excited about ACU and look forward to an exciting year in 1976-77. Abilene Christian has never enjoyed such popularity. Even though our enrollment has increased steadily for the past seven years, this year's is the largest increase ever. At the current time we are running ahead of last year's application total by over 329. Those students interested in coming to ACU who have not made application need to do so immediately.

At the beginning of the change to university designation, organizational revision was minimal. The university was simply divided into an undergraduate college, under the leadership of a new dean, Dr. Edward M. Brown of the Department of Communication, and a Graduate School, headed by Dean Floyd W. Dunn. Both deans reported to Dr. B. J. Humble, vice president for academic affairs. Today, the academic program is divided into three undergraduate colleges – Arts and Sciences, Biblical Studies, and Business Administration plus the Graduate School and the Abilene Intercollegiate School of Nursing.

The Meek School of Nursing at Hendrick Medical Center, now known as "Hendrick Health Services," was a respected school but could not award bachelor of science in nursing degrees. It prepared nursing students for their professional activities. After completing the prescribed course of study at

Meek, a student could take the state board examinations and, upon passing, was licensed as a Registered Nurse, "R.N." With the R.N. diploma, a nurse could get a job nearly anywhere. However, some shortcomings were connected with that procedure. Without a bachelor's and preferably a master's degree in nursing, one could not normally expect promotion to administrative or supervisory positions. An increasing number of nurses desired the additional opportunity to rise within the profession. They began visiting the presidents of the three local institutions of higher education, hoping that one of the three would set up a degree program in nursing. Several discouraging factors were confronted.

First, in order for the offering to be accredited by the National League for Nursing (degrees without such accreditation would not be recognized) the student-to-teacher ratio could be no larger than twelve to one, and preferably ten- or even eight to one. Colleges and universities accustomed to having twenty to one ratios or thereabouts found nursing programs considerably more expensive to operate than those from most departments.

Second, a shortage of faculty members with master's and doctor's degrees in nursing meant that nursing teachers commanded higher salaries than most disciplines.

Third, no one of the three schools wanted to set up a degree program to compete with the Meek School of Nursing and its excellent diploma program. The people at Hendrick were most cooperative and offered to merge the Meek school into a degree-granting program if that seemed to be the way most of the nursing students wanted to go.

A unique solution came about. The three Abilene universities – Abilene Christian, Hardin-Simmons, and McMurry – established an entity known as the Abilene Intercollegiate School of Nursing and, in cooperation with Hendrick, began offering the bachelor of science in nursing degree. The plan of operation was for the nursing student to matriculate at the chosen parent university and remain a student at that university until graduation. The student would take the first two years on campus doing the core courses required of all students plus nursing support courses. If admitted to the nursing program, the student would do the last two years at AISN on the Hendrick campus, including nursing studies as well as experience in the various clinical specialties and in community agencies. At the end of four years, the successful student would receive the bachelor's degree in nursing from the parent university.

Students began enrolling in pre-nursing at the three universities in the fall of 1979. This did not mean that they would be automatically admitted to the School of Nursing for their upper level work. They had to make high marks during their first two years and pass a battery of tests for admission to the last two years. The first group in the upper division was admitted in 1981, and the first degrees were awarded in 1983.

The School of Nursing has been eminently successful. During the first years, sizable deficits had to be covered by the universities. Over the years, however, generous gifts have been made to an endowment, the income from which offsets costs not covered by tuition. Founding dean of the School of Nursing was Dr. Elaine Forrest, who came in 1979 and set up such a rigorous program that some students thought it was much too difficult. But by the time they completed their work and went to take the national licensing examinations, and especially when they went out into the work force, they appreciated the good education they had received at AISN. Dean Forrest served until 1988, when she resigned and was succeeded by Dr. Corine Bonnet, who has served effectively for a decade and will resume full-time teaching in the fall. The third dean, effective in the fall of 1998, is Dr. Cecilia Tiller, who was on the faculty of the School of Nursing of the University of Georgia in Augusta.

As of May 1997, 393 bachelor of science in nursing degrees have been awarded. In addition, thirty-seven students have received the graduate degree of master of science in nursing. For a number of years, a two-year program led to the associate of science in nursing degree. Students who took that route did thirty-four semester credit hours in non-nursing courses and thirty-four hours in nursing courses, an abbreviated curriculum. The student who went that way received the associate science in nursing degree, was eligible to take the national licensing examinations, and, if successful, was licensed as a Registered Nurse. A total of 217 students completed the associate of science in nursing degree. Because that program is available at Cisco Junior College, it has been discontinued by AISN.

Coinciding with the change of name to Abilene Christian University, a movement that originated spontaneously with the faculty dealt with spiritual reaffirmation. Several interested faculty members began talking among themselves and then to others and finally to the entire faculty assembly about the subject. In fact, the pre-session faculty conference in the fall of 1976 dealt almost altogether with the spiritual reaffirmation movement.

Wendell Broom, professor of missions and an early leader in the discussion, chaired a task force which ultimately involved not only the entire faculty but the administration, staff, student body, and trustees. He was the one who pointed out that historically colleges and universities that began with spiritual commitments gradually moved away from their beginnings and ultimately surrendered to secularism. The determination of the faculty and ultimately of the entire university community, including an overwhelming majority of the student body, was that Abilene Christian University would reaffirm and add new dimensions and strengths to its spiritual goals.

A statement of the time pointed out that alcohol or illegal drug use has never been permitted. The New Testament code of sexual conduct has always been required. Every student in a bachelor's degree program is required to include Bible in the course of study. Daily chapel is required as has been the case since 1906. Smoking is not permitted anywhere on campus. The statement continued,

> But, we realize that these outward things are not all that Christian values must be concerned with. We feel the unique contributions of Abilene Christian University to the field of higher education will be in providing excellent educational opportunities in all fields offered, while reaffirming and giving even more emphasis to our spiritual goals.

The movement received enthusiastic and prayerful support and has been reaffirmed every year since 1976. In fact, the

"Centennial Vision" for the twenty-first century, which will be discussed in the last chapter of this history, restates and strengthens the historic commitments of the institution since the days of Childers Classical Institute.

(AUTHOR'S NOTE: This part of *No Ordinary University* is told in the first person because the author of the book was so closely involved with it.)

Actually, I came in on the Masten estate deal rather late, but because I was in at the finish, which was exciting, and sometimes threatening, I will summarize it.

B Sherrod met Francis Oral "F. O." Masten in 1934. He read in newspapers about this big-time farmer, and heard that Masten was interested in buying twelve four-row tractors. Sherrod had the Massey-Harris dealership in Lubbock and decided to go for the order with his line of tractors. He met the prospective customer at the Citizens National Bank in Lubbock and gave his best sales pitch. He did not make the sale. Masten gave the business to Minneapolis Moline. When the tractors were delivered to him in Lubbock, Sherrod said that Masten staged a parade through town. He brought his armada of tractors down the street in front of Sherrod's business and waved merrily as he passed the store.

After the war, Sherrod introduced Masten to Don Morris. Masten's wife was a devout member of the Church of Christ, and he himself had a tendency to talk as if he were a member although it is not certain that he ever was. Whatever the truth may be on that score, no doubt exists about the fact that he was not an active member. But when the Development Office began operations in 1948 and announced the first long-range campaign for operational funds, building programs, and endowment, Sherrod and Masten were co-chairmen. Masten pledged 100 bales of cotton to the campaign, but when the price of cotton exceeded $100 per bale, he gave $10,000 cash instead. I had the privilege of meeting him during one of his visits to the campus in those days. Through the years after 1948, Sherrod and Morris paid a great deal of attention to Masten. Because he and his wife had no children, it was obvious that he would sooner or later do something with the huge estate he was building. Masten always seemed interested in what was happening on campus. He welcomed visits. He spoke in chapel and made a big hit with the students. He suggested once to President Morris that he would like for him to meet Mrs. Masten and get her support for the college. That meeting was arranged, and Morris found Mrs. Masten to be a gracious person. Masten's home was in Sudan, where he had large land-holdings, and she stayed at their home in Wellington, where they had a showcase farm. They were not divorced. He would visit her and take her on trips, but not a great deal of communication occurred between them. Hence, the request he made of President Morris was rather strange.

Mrs. Masten died in 1967, apparently intestate, or without a will. Four years later, a representative of another educational institution related to Churches of Christ filed for probate a document that purported to be the last will and testament of Mrs. Lily B. Masten. This document provided that, at her death, her half of the Masten estate would be divided among ten institutions, including Abilene Christian. It is not clear how many people knew of this document, but certainly nobody at Abilene Christian knew of it. Inasmuch as Mrs. Masten had been dead four years when the document surfaced, time had expired for filing for probate. However, the individual who had the will showed that he had been overseas doing mission work and had not heard of the death until recently. An extension for filing was granted.

Masten was devastated on learning of the existence of such a will. He had not been informed that his wife had signed such a document. He immediately announced that he would contest the effort to get the will admitted to probate. Sherrod and Morris were likewise surprised that such had been done and recommended to the Board of Trustees that although Abilene Christian was listed as one of the beneficiaries, we should not have anything to do with the effort to get the document admitted to probate. The board agreed.

Sherrod and Morris sincerely believed that Mrs. Masten was not competent to make a will. Consequently, when called as witnesses, they had to tell the truth as they saw it. They were only two of several witnesses. After two trials the case was decided in Masten's favor. The college's position in this case caused some hard feelings. The board chairman of one of the institutions wrote,

> This does not leave me with a very kindly feeling toward Abilene Christian College and its present administration. According to those present at the trial in Wellington, it appeared that ACC thought that by giving such testimony that they would gain considerably more through siding in with Mr. Masten.

Chancellor Morris explained his situation:

> I have felt from the time I first heard about the will some fifteen months ago and how it was obtained that the will was really not Mrs. Masten's because, for one thing, I did not think that she was competent to make a will. And now I have been called to testify in the trial, which I am compelled to do. This makes it so that I will be appearing on the side opposite to some of my best personal friends in the church and on the side opposite from several institutions that I have been interested in and have tried to help. Of course, when I am questioned, I can do nothing but give the facts as I know them.

Actually, Chancellor Morris and I did our best to work out a settlement with Masten whereby all ten of the entities would have received a substantial gift from him, but we could not put it over. He had too many projects and was too busy making money to talk about what he would do with all of it. So far as I know, none of the institutions hold continuing bitterness toward us.

After the death of Chancellor Morris in 1974, I took over the responsibility of visiting Masten now and then. I would always call before a visit. He was always cordial. Bob Hunter and Gus Bowman, a Dallas banker, a trustee of the college, and a friend whom Masten trusted, worked with him in trying to get a book written about his extraordinary life, but it did not work out. However, he always liked to have Bowman visit him, and he liked Hunter. Bill Decker, as development director, visited him occasionally. He liked Decker.

Gilbert McLeskey, an ACU trustee who was head of the trust department of Gus Bowman's bank in Dallas, was another welcome visitor. He and Masten talked estate planning and quail hunting. Masten had a large estate, with no plans for its future other than a large estate tax and distribution among relatives. Ed Wishcamper, editor of the *Abilene Reporter-News*, wrote a story for the paper on Sunday, November 7, 1965, in which he described the estate as "a fabulous 120,000-acre empire of farming, ranching and oil sprawled over six counties of the Panhandle and South Plains."

To tell the truth, I had about decided that he would never plan his estate. He would die without a will, but on Friday, February 9, 1979, he called me. That was a first. I had always called him. But Betty Whiteside said, "F. O. Masten is calling." I picked up the phone, and after an exchange of greetings, he said, "John Stevens, you haven't been out to see me now in quite a while." I thought he was just passing the time of day, so I replied, "That's right. I will try to get out there before long."

His next question showed that he was not just passing the time of day: "When can you come?" I looked at my calendar, which was desperately crowded, and said, "Well, this week we are getting ready for Lectureship and the annual board meeting, and then the following week we have Lectureship and the board meeting. Suppose I came out there about March 1?" He replied, "That's too long. The world may not stand that long." I began looking at page after page of my desk calendar, and a thought occurred: "What would you think of day after tomorrow – Sunday? I could be there about one o'clock Sunday afternoon." He agreed to that. I asked him if he could have somebody meet me at the little airstrip at Sudan, and the meeting was set.

After church services Sunday morning, I went out to the Abilene airport, where a pilot and a small airplane were ready to go, and we took off for Sudan. Landing on time, I found Curtis Savage, Masten's longtime bookkeeper and right-hand man, waiting, and we drove to the house. Masten was in the house alone. We visited for approximately three hours. I wrote this narrative while the visit was fresh in my memory:

There was a brief period of time that we simply exchanged pleasantries and talked about old times. Finally, he made me this proposition. He said that his properties were now getting too large for him to manage and that he did not have anybody working for him who could manage them.

He had therefore decided that he would consider deeding everything he had to Abilene Christian University. He wanted us to sell the properties because he was convinced that we also could not manage his estate. We should sell the properties for cash and good notes. He said that he had some people related to him and others who worked for him that he would need to take care of. He estimated that there would be possibly as many as thirty of these. To some he would like to provide $10,000 per year. To others $15,000. Maybe to some there would be as much as $25,000. For his brother, Robert, he would like to leave enough money for Robert to buy the land he is now farming. He mentioned 800 acres. He added, "You will have to take care of me, too."

He said, "I know you have been planning for this at least two years, so you ought to be able to come up with a plan very soon."

I asked him if he had his complete list of names. He said that he did not have it yet but that he would supply it in due time. He wanted to know what our plan would be for taking care of it.

I told him I would get back to Abilene, have our people together for breakfast the next morning, and go to work on a plan. I left his house about 4 p.m. and rode with Curtis back to the airstrip.

The next morning's agenda began with breakfast at seven in the President's Dining Room in the McGlothlin Campus Center. I was surrounded by legal and tax specialists and members of the administration and staff who were involved in financial affairs, and we spent the day working on a plan for this multi-million dollar estate.

On Tuesday morning, I called Masten and said we were ready with a plan. He said for us to come on.

Accompanied by the university's attorney, Gaston Welborn, I arrived at Sudan's airstrip shortly before three in the afternoon. We were met by Curtis Savage and driven to the house. We met with Masten alone.

I outlined a plan for setting up a series of unitrusts to be sure that we could pay all the people that he wanted us to pay. We proposed to fund the unitrusts with twenty times the annual payment requirement. In other words, if we were to pay somebody $10,000 a year for life, we would, after selling the land, set aside $200,000 to be the principal of the unitrust. I went on to suggest that, prior to completing the land sale,

ACU could begin paying the annuities if desired and gave him a financial statement showing that we had the cash reserves to do that. I told him that if he liked the plan, we were prepared with all the necessary papers for him to sign.

He invited us to step out to the office and to repeat for the group assembled there what I had proposed to him. There we found Robert, his brother; Curtis Savage; Al Harrison, his office manager; J. K. Griffith, who farmed a large tract of Masten land; and Griffith's son, Curtis – a lawyer. I went over the plan with them. Everything seemed calm enough, but then Masten threw a surprise at us. My notes say:

> F. O. said he would like to provide a large enough annuity to enable J. K. Griffith to buy the land he was farming. We learned that for 39 years Griffith had farmed about 12,000 acres of Masten's best cotton land, which Masten valued at about $750 an acre.

We did some fast calculating and saw that the land would be worth approximately $9 million. If it were to be sold to Griffith for, say, seven per cent interest, an annuity that would pay interest alone would be $630,000 per year. And yet an annuity that large would result in such a huge income tax that there would not be enough money to pay the interest and principal. So we said that we would have to do some more figuring for that one.

At the conclusion of our meeting, Masten was all smiles. He asked, jokingly, "Can I get any of you fellows a drink of whiskey?" He said that he would talk with some other people, including the Baptist Foundation, but he would be back in touch. We left Sunday about 6 p.m.

On the way home, Welborn told me that Curtis Griffith had taken him aside and assured him that the Griffiths did not want or need an annuity of any kind from F. O. Masten. All they wanted was an opportunity to buy the land they had been farming for a reasonable price. They thought a reasonable price was in the neighborhood of $350 to $400 per acre rather than the $750 Masten had mentioned.

The next day, our group met and decided our original proposal was the best way to go, plus the Griffith proposal concerning their land instead of the impossible annuity Masten had proposed but which the Griffiths did not want.

Thursday, February 15, I called Masten and told him we were ready to present our amended proposal. He said he was not quite ready. He had to see some other people. Ten days went by. Sunday, February 25, I was in Dallas, preparing to speak at the morning service of Skillman Avenue Church. During the Bible class period, I was in the minister's office and decided to give Masten a call. That was when he unloaded on me.

He said,

> John Stevens, that plan you brought out here is the worst thing I have ever seen. You fellows do not know how to handle any estate. I'm going to give this whole thing to the Baptist Foundation. Those people are smart. You should go and spend some time with them, and maybe you could learn how to do things. I have no more time to waste on you.

I had to compliment him on his forthrightness. I said, "F. O., I'm sorry if we failed you. I hope we are still friends. Let us know if we can ever be of service."

I thought, "Stevens, you have lost it. B Sherrod and Don Morris worked with this man for decades, and you have destroyed the relationship." When I returned to Abilene, I called board Chairman Ray McGlothlin and told him about the call. I said, "Ray, you have my resignation. I have failed in carrying out my responsibilities." He said, "John, don't worry about it. It's only money." I said, "It is a big endowment." He replied, "I meant what I said. It's only money. You don't need to resign. Quit worrying about it." So I had no more contact with F. O. Masten until he began sending messages to me. Gus Bowman went to see him. He reported to me that the problem was not with our proposal but that Masten was simply not ready to decide yet. Meanwhile, Curtis Savage told me that Masten had also dismissed the Baptist Foundation people rather abruptly.

Three months to the day after the ill-fated telephone call, I received a call from Bernard Wilson, an elder of the Church of Christ in Sudan and a good friend and patron of Abilene Christian University. He told me that there had been a big misunderstanding between F. O. and his six-foot-six-inch nephew, W. C. Masten, and that after each had threatened the other,

NO ORDINARY UNIVERSITY – 355

F. O. had locked himself in his house and was not letting anybody in. For their part, W. C. Masten and Al Harrison had arranged to have his telephone disconnected so that he had no telephone connection with the outside world. However, at five o'clock that morning, May 25, 1979, F. O. had sneaked out of his house and had gone to Curtis Savage's house nearby to call Wilson. He asked him to come to see him as quickly as possible.

Wilson was there at 6 a.m. Masten told about his troubles with his relatives and that they were holding him prisoner. He asked Wilson to call me in Abilene and ask me to come to see him. Wilson called. I could hardly believe it. Wilson went on to tell me, however, that when he emerged from the house, W. C. Masten stopped him and they had a conversation. It ended when W. C. told him, "I don't want you or your bunch to come around here any more." Wilson assumed that by "your bunch" he meant ACU people.

He said he was relaying F. O. Masten's urgent message asking me to come to see him, but he was also saying that after his confrontation with W. C. Masten, he would not be in position to go with me.

The same day, I had another call from Wilson. He had heard from W. C. Lewis, a nephew of the late Mrs. Masten. Lewis, being a relative, was permitted to visit F. O. He had seen him later in the day. Lewis reported that Masten insisted that he get word to John Stevens to come to his house to see him as soon as possible. I asked Wilson, "How can I get in to see him?" He said that Hugh Vincent, Masten's oldest and closest friend, had volunteered to take me to the house. Vincent had said, "I am concerned about F. O.'s health, and nobody can tell me not to go see him." I arranged for Wilson to meet Bob Hunter, Gaston Welborn, and me at the Littlefield airport late Monday afternoon, May 28, and we would plan to visit F. O. that evening.

We did not get to see Masten. When Hugh Vincent went out to tell Masten that he was bringing us out that evening, he was accosted by W. C. Masten and told to keep us at his house until he could get there. Vincent, who had been so confident, found that there was someone who could tell him not to visit his friend, F. O. At Vincent's house, we were met by Robert Masten, F. O.'s brother; W. C. Masten, F. O.'s nephew "but not the son of Robert"; and Al Harrison, F. O.'s office manager and son-in-law of W. C.

W. C. told us that F. O. was never going to do anything for Abilene Christian University. It was all just a game with him. Now that F. O. was getting old and sickly "in his 89th year," he did not need anybody bothering him. The family had set up a twenty-four-hour surveillance of the house, and nobody could get in to see him without his, W. C.'s, clearance. "Besides," W. C. told us, "if he tries to write a will, we will go to court and have him declared crazy, just like he had his wife declared crazy when her will turned up."

We returned to Abilene. My chief regret was that F. O. might not ever learn that at least we had tried. It turned out that he did know. I was inclined to think that W. C. was correct in saying that F. O. was never going to do, or maybe be able to do, anything about his estate planning. Five months passed with no further contact. On Tuesday, October 23, 1979, a man who identified himself as Joe Salem from Sudan called my office. I was not in, but he gave his message to Betty Whiteside. He said he was calling from a pay phone in the Methodist Hospital at Lubbock. He had been visiting with F. O. Masten, who was a patient there. Masten had asked him to get in touch with John Stevens, president of Abilene Christian University, and to inform him that Masten wanted to see him the next morning at ten o'clock.

At three o'clock that afternoon, Salem called again. I happened to be in at that time. He told me that he just wanted to be sure I had received his message and wanted me to promise to be in Masten's hospital room the next morning. At nine o'clock that evening, Salem called again. This time he called Betty Whiteside at her home and left an urgent message to the effect that I should not, repeat not, go to see F. O. Masten. He left his home number in case there were any questions. Betty called me immediately. I phoned Salem and asked him, "What's the matter, Mr. Salem? Did members of the family get to you?" He confirmed that they had convinced him that I had better not try to see Masten and that his hospital room was guarded.

Again I was shut out. This did not trouble me very much, as I was still inclined to think that F. O. was, as his nephew had said, "playing games."

I was able to learn that he had advanced carcinoma of the tongue, involving the entire tongue and extending to the floor of the mouth. He could not talk much but could still write; hence, most of his communication was in written notes.

Wednesday evening, October 24, I received a call from a young woman who did not identify herself. She said that F. O. Masten wanted me to be in his room at 10 o'clock the next morning. He said for me to come unannounced so that I would be admitted to his room, which was number 324. At this point I called Willard Paine in Lubbock. I reviewed the situation for him and explained why I thought it would be hopeless for me to get in to see him. Then I said, "Now, Big Freight," a nickname he had acquired when he was a 240-pound tackle in an age of 160-pound running backs, "you have not been forbidden to see him, as I have been, directly and indirectly. Furthermore, members of the family who are guarding him may not know you, whereas they know me. And, besides, you are as big as those fellows are." And finally, jokingly, I said, "If anybody is going to get a whipping over this, I would prefer it to be you instead of me." Then I asked him if he would be willing to go to the Methodist Hospital and go by room 324. He might be able to see Masten, visit with him, explain why I had not been able to see him, and try to ascertain what he had in mind. He said he would be there at ten o'clock the next morning. Paine found the family guard missing although some hospital personnel were in the room. As soon as his visit was over, he called me, and with Betty Whiteside on the line, he dictated this message:

> I went in room 324 to see F. O. Masten. Mentioned my name and he knew me immediately. I said, "I bring greetings from John Stevens." He cautioned me to be quiet until he got everybody out of the room, and then he wrote the following messages – each message was on a separate slip of paper:
>
> Tell John Stevens to come see me for sure. Come unannounced."
>
> I got to do something now. Don't try to make appointment.

They will not let him in. It's my own folks. I want to give it all to the college – ACU.

I have six or seven million now. Between now and the first of the year – cotton two million. Oil leases. Cattle to sell.

I'm not Howard Hughes, but next man to him."

I have the CO2 gas that will unlock the Sanandres Lime. It [is] going to be millions.

Paine concluded his report to me by saying,

With talking and sign language, I told him that John Stevens said that if F. O. Masten wanted to see John Stevens, he would come if he had to bring the sheriff, and he nodded real vigorously and said, "Yea, yea." And then at the end he pointed toward Abilene and toward John's name again and waved both of his arms and indicated very vigorously that he wanted him to come and come sure enough.

Friday, Paine called to say that he went by room 324 again Thursday afternoon but saw somebody beside the nurse, so he passed on. Friday morning was the same story. It was not going to be easy to get in to see Masten. He had always been a powerful man who could give orders to his nephews and everybody around him, but now he was dying and in effect a prisoner.

Friday evening, October 26, the same young woman who had called me on Wednesday evening called again. This time she identified herself. She was Karla Moore, daughter of the W. C. Lewis who was the late Mrs. F. O. Masten's nephew. Karla and her husband, Lee, genuinely cared for "Uncle Oral," as they called him. They did not expect to receive anything at all from his estate. They simply thought he ought to be free to do what he wanted to do with what he had built up. They were in their mid-twenties. She told me that Uncle Oral had been giving notes to her. That very evening, while she and Lee were visiting, he had written these messages to her:

Hang around. I might want you to carry message for me.

John Stephens (sic) go to abstract office and draw deeds of all my properties. Go to abstract office Lubbock, Wellington, Dimmit, Amarillo. Every county seat.

I cannot do more than I am doing now. Your good friend.

(signed) F. O. Masten. (printed) F. O. MASTEN.

Mail this to John Stephens Abilene Christian University Abilene.

I'll be asking for concessions later but not unreasonable not unreasonable. Wake up and get on the ball. It is yours if you will get with. I don't need say more. I am a prisoner locked in from the world.

In an administrative session, we considered the question: "Why didn't you get a court order and if necessary a deputy sheriff and gain entrance to his room?" The answer was that he was obviously having to keep his plans confidential. If he had failed to keep his plans confidential, he might have been deprived of pen and paper or any opportunity to sign anything. For an estate valued at between $30 million and $40 million, a great many things could happen. If he wanted his people to know what he was going to do, it was his right to tell them, not ours. His old friend Hugh Vincent had said that nobody could keep him from going to see F. O. Masten, but he had found that even he could be stopped.

Karla Moore had a solution. She said that all members of the family had a practice of leaving the hospital about six o'clock on Sunday evenings, to return Mondays. In all probability, only the special nurse who was sitting with him would be in the room. We decided to go to see him Sunday evening, October 28, 1979, accepting the invitation that had been coming from him off and on since May 25. Willard Paine had consulted a Lubbock attorney who had done some work for him and his bank – Alton Griffin. I called Karla and Lee and Willard and made arrangements for Gaston Welborn and me to meet them on Sunday afternoon in Griffin's office. In that session we planned procedures and agreed to meet at a certain location on the parking lot of Methodist Hospital shortly before 8 p.m. We were all on time for the meeting.

The plan was that Willard's wife, Billie, would go first. Her job was simply to walk down the corridor past room 324 and see whether anyone except hospital personnel were in the room. She came back to the parking lot and reported that she did not see anyone. Karla and Lee Moore then went to room 324 because they were entitled to visit. As soon as they entered the room, Masten took a sheet of paper from under the blanket and handed it to Karla. She saw my name written on it and put it in her purse. Lee left the room to get me. He, Griffin, and I went to the room. Masten greeted me warmly. He was crying. Karla stood at the head of his bed on his left side, wiping tears from his eyes, while I was on the other side, trying to help but was not much help. We shook hands and greeted each other. He then signalled the duty nurse to step out of the room, and Griffin went with her. Karla then handed me the sheet of paper from her purse. I read it silently Karla says that I said, "God bless you, F. O." He then signalled for me to read it aloud, and I did. He had written on a sheet of paper labelled "Methodist Hospital, Lubbock, Texas, PROGRESS NOTES":

> At Methodist Hospital
>
> Sunday, Oct. 28th, 1979
>
> Dr. John Stephens
>
> My dear friend:
>
> It is now my will and testimony to leve [sic] Abilene Christian University all I have in this world. Take over as soon as possible. Yours truly,
>
> [signed] F. O. Masten
>
> [printed] F. O. MASTEN
>
> W. C. Lewis my executor of Quanah, mailing address is Medicine Mound, Texas

After reading the document aloud, I asked him, "Is this what you want, F. O.?" He gestured affirmatively and said, "Yes." Masten then asked for pen and paper and spent quite a bit of time writing a sheet of instructions to accompany his will. When he had completed it, he asked me to read it aloud:

> I just now got through writing my will again to the university. That will get if you will handle it right. I want all my nieces and nephews to have someng [sic] like enough to look well. My hired men some Mexicans, Negros, some are just plane [sic] working white people. Dr. Stephens, there will be plent [sic] if handled right.
>
> On Canadian River rance [sic] is CO2 gas that unlocks all my hard formations. There are millions there. You might need let the CO2 gas go to sell ranch but retain right to be used on my

other ranch."

Yours truly,

[signed] F. O. Masten

[printed] F. O. MASTEN

October 28, 1979

Methodist Hospital

F. O. Masten

After reading this document aloud, I again asked, "F. O., is this what you want?" When he nodded affirmatively, I said, "Then that is exactly what we will do."

At this time, the nurse came in to take a blood sample, and Karla, Lee, and I stepped out of the room. I went to Alton Griffin, handed him the two documents, and told him to head for the group in the parking lot with them. I would join them later.

After the nurse had finished, Karla, Lee, and I went back into the hospital room. F. O. wanted pen and paper again, and this time he signalled for Karla to leave the bedside. He had something confidential he wanted to write to me. Here was that message:

> I have a friend in Amarillo at 102 Rosemont that I want her to have the house that she now lives in and my log house on ranch at Morton and the unit houses and farm there.
>
> The Morton house is where my nephew Bob lives in now.
>
> I want her to have Twenty Five Thousand per year. She thinks she does not like the university.
>
> She has two sisters that will live with her.
>
> If you will go to abstract office in Lubbock and Amarillo and fix all the deed I'll turn it to you now. I mean now.
>
> [signed] F. O. Masten
>
> [printed] F.O. MASTEN

Oct. 28, 1979

F. O. Masten

He did not want me to read that one aloud. It was not for Karla and Lee to know. We concluded our visit about 9:30 p.m. that Sunday evening. Gaston Welborn and I flew back to Abilene, and the others went to their Lubbock homes. It had been a successful Sunday evening.

Three comments can be made about the three documents that were handed to me that evening:

First, there seemed to be no doubt in Masten's mind that he had written a bona fide will. It was a holographic will. It is noteworthy that he wrote, "Abilene Christian University." Nearly everybody was still saying "Abilene Christian College." This helped to show that he knew what he was doing.

Second, he intended for us to share with his relatives. He did not intend to cut his family out of his will. A compromise of some kind would be necessary.

Third, he wanted us to get busy and start preparing deeds for him to sign. This would have created a storm of controversy centered around the bedside of a dying man. He had less than two and a half months to live, so we simply filed that request.

Karla Moore was the real heroine. She was ably supported by her husband, Lee, and by her great and unselfish parents, W. C. and Mollie Lewis. Willard Paine had a very important part in the entire process. So did his wife, Billie. The two lawyers present, Alton Griffin and Gaston Welborn, did their part. Arriving in Abilene about midnight Sunday, October 28, I was in the office on Monday, dictating reports and trying to figure out what had been accomplished. A couple of days later, I was out of town and received an emergency call from Don Drennan, assistant to the president. He said, "There is considerable thought here among some of our people that we should go to Lubbock while Mr. Masten knows what he is doing and have legal people draw up these documents and have everything properly notarized and put in good shape." I said, "Don, don't let this happen. Hold everything until I get there. I will cancel my schedule here and come home immediately." I continued, "Don, I can guarantee anybody that there is absolutely no way we can get that done. We do not even want the relatives to know we have a will. We would be breaking faith with F. O. if we made this a public matter right now."

Don promised to work on the matter. I said I would wait to hear from him. Within a short time he called me back and said the problem had been solved. There would be no further action taken. I should continue my schedule.

I never did know, and did not need to know, who the individuals were who, with the best of intentions, wanted to wrap the deal up like a law school dean would possibly recommend. Don Drennan and Ray McGlothlin told me that attorney Jack Currey helped with advice that the handwritten will was probably the best thing we could have. It was most assuredly the only kind of will we could have obtained.

The next problem originated with Masten himself. He kept sending messages through Karla that I should be visiting with him. He wanted to know what we were doing about those deeds he was to sign. In one of his notes he wrote, "This is going to surprise my people. But better for all. They cannot handle a big estate like they trying to do it."

In another note to Karla, he said, "Call John Stevens and tell him to see me today alone. I might want he and Al to talk." He still wanted confidentiality as shown when he said "alone." But when he said he might want me to talk to Al Harrison, I was puzzled because Al was family.

Wednesday evening, November 14, I was in Fort Worth, preparing to go to Portland, Oregon, the next morning. Gaston called with word from Karla. She thought it essential that I should see F. O. because he might change his will. I canceled the Portland trip and the next morning flew back to Abilene. Welborn and I went on to Lubbock. Arriving in mid-afternoon, we met Karla and Lee at Griffin's office. It was decided that she would visit her Uncle Oral that evening and tell him that I would be there early the next morning. I had a terrible cold, however, and did not know whether to visit a sick man and expose him to my germs. When she visited him, he wrote this note: "Karla Moore. re: John Stevens visit unannounced. I will not take his cold. Slip in not let Al know."

I was in his room at 7:20 the next morning. I had to convince the nurse that I had a right to see him. I pointed out that he had asked to see me and suggested she ask him if he wanted to see me. He asked her to get out of the room and shut the door. Then he began writing notes to me and talking. I could not understand much of what he said. He was apparently wanting to discuss what we would do for Al Harrison and his sister, Dottie. He suggested a bonus of $50,000. Our visit was constantly interrupted by nurses and hospital aides coming in for one purpose or another. Finally, about 8:10 a.m. his nephew, Bob Masten, came into the room and instructed me to leave. He was courteous, explaining to me, "We don't mind you dropping by for a short visit, but you have stayed too long. You know he is incompetent, and these visits upset him."

So I bade F. O. good morning and started to leave the hospital room. He was saying, "No! No!" but Bob was standing with the door open, motioning me outside. I decided discretion was the better part of valor and left. Bob Masten's statement that they did not object to my dropping by for short visits was the first sign of welcome I had seen. We would see how long that would last.

That evening, back in Abilene, I received a call from W. C. Lewis. He had had a forty-five-minute call from W. C. Masten. He said Masten had been courteous enough but he had asked Lewis to ask his daughter, Karla, not to accept any more notes to call John Stevens. Masten told Lewis that my visit had been terribly upsetting. He finally admitted to Lewis, however, that the main thing upsetting F. O. was my being ordered to leave. He had refused to take medicine since the visit. He further said that Robert, the brother, had been appointed guardian six months earlier by the district court. Lewis might have misunderstood what Masten said on that point because records showed that it was just five weeks earlier that W. C. Masten, the nephew, and Robert Masten, the brother, had had themselves appointed temporary guardians by the county judge of Lamb County. Furthermore, the county judge had ruled that F. O. Masten was non compos mentis.

Later in the day of my morning visit, a letter came to me from an attorney for the family, requesting no further visits. We saw that a contest was seemingly inevitable and, remembering the Edwards case, lined up our attorneys. We were already working with **Alton Griffin in** Lubbock. We employed Stanley Wilson of **the Abilene** firm of McMahon, Smart, Wilson, Surovik, and **Suttle.** Hudson Smart of that firm had represented ACC in **the Edwards** case a quarter of a century earlier. His younger colleague, Wilson, was to take this case. To complete our team, we signed up a leading Littlefield attorney, Jerome Kirby. Our university attorney, Gaston Welborn, was with them all the way.

No matter what steps the family took to stop the flow of notes and messages from F. O. Masten to John Stevens, the notes kept coming. One said, "Someone should contact me every day from the college in person. Changes come and I have to meet with those things." Another said, "Do you talk to John Stevens. You are losing ground. You are too inactive. There is no way I can make contact except when you come or someone takes the message." That note was apparently to W. C. Lewis. He was supposed to tell Stevens that he, Stevens, was losing ground. Sunday, December 9, a note handed to Lewis said, "Feeling better. John Stevens need to be visiting me." Another said, "Have you talked John?"

I hated to ignore the wishes of a man who was dying. He was trying to do so much for us and was asking often for me to visit him. And yet I had been instructed from various sources to stay away. Finally, we decided that I must pay a visit. We got our legal people together and went to Lubbock. Monday, December 17, 1979, we filed in a Lubbock district court an application for a writ of habeas corpus, claiming that Masten was being illegally restrained of his liberty. Judge Robert Wright issued the writ, giving me permission to visit Masten provided one member of the family was in the room.

I received explicit instructions from Wilson and Kirby: "This may very well be the last opportunity you will ever have to visit this man," said Wilson. "Therefore, no matter who is in the room, you must tell this man publicly that his brother and his nephews are trying to take complete control of his estate, and they have had him declared non compos mentis – mentally unsound."

The reasoning behind the advice to make such a hard statement in the presence of a family member was tied to one or two recent notes Masten had written with an implied threat to change his will if someone from ACU did not visit him "every day." We wanted him to know that we could be depended on to tell him the truth about his estate, and we could be depended on to handle it responsibly, in keeping with his wishes, after his death.

It was a long walk down that hall for Gaston Welborn and me. Several Mastens were in the corridor. One aimed some profanity at us. I probably should have ignored it, but I said, "I have an order of the court here. Do you want to go and tell it to the judge?" Younger members of the family told him to be quiet. Robert, the brother, was the family member to accompany me into the room. After greetings were exchanged, I said, "F. O., did you know that your brother, Robert, and your nephews, are trying to take control of your entire estate? They have had you declared non compos mentis and have had themselves appointed your guardians." At this, the frail old man raised himself up on his elbows and shouted, "No! No!" which was about all he could say. Robert looked at me and in a low voice, said, "One of these days, Dr. Stevens, one of these days."

Then Robert said, "You have had your visit. It's been long enough." With the court order, I knew I did not have to leave. On the other hand, I had made the visit and said what we needed to say. We did not want to discuss the will in the presence of family members or even to disclose that we had a will. So we said our goodbyes and left the room and the hospital.

I never saw Masten again. Three weeks and two days after my visit, he died. As soon as word came of his death, Jerome Kirby went to the county courthouse in Littlefield and filed our will for probate. This was an important step. We filed the first and only will available.

From that point the Board of Trustees, with skillful leadership by chairman Ray McGlothlin Jr. took charge of Abilene Christian's side of the case. Lawyers for both the university and the family began taking depositions and preparing for trial. Along the way, however, they managed to work out a compromise that was good for everybody. The estate was divided approximately half and half. Some $11 million was added to the ACU endowment.

Karla and Lee Moore, who did so much to help her great uncle accomplish what he truly wanted to do and to help Abilene Christian University serve students throughout years to come, were rewarded with a generous cash settlement that was agreeable to them. Her father, W. C. Lewis, received a nice fee as executor. These people did what they did, not for any hope of personal gain, but because they thought they were doing what was right. ACU trustees were insistent that the university show proper appreciation.

Some ACU constituents wondered whether the trustees had made a mistake in compromising the case. They reminded us that in the Edwards Ranch case, no compromise had made and we had won the entire estate. The Masten case was different. Here, the donor had specified that we should provide "something like enough to look well" for the nephews and nieces. True, he did not say how much was "enough to look well," but these considerations went into the decision-making process:

First, a heavy federal estate tax would have to be paid out of the portion going to the family, and this would come off the top. There would not as much left as might appear at first glance.

Second, eighteen individuals were recognized as heirs at law; what was left after taxes would be divided among them, plus some others for whom the testator had made provisions.

Third, if the trustees were not sufficiently generous, we faced the likelihood of a long and costly period of time in court, with the possibility that in the end everybody would lose.

Hence, the settlement was made with no regrets and with good will on all sides, as far as I can tell.

In Abilene, the wets finally voted liquor in June 17, 1978. The election was close, but, as the old saying goes, close does not count except in horseshoes. Citizens who were opposed to liquor sales in the city lost the election. The precinct in which Abilene Christian University is located voted eighty-five percent against it. The vote would have been stronger than that except that the proponents chose a time for the election between sessions when most of our students were away from the campus.

A feature paragraph of The Associated Press story that went out over the nation was that the Abilene Christian University precinct voted overwhelmingly for legalization. The Abilene paper got it straight, but newspapers all over Texas carried the AP story as it came in on the wire. President Stevens was speaking in San Angelo on the Sunday morning after the Saturday election. Bill Young was minister of the Johnson Street church. He casually mentioned that ACU students had changed over the years. When President Stevens asked what he meant, he referred to the eighty-five percent vote for liquor. The clarification was, "The vote was eighty-five percent against." He said, "Our newspaper said the vote was for liquor," and he went to get a copy of the paper. Sure enough, there it was.

A call to the regional bureau of the Associated Press in Dallas brought out the information that whoever edited the wire report could not believe that a college or university neighborhood would vote against liquor. The AP people sent a correction, which was buried deep inside newspapers that carried it.

Calls and letters began arriving from various sources. "What has happened to the Abilene Christian College of the days of Don Morris and James F. Cox and Batsell Baxter and Jesse P. Sewell and the others?" President Stevens sent the letter to ACU's entire mailing list of churches:

> Isn't it strange how wrong news reports can sometimes be? Recently there was a liquor election in Abilene. The "wets" put an amazing amount of money together and worked diligently in order to provide for unrestricted sale of liquor in Abilene.
>
> The rest of us worked against it as hard as we could. The "wets" won the election by approximately 131 votes out of 23,000. They picked a time when the students of ACU were not enrolled. If our full 4,000 students had been here, the "wets" would not have won.
>
> The boxes around ACU voted 85% against, repeat, against, the "wet" proposition. That means our neighborhood was nearly six to one against it.
>
> But for some reason the AP story went out saying, "College boxes voted largely for the proposition, particularly at ACU, where the vote was about 85% to 15% in favor of the measure." The story appeared all over Texas and perhaps in other states.

> We have had telephone calls from our friends in these cities, asking what has gone wrong!
>
> The fact is that the story was totally, absolutely, completely false. Our boxes voted dry, not wet.
>
> Let me say that ACU today, as throughout its history, is opposed to the liquor business in all of its aspects.... We simply think there is a better way to live. And we think that part of our educational responsibility is to do what we can to show our 4,000 students each year how a person can live in sobriety and enjoy a happy, useful, productive, and serviceable life.

The letter was well received. Church bulletins in many cities printed the letter. The mail was favorable. The Associated Press error may have been turned to the advantage of the university.

Tuesday evening, September 9, 1980, while preparing to interview for the university's oral history project an ex-student in Colorado City, Lawrence Smith died of a heart attack. Many remarkable individuals have made up the history of Abilene Christian University, but this man filled a unique place. He was the bursar, or business manager, from 1927 until September 1, 1969. Many people have said through the years that if it had not been for the management of the money by Bursar Smith, Abilene Christian would have gone down as just another statistic in the list of Christian colleges in Texas that were established, flourished for a brief time, and then closed their doors – not because they lost the faith but because they went broke. For many years Smith had to work with no annual budget. The school simply had to operate with whatever money came in. He had to make a decision on nearly every dollar that was spent. And he could squeeze a dollar. But this financier had another side; he was deeply spiritual. He liked to preach. He drove for many years every Sunday to Cross Plains and then to Dublin to preach. There he delivered carefully crafted sermons. He was also an outstanding classroom teacher, whether of business courses or Greek.

Smith had a tremendous sense of humor. He could entertain students and faculty in chapel in Sewell Auditorium with humorous stories. People could not fail to appreciate a financier with a sense of humor, tight-fisted with money but warm-hearted with people. The youngest of his six children, Sharon Lynn, Mrs. Steven Miller, wrote this humorous, sensitive, touching memoir of her father some years ago:

> One of the most outstanding memories of my daddy, and prob-ably the one I will always remember, was his ability to 'pinch a penny.' Along with this idea was his talent to convince his fam-ily and others he came in contact with that our family was on the brink of poverty. A prime example of this was when ACC displayed a Christmas tree in the Administration Building. When the students left for Christmas break, the tree was given to our family. The rumor later spread around that the Christmas tree was given to a 'needy' family. Why, I was almost 14 years old before I found out that not everyone's daddy reused the coffee grounds four times. Even family cars became almost like family members, if years of service were recorded. After eight years and 170,000 miles, I drove up in our driveway only to discover that the old vehicle was on fire. Upon entering the house to bear the bad news, mother's only reply was, "Good." Never again will there be anyone quite like Lawrence L. Smith, and I will proudly treasure his memory as my daddy forever.

His loving wife, Lula, wrote this appraisal of her husband. It will be affirmed by all who knew him: "Lawrence helped many, many people – students, the sick, friends, widows, downtrod-den people, people rejected by others. He was devoted to his friends and he was loyal to the administration he worked with and for at ACU.... Only the Master knows what a great servant he was."

Here were some of Smith's favorite one-liners:

"Our little angel grandchildren came to see us on Monday and the little devils left on Friday."

"My daddy can whip your daddy," and, "That's no big deal. My mother can whip my daddy."

"He is one of the finest speakers in the country. In the city he's not so hot."

"Man to life insurance salesman: No life insurance for me. When I die I want it to be a sad day for everybody."

"He's got a winning smile; too bad it's on a losing face."

"Neighbor asked a six-year old boy what he thought of the new baby at his house: 'Oh, he's all right, but we needed a lot of other things worse.'"

"One good thing about being poor: it's inexpensive."

"Teacher: I want nothing but silence, and mighty little of that."

In the fall of 1978, a questionnaire was sent to trustees and to some other groups concerning the upcoming seventy-fifth year of Abilene Christian University. Should there be a yearlong celebration during the academic year 1980-81, and, if so, what suggestions did they have? The response was overwhelmingly affirmative, and suggestions were numerous. One suggestion was unanimous: appoint Bob Hunter as chairman of the task force. He was assisted by John Duty.

Hunter assembled a working group and planned activities for the entire year. The theme for the year was "Celebrating an Uncommon Commitment." The first event was an academic convocation on Saturday morning, August 30, the beginning of the fall semester in 1980. Colleges and universities throughout the nation were invited to send delegates in academic regalia, and some 100 did. Three thousand or more greeted the delegates in Moody Coliseum. Principal speaker for the convocation was Leon Jaworski of Houston, famed as the Watergate special prosecutor. At the Abilene Civic Center luncheon, Dr. William S. Banowsky, president of the University of Oklahoma, was the speaker. Sunday evening at a citywide church service in Moody Coliseum, Ira North, of Madison, Tennessee, preached to an overflow crowd. The next morning, Monday, September 1, the official opening of the seventy-fifth year at the ten o'clock chapel featured nine elderly men and women who had been in school at Childers Classical Institute during the 1906-9 period. Present that morning as honored guests were Beulah Cain Arvin, Leslie Cranfill, Roy Estes, Nora Powers Hendrix, Viola Zellner Reddell, Roy Savage, Claude Sikes, and Torksey Cranfill Wood.

The next special event was at Homecoming, "A Celebration of Remembrance," featuring the magnificent seventy-fifth anniversary musical pageant *Like Stars Shining Brightly*. This production, with music composed by Robert Page, lyrics co-authored by June Bearden and Lewis Fulks, and designed and directed by Fulks, played to full houses Thursday, Friday, and Saturday evenings, and at a Sunday matinee, October 23-26.

Lectureship in 1981 featured a Sunday, February 22, luncheon honoring trustees of the university since its beginning as Childers Classical Institute. This message was on the cover of the program for the day:

> Abilene Christian University stands today on the same precepts that inspired the creation of Childers Classical Institute seventy-five years ago. A legacy of leadership has been perpetuated by those trustees whose guidance and selfless service has made possible the growth of Abilene Christian from school to college to university. Today we honor all those who have given of themselves in this tradition of excellence.

Speaker for the luncheon was Dr. William J. Teague, then administrative vice president of the Kerr-McGee Corporation of Oklahoma City. Benediction was by John Tyson, then president of the Students Association and now vice president for development.

Grand climax for the year came in the summer of 1981. A National Christian Education Conference filled the days from Sunday, July 19, through Wednesday, July 22. There were work sessions through the days for representatives of Christian colleges and universities, elementary and secondary schools, preacher training schools, recreational and youth camps, Bible chairs, Bible schools, preachers, elders, deacons, youth directors, Bible school teachers, and others. Each day there was an outstanding luncheon or dinner speaker who drew crowds. Speakers included Roger Staubach, famed Dallas Cowboys quarterback and a decent family man; Dr. Abner McCall, president of Baylor University, who had recently made headlines by refusing access to the Baylor campus by photographers from *Playboy* magazine; Senator Orrin Hatch from Utah; and Bill Banowsky, president of the University of Oklahoma.

The Stevens era produced seven members of the ACU Sports Hall of Fame, including the first woman voted the honor. They are profiled here.

Roger Colglazier, a 1972 graduate, is now a businessman in Cookeville, Tennessee. He earned all-America honors in 1969, 1970, and 1971 in NCAA Division I for the mile relay, and he captured the Bud Clanton Memorial Award at ACU in 1971 as the track and field member with the best grade point average.

He was the first ACU student athlete to compete in the World University Games, and he ran on the winning USA 4x400 relay team at the games in Italy in 1970. He was a three-time winner of the John Sasport Memorial Award as Abilene Christian's outstanding track and field performer in 1970, 1971, and 1972.

Bonnie Buchanan Gray was first team all-America in 1980-81 after leading Coach Burl McCoy's Wildcats to the Division II national women's basketball quarterfinals with a 31-7 record, the best season in the history of Wildcat women's basketball. Before transferring to ACU, she played for Tyler Junior College, where she was a National Junior College Athletic Association All-American. In 1977, she won a gold medal with the United States women's team at the Pan American Games.

Cle Montgomery was a four-year letterman in ACU football, 1974-77. He was co-captain of the 1977 NAIA Division I national championship in the Apple Bowl game in Seattle's Kingdome. Cle was chosen as a member of ACU's all-decade team of the 1970s. He was all-Lone Star Conference and honorable mention all-American. During his Wildcat career he caught 113 passes for 2,104 yards and eighteen touchdowns. He also competed in track and field. He received his B.S. in education in 1978. After college he was a wide receiver and kick returner for the Los Angeles Raiders. He was a member of the Raiders' team that defeated the Washington Redskins in the Super Bowl in January 1984. He is the only former Wildcat to play on the winning team in a Super Bowl game. He also played for the Cincinnati Bengals. He taught and coached at Brownwood High School in Texas for a time and is now in business in Irving, Texas.

Wilbert Montgomery dazzled the nation as a running back for the Philadelphia Eagles after playing for ACU. His thirty-one touchdowns in one regular season at ACU and his seventy career touchdowns were the most TD's scored by any player in the history of intercollegiate football. He was first team all-America at ACU in 1973 as a freshman. He led the Philadelphia Eagles to the Super Bowl in New Orleans in 1980. He is now back with his coach of Philadelphia days, Dick Vermeil, as running backs coach of the Saint Louis Rams.

Billy Olson was the first American to vault nineteen feet. *Track and Field News* named him the top pole vaulter in the world in 1982. He would have been a prime candidate for the top spot in the 1980 Olympics. He was at his peak and was in good health, but that was the year the United States boycotted the Moscow Olympics because of the Soviet Union's invasion of Afghanistan. He won a bronze medal at the 1981 World Cup in Rome. He represented his country in IAAF World Championships, World University Games, Pan American games and USA-USSR dual meets. During his collegiate career at ACU, he won four Lone Star Conference titles and eight NAIA national championships indoors and outdoors. Between 1982 and 1986 he set eleven world indoor records in the vault.

Johnny Perkins was a three-year letterman in football at ACU. He made all-Lone Star Conference as a wide receiver and punter for the Wildcats. He was also first team NAIA All-America and second team Associated Press All-America. He was a member of ACU's all-decade team for the 1970s. He was drafted in the second round by the New York Giants in 1977. He played wide receiver for the Giants for eight years, and he is now in business in his hometown of Granbury.

Allen Wilson was a defensive back on the 1973 ACU team that won the NAIA Division I national championship and the Lone Star Conference championship. As a senior in 1973, he was captain of the team. He stayed on as a graduate assistant coach in 1974. After that experience, he has had a remarkable record as a high school coach. His teams at both Paris and Tyler have won state championships; Paris won the 4A championship in 1988, and John Tyler High School won the 5A trophy after defeating Plano East, 48-44, in Texas Stadium in 1994.

The Robert A. Welch Foundation of Houston was established to support scholarly research in chemistry. When the Foster Science Building was enlarged in 1969, providing room for research laboratories, six chemistry faculty members made research proposals to the Welch Foundation that caught the attention of Dr. W. O. Milligan, research director for the foundation, and his board of directors. Working in pairs, Floyd Dunn and Donald Lewis, Tommy McCord and Alvie Davis, and Bennett Hutchinson and Robert "Cotton" Hance received generous three-year renewable commitments in support of their work. Once, Dr. Milligan said in his Houston office, "Stevens, the Abilene Christian scientists have won approval for 100 percent of their proposals. Not another college or university in Texas has had that acceptance rate."

The Welch success demonstrated that what Paul Witt had started was continuing to flourish on this campus. The foundation, with Dr. Norman Hackerman as present director of research, now has a policy of making block grants to selected institutions, including ACU. The grants had been running $25,000 per year but have now been raised to $35,000. The foundation leaves it up to the chemistry department, now chaired by Dr. Eric Hardegree, to make wise use of the funds. Most of the money is used as stipends for student workers – future chemists.

Other science departments – biology and physics – are also involved in serious research. The fact is that after World War II, Dr. Robert T. Clark set a high standard of scholarly research in the acclimatization of animals to high altitude and carbon monoxide. The work of Abilene Christian biologists with mice, rats, and hamsters was part of American research designed to help airmen fly higher than had been thought possible. In fact, the research was of such high order that the Air Force hired Professor Clark away from Abilene. After Clark's departure, research projects of biologists continued, and especially during the eighteen-year chairmanship of Dr. W. Clark Stevens, 1966-84, followed by Dr. John Little, 1984-90, and by Dr. Daniel K. Brannan since 1990.

The same is true of physics. In fact, Dr. Michael Sadler has a continuing research relationship with Russian physicists at both the St. Petersburg Physics Nuclear Institute and the Los Alamos, New Mexico, Meson Physics Facility. Sadler points out that ACU is one of the few universities incorporating undergraduate students into high-level research projects, and adds, "If ACU's is not the best program, then it is one of the best for research participation that I know of."

The 1960s and 1970s saw much unrest on college and university campuses across the country. Students who were disillusioned largely because of the Viet Nam War, which seemed to be going nowhere, were besieging offices of university presidents and deans with various complaints, including student regulations, course requirements, and why we were in Viet Nam anyway – as if there were anything academic officials could do about that. ACU was largely spared in this matter, although there were a few students who decided it would be hypocritical to speak to people they did not know; hence, a campus that had always been known for its friendliness to everybody became somewhat withdrawn, with people passing one another with unseeing eyes and non-smiling countenances. In three or four instances, a student at commencement exercises, walking across the stage to receive his diploma, refused to shake the outstretched hand of the university president who had conferred upon him the degree to which he was entitled. But this was exceedingly mild compared to what was happening on many campuses. In 1974-75, Kelly Utsinger, a pre-law senior and president of the Students' Association, took exception to the fact that the administration cancelled a proposed Students' association-sponsored show at Shotwell Stadium, largely because of the financial guarantee required. Utsinger thought this was an affront to student government. Several other disagreements between the student president and the administration occurred during the year until, in January 1975, Utsinger called for the cancellation of the popular annual production by students, Sing Song. He said the basic issue was the "efficacy" of the student body. Sing Song was certainly one of the big events on campus each year, with more than a thousand students involved and several thousand paying customers on hand for three performances. Proceeds went to causes that the student body voted to support.

The administration did not react as anticipated. Dean Garvin Beauchamp simply told an *Optimist* reporter, "Sing Song is a great project for students, but if they decide not to participate, we won't force them. The school was in operation before Sing Song, and we'll make adjustments if students cancel the show." To make a long story short, the students proceeded to present Sing Song that year to the largest crowds ever, and the year ended on a good note. Kelly Utsinger today is a successful Amarillo lawyer, a loyal alumnus of Abilene Christian University, and a faithful member of the Central Church of Christ.

In 1969, a group of thirty Abilene women led the way in forming an organization that now has nearly 1,000 members nationwide. It is called Women for Abilene Christian University. National headquarters of the organization is the Jennings House, across the street west of Sewell Auditorium on Campus Court. The house, built by Mr. and Mrs. G. L. Jennings, was the fifth home erected in Abilene Heights during the 1928-29 period. Jennings was for many years Abilene's Oldsmobile dealer. He served for a number of years on the Board of Trustees. In 1976, Abilene Christian University acquired the house from Mr. and Mrs. Leao McDaniel. Mrs. McDaniel is the daughter of the late Mr. and Mrs. Jennings. The ACU Board of Trustees made an excellent decision in voting to turn the house over to the Women for ACU to be developed as a museum. WACU makes full use of the facility. A gift shop is operated out of the garage apartment. During special occasions, such as Lectureship and Bible Teachers Workshop, meals are prepared by expert volunteer cooks headed by Mrs. Betty Nelson and are served to guests for a reasonable price. The chief cook is the wife of artist-in-residence emeritus Charles Nelson. All profits go into the WACU scholarship program for deserving and needy students and other worthwhile causes.

The *WACU Yearbook* described the work of the organization:

> These hard-working women have been responsible for the automatic lawn sprinkling system, beautiful landscaping, and other projects that have enhanced the campus. They have presented outstanding gifts to various departments of the University and provided many other items greatly needed but beyond the school's budget. Of primary importance are the great contributions to scholarships through the WACU Scholarships for Women Endowment Fund and the WACU Biblical Scholarship Fund.

Clifford and Jana Thornton gave a great boost to the WACU Biblical Scholarship Fund in 1979. When they learned that Bible majors are not eligible for Tuition Equalization Grants from the state of Texas, they donated funds to be administered through WACU for financial aid for Bible majors, and these scholarships have become one of the most useful projects of WACU.

One of the best sources of revenue for scholarships has been sales of the two editions of the *WACU Cookbook*. The first edition came out in 1974 and was an outstanding success. The second edition was published in 1983, led by co-chairs Sylvia McCaleb and Leslie Carvey, with the title *Tasteful Traditions* created by Cheryl M. Bacon. The art work on the cover and throughout the book was contributed by Juanita Tittle Pollard, who was head of the Department of Art of ACU from 1938 until 1958. She resigned during that year to move to Lubbock, where she put in her own art shop and school, taught part time at Lubbock Christian College, and married R. E. "Polly" Pollard. In 1966, she joined the art faculty at Texas Tech University, where she taught until retirement. At that time she and her husband moved back to the Abilene area and to a dream home designed by her architect brother, James D. Tittle, and located in the Buffalo Gap hills twenty-seven miles southwest of Abilene. Famed as a teacher, she was even more noted for her works of art. Bob Lapham's story in the *Reporter-News* after her death in September 1994 cited the fact that her paintings may be found in more than 4,500 collections from New Mexico to New York.

At the present time, other money-raising events of WACU are membership dues at four levels – Founders, Heritage, Life, and Annual; Walk with Money, a walkathon with President Royce Money and wife, Pam; call-in orders to Betty Nelson and her "Heavenly Kitchen Crew"; "For Ladies Only" Lectureship dinner and speaker; garage and plant sale at the Abilene Garden Club; a used book sale at the museum; and rental of the museum for other activities. The amount of money WACU has contributed for scholarships and other good causes over the past twenty-eight years is approaching a million dollars.

Cullen Auditorium, undoubtedly, is one of the busiest places on campus. Under the capable management of Kevin

Weems, Cullen has excellent acoustics, a large stage, the largest screen on campus, a fine public address system, and seating for 850, a worthy complement to Moody Coliseum next door. Weems reserves the auditorium for one or more uses of the auditorium some 300 days a year.

Cullen was planned to do double duty as a fine arts auditorium and a large classroom facility. Electrically controlled partitions can be activated to divide it into two or three large class areas. Carl Brecheen and Paul Faulkner taught some supersize Bible classes in it for years. Lewis Fulks used it for his film appreciation classes, which would consistently attract up to 200 students. Large classes in business administration used it. Over time, however, it was in such demand for groups that needed it during the day that it was not practical to use it for a few classes. Besides, with the completion of such magnificent facilities as the Mabee Business Administration Building and the Biblical Studies Building, it was no longer needed for classrooms.

The Department of Music uses Cullen for dozens of recitals and concerts each year. Two or three of the largest final examinations are given there. The May Graduate School commencement is conducted there. New student orientations utilize it three times each summer. Lectureship and Bible Teacher Workshop classes use it each February and each July. Town meetings and guest speakers appear there.

During the 1997-98 school year, Cullen was the site of the Texas Christian High Schools one-act play competition, a forensic awards assembly, and a University Interscholastic League one-act play competition – all effective opportunities to acquaint outstanding high school students with the campus.

One of the most popular graduate-level programs was started in the Stevens years, in 1979, as an institute not connected with any academic department. Today it is the Department of Marriage and Family Therapy in the College of Biblical Studies. Students who are admitted to the program and successfully complete it are awarded the master of marriage and family therapy degree. This means they have completed the rigorous course work, have finished 500 hours of clinical experience, and have endured 100 hours of approved supervision. A graduate can apply for associate membership in the American Association for Marriage and Family Therapy and can begin the marriage counseling licensure process. Dr. Paul Faulkner was the first director of the institute. Dr. Tom Milholland joined the faculty in the first year of the institute as assistant director. When Faulkner relinquished the chairmanship in 1990, Milholland succeeded him, and when Milholland became associate dean of the College of Biblical Studies in the fall of 1997, Dr. Waymon Hinson became chairman.

(AUTHOR'S NOTE: The close of this chapter, like the Masten story, is told in the first person because of its personal nature.)

The writing of *No Ordinary University* gives me an opportunity to pay tribute to my colleagues in the Department History of through the years. When I joined the faculty in the fall of 1948, the History Department comprised Earl Brown, Harry Payne, and me. Brown had been at the college since 1922. Payne was beginning his second year. He taught two more years and then resigned to do mission work in Holland. I could not have had more agreeable fellow workers. My assignment was an impossible one for a new teacher, but it was fun for me: two sections of civilization past and present, a section of American history, an American government class, and a class in the history of the Far East. When taken into consideration that I was starting a new career as a college teacher and was busy getting myself married during that semester, one wonders what caliber of teaching was done. Our faculty "office" consisted of three small desks and straight chairs in one barracks room. When a student came by to see Brown, Payne or me, he or she automatically was meeting with the entire Department of History. In January 1950, I was named dean of men, and my teaching load was reduced. In 1956, I was appointed assistant president and was relieved of all teaching assignments in order to travel for the college.

In 1950, with Payne's departure, two scholarly historians arrived: Ralph Smith and Frank Rhodes. Smith had a passion for research, particularly in the history of the southwestern part of the United States and in Mexican history. Rhodes loved to teach the history of the French Revolution and Napoleon, but his specialty was American history. He succeeded Earl Brown as department head in 1966 and served until his retirement. Both Rhodes and Smith retired from the faculty in 1980.

Tommy Shaver joined the department in 1955 and taught three years. He then took a leave of absence to do his doctorate in Bible, in which department he taught until retiring in 1992. Taking Shaver's place in 1958 was Benny Gallaway, who became a recognized authority on the history of Texas and the great Southwest. His book *Texas, the Dark Corner of the Confederacy* has gone through three editions since 1968, the latest by the University of Nebraska Press in 1994. His *The Ragged Rebel: A Common Soldier in W. H. Parson's Texas Cavalry, 1861-66* is now in its fourth printing at the University of Texas Press.

In 1959, Bea Speck came aboard and taught, with time out while earning her doctor's degree at Texas Christian University, until retiring in 1989. Dr. Speck was a popular teacher and speaker and in demand especially as a book reviewer. She chaired the department from 1980 to 1984. It was during her time as the leader of the department that I returned to teaching, including one semester when I had an upper division class in the American presidents. I have enjoyed immensely being back in teaching during these past sixteen years.

Norman Hogan came from Freed-Hardeman College in 1961 and taught courses in American history for eight years before going back to Freed-Hardeman. He was always a popular teacher.

Joe Spaulding joined the department in 1964 and taught for eighteen years. He was a popular teacher. Spaulding especially liked to teach the course in Western civilization although his doctoral program primarily dealt with American diplomatic history.

John Robinson was added in 1965. His interests were primarily in Latin American, Asian, and United States history. He had a background as an operational intelligence specialist with the United States Air Force, 1953-57, and as an instructor in history and theology in the Philippine Bible College, 1962-65. He has written scholarly articles for a number of journals through the years, in addition to several books: *David*

Lipscomb: Journalist in Texas in 1971; *Living Hard: Southern Americans in the Great Depression,* published by the University Press of America in 1981; and *Bartolome Mitre: Historian of the Americas* by University Press in 1982. In 1998, he is completing a book on ways in which American culture portrays Hispanics in a negative light. He was department chairman 1986-96.

James G. Burrow came in 1969 and taught for twenty-two years until retirement in 1991. He also taught one semester in the fall of 1947. He was a scholar with a national reputation. He wrote in the field of the history of American medicine. His two books, *Voice of American Medicine* in 1963 and *Organized Medicine in the Progressive Era* in 1970, were published by the Johns Hopkins University Press. He was outstanding in the classroom. His lectures were so well prepared that he needed no notes.

Arlie Hoover came to the department in 1980. With a solid background in European history, including a Fulbright Fellowship for a year of study and research in the Free University of Berlin, 1963-64, and a research grant from the National Endowment for the Humanities for post-doctoral research at the University of Heidelberg in 1968, he was a tremendous addition to the European history offerings of the department. With research grants, he studied in European universities and libraries virtually every summer from 1985 through 1997. His publications are numerous; probably the three most in demand are *The Gospel of Nationalism: German Patriotic Preaching from Napoleon to Versailles, 1806-1918,* published by Steiner of Stuttgart in 1986; *God, Germany and Britain in the Great War: A Study on Clerical Nationalism,* published by Praeger in 1989; and *Friedrich Nietzsche: His Life and Thought,* published by Praeger in 1994.

Joining the department for a brief tenure was Richard Hughes. His first love was church history. In fact, he was much involved in writing his massive work *Reviving the Ancient Faith,* which was published by Eerdmans in 1995. He served as chairman of the department from 1984 to 1986, but when he was offered a chair in church history at Pepperdine University, he accepted the California offer.

Fred Arthur Bailey (a painstaking historian and prolific writer) arrived in 1984. His field is primarily Southern history, American social and intellectual history, and the American Civil War. His published books are *Class and Tennessee's Confederate Generation* published by the University of North Carolina Press in 1987, *William Edward Dodd: The South's Yeoman Scholar* published by the University of Virginia Press in 1997. He is currently working on a book, "The Southern Quest for a Suitable Past." His journal articles are too many to mention, as are his awards. He received a one-year appointment by Johns Hopkins University to teach at the JHU-Nanjing Center for Chinese and American Studies. He and his family enjoyed their year in the Peoples' Republic. Bailey was named chairman of the department in 1996.

The latest historian to arrive, in 1989, is Vernon Williams. He teaches courses in American history. His specialty is military history. He has written numerous scholarly articles and has two books in progress. One is *Empire Marine: General Littleton T. Walker and the Growth of American Imperialism, 1856-1920*, a full-length biography under contract with Praeger Publishers, and the other is *Admiral of the Navy: George Dewey and the Development of the New American Navy, 1856-1917*, a biography under contract with the Naval Institute Press. He is currently working to establish a museum in Abilene to house the papers and artifacts of the 12th Armored Division.

Through the years numerous part-time instructors have taught in the Department of History. One of the most distinguished in the 1990s is Abilene's superintendent of schools, Charles Hundley, who during the fall semester teaches a three-hour class on Tuesday evenings to a roomful of students who enjoy his enthusiastic and skillful teaching.

Gone are the days when ACU history teachers simply taught classes and graded papers. Members of the department now are researching and writing books and scholarly articles.

In mid-1980, with the Masten case well on the road to settlement, I told Ray McGlothlin that I would be clearing out of the president's office no later than June 1, 1983, and sooner would be all right with me. My plan was to go back to the history classroom. My coming to Abilene Christian in the fall of

1948 was for the purpose of teaching history, and although I had enjoyed administrative work, beginning as dean of men in 1950, serving as assistant president, 1956-69, and winding up my administrative career as president, I thought that after thirty years, the time had come for a return to the classroom.

Hence, the chairman of the board appointed a search committee to look for the person to nominate as the next president of Abilene Christian University. Dr. Roy Willingham was named chairman of the committee. It was interesting to me that a physician had been chosen to chair the committee. The chairman of the committee that nominated me was another well-known Abilene physician, Dr. John Paul Gibson. Other members of the Willingham committee were Bob Bailey, Oliver Jackson, Bill Johnson, Ray McGlothlin Jr. Tommy Morris, Wilson C. Orr, Lynn Packer, and Jack Pope. The committee went about its work methodically, considering persons on campus as well as elsewhere. The choice fell upon Dr. William J. "Bill" Teague. At the February 1981 meeting of the board, an official invitation was extended to him to accept the presidency, and at the May meeting, he was formally elected, with his appointment to become effective August 27, 1981. At the same meeting, I was elected to become chancellor, effective the same date as Teague's accession to the presidency. As chancellor I continued involvement in some travel, fund raising, and speaking for the university, but had no executive or administrative responsibilities. After twelve years as the chief executive, the chancellorship was a pretty nice job. This is not to say that the office of chancellor is a non-executive job on all campuses. In some universities, such as Texas Christian, the chancellor is the chief executive, but at Abilene Christian the president is the chief executive.

As for John and Ruth Stevens, we were glad to turn the presidency over to Bill and Peggy Teague. As stated, the first year out of office I did a good deal of traveling among our constituency in my role as chancellor. During the year, I mentioned to Dr. Speck, who was head of the Department of History, that I would like to teach a class beginning with September 1982. She mentioned that Spaulding was retiring and she could use me in a class of Western civilization. I had to get busy preparing to teach. A quarter of a century had passed since I had taught classes on a regular basis. After that much of a layoff, it is amazing how much work is required in preparing lectures and examinations. I had to hit the books again. It was, however, a real pleasure.

My good wife, Ruth, volunteered to grade papers for me. Then, after seeing a test or two that I had prepared, she volunteered to write the tests for me. She attended the class, took notes on the lectures, read my lecture notes, and spent a great deal of time reading the textbook and preparing questions. Then we would go over her tests carefully. I could discard any question that I did not like or could not answer, and that is the way it has been for the last fifteen, going on sixteen, years, although after the first year, she no longer attended my lectures. She had heard them. During these years, in addition to Western civilization, I have taught at various times the history of England and American history. Two other roles have come my way of late. When Bill Teague retired from the presidency, in 1991, the board elected him chancellor, and I became chancellor emeritus, and the new president, Royce Money, enlisted me as the researcher and writer of *No Ordinary University*, which meant he also enlisted Ruth for the book.

The end of the Stevens presidency, much like the end of the Cox presidency, returned an administrator to his first love, teaching – in this case, the teaching of history.

A great honor that came my way was the announcement by President Money at the conclusion of the Christian Service Luncheon during the 1998 Lectureship of the establishment of the John C. and Ruth Stevens Chair of History. Ruth and I were especially pleased to learn that our son, Clark, had made the first commitment to the chair.

Another overwhelming honor was the turnout of students, faculty, staff, administrators, and guests lining the street as I walked from my Brown Library office to my classroom on the top floor of the Administration Building for my final class May 1, 1998, after fifty years on the ACU faculty. Words cannot express my appreciation. Thanks for the memory.

A 1928 aerial photograph shows the old downtown campus developed from 1906-29.

The College Building on the old downtown campus in 1906.

The home of J.W. Childers served as the first dormitory and president's residence on the old campus.

A.B. Barret, first president of the university.

J.W. Childers, whose property made a campus possible.

The Administration Building on the old downtown campus was used from 1919-29. It burned in 1929.

An aerial photograph of the new campus, approximately in 1932, looking north along Washington Boulevard.

J.P. Sharp served as chairman pro tem at the organizational meeting of the Board of Trustees in 1906.

T.G. Moore served as the first chairman of the Board of Trustees, from 1906-11.

M. Zellner was board chairman from 1911-16.

J.S. Arledge was board chairman from 1916-33.

J.E. McKinzie was board chairman from 1933-36.

W.H. Free was board chairman from 1936-42, and a member of the original board in 1906.

E.D. Chambers was board chairman from 1942-43.

J.B. Collins was board chairman from 1943-47.

B Sherrod was board chairman from 1947-67.

Willard Paine was board chairman from 1964-74.

Ray McGlothlin Jr. ('49) was board chairman from 1974-84.

H. Lynn Packer ('50) was board chairman from 1984-92.

Don W. Crisp, board chairman from 1992 to present.

H.C. Darden was president from 1908-09.

R.L. Whiteside was president from 1909-11.

James F. Cox was elected president in 1911 but was unable to serve during the 1911-12 school year. He later served from 1932-40.

Jesse P. Sewell was president from 1912-24.

Batsel Baxter was president from 1924-32.

Don H. Morris ('24) was president from 1940-69.

John C. Stevens ('32) was president from 1969-81.

William J. Teague ('52) was president from 1981-91.

Royce Money ('64) was elected president in 1991 and continues to serve

The Student Alumni Association sponsored the first "Big Switch" day in 1992 so ACU's president, Royce Money, and a freshman could exchange roles for a day. Part of the bargain in April 1994 with first-year student Ann Francis was for Money to fill a spot in her women's aerobics class in Scruggs Gym.

West Texas rancher and benefactor William M. Edwards was generous toward Abilene Christian.

METHODIST HOSPITAL
Lubbock, Texas

PROGRESS NOTES

VOL **70** PAGE **199**

Date	Notes Should Be Dated and Signed by Physician

at methodist Hospital

Sunday Oct 28 1979.

Dr. John Stephens.

My dear friend;

It is now my will and testimony to leve Abiline Christian University all I have in this world take due as soon as possible   yours truly

— F Masten

Printed F.O. Masten

I want W.C. Lewis to be my Executor here

F.O. Masten   F Masten

W.C. Lewis my executor of guenation mailing address is Masten — mud Tey

APPLICANT

#12

06153-1   11-72   PROGRESS NOTES

The handwritten Will of F.O. Masten was contested by family members and was settled out of court.

The estate of Grace L. Woodward (1905-97) is dedicated to serving God as she did during her lifetime.

John G. Hardin, whose help saved the college in 1934.

J.C. Reese, board vice chairman who convinced fellow trustees to move the campus to its current location in 1929.

Mr. and Mrs. L.P. Bennett gave 1,600 acres that produced millions of dollars for Christian education.

Mrs. L.P. Bennett

B Sherrod and F.O. Masten, rugged West Texans who teamed up to lead ACU's development program in 1948.

Lawrence Smith ('29), Walter H. Adams ('25) and Don H. Morris ('24) were a team of administrators who helped lead ACU throughout the 1940s, 1950s and 1960s.

Robert and Katherine Bell were major donors to the Biblical Studies Building.

Joe Mabee, vice chairman of the J.E. and L.E. Mabee Foundation, and his good friend, vice chancellor Dr. C.L. Kay.

Trustee J. McDonald Williams ('61) was chair of the campaign for the Mabee Business Building.

Trustee Robert Onstead was co-chair of the College of Biblical Studies campaign.

Trustee James Muns ('53) is co-chair of the $100 million "To Lead and To Serve" campaign.

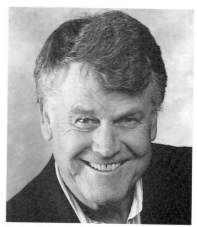

Trustee G. Randy Nicholson ('59) is co-chair of the $100 million "To Lead and To Serve" campaign.

Mary Frazier Clark ('44) was the first woman appointed to the Board of Trustees.

Professional golf great Byron Nelson was a longtime trustee. ACU's golf program is endowed in his name.

Henry E. Speck Sr. was dean from 1914-24.

Jack Pope ('34) was Chief Justice of the Texas Supreme Court and a longtime trustee.

Gary D. McCaleb ('64) is vice president of the university, executive director of the Center for Advancement of Community, and longtime mayor of Abilene.

Robert D. Hunter ('52) was a Texas State Representative and innovative administrator responsible for creating some of ACU's greatest traditions, such as Sing Song.

Daisy Sewell, wife of president Jesse P. Sewell, taught art classes and served as dean.

G.C. Morlan was chair of the education department and wrote the words to "O Dear Christian College."

Leonard Burford ('25) was a longtime music department chair and founder of the A Cappella Chorus.

Overton Faubus was professor of business administration from 1952-85 and department chair for many years. His father, D.A. Faubus, taught business courses in 1912.

Rex Kyker ('43) was chair of the communication department and a noted orator.

Paul Witt ('22) was the founding chair of the chemistry department.

Devotionals, like this freshman gathering at Welcome Week each August, are now traditionally held in Beaucham

(INSET) Devotionals on the Administration Building steps were an Abilene Christian tradition.

Lemoine Lewis ('36) was a much-loved Bible scholar, professor and church historian.

James Culp ('49) was a popular English teacher. The first endowed teaching chair was named in his honor.

Lowell Perry ('47) was a longtime communication professor and founder of KACU, the campus radio station.

Lewis Fulks ('48) was professor and director of ACU Theatre for 41 years.

Marie Wilmeth was a longtime chair of the home economics department and the first female faculty member to earn a Ph.D.

Paul Faulkner ('52) and Carl Brecheen ('52) taught a popular Marriage and Family class during three decades and conducted seminars around the world.

M.L. Daniels ('55) was a talented composer who taught on the music faculty for 34 years, including service as department chair.

For 31 years, Betty Whiteside was secretary to three ACU presidents – John C. Stevens, William J. Teague and Royce Money.

E.W. McMillan spoke at the ACU Bible Lectureship just before his 100th birthday.

J.S. "Sheriff" Burgess was a longtime night watchman and gardener who helped plant many of the stately trees on campus.

L.D. "Bill" Hilton ('48) served 42 years as assitant bursar, business manager and vice president for finance and administration.

Earl W. "Pop" Bailey, champion booster of Wildcat athletics, was named to the Sports Hall of Fame in 1988.

A tent for publishers and other exhibitors to sell their merchandise was a fixture at the annual Bible Lectureship until 1995.

What would Homecoming be without a bonfire?

Sewell Theater was once the site for daily chapel and other public lectures and presentations.

Daily chapel now takes place in Moody Coliseum. The patriotic Opening Ceremonies on the first day of school each autumn are highlighted by a Parade of Flags and unfurling of Old Glory.

Prospective graduates (dark gowns) and their guests (white gowns) file past an under-construction Moody Coliseum for Summer Commencement in 1967, which was held at Elmer Gray Stadium.

Moody Coliseum became the site of Undergraduate Commencement beginning in 1968.

A.B. Morris was Abilene Christian's first athletic director, also serving as a football and basketball coach.

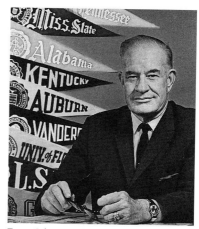

Tonto Coleman was an ACU coach before becoming commissioner of the NCAA's Southeastern Conference.

Garvin Beauchamp ('41) was an athlete and administrator at ACU who coached the undefeated, untied football team in 1950.

Wally Bullington ('52) succeeded A.B. Morris as athletic director in 1969 and was head football coach from 1968-76.

Abilene Christian's football team, circa 1920s, practiced on the old downtown campus

V.T. Smith ('49) starred as a Wildcat runningback before a career with the Los Angeles Rams that included an NFL title.

Sprinter Bobby Morrow ('59) set world records, won three Olympic gold medals in 1956, and became a national celebrity.

Pole vaulter Billy Pemelton ('64) competed for the United States in the 1964 Olympics in Tokyo.

400-meter star runner Earl Young ('62) won a gold medal in the 1960 Olympic games and made national headlines for the Wildcats.

Coaches Wes Kittley ('81), Oliver Jackson ('46) and Jerry Dyes ('64) have helped ACU earn international track and field fame.

High-scoring basketball guard John Ray Godfrey ('68) was first team all-America and powered his team to the NCAA playoffs.

Jim Lindsey ('71) set five NCAA career passing records as an ACU quarterback.

Bill Gilbreth ('69) led the nation in strikeouts, pitched for two major league teams and later coached at his alma mater.

Wilbert Mongtomery ('77) led ACU to a 1973 NAIA title, earned a spot in the College Football Hall of Fame, and helped the Philadelphia Eagles to the 1981 Super Bowl.

Ove Johannson ('77) kicked a world record 69-yard field goal in 1976.

Billy Olson ('82) set 11 indoor world records in the pole vault, was the first vaulter to clear 19 feet, and made the 1988 Olympic team.

Tim Bright ('83), a decathlete, competed in three Olympics for the U.S, setting an Olympic record in the decathlon pole vault in 1984.

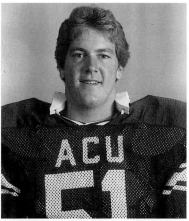

Grant Feasel ('83) played 11 years in the NFL and was named in 1977 to the NCAA Division II Football Team of the Quarter Century.

Michelle King ('92) won the NCAA Division II national title in women's singles in tennis.

Jeev Singh was national medalist while leading the Wildcats to the 1993 NCAA Division II national championship in golf.

Jennifer Clarkson ('96) was a two-time all-America who led her team to the 1996 NCAA Division II national tournament.

ACU was host for the 1996-97 NCAA Division II south central region women's basketball tournament. The Wildcats beat West Texas A&M in the championship game before a near sellout crowd in Moody Coliseum and advanced to the Elite Eight national tournament.

Cheerleaders perform at a pep rally in Bennett Gym.

Big Tex, on loan from the Texas State Fair, towered over trees and visitors to Homecoming in 1955.

The A Cappella Chorus showcases ACU's finest student vocalists and has toured the world.

The Big Purple Band provides halftime entertainment during football season.

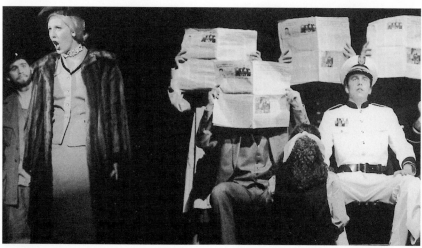

Talented students entertain loyal patrons of the theatre arts each year.

Welcome Week provides plenty of fun activities first-year students use to build friendships with each other.

Welcome Week also shows first-year students the spiritual emphasis upon which Abilene Christian was founded.

Sing Song involves as many as 2,000 students and draws large crowds to performances in Moody Coliseum each February.

The Nauseating Nine.

The World Missions Globe in the Biblical Studies Building's Esther Sowell Rotunda is a popular campus feature.

The Hope for the Future sculpture was located on campus in 1989.

The Brown Library is the academic heart of the university and the home of the state-of-the-art Walter H. Adams Center for Teaching Excellence.

Study of the sciences thrived in "The Old Chemistry Shack" from 1929 to 1946.

An aerial photograph of the campus after World War II (1947), which included military hutments.

An aerial photograph of the campus in 1968, as construction was underway on Moody Coliseum, Gibson Health Center, and McGlothlin Campus Center.

Dedication of the Biblical Studies Building in 1989 created a new eastern "front door" to the campus from Judge Ely Boulevard, via the new Teague Boulevard entrance.

An aerial view of the campus in 1997.

CHAPTER SEVEN

PERFECTING THE CAMPUS

William J. Teague had the most versatile background of any person ever to serve as president of Abilene Christian, whether institute, college, or university.

He was born July 12, 1927. His parents lived on an oil lease near Olney, Texas, but soon moved to other oil patch towns, Archer City and then to Nocona, where he grew up. After graduation from Nocona High School in 1944, he enrolled in the University of Texas. A year later he enlisted in the Navy and wound up stationed in San Diego, where he met Margaret Louise "Peggy" Newlin, a young woman with a Southern background. They were married in June 1948. The Teagues have a son, Tom, and two daughters, Susan and Helen, and two grandchildren.

After Teague received his separation papers from the Navy in September 1949, he drove with his wife and three-month-old son, Tom, to Texas. This time, instead of heading for Austin to resume his college studies, he drove into Abilene, where he enrolled in Abilene Christian College. He supported his young family and earned his bachelor of arts degree with a Bible degree within two years and a semester with the help of the GI Bill of Rights, plus preaching on Sundays for expenses and a modest stipend, officiating at high school basketball games, and serving as the first student manager of the campus radio station.

Making an appointment with President Don Morris was never difficult for a student, but Teague's work as manager of KACC gave him a better-than-average acquaintance with the head man. So he went to see him. "I would like to be of assistance to the college if there is any opening," Teague said. And he adds, "He thought I had asked to be his assistant." Teague was hired on the spot, and his first assignment was as secretary of the Alumni Association. From that post he was moved to the position of executive assistant to the president in the area of development.

He made many trips with Don Morris, developing his skills in fund raising and public relations, for which he already possessed a natural talent. In the campaign for the north wing of the Administration Building in 1955, he gained much experience. In 1957, he resigned to become vice president for development at Harding College in Searcy, Arkansas. The draw for Harding was that he could live in the New York City area and work on a graduate degree from Columbia University while calling on New York foundations in the interest of Harding College, a natural position for him. Dr. George Benson, long-time president of Harding, had spoken to congressional committees and to meetings of foundation directors, corporation executives, civic clubs, and chambers of commerce all over the nation. He almost always began his speeches with words such as these: "My name is George Benson. I am president of a small college, in a small city, in a small state." He would go on to say that any student who was willing to do some work on the campus could afford to attend Harding. New Yorkers were receptive to the message of this small college in Arkansas. Teague's job was especially to visit foundation executives and lay before them proposals for helping this small Arkansas college.

On the other hand, although Abilene Christian attracted some support from New York City, which was the foundation capital of the world, its claim to smallness did not go over very well with foundation executives. They were apt to respond, "According to our information, Texas is a land of flowing oil wells, big ranches, and large foundations of its own."

So, Teague began making acquaintance with large gift possibilities while completing a master's degree at Teachers College, Columbia. After his work in New York, he moved to Los Angeles and became vice president of Pepperdine University. During ten years in that position, he was instrumental in recruiting large financial resources for Pepperdine and helped make possible Pepperdine's move from its inner city location to the magnificent campus at Malibu. During those years, he earned a doctor's degree in administration from the University of California at Los Angeles.

In 1968, he added another dimension to his portfolio. He took a year's leave of absence from Pepperdine to run for the United States House of Representatives as a Republican against an incumbent Democrat. He lost by a small margin. At the end of his year's leave of absence, he resigned from his Pepperdine position to establish his own company, William J. Teague Associates, a management services company. He made another race for the congressional seat that had been denied him two years earlier but lost again. A footnote to the Teague political history is that Congressman Richard T. Hanna, who beat him twice was forced to resign four years after his second election. In fact, he did time in prison for accepting money from a South Korean businessman to influence fellow members of Congress to vote for South Korean interests. This scandal was called "Koreagate."

A day came, while Teague was running his own company, when he was offered a position as administrative assistant with the Purex Corporation, a Fortune 500 company. He took it and was soon promoted to administrative vice president. After several years at Purex, he accepted a position as administrative vice president of the Kerr-McGee Corporation of Oklahoma City, another Fortune 500 company. In addition to his work at Kerr-McGee, he was serving as an elder of the Church of Christ in Edmond, Oklahoma, when he was offered, and accepted, the presidency of Abilene Christian University.

William J. Teague began his work as president of ACU on August 27, 1981, and the grand inauguration ceremony took place Saturday morning, February 20, 1982, in Moody Coliseum. Gary McCaleb chaired the inaugural committee, and John Duty was coordinator of the event. In Teague's inaugural address, he gave a clear definition of what Christian education is all about: "One individual with conviction can and does make a difference in our world. Our heritage proves it. And education that is content simply to free man's spirit is deficient; we must educate to empower the spirit as well.... If the purpose is to conquer ignorance, then the mission of Christian education is to supply purpose and motive for the conquest."

The luncheon after the ceremony was at the Civic Center with Justice Jack Pope as the speaker. Pope said two goals of higher education must be "high standards of teaching and the teaching of high standards." Speaking of Christian universities, he said:

> It is they who will, who must, nurture and sustain Christian values. It is they who must confront in the classroom, on the campus, and our whole society, the blandishments of humanism, materialism, relativism, mechanism, nihilism, and positivism. It is they who still supply the standards for our educational compass.

The inauguration was a day of triumph – and of challenge.

When Teague came into the presidency, a most fortunate circumstance was just underway about the Xenia Miller land, the history of which went back to the 1928 purchase of some of the Hill land from her. The problem was that the college had been forced to turn the land back to her, along with a $3,200 note that she owed on the land and which the college had assumed in 1928. Especially after the war, the trustees were anxious to buy the land back. When B Sherrod and Don Morris visited her, she told them that she had been forced to lose something else in order to take care of the note. As Sherrod reported, she said that her son who lived in Wichita Falls would have to agree to a sale, and he was "pretty bitter" about having to take the land back "when they needed the money so badly to pay other bills."

After Mrs. Miller's death September 29, 1968, Buck Miller came by the campus and visited with Lawrence Smith about the 245 acres of land, but no agreement was reached. During the Stevens presidency, cordial visits transpired without any results. About the time of the Stevens-Teague transition, however, a demand by one of the Miller heirs brought about a partition of the estate. Then a truly remarkable development occurred.

First of all, when Buck Miller was faced with an immediate need for cash, he sold the option to buy to a group of Abilene investors. This was at first a considerable disappointment to the university leaders because of the realization that with a group of investors involved, the price would go considerably higher than if it could have been bought directly from the Miller estate. However, the trustees, realizing the great need of the university for the land, or at least a sizable portion of it, decided to march up to the cannon's mouth and buy the option. Then, with astute guidance of board members Ray McGlothlin, Wilson C. "Dub" Orr, and Randy Nicholson, with Nicholson in the lead, the university recovered the Miller land, all 245 or so acres of it. By reserving approximately 110 acres of it for campus expansion and selling the remaining acreage for development, the university came out with some new campus land, free and clear, plus nearly a million dollars to add to the endowment.

Now, Teague was ready to go to work with an overall plan that was ambitious and daring on the order of the 1928 decision to build an entirely new subdivision of the city to have enough room for the campus. He knew that sums of money far in excess of anything the university had ever set out to raise would be needed, more than the 1960s Design for Development. The first project calling for attention was a major addition to the Margaret and Herman Brown Library. Stevens had secured a pledge for $500,000 from the Brown Foundation, contingent on the completion of the $1.5 million campaign. The foundation put a time limit on how long the challenge grant pledge would remain available, and the time was about to expire.

That problem was quickly solved when C. L. "Casey" Kay of Lubbock agreed to accept appointment as vice chancellor of ACU with primary responsibility for contacting foundations. When he arrived in Abilene to take up his duties May 3, 1982, he brought with him a Mabee Foundation commitment of $1 million to meet matching requirements of the original pledge. While they were at it, Teague and Kay raised an additional million dollars to meet unforeseen needs and strengthen the holdings of the library.

Casey Kay was an individual with a remarkable background. He grew up in Cleveland, Ohio, in a family plagued by poverty. His father moved the family to Cleveland from the Appalachian Mountain region in Pennsylvania, where he had been a coal miner. During his high school years, Casey had an early morning paper route, attended school until 3:30 in the afternoon, and worked in a defense plant after school. He had no thoughts of college. After military service during World War II, he married a young woman he met at church. Ruth Kay convinced her new husband that they should move to Tennessee, where she had made arrangements for him to enter college. On the day they left Cleveland, his father told him, "Son, you'll never make it." Ruth Kay admits that she sometimes wondered how long Casey would stay with his college endeavors. He stuck it out. After graduating from Freed-Hardeman, which was then a two-year college, he and Ruth drove a thousand miles west from Henderson, Tennessee, to Portales, New Mexico. Casey had read in some church papers about the Church of Christ Bible Chair at Eastern New Mexico University and thought he would like that setup. He did. While completing his bachelor's degree, he was approached by the dean, who asked him, "Casey, do you want to be of great service to your church and country?" The answer was, "Yes." Then the dean suggested that he use the next year to get his master's degree. With his wife working, he was able to do it.

Then began a remarkable career in the college and university world. For three years, he was head of the Department of Religion at West Texas State University. In 1957, he accepted a position with Lubbock Christian College, which was just starting up. During the next twenty-five years, he served at various times as dean of students, lecturer in political science, vice president for public affairs, assistant president, and executive director of the Center of Business and Economic Education. He became widely known for speeches in the field of free enterprise and the American way. He made some 5,000 speeches along the way, which is no exaggeration. He kept meticulous records and was systematic in all of his activities.

He avoided pitfalls that some free enterprise speakers of the time fell into, in that he was always positive, buoyant, and forward-looking. After a speech in Midland, he met Joe Mabee, president of the Mabee Foundation, and they became friends.

The Mabee Foundation had helped many institutions through the years. It has been especially helpful to Lubbock Christian University and Abilene Christian University. In every major project of the Teague administration, the Mabee Foundation rendered invaluable service by making a challenge grant that served as a catalyst to bring in the total funds needed, whatever the ratio might be.

Casey Kay had numerous other contacts in the world of corporations and foundations. During his nine years with ACU, he left an indelible imprint on the university. His concern went far beyond money to deep involvement in helping students. For instance, he and Dr. Aubrey Green, professor of English, led in establishing in 1983 the Learning Enhancement Center, which has been a force in helping students and is located in the west wing of the Brown Library, his first project at ACU. This forward-looking program was designed to help two groups of students: first, the under-prepared who might otherwise be lost because of academic failure but can be greatly aided by tutoring, and, second, the gifted who seek greater challenges to excellence and who can profit from help in organizing their study habits and time. Hundreds of students have found this program made a difference in their lives.

The west library wing, consisting of 38,703 square feet of floor space, including the Learning Enhancement Center, was named the John C. and Ruth Stevens Wing. At the same time, the trustees voted to rename the Main Room in the McGlothlin Campus Center the Hilton Room, honoring Bill and Alvah Jean Hilton. The new east wing of the Brown Library was named the C. L. Kay Wing after Kay's June 1991 death, which was a profound loss to the university community.

Obtaining the Miller land made possible the second bold – some thought outrageous – Teague initiative. He wanted to move Judge Ely Boulevard, which once had been Farm-to-Market 1234, eastward, incorporating the newly acquired land so all of the campus would be located on the west side of the boulevard. A five-lane, busy thoroughfare, which Judge Ely is, piercing the heart of the campus, was undesirable. He proposed to move the boulevard so that it would skirt the eastern bound-ary, leaving the entire campus west of the boulevard.

Judge Ely extended from Interstate 20 on the north to Highway 80 and beyond at its southern extremity to East South Eleventh Street. With businesses built at intervals all along the way, it was obvious that moving the entire boulevard was impossible, and nobody suggested that. However, begin-ning at the intersection of East North Fourteenth Street with Ely, and all the way north to the interstate, all of the land east of Ely now belonged to Abilene Christian University. Hence, beginning at about East North Fourteenth, Ely Boulevard could be curved gently eastward to a central point and then curved back to reconnect with the original road bed about 250 yards north of Ambler Avenue. The plan would keep about sev-enty-five acres of the new land west of the boulevard and con-tiguous with the existing campus.

With the support of trustees McGlothlin, Nicholson, and Bob Onstead, among others, Teague turned to trustee Bob Bailey to help with the technical aspects of the proposed move. Through many years, Bailey Bridge Company had bid, won, and completed projects for the Texas Highway Department. Bob Bailey knew the people involved and was an effective con-tact person. Necessary permits were secured with the complete cooperation of state, county, and city officials. The new portion of the boulevard involved approximately one mile. The univer-sity furnished the right-of-way and cost of the new construction for the "million dollar mile."

Board members were so enthusiastic about the project that pledges and cash payments came in immediately. Some faculty members were not so enthusiastic. They maintained that the money was needed for faculty salaries. They were overlooking two factors: first, that money was specifically given for one proj-ect; it probably would not have been available for any other project, including salaries; and, second, opening the opportuni-ty to develop a truly magnificent campus with the unified land feature would attract both students and financial support in the future that would be worth many times a million dollars. It would give the university a whole new set of opportunities.

Other than the purely financial aspect, other positive factors were embedded in the plan, not the least of which was safety. University Park, the newest residence for students, housing 400 of them, is located on that land. These students and users of the new performing arts center planned for the corner of Judge Ely Boulevard and East North Sixteenth do not have to cross Judge Ely, navigating through the 26,000 vehicles of the daily north-south traffic. A. B. "Stormy" Shelton, publisher of the *Abilene Reporter-News*, told that the Ely move was one of the best things the president had done for the university. Moving Judge Ely was a move for the future.

The Miller-Ely projects made possible an entirely new so-called "front door" for the campus. The Hardin Administration Building, facing west, with its six two-story columns atop twenty-two steps leading up to a landing and the front door, was a good, central front-of-the-campus feature for years, the architectural metaphor for the college. However, College Drive was no longer the main artery to the campus. The commercial buildings across the street on Campus Court were just that – store buildings. The university owned all of them except one. They are all serviceable and useful – and are in use – but definitely not front-of-campus quality.

Teague thoroughly sold the board on the idea of a new campus front with acres of professional landscaping crowned by the two most majestic and beautiful buildings ever built on the campus. These would be the Mabee Business Administration Building and the Biblical Studies Building. In planning the Biblical Studies Building, some of the board members took the lead and demanded even more than Teague had recommended. They wanted not only a fine physical structure but a statement to the world that at Abilene Christian University the Bible is first.

The next decision was a controversial one but was essential to the entire Teague building program that came after the Stevens wing of the library. The maintenance building, a concrete and steel facility comprising nearly 20,000 square feet of floor space, was built to last for centuries, but it was in the wrong location. With the goal of building a new front for the campus, facing Judge Ely and featuring two magnificent new buildings, maintenance, which faced the old Ely, was simply in the way. Building a new front to the campus with maintenance in the center would have been as inappropriate as a family building a new house with the front door opening into the laundry room. So the building erected in 1970 was taken down, and a new maintenance and central stores unit, comprising 28,416 square feet, was erected on what was formerly Miller land on the east side of Judge Ely with an entrance from Ambler Avenue. Under the administrative direction of Kevin Watson and the supervision of Carlos Rodriguez and Byron Patterson, the university has demonstrated that with electronic mail, mobile phones, and two-way radios, efficiency can be maintained by campus maintenance personnel. This physical plant plan cleared the way for the remainder of the Teague decade of construction, which made the campus attractive, appealing, and more useful – ready for the twenty-first century.

Funds recruited during the Teague decade for the university's total program amounted to $78,199,284. With these funds, four major building projects were accomplished, plus a number of lesser but important developments. The permanent endowment of the university was increased from $18 million to $56 million, including $11 million from the Masten estate, a carryover from the Stevens administration, which was not officially recorded until 1983. The remarkable Teague achievement was possible because some individuals and couples made gifts ranging from a million dollars up to several million. Others gave hundreds of thousands. Many more gave thousands. The million-dollar and multi-million-dollar gifts were essential to a program of such magnitude, but all donations were and are important. As Don Morris expressed it, "There are no small gifts given to Abilene Christian. Gifts that come from the heart loom large in the heart of one individual and mean so much to the inspiration and motivation for others to give."

Max Dillard of Houston played a leading role in arranging for the University of Oklahoma School of Architecture and Environmental Studies to prepare a master plan for campus expansion.

First came the addition of 38,000 square feet of floor space on the west side of the Margaret and Herman Brown Library completed in 1984. Initial planning for this called for an unfinished first floor, a second, and a third floor. The two top floors would make possible a two-story atrium to provide a much-needed meeting place and space for relaxed reading and refreshments for library patrons, the only place in the library where food or a cup of coffee or a cold drink is permitted. The atrium is an inviting place for students and faculty to select a comfortable chair and do some necessary or recreational reading while ministering to a sense of hunger or thirst. The library atrium is also an attractive place for receptions.

Teague said the atrium was

> ... really my first opportunity to confront some very traditional thinking on the part of trustees. Money was too hard to come by to be 'frivolous' with it. Giving up this much square footage on the third level was not prudent in the minds of some very thoughtful trustees. The majority of the trustees, however, saw the practical as well as aesthetic value of this provision. It made a statement for all observers that the dimension of beauty would be considered in future campus expansion.... Once it was in operation, no one boasted of having opposed the atrium.

The third floor of this new wing provided space for government documents. The main floor is the location of the Callie Faye Milliken Special Collections, including the archives of the university. The ground floor, originally unfinished, has been developed as the location of the Learning Enhancement Center. It would be logical to think that when the LEC has a home of its own, the ground floor will be available for future library expansion. A requirement of the $1 million Mabee grant was that an extra $1 million be raised toward an endowment for the library. For the first time in the history of building projects at ACU, this extra endowment money was raised, and this has become standard procedure for building projects since that of the 1992 John C. and Ruth Stevens Wing.

Next came the campaign for the $10 million Mabee Business Administration Building. The Mabee Foundation launched the drive with a $2 million challenge gift, and the remaining funds were secured in a campaign led by J. McDonald Williams, chairman of the Trammel Crow Companies of Dallas. Associated with him in the early stages of the campaign were two other alumni and Dallas businessmen, William R. Waugh, president of Waugh Enterprises, and Samuel D. Ware, president of Dabney Companies.

The Business Administration Building is indeed a majestic structure. It has three components. First and largest of the three is the academic center, with classrooms, laboratories, lecture halls, a technology learning center with ninety-four computer work stations, seminar rooms, a student concessions area, and a Quiet Place for student reflection and study. The second component is the faculty center, with faculty and administrative offices, work area for support staff and student workers, reading rooms, conference room, and a faculty lounge. The third component is the student-faculty commons, which is an attractive atrium, a three-story structure connecting the three-story academic center to the two-story faculty center, and is designed to facilitate faculty and student interaction outside the classroom.

Of the $10 million subscribed for the business campaign, $6 million went into the building itself. The remaining $4 million went to endow scholarships, professorships, and library expansion. The Mabee Business Administration Building was located facing east as a graceful and imposing part of the new front door to the campus. Dean J. William Petty of the College of Business Administration joined wholeheartedly with the chairman of the drive, the president of the university, and the steering committee in planning the facility and raising funds to make it possible.

Next came the climax of the Teague campus development. Coming hard upon the heels of the successful completion of the Business Administration campaign was a drive more than twice as large for the Biblical Studies Building.

Plans were drawn by Tittle, Luther, Loving of Abilene, the university's architects of choice over the years, and with a challenge grant from the Mabee Foundation of $3 million, a campaign was begun for $10 million to meet the Mabee challenge, and $10,750,000 more for endowment, making the total drive $23,750,000. Chairing the drive were board members Robert R. Onstead of Houston and H. Lynn Packer of Dallas. How soon the goal was reached was amazing, reminiscent of the response of the people of Israel to Moses' call to build a tabernacle for the Lord in Exodus 35. The challenge was issued in January 1987, and the remaining funds necessary to complete the drive were ready seven months later. The architects came up with the crowning work of their careers, and ground breaking for the new building took place August 31, 1987. Two years later, almost to the day, the building was officially opened for the beginning of the fall semester in 1989.

The Chapel on the Hill is one of the most popular components of the Biblical Studies Building. It honors the late Robert S. Bell and his devoted wife, Katharine. The brochure prepared for the opening day of the new facility said about Mr. Bell: "Although he was not an alumnus of the university, he adopted ACU as his alma mater." The Bells sent their two daughters to ACU, where they earned degrees and married Christian men. The two men whom the Bell daughters – Barbara and Betty – married were Lynn Packer and James Muns, both of whom are trustees of the university. The Bell, Packer, and Muns families have been constant in their loyalty and support for Abilene Christian University. All of the grandchildren of Robert S. and Katherine Bell are graduates of Abilene Christian. The Chapel on the Hill appropriately perpetuates the Bell name at ACU. The chapel is a 350-seat auditorium that is used for many purposes and is especially popular for weddings, generally being reserved a year or so ahead of time. The 54-by-24, floor-to-ceiling, stained glass windows on the right and left contain 280 shades of colored glass. A two-story wall of Leuders limestone rises above the stage.

Robert S. and Katharine Bell, Lynn and Barbara Packer, James and Betty Muns, Bob and Kay Onstead, and Randy and Barbara Nicholson filled a role in the development of the Biblical Studies Center that could be compared to what the Apostle Paul said of the Macedonians, "They gave themselves first to the Lord, and then to us in keeping with God's will." Bob and Cheryl Gowens of Houston were responsible for the

Tower of Light and the Tower Chimes. This 150-foot shaft is visible for miles from the campus by day or by night. The Westminster Chimes that are heard at the quarter hours add to the academic tone of the campus.

A touching and heartwarming story is attached to the decision of Don Baker, an Austin trustee, and his wife, Lavon, to donate the globe in the rotunda. Baker, six feet five inches tall, fifty-one years of age, apparently in the best of health, came by Bill Teague's office in August 1988 to inform him of their decision and how he was going to pay the pledge. Teague replied that the university would be happy to work with him on any plan he might have. Baker said that he would make a cash donation to start with and pay the balance with proceeds of an insurance policy. "The policy is on me," he added, calmly. "You will collect before the first of the year." He explained that he had rapidly-spreading cancer of the liver and pancreas, and it was untreatable. He died on December 6. He had spent his weeks after receiving notice of his condition in getting all of his affairs in order, including funeral arrangements. The eight-foot diameter globe slowly rotates in the sixty-five-foot tall rotunda, which architecturally echoes the Mosaic tablets. Bright points of light shine out from the globe indicating locations where the church has engaged in mission work. White lights indicate nations where American missionaries are at work, and rose-colored lights mark native churches. The construction of the globe was overseen by Dr. Ian Fair, dean of the College of Biblical Studies.

Dr. Fair was a civil engineer in South Africa years earlier, a happily married man with three young children, when he met Robert H. "Tex" Williams, who was doing missionary work for Churches of Christ. Williams and his family moved into a house next door to the Fairs. Neighborliness developed into friendship and opportunities to study the Bible together. The Fairs became members of the church. Before long, Fair sold his home and moved his family from South Africa to Abilene and enrolled in Abilene Christian University to major in Bible. After graduation, the family returned to South Africa, where Fair continued his studies in the University of Natal and completed master's and doctor's degrees in New Testament studies and systematic theology. After some years he was back in Abilene as a member of the Bible faculty, and when the Department of Bible became the College of Biblical Studies in 1986, he was named the first dean. When a $140,000 contract was signed with a Los Angeles area firm for the globe, Fair's engineering background made him the ideal liaison between the company and the university.

Between the Chapel on the Hill and the Tower of Light is the Beauchamp Amphitheatre, named in honor of Garvin and Judy Beauchamp. Beauchamp was a good friend of students as coach, dean of students, and vice president for campus life. The amphitheatre has a seating capacity of about 1,000 and is the scene of the Tuesday night devotionals that for many years were conducted on and around the steps of the Administration Building. The amphitheatre is also where summer Shakespearean productions are staged annually by the Department of Theatre.

Hart Auditorium, below the Chapel on the Hill, is described as a teacher's dream. It is named in honor of Mr. and Mrs. H. E. Hart, the parents of Barbara Hart Nicholson, who is the wife of Randy Nicholson. Hart Auditorium has 300 upholstered chairs set on a tiered floor structure, which makes it possible for students on the back row to have a clear view of the teacher down front.

The Hall of Servants is an atrium 240 feet long and twenty-six feet wide, a favorite location for large receptions and exhibits during the Bible Lectureship. At its center, two unique brick pylons stand. The bricks in it came from the original Administration Building erected on the South First Street campus in 1906. When a second Administration Building was constructed in 1919, it incorporated the original forty-eight-foot by forty-eight-foot structure. When the building was destroyed by fire in 1929, these bricks were saved and for years reposed in a side room beneath the stands of Bennett Gymnasium. Their presence in the Hall of Servants celebrates the link of the past, present, and future. These bricks in the pylons bear plaques with the names of individuals who have been honored by family or friends with $10,000 donations.

The Marriage and Family Institute is part of the College of Biblical Studies. Facilities provided for this vital program include, in addition to classrooms and faculty offices, eleven counseling rooms, a closed-circuit television system, and other high-tech devices for the preparation of students as marriage and family counselors. This section honors James and Betty Muns. Dr. Betty Muns is a licensed marriage and family therapist.

The Biblical Studies Building is at the center of the new campus front door. At any given time of the day, up to 1,000 students can be studying in its classrooms. As President Teague was quoted in the dedicatory brochure,

> The College of Biblical Studies Building will never be surpassed on the ACU campus. The trustees and administration intend this building to be the ultimate standard in teaching and serving. The building is also a call to serve God and man around the world.

In appreciation for the leadership President Teague provided for the project, the board voted to name the boulevard leading from Judge Ely up to the building Teague Boulevard.

The final major construction project of the Teague decade was a $3.5 million job of renovating and improving the Foster Science Building. This project was another example of the vital role played by the Mabee Foundation, a $2.5 million challenge gift this time. Other friends donated an additional million dollars. The central core of the building was erected in 1946; east and west wings and the Walling Lecture Hall were added during the first phase of the Design for Development in 1969, more than doubling its size. Because the central core was built at World War II's end, the plumbing was obsolete and had to be completely redone. Laboratories and classrooms were updated, and space was organized for some new facilities: a science education room, a lecture room and laboratory for teacher preparation, a high-security computer laboratory, and numerous conference rooms. The facility was tied into the Central Plant for year-round climate control. One of the most appreciated additions was a laboratory for living organisms such as birds, fish, and reptiles. No longer does a casual visitor chance to meet a large snake wriggling down the stairway to possible freedom from the top floor, where the biologists hold forth. Dr. Finis Cavendar, development officer for the project, called it and the grants that made it possible "a godsend." He said that before the renovation, the building would not have passed government inspection, but now, he said, "It passes easily." The project was completed and dedicated in February 1992.

President Teague chose an outstanding group of administrators to work with him during his years in the chief executive's post.

Robert D. Hunter continued in his position as vice president of the university. Hunter was a persuasive liaison person with the legislature and governor of Texas. He was responsible for the Tuition Equalization Grant. Quite probably – almost certainly – Hunter knew more of the alumni of the university than any other person. He was the ideal ambassador-at-large. Halfway through the Teague decade, he ran for the Texas House of Representatives – with Teague's blessing, of course – and was elected. He has been reelected every two years since his first race in 1986. Although he is now officially retired from ACU, he maintains his office on the campus and represents the university at all times.

Teague appointed as vice president for academic affairs Dr. C. G. Gray, who had been a member of the ACU faculty and dean of the College of Professional Studies just one year before this appointment. Gray was an experienced administrator. With bachelor's, master's, and doctor's degrees in education from Texas Tech University, he came to ACU with a broad background of experience in the educational and business world. After completing his bachelor's degree in 1950, he spent ten years with the Lubbock public schools, beginning as a mathematics teacher at both the junior and senior high school levels, then as a counselor, next as assistant principal at Monterey Senior High School, and for the last three years as systemwide director of guidance. In 1950, he joined Science Research Associates, a division of IBM, and during the next fourteen years, he moved from staff associate for West Texas to district director for South and West Texas and New Mexico to Midwest regional manager and completed his SRA years as director of sales and product sales and manager of state adoptions. During those years he and his wife and three sons lived in Lubbock; Prairie Village, Kansas; Austin; Chicago; Dallas; and Los Altos, California. Of those fourteen years, he says, "I traveled in forty-nine states and Guam, missing only Alaska. I wish they had been giving advantage miles during that time." In July of 1974, he left SRA to become associate director of Region 10 Education Service Center of Richardson, Texas. After four years there he became assistant superintendent of the Dallas Independent School District, from which post he came to Abilene Christian University in 1980.

Dr. Gray's wife is Barbara Jeanne Morlan, whose parents, Dr. Grover Cleveland Morlan and Alma Adams Morlan were early faculty members, and whose uncle is the longtime, incomparable Dean Adams. The Gray's three sons are all ACU graduates, and one, Dr. Cary G. Gray, a Stanford Ph.D., is chairman of the Department of Computer Science. Dr. C. G. Gray continued as vice president for academic affairs until 1988, when he resigned to return to teaching and to service as vice president for information services, 1988-91. He was cited for his work in developing the Learning Enhancement Center, the Honors Program, the General Studies Department, improved recruiting, increased benefits for the faculty, and the campuswide academic computing program. Today, he is in so-called retirement but has a small office in the library and is on campus almost daily.

A faculty search committee was appointed to seek a replacement for Dr. Gray, and the man chosen was Dr. Royce Money, who was given the new title of vice president and provost, and his appointment became effective August 15, 1988.

Faculty members added during the C. G. Gray years as chief academic officer, 1982-1988, and who stayed at least ten years are Rae B. Adams, sociology and social work; Stephen H. Allison, psychology and counseling center; Linda Appleton, English; Fred A. Bailey, history; Joe Bell, exercise science and health; Gloria Bradshaw, learning enhancement; Larry L. Bradshaw, journalism and mass communication; Daniel K.

Brannan, biology; Joseph James Cardot III, communication; Elizabeth Marion Cawood, music; Richard Chowning, missions; Bruce Davis, gerontology; Glenn G. Davis, agriculture and environment; David L. Dillman, political science; Colleen Durrington, education; W. Valdy Eichmann, foreign languages; Roger D. Gee, education; Klaus Dieter Goebel, foreign languages; Robert Green, art; Eric Hardegree, chemistry; Lucy Hatch, education; Karen Hendrick, library; Roger Hines, Learning Enhancement Center; Waymon Hinson, marriage and family therapy; Jeff Hobbs, communication; Donald Isenhower, physics; Don C. Jackson, management sciences; Paul Lakey, communication; Erma Jean Loveland, library; Monty L. Lynn, management sciences; Joe McKissick, family and consumer sciences; Keith McMillin, journalism and mass communication; Jim Mankin, Bible and ministry; Jack Maxwell, art; Emmett Miller, agriculture and environment; Matthew C. Morrison, Learning Enhancement Center; Charles W. Nelson, music and artist-in-residence; Carroll D. Osburn, Bible and ministry; T. Scott Perkins, psychology; Paul Piersall, music; Gregory Powell, chemistry; Ted W. Presley Jr., international studies; Julie Pruett, music; Jack Reese, Biblical and family studies; Charles Siburt, Bible and ministry; Allen Teel, music; Darryl Tippens, English; Gailyn VanRheenen, missions; David Wallace, Bible and ministry; Kathryn Wasemiller, family and consumer sciences; Stephen R. Weathers, English; Dan A. White, education; Lorraine Wilson, exercise science and health; and Thomas L. Winter, sociology and social work.

Gary D. McCaleb was appointed vice president and dean of campus life, and Garvin Beauchamp became vice president for special services, a less pressure-packed post, but important. McCaleb, with a bachelor's degree from ACU and two graduate degrees, the master of business administration and the Ph.D., from Texas A&M University, continued teaching a course or two in the College of Business Administration, but his time was largely devoted to student life.

Finally, for the vice president for finance, L. D. "Bill" Hilton was the man. He had been in the business office since

1950 and had a superb grasp of the financial situation of every aspect of the university.

The Office of Vice President for Development, or University Advancement, as it came to be called, began under the supervision of Bob Hunter, but he was called away by his other duties. Dr. Bruce Evans had the title for a time and served valiantly, but he chose to accept appointment as dean of the Graduate School. Patsy Powell Duncan, the only woman to have served as a vice president at ACU, led the University Advancement division with distinction until her retirement.

Gaston Welborn continued as vice president for legal services and general counsel, with Charles Trevathan as associate counsel after Teague persuaded him to move to Abilene.

All in all, it was a strong team.

The tenth person to occupy the crucial position of chairman of the Board of Trustees – Ray McGlothlin Jr., of Abilene – handed the responsibility over to H. Lynn Packer of Dallas in August 1984. McGlothlin had done a superb job of guiding the institution through some great decisions.

Lynn Packer was an able successor to the chairmanship. As chairman of the board and chief executive officer of Wyatt's Cafeterias, Inc., of Dallas, he was a man with a broad background in business and an extensive acquaintance with corporate and foundation executives of the Metroplex and beyond. He was an elder of the Walnut Hills Church of Christ in Dallas. He and his wife, Barbara, were both members of Abilene Christian's 1950 graduating class, and their two sons and one daughter were all ACU graduates. McGlothlin said of him, "I know of no one more intimately familiar with the assets, operations, and personnel of ACU or of one who is in closer touch with the spiritual foundation of the school than Lynn Packer."

The new chairman had the responsibility of teaming up with the university's president in leading the institution through the bold and far-sighted program of campus expansion, including the rerouting of Judge Ely Boulevard, moving the maintenance facility, and building the new, east front door to the campus. During his tenure as chairman, 1984-92, the first African-American was named to the board, Terry Lee Childers of

Oklahoma City, in 1988. Packer was a prime mover in planning and making possible both the Mabee Business Administration Building and the Biblical Studies Building. He also provided steady and strong leadership for the board in dealing with the evolution controversy.

In late January 1985, Mark Scott, a twenty-five-year-old transfer student, came by the office of Dr. Kenneth Williams, professor of biology, and made the blunt statement, "I'm going to get you fired." When Williams asked what the problem was, Scott replied that he was teaching organic evolution. Williams explained that he was by no means teaching evolution as a fact but he was explaining what the theory is. Scott was not satisfied with that explanation and took his complaint to Dr. Perry Reeves, dean of the College of Natural and Applied Sciences. Scott included another biology professor, Dr. Archie Manis, in his accusation, and in conversation with Manis made a some-what similar threat by saying, "You'll be sorry." Dean Reeves talked with the two professors, with other professors in the Biology Department, and with other students in classes taught by Williams and Manis. He found no evidence that either of the teachers was advocating acceptance of the theory and so informed Scott.

On February 22, 1985, Scott wrote to Dr. Bert Thompson, who, with Wayne Jackson, represented Apologetics Press, Inc., of Montgomery, Alabama. The letter stated, "Evolution is being pushed on the students here at Abilene, by two teachers anyway – Archie Manis and Kenneth Williams."

March 27, 1985, Thompson sent a certified letter contain-ing thirty specific questions to each of the professors. When Williams received his letter he turned it over to Dean Reeves. Because of the threatening tone of the questions, Manis refused to accept the one addressed to him, and both men decided that this problem had best be dealt with by the administration. Reeves replied to the letter on April 12, explaining that the intent of the two biology professors was to expose their stu-dents to the way in which evolutionists think and to expose them to evolutionists' claims so that students will be better equipped to face attacks on their faith when they leave ACU and enter professional or graduate schools or the business world.

April 29, Thompson replied, stating that he would not be satisfied until he had replies from the two professors themselves. Since Manis had refused to accept his certified letter, Thompson had sent him a postcard "acknowledging his refusal of our letter and putting him on notice that unless he corresponded with us within two weeks from the date on the postcard, acknowledging his refusal of our letter, we would begin making public our inquiry into this matter."

He announced the agenda he planned to follow:

If he did not hear from Manis and Williams within two weeks he would write to Dr. John Little, head of the department, sending him copies of the correspondence. If he did not hear from Little, he would write to Dean Reeves. His letter to Reeves, he said, would include the question of "how it is that a Christian university, supported in large part by funds from members of the churches of Christ, can allow the destructive teaching of organic evolution to occur, and continue, in its science department?" If he did not hear from Dean Reeves, he would write to President Teague. If the president did not send an "adequate" response, he would write to the Board of Trustees, "and if they are unable to assist us in finding a way to stop the teaching of the atheistic system of evolution by Drs. Manis and Williams, we will then have no choice but to publish for widespread distribution the results of our attempts, through proper administrative channels, to halt the teaching at ACU of atheistic or theistic evolution in the biology department."

He went on to explain that an adequate response would include "answers to our questions," which included, "Are the days during which creation occurred ... accepted by you as being literal days of approximately 24 hours each?" Another question was "Are you using in your classes materials (books, portions of books, articles, etc.) written by humanists and/or evolutionists?"

A complete report of the situation was given by the administration to the Academic Affairs Committee of the Board of Trustees at its April 1985 meeting. The committee gave unanimous approval of the way the situation was being handled. Efforts were made to heal the breach.

September 13, 1985, a meeting was conducted involving Thompson, accompanied by James Willeford, with a member of the ACU Board, Wilson C. Orr ; Dean Reeves; the vice president for academic affairs, Dr. Gray; and the dean of the College of Biblical Studies, Dr. Ian Fair. No progress was made, but Gray promised to send Thompson written statements from the two professors by October 31.

Dr. Gray sent the letters as promised. He wrote:

> Enclosed are the statements from Dr. Williams and Dr. Manis. These statements are for your information and should not be duplicated for distribution. Your letter of October 13 indicates several areas that need further discussion. I will be happy to discuss these with you by telephone or meet with you....

Williams' statement wasas follows: "Let me state unequivocally that I believe in the Bible, in Christianity, and in the biblical account of creation as recorded in Genesis, and I do not advocate organic evolution."

Manis wrote:

> To Whom It May Concern: 1. I believe in God, the God of the Holy Bible. 2. I believe the Bible is God's inspired word. 3. I believe in the Genesis account of creation. 4. I have believed in all the above since I was about eleven. 5. I do not advocate organic evolution and I never have. 6. "Evolution Notes," a four-page handout, is simply my summary of many different readings in evolutionary theory. It was intended exclusively for my students, for their reference use; it was not used as a basis for discussion; it was designed to inform those who were quite ignorant of basic evolutionary theory.

The statements were not enough for Thompson. He wrote Gray as follows, November 1, 1985: "You of course fully realize (and your cover letter indicates that you realize) that these documents do not even remotely conform to what we all agreed on in our meeting.... It is clear from the contents of the document, that you are not a man of your word. Apparently, you had, from the very beginning, no intention of keeping your promise(s). This being the case, further discussion would be futile."

Then began a flurry of letters from various sources. Gray was assigned the task of answering these letters, and he painstakingly replied to every letter. Articles began appearing in brotherhood publications to the effect that evolution was being taught at ACU. From Apologetics Press, letters were sent to the home addresses of all students then enrolled in ACU. These letters warned the home folk about the "dangerous teaching" their students were receiving. It is not certain that any students withdrew on that account. It is known that some students who were planning to attend ACU changed their minds. On the other hand, perhaps some students who had not planned to attend ACU decided to do so upon learning that at a Christian college controversial subjects could be discussed.

In November 1985, a committee of the board was appointed to investigate the situation. Wilson C. Orr was chairman of the committee. Other members were Dr. Roy Willingham and William E. Young. The committee interviewed the accused faculty members and their colleagues in biology and made contact with 137 present and former students of the professors. Only three of those contacted thought there was any degree of advocacy by the professors, and one of those was the student who brought the accusation in the first place. Another one had studied with one of the professors in the early 1970s.

December 13, 1985, Cindi Patterson, editor of the *Optimist*, came out with a masterfully written editorial in which she summarized the history of the controversy, the investigation that had been made into the situation, and the facts that had come out of the search for truth. She wrote,

> However, the accusers have shown an incredible persistence despite the fact that the professors, the students in the professors' classes, the department head, the dean of the college, the Board of Trustees, and the university as a whole have refuted the charges and attempted to quell these debilitating accusations.

She cited a questionnaire that had been circulated among the students concerning the teaching in ACU biology courses, and printed excerpts from the returns. One student wrote: "The material was not presented as fact, but as a theory of knowledge that all well-informed, well-educated people should have some knowledge of...." Another wrote: "Evolution should, perhaps, be presented to a greater extent than it is being presented, especially in a Christian college. Christians, especially students, should not be sheltered or shelter themselves from the outside world." Another wrote: "Here at ACU the subject of evolution is avoided so often and pussy-footed around so much, it gets ridiculous at times. The professors are almost afraid to deal with it, most likely for fear of reprisals from parents and administration.... [w]e should at least be familiar with these theories." This student response summed up the matter succinctly: "Studying evolution and believing evolution are two different things."

The editorial concluded with this wise counsel:

> The accuser should not be allowed to influence the content of biology courses at ACU. The Genesis account of creation is the only account of creation advocated by the faculty on this campus. Therefore, these rumors and unjustified accusations must be corrected before the damage is irreparable.

The word was getting around the world, for sure. The January 11, 1986, issue of the *Optimist* carried a letter to the editor from an Australian student:

> Some months ago, I received a letter from my mother urging me to be careful because the talk was that there were professors teaching evolution here at ACU. I answered her letter and strongly pointed out that what I had been taught in my classes was what the textbook said but not what my professors believe. I assured her that my professors had made clear to the classes that they needed to mention it and make us aware of the theories but that they as Christians believed in and supported creation. Well, my family is not from the United States; in fact, my letter had come from Australia.... I am disgusted that one obviously disturbed student can cause such a tide of anger to spread across this globe.

President Teague and board Chairman Lynn Packer issued a formal statement during Lectureship week of 1986: "Abilene Christian University does not, has not, and will not advocate evolutionary theory, either organic or theistic, as fact.... In every field of study, the foundation of our teaching is the unshakable belief that God's Word is true, inspired, and inerrant. We believe and teach that God created the world as described in the Scriptures, including the literal creation of man, as recorded in the first and second chapters of Genesis."

Thompson came out with a 200-page book titled *Is Genesis Myth? The Shocking Story of the Teaching of Evolution at Abilene Christian University*. This volume recited a history of the controversy and in its concluding paragraphs alleged that several points had been established, including these:

1. That evolution was being taught at ACU as "a fact beyond dispute."

2. That one of the professors "the same one who issued the statement of faith quoted above" had said in class, "I'm an elder in the church, and I believe in evolution. I'm going to teach it to you, and you're going to believe it as well."

3. That the Genesis account of creation was called a "myth."

4. That "this detestable condition has been known and protested for a number of years, but it has been repeatedly ignored and concealed."

5. That students "who dared to protest this vile teaching have been harassed, intimidated, and threatened by faculty and administrators."

The book made it clear that the professors would have to affirm that the six days of creation were twenty-four-hour days and they would have to believe in a "young" earth "that is, not more than 10,000 years old" to pass the test. The author of the book and some preachers began challenging one and all to debate the issues publicly and in print. They were ready at any time. Nobody at ACU wanted to debate because nobody taught evolution as a fact.

A decision was made for ACU to begin answering its accusers by other means. In February 1986, a letter with enclosure of several *Optimist* articles was sent to all parents. At the same time, the president spoke in Chapel, informing students of the mailing their parents had received from Apologetics Press and telling them that parents would be getting a mailing from the university. He asked all students to join him on the floor of the coliseum, join hands, and be led in prayer by Abilene board member Dub Orr. Next was the report of the Board of Trustees chairman and President Teague to some 5,000 attendees at the Lectureship. Then came a mailing to more than 80,000 Church of Christ households and advertisements in brotherhood journals. The volume of critical letters dropped rapidly, and the number of supportive letters increased. Help also came after the Lectureship speech and mailings from an unexpected source east of the Mississippi.

How Charles Trevathan of Louisville, Kentucky, became involved in the controversy is an interesting sidebar. The visit of Trevathan and his wife, Phyllis, to the Bible Lectureship in 1986, played a major role in his decision.

Trevathan had never been to Abilene. He had always lived east of the Mississippi River. He had some exposure to the attacks being made against ACU when he heard some church members in the metropolitan Louisville area giving some credence to the attacks without thinking them through. He also had noticed that some church bulletins in the East were carrying the word and warning students against going to such a place. As an elder and long-time lawyer, he was uncomfortable with what he suspected was a case of extremism run amok.

George Ezell and his wife, Ann, were and are close friends of the Trevathans. The Ezells are loyal alumni of ACU, as are Ann's parents, Arnold and Ruby Mae Watson. George was and is an executive with the Ford Motor Company Truck Division of Louisville. He had tried for a long time, but unsuccessfully, to interest the Trevathans in a trip to Abilene. Ezell finally prevailed in 1986.

When the day for departure came, a six-inch snow was on the ground in Louisville, and more was falling as they headed slowly south. Several hours later, they were still in Kentucky, and Trevathan announced that he was ready to go to Flordia for a vacation. He was so persistent that Ezell agreed that if it was still snowing when they got to Franklin, they would change plans and drive to Florida. The snow stopped five miles from Franklin.

Dr. Matthew C. Morrison, who had once preached for the Louisville congregation attended by the Trevathans, was in the middle of his first year on the ACU faculty. His wife, Betty, had not been in position to move to Abilene yet, but Matt had an apartment and invited the Trevathans to attend the ACU Lectureship and be his guests.

When the travelers arrived, the Trevathans decided to debark at the McGlothlin Campus Center with suitcases in hand to try to locate Morrison. The Ezells were free to go on to their lodgings with family members who lived in Abilene. The Trevathans telephoned Morrison's number, but had no success. They looked over the Lectureship crowd after the evening session in Moody Coliseum confident they could find their host but had no luck. They resumed the search in the Campus Center.

While at the reception desk trying to locate Morrison's whereabouts, the Trevathans encountered, a short, balding but still red-haired man who stood there and listened to their troubles. He said, "I'll take you by Matt Morrison's, and if he's not home, you can stay with us. My wife and I don't have any Lectureship visitors this year, and you'll be welcome. We can find Matt tomorrow." As it turned out, they found Morrison at home, so they stayed with him as they had planned and as he was expecting. But they appreciated the proffered hospitality of Dr. Archie Manis.

Lectureship was the key for Trevathan. He discussed the issue with a good many people. He was grateful to Dr. Manis, who impressed him as a straight-shooting Christian gentleman. He thought the position of the board on the evolution controversy as presented to the Lectureship crowd by President Bill Teague was clear and fair. He found Teague's speech so inspirational that he said he kept wanting to stand up and cheer. After he returned to Kentucky, he began to hear from concerned faculty members from other Churches of Christ colleges, and he decided to get involved.

President Teague soon received a letter from Trevathan with a copy enclosed of a letter he had sent to the leadership of a congregation in Tennessee in which he criticized the church bulletin's endorsement of some of the attacks on ACU. Trevathan told Teague that he wanted to challenge the accusers by attacking their book, *The Genesis Myth*. He made it clear that he was not attempting to represent ACU but that he had concerns about the implications of the accusations, not only for ACU, but for other Christian colleges and the brotherhood at large. He stated that he did not wish to do anything that would add to the university's burdens and that, if the president wanted him to, he would reluctantly withdraw from the field. Teague told him that the university had no basis on which to ask him either to continue his plan or to abort it.

Trevathan's focus was two-faceted. First, he did not think that the issues pertaining to the age of the earth and length of creation days were nearly as critical as did ACU's accusers. In his opinion, as a test of fellowship neither of those matters rose to the occasion, or even came close. Second, Trevathan thought that the accusers used wholly unacceptable exaggerations in their book in their characterizations of those with whom they differed.

Trevathan began mailing letters to the book's endorsers. He said he was ready to take on anyone who had been challenging someone to a debate. He wanted to affirm the proposition that because of its extremist nature, the book was unworthy of endorsement by anyone. He said his opponents could make any arguments they wished in defending the book against his charge of extremism. Nobody seemed to want to debate this proposition with Trevathan. Before too long, the attacks stopped.

The Board of Trustees and the administration assured faculty members that they would receive full support as long as they were in fact operating within the terms of the charter and the stated mission of the institution: "to educate its students for Christian service and leadership throughout the world."

Some good came out of the attack on the alleged teaching of evolution as a fact and not as a theory. Faculty members were, so far as is known, unanimous in support of their embattled colleagues. The faculty appreciated the solid support of the administration and the board. The student body rallied to the support of their alma mater. Faculty members dealing with controversial subjects resolved more firmly than ever to leave no doubts in the minds of their students as to how they stood on basic matters involving faith in God's Word.

An editorial in the *Abilene Reporter-News*, February 19, 1986, summed up community support:

> Abilene Christian University has exhibited its integrity in the

way it has rallied around two of its faculty members. Two biology teachers were besieged by accusations that, after careful
review by an investigating committee, were determined to be
unfounded. The issue was a controversial one – evolution – but
students, faculty, administration, and trustees confronted it
head-on. On Monday, trustees voted their support of the two
professors, and the decision was announced publicly during the
largest university event of the year. ACU President Dr. William
J. Teague made the announcement at the end of Monday's session of ACU's annual Bible Lectureship.

The handling of this delicate issue can only add to the already
significant reputation of ACU.

Trevathan and his wife, Phyllis, were both graduates of
David Lipscomb University. One daughter had already graduated from Harding University. The other two would become
graduates of ACU. When Bill Teague and Charles Trevathan
finally met in person, Teague invited him to move to Abilene
and become associate general counsel for ACU. He gave up his
law practice in Louisville and moved his family west. He was
associate general counsel for the remaining years of the Teague
administration. When Dr. Royce Money became president in
1991, Trevathan was named vice president for campus life and
associate general counsel. After several years of distinguished
service in that office, he is now a popular teacher in the
Department of Sociology and Social Work and has retained his
work in the university attorney's office.

A major academic development of the Teague decade was
the addition of the College of Biblical Studies to the university's organizational chart. When the Board of Trustees voted in
1976 to change the name of Abilene Christian College to
Abilene Christian University, it was considered essential to
organize into colleges gradually. At first, the university consisted of the undergraduate college and the Graduate School. After
a few years, the decision was made to have four colleges for
undergraduates plus the Graduate School. At the undergraduate level there would be the College of Liberal and Fine Arts,
including the departments of art, Bible, English, political science, history, foreign languages, and music; the College of

Natural and Applied Sciences, including the departments of agriculture, biology, chemistry, computer science, industrial education, mathematics, physics, and psychology; the College of Professional Studies, with the departments of communication; education; health, physical education, and recreation; home economics, marriage and family studies; and social work and sociology; and the College of Business Administration.

In 1981, the School of Nursing was added. This, as explained earlier, was a cooperative undertaking, involving ACU, Hardin-Simmons University, McMurry University, and Hendrick Health Services.

In 1984, because of the significant growth of the Bible Department, qualitatively as well as quantitatively, the College of Biblical Studies was added.

As previously mentioned, Dr. Ian Fair was the first dean of the College of Biblical Studies, which was organized in 1984. With this new College of Biblical Studies in operation, there was a growing demand on the part of Gospel preachers for graduate studies leading to the doctor of ministry degree, which is essentially a preaching degree designed to strengthen preachers for pulpit work. The degree was initiated in July 1987 with fifteen students. It may very well be one of the principal achievements of the Teague administration. Ten of the first group graduated in 1990. It continues to grow. Several factors have contributed to the outstanding record of this program:

1. A superior faculty. An effort has been made, with success, to recruit faculty members who are scholars of the Word and who are successful in the pulpit.

2. Students with outstanding credentials for advanced study. In order to assure that applicants who qualify for admission to the program can afford to finance their studies, millions of dollars of scholarships are being made available.

3. Growing library resources. Admittedly, this has been the weakest part of the doctor of ministry program. There is, however, a significant upgrading process under way. This has been stimulated by the decision to apply for accreditation by the Association of Theological Schools, whose requirements for library holdings are strict. Also, more donations for library improvement are helping. Craig Churchill is the theological

librarian. He is available to assist doctor of ministry candidates in obtaining materials they need from other libraries if the materials are not on hand here. The Center for Restoration Studies has an outstanding collection of more than 5,000 titles in the field of the early nineteenth-century Back-to-the-New Testament movement. Meanwhile, it should be noted that library holdings of the three Abilene University libraries, plus the Abilene Public Library and the Howard Payne University Library amount to one million titles available to be checked out by ACU students.

4. An unsurpassed place to work and study. The Biblical Studies Building, completed in 1989, is a place for work as well as a place of beauty and grace.

Teague also led the way in the initiation of endowment of faculty chairs, thus making possible the recruitment and retention of exceptionally well-qualified teachers. The first of these was the Louie Welch Chair of Business Management, established in 1983 with an initial gift of $400,000. Assets of this endowment now exceed $1 million. Income from the fund goes for a faculty salary and to help with research costs and educational travel. This endowment became the model for additional chairs. Total endowment for chairs, professorships, library, and general academic support was valued in 1997 at nearly $17 million.

Another important factor in strengthening academics is the Board of Visitors program, begun in 1983. Dr. Ira Hill, an alumnus of Locust, New Jersey, who was at the time a member of the National Board and is now a trustee, introduced this concept, based on a program with which he had become acquainted at the Massachusetts Institute of Technology.

Each academic department has a Visiting Committee of skilled professionals and academics from throughout the nation who visit the campus, meet all faculty members, check on their research and library needs, hear their problems, listen to students, and suggest ideas for improvements.

One benefit of the Board of Visitors has been the reassurance of the quality of the university's academic programs. Too, the board has helped identify and recruit several of the university's finest teachers who have left older and better-known universities to serve Abilene Christian University.

Teague and Casey Kay collaborated in making arrangements for artists in ACU's Department of Music to perform for the benefit of friends and patrons of the university in the northeastern part of the United States. The Carnegie Recital Hall in New York was the locale for the first performance on Saturday evening, February 22, 1986, followed two days later by the second performance at the Terrace Theater of the John F. Kennedy Center for the Performing Arts in Washington, D. C. Dates set were Saturday evening, February 22, 1996, in the Carnegie and Monday evening, February 24, in the Kennedy. Members of the department presenting numbers were Dr. Charles Nelson, bass; Dr. Marion Cawood, soprano; Dr. Ronald Rathbun, piano; J. David Brock, piano; and John Daniel, trumpet. They were accompanied by President Teague; Senior Vice President Hunter; Suzanne Allmon, coordinator for university outreach; and Cheryl Mann Bacon, assistant to the president. The musicians played to a packed and applauding house at the Carnegie, but attendance at the Kennedy was down because of a snowstorm and blizzard. All in all, the trip was successful and gave many Northeasterners a new perspective on the quality of life at ACU. Teague had made arrangements for expenses of the trip to be reimbursed by an anonymous donor.

Endowment growth was a significant factor of the Teague years, as mentioned in connection with buildings and faculty chair endowments. Additionally, nearly $6 million was contributed specifically to endow athletics. A sizable portion of the money for this purpose came from sources outside the regular constituency of the university; hence, the project did not take away from academic budgets. In fact, it has been beneficial to the academic program in that it has provided support for the athletic program, which might otherwise be affecting academic budgets. Athletics has been a major factor in campus life at this institution since the early years of Childers Classical Institute. With the strong program of athletics nowadays and with superb facilities for football, basketball, track and field, baseball, volleyball, tennis, golf, and softball, athletics is a big-time operation. Large operating budgets are required. Today's athletic director, Stan Lambert, keeps his computer busy tracking budets. The Teague administration's initiative in recruiting endowment funds for intercollegiate athletics was a major step forward.

The largest endowments for athletics at the present time are the A. B. Morris Endowment, the Byron Nelson Endowment for golf, and the program of endowed scholarships in football. Two world-famous athletes, Byron Nelson and Nolan Ryan, were influential in helping with endowments in golf and baseball. Among pacesetting major donors to this program were William A. and Nancy McMinn and the youngest member of the group, Thomas R. "Tom" Teague, son of Bill and Peggy Teague. Tom was a principal donor and led others to participate. The program of athletic endowments has a bright and important future.

The ACU Sports Hall of Fame was organized in 1986 when a committee was named to come up with a plan for perpetuating the memory of outstanding sports figures from ACU's history. The hall began honoring individuals for character and integrity as well as athletic prowess and service. The list of honorees includes coaches and players, plus some individuals who have made outstanding contributions to athletics in other ways. The first year ten athletes and coaches who were outstanding before 1950 were honored; since then, four or so per year have been chosen. The first Hall of Fame induction dinner was conducted September 6, 1986, in Moody Coliseum. Of the original group of ten men inducted, five were honored posthumously: A. B. Morris, A. M. "Tonto" Coleman, J. Eddie Weems, Eck Curtis, and Willard Paine. The other five were Elmer "Bulldog" Gray, Howard Green, Thurmon "Tugboat" Jones, Lee Powell, and Guy Scruggs. All of these five are now deceased. Since that charter class, some sixty others have been added to the Hall of Fame, including nine who were chosen for Lifetime Achievement Awards. Of the fifty-one others, all but one were alumni of the earlier presidential eras.

Willard Tate, chosen for the year 1996-97, is an alumnus of Alabama Christian College, now Faulkner University, and of Auburn University. His master's degree is from Troy State University in Montgomery, Alabama. He came to ACU in 1973 as head coach of men's basketball and coached for seven seasons, compiling an outstanding record and representing the highest standards of coaching and teaching. He retired from coaching after the 1979-80 season to pursue his successful work as associate professor of communication, minister of the Hamby Church of Christ, and a popular speaker at workshops, seminars, and churches throughout the nation. He and his wife, Bobbie, have become vital members of the ACU community.

The lifetime achievement honorees were the following:

Earl M. "Pop" Bailey was selected for 1988-89. His citation describes him as "one of the greatest fans of the Wildcats in the history of intercollegiate sports at Abilene Christian University." He was a founder of Bailey Bridge Company and a pioneer in Texas bridge and highway construction. He was known as an "honorary assistant coach" for ACU football and baseball and the father and grandfather of Wildcat lettermen Bob in the 1950s and Brad in the 1970s, respectively.

Glen Terhune was named in 1989 and was described as one who had been "involved with Wildcat athletics for more than sixty years." He was an athlete in his student days and later was especially active in support of ACU football and track and field.

Chesley McDonald was the third person chosen for the Lifetime Achievement Award. Although he was a three-year letterman in football at ACU in the latter 1930s, he was selected for the Lifetime Achievement Award because of distinctive support of the athletic program and all other phases of the work of ACU. He and wife, Cecile, received the university's Christian Service Award in 1989. For many years he was a member of the Board of Trustees and received the Outstanding Alumnus Award in 1975.

W. E. "Mose" McCook was the fourth person chosen. He had already been noted as an honoree for his athletic prowess as a football and track letterman from 1934 to 1938. He and his wife, Mary Alice, who died in 1997, rendered distinguished service in the support of the total ACU program and in his role as an owner of Athletic Supply in Abilene.

Crutcher and Vickie Scott were named in 1994. Crutcher died in 1979 but was well represented by his wife and by their son, Al, at the function during which the Scott name was enshrined in the Hall of Fame. The ACU baseball field is named in their honor. Their lifetime of support and major donations made the field possible. It is one of the finest in college and university circles. Crutcher Scott was for many years secretary of the ACU Board of Trustees.

Roy Lewis was the seventh person to receive a Lifetime Achievement Award. He was honored in 1996. He was an engineer, now retired, for the United States Post Office in Abilene. For a quarter of a century he has volunteered to film home and road football games and officiate at track and field meets at Elmer Gray Stadium. He also was the pilot for charter trips and driver of the team bus for shorter trips. He and his wife, LuGene, and their four children are all ACU alumni.

Dr. Orval Filbeck was the eighth person chosen for the Lifetime Achievement Award. He was honored at the February 1997 Hall of Fame luncheon. He retired as a professor in the Department of Education in 1982 after thirty-seven years of teaching at ACU; he was chairman of the department 1954-78. During all of his years on the campus, he has been an avid fan of the Wildcats. His grandson, Corey Stone, is the career scoring leader in ACU men's basketball.

Rebecca Morris was the ninth Lifetime Achievement Award recipient. Her citation states, "A retired teacher, Mrs. A. B. (Rebecca) Morris has been a loyal, model fan for more than seventy-five years." Graduating from Abilene Christian in 1925, Rebecca McKay married Coach Morris and later taught drama and directed theatre productions at the university. Two endowed scholarships at ACU bear her name: a fund to benefit students who are active and show outstanding ability and potential in the performing arts and a fund for women's basketball. The Morrises' son, Charles, had a successful career in athletics at Abilene Christian and later was a coach and administrator of intercollegiate athletics. He died December 22, 1997.

When Lowell Perry joined the faculty in 1948, he brought with him a dream of a campus radio station. As the fulfillment of his dream, radio station KACC went on the air on Monday evening, January 8, 1951, from studios in the basement of McKinzie Dormitory. Bill Teague was the first student manager, and Dr. Perry its faculty adviser. Its signal was limited to the Hill. KACC's announced purpose was twofold: first, to provide a laboratory for students studying radio, and, second, to provide a type of entertainment most students preferred as well as campus, local, and world news. When the journalism and mass communication program moved into the Morris Center in 1978, the carrier-current status of the station and its limited audience provided less than an ideal training environment for future broadcasters. The city also needed a station that would bring National Public Radio and better music programming to the market. With the blessings of the Teague administration, work began to secure an FM license, but the remaining frequency had been allotted to Criswell Broadcasting of Dallas. The university bought the rights to the frequency, and David Spiceland, Gaston Welborn, and Dr. Charlie Marler nursed the application through the Federal Communications Commission and a construction grant application through the National Telecommunication Information Agency of the U.S. Department of Commerce. An NTIA grant of $290,000 was received with the provision that matching funds of one-fourth of that amount be raised. Fred and Iva Lee Barton and David and Melinda Worley were the pacemaking donors in the campaign for additional construction funds.

June 1, 1986, thirty-five years and five months after the founding of KACC, KACU-FM went on the air as an affiliate of National Public Radio from the Barton-Worley Studios and the tower and transmitter located on the Allen Farm. By this date, Dr. Bill Teague was president of the university, and his was the first voice heard as the KACU-FM broadcast began. The station can be received up to a hundred miles from Abilene. Dr. Larry Bradshaw was chosen as general manager and has filled that position with great success ever since, except for a three-year leave of absence while his wife, Gloria, was working on a doctor's degree at Vanderbilt University. During that interim, Dr. Dutch Hoggatt was acting manager.

The station is supported by ACU, and half of the budget comes from twice-a-year drives for membership and from underwriters of programming. An amazing feature of these membership drives is that from 200 to 300 volunteers from the community go on the air to help solicit gifts, reminiscent of the early days of the college when widespread support helped the young school. Surveys indicate that KACU-FM regularly has one-fourth of the listening market in metropolitan Abilene. Only one professional announcer is employed by the station. Gary Vaughn, director of operations, is that announcer. All of the other announcers are students. The news programs of National Public Radio are outstanding. The station also furnishes local news and weather reports throughout the day. Contemporary music is featured during the daytime hours and classical music during the evening hours except Sunday evenings, which feature jazz. The station is a huge success in the community and as an educational lab; its announcers regularly win regional intercollegiate radio announcing contests.

Teague recalls an attempted escape through the "slide and glide" chapel phenomenon "one of the funniest things that happened during my ten years as president." Daily chapel has always been a requirement at Abilene Christian. Now that university status has been achieved, that part remains the same. For seventy-five years, student checkers were stationed at various locations, checking assigned seating and recording absentees; cameras were used for a while when Moody was new. During the Teague years, improved technology made it possible for students to insert identification cards into electronic readers at the entrances leading into the coliseum, and their presence was recorded by the computer in the chapel secretary's office. Obviously, soon some students were sliding their cards through the electronic readers and then gliding away in the opposite direction. "Slide and glide" became quite a catchy phrase. To deal with the problem, members of the student life staff occasionally stationed themselves at various exits. When a student was seen walking away instead of into the coliseum, clearly he or she was a glider.

One day Dr. Gary McCaleb, vice president for campus life, worked one of the entrances and saw a burly young man walking away. He fell in behind him and called to him to wait up, but he did not slow down. Indeed, he began to quicken his pace. McCaleb continued to call to him, but he continued to accelerate his speed of departure. Approaching students told him, "Dr. McCaleb is calling to you," but he continued to move away and began to run. Dr. McCaleb, who at that time was running in either the Boston or New York marathons every year, had no trouble maintaining the pace. A campus security officer, seeing McCaleb in hot pursuit, fell in behind with his patrol car and was on the scene when McCaleb overtook the now severely winded football player. When questioned by McCaleb and the security officer, he gave a phony name. The officer returned with McCaleb and the athlete to the coliseum. As they entered, a football coach recognized the student and called him by his correct name, which set in motion the dialogue one might expect to take place. The coach appealed to Dr. McCaleb to "let me impose discipline." McCaleb agreed. For many days the student did untold laps to the top of Elmer Gray Stadium and around the track to the demeaning shouts of his teammates, who chided him for being unable to outrun a man as old as Dr. McCaleb. As Teague says, "The moral of the story is that when one plans to escape from a dean, he should be sure the dean is not a marathoner."

Food services, a tough challenge on any campus, and landscaping, a critically difficult one in West Texas, were taken on by Teague. His background in industry suggested to him that wherever possible it is best to out-source services and production to experts. The first application of the principle was in the operation of the campus food service. He says, "The in-house operation was probably as quality-efficient as it could ever be within the parameters of a university schedule. There are simply too many days in a calendar year when your overhead keeps running but your income is nil." So he negotiated a contract with an outside provider who accepted the responsibility of providing full-time jobs for key people. In the long term this resulted in a considerable improvement in every aspect of the food service performance. Two companies had the contract before the present provider, ARAMARK, began an association with the university that has proved to be quite satisfactory. Landscaping budgeting, says Teague, was one the toughest challenges during his ten years as president. He was convinced that ACU was losing students because of the appearance of the campus. He was able to convince the board to approve landscaping dollars in the budget and succeeded in an unprecedented campus beautification program.

A notable event of 1987 was the amicable separation of Abilene Christian Schools from Abilene Christian University. Students who enrolled in Childers Classical Institute in 1906 signed up for courses at the elementary and secondary level. Hence, Abilene Christian Schools existed before Abilene Christian University or College. In the first catalog, prepared by A. B. Barret in 1906, this affirmation is found: "It is far more important for the future man that he should find the right school, than the right college. What can college or a counting room do for the person where preparatory opportunities have been abused?"

The first college-level course was offered in 1909, according to a study made by L. D. "Bill" Hilton in 1980. From the beginning, however, the name "Christian College" predominated on the campus and in the Abilene newspapers. When James F. Cox was elected president in 1911, he announced that the name would be "Abilene Christian Training School," which was actually what it was. Of course, the charter name was still "Childers Classical Institute," but, although that name was technically correct, it was seldom used.

When Jesse P. Sewell became president in 1912, he changed the name to "Abilene Christian College," with the fine print reading "Charter Name Childers Classical Institute" because, he announced, it would actually be a junior college. By 1914, it was accredited by the University of Texas as a junior college. Hence, a college developed apart from the school. By 1917, the high school was called the Academy, while the elementary school was called the Training School. These designations continued when the college became a four-year degree-grant-ing institution in 1919.

Through the years, the school was closely connected with the Education Department of the college. Future teachers could do their practice teaching there, and the latest ideas of educators could be tried there. In 1932, the Training School and the Academy became the Demonstration School, an integral part of the Education Department of the college. In 1957, the name was changed to Campus School. By 1974, it was clear that Campus School was not an adequate title, so it was changed to Abilene Christian Schools, which is the name it bears today.

In the 1980s, Abilene Christian Schools clearly had enough of a constituency to justify an independent existence. With the growth of the university to a student body in excess of 4,000, the elementary and secondary schools were treated as somewhat of an afterthought. A number of members of the Board of Trustees of the university had Christian schools in their own cities to support. They seemed to ask why Abilene was not large enough to support its own elementary and secondary school. This coincided with opinions of local supporters of Abilene Christian Schools.

Hence, trustees of the university led in organizing a self-perpetuating board of trustees for the schools. The newly-appointed board obtained a charter and recognition by Internal Revenue as a tax-exempt educational organization. University trustees gave 30.3 acres of land on Judge Ely Boulevard north of the university campus, plus a commitment of $700,000 in cash. This money became available when trustees of the schools succeeded in raising a matching sum of $700,000, for a total of $1.4 million, to build a physical plant on the new campus for an institution offering pre-school through high school education for about 350 students.

The contract representatives of both boards signed stipulated that the property would always be used for primary and/or secondary school purposes, that there would always be regularly scheduled chapel and Bible classes for all school grades, that the Board of Trustees would always consist of faithful members of a congregation of the Church of Christ, and that the tax-exempt relationship of the schools with Internal Revenue would always be maintained. In the absence of any one of these provisions, the land given to the schools by the university would revert to the university, and the sum of $700,000 would be due and payable.

Abilene Christian Schools is thriving as an independent educational institution with a waiting list of students desiring admission. Steve Cunningham is doing a great job as executive director. Steve Woods is principal of the high school, and Roger Thomas is principal of the elementary school. These men preside over the work of a strong faculty and staff. Dr. David Bailey, Abilene physician, served as chairman of the board from the time it became independent in 1987 until 1994. Gaston Welborn, attorney for the university, has been chairman since 1994. A spirit of wholehearted cooperation exists between Abilene Christian University and Abilene Christian Schools. Plans are underway for an expansion of facilities to accommodate more students.

When Lewis Fulks announced he would retire January 1, 1990, as theatre director, consternation settled in because he *was* ACU theatre. A review of the Fulks record, covering some forty-one years, awes the senses.

He enrolled as a freshman in ACU in the spring of 1945. His first live drama experience at his new school came during the next summer. The play was *Moor Born*. He was a member of the stage crew. He declares that his love affair with ACU began with that very first production. In his second show, *The Truth about Blayds*, in the fall of 1945, he had a major acting part and was again a member of the stage crew. From that time on through his years as an undergraduate student, he was the designer for sixteen major productions. In two plays, *Holiday* and *Beyond the Horizon*, he had a major role in each in addition to being the designer. He was named Best Actor for *Horizons*.

After receiving his bachelor's degree from ACU in 1948, Fulks went west for graduate study at the University of Southern California. While there for a year, he was designer for Moliere's *The School for Wives* and *Anna Christie* and a member of the stage crew for *Pygmalion*. He came back to ACU in the fall of 1949 to begin his work as an instructor in the Speech Department and designer for the theatre. Sometimes, in addition to designing the sets, he was also director. At other times he was a major actor. But always he was the designer. December 15, 1949, he and Jerelene Warren were married. Jerry worked in the finance office while Lewis worked on his plays and as a teacher, and theirs has been a beautiful marriage. When people have through the years asked Lewis why he chose to stay at ACU instead of going on to Broadway or Hollywood, he has told them that one of the reasons is that he fell in love with his wife at ACU.

Beginning in the summer of 1949 and for the next nine years, he designed sets for the operas *LaTraviata, Martha, Madame Butterfly, Aida, Rigoletto, Lakme,* Shakespeare's *Much Ado About Nothing, The Taming of the Shrew,* and many delightful and lighthearted productions and heavy dramas. He was often director as well as designer. In 1956, he designed and directed ACU's fiftieth anniversary pageant highlighting scenes from its history. It was titled *A City Set on a Hill,* written by June Bearden of Lubbock of the class of 1942 and composed by Robert Page, class of 1948, who was a member of the faculty of Eastern New Mexico University.

Fulks was technical director for the first Sing Song in 1957. He was co-designer for the first Homecoming musical, *The Wizard of Oz,* in 1958. He designated himself "co-designer" because he and Jerry had to leave for California before the production actually came off. He spent three years directing theatre at Pepperdine while working on a doctorate at Southern California. His student assistant, Frank Morris, took over and finished *The Wizard of Oz* sets. Back in Abilene in 1961, Fulks began designing and directing a series of unbroken successes on the stage. In 1970, he moved the Homecoming musicals to the new Abilene Civic Center. In fact, his was the opening performance at the new center; *The Sound of Music* drew audiences of 7,700 for the three performances. The Civic Center was sold out four weeks before opening night. He added a Friday matinee in response to the demand.

In the winter of 1971, he began renovating Sewell Auditorium and converted it into Sewell Theatre, a dinner theatre, which apparently was a first in collegiate circles. He reduced the seating capacity of Sewell by about two-thirds and greatly expanded the stage. He paid for the improvements primarily with money the theatre had made. The first dinner theatre production was *Once upon a Mattress* in 1972. All performances were sold out, and that has been the story. A great many Abilene non-ex-students are connected to ACU because they buy theatre tickets, and people from other West Central Texas cities buy tickets in blocks.

Fulks, in 1967, started a children's theatre program. More than fifty area schools bring children to performances, which originally were staged in Cullen Auditorium. It grew to the point that seventeen performances were given each year for some 12,000 children. Since Fulks' retirement, the program has been continued under the present director of theatre, Adam Hester, and his staff. Four years ago, scheduling problems necessitated moving the production to the Paramount theatre in downtown Abilene. The Paramount, with a seating capacity of about 1,000 was packed for nine to twelve performances each year. In 1997, the children's theatre was moved to the Civic Center auditorium, with a seating capacity in excess of 2,000. The number of school buses converging on the parking lots bringing children to the shows create a show in themselves. Under the oversight of the theatre director, freshmen and sophomores are generally in charge of these productions, which provide a great experience for budding theatre majors. It is also a fruitful point of contact for prospective students.

While all of this was going on, Fulks made another major contribution to the cultural life of ACU. In the spring of 1976 he began offering a film appreciation class, using classic films as assignments. His first class attracted 283 students. When students signed up for it as a so-called easy course, they soon found that he regarded the subject as literature and as art. As long as he was teaching the course, offered twice a year, it drew more than 200 students each time it was offered.

In the summer of 1990 he began another tradition by producing and designing Shakespeare's *Othello* in the Garvin and

Judy Beauchamp Amphitheatre. Many people look forward to the annual midsummer Shakespearean play, staged out-of-doors and featuring complimentary admission.

Fulks' final production – the 187th of his career – was the Homecoming musical for the fall of 1990, *Man of La Mancha*. After that show, his retirement went into effect, and when he had time to check all of his records, he found that between 1948 and 1990, more than 500,000 patrons had seen his shows.

Fulks always was especially appreciative of his undergraduate mentors at ACU – Rebecca Morris, Chris Kyker, and Rex Kyker. He was succeeded as director of theatre by Adam Hester, a talented director who studied under Fulks, acted for the director, worked with him, and was recommended by Fulks for the position. Adam and his wife, Donna, along with Gary Varner, Steven Pounders, and others are today continuing the Fulks theatre tradition.

Rex Kyker, under whom Fulks was initiated into the theatre, pointed out in recommending him for an honorary doctorate that Fulks was a good business manager as well as a genius at directing. During his tenure as director, the ACU theatre grossed more than $2 million. This enabled him to finance the renovation of Sewell Auditorium and its conversion to Sewell Theatre and to pay many of the salaries of his staff and assistants.

Lewis Fulks considered theatre his Christian ministry. As Dr. Kyker pointed out, "Students have been deeply moved spiritually by his devotion to Christian standards, and wept together when the cast and crew met for devotionals for a rehearsal or show." The Board of Trustees voted unanimously, upon the recommendation of President Teague, to bestow the honorary degree, doctor of fine arts, upon the long-time ACU theatre director. The president conferred the degree at a dinner in Sewell Theatre, with actor McLean Stevenson as special guest, before the performance of *Man of La Mancha* October 27, 1990. If ever an individual earned an honorary doctor's degree, Lewis Fulks earned it.

Gerontology, a relatively new discipline, was born on the campus in 1984. Dr. Rae B. Adams joined the faculty of sociology and social work and was asked to set up the Center on Aging, which was soon done, and by 1986, a master's degree program in gerontology was offered. Surveys indicated that not more than thirty universities in the world were offering such a program. In 1987, Bruce Davis, with a Ph.D. in gerontology from the University of Nebraska, was added. When Dr. Adams decided to return to full-time teaching in the Department of Sociology and Social Work, Davis became director of the Center on Aging.

Soon he had an energetic helper. C. D. Pruett was a preacher in San Antonio. Over the years, he had been impressed with the need for ministers to give more attention to senior citizens in their congregations because of what they had to offer in the way of talent, wisdom, and the desire to serve. When he learned of the graduate program at ACU, he gave up his San Antonio pulpit and moved his family to Abilene to become involved as a student. Later, with master's degree in hand, he was asked to serve as assistant director of the Center on Aging, and, in 1994, when Dr. Davis resigned as director to become a gerontologist-in-residence and pursue some other interests, Pruett was named director. Pruett is pursuing a doctorate in gerontology at the University of North Texas while teaching and supervising twelve to fourteen master's degree candidates at ACU. Demand is strong for qualified people to operate facilities for the aged, nursing homes, and retirement centers in these years of increasing life expectancy. The master's degree in gerontology is an interdisciplinary study, involving courses in psychology, sociology, social work, biology, exercise science and health, and other fields of study. At the present time, gerontology is assigned to the Department of Family and Consumer Sciences and is expected to grow to departmental status. Meanwhile, Pruett has secured a $1 million endowment from an uncle, Zach Pruett, to ensure continued growth in numbers and quality. What was the Center on Aging has become the Pruett Gerontology Center.

An unsung hero was involved in achieving the campus masterpiece that is the Biblical Studies Building; the Board of Trustees mandated that it should make the most majestic, aesthetic architectural statement on the campus because it was the home of studies of the Bible. But one new building – the Mabee Business Building – had already raised the standard higher than for any other building on the campus because of one man. His name is William R. "Bill" Waugh, and an explanation is required.

When President Teague recommended to the board that a campaign be undertaken to secure funds to build the business administration building, a committee was named to take the lead. Don Williams was the chairman of the drive. His co-chairmen were Sam Ware and Bill Waugh. Don Williams was a strong campaign chairman and major donor, but he announced from the beginning that he would defer to Waugh on the matter of appearance of the facility. Waugh was the right man at the right time. He was not a business major. He had graduated from Abilene Christian in 1959 with an art major and had taken his knowledge of art and beauty into the business world and had made a fortune with his Taco Bueno, Crystal's, and Casa Bonita restaurants. Part of the secret of his success was his ability to make the interiors as well as the exteriors of his eating establishments attractive.

Waugh took one look at the plans and announced, in effect, "This will not do. We must have something more creative than this." So back to Abilene and the drawing board came the architects and the university president. A second set of drawings was rejected. Waugh was not known for beating around the bush. He described for the architects in some detail what he was looking for. He wanted a timeless quality, a contemporary interpretation of the classical look. On the way back to Abilene, architect Jack Harkins told architect Jimmy Tittle, "I believe I know what it is he is looking for."

After a time of concentrated work, a third set of business building plans was ready, and another trip to Dallas took place. On the way over, Tittle told Teague, "We have done the best we can do. If this doesn't work, I think our firm will resign from the project." Teague predicted that Waugh would be pleased. He was. As soon as Waugh walked into the room where the plans were laid out, he announced approval. The campaign was a success; the Mabee Business Building is remarkable.

Bill Waugh's insistence that the architects reach a higher standard for the Mabee Business Building inspired the even more majestic, aesthetic architectural quality of the Biblical Studies Building, the crowning achievement of the campus. So Bill Waugh is the unsung hero.

In 1984, a program honoring couples who have worked together in Christian service was inaugurated. First recipients were Ray and Kay McGlothlin Jr. They were honored at a luncheon February 19 at the beginning of Lectureship. The complete list of other couples who have been recognized for their teamwork in Christian service are 1985, Trine and Malissa Starnes, Houston; 1986, Paul and Margaret Southern, Abilene; 1987, Burton and Thelma "Sissy" Coffman, Houston; 1988, Wade and Thelma Banowsky, Fort Worth; 1989, Chesley and Cecile McDonald, Sterling City; 1990, Homer and Betty Gainer, Houston; 1991, Joe and Janelle Baisden, Belton; 1992, Lynn and Barbara Packer, Dallas; 1993, James and Jackie LeFan, Temple; 1994, Gene and Ruth Ann Stallings, Tuscaloosa, Alabama, and now Powderly, Texas; 1995, Ed and Barbara Bonneau, Farmers Branch; 1996, Wendell and Betty Broom, Abilene; 1997, Bob and Myrt Davidson, College Station; and 1998, John and Ruth Stevens, Abilene.

Peggy Teague, in 1984, helped launch the For Ladies Only dinners. These annual fellowship occasions are scheduled for the Tuesday evening of Lectureship and provide a good situation for wives of men attending the Preachers, Elders, and Deacons dinners in Scruggs Gymnasium. At first, the ladies' meetings were conducted in Cullen Auditorium, but in recent years they have been scheduled for the Hilton Room in McGlothlin Campus Center. The newly finished Margaret L. and William J. Teague Special Events Center promises a more spacious location for the ladies' dinners and the ever-increasing number of women who attend the dinner.

About midway through the Teague decade, he was visited by Dr. E. W. McMillan, a spiritual giant of a man who was in his mid-nineties and going strong. Teague invited him to speak on Lectureship when he reached his 100th year. McMillan accepted the invitation. There might have been some doubt as to whether he would live to be 100, or, if he did, whether he would be able to be a major speaker. He did live to be 100; in fact, he saw his 101st birthday before departing this life. So it was, that Edward Washington McMillan was scheduled as a major speaker on Sunday evening, February 19, 1989. His 100th birthday would not be until September 27 of that year. But he was in his 100th year, and it was decided that his lecture should be delivered then. He was allotted forty minutes, as was the case with all Lectureship speakers, but some concern was expressed as to whether he would be able to fill his time. His voice was strong, but he would have to sit in his wheelchair while speaking. The decision was made that John Stevens would sit on the platform with him and ask questions. It was thought that the question-and-answer format might be comfortable for him.

About two weeks before the event, his daughter, Elizabeth McMillan Randolph, came by the campus and expressed some concerns about the speech. When she was asked whether she feared he would not be able to take the time allotted, her answer was, in effect, "Quite to the contrary. I asked him a biblical question the other day, and two hours later he concluded his answer." That confirmed us in the opinion that a question-and-answer format might be practical after all, except that it might be useful to provide a way of bringing the meeting to a close.

A Dallas friend sent McMillan to Abilene in his private airplane. He was accompanied by his physician, Dr. Seth Cowan and Dr. Cowan's wife, Tommye. More than 2,000 people crowded into the University Church auditorium. Brother Mac was in great shape that Sunday evening. He spoke for approximately one hour, but nobody objected. No one left the auditorium. Stevens spent the last twenty minutes trying to bring closure, but the wily centenarian was too smart for Stevens to close him out. The aged soldier of the cross thrilled the audience, exhorting people to "preach the gospel and keep it simple." Dr. McMillan was the only Lectureship participant who has spoken during each of seven decades since its beginning in 1918.

At the August 27, 1990, meeting of the Board of Trustees, Teague asked the board to begin the process of selecting his successor. When he was being interviewed in 1980 about the job, the question had arisen as to how long a period he thought he would like to occupy the office. He replied that in his opinion ten years was a good length of time. His ten years would be up in August 1991. His time in office had been a period of solid – in fact, brilliant – accomplishments. Along the way he had stirred up a measure of discontent, as any intensely active president is likely to do. He tells about the day a senior staff member told him, "I wish you well. Keep up the good work. Don't be discouraged by the comments that are made in the faculty lounge." No question about it, Bill and Peggy Teague came along at exactly the right time in the history of Abilene Christian University.

At a board meeting October 26, 1990, chairman Lynn Packer appointed immediate past chairman Ray McGlothlin Jr. to chair a search committee to select Dr. Teague's successor. Board members appointed to serve with him were Dale Brown, Midland; Mary Prudie Brown, Stanton; Don Crisp, Dallas; Homer Gainer, Houston; Stanley Lockhart, San Angelo; and Richard Lunsford, Olney. Faculty members chosen were Dr. Michael Sadler, physics, chairman of the Faculty Senate, and Dr. Marianna Rasco, chairman of the Family and Consumer Sciences Department. The president of the Students' Association, Gary West, was a member. Dan T. Garrett of Kennedale and Kara Cobb of Stamford represented the alumni. Shirley Riley, controller, was chosen to represent mid-management. Dr. John C. Stevens and Dr. William J. Teague were named as internal advisers. Dr. Charles Neff of Washington, D. C., representing the Association of Governing Boards, was chosen as external adviser. Attorney Gaston Welborn was named to serve as resource person for the committee. The chairman of the board served as an ex-officio member.

The search was remarkably well organized. A large number of names came in. All nominees were contacted, and all persons desiring an appointment were interviewed. In the interest of confidentiality, the committee interviewed the nominees off-campus. When the process was completed, the committee was unanimous in recommending to the Board of Trustees, and the board was unanimous in electing, Royce Money tenth president. Stevens was named chancellor emeritus, and Teague was elected chancellor. The committee report and the board vote occurred May 10. The changes became effective three weeks later, June 1, 1990.

Teague's legacy as a campus builder is no less significant than the 1929 ACC builders; they gave it a campus worthy of a young college; he reformed their handiwork into a campus worthy of a university.

Chapter Eight

"It's a Kingdom Matter"

The tenth president of Abilene Christian University – Royce Lynn Money – began his official duties June 1, 1991, six weeks before his forty-ninth birthday. He was born in Temple, Texas, July 13, 1942. During his first interview as president published in *ACU Today*, he jokingly informed the reporter that John Stevens' birthday was July 15, Bill Teague's was July 12, and his was July 13. The reporter's comment was, "The next man who wants to be ACU president better check his birth certificate." To which Money responded, "Yes, only July applicants need apply!"

After graduation from Temple High School, Money enrolled as a freshman at ACU in the fall of 1960. He was a Bible major. As an undergraduate student, he was busy with extracurricular activities as well as his studies. During his sophomore year, a freshman from San Antonio named Pamela Joy Handy arrived on campus and soon caught the attention of the tall sophomore.

Money graduated in 1964, but he stayed on for graduate study leading to the master of divinity degree. He secured employment as assistant to the dean of students, Garvin Beauchamp, an education within itself. He had a mixture of motives for staying on: one was that he was ambitious for more education; the other was that Pam Handy had promised her father she would not get married before graduating from college. She did not promise her father that she would not speed up her studies leading to graduation. Hence, she was, as Money told an *Optimist* reporter in February 1992, a "three and a halfer," meaning that she did four years of college work in three and a half years. Her last semester ended January 21, 1965, and the wedding was January 23.

After two years in the office of the dean of students, Money was associate minister for a year with the Westgate Church of Christ in Abilene, and, in 1967, with his master of divinity degree completed, he went into the ministry in a major way. He was pulpit minister for a year in Silver Spring, Maryland; youth minister for two years in Waco, while working on a doctor of philosophy degree in religion at Baylor University; pulpit minister for a year in Dallas; pulpit minister for three years in Montgomery, Alabama; and pulpit and family minister for five years in Springfield, Missouri, where he was also a lecturer in the Department of Religious Studies at Southwest Missouri State University. Along the way, he acquired a master's degree in human development and the family from the University of Nebraska to add to his doctor's degree from Baylor.

Two daughters were born to Royce and Pam Money. Alison is now Mrs. Stefano Elliott, and Jennifer is Mrs. Brad Crisp. They and their husbands are ACU graduates.

In 1981, the Moneys accepted an invitation to move back to Abilene, where he would teach in the Marriage and Family Institute and his wife could teach in the public schools. His talent for administration was quickly spotted, and he moved rapidly up the administrative ladder. After three years in the Marriage and Family Institute, he accepted a transfer to the ministry division of Biblical studies and was named director of the division. Emphasis was being given to appointing professors in that division who had successful backgrounds in the practical experience of preaching, and Money had certainly had that. Two years later, he was appointed chairman of the Graduate Bible Department and director of the doctor of ministry program. Two years after that he was named executive assistant to the president. He was in that position from January to July in 1988 and then was appointed vice president and provost of the university, the first provost in the history of the university. The office of provost included the work of vice president for academic affairs, but it covered a wider range of responsibilities than the former position had encompassed. One month short of three years later, he moved into the office of president of Abilene Christian University.

Meanwhile, Pam Money did further graduate work. She already had a master's degree in education, but in 1986 she completed a second master's degree, this one in marriage and family therapy. Within a couple of years, she had developed quite a clinical practice. Dr. and Mrs. Money became the only presidential couple in the history of Abilene Christian University, and probably in the history of any Texas university, to be licensed marriage and family therapists. However, when her husband became president, she gradually eased out of her private practice in order to be free to work with her husband, travel with him, and use her expertise as a friend and counselor to students.

In working at Abilene Christian University instead of full-time pulpit work, Money did not consider that he was out of the ministry. In fact, when a visitor asked him once whether he thought he might ever return to the ministry, he answered, kindly, "I have never left it." When he announced his first major campaign for funds, with a goal of $29.5 million, he quoted two immortal statements from ACU's history, and added one of his own to the rationale for the campaign. First, he quoted from the speech President A. B. Barret gave to the chapel audience on the first opening day, September 12, 1906: "What Man Has Done, Man Can Do." Then he cited the unforgettable address Don Morris gave during his last chapel appearance, September 27, 1973, when he declared, "Ladies and gentlemen, this is no ordinary college that you and I have the privilege of being a part of."

Finally, he added a statement of his own to remind his hearers of the eternal implications of their work: "This is a Kingdom matter: Our goal in this campaign is not simply dollars and cents. It's not facilities or technology. Our purpose is the same as it has been since 1906: to educate students for Christian service and leadership throughout the world…. Advancing the Changeless is a kingdom matter – worthy of our highest effort." In considering his work a continuation of ministry in Christ's Kingdom, he pointed out that he planned to do essentially the kind of things he had been doing, "but maybe at a little bit more rapid pace." He declared, "I've preached in hundreds of churches in the last ten years, and I want to continue to do that." No question about it, first and foremost among the goals of Royce Money was a determination to keep a close relationship between Abilene Christian University and its religious heritage.

Two days after Money became president, Vice Chancellor C. L. "Casey" Kay died of complications after surgery. He was sixty-four, apparently in good health, energetic, optimistic. His death was a great loss. Since 1982, Dr. Kay had filled a crucial role in the development of the university in the expansion of physical facilities and in strengthening academics with the Department of Learning Enhancement and its Academic Advance Program. He had worked effectively with Bill Teague, and he was ready to continue his work under the direction of the new president and chief executive officer, Dr. Money, but that was not to be. He left a legacy of achievement on this campus just as he had done at Lubbock Christian University before coming to Abilene. His widow, Ruth, and two of their four daughters live in Abilene.

Money set about the task of appointing an administrative team. First, he had the post to fill that he had vacated in moving up to the presidency. He named Dwain M. Hart as the new vice president for academic affairs. Dr. Hart had been a member of the faculty since 1955. He held bachelor's, master's, and doctoral degrees from Baylor University. For twenty years, he chaired the Department of Health, Physical Education, and Recreation now known as the Department of Exercise Science and Health. He played a major role in planning Moody Coliseum and Gibson Health and Physical Education Center during the 1960s. He was known for his high academic standards and his congenial disposition. He enjoyed the confidence of the faculty and the respect of students. Hart had served as dean of the College of Professional Studies, 1982-91. He was soft-spoken but firm and unflappable in dealing with problems.

An interesting experience Hart encountered with the late H. R. Gibson in connection with the opening of the great coliseum-physical education center illustrates Hart's composure. Franchisees and suppliers of the Gibson Discount Centers across the nation had donated several hundreds of thousands of dollars for the construction of the facility named for Herbert R. and Belva Gibson. Sam Walton credited the Gibson stores as being among models he used in building his Wal-Mart stores. When the H. R. and Belva Gibson complex was finished in February 1968, the Gibsons were given a private tour before the public open house. Dr. Hart conducted the tour. After showing them the three basketball courts, the handball courts, the NCAA-size swimming pool, the weight rooms, classrooms, and the large dressing room for men, Hart led them through the spacious dressing area for women, with its array of hair dryers and twenty-one dressing tables, complete with lights and mirrors. Gibson quickly spotted something wrong. "What," he asked, with typical Gibsonian volume, "are Sears, Roebuck hair dryers doing in a Gibson building?" Hart, unflappable as usual, replied calmly, "They gave us the best bid, Mr. Gibson." This silenced the noted entrepreneur for a short time. Then, in a quieter voice, he said, "That will never happen again." One who knew Mr. Gibson can well imagine the discussion he had later with local Gibson management. With Hart in charge, the academic division was in good hands.

The second appointment made Dr. Gary McCaleb vice president of the university. During the Teague administration, he had served as vice president and dean of campus life. This new assignment gave McCaleb an opportunity for reinvolvement in public relations. One of his uses of this situation was in the field of city government. He was already in his second term on the Abilene City Council, and one year before the expiration of his second term, he was elected mayor of the city. He was reelected in 1993, and again in 1996. Glenn Dromgoole, former editor of the *Abilene Reporter-News*, recently referred to him as "mayor for life." In McCaleb's travels, he has met with powerful people and humble people in various parts of the world and has left an acquaintance with Abilene and ACU wherever he has gone. In addition to his outstanding public relations work, he teaches approximately 200 students per year in large classes in business management and founded the

Center for the Advancement of Community, which coordinates an interdisciplinary minor in community studies.

Third, Dr. Charles Trevathan was appointed vice president for student services. He held the position for six years before resigning in order to teach classes in sociology and to continue his work in the legal office. During his tenure, Trevathan presided over daily chapel in an effective manner, redirected some of the social clubs into more service-oriented channels, organized a campus activities group dedicated to offering more entertainment on campus, and provided administrative support for the university counseling and health services. He also oversaw the coordinator of spiritual life, the campus security force, the student housing service, and the two deans of students. With Trevathan's transfer, the division of campus life was integrated with the division of academic affairs and reports to the provost of the university.

Fourth, Jack Rich was appointed vice president for finance and administration, succeeding L. D. "Bill" Hilton, who had served as chief financial officer since 1969 and had worked in the business office since 1950 under Lawrence L. Smith. Mrs. Jerry Fulks, who worked in finance with Hilton all of those years, described him as "an absolutely phenomenal business manager, a financial genius," so Money faced no easy task in replacing Hilton.

In naming Jack Rich vice president for finance and administration, and later executive vice president, President Money picked a man with the credentials and experience equal to the task. Not the least characteristic of Jack Rich is his imposing size, six feet five inches. He is a 1976 summa cum laude graduate with a bachelor of business administration degree in accounting. He comes from an ACU family. His mother and father and his sister and two brothers are all alumni. His wife, Karen, attended ACU for two years and completed her bachelor's degree at the University of North Texas in 1978. After Rich graduated, he worked for a year and a half as an auditor with Arthur Andersen & Company in the Dallas office. In 1978 he became a Certified Public Accountant and began work as a senior vice president of InterFirst Bank of San Antonio, where his responsibilities included management of the loan review, loan recovery, credit administration, marketing, and investment departments. He was also responsible for joint venture negotiations on and building of InterFirst Plaza. Afterwards, he was president and chief operating officer of the Morton Companies of San Antonio and responsible for management of assets in excess of $100 million. He had the oversight of undeveloped land, residential construction, commercial properties, nursing homes, ranches, and banking interests. He is ably assisted by a competent staff, including three other CPA's. Abilene Christian University, with assets totalling $166 million, is a sizable operation and is being run according to sound business principles.

While selecting members of his administrative team, Money made an appointment that showed the direction he was taking in his work. He appointed William E. Young director of church relations. Young had spent thirty-three years preaching for churches in California, Colorado, and Texas. He knew and loved the brotherhood of Churches of Christ. He had been a member of the ACU Board of Trustees for six years when Bill Teague persuaded him to give up his board membership and join the ACU staff as assistant vice president and director of development in 1990. Money wanted him to work full time among the churches. In Young's new role, he provides administrative and public relations support for the College of Biblical Studies and is responsible for the annual Bible Lectureship and the annual Preachers' Fellowship Day. He schedules preaching appointments for ACU speakers through a revived Christian Education Sunday program.

Another individual who came in with Money on June 1, 1991, is Joe L. Cope, who was named executive assistant to the president. He is a graduate of Lubbock Christian University and the Texas Tech University School of Law. He was invaluable in keeping things moving with efficiency and timeliness. In early 1998, he was named executive director of the ACU Foundation, and James C. Holmans, a retired U.S. Air Force colonel, was named executive assistant to the president.

With all of the business of organizing a staff, dealing with faculty, students, trustees, alumni, and the community at large, and planning the largest fund-raising campaign in the history of the institution, President Money had to take time out for an inauguration. Apparently, he gave some thought to skipping it. But he bowed to the wishes of the faculty and students. As he said, "I have learned the significance of marker events, whether in the life of an individual or an institution." So the inauguration was set for Sunday afternoon, February 23, 1992, opening day of the annual Bible Lectureship.

After the inaugural academic processional, special music, and greetings from representatives of various groups, the new president gave an unusual but effective fifteen-minute address to the large crowd in Moody Coliseum. Dr. Lamar Reinsch, professor of business administration, gave his students the assignment of writing what they thought the new president ought to say. The composite recommendation was that the speech should have three main points: first, "Abilene"; second, "Christian"; and third, "university." The president began by thanking the students for outlining his speech. He said much in fifteen minutes.

Under the first point he declared, "From the time A. B. Barret stepped off the train in Abilene to this good day, the relationship of ACU with the people of Abilene has been a good one." He continued by praising Abilene as a place to serve, to lead, to follow, to work for the common good, to hold up solid values.

Under the heading of "Christian," he promised, "ACU will remain loyal to the biblical and historical principles that have distinguished our religious heritage." He expressed the hope that observers would judge the institution "by the worthiness of our goals and our commitment to them" and not by the struggles and frustrations experienced while pursuing those goals. He made the correct assertion that "ACU loses when people judge the whole of our enterprise by the perceived failings and shortcomings of any of its parts. ACU wins when people see the overwhelming greater good of our enterprise, tolerate our shortcomings, and help us grow." He added, "As a Christian university, ACU is not for sale. Not to the right or to the left. Not to sectarian spirits who set themselves up as standards of orthodoxy or to any spirits who would have us sell our spiritual birthright. We will not sell out to any special interest group."

Under the "university" heading, he declared, "ACU is a university, not a church. We know the difference. We grant degrees, we educate people.... We know the difference between education and indoctrination." He concluded his attention-getting address with these words: "We are people with a purpose. And we must not fail. To that end may God help us. God bless you, and God bless Abilene Christian University."

The inauguration was popular, and it was good the president decided against omitting it. To show his devotion to economy of operation, however, by scheduling it Sunday afternoon, he avoided the necessity of providing lunch for a thousand or so delegates and guests who would have attended a post-inaugural luncheon as is customary when the exercises are set for 10 o'clock Saturday morning.

Bestowing the Presidential Medallion on President Money was the last official act of board chairman Lynn Packer. He had presided over the board skillfully and effectively since August of 1984. Don Crisp, president of the Rosewood Corporation in Dallas, succeeded him. Crisp graduated from ACU as an accounting major in 1964. He is a Certified Public Accountant and was audit manager for Arthur Andersen and Company in Dallas from 1964 to 1972. Crisp was senior vice president and treasurer for the Dallas Federal Savings and Loan Association from 1972 to 1976 and has been with Rosewood since that time. Crisp as board chairman and Money as president of the university make a good team. They were both members of the graduating class of 1964. Don and Carol Crisp have a daughter, Lisa, who is married to Clifford Rhoden, and two sons, Brian and Brad. Brad married Money's daughter, Jennifer. Crisp and Money are good friends; each is a dedicated Christian; each is a good businessman. New board members named during Crisp's tenure have included a second African-American, Hubert Pickett Jr., of Abilene and the first Hispanic, Steve Carrizal of Round Rock, who served in 1993-98.

A major accomplishment of the Money administration was the revision of the basic legal document of Abilene Christian University, the Articles of Incorporation, otherwise known as the Charter. Revision had been discussed for years and after much consideration was accomplished in 1997. In fact the effective date of the Restated Articles of Incorporation, as issued by the office of the Secretary of State of Texas, was May 8, 1997.

The original charter was hurriedly adopted during the first meeting of the five-man Board of Trustees of Childers Classical Institute, November 3, 1906. The minutes of that first board meeting state that the trustees were adopting the charter that had been prepared for Gunter Bible College, a small school founded near Sherman, Texas in 1903. The Childers trustees changed two features of the Gunter charter. One was that whereas Gunter had eleven trustees, Childers had only five. And whereas Article XII of the Gunter charter provided that it could never be amended in any way except to extend the term of the corporation, the Childers Trustees provided that the charter could be amended in any way except as to the qualifications of board members as contained in Article VI. This article declared that a trustee must be (a) a member of the Church of Christ, (b) in good standing with a local congregation, and (c) a citizen of the state of Texas. Article XII further declared that all donations to the institution "shall be given and shall be considered in law to have been given on this condition." The Gunter charter was written by William B. Gano and Jesse P. Sewell, as described in chapter one.

The 1906 charter served well through the years. Amendments primarily dealt with the number of board members and how many board members would constitute a quorum for doing business. An amendment in 1920 changed the name to Abilene Christian College. An amendment in 1976 changed it to Abilene Christian University. Several problems existed, however. For example, the number of trustees at any given time should not be a charter matter at all. Whether there were five or nineteen or thirty-five or forty-five or sixty should be a matter for the board to determine from time to time and to be dealt with in the by-laws.

The major problem, however, and a serious one, was the requirement of Article VI that every trustee "shall be a citizen of the state of Texas." The same article contained the requirement that every member "shall be a member of the Church of Christ ... in good standing." Nobody on the board or in the administration of the university wanted to change that because it was of the very essence of the institution. But nobody knew why the matter of Texas residency had anything to do with building and maintaining a Christian institution of higher education. So far as a search of the archives of the institution showed, Jesse P. Sewell never explained why he and William B. Gano had included it in the Gunter charter. It was apparently not a subject of discussion among the original five trustees of Childers Classical Institute; they simply adopted the Gunter charter. For a small school that, by the time of the first board meeting had already registered a pitifully small student body – twenty-five on the first day – who would have thought that the school would ever involve a constituency larger than Texas? So for ninety-one years, the charter required Texas residency and Article XII still stated, "This Charter shall never be changed or amended as to qualifications of the Board of Trustees."

In 1995, board chairman Don Crisp appointed an ad hoc committee of lawyers who were members of the board to study the problem and come up with recommendations. Crisp, a non-lawyer, would serve as chairman. Senior member of the group was the retired Chief Justice of the Supreme Court of Texas, Jack Pope, who had been a member of the ACU Board since 1950. Other committee members were Jane Varner Beard of Abilene, Michael M. "Mike" Boone of Dallas, Jennifer Haltom Doan of Texarkana, and Warlick Thomas of Amarillo. Gary Thornton of Austin, though not officially a member of the committee, worked with the group.

The result of the committee's work was that a petition to Amend Its Articles of Incorporation was filed with the 104th District Court in Taylor County, Texas, June 13, 1996. There was no defendant in the case; in other words, nobody opposed the changes the university desired to bring about. The petition pointed out that the purpose of the university, as defined in Article II of the original charter, was "the establishment and maintenance of a college for the advancement of education in which the arts, sciences, languages, and Holy Scriptures shall always be taught, together with such other courses of instruction as shall be deemed advisable by the Board of Directors." Having stated that, the petition declared the existing Article VI of the charter, limiting board membership to residents of Texas, "materially and substantially retards the fulfillment of that purpose."

The petition then listed some differences in the 1906 situation and that of ninety-one years later. Whereas, in 1906, the trustees had the responsibility of operating a small educational institution "with goals and needs that were focused upon Abilene and West Texas," the 1997 enrollment at Abilene Christian University included students from every state in the United States and from approximately sixty foreign countries. Almost twenty-five percent of the 4,400 students "are from outside Texas." Further, it was pointed out that of the 43,927 living alumni of the institution, more than thirty-two percent lived outside Texas. During the previous five fiscal years, twenty-eight percent of the individual donors to the university were living outside Texas. Clearly, the petition stated, ACU is more than a regional university and needs to be able to add to its governing board able people from a far wider area than Texas.

The petition involved not only abolishing the requirement of Texas residency for board members, but a number of other improvements that would strengthen the charter. The court ruled favorably on the overall Restatement of the Articles of Incorporation, so that since May 8, 1997, Abilene Christian University operates under the articles printed in Appendix A of *No Ordinary University*.

In addition to making plans to raise money, the Money administration was studying ways to economize; this was not an uncommon step for universities to take at the time. Problems in the oil industry and other segments of the economy were among the causes. Fall enrollment had dropped from 4,627 in 1983 to 3,946 by 1991, the year Money became president. In the fall of 1993, the five colleges created in 1986 were reduced to three, and the eight vice presidents were reduced to five. The colleges of Liberal and Fine Arts, Professional Studies, and Natural and Applied Sciences were combined into one college, which would be known as the College of Arts and Sciences; the other two, Biblical Studies and Business Administration, were retained. These changes and other reorganization resulted in a reduction of about seventy-five employees, which meant considerable operational savings. Virtually all of these reductions came from either normal or voluntary retirements or resignations, in order to minimize hardships in the process.

Two vice presidents – Bob Hunter and C. G. Gray – retired from the administration in 1993, but both were given special assignments. Hunter built upon his highly effective work in the state capital. Jack Rich explained Gray's assignment after he left the vice presidency for academics:

> Dr. C. G. Gray helped put in motion a technology plan that has placed ACU in the forefront of information technology. The hardware and software we have on campus will unlock tremendous potential in administrative work, in academic pursuits, and in communications. Dr. Gray is now overseeing the completion of our campus-wide fiber optic network and the expansion of our library resources through technology.

Fall enrollment has rebounded from the 3,946 of 1991 to 4,542 in 1997, clear evidence that the Money administration's economies, increase in scholarships, overhaul of student recruiting strategies, and fund-raising successes are giving the 1990s one of the brightest decades in the history of the university.

One of the most interesting accomplishments of the Money administration has been the dazzling and spectacular transformation of the cafeteria into the "World-Famous Bean," as its management now modestly calls it. President Teague began the practice of utilizing outside contractors for the food service, housekeeping, and the copy service. Now with the Money administration, and especially at the initiative of Executive Vice President Jack Rich, working with the ARAMARK Company's Ed Jenkins, the concept has been developed so that ACU is used by the company as a showplace. People from other universities now visit ACU to see how it is done.

Entering the World-Famous Bean, the diner notices an open area in front of the Bean proper, where the hungry customer can have a Pizza Hut pan pizza, topped off by a cone or a cup of TCBY, "The Country's Best Yogurt." The ACU TCBY dishes out some 3,000 gallons of yogurt per week.

Across the way is a Chick-Fil-A station, which serves its famed sandwiches or a plate of sliced breast of chicken on a bed of green salad. Students wanting the full meal find a sumptuous salad bar and a food court arrangement, with different areas offering Mexican food; Chinese food, "Wok 'n' Roll"; Healthy food, grilled chicken or fish plus veggies and pasta; and various other types of delicacies, including cheeseburgers and fries and regular cafeteria food. Several types of breads are grouped in one corner with large jars of peanut butter and jellies. A diner can have as much as he or she wishes from any one station, or can sample the various stations. For dessert, the diner can have hand-dipped ice cream and/or fresh pastries. From the heartiest to the finickiest appetites, the "World-Famous Bean" finds a way to satisfy its student customers.

Fund raising in the Money era was launched at an Abilene dinner August 27, 1993, a campaign called "Advancing the Changeless" for $29.4 million. In making the announcement, President Money said, "The Advancing the Changeless campaign is a milestone for Abilene Christian University, not just because of the size of the campaign, but because of what it will enable us to do for our students." The Mabee Foundation again came in with a $1.5 million challenge. Robert J. Hall of Jasper, Robert R. "Bob" Onstead of Houston, and H. Lynn Packer of Dallas were national co-chairmen of the campaign.

The largest component of this campaign was $10 million for endowment, including scholarships and operations. A figure of $4 million was included for operational needs. The sum of $3,685,000 was set aside for a 21,000-square-foot addition on the east side of the Margaret and Herman Brown Library, to be known as the C. L. Kay Wing. It would provide additional space for library holdings and the Walter H. Adams Center for Teaching Excellence. More than half a million dollars was set aside for library acquisitions, and a nice sum for science equipment was included. The balance of the money would be used for renovation projects on the campus, including the twenty-five-year-old and much used Moody Coliseum and the sixty-five-year old Zona Luce Building. Other projects involved funds for renovating residence halls to make them more accommodating to students, completion of Crutcher Scott Field for baseball, additional equipment for the Lee Powell Fitness Center, new computers for the College of Business Administration, improvements on the 129-acre farm Kenneth Musgrave of Abilene gave for the use of the Department of Agriculture, and completion of the campus fiber optic network. The latter would enable students and teachers to communicate from their offices or dormitory rooms with one another and with other individuals around the world, using computer data, video, and voice messages. Truly, to be a distinguished university today required getting ready for the twenty-first century.

In February 1996, announcement was made that more than $30 million dollars had been contributed to put the campaign over the top, and all of these projects have been completed. The resounding success of the "Advancing the Changeless" campaign had some clearcut lessons. Never in the history of Abilene Christian University had there been such a demonstration that alumni, trustees, parents, and other friends and supporters of ACU were willing and able to provide resources needed by the university when a cogent showing of the need was presented. It was also clear that people are willing to contribute to endowment funds and not just to buildings. Some $12 million dollars was given for endowment.

Upon Money's recommendation, the Board of Trustees authorized the establishment of the ACU Foundation "to encourage, solicit, promote, and receive estate, deferred, and current gifts for the continuing development and endowment" of the university. Dr. Milton Fletcher, with years of experience in college administration and estate planning, was its first executive director, assisted by Bill Spann, also an experienced estate planner. Soon, Money invited Dan Garrett, a certified financial planner, who had been for some years on the staff of Baylor Medical Center in Dallas, to rejoin the ACU force as vice chancellor. The development force was greatly augmented with the appointment of Dr. John Tyson Jr. as vice president for development. Tyson is dedicated to his work. He is an effective organizer and executive.

Dr. Dwain Hart, after forty-one years on the faculty, including service during the last five years of that time as chief academic officer of the university, announced in 1996 that he was ready to assume emeritus status. From 1991 until the spring of 1995, he did double duty as vice president for academic affairs and dean of the College of Arts and Sciences. During those years, he had an office in the Administration Building and an office in the Don H. Morris Center. Effective June 1, 1995, Dr. Colleen Durrington was named dean of the College of Arts and Sciences, and Hart became the second provost in the history of the institution. The difference between a vice president for academic affairs and a provost, as Hart explained it to an *Optimist* reporter in August 1995, is that as provost he had oversight of all academically related matters, such as the library, registrar's office, Learning Enhancement Center, testing and university assessment, and career planning and counseling. Hart was efficient, as always, in running the provost's office, but after a year in the job, and having reached retirement age, he heard the call of the golf course, which he had not had time to visit during all his busy years at ACU, and announced his retirement.

President Money appointed a faculty search committee, chaired by English professor Darryl Tippens, to launch an all-out quest for the best possible candidate for the position. After extensive investigation and many interviews, the committee recommended Dr. Dwayne VanRheenen. The president and board approved, and VanRheenen accepted the offer. A 1966 speech and biblical studies graduate of Harding University, he earned a master of arts and a doctorate in communication from the University of Missouri at Columbia. He taught at the University of Maine from 1970 to 1985 and chaired the Department of Speech Communication, coordinating both graduate studies and basic courses. He left Maine in 1985 for the Pepperdine University faculty. At the time of the ACU appointment, he was dean of the faculty of Seaver College of Letters, Arts, and Sciences at Pepperdine. Dwayne and Joan Van Rheenen are strong additions to the campus. The name is not new here. Gailyn Van Rheenen, Dwayne's brother, has been a member of the missions faculty in the College of Biblical Studies since 1986.

Since Provost VanRheenen joined the university, one more responsibility has been added to his portfolio. The office of vice president for student services has been discontinued, and the student life program is now a part of the provost's responsibilities, harking back to the days when Dr. Walter Adams was dean of the college, of the faculty, and of the students. To be sure, the student body was about one-tenth the size it now is, but on the other hand, the provost has quite a sizable staff helping him, whereas Dean Adams had himself and a secretary. Good reasoning stands behind the integration of student life and academic affairs; the one has a great deal to do with the other. Among the earliest of VanRheenen's initiatives has been the activation of the first ever competitive faculty renewal leave program in the spring of 1998, which is designed to support faculty members in significant research and creative scholarly activities.

President Money has instituted the practice of meeting with his cabinet on a weekly basis. Cabinet members are Provost Van Rheenen, Executive Vice President Rich, Vice President for Development Tyson, and the president's executive assistant, now Jim C. Holmans since Joe Cope has become the administrator for the ACU Foundation. Once a month, Money combines the cabinet with three other senior executives and calls it the Administrative Council. The additional administrators are Vice President of the University McCaleb, Vice President and General Counsel Welborn, and Dan Garrett, who is vice chancellor of the university and president of the ACU Foundation. All in all, the Money administration is an efficient organization geared to accomplishment.

When the campaign for $100 million – the "To Lead and to Serve" campaign – was announced in February 1998 to be concluded by the end of the calendar year 2001, the trustees, administration, and staff were confidently ready to present the case for continuing to build a distinguished Christian university, while standing for eternal truth in the twenty-first century.

When Money's presidency began, he was asked by an interviewer about new buildings during the next decade. He said remodeling would be emphasized, rather than construction, but as things have turned out, a good deal of both has happened.

Moody Coliseum was renovated extensively during the 1992-93 school year. After a quarter of a century of hard daily use, the time had come for refurbishment. Studies showed that an estimated 25 million head count had used or visited the coliseum within the previous twenty-five years of heavy usage. The coliseum is used for basketball and volleyball practice and games; daily chapel; commencements of ACU, Abilene High School, and Cooper High School; Sing Song and other entertainment events; and Bible Lectureships, inaugurations, and other large gatherings. Besides, considerable traffic of senior citizen daily hikers, athletes, and students use the concourse for exercise. About $1 million dollars was required to refurbish the 4,000 seats, modernize the lighting and the sound system, paint the interior and exterior of the structure, and resurface the floor. The Tartan floor was replaced with a top-grade maple floor, comparable to that used by most National Basketball Association teams. The coliseum was readied for another twenty-five years.

The Zona Luce Building renovation was popular with older alumni, former students of the Campus School, and the Department of Agriculture and Environment. Certainly one of the most attractive of the 1929 buildings, Zona Luce was named for the distinguished lady who, with her husband, J. N. Luce, deeded to the college 620 acres of ranch land in 1928, which represented one of the first major gifts to the school. For many years, the Zona Luce Building was home to the Campus School, as the high school and elementary school came to be called. When Abilene Christian Schools moved to a new campus on Judge Ely Boulevard north of the university campus, the building was turned over to the Department of Agriculture and Environment, which had suffered through years in the Ag Annex, which had been an Army barracks, and various shared spaces. A drive was soon organized by friends of the department to refurbish and rejuvenate the seventy-year-old building, which is on the National Register of Historic Places and retains its historic outside appearance. The renovation process began in

August 1996. The Zona Luce Building exterior was sandblasted, and the interior was gutted and renovated. New wet and dry laboratories were installed; wheelchair access was improved; a new front porch area complemented the classic look; and computer capabilities were installed. Floodlights illuminating the building at night make a drive down Campus Court worthwhile.

A rededication ceremony and open house were conducted August 23, 1997. Four longtime faculty members were honored: Dr. F. M. "Doc" Churchill, Dr. Keith Justice, the late Dewey Davis, and the late T. W. Colby. Important documents, photographs, and memorabilia of these four early leaders of the department were placed on permanent display in cases in the building. More than 135 donors helped make the renovation possible. Leaders in the drive were Jane Varner Beard and her family, in honor of her parents, Sterling and Paula Varner; Sam and Seanne Sparks; Nina Christian; and an anonymous donor. Classrooms on the east side of the building on the first floor and second floor can be used for general purposes. The departments of history, psychology, and English share the rooms with agriculture. The west side of the building, first and second floors, has the specialized laboratories restricted to agricultural and environmental projects.

Dormitory renovation is an ongoing process; the goal has been to refurbish thoroughly one per year. Some dormitory projects have been major, as, for example, the conversion of Edwards from a typical residence for men, that is, a bedroom for two men with community baths down the hall, to a suite concept, with a bedroom, a study room, and a private bath for two men to the suite. This approach reduced the capacity of the dormitory from 312 men to 200, but it resulted in full occupancy and a more satisfactory living situation, which is the ultimate goal for all student residence halls. Another major reconfiguration took place in A. B. Morris Dormitory, converting it from a regular residence hall for 160 men into a thirty-nine-unit apartment complex for non-traditional students – older students, married couples, or those with a physical handicap, such as a blind student who needs a guide dog. This conversion was a success. McDonald, one of the original 1929 dormitories, has been converted to a single occupancy facility. A room with two small closets and a lavatory was too small for two students in today's world, but for one-student-to-the-room, it has been quite popular.

One of the most popular contributions to the dormitory scene was the 1995 installation of a computer lab in each dormitory, an immeasurable benefit to the students. In 1998, refurbishment is somewhat behind schedule, and one of the reasons has been the full occupancy of the dormitories – even during the summer months with a heavy slate of popular camps – a good problem for housing director Scott Galloway.

First of the new construction in the Money era was the completion of the unfinished basement of the west wing of the library in the fall of 1991. Nearly $1 million was used to prepare 12,500 square feet of space for the Learning Enhancement Center. When the original center was opened in 1984, it occupied a second floor room in the west wing of the Brown Library. By 1989, it had three rooms, and the name had been changed from Learning Assistance to Learning Enhance-ment. Usage through the years has been amazing. Each student who visits logs in at the desk. The record indicates that from 1984 through the summer of 1997, more than 21,000 students had signed the logbook. Of course, there were multiple visits by most users, but they are not counted in this figure. The record indicates that the average length of stay per visit is about one and one-half hours. Vice Chancellor Casey Kay and English Professor Aubrey Green worked together on the project. Sadly, Kay, who raised the money for the center, died in June 1991 before it was finished, and Green, who planned and operated the center, died in April 1992 after it was finished. Their work lives after them.

The east wing of the Brown Library was named the C. L. Kay Wing and includes the Walter Adams Center for Teaching Excellence. The Mabee Foundation issued a challenge grant of $1.5 million to get the drive for nearly $30 million underway. The Mabee grant was earmarked primarily for the library addition. To receive the grant, ACU agreed to raise $10.5 million in capital funds by April 14, 1994 – a year away – which was accomplished. In expressing appreciation to the Mabees for the challenge, Dr. Money also recognized thousands of friends who made the success possible. The groundbreaking ceremony was conducted August 29, 1994, and the building was officially opened February 17, 1996.

Included in the C. L. Kay Wing are two floors of space for book stacks and study rooms and one floor for the Adams Center for Teaching Excellence, designed to benefit students, faculty, and staff. The Adams Center has a digital media production center, a training center to help professors enhance their teaching, and an interactive classroom in which a professor from a distant university can speak by closed circuit television to a class, with two-way discussion between professor and students. The first class offered to ACU students via the interactive classroom was a course in engineering economics originating from Texas A&M University in the spring of 1996. Students in the classroom at ACU saw the professor teaching his course at College Station on monitors in the classroom. They asked questions via microphones suspended from the ceiling while they directed their attention to a video camera situated above the monitor with the professor's image on it. At A&M, the professor saw and heard the student asking the question and responded. In the same way, a class being taught at ACU can be picked up wherever the technology is in place. Dr. Dwain Hart predicts that the facility will assist ACU "in becoming a technology leader in the Southwest and to continuing our quest for academic excellence."

University Park, with 200 apartments with a capacity of up to 478 students, was officially opened for occupancy August 21, 1994 at the northeast corner of the campus south of Crutcher Scott Field. The apartments are a new concept among private Texas universities for student housing. The university owned the land – a strip just west of newly routed Judge Ely Boulevard. Century Development of Houston leased the land from the university, financed the project, and built the apartments. When completed, the project was deeded to the University; in return, the company received a long-term lease to operate and maintain the complex. At the expiration of the forty-year lease, the university can renegotiate the lease with Century, deal with some other company, or take over the operation. The company sets operational rules and procedures except that ACU's behavioral rules, such as the no-alcohol-or-drugs policy, must be observed. Juniors, seniors, and graduate students, singles or married, are eligible to live in the apartments, which are arranged as efficiency, two-bedroom, and four-bedroom units. When apartments are available, sophomores with a suitable grade point may be admitted. University Park offers the advantage of apartment living, which many students prefer, without the disadvantages of the average apartment complex. As the first manager expressed, "In other apartment complexes, you never know who will be living next door. At University Park, you know everyone you are living next to is an ACU student." "U.P.," as the students call it, has proved to be immensely popular.

The Powell Fitness Center, named in honor of distinguished alumnus and national board member Lee Powell of Paducah, Kentucky, was opened and officially dedicated August 27, 1993, with about $100,000 worth of fitness equipment, including a full free-weight area, mainly used by athletes, with power and Olympic platforms, bench presses, inclines, a dumbbell area, other free-weight machines, stair-steppers, bicycles, cardiovascular areas, and Nautilus machines. The project was made possible by a gift from Lee and Dorris Powell, who flew into Abilene for the dedication. He was speaker for the occasion; though frail, he still had the enthusiasm characteristic of him throughout life. He died the next year, April 6, 1994. Cliff Felkins, class of 1990, ACU strength coach and former NCAA Division I discus champion, manages the center. He says that for its size, the Powell Fitness Center cannot be excelled. It has the same quality of equipment the largest universities have and is a great contribution to the strength and fitness program of ACU athletes and others who use it.

The Margaret L. and William J. Teague Special Events Center is nearing completion in mid-1998. The Teague Center is a 43,500-square-foot, "one acre," $3.5 million facility, which will include a large multipurpose room seating up to 1,500 people for luncheons and dinners; special events during Homecoming, Lectureship, and Commencement; regional seminars and testing sessions; and a lecture hall for major speakers. There are three indoor tennis courts; conference and meeting rooms; offices for the director of athletics and coaching staff; offices and work areas for the athletic training staff; locker rooms for Wildcat athletic teams; a catering kitchen; and storage areas. ACU is grateful for the generous support and leadership of Tom Teague in making this much-needed facility available; in appreciation, the trustees voted to name it in honor of his parents.

The Money-led administrators and Crisp-led trustees have brought about a transformation in investment policy. Before 1993, university investments were heavily weighted toward fixed income assets. The policy was to use all current endowment income as the money was earned. Beginning in 1993, significant changes were made to ensure the long-term viability and growth of the endowment. One of the key changes was to adopt a five percent spending rule. This rule allows a look at the total return of the investment portfolio. Only five percent of the total return – cash yield as well as capital appreciation – can be used within a given year. Any earnings above five percent are added back to the endowment. The effect of this change is twofold: first, because the investments committee of the Board of Trustees looks at total return, more funds can be invested in a wider variety of assets, and, second, the new policy builds the endowment and makes it more likely that the endowment will grow at a rate that will at least keep up with the rate of inflation. The effects of these changes have been dramatic; grew the endowment from $55 million in 1994 to in excess of $73 million in 1997. Kevin Watson, director of business services and investments, is the key internal resource in the investment area. Another change in investment management policy was the hiring of an investment adviser and professional investment managers. The investment adviser helps with the selection of investment managers and assists in establishing allocation of assets.

The strong financial accounting team at ACU in the 1990s includes four CPA's, including their leader, Executive Vice President Jack Rich. Phil Schubert, CPA, is director of financial operations with overall responsibility for financial accounting, accounts payable, student financial services, and billing and collections. Schubert has two years of public accounting experience and has been at ACU since 1993. Dale Crawford, CPA, is controller and has nine years in public accounting and ten years in private industry experience. He started at ACU in August 1993. Ken Rideout, CPA, director of trust and endowment accounting, is responsible for the management of endowment accounts – and of trust accounts that do not become endowment until the trusts mature – totalling more than $100 million. He has six years of public accounting experience and four years in private industry. He started work at ACU in 1995.

Upon Money's recommendation, the board authorized the establishment of the ACU Foundation. An ACC Foundation had been chartered in the days of B Sherrod and F. O. Masten, in the 1940s, but it had become dormant. The ACU Foundation received a new charter in 1993 and an internal revenue classification as a charitable entity, and was established "to encourage, solicit, promote, and receive estate, deferred, and current gifts for the continuing development and endowment" of the university. Dr. Milton Fletcher, retired president of Michigan Christian College, which is now Rochester College, became the first executive director of the new foundation. With his years of experience as an administrator and estate planner, he did a successful work as head of the foundation. At the end of the spring semester of 1998, he relinquished his position as executive director and will work with the foundation on a half-time basis. Bill Spann, also an experienced estate planner, has worked with Fletcher since the foundation was chartered. Joe Cope has become the foundation's executive director.

Dan T. Garrett, a certified financial planner who was associated for ten years with Baylor Medical Center in Dallas before organizing his own company in 1994, rejoined the work at ACU as vice chancellor in the Money administration in 1995. He was named president of the ACU Foundation, effective June 1, 1998. He will continue also as vice chancellor of the university.

The development force was greatly augmented by the 1994 appointment of Dr. John Tyson as vice president for development. Tyson is dedicated to his work and is an effective organizer, executive, and spokesman for the university.

During Dr. Dwain Hart's idea-rich tenure as chief academic officer of the university, he came up with the idea of an integrated international program, which became known as World Class. Through the years, various faculty members had led groups of students on study tours to various parts of the world, with provisions for college credits to be earned. Hart believed that the time had come to organize the program as an ongoing part of the university's offerings. He thought an increasing number of students would like the opportunity of studying abroad during a part of their college years.

With the concurrence of President Money, Hart convened a faculty group to explore the matter. He found wholehearted concurrence, and in October 1993, planning began in earnest. Henry Speck III was selected as the logical person to head the program. Speck holds the doctorate from Oxford University and spent thirteen years teaching in Europe and the Middle East before coming to Abilene in 1980. He can handle the required linguistics. He knows European ways of thinking and has a good understanding of the Arab world and Islam. Speck agreed to direct the program along with teaching a reduced load in the History Department. The program has been so successful that he is now full time with World Class.

The program was based in Oxford, and classes began in the summer of 1994. Courses have been taught for groups of students – in addition to the yearly schedule at Oxford – in Prague and Central Europe, Germany, Switzerland, Belgium, Spain, Greece, Japan, Mexico, Costa Rica, Nicaragua, Kenya, and the Holy Lands. Forty faculty members and hundreds of students have participated.

The catalog description of the program states: "Not only have the students learned in the basic courses in the culture, history, literature, and languages of the host countries, but they have also studied journalism, management, government, and religion." World Class is thoroughly supportive of the stated mission of Abilene Christian University: "… to educate its students for Christian service and leadership throughout the world."

Another of the Money-Hart-Rich initiatives has been the LINK team, which was started to coordinate the proliferation of academic computer technology. The work of this group has been a landmark development in the history of the university. Its comprehensive policy planning and broad allocational use of the new technology and academic enhancement fee has changed the university from an average user of digital technology to one of the finest in the country. It certainly is one of the major achievements of the Money administration.

Only four of the ten presidents of the university have had occasion to appoint an athletic director. At ACU, athletic directors tend to stay in place longer than presidents do. When Batsell Baxter became president in 1924, he went hunting for the best man he could find to take charge of the athletic program, and he found Asbury Bratten "Bugs" Morris. At first, A. B. Morris was not called the athletic director. He was simply "coach." He coached football, basketball, baseball, and track, although track had not yet become big. As more coaches came along, Baxter had to put someone in charge, and Coach Morris was the man. The title director of athletics was not officially conferred upon him until James F. Cox became president in 1932, when Morris was so designated in the catalog. He did the job for forty-five years and was as nearly universally admired and respected as any man could be. During the long session of 1968-69, he announced his retirement, effective June 1, 1969, meaning that President Don Morris, during the last three months of his twenty-nine-year presidency, had the responsibility of appointing a new athletic director. He chose head football coach Wally Bullington, who took over June 1, 1969. Bullington served with distinction for the next nineteen and one-half years, a grand era for Wildcat athletics.

When Bullington announced that he was stepping down, effective February 1, 1988, President Teague had the responsibility of selecting an athletic director. The man he turned to was Don Drennan. He was well qualified for the post. He was not a coach, but during his years in the business office and as assistant president and director of the budget in the Stevens administration, and as a member of the accounting faculty afterward, he was for years ACU's institutional representative to the NCAA and the Lone Star Conference and chairman of the faculty athletic committee. He was a good choice. He served effectively as athletic director for two and a half years. In July 1990, he resigned to return to the Colorado ranch that he and his wife, Rudith, and their children so much enjoy. In the fall of 1993, Drennan and his family were back in Abilene, between visits to the Colorado ranch, and he has been teaching one class each semester since for the remuneration of two dollars per year. He is also a valued member of the Board of Trustees and the Abilene City Council.

President Teague, for the second time, had the responsibility of choosing an athletic director, and this time tennis coach Cecil Eager was the man. During his nearly five years in office, Eager's accomplishments were many. He resigned, effective June 1, 1995, to go into business and is now the successful general manager of T Bar M Resort and Conference Center at New Braunfels.

President Money, only the fourth president to choose an athletic director, turned to Standard Dwight Lambert as his choice. Stan Lambert grew up two blocks from the campus. His father, Ira M. "Top" Lambert, spent his early years growing up in the neighborhood of the old campus. Stan was an outstanding baseball player during his college days. He also played basketball, but his principal interest was in baseball. A former banker, he was director of student financial services when he was tapped for the athletic directorship. Having had several years of experience as a bank president, he was good at that job and is also good at keeping up with budgets while presiding over the continued growth of Wildcat intercollegiate sports. As athletic director, Lambert oversees an impressive program, one of the outstanding NCAA Division II universities in the nation. Track coach Wes Kittley is associate athletic director. In excess of 300 students are certified each year to the NCAA and to the Lone Star Athletic Conference.

Intercollegiate sports and coaching staffs are the following:

Football: Jack Kiser, head coach; and assistant coaches Victor Randolph, Rickie Harris, and Ken Collums.

Men's basketball: Shanon Hayes, head coach; Mike Martin, assistant coach.

Women's basketball: Wayne Williams, head coach; Deonna Shake, assistant coach.

Baseball: Britt Bonneau, head coach; Brad Holcomb, assistant. Korey Keiling is part-time assistant in baseball.

Men's and women's track: Wes Kittley, head coach; Jon Murray, assistant coach; Sylvia Dyer, women hurdlers and jumpers coach; and Cliff Felkins, strength trainer, director of the Powell Fitness Center, and assistant coach for the javelin and discus. Kelly Smith, sprinters, and Chris Beene, decathlon, are part-time coaches who have other jobs on campus.

Women's volleyball: Cathe Bragg, head coach; Christine Martin, assistant coach.

Women's softball: Carol Tabor, head coach; Rita Jordan, assistant coach.

Men's and women's cross country: Jon Murray, coach.

Golf: Vince Jarrett, coach.

Men's and women's tennis: Hutton Jones, coach.

Projections call for the next intercollegiate sport to be women's soccer.

In coordinating all of these activities, Lambert has some good help. For instance, Sylvia Dyer coaches women hurdlers and jumpers, and is compliance coordinator, who sees to it that ACU is in compliance with NCAA and Lone Star conference rules. Jeff Bass is an expert trainer and rehabilitation specialist. Bass and the assistant athletic trainer, Danelle Hayes, utilize nine or ten student trainers in helping keep athletes healthy and in top form. Their work, along with that of strength coach Felkins, is credited with bringing about a dramatic decrease in all kinds of injuries during the last several years. Peggy Shields is administrative assistant, and Brent Rose is events coordinator.

When Don Drennan was athletic director, he conceived the idea of writing an athletic philosophy for the university; he produced a rough draft and passed it on to Cecil Eager, who fine-tuned it and passed it on to Lambert, who added a few touches here and there. The document as it now stands gives a good picture of what the program of athletics at Abilene Christian University is designed to be. Friends of the university can be assured that when they encourage student-athletes to attend ACU or when they decide to add to the endowment for athletics, they are supporting this five-point program:

First, the athletic department will have strong spiritual emphasis. The coaches and professional staff will be active Christians who serve as mentors. The student-athletes will have spiritual goals compatible with those of the university. Christian principles will be deliberately and systematically incorporated into all activities.

Second, the athletic department will encourage, endorse, and emphasize the academic mission of the university. Prospective student-athletes will be screened for inclination and aptitude for collegiate work. The academic progress of student-athletes will be monitored. Time allocations will be determined with academic priorities in mind. Academic excellence of student-athletes will be rewarded.

Third, the athletic department will recruit student-athletes who can compete successfully at the national level of NCAA Division II. Student athletes will be physically, mentally, and emotionally skillful. Practice regimens will produce opportunities for growth and development. Game competition will provide opportunities to measure the efforts of our staff and student-athletes. The physical well-being of each student-athlete will be coordinated through a qualified medical team that utilizes progressive training and rehabilitation programs.

Fourth, the athletic department will encourage participation by students, alumni, and friends of the university. Special programs and promotions will be developed to encourage the relationship between student-athletes and other students. The athletic department will sponsor events to promote alumni participation. Non-scholarship student-athletes will be encouraged to participate. The athletic department will cooperate with the Students' Association, Office of Student Services, the Alumni Association, the Department of Music, and the Development Office in promoting special events.

Fifth, the Athletic Department will comply with regulations of Abilene Christian University, Lone Star Conference, and NCAA. Athletic staff members and student athletes will be educated on ACU, LSC, and NCAA regulations. Compliance will be monitored by personnel both inside and outside the athletic program.

Intercollegiate baseball returned to ACU during the last year of the Teague administration, and its development has continued since. The first home game was played Saturday, February 23, 1991, with Tarleton State University as the opposition. ACU won in the tenth inning, 2 to 1. As a home for the revived program, one of the finest baseball fields in college and university circles was developed. It bears the name of Crutcher Scott, who was a prominent member of the Board of Trustees for nearly forty years and secretary of the board for twenty-eight years. During those years all diplomas of graduating seniors and graduate students were personally signed by the president and dean of the college or Graduate School and the president or chairman and secretary of the Board of Trustees. Hence, "A. C. Scott" will be found on thousands of diplomas around the world. Scott died in 1979, but his wife, Vickie, his son, Al, and daughter-in-law, Dottie, have been generous donors and diligent workers in developing the field and the program. Bill Gilbreth, of the class of 1972, was first head coach. Gilbreth was a good friend of Nolan Ryan when they were teammates pitching for the California Angels in the early 1970s. That friendship has continued through the years. Gilbreth, accompanied by Vice President Gary McCaleb, went to see Ryan at his home in Alvin, Texas, and enlisted his support. Ryan's endorsement and active assistance have been a tremendous boost to the program. Baseball, which was the first intercollegiate sport at Childers Classical Institute in its first year, 1906-07, is alive and well at ACU.

On the 20th century timeline, the histories of the automobile and Abilene Christian University began within two years of one another. A. B. Barrett founded Childers Classical Institute in 1906 near the end of the domination of transportation by the railroad. Henry Ford introduced the first mass-produced automobile two years later in 1908. Ford's application of the internal combustion engine to the car very slowly but very certainly played a major role in the outreach of the university to students beyond Texas and the fabric of student life. As late as the early 1950s, the student-to-car ratio was about 6-to-1, and unchaperoned dates in cars were taboo. One of the primary purposes of the geographical clubs at one time was to expedite lining up rides homes for holidays and summer. Eventually, the dating uses were relaxed, and boys began to borrow cars of more affluent classmates for important dates. At some point in the early 1960s students stopped coming to Abilene by railroad and bus.

The increase in the ratio of cars to students certainly changed where students wanted to live, their mobility, the system of riding home with friends, where they could work in the city, and dating. These changes were markers of the changes in family income in the nation and among the college's constituency. Today the car is a necessity; a university's student body can be profiled by looking at its student parking lots. The continuum from early parking lots to today's parking lots is interesting: from mainly used cars before the 1980s to sleek, shiny, sporty new cars, to parking lots dominated by pickups and four-wheelers. Faculty wags, of course, are fond of saying the student lots look better than the faculty lots.

The stories related to the car are endless. Gripes about parking are ubiquitous; such cycles seem obligatory. As the university grew, the building of enough parking spaces was an ever present struggle, enhanced lately by the need to meet city code for runoff water. In the early days, a car found its way on top of the Ad Building. One of the all-time most creative stunts was perpetrated when unknown students numbered every car parked on campus overnight in consecutive order with white shoe polish. Over the years the security force changed from Sheriff Burgess to a staff of uniformed campus police, who are authorized to ticket parking violators. In the 1970s Garvin Beauchamp devised a method to slow down campus speeders with the now famous Beauchamp's Bumps. Teachers frequently hear excuses for absences couched in car terms, such as "My car wouldn't start." "I had a fender bender this morning." "My car broke down in Arlington last night." "I had three flats this morning." More than one alumnus can tell about a time when a team of city and campus police came to a classroom to find a student with unpaid parking or speeding tickets. And then the car is at the core of the sad, tragic, inevitable times for a community the size of a small town when students are killed or injured en route to and from the campus in auto accidents. The need to drive defensively is rescored. Chapel memorial services at these times are emotionally searing, spiritual experiences.

Social clubs also continue to thrive in the Money era. The 1997 edition of the *Prickly Pear* edited by Mark Houston has a scholarly chart of the clubs since the earliest were chartered in 1919 and 1920. Inasmuch as these clubs have been dear to the hearts of many students through the years, *No Ordinary University* includes a tribute to the flourishing clubs and the ones that have fallen. In a sense, the clubs that no longer exist can be compared to small Christian colleges that once lived but are now only a memory. Inasmuch as once upon a time these clubs helped some students adjust to college life, enjoy a successful campus experience, and perhaps form some lifelong friendships, they deserve to be remembered.

This synopsis of the social clubs is arranged alphabetically; the words "on campus" mean that the club currently operates.

Alpha Theta Chi Omega, women; adopted by Tri Kappa Gamma, 1996; on campus.

Cadettes, women, see Kappa Chi below.

Delta Theta, women; originally Lucky 13, 1925; name changed to PALS, 1933; name changed to Delta Theta, 1944; rechartered as Xi Beta Chi, 1989; folded, 1991; rechartered Delta Theta, 1996; on campus.

Frater Sodalis, men, 1943; on campus.

Galaxy, men, 1955; on campus.

Gamma Sigma Phi, men, 1988; on campus.

GATA, women, 1920; on campus.

Hi A Club, women, 1919; name changed to Ko Jo Kai, 1920; on campus.

Kappa Chi, Cadettes, women, 1934; folded, 1973, most members joined Zeta Rho.

Kappa Delian Shri, women, 1980; folded, 1987.

Kinsmen, men, 1968; rechartered as Gamma Sigma Phi, 1988; on campus.

Knights, men, 1958; folded 1980; rechartered, 1989; on campus.

Ko Jo Kai, women, originally Hi A Club, 1919; name changed to Ko Jo Kai, 1920; on campus.

Kyodia, men, 1965; folded 1969.

Lamba Phi Omega, men, 1984; folded 1986.

L'Amitie, women, 1969; folded 1974.

Lucky 13, women, 1925; name changed to PALS, 1933; changed to Delta Theta, 1944; rechartered as Xi Beta Chi, 1989; folded, 1991; rechartered Delta Theta, 1996; on campus.

Maitta, men, 1969; folded 1971.

PALS, women, originally Lucky 13, 1925; renamed PALS, 1933; changed to Delta Theta, 1944; rechartered Xi Beta Chi, 1969; folded, 1991; rechartered Delta Theta, 1996; on campus.

Pandora, women, 1958; changed name to Phi Alpha Sigma, 1966; folded 1968.

Phi Alpha Sigma, women; originally Pandora; renamed Phi Alpha Sigma, 1966; folded 1968.

Phi Delta Psi, men, originally Phi Omega Chi, 1938; rechartered Phi Delta Psi, 1951; kicked off campus, 1973, rechartered 1982; folded 1986.

Phi Omega Chi, men, 1938; rechartered Phi Delta Psi, 1951; kicked off campus, 1973; rechartered Phi Delta Chi, 1982; folded 1986.

Phi Quag Mire, men, 1983; on campus.

Pi Kappa, men, 1996; on campus.

Sigma Tau Omega, women, 1969; name changed to Sigma Theta Chi, 1969, a week after being chartered; on campus.

Sigma Theta Chi, women, originally Sigma Tau Omega for one week; 1969; on campus.

Sub T-16, men, 1923; on campus.

Titans, men, 1992; folded 1996.

Tri Kappa Gamma, women, 1986; on campus.

Trojans, men, 1930; folded 1954; rechartered 1958; on campus.

Xi Beta Chi, women, originally Lucky 13, 1925; PALS, 1933; Delta Theta, 1944; Xi Beta Chi, 1989; folded, 1991; Delta Theta, 1996; on campus.

Zeta Rho, women, 1944; folded 1985; rechartered 1990; on campus.

The lifelong loyalty of so many alumni stands as a significant factor in the continued growth and development of this university. Byrd Ray Lewis of the class of 1923 was an example. As explained in the fall 1993 issue of *ACU Today*, Lewis published a report in 1953 titled "Class of 1923, 30 Years After." In 1983, he had a sixtieth anniversary dinner in his home in Abilene. Eight classmates attended. On the seventieth anniversary of their graduation, he sent letters to all of his nineteen remaining classmates. He received replies from six of them. Some were doing well, and some were not. He sent a report to the group with news about the classmates from whom he had heard. Responses indicated their pleasure at hearing about classmates and friends of seventy years ago.

That was his last report.

August 2, 1994, not quite a year after his final report, Byrd Ray died, shortly before his ninety-first birthday. He had proved the statement true, "The friends you make at ACU will be your friends for life."

The Brown Library has some 450,000 books; 118,000 government documents are excluded from the book count; also available are 915,000 microform units and 39,000 sound recordings, plus other categories of materials. The 450,000 books are primarily in open stacks, meaning any library user, from the beginning freshman to the professor who has written a dozen books, has access to the books he or she needs. When the individual is through with a book, the proper thing to do is simply to leave it on a table and allow a library staff member to reshelve the volume according to the Dewey decimal number marked on the spine. Occasionally, a helpful soul will try to assist the library staff by reshelving the book himself; no doubt these are people who were reared to be neat at home and "put things back where they came from." During the course of a year's time, hundreds of books may be misshelved. When a scholar in need is surrounded by almost half a million volumes, a book that is not shelved in its proper order is for all practical purposes a lost book.

During August 1997, all the shelves in the entire library were "read," that is, checked to locate books shelved out of order or with some other problem. This was called a "shelf-reading party." Librarians, staff members, student workers, and volunteers tackled the job with determination. They worked all week and spent another week mopping up. They worked through lunch but had pizzas, sandwiches, and other forms of nourishment brought in. That may explain why they called it a "shelf-reading party." They found books shelved in the wrong place, hundreds that needed repair, and some in such condition that they were withdrawn. New signs now adorn all reading tables, with the words "Please do not reshelve the books. Leave them on the nearest table. Thanks. ACU Library." For maybe the first time in their lives, non-neatniks can feel good about just leaving things where they were last used.

The university has been fortunate through the years to have strong directors of the library. Dr. Howard L. Schug prepared the first accession book and has been called the "Father of the ACU Library." In addition to his work as head of the Foreign Language Department, he was library director from 1917 to 1928, supervising an all-student staff. Margaret Bishop, who followed Dr. Schug, was the first director with a degree in library science. She received the degree from Vanderbilt University in 1927. She added rare books to Special Collections, including copies of the Bible in twenty-five languages. She was director from 1928 to 1934. Elizabeth Nelson, 1934-42, was the first librarian to get to move the library out of the Administration Building. She directed the transfer to the main floor of Chambers Hall in 1937. She died in September 1942, just as the fall semester was getting underway. She had been active on the campus until three months before her death. Marguerite Anderson was the first alumnus to become director. She was assistant librarian, 1942-43, and took charge when Nelson died in September. She was director from 1943 to 1953. She had the privilege of taking over the top floor of Chambers Hall to add to the main floor in 1948. Dr. Callie

Faye Milliken, 1953-77, was the first director to plan a totally new library building – the Margaret and Herman Brown Library. She was the first and so far the only director to earn a doctor's degree in library science. Kenneth Roach, 1977-88, was the first to secure designation as a federal depository for the ACU library. He also formalized the Abilene Library Consortium with the other Abilene libraries: Abilene Public, Hardin-Simmons University, and McMurry University. Marsha Harper, 1988 to the present, brought the computer age to the library. As the October 1977, issue of *Friends* states,

> Harper has directed the online, CD-ROM, and Internet enhancements to the Brown Library. ALCON funds have been raised, the system selected and installed, and updates have been added on a regular basis. Resources that were unavailable just a few years ago are now commonplace for the ACU undergraduate and graduate students and friends.

Nine professional librarians now assist Harper and are available to help the seeker of information at Brown Library. These are the professional librarians with the master of library science degree: Harper; Lewis Armstrong, technical services; Laura Baker, government documents; Craig Churchill, theology; Karen Hendrick, public services; Erma Jean Loveland, special services; Mark McCallon, periodicals; Gary Oliver, cataloger; and Bonnie Walker, senior cataloger.

"Evenings" at the Myerson and the Wortham – the symphony and theatre centers in Dallas and Houston – were introduced by the Department of Music during the Money presidency. Sunday, April 10, 1994, ACU musicians and a capacity crowd of friends took over the Morton H. Meyerson Symphony Center in Dallas for an evening of great music. It was a sellout triumph. The only disappointed people were alumni and friends who could not get tickets. Organizations featured were the ACU Symphonic Band, directed by Fred Allen; the A Cappella Chorus, directed by Dr. Paul Piersall; and the Alumni Chorus, with Dr. Jack Boyd directing. Dr. Ron Rathbun, professor of music and director of the piano division, performed Gershwin's *Rhapsody in Blue*, accompanied by the band. The A Cappella Chorus, the Alumni Chorus, and the band united to present "Peace Hymn of the Republic" by Dr. M. L. Daniels, professor emeritus of music. Faculty soloists for the evening were soprano Dr. Marion Cawood, professor of music; bass Dr. Charles Nelson, professor of music and artist-in-residence; and mezzo-soprano Julie Pruett, assistant professor of music. Professors Nelson and Piersall sang a bass duet. J. David Brock accompanied all vocal soloists. Some 200 musicians from ACU performed during the evening.

Such a resounding success deserved an encore Meyerson performance. Hence, a return engagement was scheduled February 4, 1996. This time a February blizzard resulted in a few empty chairs, but the musicians delighted the large crowd of people who had dared the ice and snow to attend. April 13, 1997, more than 200 ACU musicians presented "An Evening at the Wortham" in the Wortham Theater Center in Houston to appreciative friends from the metropolitan Houston area. These "Evenings" have acquainted a large number of people away from Abilene with the university's talented music students and faculty.

A unique feature of the Money presidency is the annual President-for-a-Day and Student-for-a-Day exchange. The first of these annual swaps was on April 14, 1994. It was the brain child of Bob Gomez, director of alumni relations, and was carried out by Patrice Natalicchio, now Mrs. Cayce Powell, who was coordinator of alumni activities.

Ann Francis, a freshman communication disorders major from Hockessin, Delaware, bought a ticket to see a Students' Association movie on Saturday evening, April 9. Her name was drawn in chapel the next Monday from a list of students who had attended the movie, and she was announced as the first President-for-a-Day.

On the next Thursday morning she moved into the president's office. During the day, she presided over a meeting of the vice presidents of the university, discussing student concerns, interests, and problems with a group of students President Francis had invited. She chaired a luncheon in the president's dining room, visited in the office with the retired Chief Justice of the Texas Supreme Court, Jack Pope, and transacted various

items of presidential business, using great restraint as to promises made. Friends in Nelson Dormitory affixed the sign "The
Prez" to the door of her room.

As for Dr. Royce Money, he came to school that morning
wearing jeans and loafers. He attended all of Miss Francis' classes, sat by her roommate in chapel, took a pop quiz or so, and
attended a meeting of the freshman council. A highlight of the
day was when he donned knee-length gym shorts and was a full
participant in a women's step aerobics class. A photograph of
this activity is included in this volume. "The old guys thought
I couldn't make it," he said, "but I did." After graduating
summa cum laude from ACU in 1997, Miss Francis is now
enrolled in graduate studies in communication disorders at the
University of Texas at Dallas.

The day was so popular with the university community that
it has become an annual affair. Presidents-for-a-Day since 1994
have been Shannon Clarkson of Walnut Springs in 1995, Jacob
Young of Conroe in 1996, Staci Lemons of Amarillo in 1997,
and Shanta Pandit of Nashville, Tennessee in 1998.

Parents of the Year awards were introduced during the
Money administration, the latest development of the Parents
Association, which has roots in 1962 when Max Iverson "Ike"
Summerlin of Port Arthur became the first president of the new
association. He and his wife, Dorothy Merwin Summerlin, had
six children, three of whom had already attended Abilene
Christian. The other three came along, and today all six are outstanding in their careers. Summerlin was assistant manager of
the Gulf Coast Marine Department of Texaco, Inc., and was a
member of the Board of Trustees, 1965-85. He announced
three objectives of the new organization: first, to generate and
maintain the interest and good will of parents of current and
former students; second, to inform parents about the college,
its background, present program, and future plans; and third,
to promote the advancement and development of the college
and assist in its financial support.

The first announcement of the organization resulted in a
large gathering of parents at a special reception held in their
honor in connection with Homecoming in 1962. It was decid-

ed that a feature of Homecoming each year would be a reception for all parents and their students. The first Homecoming reception drew a crowd of about 800 parents and students. The receptions went on for some years, supplemented by workshops, seminars, and discussion groups dealing with different aspects of the college. Gene Linder, of the development office, accepted an assignment as executive secretary of the Parents Association and editor of the *Parents' Newsletter.*

After some years, the Homecoming reception gave way to Freshman Follies, inasmuch as parents who were most eager to attend were parents of freshmen. When Freshman Follies was moved to September in 1989, parents were still enthusiastic supporters. In addition to sending their sons and daughters, the parents donated generously to the unrestricted giving program of the institution.

The second president of the Parents Association was Harvey Baker, who kept an active program going. Third president was Leroy Brownlow. After Linder was assigned to the Design for Development program, the Alumni Office assumed responsibility for staffing the Parents Association. And so the association has helped many parents feel a part of the university family. In recent years, the program has been stepped up considerably with these activities: summer orientation program for parents of incoming freshmen; birthday cakes baked by Paula Goodman Hall, the incomparable pastry chef of the World Famous Bean, and delivered to students' rooms by local members of the Parents Association; exam-week care packages delivered by parent volunteers to students whose parents have paid ten dollars for the care package; and an appreciation dinner each semester for all dormitory supervisory personnel to thank them for taking care of the student residents.

A major event occurs on Dead Day each semester, the eve of final exams. Parent volunteers deliver loads of doughnuts and other pastries, plus plentiful supplies of coffee and cocoa, to lobbies of all campus student residences. These goodies are furnished free of charge by the ARAMARK Corporation, operators of the World Famous Bean. Local parents, augmented by some out-of-town volunteers, handle the business of getting the goodies to Sikes, Gardner, Nelson, McDonald, McKinzie,

Smith, Adams, Mabee, and Edwards dormitories, and to University Park and A. B. Morris apartments. These are generally delivered about 9:30 p.m. On Tuesday night of final exams, parents sponsor a midnight supper in the Bean from 10 p.m. to midnight. The student pays three dollars – cash or unused debit card credits – for all he or she can eat. The Bean furnishes the food; parent volunteers staff the serving counters.

The Parents of the Year Award began in 1993-94. Students are invited to nominate their parents; a committee is appointed to read all the letters and select one couple to represent all of the other parents as Parents of the Year. Honorees have been: Winston and Mardell Hamby, Beaumont, Texas, 1993-94; Mack and Kathleen Hylemon, Toano, Virginia, 1994-95; Roger and Andrea Kondrup, Riverhead, New York, 1995-96; David and Beth Phillips, North Richland Hills, Texas, 1996-97; and Bill and Betty Tate, Grapevine, Texas, 1997-98.

The eleven most unusual visitor attractions on the ACU campus today are described here in alphabetical order:

1. Bible Times Lamps – This collection of oil lamps, ranging from the year 2000 B.C. down to the Muslim period during the Middle Ages, was put together by Dr. Bill Humble and Dr. Roy Willingham. It is displayed in the Hall of Servants of the Biblical Studies Building.

2. Chapel on the Hill – The chapel's east and west stained glass windows and north Leuders limestone wall create a unique, spiritually rich setting for worship, weddings, and other events.

3. Cracked Bell – The bell on display in front of the Women of ACU Museum at the corner of Campus Court and East North Sixteenth, which had been used to call students to meals, was cracked February 11, 1934, during the celebration after the announcement of the Hardin gift, which saved the university.

4. Echo Point – The Biblical Studies Building architects designed a unique Echo Point into the west porch of the upper rotunda of the Biblical Studies Building. When the visitor stands at the point and speaks, his voice echoes.

5. "Hope for the Future" sculpture – This sculpture of a family was done by Charles Umlauf and is a gift to the univer-

sity from Gayle Potter. It is located between the McGlothlin Campus Center and the Biblical Studies Building.

6. Missions Globe – The Missions Globe in the Biblical Studies Building rotunda was donated by Mr. and Mrs. Don Baker of Austin. The eight-foot diameter globe rotates, and lights show mission work locations of Churches of Christ.

7. Noah's Ark model – The model was built by Maurice Brown of Lamesa and is displayed in the Hall of Servants.

8. Quiet Places – The first Quiet Place, in the Mabee Business Building, was the idea of an alumni couple, Richard and Dema Lunsford. The Quiet Place was so popular with students, that another was built in the Biblical Studies Building.

9. "This Is a Good Site" plaque – This small plaque by the sidewalk between Zellner Hall and the Ad Building commemorates the proposal that resulted in the marriage more than forty years ago of an alumni couple, Jim Paul, class of 1957, and Sue Bassham, class of 1958. The plaque was installed at night by grandchildren of the couple and greeted passers-by the next morning.

10. Tower of Light – The top of the 150-foot tall tower is one of the highest points in Abilene. Its carillon chimes every fifteen minutes and can play patriotic music and the university's alma mater.

11. Waynai Bible – Lewis Waynai's Bible is billed as the world's largest Bible by Ripley's Believe It or Not. The Waynai Bible is exhibited in a large cabinet in the Brown Library. Waynai created the Bible in two years with a custom wooden typewriter with one-inch letters. He finished the 8,048-page, 34-inch thick, 1,094-pound Bible in 1930 in Pasadena, California.

(AUTHOR'S NOTE: Because the establishment of the Grace L. Woodward Memorial Endowment Trust is a development with which I have been closely associated, I shall once more use the first person in telling the story.)

My first knowledge of the Woodward family of Houston came while I was a sophomore at Abilene Christian College in the spring of 1936. Inasmuch as I had been a regular reader of *The Firm Foundation* since the age of twelve, it was a routine matter for me to go to the library and look through it each week. One feature I always checked was the editorial page written by G. H. P. Showalter. In the issue of March 24, 1936, Showalter devoted almost the entire page to a writeup of Harley Emerson Woodward's death in an airplane crash. The crash occurred March 5 on Rich Mountain, a few miles north of Mena, Arkansas. Woodward was an experienced pilot. In fact, the photograph Showalter ran of him showed him in his Army Air Corps Reserve uniform with his wings insignia. On the fatal day, he was flying by instruments because of fog. A faulty altimeter led him to think he was flying at a higher altitude than he actually was; hence, he crashed into the side of a mountain, killing him and his passenger, a cousin named Edward Martin.

Harley Woodward was thirty-three. He was survived by his wife, Grace, an eight-year-old son, Robert "Bob," and his parents, Bessie and Emerson Woodward. Harley's parents were people of great wealth. His father was not a member of the church, but his mother was a devout member. Emerson Woodward built the Heights Church of Christ building in Houston so that his wife could have a location near their home in which to worship. It was one of the finest church buildings in the city. Bessie Woodward had seen to it that her son Harley grew up in the faith. In fact, Showalter's title for his article concerning Harley's death was "Died in the Service of Our King." He pointed out that Harley Woodward was "known for his faithfulness and benevolence in the Lord's work for many years." The article reported that at the time of the tragedy, Woodward was on a mission of benevolence and mercy. He had flown to western Arkansas to see about helping an orphan home that was opening there.

While Harley was in high school, he had fallen in love with Grace Logan, daughter of Gertrude and Herbert Shelby Logan Sr. She was a dedicated Christian, as he was. When he was twenty-one and she nineteen, they were married, September 1, 1923. Their first child was a daughter, who died at the age of five. In 1927, a son was born to them. They named him Robert. By the time he was eight, and soon to be nine, Robert had lost a sister and his father. However, as the apostle Paul told of how the young man Timothy was taught by his grandmother, Lois, and his mother, Eunice, so Bob was brought up in the faith by his mother, Grace, and his grandmother, Bessie. He was baptized into Christ at the Heights Church in 1941 at the age of fourteen.

Grace Woodward's life after the loss of her husband was devoted to the church. Her mother-in-law, Bessie Woodward, gave her a set of Adam Clarke's commentaries and some tips on how to teach and told her, "You can teach." That set of commentaries is now in the office of President Money. Grace Woodward began teaching and continued to teach a Bible class for women for more than fifty years. Bob says, "I may be prejudiced, but I thought she was a brilliant teacher. I know the women in her class thought as much of her as you could think of another human." Along with teaching large numbers of appreciative women, she did a good job of bringing up her son. She had help from Mr. and Mrs. Woodward and her own parents, whom she and Bob visited every Thursday at their home in the Heights section of Houston.

Although Grandfather Woodward left young Bob's Bible teaching and churchgoing up to the two women, he made a distinct contribution to the upbringing of his grandson. He owned a ranch, called "Valdina," near Sabinal and Hondo. Bob loved to spend his summers and any other time that he could on that ranch. He grew up out-of-doors and in the saddle. He could do whatever was needed on a ranch. Along the way, he became an expert marksman, as was his grandfather. During those years, his Grandmother Woodward made contact with Abilene Christian College. At the annual meeting of the Board of Trustees February 22, 1939, President James F. Cox made the following low-key, matter-of-fact announcement: "With an initial gift of $2,500 on February 1, 1939, Mrs. E. F. Woodward, of Houston, Texas, has established a Harley Woodward Foundation for Christian Evangelism in memory of her only son, Harley Woodward, who was killed in an airplane wreck about three years ago."

That was the beginning.

Mrs. Woodward sent another $2,500 in April 1939, a third installment of $2,500 in January 1940, and a fourth gift of

$2,500 in May 1941, making a total of $10,000 for the Harley Woodward Foundation for Christian Evangelism.

Meanwhile, Bob Woodward, after attending school in Houston until he was fifteen, became a student in Texas Military Institute in San Antonio and was there for three years. While he was there, tragedy struck again. May 22, 1943, his Woodward grandparents, Emerson and Bessie, were killed in an automobile-train collision near the town of D'Hanis, Texas. Before he was sixteen, Bob and his mother Grace were left with a large estate, including Valdina, to manage. He finished his schooling at TMI in May 1945, in time to serve in the U. S. Navy before World War II ended. After that, he enrolled in Texas A&M. His Grandmother Woodward had given the money to build the first building for the A&M Church of Christ and had for years supplied the funds to support the minister there. Of course, this was done with her husband's hearty concurrence. One of Bob's favorite stories is of the time his grandmother's sister asked her, "Bessie, what do you get the most fun out of doing?" The answer: "Fooling Emerson into building churches and orphan homes." A few days later, the sister's husband asked Mr. Woodward what gave him the most pleasure in life. He replied, "Letting Bessie think she is fooling me into building churches and orphan homes!"

Bob's love was the ranch. He became engaged in raising Polled Herefords and operating a wild game preserve. His four daughters grew up at Valdina. They are all happily married and faithful members of the church.

I first met Bob Woodward more than two decades ago when I drove up to the Valdina and found him trapshooting. He was an unerring marksman. We became acquainted, and I learned that this man was a champion at whatever he undertook. He could shoot par golf with the likes of Byron Nelson. He was an ace tennis player. He was successful in business. I learned one other thing about him: he was a close student of the Bible and a most capable Bible class teacher. For several years he taught a class each Sunday at Concan, in the hill country of Texas, about twenty-five miles from the ranch. I visited the class one Sunday and was greatly impressed by his analysis of the scriptures and the rapt attention of members of the class. I saw the copious notes he prepared for his classes and learned of his study habits. He would arise each morning at four o'clock, go straight to his study, and spend several hours working at his desk. There was nothing fancy about his methods. He simply took the New Testament, book by book, chapter by chapter, verse by verse, and word by word, and tried to ascertain the message and the meaning and its significance for people in today's world.

In 1977, he and his wife, Mary, left the ranch and moved to Kerrville, but they continued to drive to Concan each Sunday, although the drive was about three times as far as from the ranch. To shorten a long story, with Mary's hearty support, I finally persuaded Bob to publish the notes. To his objection that they were in rough form, I volunteered to edit them for him. The process became a routine as follows: He would do the preparation. Mary would type the notes and send the pages to me. I would go over the pages, make suggestions, and raise questions where the meaning was unclear to me. My materials would go back to Kerrville for Bob's approval. The final approval was his to give.

The ACU Bookstore published the books. Bob furnished the money. One thousand copies were printed. He gave ACU a supply. Those books have gone to preachers, especially to young preachers, who requested them. Bob gave sets to his family and close friends and to churches and others from whom he received requests. As far as I know, all copies have been distributed. I treasure the set that I have. There are twelve volumes, beautifully bound, covering all of the New Testament books. In appreciation for the massive work Woodward did in writing a commentary on every book in the New Testament, President Teague recommended, and the board approved, an honorary doctorate in Christian service for Robert K. Woodward in 1987. The commentary project and the Woodwards' visits to the campus helped build his confidence in the people at Abilene Christian.

One factor in decision-making by Bob and his mother was that the original Harley Woodward Foundation for Christian Evangelism has been used through the years to help students attend Abilene Christian University and prepare themselves for Christian service throughout the world. It has been used very efficiently. According to the records, every student who has received a loan from the Woodward fund has repaid it. And the audit of 1997 shows that the fund now amounts to $55,225, the result of interest payments by borrowers and of wise investments.

Bob Woodward appreciates wise investments. Some years ago, he took over management of his mother's estate and increased it more than tenfold. As he saw his mother becoming frailer in her nineties, he knew that the ultimate disposition of her large estate was on her mind. Finally, he made a bold suggestion to her. He said, "Mother, if it would make you feel any better, why don't you go ahead and leave your entire estate to God's work?" She at first replied that it would not be right for her not to leave it to her son. Bob says, "I don't know if this is a little irreverent or not, but I told her I didn't want her money." Then he adds in a light-hearted vein, "I told her that I didn't want to be in a place where she could disinherit me."

She gave her approval to the plan, and Bob went to work. He called me and asked, "Do you suppose the Board of Trustees of Abilene Christian University would be willing to administer a trust that would be established with my mother's estate and dedicated to God's work?" I said, "Well, Bob, there is not a more stable group of people in the whole brotherhood than the Board of Trustees of Abilene Christian University. We have members who handle large trusts all of the time. And we have members who have their own large estates and trusts. I would certainly think they would work with you." He then told me the estate was approximately $18 million.

The next day, I met with President Royce Money, and arrangements were made to meet with Bob and Mary Woodward and their son-in-law, Carl Jones, an attorney, on Saturday afternoon, February 15, 1997. Those representing ACU in the meeting were Don Crisp, chairman of the board; Royce Money; Gaston Welborn, ACU's attorney; Dan Garrett, financial planner; and my wife and me. March 19, 1997, papers were signed at Woodward's office, which is a wing connected to his home, in Kerrville.

Mrs. Grace Woodward died Thursday, April 24, 1997, at the age of nine-two. She served the Lord throughout her long lifetime, and her estate, now valued at approximately $26 million, will be used in the service of the Lord throughout the years to come, and we are confident that will be until Jesus comes.

Daughter Beverly enrolled as a freshman in 1969 and graduated with a bachelor of science degree in home economics in 1973. While she was enrolled in ACU, the Department of Agriculture was engaged in an all-out campaign to build a herd of registered Polled Hereford cattle. Because Polled Herefords were the specialization of Valdina Farms, Bob Woodward offered to give to the department fifteen heifers if members of the department would drive to the ranch and pick, as he expressed it, "the best of the herd." The offer was accepted with alacrity. Drs. Keith Justice and Edwin DuBose led the way and with expert help of the owner came away with some fine additions to the Abilene Christian herd. Beverly Woodward Starr and her husband, Neal, have a son, Kenneth, who is enrolled as a freshman in ACU in the fall of 1998.

Now that we have completed a survey of the first ninety-two years of Abilene Christian University, what is in store for the future? In the year 2005-2006, the university will celebrate its 100th year of service for this institution. Alumni and friends of the university can expect a banner year.

President Money and Provost VanRheenen initiated a study looking to the second century of ACU and to the twenty-first century and the third millennium of the Christian era. The study involved administrators, faculty, students, alumni, and trustees of the university. A summary of the salient points of the Centennial Vision are the following:

The historic ties of Abilene Christian University with Churches of Christ will be maintained and will continue to be a key resource in preparing future church leaders. The university has been and will remain centrally and wholeheartedly Christian. Inasmuch as daily chapel focuses the hearts of the ACU family, it will continue. While most of our students will be drawn from the Churches of Christ, we will continue to welcome all students of character and ability who share our Christian values.

The size of the university is projected to stabilize between 4,800 and 5,200 students, including 800 graduate students.

That appears to be the optimum size for ACU in order to offer the advantages of a comprehensive university without losing the ability to give personal attention to the students. In order to expand the globalization of the campus, the plan is to increase the international student population to ten percent of the full-time enrollment. ACU will encourage diversity by increasing the combined international and minority population to a quarter of the student body.

The academic quality of students entering ACU will increase, as measured by national entrance examinations, with the average Scholastic Aptitude Test score for undergraduates increasing to 1,100 by 2001 and the average Graduate Record Examination score increasing to 1,000 for students admitted to graduate school.

Endowed scholarship funds will have high priority in ACU's objective to excel in full-time, residential, undergraduate education. High-achieving students will be recruited through scholarships and honors programs.

Faculty with national reputations will enhance the university's national reputation. Outstanding teachers who are committed to the stated mission of the institution will be recruited. These Christian professors will be rewarded with more opportunities for renewal and professional growth, including conferences, scheduled leaves, endowed global experiences, and grant funding. Their average compensation must be raised to the national norm for similar positions at comparable institutions. The academic division will provide regular evaluation of current programs and personnel and encourage experimentation with innovative programs and approaches to the teaching-learning process.

A new performing arts complex and possible additional classroom space will be given construction priority; otherwise, most capital dollars will be used to renovate existing buildings, enabling the university to use its growing resources to fund academic enhancements without allocating significant resources for new facilities.

Significant endowment enhancement will occur to achieve the goal of providing scholarships to an increasingly capable student body and properly compensating outstanding faculty and staff. The plan is for it to grow from the January 1998 total of $73 million to $125 million in 2001 and $250 million in 2006. Furthermore, it is expected that alumni support should increase by thirty-five percent by 2006. The Annual Fund will provide $2.5 million annually to the operating budget by 2006. Also, the university plans to maintain its reputation for being a great value by keeping tuition levels in the bottom quarter of price among similar universities.

Student-athletes will continue to be recruited for their commitment to academic growth, Christian ideals, and their physical abilities. ACU will have coaches who are academic, spiritual, and athletic mentors to student-athletes. The ACU program will continue to be one of the strongest in NCAA's Division II. All men's and women's sports will have an equal opportunity to compete at the national level. In keeping with this commitment, women's soccer will be added by 2002.

The Centennial Vision closes with this paragraph: "ACU is no ordinary university. We offer an exceptional education from a uniquely Christian perspective at an affordable price. But above all, we are in the business of transforming lives into the image of Christ. This is our vision and our dream."

On the cornerstone of the Hardin Administration Building, these words were engraved in 1929: "We believe in the divinity of Christ and in the inspiration of the Holy Scriptures. 'Contend earnestly for the Faith once for all delivered to the saints.'"

So may it ever be!

APPENDICES

APPENDIX 1

RESTATED ARTICLES OF INCORPORATION
OF ABILENE CHRISTIAN UNIVERSITY
May 8, 1997

ARTICLE I.
The name of this corporation is "ABILENE CHRISTIAN UNIVERSITY."

ARTICLE II.
The corporation is a non-profit corporation.

ARTICLE III.
This corporation is created for the following purposes, to wit: the establishment and maintenance of a university for the advancement of education in which the arts, sciences, languages and Holy Scriptures shall always be taught, together with such other courses of instruction as shall be deemed advisable by the Board of Trustees and which shall be managed and controlled as hereinafter set forth by a Board of Trustees, each of whom shall be a member of a congregation of the Church of Christ, which takes the New Testament as its only and sufficient rule of faith, worship and practice, and rejects from its faith, worship and practice everything not required by either precept or example, and which does not introduce into the faith, worship and practice, as a part of the same or as adjuncts thereto any supplemental organization or anything else not clearly and directly authorized in the New Testament by either precept or example.

ARTICLE IV.

The location of this university and the business office of this corporation shall be in the county of Taylor in or near the City of Abilene, State of Texas.

ARTICLE V.

This corporation shall have perpetual existence.

ARTICLE VI.

This corporation shall have power through the Board of Trustees to do all lawful acts including to grant diplomas, appoint officers and employ teachers or other agents; to procure grounds suitable for the university and to procure donations and subscriptions; and shall have the right to exercise all such powers as may be necessary or desirable to execute the purposes for which it is created and such as are usually exercised in the establishment and maintenance of first class institutions of learning.

ARTICLE VII.

The number of members of the Board of Trustees shall be determined from time to time by the Board of Trustees either by resolution of the Board of Trustees or by provision in the Bylaws of the corporation. A majority of those serving at any given time shall constitute a quorum. No meeting of the Board, either regular or special, shall be held without a quorum as herein defined. Every member of the trustees, at the time of his or her election and during his or her entire term of office, shall be a member of a congregation of the Church of Christ, as defined in Article III hereof, in good standing, said standing to be determined by the congregation of which the Trustee is a member.

The Board of Trustees shall have the power to appoint an Executive Committee of seven or more trustees who shall exercise all powers of the Board between meetings of the Board, except that the Executive Committee shall not elect members of the Board, Officers of the Board, or Officers of the University, other than an interim Chief Executive Officer of the

University, and except that the Executive Committee shall comply with the Bylaws of the University.

ARTICLE VIII.

The names and places of residence of members of the Board of Trustees of this corporation who are serving at the present time are: [Names and addresses are in the original document.]

The Board of Trustees of the corporation shall be self perpetuating, with the members of the Board electing their successors pursuant to the Bylaws.

ARTICLE IX.

The street address of the registered office of the corporation is 111 Hardin Administration Building, Abilene Christian University, Abilene, Texas 79699, and the name of its registered agent at such address is Gaston Welborn, Jr.

ARTICLE X.

There shall be elected by a vote of the Board of Trustees a Chair of such Board, a Chief Executive Officer of the University, and such other officials as the Board may deem advisable. Any officer or employee may be removed from office or from employment at any time by a majority vote of a quorum of the Board of Trustees.

ARTICLE XI.

The Board of Trustees shall have the power and authority to incur debt for all corporate purposes and to issue and execute appropriate evidences of such debt, and as security therefor may mortgage or otherwise encumber any property owned by the corporation.

ARTICLE XII.

The corporation will not have members.

ARTICLE XIII.

No part of the net earnings of the corporation shall inure to the benefit of any trustee of the corporation, officer of the corporation, or any private individual (except that reasonable compensation may be paid for services rendered to or for the corporation affecting one or more of its purposes), and no trustee or officer of the corporation, or any private individual shall be entitled to share in the distribution of any of the corporation assets on dissolution of the corporation. No substantial part of the activities of the corporation shall be the carrying on of propaganda, or otherwise attempting to influence legislation, and the corporation shall not participate in, or intervene in (including the publication or distribution of statements) any political campaign on behalf of any candidate for public office.

Notwithstanding any other provisions of these Articles of Incorporation, the corporation shall not conduct or carry on any activities not permitted to be conducted or carried on by an organization exempt from taxation under Section 501(c)(3) of the Internal Revenue Code and its Regulations as they now exist or as they may hereafter be amended, or by an organization, contributions to which are deductible under Section 170 of the Internal Revenue Code and Regulations as they now exist or as they may hereafter be amended.

Upon dissolution of the corporation or the winding up of its affairs, the assets of the corporation shall be distributed exclusively to charitable, religious, or religious educational organizations associated with the Church of Christ which would then qualify under the provisions of Section 501(c)(3) of the Internal Revenue Code and its Regulations as they now exist or as they may hereafter be amended.

ARTICLE XIV.

This Charter shall never be changed or amended as to religious qualifications of the Board of Trustees defined in Article VII of this Charter, but in other respects, said Charter may be amended as occasion may require upon notice to the Board of Trustees mailed at least fourteen (14) days prior to the meeting at which the amendment is to be presented and provided the amendment is approved by a two-thirds majority of the Trustees present at a meeting where a quorum is present. The notice shall state the nature of the proposed amendment.

ARTICLE XV.

To the fullest extent permitted by the Texas Miscellaneous Corporation Law Act or any other applicable laws as presently or hereafter in effect, no person shall be liable to Abilene Christian University for monetary damages for or with respect to any acts or omissions in his or her capacity as a Trustee of Abilene Christian University. No amendment to or repeal of this Article XV shall apply to or have any effect on the liability or alleged liability of any Trustee for or with respect to any acts or omissions of such Trustee occurring prior to such amendment.

APPENDICES

APPENDIX 2

CHAIRMEN (PRESIDENTS) OF BOARD OF TRUSTEES

1. J. P. Sharp, pro tem (first meeting, Nov. 3, 1906)
2. T. G. Moore, 1906-11
3. M. Zellner, 1911-16
4. J. S. Arledge, 1916-33
5. J. E. McKinzie, 1933-36
6. W. H. Free, 1936-42
7. E. D. Chambers, 1942-43
8. J. B. Collins, 1943-47
9. B Sherrod, 1947-67
10. Willard R. Paine, 1967-74
11. Ray McGlothlin Jr., 1974-84
12. H. Lynn Packer, 1984-92
13. Don Crisp, 1992-

SECRETARIES, BOARD OF TRUSTEES

1. W. H. Free, 1906-13; 1914-32; 1945-47
2. L. C. Denman, 1913-15
3. Hollis L. Manly, 1933-45
4. A. C. Scott, 1947-75
5. Wilson C. Orr, 1975-84
6. Roy Willingham, 1984-96
7. Jane Varner Beard, 1996-

TRUSTEES SINCE 1906

Inasmuch as the original charter specified that board members must be Texas residents, there were no out-of-state trustees until 1976. Beginning that year, individuals from other states were selected as national trustees, with all rights and responsibilities of regular board members except the right to vote in meetings of the board. A charter revision in 1997 eliminated the residency restriction, and all national trustees then serving were added as members of the regular board. All who have ever served as national trustees are included in this list. Place of residence is as of the date elected to the board.

• Designates members of the Senior Board.

* Designates the original five board members.

** Designates board members who served before a charter was granted.

•	Acuff, Grady	Lamesa	1958-1977
	Acuff, M. S.	Austin	1912-1916
	Akin, J. W.	Longview	1922-1926
	Akins, Thane	Midland	1982-Present
	Allen, S. N.	Christoval	1929-1951
	Anderson, W. F.	Stephenville	1921-1922
•	Anthony, James E.	Fort Worth	1979-1997
	Arledge, J. S.	Maryneal	1911-1937
	Arnold, W. H.	Winters	1916-1929
	Atkisson, Dr. J. A.	Merkel	1911-1913
•	Ator, Joe T.	Los Angeles	1984-1995
	Bacon, Sam A.	Abilene	1937-1963
	Bailey, Bob G.	Abilene	1973-1991
	Baisden, Joe B.	Belton	1991-Present
•	Baker, Harvey	Abilene	1971-1986
	Banister, John	Dallas	1950-1984
•	Bankes, Robert D.	Fort Worth	1968-1994
	Banowsky, A. B.	Houston	1951-1964
	Barfield, Dr. F. Todd	Columbus	1991-Present
	Beard, Jane Varner	Abilene	1993-Present
	Bell, Robert S.	Dallas	1947-1969
	Bell, Walton E., III	Vienna, Va.	1986-1989

Bennett, Gene	Denver City	1952-1977
Bennett, L. P.	Denver City	1941-1956
Birchfield, G. W.	Fort Worth	1916-1939
Bonneau, Edwin V.	Farmers Branch	1991-Present
Bonner, O. E.	Sweetwater	1916-1931
Boone, Michael M. "Mike"	Dallas	1986-1996
Bowman, Gus	Dallas	1969-1974
Brockman, J. C. "Jay"	Angleton	1977-1992
Brown, Dale A.	Midland	1988-Present
• Brown, Mary Prudie	Stanton	1986-1994
Burden, A. L.	San Antonio	1958-1981
Burleson, Omar T.	Anson	1938-1978
Byars, Lon	Vernon	1920-1921
Caldwell, Royce	San Antonio	1998-Present
Callan, Dr. Chester	Rotan	1928-1978
Calvert, Mike	Missouri City	1996-Present
Campbell, Truvis	Dimmitt	1954-1986
Carlile, Marvin	Tulia	1956-1977
Carmichael, Art	Abilene	1964-1973
Carrizal, Steve G.	Round Rock	1993-1998
Carter, J. Q.	Abilene	1945-1956
Cayce, W. B.	Fort Worth	1953-1964
Chambers, E. D.	Afton	1929-1945
Chambers, Virginia Palmer	Tyler	1994-Present
Childers, Terry Lee	Oklahoma City, Okla.	1988-Present
• Clark, Mary F.	Abilene	1984-1993
Cockrell, C. M.	Dallas	1927-1928
Coffee, Roy C.	Dallas	1965-1972
Coffee, T. J.	Loraine	1914-1916
Collins, J. B.	Abilene	1933-1973
Conder, Don R.	Granbury	1983-Present
Cooner, R. L.	Gorman	1921-1934
Copeland, David	Abilene	1998-Present
Cornutt, C. E. "Doc"	Dallas	1989-Present
Cox, G. W.	Canyon	1938-1965
Cranfill, J. B.	Abilene	1911-1915

	Crawford, E. L.	Stamford	1922-1937
	Crisp, Don W.	Dallas	1984-Present
	Crowder, G. W.	Quanah	1916-1918
	Crowe, Marvin N.	Aurora, Colo.	1986-1991
	Dabney, Allen D.	Eastland	1917-1963
	Dabney, J. S.	San Angelo	1911-1916
	Dale, J. W.	Winters	1911-1916
	Daniel, James	Eden	1952-1972
	Dean, O. J.	Anson	1911-1912
*	Deaver, J. H.	Buffalo Gap	1906-1907
	Doan, Jennifer Haltom	Texarkana, Texas	1993-Present
	Dobbs, R. A.	Crosbyton	1916-1920
	Drennan, A. Don	Abilene	1991-Present
	Drennan, L. C.	Abilene	1912-1914
	Duncum, John M.	Dallas	1984-Present
	Echols, Clyde	Abilene	1933-1967
	Ezzell, Charles	Abilene	1995-Present
	Fisher, E. L.	Dallas	1925-1928
	Ford, R. G.	Marshall	1956-1976
	Foster, Dr. J. B.	Houston	1940-1950
	Foster, Otto	Cleburne	1921-1937
*	Free, W. H.	Abilene	1906-1947
•	Gainer, Homer O.	Houston	1976-1993
	Gibson, Dr. J. P.	Abilene	1947-1974
	Gibson, H. R., Jr.	Dallas	1974-1992
	Gowens, Bob	Missouri City	1988-Present
	Griggs, Jack A.	Dallas	1974-1991
	Gunn, William	Amarillo	1934-1947
	Hall, E. F.	Hallsville	1916-1917
	Hall, J. D.	Tyler	1946-1948
	Hall, Robert James	Jasper	1972-Present
	Hansen, Ray V.	Memphis, Tenn.	1976-Present
	Hardegree, R. V.	Temple	1970-1986
	Harrell, Tom	Eastland	1919-1922
	Harvey, Dabney	Abilene	1920-1933
	Harvey, H. C.	Abilene	1933-1940
	Harvey, Ralph L.	Oklahoma City, Okla.	1983-Present
	Hatfield, W. C.	Dallas	1976 1986

	George W. "Bill" Lawrence, John	Corpus Christi	1956-1965
	Layfield, Lavelle	Sweetwater	1977-1994
	Lee, E. S.	Spur	1938-1971
	Lee, W. B.	Spur	1922-1937
	Leggett, C. B.	Abilene	1917-1926
	Lemmons, Reuel	Cleburne	1953-1984
	Lewis, Dr. Guy "Mojo"	The Woodlands	1995-Present
	Lewis, W. B.	Plainview	1918-1933
•	Locke, Leon	Hungerford	1958-1980
•	Lockhart, Stanley A.	San Angelo	1982-1998
	Logan, B. W.	Rhome	1911-1934
	Loop, John	Leuders	1911-1916
	Loving, C. C.	Amarillo	1927-1934
	Lunsford, Richard	Olney	1978-Present
	Lyons, Tommy	Glasgow, Ky.	1990-Present
	Kirkpatrick, J. S.	Abilene	1916-1919
	Manly, Hollis	Abilene	1929-1970
	Manly, J. E.	Abilene	1933-1950
**	Manly, J. S.	Nugent	1906
	Martin, Raleigh	Lubbock	1921-1947
	Mason, J. F.	Irene	1919-1920
	Massey, Dr. Janice M.	Durham, N.C.	1990-Present
	McCartney, E. C.	Waxahachie	1919-1921
*	McDonald, A. F.	Abilene	1906-1947
	McDonald, L. Chesley	Sterling City	1974-1989
	McGee, L. M.	Hereford	1954-1974
	McGinty, J. B.	Terrell	1919-1965
•	McGlothlin, Ray, Jr.	Abilene	1964-1995
	McKay, R. H.	Ferris	1919-1935
	McKinzie, J. E.	Hillsboro	1919-1937
	McLeskey, Gilbert T.	Abilene	1968-1989
	McQuigg, J. Y.	Denton	1912-1918
	Mead, J. H.	Abilene	1914-1916
	Meador, Prentice A. Jr.	Springfield, Mo.	1986-Present
	Meggs, R. G.	Dallas	1945-1968
	Michener, John W., Jr.	Hurst	1985-Present
	Miller, C. Todd	Dallas	1985-Present

	Miller, Robert	Ozona	1929-1953
	Mitchell, E. V.	Midland	1956-1976
*	Moore, T. G.	Abilene	1906-1911
	Morgan, J. I.	Gladewater	1935-1937
	Morris, Tommy	Abilene	1974-Present
	Morrow, B. F.	San Benito	1956-1966
	Muns, James	Plano	1981-Present
	Murphy, W. B.	Crandall	1919-1922
	Myers, W. M.	Ranger	1919-1921
	Nelson, Byron	Roanoke	1965-1974
	Nelson, W. H.	Mt.Calm	1919-1921
	Nicholson, G. Randy	Abilene	1981-Present
	Offutt, George Q.	Lubbock	1990-Present
	Oglesby, Robert K., Sr.	Richardson	1988-Present
	Onstead, Robert R. "Bob"	Sugar Land	1978-Present
•	Orr, W. C. "Dub"	Abilene	1970-1998
	Overby, John T.	Iowa Park	1919-1921
•	Owen, Harrold D.	Fort Worth	1969-1994
•	Packer, H. Lynn	Dallas	1972-1998
	Paine, Willard	Monahans	1956-1983
	Payne, W. R.	San Saba	1948-1952
	Pepper, George	Junction	1929-1951
	Pepper, J. D.	Sweetwater	1921-1929
	Pickett, Hubert, Jr.	Abilene	1994-Present
	Poe, Judge Ted	Humble	1990-Present
•	Pope, Jack	Austin	1954-1983
	Porter, James "Jim"	Danville, Calif.	1990-Present
	Porter, William Harvey	Albuquerque, N.M.	1984-1997
	Powell, J. R.	Tuscola	1913-1938
	Powell, Joe A.	Paducah, Ky.	1984-Present
	Powell, Lee	Paducah, Ky.	1976-1986
	Pratt, D. C.	Abilene	1921-1922
	Puckett, J. A.	Vernon	1919-1920
	Pyeatt, R. M.	Clyde	1938-1952
	Rambo, D. B.	Huntsville	1933-1946
	Rancier, Will	Killeen	1919-1921
	Reagan, R. C.	Houston	1912-1914

	Redd, J. C.	Jackson, Miss.	1976-1992
	Reese, J. C.	Mineral Wells	1918-1937
	Reynolds, Noel	Abilene	1952-1957
	Rhoden, Don Clifford	Garland	1989-Present
	Rhoden, W. C.	Abilene	1950-1979
	Richards, J. H. Sr.	Fort Worth	1946-1970
	Riehl, John James "Jack"	Chicago, Ill.	1986-Present
	Rigney, J. C.	Lubbock	1947-1969
	Ritchie, Joe T.	Okemos, Mich.	1989-Present
	Roberts, Verne	Waxahachie	1921-1925
	Rose, Arthur	Merkel	1916-1917
	Russell, T. A.	Abilene	1911-1937
	Sanders, R. L.	Houston	1970-1986
	Scott, A. C.	Abilene	1938-1975
	Sedberry, J. M.	Hamlin	1917-1921
	Sewell, J. P.	San Angelo	1911-1916
*	Sharp, J. P.	Merkel	1906-1908
	Sherrod, B	Lubbock	1933-1971
	Shipman, J. K.	Stamford	1911-1916
	Shultz, Don M.	Dunwoody, Ga.	1986-Present
	Smith, A. J.	Colorado City	1911-1916
	Smith, Ed S.	Vernon	1920-1921
	Smith, R. J.	Temple	1963-1977
	Smith, S. Douglas "Doug"	Nashville, Tenn.	1986-Present
	Smith, W. R.	Goose Creek	1933-1940
	Sorrells, James C. "Jim"	Waco	1977-1996
•	Sosebee, Otto	Anson	1938-1970
	Spain, L. A.	Woodson	1927-1929
	Sparks, Sam	Santa Rosa	1970-Present
	Stallings, Eugene C. "Gene"	Phoenix, Ariz.	1988-Present
	Strader, Robert J. Sr.	Abilene	1984-Present
	Summerlin, M. I.	Port Arthur	1965-1985
•	Talbot, Joe	Lake Jackson	1979-1996
	Teague, William J. "Bill"	Edmond, Okla.	1980-1981

Thomas, Warlick	Amarillo	1970-Present
• Thornton, A. Clifford, Sr.	Abilene	1978-1984
Thornton, Gary	Austin	1994-Present
Tidmore, J.	Abilene	1921-1923
Tidwell, B.	Abilene	1916-1920
Tittle, G. B.	Abilene	1916-1923
Travis, R. L.	Ralls	1921-1933
Underwood, I. C.	Gorman	1919-1921
Wade, C. A.	Sweetwater	1926-1957
Wakefield, W. A.	Corpus Christi	1926-1933
Walker, Ross	Tyler	1956-1965
Walling, Dean	Glendale, Calif.	1976-1983
Warren, David M., Jr.	Borger	1966-1973
Watson, J. W.	Colorado City	1926-1965
• Waugh, William R. "Bill"	Dallas	1982-1997
• Weber, O. J.	Beaumont	1983-1991
• Welch, Louie	Houston	1953-1989
West, Robert Lee "Bob"	Saratoga, Calif.	1986-Present
Wheeler, A. N.	Windom	1921-1933
Whitacre, Dr. Stanley	San Antonio	1938-1958
Wicker, E. J.	Midland	1956-1970
Williams, J. McDonald	Dallas	1981-Present
• Willingham, Roy	Abilene	1974-1996
Worley, Melinda	Austin	1995-Present
Wright, John	Abilene	1965-1981
Yearwood, Randall N.	Nashville, Tenn.	1986-1988
Young, M. Norvel	Lubbock	1950-1957
Zellner, M.	Abilene	1908-1916

PRESIDENTS OF THE INSTITUTE/COLLEGE/UNIVERSITY

1. Allen Booker Barret, 1906-08
2. Henry Calhoun Darden, 1908-09
3. Robertson L. Whiteside, 1909-11

(James F. Cox was elected president in 1911. He worked all summer getting the campus ready for school to begin in September, but was never on campus one day during the school year. His brother, A. B. Cox, was acting president during the year.)

4. Jesse Parker Sewell, 1912-24
5. Batsell Baxter, 1924-32
6. James Franklin Cox, 1932-40
7. Don Heath Morris, 1940-69
8. John Christopher Stevens, 1969-81
9. William J. Teague, 1981-91
10. Royce Lynn Money, 1991-

CHIEF ACADEMIC OFFICERS

(Until 1912, the president was also chief academic officer.)
1. Carl Gardner, 1912-14*
2. Henry Eli Speck, 1914-24
3. James Franklin Cox, 1924-32
4. Walter Harris Adams, 1932-69
5. Bill J. Humble, 1969-76
6. Edward Marcus Brown, 1976-82
7. C. G. Gray, 1982-88
8. Royce Money, 1988-91
9. Dwain M. Hart, 1991-96
10. Dwayne Van Rheenen, 1996-

*George Klingman was dean of Bible before 1912, but Carl Gardner was first dean of the college.

Chief Financial Officers

1. Paul C. Witt, 1922-24
2. L. G. Kennamer, registrar and bursar, 1924-27
3. Clara Bishop, registrar and bursar, 1927-28
4. Lawrence L. Smith, 1928-69
5. Leo Dale "Bill" Hilton, 1969-1992
6. Jack Rich, 1992-
(From 1906 to 1924, all funds – income and expenses – were handled by the president of the college.)

Registrars

1. Hosea H. Lewis, 1921-24
2. L. G. Kennamer, 1924-27 (registrar and bursar)
3. Clara Bishop, 1927-50
4. Kenneth Hugh Rasco, 1950-1985
5. Don Stafford, 1985-1990
6. Charles Rudolph, 1990-91
7. David B. Merrell, 1991-January 1, 1998
8. Danelle Brand, 1998-

Student Life Officers

Deans of Women/Associate Deans of Students

1. Daisy McQuigg (Mrs. J. P.) Sewell, 1912-24
2. Elizabeth Nelson, 1927-34
3. Susan (Mrs. B. H.) Cogdell, 1934-41
4. Retta Scott (Mrs. J. O.) Garrett, 1941-44
5. Anna (Mrs. Luther G.) Roberts, 1944-48
6. Vera (Mrs. W. C.) Sikes, 1948-63
7. Willie (Mrs. Harold) Wilkinson, 1963-70
8. Ann (Mrs. Paul) Rotenberry, 1970-74
9. Winnie (Mrs. J. B.) Gibbs, 1974-85
10. Cynthia (Mrs. James C.) Cooke, asssociate dean of students, 1985-

DEANS OF MEN, DEANS OF STUDENTS, AND VICE PRESIDENTS FOR STUDENT SERVICES

1. Jesse Fox, dean of men, 1945-46; dean of students, 1946-47
2. Morris M. Howard, dean of men, 1947-50
3. John C. Stevens, dean of men, 1950-51; leave of absence, 1951-52; dean of students, 1952-56
4. Lowell G. Perry, dean of men, 1951-52
5. Garvin V. Beauchamp, dean of students, 1956-69; vice president for student personnel services, 1969-83
6. Douglas W. Warner, dean of men, 1968-71
7. Eugene L. Linder, dean of men, 1971-81
8. Norman Archibald, director of campus life, 1981-82; associate dean of students, 1982-88
9. Gary D. McCaleb, vice president and dean of campus life, 1983-91
10. Bob Strader, associate dean of students, 1988-92
11. Charles Trevathan, vice president for campus life, 1991-97
12. Major L. Boglin, associate dean of students, 1993-96
13. Wayne Barnard, associate dean of students, 1996-

TRUSTEES AWARD FOR OUTSTANDING TEACHER OF THE YEAR

1953	Mrs. Penn Gilbreth, education
1954	J. Roy Willingham, biology
1955	Paul C. Witt, chemistry
1956	LeMoine Lewis, Bible
1957	Orval Filbeck, education
1958	Frank Pack, Bible
1959	W. C. Sikes, mathematics
1960	Norman Whitefield, art
1961	Keith Justice, agriculture
1962	James Culp, English
1963	J. W. Treat, foreign languages

1964	Zelma Odle, English
1965	Troy Caraway, art
1966	Ed Brown, communication
1967	Abe Malherbe, Bible
1968	Tommy McCord, chemistry
1969	Clark Stevens, biology
1970	Carl Brecheen, Bible
1971	Juanita Avinger, education
1972	Overton Faubus, business administration
1973	B. E. Davis, mass communication
1974	John T. Willis, Bible
1975	Rex Kyker, communication
1976	J. W. Treat, foreign languages
1977	LeMoine Lewis, Bible
1978	Neil Lightfoot, Bible
1979	F. M. Churchill, agriculture
1980	Bea Speck, history
1981	Sam McReynolds, mathematics
1982	Paul Faulkner, marriage and family
1983	Herschel Avinger, education
1984	Benny Gallaway, history
1985	Elizabeth Campbell Rotenberry, exercise science and health
1986	Jozell Brister, business administration
1987	Charlie Marler, journalism and mass communication
1988	Perry Reeves, chemistry
1989	Jim Nichols, biology
1990	Monty L. Lynn, management sciences
1991	Mel Hailey, political science
1992	Don C. Jackson, management sciences
1993	Rick Lytle, management sciences
1994	Chris W. Willerton, English
1995	John Little, biology
1996	Stephen Weathers, English
1997	Jim Nichols, biology
1998	Perry Reeves, chemistry

DIRECTORS OF THE LIBRARY

1. Howard L. Schug, 1917-28
2. Margaret Bishop, 1928-34
3. Elizabeth Nelson, 1934-42
4. Marguerite Anderson, 1942-43 (acting); 1943-53
5. Callie Faye Milliken, 1953-77
6. Kenneth Roach, 1977-88
7. Marsha Harper, 1988-

ATHLETIC DIRECTORS

1. A. B. Morris, 1924-69
2. Wally Bullington, 1969-88
3. Don Drennan, 1988-90
4. Cecil Eager, 1990-95
5. Stan Lambert, 1995-

DIRECTORS OF DEBATE

1. Walter H. Adams, 1925-30
2. Don H. Morris, 1930-40
3. Fred J. Barton, 1940-47
4. Rex P. Kyker, 1947-56
5. Edward M. Brown, 1956-70; 1941-77
6. Gaston Welborn, 1970-71
7. Mike Ross, 1978-79
8. Joe Cardot, 1980-90
9. Jeffrey Hobbs, 1991-

THEATRE DIRECTORS

From the very first year of ACU, dramatic presentations were staged. A feature of the first commencement excercises in May 1907 was, as mentioned in the *Abilene Reporter*, "a three-act play, 'A Case of Suspension,'" presented by the students and faculty. During the 1920s and 1930s, the Dramatic Club and the Melpomenean Players presented student-directed plays. The first faculty director of theatre was Rebecca Morris in 1938.

1. Mrs. Rebecca (A. B.) Morris, 1938-43
2. Virginia O'Neal, fall, 1943 (She resigned in 1944 to enlist in the WAVES.)
3. Rex P. Kyker, 1944-50
4. Gaylan Collier, 1950-60
5. Chris (Mrs. Rex) Kyker, 1960-61
6. Lewis Fulks, 1961-91
7. Adam Hester, 1991-

BAND DIRECTORS

The *Optimist* of January 18, 1923, had this statement: "Heretofore, there has been a small band in school but this is the first attempt to engage a Director who is competent to instruct beginners in the playing of band instruments." This director was Iven H. Hensley.

1. Iven H. Hensley, 1921-24
2. J. Sullivan Gibson, 1925-28
3. Hughey Adams, 1928-30
4. Maurice Roberts, 1930-32
5. A. C. Cox, 1932-34
6. D. W. Crain, 1934-45
7. Bill Davis, 1946-48
8. Robert Holland, 1948-53
9. Douglas Fry, 1953-69
10. Charles Trayler, 1969-81
11. John Whitwell, 1981-87
12. Gary Lewis, 1987-90
13. Fred Allen, 1990-94
14. Blaine Hinton, 1994-

ORCHESTRA DIRECTORS

From early days, the school had an orchestra. The *Prickly Pear* for 1918 carried a group photograph of the orchestra, listing Orban Phillips, a piano and voice teacher, as "directress." Now and then, the individual who was band director would also be listed as director of orchestra, but it was understood that band was the principal activity. A major push toward having an orchestra came when John D. Anderson became director in 1950.

1. John D. Anderson, 1950-54; leave, 1954-55; 1955-61
2. James Benton, 1954-55
3. Douglas Fry, 1961-63
4. Erwin Daugherty, 1963-65
5. M. L. Daniels, 1965-69
6. Ed George, 1969-83
7. John Whitwell, 1983-84
8. David Brock, 1984-85

COLLEGIATE ORCHESTRA (ACU AND HARDIN-SIMMONS UNIVERSITY)

1. Scott Mather, HSU, 1985-91
2. Celeste Myall, HSU, 1991-

DIRECTORS OF A CAPPELLA CHORUS

1. Leonard Burford, 1932-50; (leave, 1950-51); 1951-58
2. Bill W. Davis, 1950-51
3. Vernon Moody, 1958-61
4. Rollie Blondeau, 1961-63
5. Vernon Moody, 1963-65
6. Richard Fulton, 1965-67
7. Bill W. Davis, 1967-68
8. Jack Boyd, 1968-80
9. Milton Pullen, 1980-86
10. Charles Nelson, 1986-87

11. Paul Piersall, 1987-94
12. Michael Scarbrough, 1994-

EDITORS OF THE *OPTIMIST*

1. Arthur Slater, 1911-12
2. D. L. Petty, 1912-13
3. Milton Cranfield, Bellah Philpott, V. McCasland, T. Arledge, 1913-16
4. Roy Coons, 1916-17
5. Hettye Randolph Summers, 1917-18
6. Willie Pritchett Witt, 1918-19
7. Vincent Sikes, 1919-20
8. Elmer Berry, 1920-21
9. Wendell H. Bedichek, 1921-24
10. Aubra "Peter" Banowsky, Burton Coffman, 1924-25*
11. Burton Coffman, 1925-27
12. Lloyd Nelson, 1927-28
13. Paul Southern, 1928-30
14. Leon Carter, 1930-31
15. Olan Hicks, 1931-32
16. Everett Maxwell, 1932-33
17. William Gray, 1933-34
18. Trine Starnes, 1934-35
19. Marlin Carruth, 1935-37
20. Samuel E. Blackwell, 1937-39
21. Leon Henthorn, 1939-40
22. Ed Sewell, 1940-41
23. Robert Findlay (fall), Don Findlay (spring), 1941-42
24. Lea Short Blauvelt, 1942-43
25. Patsy Powell Duncan, 1943-44
26. Robert Page, 1944-45
27. Kitty Hanks Owings, 1945-46
28. Eugenia Scott Fore, 1946-48
29. Kenneth Overton, 1948-49
30. Bettye Elrod Nichols, 1949-50
31. Edwin Broadus, 1950-51
32. Gary Moore, 1951-52

33. Clark Potts, 1952-53
34. Betty McDermett McLemore, 1953-54
35. Charlie Marler, 1954-55
36. J. W. Campbell, 1955-56
37. Mac Bedichek, 1956-57
38. Bob Johnson, 1957-58
39. Dennis Renner, 1958-59
40. Howard Straughn, 1959-60
41. Dudley Lynch (fall), James Batts (spring), 1960-61
42. James Batts (fall), Charlie Smith (spring), 1961-62
43. Bobby Smith (fall), Carole Stone Straughn (spring), 1962-63
44. Bobby Smith, 1963-64
45. Billie Wesley Silvey, 1964-65
46. Lola Sue Scobey, 1965-66
47. Mary Hance Stelzer (fall), Bill England (spring), 1966-67
48. Bill England, 1967-68
49. Pam Estes Padget, 1968-69
50. Garner Roberts, 1969-70
51. Raymon Fullerton, 1970-71
52. Mark Cunningham, 1971-72
53. Karen Hughes Strong, 1972-73
54. John Williams, 1973-74
55. Alan Miller, 1974-75
56. Rick Hagar, 1975-76
57. Brent Stutzman, 1976-77
58. Ron Hadfield, 1977-79
59. Cindy Stocking, 1979-80
60. Doug Mendenhall, 1980-82
61. Robin Ward Saylor, 1982-83
62. Jay Friddel, 1983-84
63. Key Payton, 1984-85
64. Cindi Patterson, 1985-86
65. Thomas Graham, 1986-87
66. Candy Holcombe Reagan, 1987-88
67. Ken Pybus, 1988-89
68. Rebekah Gibbs Sunder Raj, 1989-90
69. Gretchen Schultz Allan, 1990-91

70. Keith Alewine, 1991-92
71. Michael O'Connor, 1992-93
72. Sharla Stephens Green, 1993-94
73. Kelly Davidson Perkins, 1994-95
74. Amy Daugherity Warren, 1995-96
75. Jeremy Parish, 1996-97
76. Jessica Gray, 1997-98
77. Julie O'Neill, 1998-99

*Banowsky graduated in the middle of the year, which was divided into quarters; Coffman succeeded him as editor.

THE *OPTIMIST* FACULTY ADVISERS

1. Crawford Allen, 1935-36
2. Paul Southern, 1937-40
3. Homer F. Howk, 1941-45
4. Max Leach, 1945-47
5. Wendell Bedichek, 1947-50
6. Heber Taylor, 1950-52
7. Mima Williams, 1952-53
8. Walter E. Burch, 1953-54
9. Heber Taylor, 1954-56
10. Heber Taylor and Reginald Westmoreland, 1957-59
11. Heber Taylor and Charlie Marler, 1960-61
12. Reginald Westmoreland, 1961-63
13. Clark Potts, 1965-66
14. Bob Armistead, 1966-67
15. Irvin D. Hiler, 1967-68
16. B. E. Davis, 1969-74
17. Charlie Marler, 1974-96
18. Merlin Mann, 1996-97, 1997 fall
19. Charlie Marler, 1998 spring
20. Merlin Mann, 1998-

EDITORS OF THE PRICKLY PEAR

1. Bellah Philpott, 1916
2. W. C. Sikes, 1917
3. Hettye Randolph Summers, 1918
4. Inez Norton Rambo, 1919-20
5. Roy A. Johnson, 1921
6. W. Earl Brown, 1922
7. James H. Childress, 1923
8. Don H. Morris, 1924
9. R. L. "Red" Williams, 1925
10. Schley Riley, 1926
11. Henry T. Hogg, 1927
12. Millard Humphrey, 1928
13. Emmett L. Bryan, 1929
14. Elden Busby, 1930
15. James Chambers, 1931
16. Clovis Watson, 1932
17. C. W. Cecil, 1933
18. Leo McClung, 1934
19. Bert Ezzell, 1935
20. Homer Utley, 1936
21. Batsell Barrett Baxter, 1937
22. Carl Spain, 1938
23. G. C. Morlan Jr., 1939
24. Leslie King, 1940
25. Billie Yater Prior, 1941
26. J. B. Ellis, 1942
27. John Plunket, 1943
28. Dorothy Jean Martin Sanders, 1944
29. Barbara Morlan Gray, 1945
30. Norma Qualls Palmer, 1946
31. Edgar A. Herring, 1947
32. Betty Buford, 1948
33. Charles S. Chandler, 1949
34. Jodie Carter Decker, 1950
35. Harvie Pruitt, 1951
36. Rita Ann Walker Diller, 1952
37. Bo Dean Parham Kruse, 1953

38. Charlie Marler, 1954
39. Carol Hamm Cauthern, 1955
40. Roy Ward, 1956
41. Glenn Webb, 1957
42. Audrey Hamilton Stewart, 1958
43. John Little, 1959
44. Mickey Ligon, 1960
45. Mike Fanning, 1961
46. James Foster and Mary Ann Jackson, 1962
47. Carolyn Cunningham, 1963
48. Ron Pauls, 1964-65
49. David Riemer, 1966
50. Marcia Beazley Chitwood, 1967
51. Vicki Cardwell Goode, 1968
52. Jane Ann Wise Thomas, 1969
53. Floy Beth Conley Chambers, 1970
54. Janice Kennon Jackson, 1971
55. Stephanie Starling Smith, 1972
56. Jud Thurman, 1973
57. Wayne Gurley, 1974
58. Cheryl Mann Bacon, 1975
59. Sandy Jones Secor, 1976
60. Mark Flippin, 1977
61. Kent Hunter, 1978
62. Jan Taylor, 1979
63. Bob Nutt, 1980
64. Dana Williams Robinson, 1981
65. Suzetta Hance Nutt, 1982
66. Charles Pullen, 1983
67. Rachel Rainwater McClure, 1984
68. Betsey Bolin Craig, 1985
69. Andra Bolin Bennett, 1986
70. Julie Manis Cunningham, 1987
71. Tom Craig, 1988
72. Vonda Dietz, 1989
73. Katie Hooten, 1990-91
74. Denis McGinnis Thomas, 1992
75. Wendy Greiner Abel, 1993
76. Deana Hamby Nall, 1994

77. Marty Reves, 1995
78. Mark Houston, 1996 and 1997
79. Carol Mattei, 1998
80. Wendy Huff, 1999

STUDENTS' ASSSOCIATION PRESIDENTS

1. Wendell Bedichek, 1923-24
2. Walter Adams, 1924-25
3. Ernest Walls, 1925-26
4. Burton Coffman, 1926-27
5. J. Willie Treat, 1927-28
6. Lawrence L. Smith, 1928-29
7. Paul Southern, 1929-30
8. Alfred E. "Poly" Wells, 1930-31
9. Clovis Watson, 1931-32
10. C. W. Cecil Jr., 1932-33
11. Jack Pope, 1933-34
12. Trine Starnes, 1934-35
13. Norvel Young, 1935-36
14. Morris Howard, 1936-37
15. John Stevens, 1937-38
16. Earl McCaleb, 1938-39
17. Chesley McDonald, 1939-40
18. Garvin Beauchamp, 1940-41
19. P. H. Hill, 1941-42
20. Bill Hay (fall), Foy Short (spring), 1942-43
21. Ernest Finley, 1943-44
22. Wendell Broom, 1944-45
23. Tex Stevens, 1945-46
24. Orville McDonald, 1946-47
25. Bill Decker, 1947-48
26. Don Hardage, 1948-49
27. Robert "Tex" Williams, 1949-50
28. Jimmy Jividen, 1950-51
29. Robert "Bob" Davidson, 1951-52
30. Clyde Austin, 1952-53
31. Jack Scott, 1953-54

32. Richard "Fuzzy" Lunsford, 1954-55
33. Don Bowen, 1955-56
34. Howard Norton, 1956-57
35. Don Drennan, 1957-58
36. David Malone, 1958-59
37. David Karney, 1959-60
38. Cullen Johnson, 1960-61
39. Charles Nelson, 1961-62
40. Charles Groves, 1962-63
41. Gary McCaleb, 1963-64
42. Hubert Gill, 1964-65
43. Edward Massey, 1965-66
44. Ron Price, 1966-67
45. Charles Nakamura, 1967-68
46. Bill Cannon, 1968-69
47. Walt Cabe, 1969-70
48. Thomas Teague, 1970-71
49. Rodney Dunn, 1971-72
50. Art McNeese, 1972-73
51. Kenny Wilson, 1973-74
52. Kelly Utsinger, 1974-75
53. Steve Allison, 1975-76
54. Don Garrett, 1976-77
55. Barry Packer, 1977-78
56. Doug Williams, 1978-79
57. Ron Holifield, 1979-80
58. John Tyson, 1980-81
59. Bart Castle, 1981-82
60. Rob Sellers, 1982-83
61. Brad Cheeves, 1983-84
62. Robert Pitman, 1984-85
63. Jennifer Haltom Doan, 1985-86
64. Scott Sager, 1986-87
65. Blain McCormick, 1987-88
66. Lance McAlister, 1988-89
67. Wes Smith, 1989-90
68. Gary West, 1990-91
69. Brent McCall, 1991-92
70. Matt Murphy, 1992-93

71. C. B. Barber, 1993-94
72. Tye Lamberth, 1994-95
73. Stephen Haynes, 1995-96
74. Caleb Kelso, 1996-97
75. Matt Moreland, 1997-98
76. Kevin Linderman, 1998-99

A. B. Morris Wall of Honor

"In tribute to Wildcat student athletes who earned national championship berths on United States Olympic teams or held world records in track and field, or those named first team All-American in other sports at Abilene Christian University."

TF – Track and Field
FB – Football
XC – Cross Country
Tn – Tennis
G – Golf
WBB – Women's Basketball
MBB – Men's Basketball
Bb – Baseball

Selections for 1994

Adrian, George (TF)
Amos, Crian (TF)
Ator, Wendy (TF)
Bennett, Chip (FB)
Berryman, Neal (Tn)
Bright, Tim (TF)
Brown, Dennis (FB)
Brown, James (TF)
Brown, Marvin (TF)
Buchanan, Bonnie (WBB)
Bullington, Wally (FB)
Clarke, Vida Alexandra (TF)
Clanton, Bud (TF)

Clardy, Judy Kniffen (Tn)
Clay, Ben (TF)
Conder, Don
Cooley, Calvin (TF)
Cowart, Lance (Tn)
Cox, Larry (FB)
Craig, Justine (TF)
Crooks, Vicky (Tn)
Cross, Lisa Ward (Tn)
Davidson, Kenny (FB)
Darville, Donny (G)
Dixon, Kelly (TF)
Dyer, Sylvia (TF)
Edwards,Wendell (TF)
Estes, Frank (TF)
Faulkner, Paul (TF)
Feasel, Grant (FB)
Feasel, Greg (FB)
Fedell, Rodney (MBB)
Felkins, Cliff (TF)
Foster, Ann (TF)
Fullwood, Hope (XC)
Gridley, Kim (Tn)
Godfrey, John Ray (MBB)
Goodspeed, Chris (G)
Griggs, Waymond (TF)
Guerrerro, Martin (TF)
Harvey, Dafne (TF)
Haver, Denise (Tn)
Henry, Yolanda (TF)
Hill, Frankie (TF)
Howell, Shane (TF)
Istre, Chelsa Lancaster (TF)
Jay, Brad (Tn)
Jenkins, Dale (TF)
Johnson, Greg (TF)
Jones, Jay (FB)
Kebiro, John (TF)
Kendrick, LeRhonda (TF)

King, Michelle (Tn)
Klapprott, Brent (Tn)
Lawler, John (TF)
Lawrence, Albert (TF)
Layfield, John (FB)
Ledsome, Mike (TF)
Lewis, Denise (TF)
Lewis, Marlene (TF)
Lindsey, Jim (FB)
Longley, Clint (FB)
McClellon, Bill (TF)
McCoy, Burl (TF)
McLeod, Robert (FB)
Mahaney, Lara (Tn)
Martin, Carla (Tn)
Martin, Chip (FB)
Mayfield, Tracy (TF)
Mehgoo, Greg (TF)
Miller, Cam (TF)
Moloto, Michael (XC)
Montgomery, Wilbert (FB)
Morgan, Von (FB)
Morris, Ian (TF)
Morrow, Bobby (TF)
Nutt, Dee (MBB)
Olson, Billy (TF)
Parker, Steve (TF)
Pemelton, Billy (TF)
Perkins, Johnny (FB)
Peterson, George (TF)
Phillips, Aaron (TF)
Phillips, Charles (TF)
Poth, Matthias (Tn)
Pursley, Brad (TF)
Remsburg, Dan (FB)
Richardson, Dennis (TF)
Rodney, Jewel (TF)
Salazar, Jose (TF)
Schleyer, Claudia (WBB)

Segrest, James (TF)
Shata, Ahmed (TF)
Shoemaker, Angie (Tn)
Shropshire, Jack (TF)
Simmons, David (TF)
Singh, Jeev (G)
Sitton, Ted (FB)
Smith, Sonya (TF)
Smith, V. T. (FB)
Steen, Bill (G)
Straughn, Yolande (TF)
Sykes, Donna (Tn)
Tabor, Carol (Tn)
Tallent, Johnny (Tn)
Taylor, Laurie (XC)
Thaxton, Steve (TF)
Thomas, Mazel (TF)
Thompson, Tommy (TF)
Tinnell, Sheryl (TF)
Trusty, Ladrick (TF)
Turner, Alesha (TF)
Van Druten, Richard (FB)
Walker, Kim (TF)
Wheeler, Les (FB)
White, Roger (Tn)
Williams, Arthur (TF)
Williams, Carl (TF)
Williams, Darren (TF)
Williams, Freddie (TF)
Wilson, Mark (FB)
Witherspoon, Mark (TF)
Woodhouse, Bill (TF)
Young, Earl (TF)

Selections for 1995

Boles, Christy (TF)
Campbell, Revoli (TF)

Joseph, Hermin (TF)
Neece, Kim Bartee (TF)
Ngidhi, Savieri (TF)
Scott, Robby (TF)
Tengelei, Joseph (TF)

SELECTIONS FOR 1996

Boykins, Dontra (TF)
Clarkson, Jennifer (WBB)
Dilworth, Kevin (TF)
Ezem, Amara (TF)
Guy, Robert (TF)
Hinkson, Donna (TF)
Jordan, Dannett (Tn)
Newhouse, Darin (G)
Sheffy, Wes (Tn)
Tombiri, Mary (TF)
Wickham, Yvette (TF)

SELECTIONS FOR 1997

Cole, James (Tn)
Cooper, Sayon (TF)
Griffin, Glenn (TF)
Haring, Ronny (Bb)
Jaime, Ruth (XC)
Korir, Thomas (TF)
Nelson, Ron (TF)
Rodgers, Trafton (TF)
Samuel, Bigna (TF)
Sommers, Katina (TF)
Vann, Karrn (XC)
Vermeulen, Jerome (TF)
White, Jeff (G)

INDEX